RUPERT BROOKE

RUPERT BROOKE

Life, Death & Myth

Nigel Jones

RICHARD COHEN BOOKS • London

First published in hardback in Great Britain in 1999
by Richard Cohen Books, an imprint of Metro Publishing Limited,
19 Gerrard Street, London W1V 7LA

British Library Cataloguing in Publication Data.
A CIP record of this book is available on request from the British Library.

ISBN 1 86066 171 8

10 9 8 7 6 5 4 3 2 1

Typeset by MATS, Southend-on-Sea, Essex

Printed in Great Britain by CPD Group, Wales

For Lally
with love

Contents

Acknowledgements

The long gestation of this book has created many debts. In no particular order I wish to thank all those who have made its publication possible.

My able agent, Andrew Lownie, supported the project through many tribulations with unflagging zeal. Richard Cohen, my publisher, was in at its conception, and the team at Metro Books – Susanne McDadd, Alan Brooke, Mary Remnant, Becke Parker, Charlotte Atyeo – and Penny Phillips saw it through to full term in the teeth of many obstacles. Richard Dawes was a quite outstanding copy-editor who scrupulously spotted many errors of fact and taste, and gently excised them. (Many doubtless remain, for which I, not he, must bear responsibility.)

The Trustees of the Rupert Brooke Estate, Professors Andrew Motion and Jon Stallworthy, distinguished poets and biographers both, supported the project from the outset – and generously allowed me full access to the enormous quantity of Brooke material at the library of King's College, Cambridge.

At the archive, the librarian, Jacqueline Cox, and her staff combined cool professionalism with kindness and knowledge.

In Rugby, I am indebted to Rugby School's librarian, Rusty Maclean, for allowing me access to Brooke material; and to local historian Dr Peter Miller, a notable authority on Brooke, for his hospitality, and for sharing his knowledge – in particular for an illuminating discussion of Brooke's health and final illness from the viewpoint of a professional medical man.

I have drawn deeply and shamelessly on the knowledge of previous Brooke biographers – who have been generous to a fault in discussing our mutual interest. Michael Hastings gave me fascinating letters and photos, and shared his own memories of meetings with Noel Olivier, one of the loves of Brooke's life. Mike Read likewise disclosed a generous fraction of his own vast knowledge of Brooke in many long conversations, and I am grateful also to Professor Paul Delany for his encouragement.

Dr Keith Clements, biographer of Brooke's nemesis, Henry Lamb, was endlessly helpful, and put me in touch with Lamb's daughter, Mrs Henrietta Phipps, who, despite the ancient antipathy, was more than kind. Frances Spurling, biographer of Duncan Grant, discussed with me his relationship with Rupert Brooke; and Richard Shone, an authority on Brooke's hated 'Bloomsberries', kindly allowed me to reproduce a rare nude photograph of Brooke's soul mate, Ka Cox.

Mr Peter Ward discussed memories of his father Dudley Ward, perhaps Brooke's closest friend.

Ann Olivier Bell, daughter of Bryn Olivier, was most frank in discussing the relations of her mother and aunts with Brooke.

Mr Mark Le Fanu, of the Society of Authors, was instrumental in securing me a writer's grant that kept the book afloat when its fate teetered in the balance.

Ms Charlotte Deane was an indefatigable picture researcher, and Mr Tim Freeborn of the *Daily Mail*'s financial staff helped me compare Edwardian currency values with those of today.

D. M. Thomas, poet, novelist, mentor and friend, showed me Brooke's grave on Skyros and greatly encouraged me when this project was but a gleam in my eye.

Mr Andrew Roberts, a historian with a special knowledge of Edwardian England, was kind enough to read the manuscript.

Lastly, it is no mere convention to thank my partner, Lally Freeborn. She lived the book with me, and, not least, reminded me to enquire into who cooked and cleaned for Rupert. I still don't know.

Nigel Jones

Introduction

What's in a name? 'Rupert Brooke – isn't it a romantic name?' trilled Lytton Strachey to Virginia Woolf after meeting the brilliant and handsome young Cambridge freshman who was about to conquer the university, just as he had cut a swathe across the sacred sward of Rugby School's famous Close.

It takes a huge leap of the imagination for us, at the end of the century whose batting he opened, to imagine what the mere words 'Rupert Brooke' conjured up for his contemporaries and the generations that followed his death *en route* to the blood-drenched beaches of Gallipoli. Those three syllables encapsulate a world: a timeless world of honeyed teas, cricket whites on greens, the rap of leather on willow and the mild ripple of applause that follows, punts languidly negotiating a river bend where weeping willows lean, girls in gypsy headscarves and floppy-haired young men; a world where – except at rural camps – someone else was always there to cook and clean. A world of class distinctions, rotten teeth and people who knew their place. But I find myself drifting into one of Brooke's 'list' poems, in which, simply by ticking off material objects in which he took delight, he attempted to summon and sum up a world to defy time, change, decay or, in one of his favourite words, 'transience'.

It is a measure of Brooke's success as a writer that it is so difficult for us to picture the Edwardian and Georgian period in which he bloomed except through the rosy-lensed prescription glasses that he provided. But the golden glow surrounding him and his friends, the misty aura that he so mysteriously casts over his era, is essentially sentimental and false. It is a myth created not so much by Brooke himself but by some of his friends, and by politicians, propagandists and a public hungry for heroes in a war of unprecedented ferocity and tragedy.

One of the many paradoxes about Rupert Brooke is that no one more bitterly loathed sentimentality than he did. E. M. Forster remarked that he did not envy anyone who applied to Brooke for sympathy, since his hatred of 'slosh' ran so deep that it had poisoned the 'eternal wellsprings' and curdled the milk of human kindness. And yet both Brooke's persona and his best-known poetry are steeped in mawkishness. 'He has clothed his attitude in fine words, but he has taken the sentimental attitude,' his fellow war poet Charles Hamilton Sorley justly remarked of the famous 1914 sonnets. Some of Brooke's lines have entered the language, certainly; but what lines – a glance at the *Penguin Dictionary of Quotations* gives the answer: 'Stands the Church clock at ten to three?/And is there honey still for tea?' 'If I should die, think only this of me:/That there's some corner of a foreign field/That is for ever England.' 'Now, God be thanked Who has matched us with His hour/And caught our youth, and wakened us from sleeping.' And so on. There is little sense here of the bitter Brooke whose sour 'love' sonnets usually ended with a spurt of vitriol at the beloved; nor of the 'sick' Brooke whose sonnet comparing seasickness to the pangs of love – "Tis hard, I tell ye/To choose 'twixt love and nausea, heart and belly' – so outraged his contemporaries; and not just for its awful closing rhyme.

Yet such paradoxes litter his life: the super-patriot of 1914, the 'chauvinistic fugelman', as Michael Holroyd characterizes him, was also the socialist who proclaimed in 1910: 'I *hate* the upper classes.' The 'Great Lover' of women was almost exclusively homosexual – in spirit if not often in flesh – at Rugby and Cambridge. The youth whose carefree charm dazzled (almost) everyone who met him could also admit that his air of easy grace was an assumed act, a careful performance: 'Oh yes, I did the fresh boyish stunt,' he boasted airily after his first meeting with a bedazzled Henry James, during which he poled 'the Master' down the Cam in a punt. Sure enough the besotted novelist joined the legion of Brooke's admirers, to the extent that his last published work was an introduction, dribbling with doting drool, to Brooke's posthumous *Letters from America*.

Brooke was a formidably energetic letter-writer – few weeks passed in his adult life without at least one, more often three or four, lengthy screeds splashing from his pen, to his biographers' mingled delight and despair – who was also permanently prey to nervous exhaustion. The Brooke whose sheer love and zest for life shines out in the scores of recollections and memoirs of him could speak and write privately with a scorn, prejudice, paranoia and downright madness that can still shock the unprepared reader. The open, smiling countenance hid a Dorian Gray face twisted by hatred of women, homosexuals, Jews, pacifists, promiscuity (except in himself);

and above all the group of former friends we now lump together under the term 'Bloomsbury'. The barefoot boy with the sun in his eyes and hair became a rabid ranter, obsessively raving about 'dirt', 'cleanliness', 'foulness' and threatening to shoot himself or his enemies. Plainly there is something wrong here; badly wrong.

Brooke was, in current jargon, 'a control freak'. Rigidly ruled and directed in his own early life by a mother whose tyrannical grip he never entirely escaped, and by the iron codes of boarding-school life, he subsequently demanded freedom for himself, yet could not bear to see the same privilege exercised by others – especially women. One of his more bizarre fantasies was the idea of kidnapping a woman who briefly obsessed him – Bryn Olivier – and 'going shares' with her with a male friend in Brighton's Metropole Hotel. Another face of his controlling tendency was his fears about Bryn taking a country walk on her own – so much so that he gravely warned her sister Noel against the danger of her being abducted in the street. So how did this hysterical bundle of prejudice, neurosis, nastiness and insanity come to exercise such a spell over so many of his contemporaries?

It was not only obviously susceptible figures like Henry James or his patron Eddie Marsh, but hard-bitten old buzzards like Herbert Asquith, Churchill, General Sir Ian Hamilton and D. H. Lawrence who fell swooning at his feet. He was welcome at the high tables of Cambridge colleges, and nursed by the Prime Minister's family at Downing Street in wartime; he conferred alone with Churchill at the Admiralty; he interviewed premiers; joined a West End chorus line; slept under the stars; seduced South Sea island maidens; and carved his name indelibly into the memories of a generation. In short, he was endowed with more than his fair share of that most intangible of all qualities: charm. He had it by the truckload.

So heavily laden with charm was Brooke that it became an insupportable burden. And it has long outlasted his brief life. One of his most critical biographers, Paul Delany, has the honesty to admit: 'There is something in Rupert Brooke and Neo-Paganism that still has power to charm, resist it or debunk it as we may.' As to what that 'something' is, Delany identifies it as 'hope. It is an emotion that, in any collective form, seems almost extinct today – deposed by its bastard child, ambition.' Delany also remarks that, from his earliest youth, Brooke was always performing before an unseen audience. Certainly, he was always painfully conscious of his place in posterity. At the end of a slightly callous letter to Eddie Marsh explaining why he would not be marrying the actress Cathleen Nesbitt – one of many women he pursued with apparent ardour only to reject when they began to look attainable – he scribbled in parentheses: 'This is the sort of letter that doesn't look well in a biography.'

Two years later, when his early death had ceased to be a possibility to be toyed with at leisure, he wrote to another lover, Ka Cox, from the ship that was taking him to extinction on the eve of the Gallipoli campaign: 'Dear child, I suppose you're about the best I can do in the way of a widow . . . They *may* want to write a biography! How am I to know if I shan't be eminent? . . . It's a good thing I die.' Brooke was right: 'They' did indeed want to write a biography; but the battles that ensued for possession of the barely cold corpse of his 'repper', as he called his reputation, would have both amused and amazed him. In the end, his friends failed him. They disobeyed his dying injunction to 'let the world know the poor truths' about him, and they buried the real Brooke beneath a heap of rubble as heavy as the marble chunks that were heaped on his tomb.

By the time he died Rupert Brooke was not just a minor poet whose charm and real, if limited, talent, had enchanted a generation of close friends. Thanks to the war's exigencies he had become a symbol of the nation's youth in arms, a name, a face and a body that could be conveniently corralled as the first steer for the slaughterhouse. Winston Churchill twirled the lasso: 'Rupert Brooke is dead,' he informed readers of *The Times* portentously: 'A voice had become audible, a note had been struck . . . more able to do justice to the nobility of our youth in arms . . . than any other . . . The voice has been swiftly stilled. Only the echoes and the memory remain; but they will linger.' After more in similar vein, Churchill concluded his propagandizing tribute: 'Joyous, fearless, versatile, deeply instructed, with classic symmetry of mind and body, he was all that one would wish England's noblest sons to be in days when no sacrifice but the most precious is acceptable, and the most precious is that which is most freely proffered.'

But the figure eulogized in this magnificent example of Churchillian rhetoric – and in countless poems and tributes by less gifted wordsmiths – was almost unrecognizable to Brooke's friends. As well as being 'joyous, fearless, versatile' and so on, the man they had known was also at times cold, cruel, pettish, weak, a poseur, anti-Semitic, anti-women, paranoid and childish. In short, he was a human being with a full flush of faults and flaws. The Brooke who was presented to the public was not a real man, but a gilded cardboard cut-out. Those who knew better kept their reservations to themselves. They shrouded the real man and refined the image, until their 'Rupert Brooke' bore as much resemblance to a living, breathing man as the outsized statue of a hunky Belgian male prostitute that was unveiled in the 1920s as a memorial to the poet on Skyros, the Greek island where he had died.

The first gilder who set to work was Eddie Marsh, whose memoir of Brooke, delayed until 1918 by the necessity of placating the dead poet's formidable mother, horrified his friends by making no mention of his intimate life at all: major friends like Noel Olivier or Cathleen Nesbitt were omitted altogether, and the central crisis of Brooke's life – the total mental and physical breakdown he suffered in 1912 – was discreetly left out of this anodyne account. By the time the account appeared, a huge wall of corpses separated Brooke's world from the grey, famished, flu-stricken, bereft post-war era. The poetry of Sassoon, Owen and Eliot more closely resembled such a wasteland – yet Brooke's poems continued to sell in spades, producing a healthy income for the three Georgian poets he had nominated as his heirs. Despite, or more likely because of, this popularity with the public, critical opinion turned irrevocably against Brooke, bracketing him with the Edwardian celebrants of an unreal England that had died with the shots at Sarajevo. His friends continued to grumble among themselves, but in the popular mind he was a sunny lightweight poet who had written a clutch of naively patriotic verses ludicrously celebrating the coming of the worst war in human history.

By 1930, when the death of Brooke's overbearing mother removed a boulder blocking the path of biographical enquiry, the world had worse things to worry about than the switchback emotions of a dead poet. Brooke's surviving friends remained reticent, and to ensure continued silence Mrs Brooke's gagging role was assumed by Geoffrey Keynes, a school friend of her son, and a man who worshipped both Brooke and his mother: 'I came to love her very dearly.' It was Keynes who wrested Brooke's papers from his designated literary executor, Eddie Marsh; Keynes who sat on his letters, until eventually producing a heavily bowdlerized version as late as 1968; and Keynes who discouraged any attempt to write an objective biography of the friend whom he described at the end of his own long life as 'quite the most wonderful person I have ever known'. An uncomplicated heterosexual who was able to overlook even the rampant homosexuality of his more famous elder brother John Maynard Keynes, Geoffrey Keynes waited until the 1950s before finding a man he felt could be entrusted to write a 'safe' official biography.

The man he and his fellow-Trustee, the even more cautious Dudley Ward, chose for this delicate task was a minor poet and opera librettist named Christopher Hassall. The Trustees were able to count on Hassall's discretion as he had written in 1955 a huge and exhaustive biography of Eddie Marsh, which, although 700 pages long, manages to avoid the topic of its subject's homosexuality. Hassall duly repaid their trust with another huge volume into which he stuffed almost every fact known about Brooke – except any mention of his sexuality, his paranoia or any other shadowy aspect of his brief existence. Although Hassall died of a heart attack just before publication of *Rupert Brooke: A Biography* in 1964, the most sensitive and secret areas of Brooke's life remained, for the time being, inviolate from enquiry. Even Hassall, however, left silent clues for a bolder biographer to follow: by colouring in the details of Brooke's everyday existence, he made the gaps stand out all the more glaringly.

In 1968 a bolder biographer did step forward: the young playwright Michael Hastings produced *The Handsomest Young Man in England*. This lavishly illustrated pictorial account of Brooke and his circle performed a necessary demolition job on both the myth of the untainted golden boy and the excessive anti-Brooke critical reaction that had damned most of his work to the limbo of the great unread. Hastings explained neatly why the Brooke myth had arisen. He pointed out how perfectly the poet embodied a pastoral dream of innocence and youth, and of a mythical pre-modern England. Finally, with the daring of youth and the sixties, Hastings hinted that the reluctance of Brooke's surviving friends like Keynes, Dudley Ward and Frances Cornford to expose the full truth about him had something to do with their fear of destroying a legend on which the foundations of their own lives rested.

Twelve years later, in 1980, the editor and critic John Lehmann published *Rupert Brooke: His Life and His Legend*, a brief and elegant account which told the story of Brooke's breakdown for the first time. Lehmann, who had known many of Brooke's friends, correctly identified the episode as the central crisis in his subject's life.

The slow process of revelation continued through the eighties and nineties with dribs and drabs of information leaking out at intervals from a variety of sources. In 1987 came a study, *The Neo-Pagans: Friendship and Love in the Rupert Brooke Circle* by Paul Delany, that began as a collective biography of the Olivier sisters and ended as the most striking revelation of Brooke's life and personality so far. Delany, the first writer to examine Brooke since the death of the watchful Keynes in 1982, gave chapter and verses from the poet's letters to illustrate his manic assault on Bloomsbury. Perhaps Delany went too far in his distaste for Brooke's ravings and slipperiness. Brooke may have often overreacted, but the Stracheys and most of the Bloomsberries were truly poisonous people, whose gossip about each other was bad enough, but whose malice about outsiders was absolutely toxic.

Brooke comes over as a surprisingly modern figure, with his emotions in such a hideous mess that the war and his death must have come as a blessed relief. This picture was reinforced by the appearance in 1990 of *Song of Love*, the inappropriately titled collection of the often blistering letters between Brooke and Noel Olivier, edited by Noel's granddaughter, Pippa Harris. Another piece from the vast jigsaw that is Brooke's correspondence fell into place in 1998 with the publication of his even more revealing letters to his oldest and most intimate friend, James Strachey: *Friends & Apostles*, edited by Keith Hale. The same year saw the appearance of *Forever England* by Mike Read, the disc jockey, an unashamed admirer of Brooke of the old school. To Read belongs the credit for discovering the existence of Brooke's probable illegitimate daughter, Arlice Raputo, by his Tahitian lover Taatamata.

Collectively, what all these books amount to is the presentation of a 'new' Brooke who is the almost complete antithesis of the sanitized super-schoolboy purveyed by Hassall and Keynes. The present book is an attempt to synthesize all this information – plus new material that I have turned up – and to give as balanced a judgement as possible on a mightily ill-balanced figure. I have been interested in Brooke since my own childhood, and the itch to discover what lay beneath the Peter Pan surface has never left me.

The legend burns on – I do not flatter myself that I have extinguished it – and it is clear that Brooke exercises the lasting appeal of a Keats or Shelley; poets whose youthful deaths in 'some foreign field' seem as potent as the verses they left behind. In an age of renewed interest in the Great War among imaginative writers and the reading public alike – witness the success of Sebastian Faulks's *Birdsong* and Pat Barker's *Regeneration* trilogy – it seems likely that Brooke's life and legend will loom still larger as he recedes into history. 'The echoes . . .' as Churchill prophesied, 'will linger' – though perhaps not in the way he had in mind.

Posterity may even prove kinder to the best of his poetry. His travel writing is vivid and leaps from the page even now, as do his letters – although not always for the right reasons. But even if neither his verse nor his prose ever returns to fashion, I believe Brooke will be remembered, like Byron, as a sexy star before his time. He was a more innocent Rimbaud, a fast-driving James Dean, a pre-rock Jim Morrison, who really did hope to die before he got old. As to why he told Ka: 'It's a good thing I die' – let's find out.

I

Breathing English Air

At 7.30 a.m. on 3 August 1887, the year of Queen Victoria's Golden Jubilee, Mrs Ruth Mary Brooke, wife to William Parker Brooke, schoolmaster, was safely delivered of a baby boy at the couple's home, 5 Hillmorton Road, Rugby, Warwickshire.

The sex of the child was something of a shock to Mrs Brooke. She had confidently anticipated the arrival of a girl, and what Mrs Brooke wanted she generally got. She had one son already, Richard, known as Dick in the family, born in 1881. A daughter, Edith Marjorie, followed in 1885, only to die the following June. The new baby, therefore, was fully intended to be a substitute for his recently dead sister; but alas, he was indisputably male.

If there was a lingering ambiguity over the new arrival's gender – his mother made no secret of her disappointment to her second son – a further dichotomy was built into his make-up by the names his parents chose for him: he was christened Rupert Chawner Brooke. 'Rupert' was his conventional father's improbably romantic choice – from the dashing Cavalier cavalry commander of the Civil War who impetuously led his forces to victory – and, more often, defeat – in that conflict. 'Chawner' was Mrs Brooke's contribution, chosen in direct contradiction of his first name, to commemorate a shadowy ancestor of her own, a contemporary of Prince Rupert who had been a fanatical Roundhead, a Puritan MP and, according to family legend, a regicide. Even if it is too fanciful to suggest, as some writers have done, that this tension between the names helped to mould Rupert Brooke's own divided nature, it is nevertheless symbolic of the splits that were to be so entrenched in the very foundations of his character.

The paternal side of Brooke's riven heritage can be traced back to the early sixteenth century and his most distinguished ancestor: Matthew Parker

(1504–75). A Norwich-born tailor's son, Parker successfully negotiated the murderous rapids of Tudor ecclesiastical politics. He rose from being private chaplain to the ill-fated Anne Boleyn to become Archbishop of Canterbury under her daughter, Elizabeth I. In this high office he skilfully presided over the Church of England's decisive schism with Rome.

The Parkers continued to live in Norfolk as wealthy gentry until November 1761, when Matthew's descendant John Parker, squire of Berry Hall, the family house at Great Walsingham, married off his daughter Anne to William Brooke from the nearby village of Geist.

The couple produced a daughter, also named Anne, who inherited Berry Hall while still a girl. The younger Anne, a woman of great wealth and status, married beneath herself in 1783 when she became the bride of a local farmer, John Reeve. At her parents' insistence, the groom changed his name on marrying to John Reeve Brooke. Their son, another John, further improved the family's economic standing and became a celebrated breeder of prize bulls. He married into another wealthy Norfolk family, the Englands. His bride, Ellen England Brooke, bore a son, Richard England Brooke, in 1821. Richard, the poet's grandfather, became the first member of the family to venture on to a wider stage than Norfolk when he inaugurated the Brookes' close connection with Cambridge University by graduating from Caius College and being ordained at Ripon in North Yorkshire in 1845.

The following year the Reverend Brooke married Harriet Hopkins, a Lincolnshire woman, and became Rural Dean at Hull (Brooke refers to 'the sly shade of a Rural Dean' in his poem 'The Old Vicarage, Grantchester') before settling as Rector of Bath Abbey, where he was to remain for 20 years. The couple produced a typically Victorian brood of children – four sons and two daughters. The boys all attained academic distinction. The eldest, Alan, became Provost of King's College, Cambridge, while the second son, William Parker Brooke, although outshone academically by his elder brother, achieved a solidly successful career as a public-school master.

William Parker Brooke was born at his father's parsonage at Sowerby, Lincolnshire, in 1850. He was educated at Haileybury, in Hertfordshire, one of a new breed of public schools dedicated, after the example of Thomas Arnold's Rugby, where Parker Brooke was to crown his career, to training the sons of Britain's governing classes to rule both the Empire and their own restless inner selves with rods of iron. A quiet, conformist boy, with a withdrawn manner, Parker Brooke still had some steel in his soul, at least as a youngster.

Although his diminutive stature – he was just five feet three – made him a target of schoolboy bullying, he was not broken by the Spartan regime of Haileybury: on the contrary, he thrived there, and chose to spend the rest of his life within similar institutions. He became Head of School, captained the First XI at cricket and won the senior prizes in Latin and Greek. This distinction in the Classics earned him a place at Trinity College, Cambridge, in 1869. After transferring to King's College, he graduated in 1873, and was considered so brilliant that he was granted the signal honour of becoming the first King's Fellow not to have been educated at Eton, King's sister foundation. Provost Okes was less than effusive when welcoming the new Kingsman to the ranks of the Fellows, commenting sourly: 'Let us hope that this new leaven will not leaven the whole lump.' By this time Parker Brooke was used to swallowing such slights.

Freighted with high academic honours, Parker Brooke had no difficulty in obtaining a post as housemaster at Fettes, known as the 'Scottish Eton', when the recently founded Edinburgh school required a co-head for its School House. The new master found a congenial colleague in one of his fellow-housemasters who came from a similar clerical background. The Reverend Charles Clement Cotterill was a robust specimen of that peculiarly English limb of the Church Militant, a muscular Christian socialist, after the model of luminaries like Charles Kingsley and the great Thomas Arnold. Although the mild-mannered Brooke must have been shocked by some of Cotterill's radical political views, he deferred to and respected his forceful new friend. Towering over Brooke physically and given to preaching his decided opinions in a harsh and grating voice, Cotterill was a naturally dominant man. Brooke was a natural follower.

Two years after Parker Brooke arrived at Fettes, Cotterill was joined at the school by his sister, Ruth Mary, who came to Edinburgh as a house matron to assist her bachelor brother in managing his responsibilities. Born in 1848, that year of European revolution, and hence two years older than her future husband, Ruth Mary Cotterill shared with him a Lincolnshire heritage, her father hailing from Brigg in that county. Also like Brooke, she was a child of the cloth. Her father, uncle and brother were all Anglican priests, and it was in her father's parish in Stoke-on-Trent that she was born and brought up. She shared her brother's domineering ways and many of his characteristics – including a commanding height, a harshly shrill voice and an imperious will. These, together with an extreme inquisitiveness, made her ideally suited to ferreting out the innermost secrets of the boys in her charge, and indeed of the little man who now, with characteristic caution and diffidence, began to lay siege to her armoured heart.

3

Ruth Mary Cotterill's physique was as striking as her character. Tall and stately, she was proud of her looks: she had a retroussé nose and small but piercing eyes, with lids that drooped down at the sides. All these genetic traits were passed to her second son. From his father, Brooke was to inherit his blue eyes, though not the goggling look of the orbs themselves; his fair hair; and his clear, almost translucent skin – variously described as 'pink', 'golden' or 'girlish' – which, to its owner's frequent humiliation, betrayed his confusion and embarrassment at moments of high stress by hectic blushes. In the years to come there would be much for Brooke to blush about.

William Parker Brooke's courtship of Miss Cotterill, as befitted his conventional personality, was stealthy and prudent. It crept steadily forward until, in the spring of 1879, Miss Cotterill graciously consented to the announcement of their engagement. On 18 December of that year the couple were married in St Mary's Cathedral, Edinburgh. The ceremony was performed by the Bishop, Henry Cotterill, who was the bride's uncle.

As there was no provision for married masters at Fettes, the school's head, Dr Potts, a former assistant headmaster at Rugby, contacted that school's headmaster, Dr Jex-Blake, and prevailed on him to give Parker Brooke, sight unseen, a job. The vacant post was that of Tutor at Rugby's School Field House. A fortnight after their marriage, the newly-weds found themselves on the endless platform – the longest in Europe – of Rugby station, as they arrived in the small town where they were to spend the rest of their lives.

Rugby was dominated, both physically and culturally, by the looming mass of Rugby School, then enjoying its heyday as the standard-bearer of the English public-school ethos that was setting the standard for lesser institutions to imitate and emulate wherever British power and influence prevailed. Founded in 1667, and content over the centuries with its relative obscurity as a school where prosperous Midlands gentlemen and farmers sent their sons to acquire some social polish and a rudimentary Classical education, Rugby was transformed in 1828 with the appointment of Dr Thomas Arnold as headmaster.

From the moment he began to rule Rugby's roost until his death in 1842, Arnold imposed his ideology upon the school with feverish energy, an iron will and a laser vision no less intense for the blinkered narrowness of its confines. He found the school a small, moribund, provincial backwater, and left it the most influential educational institution in Britain – and thus, at the height of Empire, of the world. A passionate Anglican –

in an age when this was not a contradiction in terms – Arnold saw in the seething cities of industrial England merely 'a mass of evil' – a fetid swamp of sin awaiting a health-giving drainage, a spiritual sewage system. He resolved to transform Rugby into a nursery for turning out truly Christian gentlemen. His programme was summed up in his three ideals: first, religious and moral principle; second, gentlemanly conduct; and third, intellectual ability.

The ordering of these precepts is significant. In a break with tradition Arnold, an ordained priest, made himself school chaplain as well as head-master – assuming the dual function of the school's spiritual as well as worldly leader – and proclaiming his intention of making the school chapel the hub of Rugby's life. 'Gentlemanly conduct' was instilled into the boys by a mixture of carrot and stick. Hoarse injunctions to beware of 'beastliness' were dinned into the boys during Arnold's moralizing and seemingly eternal Sunday sermons. These, coupled with savage floggings administered to backsliders, soon made Rugby a stew of sanctimonious hypocrisy, heavy with the sentimental homoeroticism so familiar from the pages of *Tom Brown's Schooldays* – a brilliant piece of special pleading for the Arnoldian view of the universe.

Arnold's vaunted 'intellectual ability' was in practice confined to screwing the rudiments of Greek and Latin into his reluctant charges. The subjects that were the real sinews of the Empire that the boys were being trained to build and rule – administration, industry and technology – were conspicuous by their absence from the school curriculum. As a result, the typical products of Rugby were long on religious repression, skilled at declaiming Horace or translating Homer, matchless at the game to which the school had given its name, but hopelessly under-equipped at dealing with their own emotions or the complex demands of the modern world.

It may not have been Arnold's intention to send out his armies of young men with hearts of stone and heads of bone; muscle-bound flannelled fools and muddied, muddled oafs – but this was often the effect of his theories so ruthlessly applied. In one field, however, the good doctor could not be faulted: he was a brilliant propagandist. Works like *Tom Brown's Schooldays* spread his message far and wide, and Rugby's image became the model for an education seen by its admirers as the acme of civilized attainment. A whole crop of new schools sprang up, overtly dedicated to copying Arnold's methods and results: Haileybury, Fettes, Lancing, Uppingham, Radley were all examples of the new breed; and older schools such as Eton, Harrow, Winchester and Westminster were forced to change their ways and conform to the Arnoldian model.

In the end, Arnold failed in his avowed mission to re-Christianize England. He was not able even to convert his own household. His son, the poet and educationalist Matthew Arnold, became one of the most influential sceptics of the late-Victorian era, hymning the ebbing of the 'sea of faith' with scarcely concealed glee. The rigid rules of Thomas Arnold's Rugby were bound to produce their own reaction – and the life of Brooke, himself a quintessential product of the Rugby system, was to embody that reaction in all its terrible complexity.

The house where Mr and Mrs Brooke began their life at Rugby adjoined the school's sweeping seventeen-acre Close, the legendary birthplace of Rugby football. Their home was a two-storey red-brick villa on the corner of Church Walk, with twin gables and a bow window on either side of the front door. It was a modestly comfortable dwelling for a schoolmaster and his burgeoning family: a small front garden and gate gave access to the pavement and the world beyond, and there was a tiny functional backyard. Here all the Brooke children were born, and here William Parker Brooke, much to his muted dismay, began to get the full measure of the formidable woman he had married.

Whatever his scholarly achievements, from the moment of his marriage William Parker Brooke became an ever dimmer presence in the life of his family, like a fading sepia print. Photographs show a miserable-looking man, with sad, flinching eyes and a face half-hidden by a luxuriant Nietzschean moustache. 'Nor,' as a biographer remarks, 'was it hard to see from whom he was hiding.' He developed eccentric habits, like taking his dog into classes, and – to the huge delight of the boys – he frequently jiggled coins and keys in his trouser pockets. The boys suspected him of playing what they called 'pocket billiards' and he acquired the indelible nickname 'the Tooler'. His wife, by extension, became 'Ma Tooler'.

The fact that 'the Tooler' was in thrall to his spouse was well known to the boys: her dominance was rumoured to extend to ordering her husband into the town's streets by night to collect horse droppings to manure her garden. Even if apocryphal, this widely believed story sums up the nature of the Brookes' marriage. There was little overt domestic discord in the household, however; if only because Parker Brooke accepted his subordinate position with at most an occasional muttered protest – 'It *is* so, after all' – after losing yet another battle of wills with his wife.

Parker Brooke retreated into himself. Henpecked and frustrated, he neglected his work, became increasingly absent-minded and dreamed of the man he might have been. The opinion of one of his pupils, Geoffrey

Keynes, contemporary and devoted friend to Rupert, can serve as Parker Brooke's epitaph: 'He was a kindly man, but without any particular understanding of, or special sympathy with, the minds of adolescent boys, and my feelings towards him were and remained indifferent.'

Brooke himself shared the prevailing contempt for his father. In a letter to another faithful friend, Dudley Ward, written shortly before his father's death in 1910, he described him as a 'very pessimistic man, given to brooding, and without much inside to fall back on'.

No one could be indifferent to Mrs Brooke. She had, says Keynes, a 'loud, harsh voice and an alarming manner. She had little sense of humour and seldom laughed . . . I quailed before her for several years, but in the end came to love her very dearly.' Keynes's devotion to Mrs Brooke's memory is not so surprising. She had taken his side in his battle with another of Brooke's admirers, Eddie Marsh, for possession of the dead poet's literary estate. In the end, with her support Keynes succeeded in wresting Brooke's papers from Marsh, in flagrant violation of the poet's wishes. Writing from the ship taking him to his death, Brooke had specifically appointed Marsh as his literary executor.

Keynes and Marsh are at one, however, in agreeing on Mrs Brooke's humourlessness: 'How someone so without humour, and narrow to that degree, could have produced Rupert, is beyond me,' an exasperated Marsh wrote after she had blocked publication of his innocuous memoir of Brooke for three years.

Whatever her qualities of mind and purpose, Mrs Brooke was a distinctly unlovable person. Severe, hard and self-righteous, she combined an unbendable will with narrow moral rectitude and an energetic determination to rule the lives of others to a very unattractive degree. Much of her second son's driving energy was devoted for too many of his mature years to evading and avoiding his mother's unceasing vigilance, and to concocting elaborate and absurd schemes to hoodwink her about the true state of his life and affections. He wrote more letters to his mother than to any of his many correspondents, yet they are almost worthless as a true record of his doings and feelings. Even as he sailed to his death in the Aegean he remained in the same state of paralysed awe of her as he had been as a child. In his last letter to his most durable love, Ka Cox, he begged her not to tell his mother the true story of their tangled relationship: 'you'd probably better not tell her much. Let her be. Let her think we might have married.' Fear of his mother ran so deep, it seems, that it followed him into the valley of the shadow of death itself.

These habits of deceit, literally learned at his mother's knee, soon seeped into all areas of Brooke's life, so that his relations with his friends and lovers were also marked by lies, evasions and deception – not least self-deception.

It is no surprise to learn that Mrs Brooke, with the heritage of her family's Evangelical radicalism and their social conscience, was an ardent supporter of the then dominant Liberal party, as well as a 'Guardian of the Poor' and Rugby's first woman magistrate. In her all the worst traits of the Victorian Nonconformist spirit coalesce to create a uniquely unsympathetic personality type: bossy, shrill, narrow, nosy – the whole armoured in an armadillo-like strait-jacket of moral righteousness. One of Brooke's greatest tragedies is that he was, with his inbred puritanism, truly his mother's son.

The surroundings in which the infant Rupert was taken by his mother for his first outings in the autumn of 1887 were dominated by the sacred sward of the Close and by the architect William Butterfield's imposing Italianate additions to the school buildings, its recent red and yellow brickwork gleaming raw. Chief among the new buildings was the cathedral-sized chapel, completed in 1872. Here, one day, an idealized plaque depicting a swan-necked, bare-shouldered Brooke would take pride of place in the chapel's own Poet's Corner, sandwiched between memorials to other literary Rugbeians, including Matthew Arnold, Lewis Carroll, Arthur Hugh Clough ('Say not, the struggle naught availeth') and Walter Savage Landor ('I strove with none; for none was worth my strife;/Nature I loved, and next to Nature, Art;/I warmed both hands before the fire of Life;/It sinks, and I am ready to depart').

Other local landmarks to which Brooke was wheeled in his pram included the gloomy Clifton Road municipal cemetery, the ultimate resting-place of his parents; and the new Clock Tower, erected in the Market Place as Rugby's contribution to the Queen's Jubilee. The tower and Rupert, Mrs Brooke liked to observe, arrived together.

With the birth of a third son, Alfred, in 1891, the Brooke family was complete. Possibly Mrs Brooke gave up after the disappointment of yet another male child. Or perhaps Parker Brooke's growing gloom and scholastic responsibilities distracted him from his marital duties. These included, in the year of Alfred's birth, the housemastership of School Field House. The family left the cramped confines of Hillmorton Road for the more commodious surroundings of School Field House, with its towering chimneys and ivy-clad walls, safe within the closed precincts of the school itself.

The change in their circumstances brought some financial improvement for the Brookes. By becoming housemistress, Ruth Brooke was able to amass a small but significant profit on the fees paid for the board and lodging of the 50 or so boys in her care. Responsibility for this extended family also gave her power-hungry instincts free rein, and even Christopher Hassall, most sympathetic to her of all Brooke's biographers, is compelled to admit: 'She was . . . not unsympathetic, so long as you were doing exactly as you were told.'

Outside the school walls Rugby, the place where Brooke was born, educated and to which until the end of his life he continually if reluctantly returned, remained essentially what it has always been: an ordinary town in a largely rural county. But, close to the geographical centre of the country, it was also the historic heartland of England, in the Warwickshire of Shakespeare, Avon and the forest of Arden.

Writing to Lady Eileen Wellesley on the eve of the war that was to take his life, Brooke describes a valedictory drive in his mother's car to the scenes of his childhood, taken on 2 August 1914, the last Sunday of the old world that was about to vanish for ever. Beneath the irony, and the playful posturing so typical of Brooke in his out-to-impress style, it is a poignant and very fond farewell:

> It's the sort of country I adore. I'm a Warwickshire man. Don't talk to me of Dartmoor or Snowdon or the Thames or the lakes. I know the *heart* of England. It has a hedgy, warm bountiful dimpled air. Baby fields run up and down the little hills, and all the roads wriggle with pleasure. There's a spirit of rare homeliness about the houses and the countryside, earthy, uneccentric yet elusive, fresh, meadowy, gaily gentle. It is perpetually June in Warwickshire, and always six o'clock of a warm afternoon . . . Here the flowers smell of heaven; there are no such larks as ours, and no such nightingales; the men pay more than they owe; and the women have very great and wonderful virtue, and that, mind you, by no means through the mere absence of trial. In Warwickshire there are butterflies all the year round and a full moon every night . . . and every man can sing 'John Peel'. Shakespeare and I are Warwickshire yokels. What a county!

This prose passage, aching with sentimental nostalgia, has clear echoes, whether conscious or not, of Brooke's two most celebrated poems: 'The Old Vicarage, Grantchester':

> The women there do all they ought;
> The men observe the Rules of Thought

and the poem he was about to write, 'The Soldier':

> A dust whom England bore, shaped, made aware,
>   Gave, once, her flowers to love, her ways to roam,
> A body of England's, breathing English air,
>   Washed by the rivers, blest by suns of home.

But, as Brooke's letter to Lady Eileen goes on to acknowledge, such tranquillity was deceptive. Just over the horizon of green woods and fields sprawled Birmingham and the Black Country:

> This is nonsense; and I will grant you that Richmond Park is lovelier than all the Midlands, and certainly better inhabited. For Hampden was just too full of the plutocracy of Birmingham, short, crafty, proudly vulgar men, for all the world like heroes of Arnold Bennett's novels. They were extraordinarily dressed, and for the most part in very expensive clothes, but without collars. I think they'd started in collars, but removed them by the way. They rolled out of their cars, and along the street, none so much as five foot high, all hot, and canny to the point of unintelligibility, emitting the words 'Eh . . .' or 'Ah, lad . . .' at intervals. They were profound, terrifying, and of the essence of Life: but unlovely.

Brooke here exhibits all the terror of the middle class when confronted by the workers and the *nouveaux riches* who were actually making the guns and screws that held together the whole Imperial edifice: they appear to him as troglodytic interlopers from another world: dark, tiny, mouthing an unintelligible language, at least as threatening as the foes he was about to confront on the battlefield. No one growing up in Rugby at the turn of the century could fail to be uncomfortably aware of the subterranean stirrings beneath the crust of the Midlands mud.

The town, cradle of Rugby football, that ritualized warfare, rough yet fair, steered uncertainly into the new century with one foot stepping hesitantly towards a fearful new world of industry, social unrest and the questioning of time-hallowed tradition, while the other remained firmly mired in the Midlands loam. Even today, on Sundays Rugby remains wrapped in the Sabbath torpor of which Brooke frequently complained. But frozen, multicoloured pools of vomit on the morning pavements tell of a different Rugby, a Saturday-night party; a more ancient and Merrier England. Another duality for an already confused boy to wrestle with. A very English place, then, where an essentially English poet might try to grow up.

In 1897 Brooke, aged ten, was released from the restraints of his governess, Mrs Tottenham, whose watch over him had been extended for longer than usual. This was due to his mother's worries about his already delicate health. He was dispatched down the road to Hillbrow, a preparatory school where boys destined for public school, especially Rugby, were readied for their fate. Brooke was spared the full ordeal of boarding school, however – he attended Hillbrow as a day boy, escorted to and from the premises by his elder brother Dick.

Hillbrow was the domain of yet another dominant female, Mrs T. B. Eden, wife of the headmaster. She had a habit of reading Dickens aloud to the assembled forty or so boys on Sunday evenings. The school's physical environment was not the best place for a delicate boy of uncertain health: its stone corridors were bone-chillingly cold in winter; and summer dust exacerbated the frequent bouts of 'pink-eye' (conjunctivitis) that often laid Brooke low.

Despite these handicaps, he seemed to make his mark, if a letter from Tom Eden to Parker Brooke is any guide: 'I send Rupert's reports. I hope he may get many as good. His work certainly promises well. He might begin Greek as he understands Latin as far as he has learn't.' Brooke's early school reports confirm this picture of a gifted and able boy; in Latin he is described as 'careful and industrious – he has used his head more than most boys'. In English: 'He works well and answers intelligently.' His general conduct is described as 'Quite satisfactory'.

In 1898 at Hillbrow Brooke made the first of many early friendships that would last for most of his life. This one was at once more passionate, more strained and more enduring than most. James Strachey, an almost exact contemporary, was the youngest of the brilliant and eccentric progeny of General Sir Richard and Lady Jane (née Grant) Strachey, who had produced five sons and five daughters. Like Brooke, James was burdened by an overweening mother similarly disappointed in her son's maleness. He seems almost pre-programmed to be Brooke's closest confidant.

The two boys' similarities even extended to their hairstyles – a fringe cut straight across the forehead. It was not a fashion designed to endear them to the heartier type of teacher. Indeed the headmaster, Tom Eden, is recalled yelling to the two friends: 'Back to the changing room, both of you, and part your hair properly! You look like a couple of girls!' Girls! Again, that accursed accusation. It was a charge doomed to haunt Brooke, even from the mouth of a friend, as in Edward Thomas's description: 'His clear, rosy skin helped to give him the look of a great girl.'

The physical impression made by Brooke on older men, particularly those homosexually inclined, was almost always striking, and often overwhelming enough to lead them to suspend critical judgement on his intellectual gifts. For example, the habitually cynical Lytton Strachey, James's eldest brother, wrote to his fellow-homosexual John Maynard Keynes – elder brother of Brooke's friend Geoffrey – after meeting Brooke in 1905 ahead of his arrival at Cambridge: 'He has rather nice – but you know – yellow ochreish hair, and a healthy young complexion.' Three years on, writing to Virginia Stephen, another future friend of Brooke's, Strachey was more smitten: 'Rupert Brooke, isn't it a romantic name? – with pink cheeks and bright yellow hair – it sounds horrible, but it wasn't.'

Given this capacity for striking his elders silly with admiration and desire, it is small wonder that Brooke would be both unhealthily aware of the effect produced by his looks and in some perplexity over his sexual identity. One way of emphasizing his masculinity was by his prowess on the playing field, though this was not to come to its fullest fruition until his public-school years. Another was in rampant male competitiveness. 'Aha!' he exults in a Hillbrow journal. 'One [mark] more than Strachey in Latin!'

Even at Hillbrow Brooke had begun a habit of winning school prizes. The Michaelmas term of 1898 ended with him taking second place in a recitation contest for his rendering of an 'Ode on the Death of the Duke of Wellington'. The first prize went to another Hillbrow boy, his senior by three years, also fated to interweave in his future life. This was the Stracheys' cousin Duncan Grant, painter and future lover of the Blooms-bury luminaries Maynard Keynes and Vanessa Bell. Like the Stracheys, the mainly homosexual Grant was to fall briefly under Brooke's spell. His attraction to Brooke was at its height in the autumn of 1911, when they dined at London's fashionably bohemian Eiffel Tower restaurant and afterwards visited a cinema to see the film *Cesare Borgia*. 'But,' notes Grant's biographer, Frances Spurling, well used to her subject's fickle attitude to love: 'It was a fleeting emotion.'

It was in 1899, during an Easter holiday on the north Cornwall coast at St Ives, that another piece of Brooke's chequered future fell into place. Here he first met the future Queen of Bloomsbury, Virginia Stephen, and played cricket with her on the beach. He was 12, she five years his senior. This was a foretaste of later shared aquatic delights when Brooke would invite her to visit him at his home in Grantchester outside Cambridge, and together they bathed nude in Byron's Pool on the Cam. Memories of the Cornish holiday inspired Brooke's fledgling literary efforts.

On his return to Rugby he compiled a hand-written magazine containing a description of a Cornish castle and a short story in which two burglars are apprehended when they rob the same house and disturb each other. These jottings show no particular promise to mark him out from the offerings of the average schoolboy, nor evidence of the themes that would come to preoccupy him – beyond a brief moan about the stultifying tedium of a typical Rugby Sunday. Nevertheless, with his new-found friends and his blossoming interest in writing, the future lineaments of his life were gathering around him.

James Strachey soon left Hillbrow to become a day boy at St Paul's School in Hammersmith, London, but Rupert met him again on his first holiday of the new century, at Easter 1900, when the Brookes and the Stracheys ran into each other on Brighton sea front. Brooke was introduced to Lytton for the first time, but the future critic and iconoclast of Thomas Arnold failed to remember this early encounter with a boy who would one day demonize him as one of his chief hate figures.

The opening year of the new century saw the first serious challenge in contemporary times to Britain's military might. The two small Boer republics of South Africa attempted to fight free of London's rule. The Boer War divided opinion at home. The vast majority fiercely supported the war effort, but a vociferous radical minority of pro-Boers argued for the right of small nations to go their own way, thus questioning the whole morality of Britain's imperial mission. Mrs Brooke, as a keen and committed Liberal, attended a pro-Boer meeting in Rugby. She was startled to see her 12-year-old son sitting among the meeting's organizers on the platform. One steely glint from his mother's hawk-like eyes was enough to persuade the boy to abandon his platform perch and join her. It was not the last time that Mrs Brooke would face a rebellion by her son, nor the last time that she would successfully stifle it.

Evidence of the diverging views of mother and son also survive in an album presented to Brooke on his thirteenth birthday. Here the pair answer a written catechism on their attitudes to life. Asked to name their favourite amusements, Mrs Brooke claims cycling and watching others play games; her son lists cricket, tennis and football – before admitting to reading and cards. As her 'favourite qualities in a man' Mrs Brooke characteristically gives 'earnestness of purpose' and 'moral courage'. Brooke, ironically, given his later penchant for carrying on multiple simultaneous relationships, names 'fidelity' – followed by 'intelligence'. His favourite reading, conventionally enough, is Kipling and the Sherlock Holmes stories, while his idea of 'misery' is 'Ignorance, poverty and OBSCURITY'. His aim in life, he writes, is: 'To be top of the tree in everything.'

2

Youth is Stranger than Fiction

Despite his subservience to his mother, Brooke, like his father, felt affronted by what he saw as his shameful servitude to her powerful personality. Indeed, his first recorded words, uttered at the age of seven, sound an authentic note of rebellion. His mother caught him bullying his younger brother, Alfred, and chided him for his 'cowardice'. She then threatened him with more severe punishment should he repeat his behaviour. 'Then you'd be the coward,' he smartly replied.

Another form of revolt against the smothering tyranny of home was his ill health, although Brooke's frequent bouts of sickness are doubtless also attributable to an inherently weak immune system. His elder brother Dick and his father both died early. But there is a psychosomatic hysteria behind the many maladies that laid him low in periods of crisis throughout his life. His first surviving letter, written in May 1901 to Owen O'Malley, a Hillbrow chum who had recently left the school – and who was destined to become Britain's ambassador to Hungary – is written from one of his many sickbeds, to which he had been consigned after collapsing during the school's Sports Day. Couched in cod Olde English and employing the boys' nicknames – Brooke was 'Oyster' for reasons that remain obscure – the letter addresses the future diplomat as 'Child', a patronizing epithet that Brooke would employ with maddening frequency in his letters throughout his life, particularly to female correspondents. It begins: 'Wherefore sendest thou strange manuscripts adorned with divers devices which bring back to the mind thoughts of a time which is past?' and continues to report the circumstances of his collapse: 'On the ninth day of May the sports for athletics were held and I did win many heats, and when I had finished running 3600 inches – a boy named B. Foote was about 70 inches behind. And the next day I was ill and unable to compete wherefore my temper was exceeding warm.' Brooke reveals that his illness also barred him from the scholarship exam to enter Rugby School, and concludes: 'Forgive my letter being strange in manner. The reason is that much trouble hath unhinged my brain; wherein I resemble Hamlet. And if you gaze closely on my portrait which I have sent you, you will see a wild look in my eyes; denoting insanity.'

In this early example of what would eventually become an enormous correspondence with a huge cast of friends, Brooke already exhibits some of the traits that would mark his entire life – including most notably the irrepressible need to both dramatize and mock himself. A devouring self-absorption is evident, along with an insistent exhibitionism. This stance, so marked at so early an age, would gradually harden until it becomes impossible to separate the poser from the pose.

Even though Brooke lacked a scholarship, his father's position at Rugby was enough to swing open the school's doors, and in September 1901 he became a new boy in Parker Brooke's School Field House. This apparently smooth progress was actually a regression. However illusory the independence Brooke had enjoyed at Hillbrow, at least the few hundred yards that separated home and school had been a step towards freedom. Now he was back under his parents' roof, and his relations with the other boys in the House were dogged by the fact that he was the son of the housemaster and housemistress, and so had one foot in the enemy camp.

This ambiguous position added another important dimension to the emerging divisions in Brooke's nature. He had to balance his sheer survival in the school, eventually earning the respect and even admiration of his peers, with holding on to his parents' approval at home. It was a precarious feat, but somehow Brooke achieved it. One strategy for survival beyond the green baize door that separated his domestic quarters from the bear garden of the school beyond was the occasional flicker of revolt against his mother. A possibly apocryphal but nevertheless revealing story has Mrs Brooke opening the dumb waiter that came rumbling up from the kitchens in the bowels of the House and finding Brooke crouched inside, with a blasphemous notice attached which read: 'Mother, behold thy son.'

Brooke's first year at Rugby was largely taken up with learning the bewilderingly complex regulations governing public-school life: attending the thrice-daily roll-call; running to address the needs of older boys whenever the bellowed call of 'Fag!' summoned the juniors deputed to act as the seniors' menial servants; understanding when and where it was permitted to stroll with one's hands in one's pockets, or meet a boy from another House: even the son of a housemaster was not exempt from the hallowed codes of Rugby life. Nor was that life a soft one.

The boys were summoned from their narrow beds at 5.45 a.m. to endure a cold shower – the proverbial remedy against libidinous thoughts and the masturbation that accompanied them – and their first lesson before breakfast. The school curriculum consisted of 11 hours daily of solid work at Latin, Greek, English, French, Scripture, History, Geography and Maths. As his schoolfellows slowly came round to accepting Brooke's curious double life – among them, yet not of them – they were also charmed into giving him their affection.

He had most of the attributes that usually make for popularity among schoolboys: fresh good looks, a tall, athletic build – his full-grown height was five feet eleven – and an appropriate prowess on both the rugby and the cricket fields. Coupled with these were a deceptively uncomplicated and cheerful disposition and the first glimmerings of that charm and self-deprecating wit that were to become legendary.

His pleasing physical appearance was now topped off by a classically handsome face with peachy, rose-petal skin. Allowed more leeway with his hair styling, he had replaced the close-cropped look of early years with a mop of hair, fair and tinged with reddish gold, which he wore increasingly long as his seniority at the school increased. This style was both a fairly safe gesture of nonconformity and a nod to the *fin-de-siècle* decadence of the 1890s; an aesthetic mode self-consciously adopted by Brooke, who was blissfully unaware that it was *passé* outside the cloistered backwater of Rugby. The radiance of Brooke's looks was only marred by his slightly short bow legs, which won him the nickname 'Bowes'. The bestowing of nicknames at public school, unless they are palpable insults, is invariably a sign of general acceptance as a 'good chap'.

Parker Brooke continued to be a dim and distant presence in his son's life. His absent-mindedness increasing, he was knocked down by a hansom cab while standing in the middle of the road lost in a fit of abstraction. He sustained a broken arm. Behind the green baize door he coached Brooke in the Classics and watched with quiet approval his son's elevation to the House First XI in cricket and First XV in rugby.

Off the Close, Brooke joined Rugby's Officer Training Corps (OTC) – an almost obligatory commitment in Britain's public schools in an increasingly bellicose era. In the short morning of his life, as in its closing weeks, he posed for group photographs with the other officer cadets, his long hair tucked tidily inside a cap, his body clad in one of the newly issued khaki uniforms currently being given their first blooding on the South

African veldt in the closing stages of the Boer War.

If his school reports are to be believed, academically Brooke was a capable rather than an outstanding student. His form master – and godfather – Robert Whitelaw commented laconically at the end of his first term: 'Has begun well.' Parker Brooke tactfully left the space for the housemaster's comments blank, though by 1903 he was emboldened to remark with forgivable paternal protectiveness: 'Where he fails it is certainly not from want of time spent on work.' In response, Rugby's headmaster, Dr Herbert James, known to the boys as 'the Bodger', noted acidly: 'He must think about his work as well as just give time to it.' 'The Bodger' also noted that Brooke was 'more of a linguist than a thinker' and, in 1905, was still nagging away at his want of application: '[He] has much ability but he needs to work harder at the parts of his work he likes least.'

By the Trinity term of 1906, with Brooke's departure to Cambridge looming, his continued lack of appetite for the grind of academic application still bothers Dr James: 'Work rather below par this term: possibly from indifferent health . . . [he] rather dislikes detail.' Then, in an upbeat closing comment, he concedes: 'Where he is good, on the purely literary side, he is capable of very brilliant results.' Though scarcely a nonconformist, still less a rebel, Brooke was apt to indulge in minor acts of subversion, as a note from one of his teachers, R. Butler, to his father plaintively complains: 'Dear Brooke, I fear I must complain of Rupert for bribing a musician to play during my 4th lesson.'

Under the seemingly tranquil surface of school life, however, unsuspected or at least ignored by Mr and Mrs Brooke, darker currents swirled. Aged 14 when he went up to Rugby, Brooke was immersed in the turbulence of puberty, and in the only outlets possible for the fevered erotic longings of adolescents in an all-male public-school environment. The practical fact that the boys – at least during term time – were rigorously segregated from female company at once created and chimed with a prevailing homoerotic ethos that had, by the turn of the century, become so marked in Britain's ruling class. The evangelizing zeal with which those hearty Christian masters hunted down physical manifestations of homosexuality within their schools, no less than the dire warnings issued from the pulpits of their chapels on the horrendous consequences of 'self-abuse' and the hypocritical homophobia shown in the Oscar Wilde trials of 1895, testified to the obsessive interest in a subject that loomed large in the collective unconscious of England's Establishment.

Brooke, an attractive boy with an active libido and literary leanings, was

17

not immune to the heavy homoerotic atmosphere that hung over the school. In succumbing to that atmosphere, he was going along with peer-group mores as he did when joining the OTC or the House cricket team. Where Brooke was unusual was in openly confessing to his homosexual feelings and activities both at the time and later. At the height of his ill-fated passion for Ka Cox in 1912 he reported a revealing exchange with his mother: '"Katherine Cox seems," she almost beamed, "to go everywhere." "Oh yes," I agreed: and then we were fairly launched on you. I felt the red creep slowly up – Damn! It's just as it always was; even from the time when the holiday mention, at lunch, of the boy of the moment, in the House (with apologies, dear!) left me the level red of this blotting paper, and crying with silent wrath.'

This passage is so replete with Rupertisms as to constitute a self-portrait in miniature. As such it is worth analyzing in some detail. The opening sentence shows his tendency to mock his nearest and dearest – especially his doting mother – but always behind their backs. 'I felt the red creep slowly up – Damn!' reveals his abiding sense of shame sitting oddly alongside his confession to Ka. His sense of embarrassment over this childish emotion is so strong that he seems unable to shake it off, even as an adult. While candidly owning up to his schoolboy homosexuality, he admits to carefully concealing it from his mother. Even as a grown man he cannot face confronting her with the true facts of his sexual – but by now respectably heterosexual – life. As his boyish blush betrays, he is still, in his mid-twenties, the guilty adolescent.

The fact that Brooke chose to express his blossoming sexuality with boys is scarcely surprising given their ready availability at Rugby and the lack of a female alternative. But there was one girl in his life, the only one before his arrival at Cambridge, with whom he enjoyed the first glimmerings of an emotional relationship, albeit largely confined to their letters. Erica Cotterill was his first cousin, the teenage daughter of the Reverend Charles Cotterill, who had played a clerical Cupid to Brooke's parents when they were courting at Fettes. Exchange visits and meetings on family holidays led to the first sustained correspondence of Brooke's young life, beginning in 1904.

His letters to Erica are apparently honest and even brave in their openness. Clearly, like his simultaneous letters to Keynes, which are frank in their candid revelations of his Rugby romances, they are not documents that he would have wished his mother to read. But there is also a distinct sense of showing-off already evident. A sort of smug hope that Erica and Keynes are going to be shocked by his confessions. His love is not only daring to speak its name – it is shouting it from the rooftops. Brooke's air of preening insouciance about feelings that were presumably heartfelt would become his characteristic hallmark when writing about his many emotional involvements. This goes a long way towards explaining why many suspected him of shallow pretence when it came to affairs of the heart, and why so few were prepared to take him seriously as a mature lover for all his passionate protestations. In his early essays in the arts of love Brooke consciously plays the capering heartsick fool; but again, this pose of youth would last a lifetime.

At Rugby, Brooke acquired a new circle of friends to replace the relationships with James Strachey, Duncan Grant and Owen O'Malley – all of whom had left for public schools elsewhere. In passing it should be noted that both Strachey and Grant would keep the homosexual colouring they had acquired at Rugby, in each case dyed a deeper shade of pink than Brooke's most severe blush. Both would also enjoy heterosexual relationships.

Brooke's new circle of friends included Geoffrey Keynes, Hugh Russell-Smith and Michael Sadler (who later called himself Sadleir to distinguish himself from his identically named father). Like Strachey, Keynes was the younger brother of a more gifted and famous elder sibling who none the less managed to carve out his own distinguished niche in later life – Strachey as a psychoanalyst and translator of Freud, Keynes as a surgeon and bibliophile. Geoffrey Keynes did not share the proselytizing homosexuality of Maynard, nor his formidable intellectual powers. He was, however, possessed of a large ego, a strong will, robust health and an uncritically hero-worshipping attitude towards Brooke that would eventually make him the longest-surviving and most industrious guardian of his friend's posthumous reputation – and thus a creator of the myth of Brooke as the boyish poet-hero, the flawless youth cut down in the springtime of life. Keynes's longevity, coupled with his role as executor of Brooke's estate and editor of his *Collected Letters* were decisive factors in shaping the Brooke legend – a fact that would have astonished Brooke himself, who saw little of him after their Rugby days. For all his upstanding morality, Keynes was not above doctoring the facts to suit the myth he wished to perpetuate, suppressing a reference here, doctoring a letter there – the whole effect being to entomb his hero behind a wall of half-truths quite as solid as the marble that covers his tomb.

Brooke's relations with Keynes were uncomplicated by sex. The same was true of his other great friend at Rugby, Hugh Russell-Smith, like Brooke destined to be a victim of the Great War. A scion of a wealthy

Hampshire family, he was described by Brooke as 'ever a dreamer . . . an idealist, a thing of shreds and patches, not wholly of this world'. The Russell-Smiths' home, Watersgreen House, near Brockenhurst in the New Forest, was a bolt-hole to which he escaped in school holidays to breathe an air less restricted than that of Rugby. The attractions there included Hugh's younger brother, Denham, with whom Brooke indulged the tentative first steps in a homosexual romance that was to burst into brief but explosive flower years later. Brooke, Keynes and Hugh Russell-Smith, formed a sort of Three Musketeers, as Keynes relates: 'We made up a cheerful trio, Brooke providing most of the entertainment with a flow of hilarious nonsense. Thus we climbed up the school in parallel until we found ourselves working in the same form, known as the Twenty, under a great classical scholar, Robert Whitelaw. Brooke was at the top of the form and I was stationed firmly at the bottom.' In an obituary of Brooke written for the school magazine, *The Meteor*, the year before his own untimely death, Hugh wrote:

> Rupert had an extraordinary vitality at school and afterwards, and it was a vitality that showed itself in a glorious enthusiasm and an almost boisterous sense of fun . . . I see Rupert singing at the very top of his voice, with a glorious disregard for the tune, the evening hymn we used to have so often at Bigside Prayers . . . I see him tearing across the grass so as not to be late for Chapel. I generally think of him with a book.

Keynes's memories, in the hindsight of old age, are tinged with the golden glow with which his memory haloed his friend: 'Rupert, though a few months younger than I, was much wiser and more clever and he soon became the friend to whom I turned with complete confidence and admiration. I was at first unaware of the physical beauty for which he afterwards became so famous.'

Michael Sadler was another Rugby contemporary and friend, who remained in fitful contact with Brooke in later life. Unlike Keynes and the elder Russell-Smith, however, their friendship was more of an *affaire*, though it is unclear how far physical relations progressed. Subsequently Sadler, too, achieved literary distinction, becoming Chief Editor at the publishing house Constable, and as such discovering two exceptional novelists: Patrick Hamilton and Jean Rhys. He was an authority on Victorian literature – Trollope in particular – and a novelist in his own right, most famously as the author of the classic account of Victorian sexual hypocrisy and low life *Fanny by Gaslight*.

Brooke's later years at Rugby were dominated by his growing enthusiasm for literature and his simultaneous affairs with three Rugby boys – Sadler, Denham Russell-Smith and a third youth, Charlie Lascelles. Although he is fairly frank – by the standards of the age astonishingly so – in describing the progress of these romances in his letters, he rarely refers to his lovers by name, and the fact that they overlapped makes it difficult at this distance to distinguish between them. His involvement with Sadler began in early 1906 when Brooke heard that the boy had asked the school photographer for a picture of him. As Brooke eagerly told Keynes:

> It began by Dean [the school photographer] catching me one day & informing me that 'a gentleman' in another House had been trying to buy a photo of me: Dean was willing, but my leave was necessary. My enormous conceit was swelled even more – and I gave leave . . . I secretly made inquiries and found it was one I knew of old – one with the form of a Greek God, the face of Hyacinthus, the mouth of Antinous, eyes like a sunset, a smile like dawn . . . Sadler. It appears that the madman worships me at a pale distance: which is embarrassing but purple . . . So I wander around, taking a huge aesthetic delight in the whole mad situation.

Brooke began to refer to Sadler by the code name 'Antinous', the beautiful boy lover of the Emperor Hadrian who was deified by the Emperor after his early death. Brooke, as he told Keynes on 4 June 1906, kept 'a framed picture of the Roman Antinous (the prototype, of course. The reincarnation's likeness is within a cupboard . . .)'. He had already candidly confessed his intention of carrying the infatuation to carnal lengths, despite the heterosexual Keynes's disapproval. On 23 March of that year he reported that 'Antinous' was ill and out of action: 'This will allay your fear of my "doing something rash" during this term. But next term you must be prepared for the worst. An English summer (and my last term) really invites one to all that is "rash".' A few days later (31 March) things are shaping up nicely: 'I have obtained Antinous's – I mean Sadler's – photograph from him; and I employ my spare time in sending and receiving letters . . . His letters are quaint and a little sad . . . It is all rather sweet and rather unusual: and he really looks very nice.'

Keynes, in his down-to-earth way, queries the flowery extravagance of Brooke's feelings, and elicits the response:

> You wonder how much of my affaire is true. So do I. (So, no doubt, does he!) It does not do to inquire too closely. It is now very pleasant. Some day, perhaps

we shall grow old and 'wise', and forget. But now we are young, and he is very beautiful. And it is spring. Even if it were only a romantic comedy, a fiction, who cares? Youth is stranger than fiction . . . At present he – the adorable, rose-crowned – is at Rome: and I receive affectionate pale letters from him whenever the Gods, and the Italian posts, permit.

A month later illness again impedes Brooke's hopes:

Antinous has got – the mumps! This is so horribly incongruous that it sounds like a line from one of Heine's most bitter lyrics. He will be back in a week or two. I am a little sorry. For though I love to look upon him – as a supreme work of art – yet he is something of a tertium quid . . . I am writing nothing, not even a Hymn to Antinous. I am content to exist. I know now whither the Greek Gods have vanished now-a-days. They are to be found in public schools. Always, in the sunshine, and the Spring, I see them, thinly disguised, rushing over the grass, supple of limb & keen-eyed, young and beautiful. Here is Olympus, and now. I feed on the nectar of Life, from Ganymede's hands, and from amidst my young unconscious gods, write to you now, ecstatically.

Whether Brooke achieved the longed-for ecstatic physical fulfilment with Sadler/Antinous that he dreamed of remains obscure; but there is evidence enough that Keynes's doubts about his friend's sincerity were soundly based. For, running parallel with his swooning over Sadler, Brooke was involved with not one, but two, rival swains. First there was Charles Lascelles, who was two years younger than himself. He was clearly infatuated with him, as a later letter to Ka Cox fondly recalls of an evening in Rugby chapel: 'I was all eyes, & straining, for Charlie's brunette radiance among them all – & he'd looked towards me a fraction of a second as he passed.' Brooke's school holiday visits to his friend Hugh Russell-Smith in the New Forest in the summer vacations of 1906 and 1907 gave him the opportunity to deepen his acquaintance with Hugh's younger brother Denham: in his remarkable confessional letter to James Strachey of 10 July 1912, in which he gives what might be called a blow-by-blow account of his later seduction of Denham, Brooke remembers how their relationship began:

We had hugged & kissed & strained, Denham & I, on & off for years – ever since that quiet evening I rubbed him, in the dark, speechlessly, in the smaller of the two Small Dorms. An abortive affair, as I told you. But in the summer holidays of 1906 & 1907 he had often taken me out to the hammock, after dinner, to lie entwined there. He had vaguely hoped, I fancy, . . . But I lay always thinking about Charlie. Denham was, though, to my taste, attractive. So honestly and friendlily lascivious. Charm, not beauty, was his fate.

Brooke's taste for sailing close to the wind is illustrated by his cheekily referring to the hammock in which he and Denham petted in his letter of thanks to Mrs Russell-Smith at the end of his stay in August 1906: 'Many thanks for tolerating me so long. I shall soon write to one of the boys. I loved it all – even the excessive physical exercise in a way – and especially one of the hammocks – the one further from the house. Please give my love to it – a delightful hammock!'

Given his sexual inhibitions, and the ferocious propaganda assault all public schoolboys were subjected to against any physical manifestation of their sexual needs, it is highly unlikely that Brooke's relations with any of his three friends went beyond hugging, kissing and perhaps a touch of mutual masturbation. But the memory of all three boys would haunt him long after he left Rugby: he had Lascelles's photo in his rooms at Cambridge as late as 1908. However, since both Lascelles and Sadler were at Oxford, they were out of reach. None the less, he continued to hanker: writing to Keynes in April 1913 he asks for Lascelles's address, and the same year meets up with Sadler again in the company of Eddie Marsh. With Denham, as we shall see, he was destined to have one even more fateful encounter.

One can make too much of Brooke's schoolboy sexual experimentation – such homosexual calf-love was commonplace in the masculine society of the public school. None the less, the fact remains that Keynes, chief guardian of Brooke's posthumous reputation, was concerned enough about it to edit out all references to Sadler from the *Collected Letters*, and neither Sadler, Lascelles nor Denham Russell-Smith is even mentioned in Christopher Hassall's massive official biography. Brooke's half-hearted homosexual dabbling continued when he went up to Cambridge, another closed male community where a homoerotic ethos reigned supreme. The fact that he reacted violently against some of his homosexual friends at the end of his life only underlines the importance it had for him. Indeed, it could be said that these relationships, powered by the high-octane fuel of adolescent hormones, were the most intense of his life. They set a template of 'pure' and 'innocent' love that he would search for in vain in his heterosexual relationships.

It was in the summer of 1904, during one of his periodic bouts of ill health – this time a throat infection – that Brooke encountered a figure who was to be instrumental in encouraging his literary aspirations. Significantly, this man, who bore the unlikely name of St John Lucas Lucas, was also a homosexual, an aesthete with a fondness for the fading decadence of the 'naughty nineties' associated with Wilde and his imitators. Lucas, a Rugby resident, had heard of 'The Pyramids', a long poem on a set theme that Brooke had unsuccessfully entered for a school prize. He found his way to Brooke's sick room at School Field House and was entranced by the vision of the stricken young poet. Lucas, an enthusiast for French literature – he would soon begin editing *The Oxford Book of French Verse* – brought with him another young local writer of similar aesthetic and sexual tastes, Arthur Eckersley, a playwright and contributor to *Punch*. The books that this precious pair left by Brooke's bedside – the poems of Baudelaire and Ernest Dowson – soon crept into the poems he was beginning to write, with their sighing nostalgia, their hints of unspoken sins, and their extravagantly purple imagery:

> Strange blossoms faint upon that odorous air,
> Vision, and Wistful Memory; and there
> Love twofold with the purple bloom of Triumph
> And the wan leaf of Despair.
> ('The Path of Dreams')

> Amid the fevered press
> Of hot-eyed men, across the desolate sea,
> Hoping a dreamer's hope, I sought for thee
> Wisdom at last I found, and weariness.
> ('The Return')

> Ah, if thou know'st this sorrow, thou art even as I;
> As one who has long outlived his joy, and would forget;
> Who nurses in his festered soul a slave's dull hate
> For this interminable hell of Life . . .
> ('Afterwards')

This is forgivable stuff – the average schoolboy stew of overheated emotions, of objectless longing, glossed with a light dusting of 'thou arts' and several garlands of wilting rosebuds and a barrel or two of sun-warmed wine. There is nothing here yet to indicate that Brooke is any different from the ordinary run-of-the-mill adolescent of scant experience and limited talent.

Brooke lost no time in reporting his meeting with Lucas to Erica

Cotterill: 'I have fulfilled one of the ambitions of my life: I have met a real live poet, who has presented me with a copy of one of his books signed with his own hand. Of course, like all poets worth counting nowadays he is Celtic and very melancholy. Last but not least he knows George Meredith quite intimately! A most enchanting man. And – quite incidentally – his poems are often readable.'

Instantly, he added the pose praised by his new mentors to the accretions of pretence already in place – growing his hair longer still, cultivating a dishevelled tie and collar and hanging about the school's library reading the Decadents. He was developing a reputation for wit and paradox, as he told Erica: 'When I say what I mean, people tell me "O Rupert, what delightful nonsense you talk!" and when I venture on the humorous, I am taken seriously and very promptly and thoroughly squashed for "saying such strange things."' The same letter offers a thumbnail self-portrait: 'washy blue eyes, tow-coloured hair, a habit of doing the wrong thing unintentionally, and a propensity for dying young . . .'

As a reward for his literary efforts, Brooke was allowed to edit a supplement to the school magazine called *The Phoenix*. It was top-heavy with the editor's own contributions: drama reviews, a mildly satiric 'Child's Guide to Rugby School' and a couple of poems. On Christmas Eve 1904 Brooke again succumbed to sickness. The Brooke family doctor recommended the traditional English remedy: a spell in the healing sunshine of the Mediterranean. In the New Year Brooke was packed off with Alfred to stay with Dr and Mrs Gibbons – family friends who owned a villa near the sea at Rapallo in north-west Italy. He planned to use the time to bone up on the Decadent writers recommended by Lucas and, under their influence, wrote more in the same style, which he duly sent back for his mentor's hopefully golden opinions ('I should like a full-grown live critic's opinion of where they are worst'). Simultaneously he kept up his correspondence with Erica: 'German, I find, sounds even worse than it looks, which is something awful'; and Keynes: he compared reading Tennyson to consuming 'three basins of bread and milk with too much sugar in it'.

Behind the adolescent posing, Brooke was more serious about his early poetic experiments than he liked to admit. In response to Lucas's critique of his verses he wrote at length about the techniques of sonnet composition and iambic pentameters, revealing a growing and quite earnest grasp of his deepening vocation. He concluded with typical self-deprecation mixed with a not-so-secret desire for approbation: 'I really have very vague notions about technique. I generally trust to luck and put down anything

25

that sounds all right. But the Italian winds though they may whisper many beautiful ideas in my ear, will not, I fear, teach me much about the structure of a sonnet.'

His convalescence in the healing rays of Italian sunshine proved slower than expected and he was forced to miss a term at Rugby. Reporting this with mock sorrow to Keynes, he gave an exaggerated account of the tedium of his days:

> 1–2 Lunch. 2–3 Lie down on a Sofa and read. 3–4 Walk up and down garden trying to compose tail end of sonnet. 4–4.30 Tea. 4.30–5.30 Walk up and down garden throwing lemons at the cats and . . . thinking . . . 5.30–6.30 . . . Letters. And so on. About 9 I retire to bed with the cheerful prospect of another happy, happy day when I wake. Half the night perhaps I lie awake thinking . . . all the time I am profoundly bored. At intervals they drag me up to Genoa and round a picture-gallery; which is wasted on me. I say 'How beautiful!' at every fourth picture, and yawn.

In March this world-weary existence was enlivened by a visit to Florence and a stay with two girl cousins, Margaret and Reeve Brooke. Rather than sample the cultural glories of the city, he spent most of the time dabbing laudanum on an aching tooth and avoiding the predatory attentions of Italian girls – clinging to his cousin's arm with the injunction: 'Promise not to let those girls get hold of me.' Another visitor was Duncan Grant, already studying art. The pair paraded around the Piazza de Signoria, talking nostalgically of Hillbrow.

In mid-March, forbidden by his mother to stop off in Paris – belatedly she had awoken to the moral danger posed by Lucas, who was in the French capital and attempting to woo his protégé – Brooke left Italy. He passed the time on the long journey home by eagerly devouring *De Profundis*, Oscar Wilde's prison letter to Lord Alfred Douglas, which had been sent to him by Lucas on its posthumous publication in 1905. As compensation for his missing out on the delights of Paris Mrs Brooke had sent Brooke money for a theatre visit in London.

He chose to spend the cash on seeing *Peter Pan*, then enjoying its vastly successful première production. It is difficult to exaggerate the effect of this play on the psyche of a boy who in many ways was to embody Peter Pan in his own life. He saw the play subsequently on repeated occasions, and while at Cambridge would fantasize that King's College chapel had been replaced by Wendy's tree house. The dictum of Peter's creator, J. M. Barrie, that nothing in life matters much beyond the age of 12 chimes perfectly with Brooke's terror of the complexities and perplexities of adulthood. One can well imagine him agreeing with Peter that 'Dying will be an awfully big adventure' – indeed it is explicit in the letters he wrote home from his last voyage.

His enchantment with the play's never-never land on this first encounter is evident in his account of the event to Keynes:

> Yesternight I was vastly happy. I saw Peter Pan. It was perfect. It is merely and completely the incarnation of all one's childish dreams – the best dreams, almost that one has. Red Indians, A Pirate Captain, Faeries, and all mixed up with Home . . . did you see it? If not, you must, next Christmas. It is wonderfully refreshing and never silly. And it brings out people's natures so – shows, I mean, if they are real children or no.

Brooke, for one, would remain a child in his essential nature until the day he died. As he told Keynes: 'I have made an epigram of it. Before the age of 25 you pull the World to pieces: after 25 the World pulls you to pieces. And we are getting on for 18, you know!'

This feeling of a life hardly begun yet already running out was much in his mind as he left for another segment of his protracted convalescence with two aged aunts at their house in Bournemouth, called, presciently enough, Grantchester Dene. Duplicitous as ever, he warned Keynes against any too explicit remarks in his letters: 'This is to say I am staying with two faded but religious aunts. They happened to be in when the post came and one of them, chancing on your letter, received quite a severe shock . . . you really must be careful! . . . I haven't as you may surmise much to do here. However, it is I think, less like Hell than Italy is. Hell is a place where there are no English books!'

Again he filled the empty hours by rereading *De Profundis*, noting in the margin: 'Most people are other people. Their thoughts are someone else's opinions, their lives a mimicry. Their passions a quotation.' Brooke was not neglecting his own writing. A poem of the time ends with God 'flinging the earth into the sun's white fires' while, as he confessed to Lucas's friend Eckersley, he had started work on a school novel – a work not destined to get beyond its first page. Its opening is soaked in the exotic perfumes of decadence:

> Chrysophase Tiberius Amaranth sat in his study, a small pale green room, reading. From one hand an opium-flavoured cigarette circled wreaths of odorous pallid smoke among the shadows. There was a knock at the door, and

the Headmaster entered. 'Ah!' he exclaimed genially, 'Studying the classics, Amaranth?' Chrysophase laid down his book. It was French, bound in dark green, and strangely scented.

'Scarcely!' he replied, 'the exact opposite, in fact. A classic is read by nobody, and quoted by everybody. This book, on the contrary, is read by everybody – in secret; and quite unquoteable.'

'Thank you,' said the Headmaster prettily: 'I see that you have learnt one of the two duties of the modern youth.'

'?'

'To embrace the world in one sentence.'

'And the other?'

'To embrace the world in one person,' answered the Headmaster with a musical sigh.

'My dear James,' exclaimed Chrysophase, 'you are magnificent tonight! May I offer you a cigarette?'

'Thank you. I never smoke them. Their shape is so banal. But if you have some absinthe . . . Yes, just a little . . .'

Before Brooke ran out of inspiration his 'novel' concluded with the portentous words: '. . . silence is older and more terrible than speech. Man speaks. God is silent. Sooner or later we shall all yield to silence.'

At this stage Brooke's writing is uneasily poised between gently satiric mocking of Rugby and its headmaster, Dr James, and his half-horrified fascination with the drugs and drink culture of the Decadent writers he was reading in secret.

In April he at last arrived back with his mother, rejoining the person who most epitomized disapproval of his every deviation from the straight and narrow. Mrs Brooke was installed at the Palace Hotel, Hastings. He took the precaution of warning her in advance about a development she would doubtless regard with disfavour: 'I haven't had my hair cut since the end of February: and it's simply grand now! But I shall have it cut today. I daren't face you as I am.'

His reading matter in the Sussex resort – certainly concealed from his mother's hawk-like eyes – was Walter Pater, a fashionable Oxford critic, who urged his readers to 'burn always with this hard, gemlike flame' while himself living a cautious life of cloistered rectitude. Brooke faithfully mimicked Pater's Nietzschean hilarities in a letter to Keynes:

The only tolerable things in Hastings are dinners at this hotel. I had some soup last night that was tremulous with the tenseness of suppressed passion; and the entrées were odorous with the pale mystery of starlight . . . the real reason for this absurd epistle is this. I wish to warn you. Be prepared. It is this: I am writing a Book. There will only be one copy. It will be inscribed in crimson ink on green paper. It will consist of thirteen small poems; each as beautiful, and as meaningless as a rose-petal, or a dew-drop. (These are not yet written, however.) When the book is prepared, I shall read it once a day for seven days. Then I shall burn the book: and die.

Why was Brooke – who, as he emphasized, was nearly 18 – writing this sub-adolescent, self-dramatizing juvenile drivel? At one level he was guying himself; realizing that the prosaic Keynes would not be greatly impressed by his art for art's sake pose, he gilded the everyday with a gloss of artifice that invited ridicule. Yet at the same time, as his poems attest, he believed in his self-created image as a doomed young poet indulging in nameless sins. ('I dared the old abysmal curse,' as one line from his verse at this time put it.) The contradiction of this Faustian figure staying quietly with his mother at a dull hotel on the south coast was, as he acutely realized, too comic for contemplation.

On 15 April 1905, after a three-month absence, Brooke returned to Rugby. His immediate task was to complete the long poem on a set theme for the school's annual poetry competition, which he had narrowly failed to win the previous year. This year the subject was 'The Bastille', of which he touchingly confessed his ignorance in a letter to Lucas: 'my knowledge of it is a little vague at present. I have only a suspicion that it was a prison, and fell in the French Revolution . . . However, facts don't really matter I suppose.' The resulting poem was scornfully dismissed by the poet himself as: 'the worst I have ever written. They [the lines] have no ideas. They don't scan. And . . . are as dull and vulgar as a Bank-holiday.' All the same, and perhaps inevitably, he won the prize.

As a result, Brooke found himself declaiming 'The Bastille' before an admiring throng at the school's prize day on 24 June. With him on the platform, to provide accompaniment on the piano, was Rugby's star music student, Denis Browne, a future composer. A contemporary and friend of Brooke, he was destined to become a fellow-officer in the last weeks of Brooke's life and to help conduct his funeral.

It was at this auspicious moment that another lifelong friend, James Strachey, absent from Brooke's life since Hillbrow days, decided to re-establish contact. James's initial letter set the pattern for their relationship with a supplicating plea for a weekly exchange of mail. Brooke's mock-disdainful reply was also characteristic: 'I promise to do my best, and if at any time my resolution lapses, pen me a few fierce vitriolic words and you shall receive by the next post a lachrymose & abject apology.' Thus began a regular – if not quite weekly – correspondence that was to follow the ups and downs of Brooke's life until 1914. Strachey's attitude was and remained idolizing – he nurtured an unrequited physical passion for Brooke, tempered by the clear-eyed cynicism that was the hallmark of his family. Brooke's side of the correspondence was by turns teasing, confessional and boastful. Through it all he casts Strachey in the role of deluded clown and himself as smilingly superior; though in truth the real roles were almost the exact reverse – it was Strachey who was worldly-wise, Brooke the cloistered, childlike romantic.

Strachey at once attempted to lure Brooke into meeting him – although Brooke's calendar for the long summer break was already full, composed of cricket matches, an OTC summer camp at Aldershot and a stay with the Russell-Smiths at Brockenhurst. On 30 July Brooke reported: 'In two days the Summer Term will be over, & already people are going about bidding sad farewells. All of which is highly mournful, & may account for the pessimistic tone of this letter. My time is at present divided between playing cricket with gigantic vigour, reading Swinburne on a grassy bank, and toying with mildly foolish examination papers . . .'

It was at this point that Brooke first became drawn into the Machiavellian machinations in which the Strachey clan delighted. James's elder brother, Lytton, who was ending his fifth year at Trinity College, Cambridge – where James himself was bound the following year – had become intrigued by his younger brother's description of his Rugby friend and asked James to set Brooke a questionnaire to determine his views on life, and whether he could be admitted to the inner circle of the Stracheys and their intellectual, cynical friends. The questions James posed to Brooke were: 'Do you approve of the Royal Academy? What are your views on Wagner, Mr Chamberlain and Christ? Are you in favour of War at any Price? Why are you going to Oxford? [An error: Brooke, too, was bound for Cambridge.] Does Jackson play such a good all round game as [C. B.] Fry?' Ignoring the cricketing question Brooke replied that he approved of the Royal Academy and all other 'forms of charitable institution'. He continued:

Certainly I approve of war at any price. It kills off the unnecessary. As for Mr [Joseph] Chamberlain I detest him. He is a modern politician, and I hate modern politicians; he comes from Birmingham and I abhor Birmingham; he makes a noise, and I loathe noises; he is utterly materialistic . . . About Wagner I have no views, I am very sorry, but I can't help it. I have tried very hard for years, but I cannot appreciate music. I recognize that it is a fault in me, and am duly ashamed. In Literature, and a little even in Painting, I humbly believe in the Beautiful, but I am born deaf. This is a Tragedy. For Christ – I am so obsessed by 'De Profundis' that I have no other views on this subject than those expressed therein. The Perfect Artistic Temperament.

His response to the Strachey catechism must presumably have satisfied the stringent requirements of his interlocutors. On the strength of Brooke's anti-Toryism, and his espousal of Oscar Wilde's artistic values, Lytton concluded that it would be worth keeping an eye on James's bright young friend with a view to welcoming him to Cambridge the following year.

Another powerful Cambridge contact with an interest in Brooke was Maynard Keynes. Brooke was not averse to exploiting the connection, and wrote to Geoffrey angling for an introduction. In the meantime he met Lytton himself face to face when he succumbed to James's entreaties and in September went to stay at the Stracheys' rented summer residence, Great Oakley Hall, near Kettering in Northamptonshire. His reported response – 'Lytton Strachey I found most amusing, especially his voice' – may have offended the languid scholar, who was often teased for his high-pitched, squeaky tones, had he got to hear of it. At all events Lytton was interested enough, as he reported to Duncan Grant, to take Brooke for a morning stroll around the Hall's park, where 'he talked about Poetry and the Public Schools as decently as could be expected'. Reporting in more detail to Maynard Keynes, Lytton recorded his impression of his brother's friend in terms of cool disdain:

> I wasn't particularly impressed. His appearance is pleasant – mainly, I think owing to youth – complexion, hair etc. Of course he's quite incredibly young [he was seven years Lytton's junior] so it's rather difficult to talk. I felt he wanted to attack the subject of Platonic Love etc. but the whole thing seemed so dreadfully commonplace that I couldn't manage it. He's damned literary, rather too serious and conscientious, and devoid of finesse. The Cambridge-Oxford question still hangs in the balance. I didn't make any great effort to obtain him.

Lytton's lukewarm response is partly explicable as a reaction to the extravagant praise heaped on Brooke by James. However, there is no doubt that initially he regarded the Rugby star as not quite up to par intellectually, describing his diction as 'vile' and his jokes as feeble. He was miffed by Brooke's popularity, his radiant good looks and the aura of effortless success that always seemed to accompany him. As a result, he determined, Brooke suffered from 'complacent egoism'. Nevertheless he suspended final judgement – Brooke's saving graces included general innocence, an acute sensitivity to character and situation and the germ of an interest in interesting things. In short, something might yet be made of him, and, while Lytton did not actively attempt to recruit Brooke into his Cambridge coterie, neither would he discourage him.

One unintended but permanent result of Brooke's brief stay with the Stracheys was the birth of his nickname 'the Ranee' for his mother. Lytton, hearing unfounded rumours that the Rugby Brookes were related to the famous Victorian Imperialist of the same name who had helped colonize Indonesia, began referring sardonically to Brooke as 'the Rajah of Sarawak'. Learning of this, Brooke promptly baptized Mrs Brooke by the title of the Rajah's wife – 'the Ranee'. In the way of nicknames that stick, the title suited her and 'the Ranee' she remained.

The Oxford–Cambridge dilemma did not long remain unresolved. In mid-September Brooke made a flying visit to King's College, Cambridge, where his father's elder brother, Alan England Brooke, had now risen to be Dean. It was agreed that Brooke should try for a Classical scholarship at King's the following year. On his return to Rugby, a Classics tutor was engaged to coach him in a subject in which, thanks to indolence and illness, he had fallen behind. Just before the melancholy Michaelmas term resumed, there was a piece of cheering news: one of his first poems appeared in public print as a prize-winner in a competition run by the *Westminster Gazette*, a leading Liberal newspaper. Brooke's effort, a sonnet titled 'The Sea', is unremarkable:

> Hushed is the homeless sea's unfinished song,
> Its treasures lie forgot in desert space

but its mere appearance in print, coupled with a tangible prize of ten shillings and sixpence, was enough to bestow on the poet a measure of glory as he returned to his unwelcome labours.

As he sweated away over Pindar and Propertius, his correspondence with Lucas continued as a necessary outlet for his literary urges. One poem written to his mentor's order, 'Vanitas', positively reeks with a summons to wild excess:

> Laugh now and live! our blood is young: our hearts are high;
> Fragrant of life, aflame with roses.

Surfacing again from his studies in late November he addressed Eranos, the Sixth Form literary society, with a paper on Swinburne. Soon after came a new sonnet, 'The Dawn', which he sent to Lucas. It begins:

> When on my night of life the Dawn shall break,
> Scatt'ring the mists of dreams, the old sad gloom,
> Before the terrible sunrise of the Tomb . . .

It concluded:

> Nor see the pale cloud of her tossing hair
> Laugh and leap out along the desolate wind.

The images of this poem would remain a constant in Brooke's verse, even though the form he used to express them grew more skilful. His mature verse is full of nights and dawns, of tossing heads and blowing winds.

That Christmas Brooke again travelled to Cambridge, this time in the company of his fellow-Musketeers Hugh Russell-Smith and Geoffrey Keynes. They stayed with Keynes's family – including Maynard – in Harvey Road while they took the Cambridge scholarship exams. Maynard, primed by Lytton's reports, took the opportunity to inspect Brooke at close quarters and refused to be bowled over by what he saw; agreeing with Lytton that Brooke's charms were overrated and chiefly attributable to his youth and beauty.

As a result of his Christmas efforts, Brooke – along with Russell-Smith, who went to St John's College – won a Classical scholarship to King's. Geoffrey Keynes opened the door to his glittering medical career with an exhibition in natural sciences at Pembroke College. However, true to form, Brooke then collapsed on Christmas Day with a fever and retreated to his bed. His sickbed reading matter consisted of Malory's *Morte d'Arthur*, illustrated by Aubrey Beardsley, and the Elizabethan dramatists, whose plays, he boasted to Keynes and Strachey, he was devouring at the rate of three or four a week.

With the exams behind him, Brooke rewarded himself with a trip to London during which he saw Shaw's *Major Barbara*, having been impressed by the same author's *John Bull's Other Island* earlier in the year. Even more to his taste was *Peter Pan*, which he saw for the second time. He raved to James Strachey: 'I found it enchanting, adorable and entirely beautiful. In reality, no doubt, it is very ridiculous. I am very aged & this mania for children's plays is a token of advanced senility.' By contrast he found Shaw's

33

study in salvationism, as he told Erica Cotterill, 'a brutal, sordid play, difficult to understand and very interesting'. Beneath the man-of-the-world role he liked to play, Brooke was still in many ways the wide-eyed provincial boy.

3

'Every hour as golden'

Nineteen hundred and six opened with a general election. The new year saw the era of Tory Imperialist hegemony end with a Liberal landslide victory that inaugurated an age of social reform and unrest that would last until Brooke's death.

The Brooke family threw themselves enthusiastically into the local electoral struggle in Rugby. Parker Brooke signed the adoption papers of the Liberal candidate, Corrie Grant, and Brooke's brothers went out canvassing while he languished in his sickbed. Moved by all the excitement, he rose before he had fully recovered, to join the fray. While the Ranee wooed wavering voters over tea and scones, Brooke edited a Liberal news-sheet, *The Rugby Elector*, specializing in roundly abusing the Tory candidate. He found time to report to Keynes: 'We are having a ferocious fight down here . . . figure me, covered with Liberal rosettes, rushing about the town . . . I have made 37 mortal enemies in 4 days. And the immense joke of the matter is that I really take no interest in politics at all.'

This dilettante attitude continued when he reported the Liberal victory to Erica: 'I fell on the neck of a whiskered and bespectacled nonconformist minister who stood near me and we both wept in silent joy.' Typically he added that he was now posing as 'a rabid Socialist' – but without knowing what the term really meant. His new-found radicalism had another outing on 27 January at the school's debating society, when he opposed a motion deploring the rise of the Labour Party. Despite Brooke's eloquence, the motion was carried. In his speech he castigated opponents of Labour and the working class for their 'ignorant prejudice and class feeling'. He concluded: 'Liberty will make its voice heard in some way. We should welcome the chance of letting it make itself felt by a peaceful and constitutional revolution.'

In March he was again felled by his recurrent complaint of conjunctivitis – a condition that he attributed to 'gazing too often on Butterfield's architecture'. Accompanied by Hugh Russell-Smith, who had the same symptoms, he was laid up in the school sickbay, where, reading being precluded by their condition, a new work by Hilaire Belloc was read to them. Belloc was a robustly patriotic poet and essayist whose writing was to have a profound influence on Brooke. By this time Geoffrey Keynes had left Rugby and was spending a miserable five months in Germany in preparation for Cambridge. Brooke continued to cheer his friend with regular letters, in one of which he jocularly reported, 'I have converted half the House to Socialism and the rest to Mormonism.'

With his entrance to Cambridge secure, Brooke was free to indulge his private interests in his final months at Rugby. He continued to excel on the sports field – though his long locks tended to flap about his face during strenuous moments on the pitch; and took to wearing a 'poetic' black silk tie, a form of floppy neckwear that he would adopt for the rest of his life. His reading was maturing: he recommended the Jacobean dramatist John Webster to Keynes – the then obscure Webster would continue to be an enthusiasm for Brooke and would form the subject of his Cambridge thesis.

Alongside sport and study, Brooke indulged his simultaneous passions for Sadler, Russell-Smith and Lascelles, and these feelings helped fuel his premature nostalgia for his schooldays as the fearful prospect of leaving loomed ever closer. He confessed to Keynes: 'It is terrible to feel that one is exchanging the cynicism of youth for the bright optimism of manhood; it is very sad to outgrow one's disillusions.'

After a delay caused by Brooke's sickness, his family set out on an Easter holiday in Italy. This time the destination was Venice; but the jewel of the Adriatic was no more impressive to Brooke's jaundiced eye than Florence had been the previous year. He wrote to Keynes: 'Venice is an American colony, chiefly peopled by Germans. There is also a small Italian element in the population. It is a little out of date, but the steamers and hotels are rapidly supplanting the old-fashioned gondolas and palaces . . . I hate it. It is hot and malodorous . . . the place is befouled by a mob of shrieking tourists. Moreover my family are extremely obnoxious people to travel with.'

A ten-day stay, prolonged by flying visits to Padua and Verona, concluded with stop-overs in Paris and Oxford *en route* to Rugby. Once there Brooke prepared for his final golden summer at the school. He told Keynes: 'The Summer Term has dawned. It is my last, and I weep. The same fantastic things happen, there is that strange throng of young beings, unconscious of all their youth and wonder. Another Spring dies odorously in Summer . . . But I am quite happy. To be here is wonderful, and suffices. I live in a mist of golden dreams. Afterwards life will come, cold and terrible. At present I am a child.'

To the older Lucas, Brooke wrote in similarly elegiac terms: 'After this term is over the world awaits. But I do not now care what will come then. Only, my present happiness is so great that I fear the jealous gods will requite me afterwards with some terrible punishment, death, perhaps – or life.' This final, Wildean paradox embodies a lasting truth about Brooke's overriding fear of life, which runs beneath his apparent eagerness to embrace it so extravagantly.

As each day passed, he told Keynes: 'I am beginning to value the things around me more every day, the good and the bad in them. This school-life, with its pathetic transience and immense vitality, calls to me with a charm all the more insistent that I am soon to lose it . . . I am both actor and spectator.'

Squeezing the last drops of juice from his glory days, he reaped the final fruits that Rugby had to offer by winning the King's Medal for Prose for an essay on the unlikely subject of William III, joining the First XI in cricket and taking unheard-of liberties in his hair and dress styles. He addressed the Eranos literary society again, this time on the subject of James Thomson, the doomed poet who wrote 'The City of Dreadful Night'. In collaboration with Denis Browne he wrote an 'Easter Day Song in Praise of Cremation', which his friend set to music. Ironically, in view of the fact that Browne would arrange his burial, the poem expresses Brooke's horror of interment:

> In that unwilling bridal of the tomb
> To lie
> Through the slow hours of stifling gloom
> In shameful, helpless agony,
> Changed by the worm's unnatural cold lust
> To slime and dust!

Following up his talk on Thomson, Brooke addressed Eranos yet again, on 'Modern Poetry'. Despite such Wildean aphorisms as 'Beauty cannot be moral or immoral: it is white or coloured: that is all', his lecture showed how seriously he took his chosen subject, and the notebooks he kept at this time, with their lists of arcane words and remarks on poets from Dryden to Keats, attest to the depth and breadth of his reading.

The effort of composing his prize-winning essay on William III inevitably brought on a collapse in health – which he variously called flu, hay fever or ophthalmia – but was probably nervous exhaustion allied to conjunctivitis, and almost caused him to miss the presentation of the prize at his last Speech Day. He capped this event with his final appearance before Eranos on the last Sunday of his last summer term. His father and Alfred turned up in honour of the event. Brooke's survey of the current state of English verse covered the waterfront, from the patriots like Henley, Newbolt and Kipling through Yeats and the Celtic revival to his own favourites, Swinburne, Housman and Dowson, who, he concluded, should be read 'on an evening like this, when the light is fading and the air is cool with late rain, and the roses, with the Summer Term, have almost come to an end'. There must have been scarcely a dry eye in the House.

Brooke now felt himself poised on a plateau of achievement which could be followed only by a long anticlimax. He was a victim of the syndrome most satisfactorily defined by Cyril Connolly years after Brooke's death – the 'theory of arrested development'. Connolly held that: 'the experience undergone by boys at the great public schools, their triumphs and disappointments, are so intense as to dominate their lives and to arrest their development. From these it results that the greater part of the ruling class remains adolescent, school-minded, self-conscious, cowardly, sentimental and in the last analysis homosexual.' Brooke is a classic case-study in all these attitudes, which were probably at their peak in the year he left Rugby.

The previous year had seen not only the birth of the deathless *Peter Pan* but the publication of the 'Reginald' stories of Saki (H. H. Munro – another Great War victim) and that early candid picture of public-school life, H. A. Vachell's *The Hill*. Whereas Walter Pater professed to believe that to burn continually with a 'hard, gemlike flame' was 'success in life', Saki commented that 'to have reached thirty is to have failed in life'. J. M. Barrie told his fellow-writer Arthur Quiller-Couch that 'the best is past by the time he is three and twenty'. A. E. Housman, the homosexual author of *A Shropshire Lad*, hymned 'lads that will die in their glory and never be old'. Brooke was clearly not alone in believing that his best days were done and that life would be all downhill from now on. In retrospect he wrote: 'I had been happier at Rugby than I can find words to say. As I looked back at those five years I seemed to see almost every hour as golden and radiant, and always increasing in beauty as I grew more conscious; and I could not and cannot hope for or even imagine such happiness elsewhere.'

Faced with the prospect of leaving home and school simultaneously,

Brooke was in a gloomy mood as he watched the school break up two days before his nineteenth birthday. He clutched desperately at the friends who would be going up with him to Cambridge – he persuaded Keynes to accompany him to one final shot at schoolboy glory, the Rugby versus Marlborough match at Lord's, where his friend witnessed Brooke make two good catches before his wicket fell ingloriously for a duck. Describing himself to Keynes as 'a pale ghost who has lived and can now only dream', Brooke escaped the 'deserted Hell' of Rugby to join his other close school friend, Hugh Russell-Smith, at Brockenhurst.

He was happy enough among the lively Russell-Smiths, playing tennis, reading his earliest literary love, Browning, and smooching with Denham in the hammock. True to form, though, he upheld his pose as the melancholy wanderer in a letter to Lucas: 'The stillness and solitude here frighten me, for there are memories and visions, and one hears other voices whispering in the heart. I should like to be in London, in the crowds and the noise, where one can be silent and alone. Write to me.' The same nostalgic spirit, the feeling of his life decaying with the waning summer – 'That gay witch, the Summer, who charmed me three weeks ago! I have looked into her face and seen behind the rouge and the smile, the old, mocking visage of a harlot,' as he put it to Keynes – pervades a poem he was writing at the time. 'The Beginning' was the first poem that Brooke felt finished and mature enough to include in his only book, *Poems* (1911). It ends:

> So then at the ends of the earth I'll stand
> And hold you fiercely by either hand,
> And seeing your age and ashen hair
> I'll curse the thing that once you were,
> Because it is changed and pale and old
> (Lips that were scarlet, hair that was gold!),
> And I loved you before you were old and wise,
> When the flame of youth was strong in your eyes,
> —And my heart is sick with memories.

It was hard, being an ex-hero, a former Head of House, a somebody, no longer 'to be among 500 people, all young and laughing . . . seated on the topmost pinnacle of the Temple of Joy'. Facing the prospect of becoming an anonymous nobody, his spirit and ego revolted and he retreated into his favourite fantasy/prophecy – that of early death. Failing yet again to join Lucas in France for the final weeks of pre-Cambridge freedom he lamented: 'I had dreams of dying quietly in France . . . my few conscious moments soothed by you reading Baudelaire. But now, alas! I shall expire vulgarly at Bournemouth; and they will bury me on the shore, near the bandstand.' He echoed the theme to Erica Cotterill: 'Come and lay a few lilies on my grave soon, it is rather bare.'

In keeping with this juvenile *Weltschmerz* he arrived to stay with his maiden aunts at Bournemouth after three days at a summer camp in Kent where working-class and public-school boys mixed and tried to learn from one another. His reading material on the promenade was suitably mournful: Baudelaire's *Les Fleurs du Mal*, which soon found its way into his writing, as he told Lucas:

> I am busy with an enormous romance of which I have written five chapters. It begins with my famous simile about the moon . . . ['The moon was like an enormous yellow scab on the livid flesh of some leper'] One of the chief characters is a dropsical leper whose limbs and features have been absorbed in one vast soft paunch. He looks like a great human slug, and he croaks infamous little songs from a wee round mouth with yellow lips. The others are less respectable.

If the aunts had caught a glimpse of this – assuming indeed that he even wrote it, since it does not survive – they would doubtless have been even more shocked than they were the previous year by Keynes's risqué letter. The passage illustrates Brooke's desire to shock by the use of grotesque imagery, albeit artificial and totally removed from his own cosy existence. His pathetic use of the closing paradox is another wearisome characteristic that palls by overuse, like a constantly reiterated dying fall. His pose of a prematurely aged and cynically moribund observer, worn out before his time, is resolutely maintained to Keynes: 'With other decrepit and grey-haired invalids I drift wanly along the cliffs . . . I have seen everything there is to see and my eyes are tired.'

Then, on 6 October, he writes to the friend of his youth with a sterner summary of his current philosophy, which owes more to Nietzsche, Wells and Shaw than to Baudelaire, Wilde and Dowson:

> tomorrow I return to Rugby for a few gloriously ghastly days. I shall be wonderful there, laughing wonderfully all day, and through the night wonderfully weeping. Then – leaving the people I have hated and loved I shall throw off, too, the Rupert Brooke I have hated and loved for so long and go to a new place and a new individuality . . . Indeed I have forsworn art and things

beautiful; they are but chance manifestations of Life. All art rests on the sexual emotions which are merely the instruments of the Life-force – of Nature – for the propagation of life. That is all we live for, to further Nature's purpose. Sentiment, poetry, romance, religion are but mists of our own fancies, too weak for the great nature-forces of individuality and sexual emotion. They only obscure the issue.

One can sense Brooke bracing himself and stiffening the sinews for the ordeal ahead as he assures Keynes, the natural scientist, that humanity's duty is merely to propagate the species and quietly await its inevitable demise 'heeding as little as possible the selfish and foolish greed for personal immortality, or the incomplete love of an individual'. The prospect before us, Brooke admits, may be 'rather grey' but is nevertheless 'quite logical and scientific'. He rounds off his atheist sermon with a quotation from another French Decadent, Villiers de l'Isle-Adam: 'Science will not suffice. Sooner or later you will end by coming to your knees . . . before the darkness!' On that chilly note, the world-weary young philosopher embarked on the central phase of his comet-like rush across life.

4

'Forward the Day is Breaking'

Brooke arrived at Cambridge in mid-October 1906. One of 50 freshmen starting at King's, he was assigned Room 14 at the top of Staircase A in Fellows' Buildings, in the left-hand corner of the college's front court, with a breathtaking view across to the chapel. Seventeen years before, the rooms had been home to one of his Decadent idols, Aubrey Beardsley. It seems odd that during his first weeks he felt lost and homesick, since he had no shortage of friends and well-wishers around him.

His uncle Alan, the college Dean, kept a watchful eye on him and had him to tea every Saturday afternoon; and he had brought with him a trio of his closest friends – Geoffrey Keynes, Hugh Russell-Smith and Denis Browne – although, since they were at different colleges, he did not see as much of them as he had at Rugby. The dons who supervised his studies were also sympathetic, although since they were all young confirmed bachelors of homoerotic inclinations they may have had their own reasons for welcoming this handsome newcomer.

His tutor was John ('Jack') Sheppard, who was destined to end his career as Provost of King's and was described as 'a man of fascinating personality and an electrifying lecturer'. His lecturer in Classical History was Nathaniel Wedd, a convinced atheist and socialist, while his lecturer in Greek was Walter Headlam, more at home with the thought and speech of ancient Athens than he was in English. Another King's Fellow was Goldsworthy Lowes Dickinson, the famed author of *The Greek View of Life* and *A Modern Symposium*. All three men, to a greater or lesser degree, were inspired by the ideals of ancient Greece, and aimed to re-create the atmosphere of Athens in its heyday, with free and unfettered exchanges between teachers and students, treating their pupils more or less as equals, as Plato, Socrates and Aristotle had done. They were agnostics, if not atheists, in belief; and pagan in spirit. It followed that their moral and political outlook, in a Cambridge tradition, would be radical and rationalist – which well suited Brooke's own budding ideas.

It did not take Brooke long to find his first new friends. On the first Sunday of term he was expected to make a courtesy call on the Provost, M. R. James, later famous as the author of the greatest ghost stories in the language. While waiting on the steps of the Provost's lodge, Brooke met a fellow-freshman who had come along for the same purpose. Hugh Dalton, later to find fame as a leading Labour politician and Chancellor in Clement Attlee's 1945 government, was the son of the Canon of Windsor, a former tutor to Queen Victoria's children. Tall, with a foghorn voice and a massive face, Dalton tended to repel people as easily as Brooke attracted them. (The Queen herself was the first of many enemies, describing the toddler as 'Canon Dalton's horrid son'.) At this time Dalton shared Brooke's enthusiasm for Swinburne and Housman, but was more radical politically. Almost immediately they decided to set up a new political discussion society, christening it 'the Carbonari' after the secret Italian society that had paved the way for the Risorgimento.

Despite this sympathetic if overbearing new friend, Brooke was slow to find his feet in the strange new world of Cambridge, with its servants, hierarchies and traditions. He was overwhelmed by the freer atmosphere he breathed, and took refuge in childish petulance. 'I do not know if it's the climate or the people: most probably it's neither, but my cantankerous self,' he wrote to Erica. 'But for some reason I find this place absolutely devoid of interest and amusement. I like nobody. They all seem dull, middle-aged, and ugly . . . In fact, I suppose I'm "growing up".'

His pose of finding Cambridge and its citizens 'ugly' was to persist, witness 'The Old Vicarage, Grantchester':

> For Cambridge people rarely smile,
> Being urban, squat and packed with guile;

He moped in his rooms, lying on his sofa, his head resting on a green bolster – a gift from his maiden aunts – and reluctantly receiving visitors. To Lucas he complained:

> They talk vivaciously for three minutes and I stare at them with a dumb politeness, and then they go away. My room is a gaunt 'Yellow Book' wilderness with a few wicked little pictures scattered here and there. At certain moments I perceive a pleasant kind of peace in the grey ancient walls and green

lawns among which I live; a quietude that does not recompense for the things I loved and have left, but at times softens their outlines a little. If only I were a poet I should love such a life very greatly, remembering moments of passion in tranquility; but being first and chiefly only a boy I am restless and unable to read or write.

Rescue from his isolation was at hand. A third-year student at Emmanuel College, Justin Brooke, although no relation, was struck by the fact that Brooke shared the name of his elder brother and sought the new Kingsman out. Justin invited Brooke to attend a rehearsal for a production of Aeschylus's *Eumenides* at the A.D.C. Theatre in Jesus Lane. One autumn afternoon, with nothing better to do, Brooke wandered into the stalls. His striking appearance was noticed, and he was instantly asked to take the part of the Herald, a non-speaking role which merely required him to pretend to blow a trumpet and look suitably beautiful.

Justin Brooke's father, Arthur, was a hard-nosed northern businessman who had built his small tea merchant's business into the Brooke Bond tea empire. He had sent his sons to Bedales, a newly-founded 'progressive' boarding school in conscious revolt against Arnold's public-school ethos. Its founder and headmaster, J. H. Badley, was a Rugbeian who had gone on to Cambridge, where he had absorbed the ethics of anti-Victorian revolt epitomized by Goldsworthy Lowes Dickinson. Heterosexual himself, Badley determined to found an unheard-of innovation: a co-educational boarding school. He bought a country house, Bedales, near Haywards Heath in Sussex, and opened its doors in 1893.

The school atmosphere was a combination of high-minded ethics and plain Spartan living with an emphasis on the great outdoors. Both boys and girls began the day with a douche in a cold tub – a baptism that set the tone for the rest of the curriculum, with its cross-country runs, outdoor camps, swims in rivers and plain vegetarian food. In 1900 the school moved to its present quarters in the Hampshire village of Steep near Petersfield.

Under Badley's firm guidance – like many progressive educationalists, 'the Chief' as he was called, was authoritarian – a recognizable Bedalian 'type' soon emerged. Staff and pupils dressed in loose-fitting clothes – believed to encourage the 'airing' of private parts – sandals and head scarves. Boys and girls were encouraged to associate freely and bathe in the nude together, but physical expression of their sexuality was absolutely banned. The intellectual spirit of the school was vaguely radical, but owed more to William Morris with his back-to-the-land, Arts & Crafts ideals than it did to Karl Marx. Country pursuits, including hiking, nature studies and ploughing, were encouraged, and there were classes for the boys in cooking, needlework and handicrafts. In its rural style Bedales was as far removed from the realities of the twentieth century as Rugby, and its fostering of rational, sexless 'comradeship' between the sexes was as psychologically deficient as the most hidebound public school.

Although in its turning away from the urban and industrial realities of the world Bedales was a reactionary place, its superficial trappings of sexual equality, the free outdoor life and its anti-religious outlook were an attractive package to someone fresh from the confines of Rugby, like Brooke. Justin, who had ended up as Bedales' head boy, told his new friend all about the place, and introduced him to another former Bedalian, his room-mate and fellow Emmanuel student, the Frenchman Jacques Raverat. Bedales put more emphasis on the arts than the classics, and Justin had discovered in himself a taste and a talent for drama during his time there. When he went up to Cambridge he continued to devote most of his energy to the stage, often playing female parts, to which his clean-cut, boyish good looks and 22-inch wasp-waist predisposed him. His beauty, like Brooke's, made him the pin-up of homosexual admirers, but – like Jacques – he remained firmly heterosexual.

Jacques described his new friend Brooke as having: 'a childish beauty, undefined and fluid, as if his mother's milk were still in his cheeks . . . The forehead was very high and very pure, the chin and lips admirably moulded; the eyes were small, grey-blue and already veiled, mysterious and secret. His hair was too long, the colour of tarnished gold, and parted in the middle; it kept falling in his face and he threw it back with a movement of his head.'

Justin, for all his interest in the arts, was an unimaginative soul, with a curiously flat, unemotional personality; but Jacques and Brooke took to each other at once, and spent many hours in feverish talk about poetry, art, sex, life and religion. They found common ground in a mutual disdain for God and 'the absurd prejudices of patriotism and decency; [and] the grotesque encumbrances called parents' – an easy set of attitudes to adopt when one's parents – as Jacques' were – were wealthy, château-owning members of France's *haute bourgeoisie*.

As rehearsals for *Eumenides* went enjoyably forward, Brooke resumed his friendship with James Strachey, who was up at Trinity, putting as much energy into his sex life as Brooke did into drama. James's promised weekly letters to Brooke had lapsed during 1906, preoccupied as he was by brief affairs with his cousin Duncan Grant and an on-off liaison with the Trinity Classics lecturer Walter 'Watty' Lamb, with whose younger brother,

45

Henry, Brooke was destined to tangle disastrously during the last years of his life. The flavour of James's *louche* life at Cambridge is conveyed in a letter to Grant on 8 November 1906: 'This is a dreary hole; where one divides one's time between buggering the senior dean's sons and hearing Donald Tovey massacre The Appassionata . . . [Among other accomplishments, James was a distinguished critic of music.] I suppose you'll be coming to see the Rajah in his tights and spangles.' The reference is to Brooke's costume as the Herald in *Eumenides*, which received its première on 30 November. Brooke, clad in a red wig, with cardboard helmet and armour and a short, sequinned skirt which inordinately excited his admirers but was so tight that he was afraid to sit down in it, duly blew on his mock trumpet and struck his statuesque pose before an audience, according to one witness largely composed of 'Hellenists and paedophiles'. The gay librettist of 'Land of Hope and Glory', A. C. Benson, noted in his diary: 'A herald made a pretty figure, spoilt by a glassy stare.' Also there was Eddie Marsh, a wealthy and influential civil servant with an equally passionate interest in the arts and handsome young men: he was to become Brooke's most powerful patron and mentor. Writing in retrospect, Marsh nostalgically recalled 'the radiant, youthful figure in gold and vivid red and blue, like a Page in the Riccardi Chapel, [who] stood strangely out against the stuffy decorations and dresses'. Instantly smitten by this vision, Marsh remained devotedly in love with Brooke until the very end.

At the post-performance party Brooke met other figures who were to play a prominent part in his future. There was Francis Cornford, a junior Classics don at Trinity, Jane Harrison, a don at Newnham, one of Cambridge's two women's colleges, who overheard Brooke coin one of his instant Wildean epigrams: 'No one over thirty is worth talking to'; and there was Charles Sayle, who worked in the university library. Hovering on the fringes was James Strachey, who gave his reaction in a note to Brooke that same night: 'Dear Rupert, In the excitement of the moment I must just write to tell you (a truism) that you were very beautiful tonight. How sorry I shall be tomorrow morning that I sent you this! How angry you will be when you read it! *Vogue la galère.* [Let's risk it.] Yours in admiration, James.' There – it was out – a first declaration of love and devotion. Another admirer was added to a lengthening list. Brooke would use the weapon that James had handed to him quite ruthlessly in the years to come.

Also with James at the party was George Mallory, a Magdalene man and protégé of the Magdalene don A. C. Benson. Mallory, 'with good looks in the Botticelli style', in Geoffrey Keynes's estimation, was an early pioneer of the sport of rock climbing and was doomed to find immortality when he died during an attempted first ascent of Mount Everest in 1924. He too had enjoyed affairs with the indefatigable Duncan Grant and the incorrigible James Strachey, and, along with James, was a member of a tightly-knit gay Cambridge coterie whose members included Oscar Browning and Charles Sayle – one of the most ecstatic of Brooke's legion of male admirers.

Browning had been the first to attempt to lure Brooke into his slightly sticky web – hardly surprisingly since he shared the top floor of Staircase A in Fellows' Buildings with him. A former master at Eton, which he had left under a cloud of suspicion for 'messing about' with the boys, Browning, universally known as 'the O.B.', was a History Fellow who enjoyed a slightly sinister reputation as a serial seducer of pretty boys. He played Beethoven on a harmonium in his rooms and is rumoured to have employed a string quartet of elderly ladies to provide a suitable accompaniment from behind a screen while he made love to James Strachey. He was apparently unable to do the same to Brooke, who dutifully reported to the Ranee: 'I went to lunch with the "O.B." on Sunday. He was rather quaint to watch but I did not much like him. He was so very egotistical, and a little dull.'

Brooke took more to Charles Sayle, the 42-year-old university under-librarian, whose home at 8 Trumpington Street was a well-known centre for the Cambridge gay crowd. Sayle, who had been a friend of J. H. Badley at Rugby, was 'small, fussy and spinsterish'; his camp persona was summed up in his nickname 'Aunt Snayle'. His tastes ran to young, working-class boys, whom he called 'Angels of Earth', though he also fell in love with George Mallory – and with Brooke. His besotted journal entries about Brooke make one understand why Bertrand Russell called Sayle 'a well-known ass': 'I do not know in what language to moderate my appreciation of this great man,' Sayle wrote of Brooke. 'Great in his ideals, great in his imagination, great in his charm. The world will learn to know him later on. It has been mine to know him now.' Brooke lapped all this up and was a regular visitor to Sayle's house as long as he lived in Cambridge – although there is no evidence that they were lovers.

After the excitement of *Eumenides* Brooke returned to the grind of his studies. With little interest in the Classics he was studying, he was in danger of relapsing into the depressed cynicism in which he had arrived. Even at this early stage he was tempted to change to English, especially under the influence of the brilliant but abstracted scholar Walter Headlam, who re-fired his interest in Elizabethan drama – particularly in Webster. Hugh

47

Dalton's breezy friendship was another antidote to his gloom, and he enjoyed the weekly meetings of the Carbonari, to whom he read his paper on modern poetry and a new poem of his own, 'The Song of the Beasts':

> Unswerving and silent follow with me,
> Till the city ends sheer,
> And the crook'd lanes open wide,
> Out of the voices of night,
> Beyond lust and fear,
> To the level waters of moonlight,
> To the level waters, quiet and clear,
> To the black unresting plains of the calling sea.

Brooke returned to Rugby, where his mood matched the flatness of the Cambridgeshire Fens: he had briefly been a star, and had attempted quite consciously to carry out the personal plan outlined to Geoffrey Keynes:

> I shall be rather witty and rather clever and I shall spend my time pretending to admire what I think it humorous or impressive in me to admire. Even more than yourself I attempt to be 'all things to all men'; rather 'cultured' among the cultured, faintly athletic among athletes, a little blasphemous among blasphemers, slightly insincere to myself . . . However there are advantages in being a hypocrite, aren't there?

Even then, the cynicism hid a nagging dissatisfaction: how many of those who eagerly sought him out wanted to know the real Brooke, and how many were beguiled by the surface charm? In a sense his speechless stage role had been appropriate – for was he not all show and little substance? His secrecy and guile, his play-acting and downright lying were all weapons aimed at deflecting the demands his appearance and 'radiance' inspired in others. Having no ready response to their expectations, he dissimulated. The ambivalence of his appearance, and his obvious attractiveness to both sexes only served to deepen his confusion. His mother's prudishness was at war with an open and healthy libido – as witness his Rugby dalliances – and the result was inner chaos. Jacques Raverat got a glimpse into this when Brooke told him of seeing a working-class woman under a lamp-post locked in the arms of her lover, with her pale, ordinary face transfigured by the aura of love. He could, he admitted, feel only 'sick with envy'.

★

Brooke arrived home to find his mother ill with flu, along with his brother
Dick, whose health had never been robust. On cue, and for the third
Christmas in a row, Brooke joined them on the sick list. In his enforced
idleness he wrote to two of his old correspondents, his cousin Erica
Cotterill and Geoffrey Keynes. He told Erica of his escapist ambition to go
and live in Paris or London 'like a great red flame'. To Keynes he narrated
a dream that would have provided rich pickings for James Strachey in his
later profession of Freudian psychoanalyst:

> I was in the Gardens of Heaven walking between great odorous beds of
> helichrys and asphodel. Turning a corner I met the present Headmaster of
> Rugby School in his shirt-sleeves. He was digging up all the beautiful flowers.
> I hit him severely on the nose, and asked what he was doing. He said he was
> uprooting the useless flowers and planting vegetables for food instead. I told him
> that in Heaven one subsisted entirely on beautiful thoughts. He replied that he
> would starve, and continued to dig, muttering. He began to swell as I gazed,
> and, still grunting 'Cabbages and Onions', grew so big that he blotted out all the
> sky . . .

Dr Herbert James figured large in Brooke's subconscious as a father-figure
in lieu of the real thing. Here he clearly represents the philistine in full
flight. While in heavenly mood Brooke enclosed a new sonnet, 'The
Vision of the Archangels', which pictures God in a 'little dingy coffin'
dropping for ever 'Into the emptiness and silence, into the night'. Keynes
responded with a weary plea for Brooke to give up his pretence of poetic
gloom. Brooke responded: 'I have thought over your idea of my at length
giving up the pose of discontent and taking to optimism in my old age. I
think not. The change might be refreshing, but I scrape along very well as
I am; and the pessimistic insincerity pleases ME at any rate, which is the
main thing.' Another sonnet, inspired by his illness, 'To My Lady
Influenza', finds Brooke in playfully grotesque mood:

> . . . so cometh now
> My Lady Influenza, like a star
> Inebriously wan, and in her train
> Fever, the haggard soul's white nenuphur,
> And lily-fingered Death, and grisly Pain
> And Constipation who makes all things vain,
> Pneumonyer, Cancer, and Nasal Catarrh.

But 'Pneumonyer' was soon to cease to be a source of light relief to Brooke. He was just packing for his return to Cambridge in mid-January when a message came from Southsea, where his brother Dick worked, to say that Dick was desperately ill with pneumonia. Parker Brooke left at once and was at his eldest son's bedside when he died on 13 January. Although as charming as his younger brother, Dick had always been emotionally and physically frail and, after beginning a business career in Southsea, had taken to the bottle, which further undermined his health. He was six years Brooke's senior and the two had never been close, but Brooke shared his parents' grief and offered to stay on in Rugby to help them bear it.

However, Mr and Mrs Brooke preferred to shoulder their sorrow alone, as Brooke explained in a note to Charlie Lascelles:

> I am very glad to get away before you all return. This sounds rude. But I am feeling terribly despondent and sad, and I feel that I could not face everybody. The only thing was if I could help Father and Mother by staying, but they say not, and I do not think so. And if I stayed I know I should break down. There is an instinct to hide in sorrow, and at Cambridge where I know no-one properly I can be alone . . . I hope you'll be gentle to my pater at first. He has had a terrible time, and is very tired and broken by it.

Indeed, Parker Brooke retreated still further into his shell, and his grief for his son probably contributed to his own early death.

To distract himself from mourning for Dick, Brooke plunged into work on his return to Cambridge. Not content with catching up on his studies, he proposed to review poetry for the *Cambridge Review* and offered this and the *Westminster Gazette* his own current compositions. On 14 February 1907 the *Review* published 'The Call', a poem saturated with feeling for his dead brother:

> Your mouth shall mock the old and wise,
>   Your laugh shall fill the world with flame,
> I'll write upon the shrinking skies
>   The scarlet splendour of your name.

The *Gazette* also printed a couple of his other offerings, signed for the first time with his own name, indicating an increasing confidence in the worth of his work. He was unimpressed by the verse he read for the *Review*, telling Lucas: 'I frequently wonder whether I have not written several of them myself under a pseudonym, and forgotten about it.' His resulting notices were so savage that the *Review*'s editor felt compelled to tone them down, although he left in scathing remarks like 'It is a relief to turn from the merely silly to the merely dull.' In March Brooke went to London and saw *Peter Pan* yet again.

Before Easter, Hugh Dalton introduced Brooke to a forceful character who was to have a decisive influence on his hitherto amateurish dalliance with politics. Ben Keeling was a third-year undergraduate at Trinity who was the driving force behind the university's infant Fabian Society, a mainly middle-class group of radicals who provided much of the intellectual underpinning of the nascent Labour Party. Shaw, H. G. Wells and Beatrice and Sidney Webb were among the Fabians' leading lights. They advocated a doctrine of peaceful and gradualist transformation of society towards socialism, in which an informed élite, armed with a 'scientific' analysis of social injustice, would slowly educate workers and government alike in the necessity of a change of course. When Keeling arrived at Cambridge in 1905 he found only half a dozen Fabians, but by the time Brooke met him his single-handed efforts had transformed the situation, and scores of students and dons were involved. Keeling master-minded Cambridge socialism from his rooms overlooking Trinity's gatehouse, which were adorned with a massive poster of workers advancing with clenched fists under the slogan 'Forward the Day is Breaking'. This later inspired Brooke's poem 'Second Best':

> Yet, behind the night,
> Waits for the great unborn, somewhere afar,
> Some white tremendous daybreak . . .

Keeling's propagandist tactics included inviting the Labour Party's founder, Keir Hardie, to address the Fabian Society. When right-wing 'hearties' threatened to disrupt the event by kidnapping the veteran socialist, Keeling countered by deploying several decoy Hardies, kitted out in authentic-looking beards and red ties, to confuse the opposition. Hardie duly completed his address.

One revolutionary feature of the Fabians' programme was its espousal of women's rights and feminism, a current hot potato, with the women's suffrage campaign getting under way. The Cambridge Fabians were the first student society to admit women as equals, and their first treasurer was Amber Reeve, the current mistress of the libidinous H. G. Wells.

At his first meeting with Keeling, an awed Brooke listened wide-eyed to his host's account of his running battles with his Tory opponents – which included, at one stage, smearing his stairs with margarine and rigging up an electrified barbed-wire barrier to deflect a determined raid by 'hearties'. Dalton had become a committed Fabian and urged Brooke to follow suit, but a cautious Brooke, conscious that such an association would not go down well in Rugby, held back. Full membership of the Fabians entailed signing a document known as 'the Basis', which set out their beliefs, but sympathizers not ready to go this far were allowed to become Associates of the Society and, for the moment, Brooke contented himself with this. He told Dalton: 'I'm not your sort of socialist – I'm a William Morris sort of socialist.'

But the seeds of socialist belief had been sown, however thinly, and Brooke began to read radical texts like William Morris's Utopian novel *News from Nowhere* and a pamphlet written by his own maternal uncle, Clement Cotterill, entitled 'Human Justice for those at the Bottom from Those at the Top'. Impressed, he wrote to the author expressing his hopes of converting the Cambridge Fabians to 'a more humane view of things . . . Of course they're really sincere, energetic, useful people, and they do a lot of good work. But, as I've said, they seem rather hard . . . They sometimes seem to take it for granted that all rich men, and all Conservatives (and most ordinary Liberals) are heartless villains.'

Adding Keeling to his growing circle of Cambridge friends, Brooke elected to spend the first half of the Easter vacation on a walking tour of Sussex with an earlier chum: Hugh Russell-Smith. Perhaps he was influenced by praise of the open-air life by his Bedalian friends Justin Brooke and Jacques Raverat. Sussex was also the heartland of one of his favourite current writers, Hilaire Belloc, whose verses were continually on Brooke's lips, especially the quatrain:

> From quiet homes and first beginning,
> Out to the undiscovered ends,
> There's nothing worth the wear of winning,
> But laughter and the love of friends.

Planning their route, Brooke revealed in a letter to Russell-Smith his ignorance of the great outdoors that was soon to form a central part of his life: 'I have never been on a "walking-tour" (damned word) before . . . describe to me the satchel I shall bear . . . on my head, what? A cap, I suppose . . . And within the napzak [sic], what? . . .' Their ramble took them through the sleepy settlements of West Sussex and Hampshire, to end up at Easter at the Green Dragon inn at Market Lavington in Wiltshire, from where he reported to Lucas: 'I am terribly Fabian; which in our family is synonymous with "atheistical", "Roman Catholic", "vulgar", "conceited", and "unpractical".'

The second half of the holiday was taken up by a trip to Italy in the company of his brother Alfred, known as 'Podge'. They travelled by train to a *pensione* in Florence, chiefly populated by elderly English gentlewomen, one of whom fazed Brooke when he playfully asked her to identify his school. After eyeing him for a minute she accurately pronounced, 'Rugby!' Brooke dutifully took Alfred round the galleries, but himself remained impervious to their glories: 'I have made the final and irrevocable discovery that I hate and am perfectly blind to all painting and sculpture.'

Before Brooke left for Italy he had received a plaintive letter from James Strachey reproaching him for having avoided him since his declaration of adoration on the night of *Eumenides* and imploring him to 'be kind'. In his reply, written from Florence, Brooke denied intending to drop or cut James, and blamed his invisibility on the depression that had accompanied his bereavement. 'All this explains my not coming to see you. No doubt it was very selfish. But as my friends will tell you, I am wholly selfish. I never think of others' feelings. I am entirely taken up with pitying myself. Indeed, if you are still foolish enough to want it, you can know me "as Mr Dalton knows" me – or more closely . . .' He concluded by inviting James to tea. When, back at Cambridge, James took up the invitation, the encounter was brief, according to his report of the event to Duncan Grant:

S: I suppose you know what's the matter with me. I'm in love with you.
B: How distressing of you! Will you have a cigarette?
S: I suppose you don't believe I have any feelings.
B: It doesn't interest me . . . besides, it annoys me.
S: I don't see why it should.
B: Because it irritates me: I AM irritable . . . I think I really ought to laugh at you.
S: I think I'd better go.
B: I should advise you to go and make yourself a drink.

The dialogue, if true, bears out the opinion of another Cambridge homosexual admirer of Brooke's, E. M. Forster, who wrote just after the poet's death: 'He was essentially hard; his hatred of slosh went rather too deep and affected the eternal water-springs, and I don't envy anyone who applied to him for sympathy.' (His perceptive analysis of Brooke did not prevent Forster from harbouring 'sloshy' feelings for him – he is reputed to have treasured a pair of the poet's underpants – provenance unknown – in his rooms at King's until he died in 1970.) Brooke's well-attested anti-sentimentality sits oddly alongside the lush sentiment of some of his poems. A closer reading of the bulk of his verse, however, reveals that the predominant mood is satire and cynicism. These strands in his character derived from his mother's scornful Victorianism and from his own annoyance at being the unwilling love-object of so many unwelcome suitors – especially men like James Strachey and Forster, to whom he was not sexually attracted. Seen in this light, his 'hardness' is at least under-standable, and even forgivable.

5

Apollo and Apostles

Brooke returned to Cambridge early in May. Before he was embroiled in the hurly-burly of the May exams, he found time to reply to a plea by Erica Cotterill which echoed Keynes's earlier advice to drop his pose of poetic *Weltschmerz* and stop 'extracting unreasonable misery from art'. 'This,' spluttered Brooke, 'is all bosh. Art isn't the thing that makes one happy or miserable: it's Life. Art is only a Shadow, a second-rate Substitute, a refuge after Life – real Life.'

Brooke feared he had not done well in his exams. His lack of interest in Classics could no longer be concealed. There was still time to make up lost ground, but his thoughts were turning to drama and literature. He had been putting more time and energy into the stage, playing the part of Stingo in Goldsmith's *She Stoops to Conquer* for the A.D.C. Theatre in February. Now he got involved in a production that was to be instrumental in widening his social circle and providing a new direction for his aimless way of life.

Inspired by the freshness and vigour displayed by Dublin's Abbey Theatre company on a visit to Cambridge, Justin Brooke suggested to the A.D.C. that it abandon its usual fare of farce for something more serious. Receiving a dusty answer, he resolved to mount his own production of Christopher Marlowe's *Dr Faustus*, and formed the Marlowe Dramatic Society for the purpose. Its members consisted almost entirely of his own friends and contacts. His first port of call was Brooke, who was already a Marlowe fan. Together they called on an Old Rugbeian Trinity man, Andrew 'Granny' Gow (later a teacher of George Orwell at Eton). Gow won permission of the university authorities for the project, and roped in another Trinity don, Francis Cornford. Justin himself played the part of Faustus and the rest of the cast and stage staff form a roll-call of Brooke's friends.

Brooke himself took on the role of Mephostophilis. Geoffrey Keynes was the Evil Angel, Hugh Russell-Smith Gluttony and Denis Browne Lucifer. George Mallory played the Pope. Although no women were permitted to take acting roles, they were actively engaged backstage. Rehearsals started, with the aim of staging the play in the autumn. Meanwhile summer was approaching, with the pleasures of the long vacation.

Brooke began by mortifying his flesh with a stay in the uninspiring company of his maiden aunts in Bournemouth, where, in between secreting the writings of the gay and atheistic Marlowe from their censorious eyes, he wrote comically despairing descriptions of his fate to his friends. 'My Evangelical aunts always talk at meals like people in Ibsen. They make vast Symbolic remarks about Doors and Houses and Food. My one aim is to keep the conversation on Foreign Missions, lest I scream suddenly,' he informed Lucas.

Bournemouth brought Brooke within striking distance of a part of Dorset that was to loom large in his future: Lulworth Cove. Poring over a map of the area, his eye was drawn to the oddly named Mupe Rocks. ('Have even *we* made a better name?' he asked Hugh Russell-Smith, whom he had recruited for a repetition of their walking tour in the spring.) Intrigued, he resolved to make Lulworth, just half a mile from the rocks, the base for their tour and reserved rooms above West Lulworth post office, mocking the illiteracy of the postmistress, Mrs Emily Chaffey, as he did so: 'Mrs Chaffey thanks me for my card and will reserve rooms "'as agreed'".' Brooke persuaded a new Cambridge friend, a dour and studious economist named Dudley Ward, to join the party.

Just before leaving Bournemouth he received the results of his exams – a disappointing Second. It was said that his 'flippancy' in his History papers had greatly contributed to his poor showing; but neither this news, nor a comic mishap on arrival at Lulworth – having forgotten his keys he was obliged to force open his trunk with a pickaxe – seem to have dampened his exuberant high spirits at the prospect of a seaside holiday in one of the most attractive and invigorating spots in southern England. Even a bout of food poisoning after sampling Mrs Chaffey's home cooking failed to depress him: 'Today I am weak but cheerful,' he told Keynes as he recuperated. 'I can sit up and take a little Plato.'

This holiday at Lulworth seems to have been beset by comic interludes. Another such saw Brooke drop his volume of Keats into the sea. After a frantic search by boat, the missing volume was spotted by Hugh 'in the midst of a roaring vortex'. 'I cast off my garb and plunged wholly naked into that "fury of black waters and roaring foam".' The bedraggled book was safely retrieved. Brooke was to discover subsequently the '*amazing*' coincidence that Keats had made his last landfall in England at Lulworth *en route* to Rome and death, and had taken the opportunity to write his last great sonnet, 'Bright Star'.

A poem written on 8 July at Lulworth, 'Pine-Trees and the Sky: Evening', indicates that the open-air life had succeeded, where Keynes and Erica had failed, in blowing away some of the cobwebs of Brooke's former melancholy. In it, he describes a gathering evening that inspired his usual thoughts of decay and transience:

> And I was sick and tired that all was over,
> And because I,
> For all my thinking, never could recover
> One moment of the good hours that were over.
> And I was sorry and sick, and wished to die.

But then all is transformed:

> Then from the sad west turning wearily,
> I saw the pines against the white north sky,
> Very beautiful, and still, and bending over
> Their sharp black heads against a quiet sky.
> And there was peace in them; and I
> Was happy, and forgot to play the lover,
> And laughed, and did no longer wish to die;
> Being glad of you, O pine-trees and the sky!

The previous term he had published another poem in the King's college magazine, *Basileon*, a sonnet entitled 'Dawn' which successfully essays his first exercise in the mood of disgust with bodily functions that he was to make his own. Inspired by his train trip to Florence with Alfred in a closed carriage, it repeats the refrain, 'Opposite me two Germans sweat and snore', and concludes:

> One of them wakes, and spits, and sleeps again.
>   The darkness shivers. A wan light through the rain
> Strikes on our faces, drawn and white. Somewhere
>   A new day sprawls; and, inside, the foul air
> Is chill, and damp, and fouler than before . . .
>   Opposite me two Germans sweat and snore.

After his apprenticeship in the purple shadows of decadence, Brooke was, however haltingly, casting off their stifling influence and beginning to find his voice.

He passed his twentieth birthday at Brockenhurst in the company of the Russell-Smiths. As the tonic of the Lulworth ozone wore off, the anniversary gave rise to predictably melancholy reflections, as expressed to Lucas:

> Now I am staying with this foolish family again . . . They are delightful, and exactly as they were last year . . . A few days ago they found I was exactly 20; and congratulated me on my birthday, giving me a birthday cake, and such things. I hated them, and lost my temper. I am now in the depths of despondency because of my age. I am filled with a hysterical despair to think of fifty dull years more. I hate myself and everyone. I have written almost no verse for ages; I shall never write any more . . .

This petulant rant shows Brooke in his worst, though sadly all too frequent, mood: that of the spoilt, self-pitying brat. Its only saving grace is that he recognizes its hysteria for the childish tantrum that it is. More miserable, though accurate, self-analysis followed to Geoffrey Keynes: 'What I chiefly loathe and try to escape, is not Cambridge nor Rugby nor London but – Rupert Brooke. And I can only do this by rushing suddenly to places for a few days. He soon overtakes me.' Brooke's rush to escape himself for the rest of the summer took him to Rugby, then on a family holiday to Belgium in September.

While in Antwerp with Alfred he witnessed a demonstration by striking workers violently dispersed by the police. This inspired a curiously reactionary response in a letter to Lucas: 'I prayed that some great archangel would smite suddenly, blazing down the street, and blast the crawling maggots. The English are the only race who are ever clean and straight and beautiful; and they rarely.' His sentiments show clearly that his recent interest in socialism was only skin-deep – in essence just another fashionable pose – and that his real instincts were deeply conservative. His fear of the inchoate masses – 'crawling maggots' – is plain, and his deep belief in the racial superiority of the English over more benighted nations, which was to surface so virulently in the last years of his life, is seen in its true inglorious colours. Ironically, the next time he would see Antwerp would be at the outset of the Great War, when he returned in uniform to defend the 'crawling maggots' from the German army.

For the moment, as he told Lucas, his heart was sick at the thought of having to 'go back to Cambridge for my second year and laugh and talk with those old dull people on that airless plain! The thought fills me with hideous ennui.' He was soon able to repay the debt of influence – albeit a mixed blessing in the progress of his poetry – that he owed to Lucas when he reviewed two volumes by his first literary mentor in the *Cambridge Review*. These were *The Oxford Book of French Verse* and *The Marble Sphinx*, a violent and exotic Oriental fantasy. Reading the latter in Rugby while laid up with a knee injury from a football game, he wrote to tell their author of his admiration: 'It has coloured my dreams for nights.' Comparing his bruised leg to Lucas's jewelled prose, he added: 'It is swollen and strangely green and black as your prose style, but not nearly so pleasant.'

Back in Cambridge on 7 October, Brooke found his second-year dwelling in Room 1 on Staircase E of Gibbs Building, in a corner of King's front court furthest from the chapel. A new friend was acquired in the shape of a freshman, Arthur Schloss – later, as Arthur Waley, a distinguished translator of Chinese poetry. But another friend, Jacques Raverat, was temporarily absent – convalescing in France after the first attack of a mysterious illness that was for a long time misdiagnosed as nervous exhaustion but eventually proved to be the cruel and wasting creeping paralysis of multiple sclerosis.

Possessed by his customary beginning–of–term blues, Brooke vented his spleen on Cambridge, variously dubbing it 'a miasma', 'a swamp', 'a wilderness' and 'a bog'. He sought distraction in renewed rehearsals for *Dr Faustus*, which opened on 11 November in the presence of Prince Leopold of Belgium. The King's don E. J. Dent, who was also there, criticized Brooke's 'thick and indistinct voice' thanks to his head being half-concealed in a Mephistophelean cowl and turned away from the audience. Despite its imperfections, the production made a handsome £20 profit, which enabled the Marlowe Dramatic Society to be established on a firm footing as a permanent addition to the university's theatrical life.

Charles Sayle threw a post-performance party for the cast, although the main attraction for the host was Brooke, who had now become a regular visitor at Trumpington Street, as 'Aunt Snayle' recorded: 'I did a little shopping and came home. Standing in my hall in the dark, and thinking of other things, I looked towards my dining room, and there, seated in my chair, in a strong light, he sat, with his head turned towards me, radiant. It was another unforgettable moment. A dramatic touch. A Rembrandt picture. Life.'

Meanwhile Brooke's involvement with socialism was deepening. He was elected to the Cambridge Fabian Society Committee with Hugh Dalton's support, and travelled to Oxford with his fellow-Fabians, 'an indecorous, atheistical, obscene set of ruffians', as he told Michael Sadler in an advance letter, for a meeting with like-minded students in 'the other place'. Back in Cambridge, he attended a meeting addressed by the Fabians' founding father, George Bernard Shaw. He was not impressed by the garrulous dramatist: 'It was the same speech as he made the night before in London and the night after, somewhere,' he told Erica. 'Mostly about the formation of a "middle-class party" in Parliament which didn't interest me much.'

Shaw was not the first eminent man of letters Brooke had encountered at Cambridge. In June his hero Hilaire Belloc had read a paper to a private group at Pembroke, and he had been able to study the massive bulk of the great controversialist at close quarters. Reporting the event to Erica, Brooke recounted how the Anglo-Frenchman 'talked and drank beer – all in great measure. He was vastly entertaining. Afterwards Gow and I walked home with him about a mile. He was wonderfully drunk and talked all the way.' Then came the characteristically Brookian note of alarm: 'You can tell Ma if you see her; but for God's sake don't say he was drunk, or she'll never read him again.'

It is easy to see what superficial attraction Belloc held for Brooke – his beer-swilling advocacy of a mythical 'Merrie England' that had been destroyed by capitalism, industrialization and the Protestant work ethic would have been instantly appealing. But there was a darker side to Belloc's politics that found an answering echo within Brooke's divided heart – his English patriotism contained a worm of xenophobia, particularly anti-Semitism, that Brooke shared. Brooke's feelings were bolstered by Jacques Raverat, who equated the modernism he abhorred with the machinations of international Jewry. With the Dreyfus affair still a recent memory, such prejudice was common in Frenchmen of Raverat's and Belloc's class, but it was a virus which crossed the Channel too – as the Marconi scandal would shortly prove.

Ever since he had been up at Cambridge, Brooke had been under the scrutiny of a secretive élite society with a weather eye out for new members – students of particular promise or brilliance, especially if they happened to be handsome too. The Cambridge Conversazione Society, better known as 'the Apostles', had been founded in 1820 as an informal discussion group to bridge the divide between colleges throughout the university. It was particularly strong in King's and Trinity. Over the years its secretiveness increased, as did its selectivity. No one could apply to become an Apostle; as with the Freemasons, suitably qualified individuals were discreetly approached to become a candidate member, or 'embryo' in Apostle jargon. If he passed a period of probation satisfactorily, the embryo would be admitted to the select inner circle, given an Apostolic number and sworn to secrecy. Membership lasted for life.

The Apostles met every Saturday behind closed doors at Trinity for tea and elevated conversation over anchovies on toast. Tennyson, Arthur Hallam and Edward FitzGerald, the translator of *The Rubáiyát of Omar Khayyám*, had been among the earliest members. By the turn of the century, the society, which had always had a homoerotic tinge, had become almost exclusively homosexual: a tendency that was confirmed when Lytton Strachey and Maynard Keynes came to be members. Almost all Brooke's teachers at King's, including Lowes Dickinson, Harry Norton and Jack Sheppard were Apostles, as was Oscar Browning, who had donated the wooden chest, known as 'the Ark', in which the papers read by members at their meetings were solemnly deposited. The ethics of the Apostles, which became the guiding spirit of Cambridge in the Edwardian era, were best summed up in the work of one of their members, the philosopher G. E. Moore, who preached a gospel of sceptical rationalism and friendship uncontaminated by passion among a civilized élite.

As is the way with secret societies, the original disinterested aims of the Apostles became corrupted by intellectual snobbery, mutual back-scratching and back-stabbing, and downright arrogance. High standards slipped when it came to electing good-looking but intellectually undistinguished youths as members. Lytton Strachey and Maynard Keynes played their part in this process, which was well advanced by the time Brooke came under their collective eye.

The main advocate of Brooke's membership was James Strachey, who had himself become an Apostle as a result of his brother Lytton's influence. James had lobbied tirelessly for his friend's admission to the elect ever since Brooke had come up to Cambridge. Lytton and Maynard Keynes, who, as already mentioned, had not been greatly impressed by Brooke when they had met him as a Rugby schoolboy, were reluctant, but eventually yielded to James's importunities. By the time the university broke up for the Christmas holiday in 1907, Brooke's elevation to the Apostles' ranks had become a certainty.

Brooke had been invited to spend Christmas with a group of Cambridge friends at Andermatt in the Swiss Alps. The party contained a strong seasoning of Fabians, including several women members. Foremost among these was the Cambridge Fabians' new treasurer, who had just replaced Amber Reeve in that post, Katharine Laird Cox, known to her many friends as 'Ka'.

Born in the same year as Brooke, Ka was a recent orphan – her wealthy stockbroker father Henry having died in 1905, leaving Ka and her two sisters, Hester and Margaret, more than well provided for. A student of Newnham College, Ka had a flat in Westminster that she shared with Hester and a substantial country house, misnamed Hook Hill Cottage, on her father's estate near Woking in Surrey. In appearance, Ka was far from beautiful, being heavy and thick-set, with unflattering pince-nez for her severe myopia and a tendency to let her mouth hang open. Her large breasts and surprisingly trim ankles were permanently concealed by long dresses. Her personality, however, more than made up for this unpromising exterior. She was one of those rare people who seems to have instinctively put the needs of others before her own. The fact that she had been forced by her mother's early death to care for her father and sisters had reinforced this innate motherly trait. Her generous, easy-going nature made her extremely popular with her friends, who looked to her for solace in times of emotional stress. One of them compared her calming presence to sitting in a field of green clover, while Brooke himself was to describe her almost submissive support as 'a cushion, or a floor'.

Another Newnhamite at Andermatt was Margery Olivier, also a prominent Cambridge Fabian, and, like Ka, used to taking responsibility for her younger sisters. There were three of these: Brynhild, Daphne and Noel, the progeny of Sir Sydney and Lady Margaret Olivier. Sir Sydney uneasily combined a career as a colonial administrator – he had been appointed Governor of Jamaica the previous April – with advanced Fabian views. Margery, less attractive than her sisters, had brought with her to Andermatt the stunningly beautiful Brynhild. Brynhild shared the film-star looks of her cousin Laurence, who had just been born, and was less intellectual than the bluestocking Margery, who enviously kept a protective shield around her siblings. Brooke instantly noticed the dazzling 'Bryn', and was tongue-tied in the presence of these bright young things skiing and sledging in the Swiss snow.

He had dreaded the prospect of being among so many free – and female – spirits for the first time in his life, writing to Erica only half-jokingly that his companions would be 'mostly young, heady, strange. Females. I am terrified.' Once installed at the Grand Hotel he reported to his cousin: 'I'm a bad person to be one of a party of merry people like these. I'm too dull and sulky.' But he grudgingly conceded: 'Even the Newnhamites and others of their sex and age are less terrible than they might be . . . several are no duller to talk to than the males.'

The group staged a reading of Wilde's *The Importance of Being Earnest* in the hotel ballroom, and as the undoubted stars of the show Brooke and Bryn were assigned the plum parts of Algernon and Cicely. Brooke was both excited and disturbed to be close to such an alluring woman. 'There is One! . . . oh there is One,' he wrote to Erica, 'aged twenty, VERY beautiful & nice & everything . . . My pen is dragging at its bit to run away with me about her.' Then comes the protective, cynical pay-off: 'I adore her, for a week.'

As he travelled back to Cambridge and the bore of more exams, Brooke was ablaze with heady memories of the Alpine holiday. Andermatt was the first of many occasions in the coming years when he would be among young men and women with 'advanced' ideas on political, social and sexual matters. The fact that such ideas – especially those concerning sex – were rarely acted upon in cold reality increased the excitement – and the frustration. Even on the ski slopes the girls kept on their long dresses, and the adult chaperones were never far away. Altogether he felt safer and more comfortable in the male-only society to which he now returned. But a door had swung ajar.

Back at King's, Brooke heard that he was about to learn his fate over admission to the Apostles. Maynard Keynes had continued to have his doubts about him as recently as that October – 'I'm damned if I know what to say,' he had written to Lytton. 'James's judgements on the subject are very nearly worthless; he is quite crazy. I have been to see R. again. He is all right I suppose and quite affable enough – but yet I feel little enthusiasm.' However, such doubts had at last been overcome and Brooke was duly elected as the first new Apostle for two years.

It fell to James to convey the good news to him. But almost immediately he too was assailed by doubt as to whether Brooke would prove worthy of the honour. He told his brother: 'How dreadful it is to satisfy a violent desire . . . I completely forgot, of course, to tell him it was secret – so he's probably retailing it all at this very moment to Geoffrey Keynes . . . it was I alone who saw, in a ghastly moment as he went away, his incredible stupidity.'

In fact it was the secrecy of the Apostles that most appealed to Brooke, particularly to the conspiratorial side of his nature. He did not, as feared, brag of his election and kept his regular attendance at meetings a secret from his friends who were outside the charmed circle. He accepted with equanimity the overt homosexuality of the group, but if James had hoped that his efforts to get Brooke elected would be rewarded by an admission to his bed he was bitterly disappointed, as Maynard Keynes indicated in a letter to his lover Duncan Grant in early February: 'James' ups and downs with Brooke seem to be almost more violent than usual . . . There is an understanding between Brooke and Gerald [Shove – a King's economics student and distant friend to Brooke] – they sit together every evening – to which he feels that he doesn't belong.'

Brooke was quite prepared to play fast and loose with James's feelings and to flirt outrageously with other men. But the sincerity of his own sexual feelings remains open to doubt. Most probably he was unsure of them himself. The almost exclusively homoerotic ambience of Rugby and Cambridge had cemented themselves around his personality, and he would remain permanently susceptible to homosexual emotions. But the experience of Andermatt had proved to him that he was attracted to – and attractive to – women as well. Although he would never be able to conduct a fully mature heterosexual relationship, and his emotions would stay mired in an adolescent swamp, his yearning to prove himself a lover of women would be as much a part of his make-up as his early homoeroticism.

For the remainder of the term, much of Brooke's energy was poured into simultaneous political and dramatic activity. On 23 January he attended his first meeting of the Fabian steering committee with Ka Cox, who, in the words of one of his biographers, began to 'slip almost invisibly into some inner room of his being, and . . . warm it like a log-fire so slow burning that he was for a long time hardly aware of it'. At the same time he was elected President of the Marlowe Dramatic Society, which was in the throes of preparing for a major production as a follow-up to *Dr Faustus*.

One of Brooke's tutors, Walter Headlam, and Dr A. C. Shipley, Master of John Milton's old college, Christ's, had independently arrived at the idea of celebrating the poet's tercentenary with a production of his masque *Comus*. Justin Brooke, with his habitual energy, seized on the idea as a perfect vehicle for the Marlowe Dramatic Society and swiftly enlisted Brooke to be stage manager and to play the part of the Attendant Spirit. Two Cambridge cousins, Frances and Gwen Darwin, granddaughters of the great scientist, were approached by the Brookes to help make the costumes and paint the scenery. Thus two more friends of Brooke were made. Frances was an able and original poet, Gwen an equally accomplished artist. As preparations for the ambitious enterprise went ahead, more friends were persuaded or bullied into joining the project – including Ka Cox, who agreed to be a dancer and help with the set design.

Brooke's absorption with the theatre still left room in his life for his deepening political interests. Invited by Geoffrey Keynes to hear H. G. Wells address a Pembroke discussion society, Brooke took the opportunity to ask the great man to give a lecture to the University Fabians. Afterwards Wells agreed to give a talk to a private meeting of Brooke's Carbonari on the subject of 'the family'.

Wells was the unofficial leader of the Fabians' more radical wing. He wished to carry the social revolution that they advocated to the wilder shores of replacing marriage by 'free love' – a shocking proposition for older Fabians like Shaw and the Webbs. Wells certainly practised what he preached, rarely passing up an opportunity to seduce any young woman who seemed remotely susceptible to his dubious charms. Not a few succumbed. Soon Wells acquired a roguish reputation, both for his revolutionary ideas and his colourful private life. The one outraged the conservative Right, the other offended the censorious Left.

Brooke was captivated by Wells's vision of a new society guided by an intelligent élite whom the tubby novelist christened the 'Samurai', after Japan's warrior caste. No doubt Brooke saw himself as a member of just such an élite, but there was with Wells, as with Belloc, a sinister side: Wells too was a convinced racial supremacist who believed in using science to repress both lesser breeds and the unenlightened masses. An enthusiastic advocate of eugenics, the elimination of the mentally and physically unfit and other proto-Nazi ideas, Wells held a vision of socialism as an authoritarian society run for the convenience of people much like himself, rather than a community of free and equal men and women. The concept appealed to him as a tidy way of eradicating poverty and ushering in a hygienic and controlled hierarchy in which the enlightened few would lord it over the ignorant many.

Listening with Brooke were fellow-Carbonari like Dalton, Arthur Schloss, Gerald Shove and Ben Keeling, along with distinguished older guests like Lowes Dickinson. As the organizer, Brooke felt he was shining in the company of his most brilliant Cambridge contemporaries. At last he was at the centre of things, and among people who mattered. 'Wells is a very pleasant little man,' he reported condescendingly to his mother, 'insignificant in appearance and with a thin voice (he has only one lung) and slight Cockney accent ("thet" for "that"). He is rather shy.'

The meeting with Wells nudged Brooke to the very brink of becoming a fully-fledged Fabian socialist by signing 'the Basis'. As he looked back on the Lent term he could pat himself on the back with a sense of real achievement. He was now a prominent and sought-after member of three university organizations that were setting the agenda of Cambridge life: the Apostles, the Fabians and the Marlowe Dramatic Society. He had made good and lasting friends – sometimes overlapping in all three spheres. The fact that he could juggle these three interests and keep them in largely separate compartments appealed to him. In short, he had conquered Cambridge and regarded the city with all the contempt of a victorious general looking down on a vanquished citadel. He wrote to the absent Jacques Raverat from 'the Hinder Parts, the faeces or crassamentum or dregs, the eastern Counties; a low swamp, a confluence of mist and mire, a gathering-place of Dankness, and Mud, and Fever; where men's minds rot in the mirk [sic] like a leper's flesh, and their bodies grow white and soft and malodorous and suppurating and fungoid, and so melt in slime.'

Brooke was having fun and, as a result, his carapace of cynicism had begun to slip. Merriment and a sheer zest for life kept breaking through, accompanied by an aching realization that he would never enjoy himself with quite the same delight he was feeling now. Portentously, he told Hugh Dalton: 'There are only three good things in the world. One is to read poetry, another is to write poetry, and the best of all is to *live* poetry.' He felt that poetry put him in touch with a current that continually powered and invigorated him in some mystical way.

After another conversation on the nature of beauty, the two friends were sitting late at night at a window overlooking Kings Parade when a group of students, returning well lubricated from a dinner, passed below, whistling and yelling as they staggered home. 'Those fellows,' remarked Brooke, 'would have thought us very old if they had been in this room tonight, but when they go down and sit on office stools they will grow old quite suddenly, and, many years hence, we will still be talking and thinking about this sort of thing – and we will still be young.'

In some sense, Brooke was right – he would never grew old as Dalton did; even so, his obsessive fear of ageing and losing his youthful *élan* would haunt him for the few remaining years he had. Also held in contempt was the vulgar herd obliged to work for a living at humdrum jobs. Brooke equated growing up and settling down, getting married and having children with a betrayal of youthful idealism and spirit. His poetry is replete with gibes against the old and shuddering diatribes about ageing and bodily decay. Lodged like a beautiful golden insect inside the amber of his inner world, Brooke welcomed an early death as his one chance of escaping the fate of decrepitude.

One of his new friends, Frances Darwin, encapsulated Brooke's image in his early Cambridge career in a verse that came to embarrass both its subject and its author. Nevertheless it contains more than a grain of truth:

> A young Apollo, golden-haired,
> Stands dreaming on the edge of strife;
> Magnificently unprepared
> For the long littleness of life.

6

Fabian Summer

It was Hugh Dalton who first learned that Brooke was ready to take another step on his faltering journey towards socialism. Writing to his friend from Torquay in early April 1908, where he was spending the first ten days of the Easter vacation, Brooke forgivably boasted that he had been invited to meet H. G. Wells at his London club and, under the great man's influence, had 'decided to sign even the present Fabian Basis, and to become a member (if possible) of the central Fabian Society'.

The meeting with Wells at the National Liberal Club – soon to become one of Brooke's own London bases – was an epochal event for Brooke. As we have seen, he was impressed by Wells's vision of a new society inaugurated by an intellectual élite which would sweep aside an effete civilization. While in Torquay he noted, 'how often it consoles me to think of barbarism once more flooding the world and real feelings and passions, however rudimentary, taking the place of our wretched hypocrisies.' Intellectually, at least, Brooke was serious in his study of socialist texts – neglecting his Greek studies, the ostensible purpose of his seaside stay, to make copious notes in the margins of William Morris's *News from Nowhere* and the Fabian tracts that Wells had pressed into his hands.

From his quayside lodgings at 3 Beacon Terrace, Brooke would set out for strolls along the promenade with his varied reading matter, which included a new play written by Erica Cotterill and sent by her for his comments. As he frankly wrote to her, it served a more mundane purpose: 'I carry it about with me and sit on it at intervals.' At the same time he wrote to Geoffrey Keynes, holidaying at nearby Lulworth: 'I am not a poet – I was, that's all.' But Brooke lied. His daily routine at Torquay informed a sonnet, 'Seaside', which contains lines of real maturity, quite foreign to the strident poses of his earlier self:

Swiftly out from the friendly lilt of the band,
   The crowd's good laughter, the loved eyes of men,
   I am drawn nightward; I must turn again
Where, down beyond the low untrodden strand,
There curves and glimmers outward to the unknown
   The old unquiet ocean. All the shade
Is rife with magic and movement. I stray alone
   Here on the edge of silence, half afraid,

Waiting a sign. In the deep heart of me
The sullen waters swell towards the moon,
And all my tides set seaward.
               From inland
Leaps a gay fragment of some mocking tune,
That tinkles and laughs and fades along the sand,
And dies between the seawall and the sea.

From Torquay, Brooke made his way to the northern edge of Salisbury Plain and the isolated village of Market Lavington, where Hugh Russell-Smith and he had ended their walking tour exactly a year before. This time the Green Dragon was to be the venue for an Apostles reading party organized by John Maynard Keynes. It was the first such gathering Brooke had attended since his election two months earlier and he must have felt some qualms about his own modest intellectual attainments in the presence of such big guns as Keynes, Lytton Strachey, the critic Desmond MacCarthy and, above all, the philosopher G. E. Moore, whose *Principia Ethica*, published in 1903, provided the guiding principles for the Apostles as well as the Bloomsbury group that grew out of them. Brooke need not have worried. Moore's principal contribution to the relaxed proceedings was to play Schubert songs on the pub's piano, accompanying himself in a high baritone voice until the sweat glistened on his egg-shaped head.

    Characteristically, Lytton Strachey refused to take part in the fun and games, withdrawing to his room to read Racine and complaining to his friend and Bloomsbury ally in cattiness, Virginia Stephen, about 'the coldest winds you can imagine sweeping over the plain, and inferior food, and not enough comfortable chairs'. Despite this whinge, Lytton concluded magnanimously: 'I was quite amused.' One element which kept him smiling was the presence of Brooke, a centre of attention among so many confirmed bachelors. 'Whenever I began to feel dull,' Lytton told Virginia, 'I could look at the yellow hair and pink cheeks of Rupert.'

    Brooke also made an impression on another guest, E. M. Forster, whose novel *The Longest Journey* had been published the year before, and whose latest story, 'The Celestial Omnibus', Brooke happened to be carrying about in his jacket pocket. As he told James Strachey, in a preparatory postcard from Torquay confirming his intended presence at the Green Dragon: 'having the pleasant tolerance of the old (or at least old-fashioned), I am not especially bored even with the wise.' James was delighted by Brooke's decision to attend. He remained passionately in love, and had even jettisoned his Conservative political allegiance to follow Brooke into the Cambridge Fabians. As such, he had accompanied his beloved to a political debate in London, where Brooke, he reported excitedly to Duncan Grant, had actually seized him by the arm. 'I felt decidedly at the time that he was deliberate . . . That he'd been meaning to do it for some time, and jumped at a chance. I can't believe that he didn't know it was important. Why else was he so absurdly shy?'

For his part Brooke heartlessly enjoyed the game of making the prematurely old, spinsterish souls of Forster and the Stracheys pine for him. In contrast to his disturbing experience at Andermatt, there were no glamorous women around to share his limelight, and he basked in the admiring attention, without, as yet, worrying too much about the implications of being a pin-up of such a desiccated group.

From Market Lavington, he returned directly to Cambridge for the new term, where his first act was to sign the Fabian Basis as promised. His sponsors in this step were Hugh Dalton and Ben Keeling. Brooke was now publicly committed – at least in theory – to a fundamentalist socialist programme, including the abolition of rent and private property, the 'disappearance of the idle rich' and the complete equality of men and women. It was a set of beliefs that he was to find easier to honour in the breach.

The newly fledged Fabian found himself invited by Ben Keeling to his rooms at Trinity on 10 May. The guest of honour was Sir Sydney Olivier, whose beautiful daughter Bryn had so bewitched Brooke at Andermatt. Following the frugal one-course socialist meal (with fruit), the company adjourned to Francis Cornford's nearby rooms for coffee. Behind the scenes at this apparently innocuous and high-minded event an emotional and sexual maelstrom was let loose that was to have unforeseen and momentous consequences both for Brooke's personal life and for the development of the Fabians.

A late arrival at the feast was Wells, who as a result had to sit in a window seat, awkwardly balancing his plate on his knee. It was noted with raised eyebrows that he was accompanied by the Newnham student Amber

Reeve, Ka Cox's predecessor as treasurer of the Cambridge Fabians. Wells was a close friend of Amber's father, William Pember Reeve, the Fabian director of the London School of Economics, which had been founded by two more senior Fabians, Sidney and Beatrice Webb. Beatrice was a great sniffer-out of political and sexual unorthodoxy, and her shrivelled nostrils were already twitching disapprovingly in the direction of the sexy young Amber: 'An amazingly vital person, and I suppose very clever, but a terrible little pagan – vain, egotistical, and careless of other people's happiness.'

On this occasion Amber confirmed Beatrice Webb's worst fears by taking Wells to her Newnham bed. Their passionate lovemaking caused them to arrive late and flushed for Keeling's party. Wells was already in deep trouble with senior Fabians – only the previous month he had stormed out of their annual general meeting after being censored for supporting Winston Churchill, the Liberal candidate in an Oldham by-election, against a socialist. His reputation for seducing nubile Fabian daughters physically and susceptible Fabian wives intellectually meant that a terminal break with the movement's leadership could not long be delayed. His open affair with Amber Reeve, begun that May evening, was to be the catalyst that caused it.

Brooke's attention, however, was distracted by the presence at the party of another guest, who was to become the main romantic focus of his life for the next four years. Sir Sydney Olivier had brought with him to Cambridge not only his wife, Lady Margaret, but three of his four daughters – Margery, Daphne and Noel; Bryn had been left in Jamaica. Brooke knew Margery already, but he had never met Daphne or Noel. Placed opposite Noel at the dinner table, he was almost instantly smitten – transfixed like one of the rabbits that the young Noel liked to pin down and dissect.

Born on Christmas Day 1892, and hence just 15 at the time of her meeting with Brooke, Noel, youngest of the Olivier sisters, had spent an idyllic childhood divided between the English countryside and Jamaica, where her father was Colonial Secretary before being appointed Governor. In contrast to Brooke's strait-laced upbringing, Noel and her sisters had felt the benefits of their parents' dedication to their radical ideals. From their privileged colonial lifestyle of polo and ponies in Jamaica, to wanderings in the woods of the North Downs near their father's cottage at Limpsfield Chart in Surrey, freedom had been the keynote of Noel's young life.

Limpsfield Chart was something of a progressive nexus in the otherwise stuffily conservative county of Surrey. The Oliviers' neighbours in the scattered rural community, with its views over Box Hill to the west and the

Weald of Kent to the south, included Fabian families like the Peases and the Hobsons and Russian exiles drawn by other neighbours, the literary critics and translators of Russian literature, Edward and Constance Garnett. The Garnetts' son, David – known from his early days as 'Bunny' – was a childhood playmate of Noel's. He shrewdly observed of the Oliviers' ruling family ethos: 'They were all aristocratic creatures, pride was the moving force of their lives; they felt contempt easily; pity did not come naturally, except for animals.' In Noel's case, even animals were excluded. From her youngest years she had a penchant for collecting the cadavers of dead creatures and dissecting them. As Bunny Garnett recalled: 'We collected skeletons, we stuffed birds; we skinned rabbits and moles and tanned their skins.' The two would go out at dead of night to collect nocturnal specimens: each kept a string attached to their big toe dangling from their bedroom windows to summon each other for their secret explorations.

The open beech and pine woodlands of the countryside around Limpsfield Chart were the sisters' element, and the liberty allowed them by their parents, coupled with the sense of being members of a gifted élite removed from the common herd, combined to produce, in Noel's granddaughter's words: 'Four self-confident, independent girls, whose clannish arrogance often led rather too swiftly to contempt of others. Like Sydney, they could be unbelievably insensitive at times, often hurting the feelings of others over issues which they considered trivial.'

Bunny Garnett, who knew all four sisters from their childhood, describes the eldest, Margery, as 'tall, brown-eyed and brown-haired, handsome, with the impulsive warmth and sudden chilliness of her father'. Brynhild, the second sister, was the beauty of the family, who grew, says Bunny, a noted connoisseur of feminine charms, 'into the most beautiful young woman I have ever known. She was rather fairer than Margery; with the most lovely bone structure, a perfect complexion with red cheeks, and starry eyes that flashed and sparkled as no other woman's have ever done.' The third sister, Daphne, soon to join Margery at Newnham when Brooke met her, was 'darker, more dreamy, and, in her childhood, wrapped in the skin of some beast, or crowned with flowers'. But Bunny, like Brooke, reserved his real fascination for the youngest sister, because, he says, 'she became far more important than any of her family . . . She was quiet and the least conspicuous of the four.' But still waters run deep, and Noel was to outstrip all three of her elder sisters in intelligence and achievement.

It is easy to see what attracted Brooke to the Oliviers. They shared his charm and physical attractiveness and his propensity to regard less favoured mortals with contempt. At that fateful dinner, Noel regarded him silently as he chatted to her sister Margery, cracked nuts and flashed her the occasional smile. When the guests decamped to Cornford's rooms for coffee, Noel dropped a precious small green coffee cup and was mortified as it smashed to pieces. Instantly Brooke saw his chance and pounced, swiftly putting the flustered schoolgirl at her ease as he swept up the broken shards.

Later that month the owner of the broken cup, Francis Cornford, persuaded Brooke to entertain forty members of St Pancras Working Men's Club in his rooms, and the young Fabian earnestly quizzed these genuine members of the proletariat on their attitudes to property and Empire. Meanwhile Brooke was deepening a tie with Cornford's future wife, the poet Frances Darwin, who expressed admiration both for his glamorous person and for his poetry.

Both Francis and Frances were deeply involved in the Marlowe Dramatic Society's production of *Comus*, the rehearsals for which were now entering their final stage. Frances recalled a conversation at this time with Justin and Brooke that showed how skin-deep Brooke's new-found commitment to sexual equality really was:

> Rupert: When I marry I shall settle absolutely everything in my own house. My wife must completely obey me.
> Justin: Oh, Rupert! I should hate that! I *do* want a wife who can stand up to me.
> Rupert: No. I shall settle everything.
> Frances: But may she not ever have her own way, even about the children?
> Rupert: I suppose she may just settle little things about them when they are quite small. That's all.

Frances, like the Olivier sisters, had a wild, outdoors side to her nature – she was prone to striking poses in diaphanous gowns in picturesque sites – and she tended to romanticize Brooke for his similarities to herself. She was pivotal in attracting him into her circle of Cambridge women, a group that provided a powerful counterpoint to his previously predominantly male society. Her cousin Gwen Darwin, Ka Cox, Sybil and Ethel Pye (by coincidence neighbours of the Oliviers at Limpsfield Chart) and the Olivier sisters themselves were all drawn into various aspects of *Comus* as June became July, and Brooke, the harassed stage manager-cum-second lead actor, chivvied his teams of seamstresses, scene painters and costume designers into ever greater efforts. The pace grew too hot for Justin, preoccupied by his Finals, and for Frances herself, always prone to the inherited Darwin weakness of depression, and both fell by the wayside. By the time the production opened, on 10 July, Brooke, energized by his responsibilities, stood almost alone as the commanding figure. For once he did not fall ill.

Brooke's own lack of stage skills were all too apparent to those who saw the piece in rehearsal. According to the critic E. J. Dent, who had also observed him in *Dr Faustus*, Brooke was an indifferent speaker of verse, with the family impediment of a harsh, grating and monotonous voice. But he was willing to learn: his new women friends gave him tips on how to hang down his head and shake his luxuriant hair loose. Frances tells how afterwards he was seen staring in a mirror, dreamily running his fingers through his hair and asking no one in particular: 'Is it right now? Will my hair do now?' On a more serious level, he was genuinely moved by his discovery of Milton; telling Frances theatrically that the Puritan poet had joined that select company who made his hand tremble with anticipation as he prepared to take down a volume of theirs from a bookshelf.

Brooke's acting abilities notwithstanding, James Strachey was smitten anew by the sight of him in costume at the dress rehearsal, as Maynard Keynes reported to Duncan Grant: 'James went to a rehearsal last night and declares that Brooke's beauty was so great that he couldn't sleep a wink last night for thinking of it.'

The day before the production, Brooke suffered a loss which affected him almost as deeply as Dick's death. His Greek teacher, Walter Headlam, the man who had originally suggested a performance of *Comus*, died after collapsing at Lord's at the early age of 42. Brooke was devastated, describing Headlam as not only the best writer in Greek since the Greeks themselves, but also the man who had awakened him to poets like Donne, Webster and Milton himself.

Brooke was so affected by the loss of Headlam and the accumulated strain of organizing almost every aspect of the production alone that he spent much of the day of the performance slumped in a chair in E. J. Dent's garden in a state of nervous collapse. He did not even rouse himself to receive his mother when she arrived to see the play, leaving James Strachey and Frances Darwin to entertain her to tea.

Brooke had pulled off an amazing PR triumph for what was essentially an undergraduate production of a fairly obscure work: apart from several representatives of the local and national press, the opening night was attended by a galaxy of the literary good and the great, including both the reigning and future Poet Laureates, Alfred Austin and Robert Bridges;

Thomas Hardy; and the foremost critic of the day, Edmund Gosse. Not all the celebrities were impressed: Bridges left before the end; and Gosse, asked what he thought now that he had heard *Comus*, replied: 'I have *over*heard it.'

The hospitable Charles Sayle gave his customary post-production party for the cast, and they assembled again the following morning at his home for a celebratory breakfast at which the guest of honour was Hardy himself. The legendary man of letters, reported Brooke, was 'incredibly shrivelled and ordinary' and 'made faintly pessimistic remarks about the toast'. The second and final performance of *Comus* was given for paying punters the same afternoon at the New Theatre.

The critics' verdicts on the performance were generally kind, although opinion on Brooke himself was mixed. In contrast to E. J. Dent, *The Academy* praised his 'voice and comely presence' while the *Cambridge Daily News* found him 'somewhat stilted'. Lytton Strachey, in the throes of an emotional crisis caused by the desertion of his lover, the fickle Duncan Grant, for the arms of Lytton's friend Maynard Keynes, rallied sufficiently to write a review for what was virtually the Strachey family's house journal, the *Spectator*. In it, he damned Brooke with faint praise, admiring the beauties of the verse but passing over the way it was delivered.

That evening the cast assembled again, in full costume, at Newnham Grange, the Darwin family's home on the Cam. The show was the talk of the town, especially for its daring innovation of using women to play the female roles. Once again Brooke found himself the centre of an attentive and admiring throng. He was unable to enjoy the adulation in complete ease since he was unable to sit down owing to the tightness of his skimpy, star-spangled sky-blue costume. But he managed to hold court standing with his back to a wall.

Keeping a watchful eye on the proceedings was the Ranee, who was introduced by her son to some of his new female friends. Her disapproval was obvious and her reaction instantaneous: she wasted no time in gathering up an admittedly exhausted Brooke and sweeping him off to Rugby, without giving him the chance to say a proper farewell to his friends or help them to strike the *Comus* set. He did, however, find the time to pose for a series of photographs in his costume taken by the Cambridge studio of Scott & Wilkinson. Brooke could never resist the temptation to back into the limelight.

Recovering in Rugby under his mother's ministrations, a guilt-stricken Brooke wrote to Frances Darwin to excuse his hurried departure: 'The fun being over, I sneaked away on Monday and left you all to clear up the mess

. . . My mother (I can plead) packed me up and snatched me here to sleep and recover . . . I felt a deserter.'

During the preparations for *Comus* Brooke had used his dominant position as *de facto* director to exact a curious promise from his fellow-Thespians. They should all, he sternly demanded, pledge not to pair off and get engaged for at least six months after the production. Feeling the tug of love himself towards Noel Olivier, his innate puritanism surfaced in a blind panic that the fragile community of young talent he had created around *Comus* would fracture into separate ties. The romance of a show played out at the end of term in the fevered heat of a Cambridge summer could, he feared, kindle warmth and loyalties that would run out of control. Still more curiously, such was the power of his winning ways that each member of the cast agreed to his bizarre request. However, unknown to him, two of them were about to 'turn with traitor breath' and break the solemn bond.

Frances Darwin and Francis Cornford had dared to become engaged. Their romance, started in Cambridge, had been carried on by correspondence while Frances was spending her summer vacation in Ireland. Cornford, at 34, was 12 years older than his fiancée, with a settled academic career. He was a safe choice, and the marriage proved an exceptionally happy one. After the initial shock of the news, Brooke forgave his friends and continued to see them and correspond with Frances, who acted as a valued mentor and adviser in his various emotional and romantic entanglements. But the couple's marriage had placed them on the outer margins of Brooke's friends, and he continued to regard matrimony as the ultimate betrayal of the friendship he fetishized. Marriage was an infallible sign of the maturity that he dreaded so deeply to attain.

However, he had his own romantic fish to fry. With little to do in Rugby, he turned his mind to a subtle plot he had developed to bring him in touch with Noel. Two women stood in the way of his plan's realization – his mother and Noel's eldest sister, Margery. Craftily, he intended to use them both to bring about his heart's desire. He suggested to the Ranee that the Olivier sisters should be invited *en bloc* to visit Rugby. An invitation was duly sent to Margery, who was acting *in loco parentis* while Sydney and Margaret Olivier were away in Jamaica. Brooke had to tread carefully, for Margery was on the lookout for a mate and was half-protective and half-jealous of male attention paid to her more attractive younger sisters. He hinted at the difficulties in a letter to his sensibly studious Cambridge friend Dudley Ward:

There is a Young Person at present in Rugby (I've not seen her) who hails from Jamaica – is, indeed, a friend of the Oliviers – is going soon to stay at Limpsfield. Mother met her; said 'Oh yes we're going to have two of the Oliviers to stay with us, do you know them?' 'My, yes!' the person shrilled. 'The Oliviers! They'd do *anything*, those girls!' Mother (whose *anything* is at once vastly ominous and most limited) is, and will be for months, ill with foreboding. She pictures, I think, Margery climbing on the roof at night, or throwing bread about at table, or kissing the rural milkman.

In the event, Brooke's planning went for naught: the Olivier girls all accompanied their returned parents to the Lake District and he had to shelve his plan. But it remained in his mind, to be fulfilled at a more propitious time. Meanwhile he turned his attention to the highlight of his summer: the Fabian summer school at Llanbedr, near Harlech, on the remote north-west coast of Wales. Political summer schools were a novelty in British political life: the first such Fabian school had been organized by Bernard Shaw and his wife Charlotte only the year before. However, Brooke felt more confident about attending the event than he had at Andermatt or among the Apostles at Market Lavington, not least because he would be with a large posse of his Cambridge friends. The party included James Strachey, Ben Keeling, Hugh Dalton, Dudley Ward, Arthur Schloss and Gerald Shove. Female Fabians attending included Margery Olivier and Amber Reeve.

The prospect of the camp cheered Brooke's otherwise muted celebration of his twenty-first birthday in the bosom of his family. The event was marred by his mother's reaction when he told her that his chief aim in life was pleasure – the confession reduced her to tears. Before setting off for Wales he entertained a group of his friends to lunch – Dudley Ward, who was coaching Alfred Brooke in history, Keeling and Dalton. The Fabian trio were under strict instructions from Brooke to keep their socialist politics concealed from his devotedly Liberal mother, and he remained in Rugby for a few more days to soothe her when they left.

Before long he rejoined his friends, and the Cambridge party found themselves staying with Sidney and Beatrice Webb at a farmhouse near Leominster. It was Brooke's first encounter with the formidable Mrs Webb, whose ferocity and belligerence made even the Ranee look mild-mannered, and he must have felt he had fallen from the frying pan into the fire in swapping one censorious middle-aged lady for another. For their part, the founding Fabians eyed up these representatives of the new university élite with a jaundiced eye. Like Wells, the Webbs believed in a secular band of warrior-priests who would inaugurate socialism, and they clearly hoped that these young Cambridge men would form the nucleus of such a group. The brief encounter at Leominster left the couple feeling equivocal, but by 1910 Beatrice had made up her mind about Brooke and his friends: 'They don't want to learn, they don't think they have anything to learn . . . the egotism of the young University man is colossal.'

It must be admitted that, from the Webbs' sombrely earnest viewpoint, the Cambridge contingent did not come up to scratch. Healthy, good-humoured, exuberant – Brooke's peer group were at least as interested in having a good time as they were in studying the sacred, and sometimes turgid, texts of socialism. James Strachey, in particular, was clearly more interested in moving his mattress next to Brooke's in the communal dormitory, while Hugh 'Daddy' Dalton, the future Labour Chancellor, was on this occasion equally preoccupied by carnal desire, as Brooke reported in a letter to Lytton Strachey:

> Daddy was a schoolboy in dormitory and conceived a light lust for James – who, I thought, was quite dignified about it. He would start up suddenly behind him and tickle him gently under the armpits, making strange sibilant cluckings with his mouth meanwhile. And when James was in bed Daddy stood over him, waving an *immense* steaming penis in his face and chuckling softly. Poor James was nearly sick.

The summer school was held in a cliff-top farmhouse, Pen-yr-Allt, which had stables converted into dormitories and a plunge bath for cold early-morning dips. The Cambridge group arrived on 30 August after a stop on the way to visit Ludlow Castle, in Shropshire, the site of the original production of *Comus*. In the absence of the Webbs, the young people let off steam with cruel mimicry of their recent hosts. The tone of the school was high-minded in true Fabian style, with vegetarian food, Swedish-style physical jerks, lectures on subjects ranging from Tolstoy to the Poor Law and plenty of time for both reading (Brooke had brought no fewer than 19 books) and rambles in the surrounding hills. It was a mind- and body-stretching programme, but Brooke was not put off, and left the school more of a convinced Fabian than ever.

7

In Arcadia

The Michaelmas term at Cambridge promised to be filled with as much hectic extracurricular activity for Brooke as the *Comus*-dominated previous term had been. He was uneasily aware that he was falling behind with his studies, and without the encouraging presence of Walter Headlam, his interest in Classics, never pronounced, had completely vanished. For the moment, he was able to shove this problem to the back of his mind, but he knew he would soon have to confront it.

Meanwhile there were friends, politics – and poetry. As always, Brooke was rehearsing his place in posterity; and, half-seriously, imagining himself as a literary immortal. Showing Hugh Dalton round Rugby chapel, he pointed to a gap beside the plaque to Arthur Hugh Clough and remarked: 'They're reserving that for me.' Sure enough, that exact place on the memorial wall was eventually to be filled by Brooke.

An even more fervent admirer was James Strachey, who had suffered wretchedly at Llanbedr when he persuaded himself that Brooke was at last returning his love. True, there were uneasy suspicions in his mind that Brooke was in love with a woman – he suspected Daphne Olivier, being as yet unaware of Noel. 'Why did we think him a sodomite?' he asked Duncan Grant piteously. Three days later his hopes revived: 'Good God – he's falling in love with me,' ran his running report to Grant. 'No, no, no. I can't bear it. This is too vast.' It was. Four days after, James was once again plunged into the depths: 'panic fell – oh, on him perhaps too – and it all dissolved into air . . . So everything's to end in utter misery, after all.'

While James retired to lick his wounds, Brooke resumed his social round in Cambridge. One new passing acquaintance was a second-year Trinity man, Vyvyan Holland, second son of Brooke's early idol, Oscar Wilde. Holland invited Brooke to a champagne supper with Ronald Firbank in honour of Robert Ross, Wilde's most loyal friend and indefatigable defender of his posthumous reputation. Very different from this homosexual trio was another casual acquaintance made this term, Herbert Morrison, later a leading Labour politician and a bitter rival to Hugh Dalton.

Brooke and Dalton continued to promote the Carbonari, who discussed topics like 'Immortality' – the former remained a firm and increasingly dogmatic atheist – and Brooke read a paper on 'Satire in English Verse', in which he lauded the poetry of Hilaire Belloc, whom he was to meet again in the New Year.

One more figure who entered Brooke's life at this time was destined to become his most powerful and influential literary mentor, and a man whose wealth, generosity and total devotion to Brooke was to last for the rest of his life and well beyond it. Eddie Marsh, at the time of their meeting, was a high-flying civil servant who had recently hitched his professional wagon to the meteoric star of Winston Churchill, whose Private Secretary he became in the Colonial Office, and later at the Home Office and Admiralty.

Marsh was born to wealth as a great-grandson of Spencer Perceval, the only British Prime Minister to have been assassinated. A shocked parliament had voted a huge sum to Perceval's many children after he was shot by a deranged bankrupt in 1812. Eddie continued to use his share of what he called 'the murder money' to promote his major interests – the arts, and particularly handsome and talented young painters and poets. Homosexual, but, because of a childhood bout of mumps, probably non-practising, Eddie had been aware of the handsome young Kingsman on previous visits to Cambridge. An Apostle in the 1890s, the 36-year-old Eddie was now an 'Angel' – Apostolic jargon for a member who had left the university but still attended meetings of the group; and it was at one of these that he invited Brooke for a tête-à-tête breakfast.

A boastful Brooke read his future mentor a new poem, 'Day That I Have Loved':

> Tenderly, day that I have loved, I close your eyes,
>   And smooth your quiet brow, and fold your thin
>   dead hands.

He went on to read a second poem, 'The Jolly Company', which had just netted him another prize in his regular outlet, the *Westminster Gazette*. Brooke was frankly cynical about the reasons for his regularly churning out inferior poems and other pieces for the *Gazette* – money. He was on a safe but not lavish income of £150 from his mother, doled out in quarterly instalments, and depended on his literary work for any monies beyond this basic allowance. As he told James Strachey, he felt he was rich when he made £7 in a single day – £2 from the *Gazette* and £5 from a prize-winning King's essay. With his tongue in his cheek, he computed that if he could keep up this rate of income, he would be earning £1895 a year.

Brooke was brooding on his unfulfilled – and apparently unfulfillable – passion for Noel Olivier. Tortured by frustration in Wales, his emotions intensified by the presence of Noel's less fanciable sister, Margery, Brooke began to dream of extreme remedies. Noel was a pupil at Bedales, the establishment that had been attended by his friends Justin Brooke and Jacques Raverat, and in late October he wrote to Dudley Ward suggesting that they kidnap Noel from the school. It was only half in jest.

Soon a more plausible plan suggested itself. Brooke learned that Margery and Noel would be taking a Christmas holiday at Klosters in the Swiss Alps, among a party of around 30. The cost of the 11-day vacation – a guinea a day – he managed to wangle out of the sceptical Ranee on the pretext that he needed to recover from his (non-existent) academic labours of the term. Any increase in his intimacy with Noel he regarded as money well spent. Noel celebrated her sixteenth birthday on Christmas Day, and the following evening the company presented the melodrama *From the Jaws of the Octopus*, which Brooke had written specially for the occasion, and in which he played the hero, Eugene de Montmorency. On New Year's Day he told James Strachey: 'Switzerland fair. (I morose). Noel Olivier superb.' At last he had lifted a corner of the veil of his secret romance to a savagely jealous James, who would enjoy a passionate physical affair with Noel some 15 years after Brooke's death.

The mountain air and vigorous skiing and tobogganing had doubtless raised Brooke's libido to new heights; but, bound by the sexual etiquette of his class and time, he was no nearer to a physical consummation of his passion for the 16-year-old schoolgirl, with her strong, chunky body and cool grey eyes. Noel, for her part, was fascinated and flattered by her handsome admirer, but she had more than her share of the Olivier family's distrust of excess of feeling and, for the moment, kept Brooke at arm's length. He consequently returned to Rugby in a foul mood, and took out his frustration in a two-hour row with the Ranee – an unheard-of insubordination.

The new term began at Cambridge with Brooke coming under fire from his elders during a general discussion at an Apostles meeting on 19 January. It was a salutary drubbing. Leading the assault was the King's don Jack Sheppard, who pitched into Brooke for daring to defend H. G. Wells's ethics, and, as Maynard Keynes put it in a letter to Duncan Grant: 'for thinking truth beauty, beauty truth. [Harry] Norton and Lytton took up the attack and even James [Strachey] and Gerald [Shove] stabbed him in the back. Finally Lytton, enraged at Brooke's defences, thoroughly lost his temper and delivered a violent personal attack.' The seeds for Brooke's later extreme antipathy to the elder Strachey were already being sown.

Three weeks later, apparently reconciled, Brooke invited his fellow-Apostles to meet Hilaire Belloc over dinner in his rooms. The evening lasted for over three hours, one of which was taken up with a monologue over the coffee by the loquacious author. Brooke still showed little sign of knuckling down to his studies, and yet again much of his time was taken up with a Marlowe Dramatic Society production of Ben Jonson's *The Silent Woman*, produced by a friend and fellow Kingsman, the future actor and author Reginald Pole.

Belloc was a clear influence on a paper read by Brooke to the Carbonari entitled 'The Romantic History and Surprising Adventures of John Rump' in Dalton's rooms later in February. Brooke took as his motto for the piece an Arnoldian precept he had heard preached from the pulpit of Rugby chapel in 1904: 'It is character we want, not brains.' His piece, retailing the life history of Rump, an archetypal middle-class Englishman, is a telling insight into the well-springs of Brooke's psychology, with obvious autobiographical roots. Rump's father is a public-school housemaster, while his mother is 'a peculiar mixture of irritable discontinuous nagging and shrill incompetence'. The family make up for the shortfalls in their income caused by their financial mismanagement by cheese-paring economies like cutting the food rations of the boys in their charge. Many of Rump's characteristics reflect Brooke's – such as his lifelong aversion to religion caused by an overdose of evangelism in the nursery. His adult life is a wilderness of dreary mediocrity until death mercifully snuffs him out at the age of 70. The satire is notable for its brutal rejection of the money-grubbing philistinism of the middle class, summed up in Rump's greeting to God as he arrives in Heaven complete with top-hat, frock-coat and, of course, umbrella:

> You long-haired aesthetes, get you out of Heaven!
> I am John Rump, this is my hat, and this
> My umbrella. I stand here for sense,

> Invincible, inviolable, eternal,
> For safety regulations, paving-stones,
> Street-lamps, police, and bijou residences
> Semi-detached. I stand for Sanity,
> Comfort, Content, Prosperity, top-hats,
> Alcohol, collars, meat. Tariff Reform
> Means higher wages and more work for all.

Dalton had succeeded Ben Keeling as President of the Cambridge Fabians, and Brooke was being groomed to follow his friend into this august office. He helped organize a visit by Ramsay Macdonald, then the fiery chairman of the Independent Labour Party, and decades away from his role as the gravedigger of socialism as Prime Minister of the first Labour government. Brooke's prominence in Fabian activities made him a target of the Tory hearty faction at the college, and he had to bribe his bed-maker to warn him of a planned raid on his rooms after the hearties comprehensively trashed the lodgings of his Fabian friend Gerald Shove.

The hearty threat was one of the reasons why Brooke began to contemplate moving out of Cambridge altogether. More pressing was the advice of his teachers to accept the inevitable and take the consequences of the realization that he would never be a Classical scholar. Two of his tutors, the brothers W. H. and C. G. Macaulay, concurred in counselling Brooke to concentrate, in his fourth Cambridge year, on his obvious preference for English literature. The Macaulays pointed out that, so long as he remained in college, he would be continually tempted to neglect his studies by the constant stream of visitors who dropped in on his rooms. They were well aware, also, of the drain on Brooke's time and energy imposed by his extracurricular activities – and successfully persuaded him to turn down an invitation to edit the *Cambridge Review*.

With his tutors' advice ringing in his ears, Brooke returned to Rugby, where his mother was laid low with illness. There he wrote his first surviving letter to Noel Olivier in his frequently employed voice of a flippant and witty show-off. The letter is full of elaborate – but abortive – plans to meet up in Devon, and Brooke cannot resist playing the didactic elder brother as he recommends a raft of new writers for Noel to read 'whose names you have never heard before I uttered them': Wells, Belloc, Algernon Blackwood and W. B. Yeats.

Kicking his heels in School Field House, Brooke was buzzing with intricate plans for the Easter holidays. He meant to squeeze in no fewer than five separate vacations, each representing a different facet of his increasingly complex and secretive life. There was a party at Becky Falls, a Dartmoor beauty spot near Manaton in south Devon; an Apostles reading group at the Lizard in Cornwall; and 'duty calls' on his surviving 'mad aunt' at Bournemouth and his parents at the resort of Sidmouth in south Devon.

Over and above these, however, was his determination to get together with Noel Olivier. He had gone about arranging this longed-for conjunction with almost serpentine care. The first move in his campaign, begun in the aftermath of his Christmas meeting with Noel at Klosters, was to initiate a weekly correspondence with her elder sister and 'minder' Margery Olivier. From these letters he had gleaned the information that Noel and Margery would be spending part of their Easter holidays at an isolated cottage at Bank in the New Forest. Brooke promptly enlisted the aid of Dudley Ward, his dull but dependable Fabian friend, as an unlikely chaperone of his wooing of Noel:

> Well! If they're in the New Forest, good, I'll go . . . But I leave it to you to learn of their arrangements, discover all, and break to them that we shall be passing their door. I do so because (a) I've been writing to Margery about once a week since January, and she'll be about sick of me, (b) I daren't do it, (c) I have no time and you have plenty. So you must settle. But oh! be tactful, be gently tactful! Perhaps they will hate us? Horrible thought! Do not intrude! apologize! apologize!

Brooke had to conceal his amatory ambitions, not only from the Ranee but also from other friends who would disapprove of him wooing a schoolgirl. He planned to enlist another old friend, Hugh Russell-Smith, as a convenient 'cover' for his journey to the New Forest, simply because the Russell-Smiths' family home was close to Bank. 'I have told him [Russell-Smith] 'I am going to "seek Romance!"' he wrote to Dudley. 'He believes I am going to wander through Surrey disguised in an Italian sombrero, with a guitar, singing old English ballads for pence! Ho! ho! But remember, a profound secret. It adds SO much to the pleasure of it all.'

With these complex schemes in play, Brooke left Rugby for the first station on his tortuous path through south-west England – Becky Falls, where he arrived in the last week of March with Hugh Russell-Smith in tow. He stayed with the Herns, a farming family whose house overlooked the Falls themselves, an impressive 70-foot waterfall tumbling over granite rocks. He described his regime in a letter to Erica Cotterill:

I am leading the healthy life. I rise early, twist myself about on a kind of pulley that is supposed to make my chest immense (but doesn't), eat no meat, wear very little, do not part my hair, take frequent cold baths, work ten hours a day and rush madly about the mountains in flannels and rainstorms for hours. I am surprisingly cheerful about it. It is all part of my scheme for returning to nature.

The regime reminds one of a combination of the Rugby and the Bedales life – clearly the pull of the old school was not one that Brooke could easily escape. He waxed lyrical about his surroundings in letters to Dudley Ward ('I dance through the rain, singing musically snatches of old Greek roundelays') and Jacques Raverat: 'The sunsets were yellow wine. And the wind! – oh! there was never such a wind to take you and shake you and roll you over and set you shouting with laughter.'

Sated with such physical boisterousness, at the beginning of April Brooke moved on, alone, to join a party of Apostles organized by G. E. Moore at Penmenner House on the Lizard, Britain's southernmost promontory. If Dartmoor had been a celebration of the body, the meeting at the Lizard was to be a more cerebral gathering. The cast was a reunion of the group from Market Lavington the previous year: Moore, Desmond MacCarthy, C. P. Sangar, R. S. Trevelyan and James Strachey. In addition, Brooke met for the first time Leonard Woolf, an intellectual civil servant, destined to woo and wed his childhood friend Virginia Stephen. Reporting to Raverat, Brooke enthused: 'Cornwall was full of heat and tropical flowers: and all day I bathed in great creamy breakers of surf, or lay out in the sun to dry (in April!); and all night argued with a philosopher, an economist, and a writer. Ho, we put the world to rights.'

Once again James Strachey suffered the sweet sorrow of having Brooke at his side, yet still strangely distant. He told Lytton: 'This afternoon, for the first time in my life, I saw Rupert naked. Can't we imagine what *you'ld* say on such an occasion? . . . But *I'm* simply inadequate, of course. So I say nothing, except that I didn't have an erection – which was . . . fortunate?, as I was naked too. I thought him – if you'ld like to have a pendant – "absolutely beautiful".'

As Brooke crossed intellectual swords with G. E. Moore, who launched a determined assault on his Fabianism; and fended off James, who mounted an equally determined, and equally unsuccessful attempt on his body, his mind was busy with the next, and most exciting stage of his pilgrimage: the meeting with Noel.

On his circuitous route to the forest idyll, he enjoyed a picnic in Devon with another group of friends – Geoffrey and Maynard Keynes and Ka Cox. He observed that Geoffrey was paying court to Ka – as was another of his correspondents, Jacques Raverat – but as yet he was too preoccupied with thoughts of Noel to pay much attention to the homely charms that had captivated his old friends. In his absence, Dudley Ward had done his work well, discreetly engineering an invitation to call on the Oliviers at the Bank cottage. Then, having made their smokescreen call on the Russell-Smiths, Brooke and Dudley departed for what Brooke called 'Arcadee'. Behind them, as they disappeared into the shade of the forest, the friends had deliberately dropped a trail of false addresses, so that the Russell-Smiths believed them to be in Surrey, his aunt at Bournemouth thought Brooke was still in Cornwall, and so on. The result was that between 10 and 13 April Brooke disappeared from the world to pay careful court to the youthful and unwitting object of his affections.

The two friends stumbled on the nest of Newnhamites as if by accident, discovering in residence at Bank not only Margery and Noel but Brynhild as well, along with two Newnham friends of Margery, Evelyn Radford and Dorothy Osmaston, who recorded the visit with her camera. The resulting photos are revealing, showing a handsome and windswept Brooke in Norfolk jacket, flannel trousers and tough boots; a bespectacled and watchful Dudley; a clearly adoring Margery; and Noel herself, in her Bedales smock, shyly averting her eyes from the camera lens.

Margery was a problem, since she had been misled by Brooke's weekly letters into believing that she, not her youngest sister, was the object of his attention. Brooke had to use all the charm and subterfuge at his command to snatch a few precious moments alone with Noel, but somehow he managed it, as he recounted to Jacques Raverat:

> But then, after the Lizard, oh! then came the Best! And none knows of it. For I was lost for four days. I was, for the first time in my life, a free man, and my own master! Oh! the joy of it! Only three know, but you shall . . . For I went dancing and leaping through the New Forest, with £3 and a satchel full of books, sleeping and eating anywhere, singing to the birds, tumbling about in the flowers, bathing in the rivers, and, in general, behaving naturally. And all in England, at Eastertide! And so I walked and laughed and met many people and made a thousand songs – all very good – and, in the end of the days, came to a woman who was more glorious than the sun and stronger than the sea, and kinder than the earth, who is a flower made out of fire, a star that laughs all day, whose brain is clean and clear like a man's and her heart is full of courage and kindness and whom I love. I told her that the Earth was crowned with wild flowers and dancing down the violet ways of Spring; that Christ had died and

Pan was risen; that her mouth was like sunlight on a gull's wing. As a matter of fact, I believe I said 'Hullo! Isn't it rippin' weather!' . . .

This impassioned compendium of Brookian delights, with its mix of high-coloured exaggeration, childlike exuberance, sheer egotism and its scorpion sting of self-mockery in the tail is typical of Brooke at his lyrical, hyperbolic best – or worst. But his affection for Noel and his delight at escaping – if only momentarily – the restrictive talons of the Ranee shine through. The discovery of love under the greenwood tree in such a historic corner of old England (Gritnam, the clearing of cottages outside Bank where they were staying is mentioned in the Domesday Book) was a revelation for Brooke. He would return to the home cooking of Mrs Primmer, the landlady (a discovery of Ben Keeling and a favourite with the Cambridge Fabians), and from now on was a convinced adherent of the simple life *à la* Bedales, with its delight in camping, vegetarianism, nude bathing and a free and easy mingling of the sexes. He left Bank a new man. To Jacques he summed up his feelings thus:

> From being sad I have travelled far; to the same goal as you, that of laughing, at times – often – for the joy of life . . . I find all things . . . admirable. Splendour is everywhere. I have come out of the Night; and out of the Past. There are a great many poems and paintings in the world, and I love them; also there are the sun on the sea, and flowers, and people's faces. I am intensely happy; and not with that Maeterlinckian happiness that always fears the gods' jealousy. For I feel certain that happiness is abiding. At least, I have had it, and known. Nothing can take that. So I dwell, smiling. The world is full of tremendous hopes. I am going to be 'a failure' in my Tripos. And they all curse me for wasting my career. I smile at them. Never was my conscience so serene. I know more than they.

In this exalted state, Brooke/Pan pranced off on his newly acquired cloven hooves to confront the suspicious Ranee at Sidmouth. An open avowal of his travels in Arcadia was impossible – Mrs Brooke's gluey grip on the strings manipulating his life, not least the purse-strings, would never be relaxed. The only answer was the long-learned habits of deception, and the practice of them that had by now become second nature.

Mr and Mrs Brooke had taken lodgings on the sea front at Sidmouth, and once Brooke had joined them he dashed off a poem for a *Westminster Gazette* contest. Brooke's effort, 'The Voice', is infused with the recent memory of his Easter rapture before a more cynical note sets in:

87

And I knew
That this was the hour of knowing,
And the night and the woods and you
Were one together, and I should find
Soon in the silence the hidden key
Of all that had hurt and puzzled me—
Why you were you, and the night was kind,
And the woods were part of the heart of me . . .

But the long-awaited beloved does not come up to the poet's expectations:

And suddenly
There was an uproar in my woods,
The noise of a fool in mock distress,
Crashing and laughing and blindly going,
Of ignorant feet and a swishing dress,
And a voice profaning the solitudes.

The spell was broken, the key denied me,
And at length your flat clear voice beside me
Mouthed cheerful clear flat platitudes.

You came and quacked beside me in the wood.
You said, 'The view from here is very good!'
You said, 'It's nice to be alone a bit!'
And, 'How the days are drawing out!' you said.
You said, 'The sunset's pretty isn't it?'

By God! I wish—I wish that you were dead!

The plodding clumsiness of the early verses does nothing to prepare the reader for the petulant savagery of the final lines. But anyone with knowledge of Brooke's inner turmoil cannot be surprised at his surprise that the real Noel, a shy, diffident, but resolutely down-to-earth teenager, should be a very different creature from the Goddess 'More glorious than the Sun and stronger than the sea' of his fevered imaginings. His feelings for Noel, however, were nothing if not changeable: after the hissing hatred about 'quacking' and 'platitudes', a very different note is sounded in a sonnet he sat down to write as soon as he had sent off 'The Voice', which won the *Gazette*'s competition. The new poem read:

Oh! Death will find me, long before I tire
   Of watching you, and swing me suddenly
Into the shade and loneliness and mire
   Of the last land! There, waiting patiently,

One day, I think, I'll feel a cool wind blowing,
   See a slow light across the Stygian tide,
And hear the Dead about me stir, unknowing,
   And tremble. And *I* shall know that you have died,

And watch you, a broad-browed and smiling dream,
   Pass, light as ever, through the listless host,
Quietly ponder, start, and sway, and gleam—
   Most individual and bewildering ghost!—

And turn and toss your brown delightful head
Amusedly, among the ancient Dead.

This poem is the first of Brooke's many love lyrics in which genuine, unforced emotion comes over in a mature way. Its feeling and control show a master's touch, and he rightly led off with the poem in the first collection of his verse that appeared three years later. The opening line, like the first stroke of a conductor's baton, leads the reader in, and the light ending, with its image of Noel carelessly and haughtily tossing her hair, is a satisfying adieu.

A few days after being clasped 'to the bosom of my sad family', as he put it to Eddie Marsh, Brooke found pressing reasons to return to Cambridge 'earlier than I thought'. *En route* he accepted an invitation from Eddie to spend a night at his bachelor chambers at 5 Raymond Buildings, Gray's Inn. The address was soon to become Brooke's unofficial London residence. Here, at the top of a stone staircase, in a comfortable apartment lined with books and pictures, where Eddie's loyal housekeeper, Mrs Elgy, looked after her master and his constant stream of young – and mostly male – visitors, Brooke would find a home more cosy and congenial than the real thing – though he was too astute not to suspect that the real agenda behind his friend's invitation was a homosexual attraction that was to remain undeclared.

The first night he spent under Eddie's roof – 23 April 1909 – was six years to the day before his death in the Aegean. Brooke's time had already begun to run.

8

Milk and Honey

Brooke's sudden infatuation with Noel begs all sorts of questions – about his sexuality, his self-regard and the sexual etiquette of the time. H. G. Wells's public affair with Amber Reeve, which he fictionalized in 1909 in *Ann Veronica*, was shocking enough to members of the Fabians to have the writer turfed out of the Society. For all their apparent devotion to sexual equality and their denunciation of Victorian hypocrisy, the young people in Brooke's set were still hidebound by the morals of their parents' generation. Why else would Brooke go to such lengths to wrap an innocent chaperoned visit to a group of female friends in such mystery? Although he enjoyed secrecy for its own sake, he remained imbued with his mother's strait-laced values, and was horrified by any open manifestation of sexuality among his friends outside the bonds of marriage.

Brooke had a healthy libido, and we know that he was happy enough to indulge it in strict privacy or when he was abroad and thought that word of his activities would not get back to the ears of his friends or family at home. His passion for secrecy only partly explains why he was so keen to keep the romance to himself and a select group of friends, for he was seriously concerned that he would not be taken seriously as a lover of women. His actual experience of women was, anyway, very limited at the time he met Noel, and it is significant that he fell for a tomboy who was still in the process of maturing. Throughout his pursuit of Noel he continued to indulge in teasing homosexual badinage with James Strachey, and met up with his former lovers at Rugby, Charlie Lascelles and Denham Russell-Smith. It seems clear that he remained confused and uncertain about his sexual identity until late in his life. The homoerotic element in his make-up was too ingrained to root out, even had he wished to.

For her part, Noel can be forgiven for her cautious response to Brooke's wooing: shrewdly, she sensed the fickle, restless and unfocused nature of his commitment. Suspicious of his intentions, she held him off, thereby heightening both his sexual frustration and his anger with her as a despised representative of all women. While he enjoyed the chase and the deceptions it entailed, one doubts the seriousness of his pursuit should push have come to shove. His frustration comes through clearly in the closing lines of 'The Voice' and it is disturbing that he should have been so ready to commit this early disillusion with her to public print in the *Westminster Gazette.*

Back in Cambridge, Brooke faced the unwelcome prospect of his Tripos exams. He took his mind off the impending unpleasantness by embarking on a series of bucolic picnics in the countryside in the unseasonably warm weather. The first of these, on 2 May, was undertaken in the wealthy Justin Brooke's newly acquired Opel car. The two Brookes piled into the commodious vehicle along with Geoffrey Keynes and a quartet of Newnhamites – Ka Cox, Gwen and Margaret Darwin and Dorothy Lamb, sister of Brooke's future nemesis, Henry Lamb. Justin drove the party out to Overcote on the River Ouse, where they laid out the victuals in a watermeadow. The setting was idyllic: a nightingale sang and crab-apple was in blossom. As they opened their picnic baskets and flung themselves on the damp grass, Brooke was moved to read aloud appropriate verses: Robert Herrick's 'Corinna's Going a-Maying':

> Come let us goe, while we are in our prime
> And take the harmlesse and follie of the time.
> We shall grow old apace, and die
> Before we know our liberty.
> Our life is short: and our dayes run
> As fast away as does the summer.

The shortness of 'summer's lease' was a leitmotif in Brooke's own poetry. He, more than most, had reason to dread growing old. The metaphor of gathering rosebuds while he might was an all too present reality informing his 'dew-dabbling', as such pastoral frolics became known. On this occasion the company was even inspired to plait chains from the riverside flowers and crown each other as monarchs of their fragile May. Later that month the same group repeated the picnic, and a barefoot Brooke was caught by a camera wrestling with Donald Robertson, later a professor of Classics at Trinity.

The picnicking continued throughout that enchanted month: one night Brooke, Dalton and a companion even stayed out through the dark reading

Swinburne by the light of a bicycle lamp. The poet's recent death and Christian burial had prompted a snort of anti-religious rage on Brooke's part. 'Did you see,' he wrote to Dalton, 'that, against his desire the bloody parson mouthed Anglicanisms of blasphemous and untrue meaning and filthy sentimentality over him?'

While the anti-orthodox mood was upon him, Brooke delivered a paper to the Carbonari entitled 'Endogamy', a bare-knuckled, full-frontal assault on the institution of marriage, which was, he argued, a futile attempt to relieve inevitable human solitude. He compared matrimony to walkers blundering about in a thick fog howling at each other with indistinct cries. Far better, he gloomily concluded, to resign oneself to loneliness than to be deceived by the illusion of true communication with another human being: 'It is something to possess your own soul.'

The same mood of disillusion pervades an impressive poem of that year, 'Menelaus and Helen', in which Brooke imagines the couple who launched the epic Trojan wars as a result of their conjugal difficulties growing old together, shackled in mundane domesticity:

> So far the poet. How should he behold
>   That journey home, the long connubial years?
>   He does not tell you how white Helen bears
> Child on legitimate child, becomes a scold,
> Haggard with virtue. Menelaus bold
>   Waxed garrulous, and sacked a hundred Troys
>   'Twixt noon and supper. And her golden voice
> Got shrill as he grew deafer. And both were old.
>
> Often he wonders why on earth he went
>   Troyward, or why poor Paris ever came.
> Oft she weeps, gummy-eyed and impotent;
>   Her dry shanks twitch at Paris' mumbled name.
> So Menelaus nagged; and Helen cried;
> And Paris slept on by Scamander side.

Here Brooke boldly goes where Homer feared to tread, and follows the protagonists of the *Iliad* offstage. The poem is remarkable in its disgust with the processes of ageing and reproduction, and its misogynistic revulsion at female mortality. Insult is piled on insult until one suspects that 'Menelaus and Helen' should be retitled 'William Parker and Mary Ruth'. Despite, or because of, this personal input of bile, the power of the poet's horror at the banality of human existence is undeniable.

As the Tripos approached, Brooke, knowing of the likely outcome, began to cast about for a new home where he could indulge in 'dew-dabbling' more freely than in frigid Cambridge, with its continual calls on his precious time. When another Kingsman, A. F. Scholfield, who had plucked Brooke from obscurity to stardom when he picked him to take a part in *Eumenides*, invited him to share lodgings, he declined the offer, explaining: 'I am passionately enamoured of solitude; and as a housemate I cannot imagine myself as anything but wildly irritating . . . I am going to try to get rooms in Grantchester . . . I passionately long to shut myself up and read only and always . . .'

Grantchester, a small village some two miles south-west of Cambridge on the upper reaches of the Cam, where it becomes the Granta stream, is the place that Brooke was to call home for the rest of his life. He had got to know the spot on walks with Geoffrey Keynes. He immortalized the village in his poetry as an emblem of England, but its history long preceded him. The site of Trumpington Mill, the setting for Chaucer's 'The Reeve's Tale', Grantchester dates back to pre-Roman times, when there was a ford below the mill. Another English poet who died in Greece, Lord Byron – a Trinity man – had bathed in the pool there that still bears his name.

A century after his lame Lordship swam that pool, Mrs J. W. Stevenson opened a tearoom at her riverside home, the Orchard, which had become a favourite of students out for a weekend stroll. Brooke heard that rooms were available at the Orchard – two bedrooms and a ground-floor sitting-room, with free use of the garden. He agreed to take them for 30 shillings a week.

Before moving in, Brooke sat the dreaded Tripos. Between taking the exams and receiving the results, he went to stay with his cousin Erica Cotterill at Godalming in Surrey. The main attraction, besides seeing his most durable pen-friend, he confided to his ally Dudley Ward: 'Oh ho! The South! The Lakes of Surrey! They call me! And I shall possibly see Noel in the distance!' Angling for an invitation to visit Noel at nearby Bedales, Brooke wrote to her on 28 May describing his academic ordeal:

At eleven o'clock this morning I finished the last paper of my Classical Tripos. There were 108 other candidates in the room, but they all stayed the full time, till noon. They write longer, better papers than mine. (They all wear spectacles.) I wrote my translation of the last Latin word (the last Latin word I shall ever translate in my life. Glory!), which happened to be 'Good-bye!' The fitness delighted me, and I screamed with laughter, suddenly; & the hundred & eight turned round & blinked. I nodded at a hairless don who was in command, &

ran cheerily out of the room, tearing the examination paper to bits as I went. I sang loudly all the way to my rooms, & annoyed all the policemen & danced a little; & when I got here I burned the paper, & I keep the ashes in an Urn. I shall never read Latin or Greek again.

The schoolboy squeak of delight at his liberation from the Classics ('No more Latin, no more French/No more sitting on the old schoolbench') is as audible here as his totemic disdain for his personal symbols of senile decay, baldness and myopia. In Brooke's world it is a sin to be old or even ageing.

He goes on to propose dropping in at Bedales during his Godalming stay, in company with Jacques Raverat, who had returned from a two-year exile in France and was living in the village of Froxfield, near his old school. Brooke is evidently on tenterhooks as to his reception: 'Shall I just . . . see you about? Or shall I definitely SEE you . . . it occasionally seems to me rather impossible, quite impossible. Schools are so mad. And my malign appearance, & influence!' He leaves his ego an escape route: 'You can, and may, evade, or stop me. (Surely we have got beyond the last insult of politeness?) . . . You understand all things in the world . . . and you are a thousand years old, and we know each other perfectly; you must decide.' Noel's third-person answer cannot have pleased Brooke: 'She wishes you weren't coming; but she daren't say so out right, for fear of offending your pride.'

Brooke's reply, from Erica's home at Godalming, Coombe Field, was written in a tone of barely controlled fury: 'God (a thing you don't believe in) burn (a sensation you've never had) you (*You!*), Madam (a title given in honour, reverence and admiration to the middle-aged) (now used in the most scathing sarcasm)! . . . You're a devil. *Beginning* by assigning a time, *going on* to water it down, down . . . and *ending* by a post-script in the third person . . . changing the whole thing, & leaving me cr-r-ushed.'

In the event, given Noel's less than thrilled response to his threatened descent, Brooke did not proceed with his plan, but instead of shelving it altogether merely postponed it. His obsession with her continued at full throttle.

Meanwhile there was the result of the Tripos to deal with. Brooke received a poor Second. Despite anticipating this, he felt as crushed in his academic hopes as Noel's rejection had left him dashed in his personal self-esteem. He sought comfort with the newly married Frances Cornford, who wisely neglected to tell him that her husband Francis had been one of Brooke's examiners, and who knew how narrowly he had escaped getting a Third. An ashen-faced Brooke confessed that he was most worried by his mother's reaction. Rallying, he resolved to put all he had, academically, into redeeming his failure over the next year by entering the King's Shakespeare scholarship – the Charles Oldham Award – with a dissertation on his favourite dramatist, John Webster. In order to concentrate on this goal in undisturbed seclusion, he moved to Grantchester without further ado.

Relieved to have got the burden of the Tripos shifted from his shoulders, however unsatisfactorily, Brooke relaxed in his new rural surroundings, and, true to form, lost no time in telling his friends, in exaggerated terms, of his exuberant contentment: 'This is a divine spot,' he informed Hugh Dalton. 'I eat only strawberries and honey.' He referred to his new home as 'Arcadee'. At the end of July he told Noel:

> I work at Shakespeare and see few people . . . In the intervals I wander about bare foot and almost naked, surveying Nature with a calm eye. I do not pretend to understand Nature, but I get on very well with her, in a neighbourly way. I go on with my books, and she goes on with her hens and storms and things, and we're both very tolerant. Occasionally we have tea together . . . I get on very well by addressing all flowers 'Hello, Buttercup!' and all animals 'Puss! Puss!' I live on honey, eggs and milk, prepared for me by an old lady like an apple (especially in face) and sit all day in a rose garden to work. Of a morning Dudley Ward and a shifting crowd come out from Cambridge and bathe with me, have breakfast (out in the garden, as all meals) and depart.

Noel responded to this torrent of burbling whimsy with a put-down as brutal as a Bedales douche. Enraged by Brooke telling her that the Ranee had disparagingly called her 'Quite a schoolgirl', Noel let fly:

> I know this is a beastly and absurd letter, but few people, and certainly not I, would be capable of answering that – what was it? – *letter* you sent. I dont quite see how it is you can enjoy breakfast – and all meals – but especially breakfast in a rose garden this sort of weather, I should think that butter would be too hard frozen and the coffee – I *beg* your pardon, of course you dont drink such poisonous stimulants, but milk – the milk too diluted with dirty rain water – dirty with Cambridge soots – to be enjoyable. But no doubt you have a tremendous capacity for enjoyment, only I wish you wouldnt talk of Nature in that foolish and innocent tone of voice – you call it making jokes, and I suppose you think its nice; but I dont like it a bit – Ive told you why lots of times.

★

She concluded: 'I'm sorry – I'm in a very bad rage – because I've been doing easy exams badly – a thing you never did, so you cant sympathise. Dont try. from Noel.'

This unaccustomed deflation left Brooke winded. With her Olivier common sense, Noel had unerringly pinpointed his irritating habit of rhapsodizing about himself, and he didn't like it. He preferred uncritical correspondents like Erica, to whom he wrote in customary self-regarding vein:

> I work at Shakespeare, read, write all day, & now & then wander in the woods or by the river. I bathe every morning & sometimes by moonlight, have all my meals (chiefly fruit) brought to me out of doors, & am as happy as the day's long. I'm chiefly sorry for all you people in the world. Every now & then dull bald spectacled people from Cambridge come out & take tea here. I mock them & pour the cream down their necks or roll them in the rose-beds or push them in the river, & they hate me & go away.

Of course Brooke couldn't really have been like this, or he would have been lynched from one of his rose trees with one of his open-necked shirts. But he felt it necessary to construct and broadcast this image of himself. In the summer of 1909 a caricature of a new Brooke was firmly in place in his own mind – and consequently in that of his friends. The previous pose of a languid Decadent was replaced by that of a whimsical wandering child of nature, a fruitarian in bare feet talking to flowers and communing with poesy. Many of the friends he gathered around him became disciples – a tribute to his ability to inspire others to devotion.

His attempt to escape from the buzz of Cambridge to the tranquillity of the countryside was only half-serious. Grantchester provided him with a wider stage on which to perform, and he went about it with gusto. Within weeks he was entertaining Eddie Marsh and astonishing his landlords, the Stevensons, with his uniform of striped blazers, loose shirts and once, embarking on a London trip, bowler hat, gloves and – shades of 'John Rump' – an umbrella.

Before moving to Grantchester Brooke rebuffed yet another advance from the indefatigable James Strachey. According to James's account to Duncan Grant, he had discovered Brooke in bed and asked for his fingers to kiss, a request which Brooke refused. James comments: 'I found out something about him which DID make me despair. He's a REAL womanizer. And there can be no doubt that he hates the physical part of my feelings instinctively. Just as I should hate to be touched by a woman.

I think also that he has to some extent a dislike of everything physical – that he has a trace at least of virginity.' James, the future psychoanalyst, here sniffs out one of Brooke's most shameful secrets – his prudishness. In early July Brooke rubbed salt in the wound by teasing James about his meeting with his old Rugby flame, Charlie Lascelles: 'You may see Charlie if you're good, for a second. But not talk to him.'

Brooke had barely settled into his new quarters when he was called upon to entertain one of the grandest of England's men of letters – none other than 'the Master', Henry James. The distinguished novelist had been lured to Cambridge after much negotiating by what he called a 'triumvirate' of admirers – Geoffrey Keynes, Charles Sayle and a colleague of Sayle's named Theo Bartholemew. After touring the university James was conveyed to Keynes's rooms in Pembroke for lunch on Saturday 12 June. One of the select guests was Brooke, and, in Keynes's words 'there is no doubt that James fell at once under the spell of Rupert Brooke'.

James had an opportunity to renew his admiration the following morning, when he was guest at a breakfast hosted by Maynard Keynes. Brooke was present again, and once more caught the author's eye. James asked another guest, Desmond MacCarthy, about the identity of the 'long quiet youth with fair hair who sometimes smiled'. When told that Brooke was a poet, but not a good one, James responded: 'Well I must say I am RELIEVED, for with THAT appearance if he had also talent it would be too unfair.' James then engaged Brooke in conversation, allegedly telling him loftily not to be afraid to be unhappy.

Clearly smitten, as so many bachelors were, by Brooke's radiance, James was delighted to discover him in attendance yet again the following morning when the novelist was persuaded to ease his bulky form into a punt for a stately progress down the Cam along the Backs. Geoffrey Keynes takes up the tale:

> The process of pushing off from the landing stage was marred when Sayle dropped the pole with a crack on the large, shiny, yellowish dome of James's bald head. Fortunately, no serious harm was done, and Rupert Brooke . . . assumed the task of poling the punt. Henry James enjoyed the unaccustomed experience to the full and an unforgettable image of him remains, lying comfortably on the cushions and gazing up through prominent half-closed eyes at Brooke's handsome figure clad in white shirt and white flannel trousers.

Asked later how he had performed in the unnerving presence of the most distinguished but possibly least-read novelist of his era, Brooke smilingly

confessed to Frances Cornford that he had pulled off what he knowingly
called his 'fresh, boyish stunt' with aplomb. It evidently worked to stunning
effect, for James remained in besotted reverence for the rest of Brooke's life.
He wept when he learned of his death, and his last published work was a
lachrymose introduction to a collection of Brooke's travel writing, *Letters
from America* (1916), in which he fondly recalled, in typical Jamesian fashion,
the vision of Brooke on the river, 'with his felicities all most promptly
divinable'.

An equally famous but far more bohemian figure appeared in Brooke's
life the following month when Augustus John came to camp at
Grantchester. The bearded, fierce-eyed portraitist, then just turned 30 and
at the height of his notoriety for his free-living, free-loving ways, had been
commissioned to paint a portrait of a Newnham don, Jane Harrison, an
acquaintance of Brooke from the Marlowe Dramatic Society. He chose to
bring his tribe of six horses, two caravans, one cart, seven children, wife,
sister-in-law and odd-job boy to roost in Grantchester meadows. Brooke
was already an admirer of John's art, having put aside part of his allowance
the previous year to purchase two of his drawings, and he lost no time in
getting acquainted with a way of life that fascinated him but in which he
was far too respectable to do more than dabble.

At this stage in his peripatetic existence, John was obsessed by gypsies,
and the arrival of his caravanserai seemed as exotic to the Grantchester
rustics as the descent of a sheikh and his seraglio. Brooke was as wide-eyed
as any, and was soon boasting to Noel:

> Augustus John (the greatest painter) (of whom I have told you) with two wives
> and seven children (all male, between 3 and 7 years) with their two caravans and
> a gypsy tent, are encamped by the river, a few hundred yards from here. I go
> and see them sometimes, and they come here to meals . . . the chief wife is a
> very beautiful woman. And the children are lovely brown wild bare people
> dressed, if at all, in lovely yellow, red or brown tattered garments of John's own
> choosing. Yesterday Donald Robertson, Dudley Ward and I took them all up
> the river in punts, gave them tea and played with them. They talked to us of an
> imaginary world of theirs, where the river was milk, the mud honey, the reeds
> and trees green sugar, the earth cake, the leaves of the trees (that was odd) ladies'
> hats, and the sky Robin's blue pinafore. Robin was the smallest. The sun was a
> spot of honey on Robin's blue pinafore . . .

Noel responded to this Peter Pannish vision with another withering put-
down: 'As for the way you and Dudley – babies both – suddenly in your

old age rediscover the charming imaginations of children of 5 and listen to and remember their obvious descriptions of imaginary worlds, when you yourselves have only just left that stage, THAT is a joke – perhaps you meant it as such, but not likely.' One begins to suspect that Brooke was attracted to Noel in part precisely because of her no-nonsense rebukes, which possibly reminded him of the Ranee. Although, ironically, she was barely out of childhood herself, her attitude was that of a worldly-wise adult 'earthing' an ethereal child. It seems to have been this cold quality in all the Oliviers that perversely attracted Brooke – certainly Noel was the one member of his circle who could be relied upon to squash his tendency to whimsy. But she could not crush it completely, and Grantchester remained in his imagination a land of milk and honey.

The other observation that can be made of the Henry James and Augustus John episodes is their demonstration of Brooke's uncanny skill at what we would call networking. He spared no effort to charm and court these very different sacred monsters – and succeeded. It is this ability to dazzle the good and the great that goes a long way to explain why he was fast becoming a legend in his own lifetime. The romantic words 'Rupert Brooke' were already becoming a rubric to conjure with in worlds beyond Cambridge and Grantchester.

Undeterred by Noel's brutal douching of his wooing, Brooke, with that dogged determination that was as much a part of his Protean nature as his whimsy, put into effect his plan to visit her at Bedales. His instrument on this occasion was Jacques Raverat, who came to visit him in his new domain at Grantchester. Brooke arranged for Jacques to lodge at the Old Vicarage, a rambling ruin of a house next door to the Orchard. He was curious about the place, and was already hatching an ambition to live there himself. The observant Frenchman, who had not seen Brooke for two years, noted the changes that had occurred in his friend: he had become a vegetarian, forsworn alcohol and tobacco, and appeared to be pursuing his studies with effort and determination.

Jacques took his friend to Bedales, unannounced, and Noel, glancing out of a window at the school, was amazed to see Brooke crossing the school yard. She rejected an invitation to take tea, but the brief meeting seems to have repaired the rift between her and Brooke that had opened in their letters. By way of a quid pro quo for this favour, Brooke agreed to do what he could to advance Jacques' courtship of Ka Cox in his capacity as a fellow-member of the Cambridge Fabians' committee. In view of Brooke's own future involvement with Ka, this is not without irony.

With his usual devious methods – using intelligence supplied by Dudley

Ward and Margery Olivier – Brooke had discovered that the Oliviers were planning to hold a Bedales-style camp on the River Eden near Penshurst in Kent. The three younger sisters – without the watchful Margery – were under canvas, along with Dorothy Osmaston and their friend and neighbour Bunny Garnett, who had brought along a trio of male friends: Godwin Baynes, a strapping medical student whom Brooke had met at Klosters; Harold Hobson, an engineer; and Walter Layton, who was soon to become engaged to Dorothy. In a reprise of their Easter adventure in the New Forest, the campers were joined by Brooke and the faithful Dudley Ward, who both pretended to be just passing by.

Edenbridge is the first occasion that Brooke encountered in practice the lifestyle of the group that was to become known as the Neo-Pagans. Although they were not all Old Bedalians, they had learned their liking for summer camps at Badley's knee, and the etiquette for such holidays under canvas had already been laid down in writing by the school's founding father:

> The Camp is always pitched near a bathing place, for Bedalians, like fish, cannot live long out of water . . . The Camp itself consists of four tents – the cook tent, one sleeping tent for the girls, and two for the boys. Bedding of straw, bracken, or heather is provided, and each camper brings with him three blankets, one of which is sewn up into a sleeping bag. Pillows most of us scorn; the most hardened do without, the others roll up their clothes, and thus make a good substitute . . . Every other day, at least, is spent in a good tramp across the country – ten or fifteen miles at first to get into training, but this may be increased to twenty, or even twenty-five, later on . . . We take sandwiches with us for lunch, thus avoiding an elaborate midday meal, and on the longer walks find tea on the way, arriving back at Camp in time for a bathe and supper. Then we adjourn to the neighbouring farmhouse (whence we get our bread, butter, eggs, and milk) and for the rest of the evening sit lazily, while the Chief [Badley] and another take turn and turn about in reading aloud some novel. After a strenuous day of walk, a slack day usually follows, with plenty of bathing and perhaps a short walk in the afternoon to get up an appetite for supper. Too many slack days, however, should be discouraged, as they mean extra work for the cook, and anyway we don't come to Camp to slack . . .

These rigorous ground rules owe much to Badley's admiration for Baden-Powell's Scout movement, then in its heroic infancy, which Badley praised for satisfying 'the universal craving for adventure and for open-air life'. Where Badley parted company with the Chief Scout was in his emphasis on sexual equality and his tolerance of healthy nudism: 'There is much to be said for the practice, where possible, of nudism as a means of mental as well as bodily health . . . amongst friends at camp for instance, it is perfectly possible and, I believe, all to the good. But I have never wished to make it the rule for all, as there are some whom it makes unwholesomely sex-conscious.'

Noel had already blotted her copybook with Badley by diving nude off a high board in plain public view – an incident which caused him to ban nudity at Bedales thereafter. At Edenbridge, removed from the Chief's vigilance, conditions were more relaxed, as Bunny Garnett recounts:

> On Sunday morning the rustics of Penshurst came down and leant in a line upon the parapet of the bridge, staring into the pool in which we were to bathe. 'Come on', said Daphne, 'They're not going to stop us.' Nor did they. We bathed, ignoring them, and Noel, not to be put off from her high dives, picked her way along the parapet between the rows of wrists and elbows, politely asked for standing-room in the middle, and made a perfect dive into the pool. With florid expressionless face, the nearest labourer shook his black Sunday coat-sleeve free of the drops which had fallen from her heel.

It was Bunny who had discovered the riverside camp-site, while on a cycling trip with Bryn from their nearby homes at Limpsfield Chart. Across the river stood the imposing edifice of Penshurst Place, the magnificent fourteenth-century mansion that had once been the home of Sir Philip Sidney, the chivalrous Elizabethan poet who, like Brooke, found an early death in a foreign field. Years later Bunny recalled Brooke's arrival at the camp:

> . . . just after we'd all retired to sleep, there were gay shouts of greeting as we all emerged from sleeping bags and tents to find two young men from Cambridge had come to join us. They were Rupert Brooke and Dudley Ward. Rupert was extremely attractive. Though not handsome, he was beautiful. His complexion, his skin, his eyes and hair were perfect. He was tall and well built, loosely put together, with a careless animal grace and a face made for smiling and teasing and sudden laughter. As he ate in the firelight I watched him, at once delighted by him and afraid that his friendliness might be a mask. What might not lie below it?

The days – and nights – passed in a welter of walking, swimming, eating and communal talks amid the scent of new-mown hay and what Brooke would call, referring to Grantchester, 'the thrilling-sweet and rotten/

Unforgettable, unforgotten/River-smell'. According to Bunny, Noel was by no means averse to the arrival of her persistent suitor:

> soon we were sitting round the blazing fire, Noel's eyes shining in welcome for the new arrivals and the soft river water trickling from her hair down her bare shoulders. And on the white shoulders, shining in the firelight, were bits of duck weed, which made me love them all the more. The moon rose full. Soon we crawled back into our sleeping bags and slept, but Rupert, I believe, lay awake composing poetry.

A poem that Brooke is thought to have written around this time gives an intriguing insight into his complicated sexual feelings. Frankly titled 'Jealousy', it portrays the poet consumed by the green-eyed monster as he contemplates a woman once so 'wise and cool' now 'Gazing with silly sickness on that fool'. If the poem is indeed – as were most of Brooke's verses – modelled on real people and events, then the description of the poet's rival's: 'red lips . . . empty grace . . . strong legs and arms . . . rosy face' would fit the muscular Rowing Blue Godwin Baynes; while the woman, or 'lover-wife' would more easily fit Brynhild than Noel. Bryn was indeed the object of Baynes's attentions; he was to propose to her, unsuccessfully, a few weeks after the camp. The poem continues with a typical Brookian rant in which he catalogues his disgust with the body and the physical manifestations of love:

> —Oh! then I know I'm waiting, lover-wife,
> For the great time when love is at a close,
> And all its fruit's to watch the thickening nose
> And sweaty neck and dulling face and eye,
> That are yours, and you most surely till you die!
> Day after day you'll sit with him and note
> The greasier tie, the dingy wrinkling coat;
> As prettiness turns to pomp, and strength to fat.
> And love, love, love to habit!

The hysterical note is maintained as the poet turns to contemplate the final stages of love's disintegration into domestic decrepitude:

> And you, that loved young life and clean, must tend
> A foul sick fumbling dribbling body and old,
> When his rare lips hang flabby and can't hold

Slobber, and you're enduring that worst thing,
Senility's queasy furtive love-making,
And searching those dear eyes for human meaning,
Propping the bald and helpless head, and cleaning
A scrap that life's flung by, and love's forgotten,—
Then you'll be tired; and passion dead and rotten;
And he'll be dirty, dirty!
                                        O lithe and free
And lightfoot, that the poor heart cries to see,
That's how I'll see your man and you!—
                                        But you
—Oh, when *that* time comes, you'll be dirty too!

It could be expected of Brooke that when in the throes of love for Noel –
and receiving some requiting from her – his attention should turn, like the
fox with his unobtainable grapes, to the sister he had so briefly desired in
the Swiss snows. As we shall see, jealousy burned like a pilot light in the
murk of Brooke's psyche, always ready to flare up into a reason-consuming
blaze. It is more than possible that this is what he felt at Edenbridge as he
watched Godwin with Bryn or Dorothy Osmaston and Walter Layton. He
and Noel had the opportunity for one long solitary talk during a walk along
the riverbank, from which they were picked up by boat at a prearranged
spot by Dudley and Daphne Olivier. The would-be lovers had a chance to
see each other naked when they bathed side by side one night by the light
of a bicycle lamp. Noel, as she confided to a sympathetic enquirer towards
the end of her life, was as impressed by her admirer in the buff as James
Strachey had been. For Brooke, as 'Jealousy' makes all too plain, sexual
experience was still a dangerous and demeaning experiment – one likely to
tar the practitioner with an indelible mark of 'dirt', a 'filthy' badge of Cain,
a stain that no river could wash off.

Before the temptations of the Edenbridge interlude, Brooke had again
travelled to Llanbedr to put in an appearance at the Fabian summer school.
Once again he fretted under stricter rules than those that governed the
Neo-Pagans – there were set times for meals, lectures and a veritable return
to Rugby-style lights out. Activities were conducted under the disapproving eye of Beatrice Webb, who was present with Sidney to talk
about the *Minority Report of the Poor Law Commission*, a Fabian tract that had
been among Brooke's reading matter in the New Forest at Easter.

The Webbs had been members of a Commission appointed to overhaul the outdated Poor Law of 1834. While the majority of the commissioners had favoured a piecemeal reform, the Webbs had been among a minority of four who had argued for a root-and-branch change to the system of relieving poverty. The Webbs proposed a mixture of public and private charity based on local Boards of Guardians who oversaw the detested workhouses, where the indigent eked out an existence little better than slavery. They favoured a centralized system of dragooning the unemployed into work while providing their families with health care, pensions and relief. Within the Fabians they formed a group to agitate for the implementation of their ideas, the National Committee for the Prevention of Destitution, and were actively looking for recruits to join and spread the word. Convinced and enthused by their arguments, Brooke eagerly signed up.

As soon as he got back to Grantchester, he threw himself into the campaign with his customary zeal: leaflets advocating the abolition of the Poor Law were placed on a table at the Orchard for visitors to the tearoom to peruse, he distributed the pamphlets by bike from door to door in the village and he entertained to tea a working-class radical MP, Will Crooks. His fellow-Fabians Hugh Dalton, Ben Keeling and Ka Cox joined the campaign, and a grand meeting was planned for the Michaelmas term. Meanwhile summer's lease still had some way to run, and further distractions beckoned.

Brooke was expected to join his parents for their annual summer holiday late in August. The Brookes had rented a large Victorian vicarage at Clevedon in Somerset, overlooking the Bristol Channel. Bored by the prospect of weeks in the unstimulating company of his parents, Brooke prevailed on the Ranee to invite some of his friends to stay in the house's many spare rooms in order to alleviate the tedium. Urgent signals were sent to James Strachey: 'There are a lot of books here that you'll like'; and to Dudley Ward: 'My only way of keeping in touch with "life" is to play tennis barefoot. It's not so effective as living in a tent and a river with three Oliviers: but it annoys the family ... the family atmosphere is too paralysing. I am sinking. Save me, or I die.'

On cue, in obedience to Brooke's imperious invitations, on 26 August a horse-drawn carriage from the local station disgorged an enormous miscellany of his Cambridge cronies, together with a smattering of Neo-Pagans. Present were Hugh Dalton, Gerald Shove, Dudley Ward, Gwen Darwin, Margery and Bryn Olivier (though not Noel); and a couple of more marginal members of his Cambridge circle – Archie Campbell, a poet and Greek scholar who had played a part in *Comus*; and Frankie Birrell, grandson of Tennyson and son of the Liberal Cabinet Minister Augustine Birrell. The younger Birrell was a homosexual who had affairs with Maynard Keynes, Gerald Shove and the cheerfully bisexual Bunny Garnett. Later arrivals at Clevedon included Eddie Marsh, Jack Sheppard, Bill Hubback, a Cambridge economist and Fabian, and his fiancée Eva Spielman. There was even a brief visit from the great Maynard Keynes himself. For one brief and shining moment, Cambridge's intellectual élite were concentrated in this corner of Somerset, clustering, like dusty moths round the flame of Brooke's brilliance.

The object of all this adoration took the influx lightly; but not so his mother, who kept a beady eye on the female members of the party, particularly the stunningly lovely Bryn. After observing Bryn at close quarters Mrs Brooke primly told Gwen Darwin: 'I prefer Miss Cox. Her wrists are very thick and I don't like the expression of her mouth, but she's a sensible girl. I can't understand what you all see in these Oliviers; they are pretty, I suppose, but not at all clever; they're shocking flirts and their manners are disgraceful.' Like Queen Victoria, Mrs Brooke had an aversion to homosexuals on the rare occasions when she recognized one for what he was – this prejudice lies behind her distrust of St John Lucas Lucas and her dislike of Marsh. But on this holiday, one of Brooke's tutors, Jack Sheppard, a closet homosexual, insinuated himself into the Ranee's good graces with such finesse that she later named him as an executor of her favourite son's Estate.

Brooke retailed his mother's outrage at his friends' *en masse* descent in comic letters to those who were missing out on the jamboree, telling Ka Cox: 'They've come and gone, singly and in batches, and the Elder Generation couldn't stand any of them.' To James Strachey, who dropped by briefly ahead of the major incursion, he reported: 'And since you left there have been recurring millions of people. All hated by my Family. "I have met so many brilliant, conceited young men" said my mother, bitterly, last night, apropos of Maynard. But she'd said, a week ago "I don't call poor James clever". Sheppard heads you, however, in popularity. There was nobody else they could *stand*.'

Of the Oliviers, Brooke told James superciliously: 'The treasurer [Margery] and her sister Brynhilde [sic] have been about; which, of course, pleased my vulgar tastes enormously. I discern a Meredithian Earth–Our Mother tint in the blood of Sir Syd. that takes me. I pine to watch dusky women snaring parakeets . . .' In fact, Margery much displeased Brooke at Clevedon by taking him aside and warning him off Noel, having belatedly got to hear of the Edenbridge escapade. Whether her motives were jealousy or a more disinterested desire to protect her sister, Margery was seriously disapproving, as a surviving letter underlining her warning makes clear:

> If . . . you went on now so that she came to love you, have you thought how it would be with her? (I think I would find a way to kill you) . . . What is clear is that you must not bring this into her life now . . . I think I see that when a woman falls in love she does so much more completely and finally, she gets quite lost & absorbed in that one thing and cannot think of other things and her development almost ceases.

It seems clear that in the aftermath of Edenbridge Noel was seriously affected by Brooke's ardour. When he returned to Cambridge after a two-day visit to The Champions, the Oliviers' family home at Limpsfield Chart, Noel sent him a telegram in German with a single quote from Schiller's *Wallenstein*:

> I have tasted the fullness of earthly bliss
> I have lived and I have loved.

The highlight of Clevedon was Brooke's own attempt to enlist his friends in a make-believe project demonstrating his own commitment to living and loving. The extraordinary idea arose during a cliff-top walk near the Bristol suburb of Portishead with Margery, Bryn, Dudley Ward and Bill Hubback. News had just reached them of the death of John Davidson, a *fin-de-siècle* Decadent poet, who had drowned himself in Cornwall, aged 51. His last poem, 'The Testament of John Davidson', had hymned the life of the open road as the best answer to decrepitude and death:

> I took my staff in hand; I took the road,
> And wandered out to seek my last abode.
> Hearts of gold and hearts of lead
> Sing it yet in sun and rain,
> 'Heel and toe from dawn to dusk,
> Round the world and home again.'

Brooke and his friends elaborated on the fantasy that Davidson had merely faked his death in order to escape his previous existence and the burden of responsibility and failure. The more they talked, the more the idea appealed to them – or at least to the persuasive Brooke – as the perfect solution to the decline of youth into the humdrum mediocrity of middle age. Brooke told Jacques excitedly:

The idea, the splendour of this escape back into youth, fascinated us. We imagined a number of young people, splendidly young together, vowing to *live* such an idea, parting to do their 'work in the world' for a time and then, twenty years later, meeting on some windy road, one prearranged spring morning reborn to find and make a new world together, vanishing from the knowledge of men and things they knew before, resurgent in sun and rain . . .

Harking back to their Swiss holidays, the hikers there and then solemnly pledged, at Brooke's urging, to make just such a new start in middle age. They made a pact to meet at breakfast time on 1 May 1933 at Basle station and vanish from their ordered lives, 'fishing for tunnies off Sicily or exploring Constantinople or roaring with laughter in some Spanish inn'. Jacques was asked to join the pact, as were Godwin Baynes (presumably at Bryn's insistence), Ka Cox and a few more of Brooke's closest devotees.

This was a key moment in Brooke's life – the point at which his whimsical Pater Pan fantasies, however briefly, became explicit and real – at least for him. The idea of a fame and spirit that can outsoar even death is a recurring Romantic notion, from Keats's 'Ode to a Nightingale' ('Thou wast not born for death, immortal bird/No hungry generations tread thee down') to a popular refusal to credit the deaths of contemporary popular heroes like Elvis and Jim Morrison. But Brooke seems to have taken the idea in all seriousness: 'The great essential thing is the Organised Chance of Living Again,' he assured Jacques. It would be far better than the future he imagined for himself as 'a greying literary hack, mumbling along in some London suburb . . . middle aged . . . tied with more and more ties, busier and busier, fussier and fussier . . . the world will fade to us, fade, grow tasteless, habitual, dull'.

No practical considerations intruded as Brooke's vision ascended into the stratosphere. What would become of the chosen few's children, partners, homes, jobs and friends? How would they live, where would the money come from? Such mundane considerations were airily swept aside:

We'll be children seventy years, instead of seven. We'll *live* Romance not *talk* of it. We'll show the grey, unbelieving age, we'll teach the whole damn World, that there's a better Heaven than the pale serene Anglican windless harmonium-buzzing Eternity of the Christians, a Heaven in Time, now and for ever, ending for each, staying for all, a Heaven of Laughter and Bodies and Flowers and Love and People and Sun and Wind, in the only place we know or care for, ON EARTH.

So attractive is Brooke's rhetoric that the ironies of what really awaited, a lifetime later in May 1933, are almost too depressing to enumerate: Brooke and Jacques and Bill Hubback would be dead; Margery hopelessly insane; Bryn terminally ill; and Ka, too, within five years of her own premature demise. As for the world they would escape to: Hitler would just have come to power; Sicily would be ruled by Mussolini and Spain teetering on the edge of civil war. Hardly the earthly paradise Brooke had promised. Mercifully all this was hidden by the veil of the future from the carefree young people at Portishead. Only in one sense was Brooke to be right, in his concluding prophecy to Jacques: 'I am NOT going to be a resident fellow of King's, nor a lecturer in Leeds, I am going to be a Bloody POET.'

9

The Old School

Brooke, by now the undisputed leader of a distinct and growing social set, returned to hold court at his Grantchester kingdom for a constant cast of friends, acolytes and casual visitors. The atmosphere of his first season in the village is captured on camera at a breakfast he gave for a group of his intimates in the garden of the Orchard, waited on by an anxious Mrs Stevenson.

The 12 disciples present at this feast – the Biblical parallel is inescapable – included Brooke's rock-like Peter, Dudley Ward; his first follower, Geoffrey Keynes; Bill Hubback, Archie Campbell, Jacques Raverat and a trio of handmaidens – Bryn Olivier, Ethel Pye and Dorothy Osmaston. Another female follower, Gwen Darwin, destined to marry Raverat after he failed to capture Ka, gives a glimpse of Brooke in his new surroundings in an unpublished fragment of an autobiographical novel: 'We used to loll wearily in armchairs and talk of Art and Suicide and the Sex Problem. We used to discuss the ridiculous superstitions about God and Religion; the absurd prejudices of patriotism and decency; the grotesque encumbrances called parents. We were very old and we knew about everything.'

According to Gwen, parents were a subject that, unsurprisingly, much possessed Brooke: 'You kiss them sometimes, and send for them when you're ill, because they are useful and they like it; and you give them mild books to read, just strong enough to make them think they're a little shocked, but not much, so they can think they're keeping up with the times. Oh you ought to be very kind to them, make little jokes for them, and keep them awake in the evening, if possible. But never, never let them be intimate and confidential, because they *can't* understand, and it only makes them miserable . . . Why, they'd die if they knew what we were really like.'

Despairingly, Brooke added: 'Calmness and firmness are no good with my mother – she's so much calmer and firmer than you are yourself.' This passage, with its mix of flipness, cynicism and open admission of duplicity is so richly representative of Brooke that it can stand as a statement of his familial philosophy in a nutshell.

Gwen, one of the most loyal of Brooke's friends, who stood by him during the paranoid dark night of the soul that followed the worst crisis of his life in 1912, described him at the Orchard in familiarly glowing terms:

> Perhaps the most obvious thing about him was his beauty . . . there was something in his appearance that is impossible to forget. It was no good laughing at him, calling him pink and white, or chubby, saying his eyes were too small or his legs too short, there was a nobility about the carriage of his head and the shape of it, a radiance in his fair hair and shining face, a sweetness and a secrecy in his deepset eyes, a straight strength in his limbs, which remained for ever in the minds of those who once had seen him, which penetrated and coloured every thought of him.

To be the recipient of so much dumb worship, to be so inordinately praised for one's surface appearance – hair, face, eyes and limbs – which were anyway outside one's own control, and to be overlooked for the achievements of the mind – would have galled a far nobler nature than Brooke ever claimed to possess. Small wonder then, that his head was turned to vanity and self-absorption. His genes and his friends laid burdens on his shoulders that were impossible to shake off.

Brooke at Grantchester was more than ever the hub of his circle now that it was beginning to break up, with several members settling in London. James Strachey was working as secretary to his uncle, St Loe Strachey, editor of the *Spectator* in the Strand; Jacques had moved to Chelsea to study printing; Gwen was about to start studying art at the Slade; Ka, too, was increasingly to be found at her flat in Westminster; while Geoffrey Keynes had begun his distinguished career in medicine as a student at St Bartholomew's Hospital. For all of them Brooke remained a magnetic attraction, drawing them back to Cambridge, where they had first come into his orbit.

But beneath the golden façade, ominous portents of the future already lurked – one such was Brooke's ever-precarious health. His delicate constitution was too fragile to sustain the demands his exuberant spirit made upon it. Particularly at times of stress or great exertion, a collapse

1. William Parker Brooke, Rupert's father –
hiding behind his moustache, 1903

2. Mother's boys: Mrs Ruth Brooke – 'the
Ranee' – with Rupert *(left)* and Alfred in fancy
dress, 1898

3. Dick, Rupert and Alfred (*front row, left to right*) with the rest of the Brooke family, *c.* 1901

4. First love: Rupert *(right)* with Denham
Russell-Smith, Brockenhurst, *c.* 1904

5. Rupert the clean-cut Cambridge student

6. Lazy days with the ladies: Rupert picnicking in May week 1908 at Cambridge with *(left to right)* Frances
Darwin, Francis Cornford, Eva Spielman and Margery Olivier *(King's College Library, Cambridge)*

7. Rupert as the Attendant Spirit in the Cambridge student production
of Milton's *Comus*, 1908

8. Ka Cox clothed, 1910

9. Ka Cox naked, *c.* 1912 *(Charleston Trust, Richard Shone)*

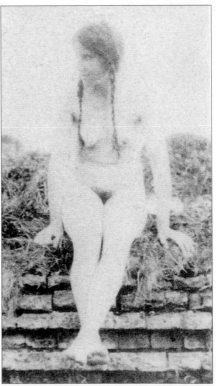

10. Noel Olivier clothed, aged 15, 1909

11. Noel Olivier naked, 1913

12. *Below:* Rupert and Dudley Ward on the Cam, *c.* 1910 *(author's collection)*

13. *Right:* James *(left)* and Lytton Strachey, 1912 *(National Portrait Gallery)*

14. 'A Young Apollo': Rupert's much-admired profile, 1912 *(author's collection)*

15. Geoffrey Keynes

16. 'Camping Out': *(left to right)* Noel Olivier, Maitland Radford, Virginia Stephen (later Woolf) and Rupert at Clifford's Bridge, 1908 *(National Portrait Gallery)*

17. Bryn Olivier and Justin Brooke under canvas at Clifford's Bridge, 1911

18. Noel Olivier *(foreground)* and Ethel Pye at Beaulieu camp where she was secretly 'engaged' to Rupert, summer 1910 *(author's collection)*

19. The Old Vicarage, Grantchester: a
woodcut by Noel Rooke, 1918

20. 'The Creature': Rupert's rival in love,
Henry Lamb, 1908

threatened. It seems that he had no reserves to fight off the infections that often laid him low. In the aftermath of the excitements of Clevedon, for example, he told Dudley Ward:

> I'll tell you . . . why this morning I'm in the worst temper I've ever been in. (Lord! I've had a scene with Mother! She *crept* out of the room, at the end – which was brought on by my choking with rage, and being therefore unable to continue.) It began 16 days ago: when you and I and admirable people were charging ridiculously down a far hill in the dark. You with the gay childish *abandon*, which is indeed your most lovable characteristic, ran up behind me and kicked my left ankle with your heavy boot, laughing the while with high hysterical delight. The hole you made was poisoned by a sock, and, they say, inflamed by tennis: and changed into a sore that grew wider and deeper with incredible rapidity. When I got home the doctor examined it. And I have been on a sofa with my left leg in bandages ever since. The wound slowly diminishes. But if I 'go about on it' before it's well, the elderly, shifty fraud who is my doctor, says it will turn to an abscess and eat the bone of my leg. *Then* I shall be a bit of a fool at wooing dryads . . .

In his enforced idleness at Rugby, Brooke was obliged not only to endure the torment of his mother's domineering ways – 'my meagre mother's nightly anti-Olivier lectures', as he described them to Dudley – but also Margery's hectoring letter warning him to stay clear of Noel. Brooke's reaction to this 'great, fierce, blazing sermon' was itself extreme: 'that made me hate her'. But it also induced a state of angst about his future prospects with Noel: 'All the same, I was torn by mistrust of myself, fear, perplexity, and despair, all that night. I didn't get to sleep till 6; having gone to bed at 11. The next night saw me awake at 3 a.m. thinking. My dear, I've had an awful time. I don't know what to do . . .' This confession of confusion and insomnia curiously presages Brooke's breakdown in 1912. It is another indication of the instability of his health and mental balance. Margery's warning also awakened his slumbering paranoia, and he subsequently told Geoffrey Keynes that he chiefly blamed her for the ultimate failure of his relationship with Noel.

Meanwhile he was continuing to publish his poetry: the influential *English Review* printed four poems; and he still wrote and reviewed regularly for the *Cambridge Review*. Now that he was something of a living legend at the university, Hugh Dalton wrote a profile of him in the Cambridge magazine *Granta*. Among the insights that Dalton vouchsafed his readers was:

On his day he is still an irresistible tennis player, preferring to play barefooted and to pick up the balls with his toes . . . He is sometimes credited with having started a new fashion in dress, the chief features of which are the absence of collars and headgear and the continual wearing of slippers. He will tell you that he did not really begin to live till he went out of college at the end of his third year and took up his residence at the Orchard, Grantchester.

Brooke himself suggested the final fictitious paragraph: 'It is said that he lives the rustic life, broken by occasional visits to Cambridge; that he keeps poultry and a cow, plays simple tunes on a pan pipe, bathes every evening at sunset, and takes all his meals in a rose garden.'

One nugget among all this dross was true – Brooke did indeed have long, prehensile toes, and performed a party piece for the artist Stanley Spencer – another protégé of Eddie Marsh – by executing a skilled drawing of a house with a pencil clasped between his toes.

On his return to Grantchester at the end of September, Brooke received a letter from Lytton Strachey – who was holidaying with James in Sweden – asking about the possibility of renting rooms in the neighbouring Old Vicarage. Their falling-out at the Apostles' meeting apparently forgotten, Brooke replied cordially with a detailed description of his own future home and its owners, Mr and Mrs Neeve:

The Neaves [sic] are 'working people' who have 'taken the house and want lodgers' . . . Mr Neave is a refined creature, with an accent above his class, who sits out near the beehives with a handkerchief over his head and reads 'advanced newspapers' . . . The garden is the great glory. There is a soft lawn with a sundial, and tangled, antique flowers abundantly; and a sham ruin, quite in a corner; built fifty years ago . . .

Brooke went on to allege that the Old Vicarage's garden was haunted by the ghosts of its former clerical residents: 'with faint lights and odd noises. We of the village hate passing.' This fancy resurfaced years later when he came to write one of his two most celebrated poems, 'The Old Vicarage, Grantchester':

And spectral dance, before the dawn,
A hundred Vicars down the lawn;
Curates, long dust, will come and go
On lissom, clerical, printless toe; . . .

Undeterred by the threat of the supernatural, Lytton visited Grantchester to spy out the land, staying for one night with Brooke at the Orchard. Brooke was amused by Lytton's curious ways, observing his habit of sitting with his back to a bookshelf then, without looking around, extending a languid arm, extracting a volume, perusing it, replacing it and extracting another by the same blind method. Lytton – a creature who loved his comforts – thought better of taking the ramshackle Vicarage and decamped to the safety of Cambridge. He was succeeded as guest at the Orchard by another old–maidish man of letters – E. M. Forster – up to read a paper to the Apostles.

When the Michaelmas term began, Brooke succeeded Dalton as President of the Cambridge Fabians. He threw himself into organizing their campaign for reform of the Poor Law on the lines advocated by the Webbs, who visited in October to address a meeting organized by Brooke. Secretly, he was scathing about the competence of his treasurer, Ka Cox, who had been assigned the tedious chore of researching possible objections to the Webbs' plans in order to brief Brooke with speakers' notes at his meeting. Not content with castigating Ka – 'a fool', he told Dalton – for failing to pay out of her own pocket for hiring the Assembly Rooms for their meeting, Brooke also criticized the unladylike language of her lecture notes.

Alongside his usual hectic activity, he was still recruiting friends for 'the Scheme', as he termed the 1933 Basle reunion. Noel Olivier received her invitation:

> Integrally, it's a device for getting out of Middle Age by secretly vanishing and starting afresh. Now, all sensible people to themselves have desired to do this, I expect. But they've never arranged it. The thing is to get some impetus powerful enough to jerk the man of 45 out of his world into a new one . . . Therefore a prearranged and much thought of date and place is essential. Secrecy, as a general rule, is also necessary, and the general feeling of starting afresh. That is the kernel of the thing.

Alfred Brooke had gone up to King's this term. The two brothers were no longer particularly close, but Alfred, like his elder sibling, soon became the toast of homosexual Cambridge – James Strachey described him to Maynard Keynes as 'pink and white, almost buggerable'. Brooke himself seems to have had few illusions about his brother's sexuality, reporting to James that Alfred was 'debauched and lascivious'. Hugh Dalton was among Alfred's many male admirers.

It was after one of the regular Saturday afternoon meetings of the Apostles at Trinity, on 29 October 1909, that Brooke's only fully documented homosexual encounter took place – documented, needless to say, by himself. Alongside his pursuit of Noel, Brooke continued with homosexual dalliances, although, since he shrouded these activities in his habitual secrecy, details are hard to come by. It is known that he met his old Rugby flame Charles Lascelles, at a London theatre, and rumour in Cambridge linked him with a number of gay contemporaries at the university, including Gerald Shove, and James Strachey's lover George Mallory. But the only concrete evidence we have for physical homosexual lovemaking comes from Brooke's own hand, in a confessional letter to James written at the height of his own nervous breakdown in July 1912, and in the aftermath of the sudden death of his partner that autumn night, another of his old Rugby loves, Denham Russell-Smith. For its time, it is an extraordinarily explicit document.

After describing his feelings for Denham at Rugby, Brooke recalls:

He was lustful, immoral, affectionate, & delightful . . . But I was never in the slightest degree in love with him.

In the early autumn of 1909, then, I was glad to get him to come & stay with me, at the Orchard. I came back late that Saturday night. Nothing was formulated in my mind. I found him asleep in front of the fire, at 1.45. I took him up to his bed – he was very like a child when he was sleepy – and lay down on it. We hugged, & my fingers wandered a little. His skin was always very smooth. I had, I remember, a vast erection. He dropped off to sleep in my arms. I stole away to my own room: & lay in bed thinking – my head full of tiredness & my mouth of the taste of tea and whales [Apostolic jargon for the sardines that were habitually served at their gatherings].

I decided, almost quite consciously, I *would* put the thing through next night. You see, I didn't at all know how he would take it. But I wanted to have some fun, & still more to see what it was *like*, and to do away with the shame (as I was taught it was) of being a virgin. At length, I thought, I shall know something of all that James & Norton & Maynard & Lytton know & hold over me. Of course, I *said* nothing. Next evening, we talked long in front of the sitting room fire. My head was on his knees, after a bit. We discussed Sodomy. He said he, finally, thought it *was* wrong . . . We got undressed there, as it was warm. Flesh is exciting, in firelight. You must remember that *openly* we were nothing to each other – less even than in 1906. About what one is with Bunny (who so resembles Denham). Oh, quite distant! Again we went up to his room. He got into bed. I sat on it & talked. Then I lay on it. Then we put out the light & talked in the dark. I complained of the cold: & so got under the eiderdown. My brain was, I remember, almost all through, absolutely calm & indifferent, observing progress & mapping out the next step. Of course, I had planned the general scheme beforehand.

I was still cold. He wasn't. 'Of course not, you're in bed!' 'Well then, you get right in, too'. I made him ask me – oh! without difficulty! I got right in. Our arms were round each other. 'An adventure!' I kept thinking: and was horribly detached.

We stirred and pressed. The tides seemed to wax . . . At the right moment I, as planned, said 'Come into my room, it's better there . . .' I suppose he knew what I meant. Anyhow he followed me. In that larger bed it was cold; we clung together. Intentions became plain; but still nothing was said. I broke away a second, as the dance began, to slip my pyjamas. His was the woman's part throughout. I had to make him take his off – do it for him. Then it was purely body to body – my first, you know!

I was still a little frightened of his, at any too sudden step, bolting; and he, I suppose, was shy. We kissed very little, as far as I can remember, face to face. And I only rarely handled his penis. Mine he touched once with his fingers; and that made me shiver so much I think he was frightened. But, with alternate stirrings, and still pressures, we mounted. My right hand got hold of the left half of his bottom, clutched it, and pressed his body into me. The smell of sweat began to be noticeable. At length we took to rolling to & fro over each other, in the excitement. Quite calm things, I remember, were passing through my brain. 'The Elizabethan joke "The Dance of the Sheets" has, then, something in it.' 'I hope his erection is all right' . . . and so on. I thought of him entirely in the third person. At length the waves grew more terrific: my control of the situation was over; I treated him with the utmost violence, to which he more quietly, but incessantly, responded. Half under him & half over, I came off. I *think* he came off at the same time, but of that I have never been sure. A silent moment: & then he slipped away to his room, carrying his pyjamas. We wished each other 'Good-night'. It was between 4 & 5 in the morning. I lit a candle after he had gone. There was a dreadful mess on the bed. I wiped it as clear as I could, & left the place exposed in the air, to dry. I sat on the lower part of the bed, a blanket round me, & stared at the wall, & thought. I thought of innumerable things, that this was all; that the boasted jump from virginity to Knowledge seemed a very tiny affair, after all; that I hoped Denham, for whom I felt great tenderness, was sleeping. My thoughts went backward and forward. I unexcitedly reviewed my whole life, & indeed the whole universe. I was tired, and rather pleased with myself, and a little bleak. About six it was grayly daylight; I blew the candle out & slept till 8. At 8 Denham had to bicycle in to breakfast with Mr Benians, before catching his train. I bicycled with him, and turned off at the corner of –, is it Grange Road?–. We said scarcely anything to each other. I felt sad at the thought he was perhaps hurt and angry, & wouldn't ever want to see me again. – He did, of course, & was exactly as ever. Only we never referred to it. But that night I looked with some awe at the room – fifty yards to the West from the bed I'm writing in – in which I Began; in which I 'copulated with' Denham; and I felt a curious private tie with Denham himself.

So you'll understand it was – not with a *shock*, for I'm far too dead for that, but with a sort of dreary wonder and dizzy discomfort – that I heard Mr Benians inform me, after we'd greeted, that Denham died at one o'clock on Wednesday morning, – just twenty four hours ago now. Rupert.

This confession is remarkable for both its honesty – what might be called its blow-by-blow account of the proceedings – and its tender innocence. For once we do not get a sense of Brooke preening and prancing before an invisible audience. Though he was still full of self-regard, frankness, for once, does shine through – perhaps prompted by the surprise of Denham's death, which came about, by morbid irony, through blood poisoning – the same condition that would one day kill Brooke.

Meanwhile Brooke's less clandestine social whirl continued. Gwen Darwin organized a group of seven of her close friends to attend the Slade's annual fancy-dress ball, all attired as the winds and leaves of Shelley's 'Ode to the West Wind'. Brooke took a childlike delight in the occasion, getting his diaphanous *Comus* costume out of mothballs for the event, and suggesting that James Strachey, as ever the butt of his jokes, attend as 'a dead twig'.

Brooke carefully maintained his contact with the influential Eddie Marsh; sympathizing with Eddie's chief, Winston Churchill, who, as Home Secretary, was the chief target of the Suffragettes' militant campaign. 'I hope you've evaded the Suffragettes so far,' wrote Brooke, adding with a typical touch of whimsy: 'What do you do when they fling vitriol at you? Is an umbrella any use?'

In the Christmas holidays Brooke journeyed to the by now traditional Swiss winter-sports holiday, this year at the Schweizerhof Hotel, Lenzerheide, from where he reported to Noël on Christmas Eve, enclosing a copy of W. E. Henley's poems as a festive gift: 'It is hot. We sit about all day and bathe in the skating rink before breakfast . . . I send a book you know because tomorrow is your and Jesus' birthday.' Romantically, the holiday ended with a long ride by sledge as they raced the dawn to reach the railway station. Passing through Basle, the intended site of the 1933 reunion, Brooke, Jacques and Dudley signed a postcard to Ka: 'We passed through Basle this morning while you slept. Ha, Ha!'

They returned via Paris. During the journey Brooke had eaten some honey, which, bizarrely given his association with the health-giving nectar, made him feel extremely ill; so much so that he blacked out while admiring the pictures in the Louvre. He dragged himself back to Rugby and was

instantly put to bed with suspected typhoid. In his self-dramatizing mode
he described himself subsisting on a diet of tapioca with 'throat and stomach
. . . raw where that accursed stuff touched them. The skin peels off like bad
paper from a rotten wall.'

Entering the convalescent stage, Brooke rallied and summoned the
energy to complete a sonnet that he had roughed out while enduring a
turbulent Channel crossing on his way to Switzerland. The finished piece,
'A Channel Passage', became one of his most successful and rightly
admired exercises in the corner of light verse that he made so much his
own: that of the disgusted, fastidious, yet self-mocking sufferer of
Weltschmerz:

> The damned ship lurched and slithered. Quiet and
>   quick
>   My cold gorge rose; the long sea rolled; I knew
> I must think hard of something, or be sick;
>   And could think hard of only one thing—*you*!
> You, you alone could hold my fancy ever!
>   And with your memories come, sharp pain, and
>   dole.
> Now there's a choice—heartache or tortured liver!
>   A sea-sick body, or a you-sick soul!
>
> Do I forget you? Retchings twist and tie me,
>   Old meat, good meals, brown gobbets, up I throw.
> Do I remember? Acrid return and slimy,
>   The slobs and slobber of a last year's woe.
> And still the sick ship rolls. 'Tis hard, I tell ye,
> To choose 'twixt love and nausea, heart and belly.

Despite the ''twixt' and ''Tis', this sounds an authentically realistic and
contemporary note. A sonnet on vomit was a new departure in English
poetry, and the poem disgusted Brooke's future publisher, Frank Sidgwick,
enough for him to plead that it be kept out of Brooke's first collection,
published in 1911. To his credit, Brooke refused to bow to Sidgwick's
queasy attempt at censorship. The identity of the lover to whom the poem
is addressed is unclear, but from internal references – 'last year's woe' – it is
most probably Noel.

A crisis was about to engulf the Brooke family that would put such bouts
of passing nausea in their true perspective. Hardly had Brooke recovered
from his sickness than his father fell ill, complaining of failing eyesight and

raging headaches. Parker Brooke asked his son to stay away from Cambridge for the coming term and help him run School Field House. Writing to excuse himself from Fabian duties, Brooke told Ka Cox: '"Duty to one's family" Ka, that you sometimes and so solemnly mention! That is what is dragging me from the place where I am happier than anywhere (no, not Cambridge – Grantchester!).' He hastily rearranged his hectic schedule: Hugh Dalton, who was visiting Rugby with Maynard Keynes to speak in the current general-election campaign, agreed to take on Brooke's campaign in favour of the Minority Report on the Poor Law; and Brooke backed out of the Marlowe Dramatic Society's coming production of *Richard II.*

Frances Cornford was planning to cast Brooke in a Yeats play, *The Land of Heart's Desire*, but he told her he would have to decline the offer:

> There are other things I'm very sick to miss, the Marlowe play . . . seeing you all – the whole life of it, in fact. Also I fear I may have confused the Fabians rather by not coming up. I'm a general nuisance. Oh! and I'm so sad and fierce and miserable not to be in my garden and little house at Grantchester all this term. I love being there so much – more than any other place I've ever lived in. I love the place and especially the solitude so much. I'd thought of being there when the spring was coming, every day this winter, and dreamt of seeing all the little brown and green things.

Frances had recently married Francis Cornford, and was busy building a new house, Conduit Head, on the outskirts of Cambridge, furnishing it with wedding presents, among them an Augustus John drawing given jointly by Brooke and Ka. At the same time she was having her first book of poems privately published. In some envy Brooke wrote back, fantasizing that he too would bring out a simultaneous volume of verse:

> But they will review us together. The *Daily Chronicle*, or some such, that reviews verse in lumps, will review thirty-four minor poets in one day, ending with *Thoughts in Verse on Many Occasions by a person of Great Sensibility*
> By F. Cornford
> *Dead Pansy Leaves: & other flowerets*
> By R. Brooke
> . . . and it will say 'Mr Cornford has some pretty thoughts; but Miss Brooke is always intolerable.' (They always guess the sex wrong). And then I will refuse to call on you. Or another paper will say 'Major Cornford and the Widow Brooke are both bad: but Major Cornford is the worst.' And then you will cut me in the street . . .

Beneath the banter, Brooke was deeply worried about his father's worsening condition. Parker Brooke was now suffering from lapses in memory, and the family doctor suspected a blood clot on the brain. On 18 January Mr and Mrs Brooke travelled to London to consult a specialist. Brooke gloomily wrote to James Strachey: 'It is supposed the specialist will say he has a clot on the brain. Then he will go mad by degrees and die. Meanwhile we shall all live together in a hut on no money a year, which is all there is. Alfred is sombre, because he thinks he won't be allowed to continue a brilliant political career at Cambridge.' (Alfred was speaking in the Liberal cause in the Rugby general-election campaign.)

'It is pitiful to see father groping about, or sitting for four hours in gloom,' Brooke went on. 'And it is more pitiful to see mother, who is in agony.' He added, puzzlingly:

> But I am not fond of them. But I rather nervously await the afternoon, with their return. Will it be neuralgia, after all? Or really a clot? Or blindness? What will one do with an old, blind man, who is not interested in anything at all, on £600 a year? Shall I make a good preparatory-school master? Will it throw me back to the old orthodox ways of paederasty . . . What does one do in a household of fools and a Tragedy? And why is Pain so terrible, more terrible than ever when you only see it in others.

After this howl of genuine anguish, torn from him by anxiety out of control, Brooke reasserted his control: 'But breathe no word. If it's kept dark, the school goes on paying us.'

That same evening, on his parents' return, Brooke wrote again to James with an update. He reported that the London doctors had been 'vague . . . but not cheering' and he feared that the family would be thrown out of School Field House by Easter. But after the gloom and the middle-class terror of destitution, the cocky, self-centred Brooke reared up again: 'The Fabians, the M.D.S. [Marlowe Dramatic Society], the . . . what a man of affairs I am! I suppose, in this place, I shall write several masterpieces by April.' Two days later he seemed to be going out of his way to cultivate his hard-man image to James. Next to an ink blot on his paper he wrote '*not a tear*' and added: 'My way of disregarding people's emotions seems to me superior to going all squashy about them. Being immensely egotistic, I am as delighted to see other people suffer, when I am suffering, as any of your common selfish sentimentalists. I can't really agree that it's a high emotion. But I am most proud if it really gives me a claim to have "a heart".'

The same cold-heartedness extended to his family in their hour of need – he wrote about his mother breaking down and praying for his father's quick death and the servants creeping about 'sniffling'. In truth, such a robust response to tragedy was more of a pose than Brooke liked to let on. For all his contempt, he was deeply affected by his parents' suffering, and donned the iron mask of derision as a defence against his own emotions being rubbed too raw to endure.

The suspense of waiting for what seemed an inevitably grim outcome was broken on 23 January by a brief cross-country trip to Grantchester to pick up mail and books at the Orchard. While he was there the blow finally fell: a telegram came from Rugby telling him his father had had a stroke. Brooke rushed back, and the family took it in turns to mount a vigil by the dying man's bedside. Remorselessly, Brooke described the scene to Dudley Ward: 'Father has had a stroke. He is unconscious. We sit with him by turns. It is terrible. His face is twisted half out of recognition, and he lies gurgling and choking and fighting for life.' A few hours later, on 24 January, Parker Brooke died. He was 59. Brooke was sparing when telling his friends about it. 'All the details are too horrible,' James was told; 'smell and so forth – And I've not seen people dying before.' To Jacques he wrote simply: 'Death's horrible . . . But death's kind.'

On cue, Brooke went down with influenza after the freezing funeral in the bleak Clifton Road municipal cemetery. He was suddenly overwhelmed with responsibility as the head of the family. Not the least of these, with a new term about to begin, was his father's academic duties. Brooke stepped into the dead man's shoes, and took over the running of School Field House on his own until April, giving his mother the chance to find a new home.

The day of the funeral, the 53 boys of the House returned and Brooke, still stricken by flu, was plunged into his duties. On 10 February he told James: 'You know I've got the responsibility of the souls brains & bodies of fifty boys of riotous character. One has yellow hair. I take prayers every night. Hymns only on Sundays.' James could not resist the temptation of seeing Brooke amid his young charges, and got himself invited to Rugby at the end of February. In advance Brooke gave him a brief lecture about school etiquette; banning the unruly James from prayers, while allowing him to talk about religion and politics but 'Scarcely anything about Sodomy'.

He went on: 'When you enter 108 – no, 106, for Turner is away this term – curious & hostile eyes will be turned on you. Can you bear it? Our surroundings will be very shy & silent, so you will have to talk. They all love me. They are very ugly: though God knows if you will think them beautiful or not.'

Once the immediate shock of his father's death had worn off, Brooke settled into the school routine – so recently experienced from the other side of the green-baize door – with apparent equanimity and even enjoyment. His carefree, self-mocking tone was soon back in use in the various accounts of his new life with which his friends were regaled: 'The boys are delightful; and I find I am an admirable schoolmaster. I have a bluff, Christian tone that is wholly pedagogic ... But a certain incisive incredulity in my voice when I mention the word God is, I hope, slowly dropping the poison of the truth into their young souls.' As he supervised 'prep' he told Geoffrey Keynes: 'The inky babes are splashing each other. I must rise and cuff them ... My love to Cambridge.' Ka Cox was given a synopsis of Rugby life that reads like a parody of Billy Bunter, and intentionally so: 'Lots happening. Gibson is still in the Sanatorium with swollen glands. Bacon mi. has got his Gym XX. House mile on Saturday and Confirmation on Tuesday. No other news.'

As 'John Rump' had indicated, Brooke's view of public-school masters was tinged with a knowing, satiric inside view of the homoeroticism preached – and sometimes practised by so many of them. His tongue-in-cheek leading of prayers betrayed a subversive attitude to another invariable accompaniment of the Arnoldian world view – and he managed to avoid the duty of preparing the boys for Confirmation.

In late March he told James Strachey: 'I caned a boy on Tuesday. It is an extraordinary sensation. He had broken his furniture to small pieces with a coal-hammer. But I had no consciously sexual emotions. I cried a little after he had gone.' At the same time he penned some doggerel verse to Dudley Ward containing the line: 'Nor buggering Bishop went to taste his boy.' The poem concluded with some unflattering views of his charges:

> They are upper-class. They do not know the Light.
> They stink. They are no good. And yet ... in spite
> Of the thousand devils that freeze their narrowing views
> (Christ, and gentility, and self-abuse)
> They are young, direct, and animal. In their eyes
> Spite of the dirt, stodge, wrapping, flits and flies
> A certain dim nobility ... So I love
> (Partly because to live it, once, I found
> All glory, and ... there are ... spots of holy ground
> —Oh, mildly holy—about the place!) each line
> Of the fine limbs and faces; love, in fine,
> (O unisexualist!) with half a heart,
> Some fifty boys, together, and apart,
> Half-serious and half-sentimentally ...

The return to Rugby had awakened Brooke's slumbering but ever-dormant homosexual side. In an honest piece of self-analysis at this time, Brooke estimated that his nature was one-quarter homosexual, and usually aroused by good-looking boys and youths (he referred to the yellow-haired lad in his House as 'My embryo' – the Apostolic term for an attractive young recruit) and half heterosexual. (Where the remaining quarter lay went unstated – but maths was never Brooke's strong point.)

In the meantime he remained acutely and embarrassedly aware that he was acting, playing a role that was expected of one of his class and paternity: 'When you see the pale men who teach you sliding wearily & alone round Bedales, pity them,' he wrote to Noel Olivier on 20 March, a Sunday, in a rare moment of free time:

> They too are human & alive (in a way). I tell you this, because I know. I am, so to speak, them. I am in charge, this term, of a houseful of youths, varying from four to seven feet in height. I like it, because I like them. They are a good age – fourteen to nineteen. (It is between nineteen and twenty-four that people are insufferable.) They look rather fresh and jolly too. But oh! the mask like faces that come before me. I am a 'master', & therefore a moral machine. They will not believe I exist. Also, I am shy. Occasionally I determine to make a great attempt to pierce to their living souls by some flaming, natural, heartfelt remark. So I summon one. And when he trots into the study, a sullen meekness. I can only say, in a mechanical voice, 'Jones mi, I hear your Latin Grammar was not sufficiently prepared. Please do me fifty lines.' And really, you know, they're quite real, individual persons, rather bloody, of course, with accretions of the public school atmosphere, but human, and therefore conceivably nice. It's really that I'm in a false position; and when I try to stretch out a jolly hand to any of them, the shades of a thousand schoolmasters rise between us, & form a black wall of fog: & we miss each other in the dark. Some of the elder ones are intellectually intelligent, if prim; & they are shocked & fascinated by the things I say about various deep, clear ulcers in their souls.

In his isolation from his friends – despite supportive visits from the likes of James and Jacques – Brooke compared himself to the Roman poet Ovid in the bitterness of his final enforced exile, although, he patronizingly informed Noel: 'of course you don't know what that means.' By this time the Ranee had rented a new home at 24 Bilton Road, Rugby, a tall house set back from the road. As they sorted out their possessions in preparation for the move, a sense of sadness for the past stole over Brooke: 'It is unpleasant, turning out. One empties cupboard after cupboard, sorts and destroys . . .' Tibby, the aged family cat, was a victim of the move – Brooke was deputed to kill her with a potion of poison in her milk.

With the Ranee safely installed in her new home, Brooke, released from his duties, eagerly left for his old Dorset haunt of Lulworth, where he was to be joined by the Strachey brothers – Lytton and James – for an Easter vacation. On the eve of his departure from Rugby on 6 April 1910 he wrote to Eddie Marsh:

> I wept copiously last week in saying good-bye to the three and fifty little boys whose Faith and Morals I had upheld for ten weeks. I found I had fallen in love with them all. So pleasant and fresh-minded as they were. And it filled me with puerperal gloom to know that their plastic souls would harden into the required shapes, and they would go to swell the undistinguished masses who fill Trinity Hall, Clare, Caius . . . and at last become members of the English Upper, or Upper Middle Classes. I am glad I am not going to be a schoolmaster for ever. The tragedy would be too great.

The impetus for the holiday had come from Lytton. Somewhat surprisingly, given the fact that the two had never been close, the older Strachey, in poor health and depressed spirits, had written to Brooke, proposing a week's vacation. Brooke responded eagerly: 'All I want is Intellectual Conversation and to avoid Rugby . . . I really don't care where I go.' Original plans to go to Holland or Dartmoor having fallen through, Brooke fell back on Lulworth and booked them in for a week at the Cove Hotel. He outlined the attractions to Lytton: 'a fishing village, which had a beautiful left-handed boy in it two years ago'.

Ironically, given the enormity of the damage his arrival would wreak in Brooke's life at this very location of Lulworth in two years' time, it was another 'boy' who was currently obsessing the ever sexually susceptible Lytton: the promiscuously bohemian artist Henry Lamb. Brooke had known Lamb's elder brother Walter, a homosexual classics don at Trinity who had had affairs with both Lytton and James Strachey. Henry, by contrast, whom Brooke was yet to meet, was an enthusiastic and voracious heterosexual – a fact that would one day cause Brooke the greatest grief. All of this lay in the future that Easter, as Brooke lent a sympathetic ear to Lytton's tales of woe.

Lytton arrived at Lulworth in a state of exaggerated gloom – a frequent occurrence in the aesthete's tortured life. His career was marking time, his friends were otherwise engaged, he feared that he was rapidly ageing and, above all, his love life was at an impasse, with Henry Lamb callously scorning his efforts at seduction. To add to his vexation, another love object, George Mallory, whose Cambridge home, Pythagoras House, he had been occupying, had invited him to Paris when he had already committed himself to Brooke and Lulworth.

Brooke, however, provided balm for his bruised soul: James briefly joined them, and after his departure Lytton, left alone with Brooke, wrote to his brother: 'Brooke read me some of his latest poems on a shelf by the sea, but I found them very difficult to make out, owing to his manner of reading.' Lytton responded by reading Brooke the first act of his current literary project – a play on the Elizabethan Earl of Essex, which he later turned into a successful biography. Brooke pleased him by his appreciative response, which delighted the crusty critic and melted his reserve: 'I found him, of course, an extraordinarily cheerful companion. I only hope, though, that he won't think me . . . "an old dear". I thought I saw some signs of it.' Brooke even persuaded the notoriously hypochondriac and anti–hearty Lytton to partake in some unfamiliar athletics: getting him to plunge into cold baths and pull ineffectually at a chest-expander.

Brooke, too, was cheered at Lulworth by a letter sent on from Rugby from *The Nation*, a recently founded radical weekly, to which he had sent a clutch of recent poems. The acting editor, H. W. Nevinson, a perceptive critic, while liking some of the verses, took strong exception to 'A Channel Passage', which he described as 'the notorious disgusting sonnet'. When he had got to know Brooke, the journalist wrote of him with sharp acuity: 'The fear of being petted and fussed over, for his beauty, the fear of falling into a flattered literary career, and of winning fame as one more beautiful poet of beautiful themes, it drove him into violence and coarseness . . .'

On his way back to Grantchester from Lulworth, Brooke stopped over with Eddie Marsh in London and took the opportunity to drop into *The Nation's* office and meet Nevinson, who, immediately after the poet's death, recalled the impression he had made:

Suddenly he came – an astounding apparition in any newspaper office. Loose hair of deep browny-gold; smooth, ruddy face; eyes not grey or bluish white, but of living blue, really like the sky, and as frankly open: figure not very tall, but firm and strongly made, giving the sense of weight rather than speed, and yet so finely fashioned and healthy . . . he wore a low blue collar and blue shirt and tie, all uncommon in those days. Evidently he did not want to be conspicuous, but the whole effect was almost ludicrously beautiful.

Marsh was beginning to introduce his adored young friend into the grand social circles that were to become increasingly important in Brooke's life. While Brooke was staying with his mentor at Raymond Buildings, they went to a performance of *Trelawny of the 'Wells'*, then moved on to an evening salon in Bedford Square presided over by Lady Ottoline Morrell, one of the great literary, political and social hostesses in an age when such creatures were abundant. Lady Ottoline, sister of the Duke of Portland, was married to a radical Liberal MP, Philip Morrell, and patronized the wilder shores of London's bohemia with generous abandon. Among those who enjoyed her hospitality were Lytton Strachey, Duncan Grant and the rest of the future denizens of Bloomsbury: Virginia Stephen, Clive and Vanessa Bell, Desmond MacCarthy and E. M. Forster. Her lovers were legion, but included Bertrand Russell and Henry Lamb.

Brooke's curiosity about his future nemesis, already aroused by Lytton, must have been further whetted by Eddie's description of Lamb at a previous salon: 'Do you know him? He was in a rough brown suit, with tails, shaped at the hips, and had a red handkerchief around his neck, but looked far more elegant and fashionable than any of the men in faultless evening dress. I'm afraid he didn't take to me much, and I'm told he has a cold and selfish nature.' Just how cold and selfish Lamb was, Brooke would one day, to his cost, discover.

While Lytton had been unburdening himself about Lamb, Brooke had been brooding about his own fruitless love: Noel. In December 1909 he had made another of his illicit descents on Bedales, accompanied by Jacques Raverat, on the thin excuse of seeing the school's annual play. He had not managed to see Noel alone, and the ever-suspicious Margery had made sure that neither Bryn nor Noel had been present at Switzerland that Christmas. While he served out his time in the housemaster's study at Rugby, a rival suitor for Noel's favours, Bunny Garnett, who had known her since childhood, was continuing to press her. With wisdom far beyond her years, Noel coolly told Bunny that the whole charm of youth lay in falling easily in love, while remaining aware that such passing passions weren't permanent and could therefore be taken lightly. This was a message that Brooke resolutely refused to hear.

On his way to Lulworth he had stopped off in Birmingham in the vain hope of meeting Noel, who was passing through the city by train on her way to a rock-climbing holiday in Wales. Brooke's physical clumsiness – the same deficiency that kept him off the dance floor – precluded him from climbing – a hobby that delighted several of his friends, including Geoffrey Keynes, George Mallory, Jacques Raverat, Godwin Baynes and the Oliviers. This was one area of Neo-Pagan activity where Brooke could, or would not, accompany his friends.

★

Back at the Orchard after his long absence, Brooke hosted a May Day breakfast for a large group of his friends, including Ka Cox and Geoffrey Keynes, who was unsuccessfully pursuing the popular Fabian treasurer. The fondness of Brooke's circle for outdoor activities had won them the derisory nickname in Cambridge of 'dew-dabblers', as Brooke explained to Noel the day after the party:

> The thing is that they insist on 'dabbling in the dew' & being 'in the country' on the first of May. I had to get up at half past seven to give them breakfast: though I had worked until 2. It rained in the morning; yet they all turned up, thousands of them – men and women, devastatingly and indomitably cheery. The world is hard, & I was very bitter. When rain ceased we put on galoshes & gathered cowslips in the fields. We celebrate the festival with a wealth of detailed and ancient pagan ritual; many dances & songs . . .

Brooke was hard at work on his studies, and applying himself with more than customary enthusiasm now that he was concentrating on English with the aim of gaining a Fellowship in 1911 or 1912. He had started work on the chosen subject of his thesis, the dramas of John Webster, and was also reading up on the effects of Puritanism on English drama. Visitors to the Orchard in May included Lytton and a new friend, the swarthy and popular contemporary romantic poet James Elroy Flecker, with whom Brooke engaged in friendly and jocular rivalry. Another frequent visitor was the future novelist Rose Macaulay, the daughter of Brooke's tutor at King's. Rose, who was six years Brooke's senior, nursed romantic desires for him, as her novels made clear.

In June Brooke and Geoffrey Keynes took a tent out to Overcote, the quiet hamlet on the River Ouse that he had discovered a year previously. Alongside this 'dew-dabbling' his academic and political activities continued unabated: he led the Cambridge delegation to the Fabian national conference in London, and was amused by witnessing one of the many rows that rent the movement in its early years – this time over the hot topic of female suffrage. Brooke, whose misogyny was never far from the surface, reported approvingly to Hugh Dalton: 'The Northern delegates were superb men. They lashed the women with unconquerable logic and gross words. There were the most frightful scenes, and the women gibbered with rage.'

Inspired by new enthusiasm for the cause, Brooke began to plan a caravan tour of the south-west with Dudley Ward, during which the two friends aimed to hold wayside political meetings in favour of Poor Law reform.

Funded by £2 12s. prised from the tight grip of treasurer Ka Cox, Brooke hired a caravan from two fellow Kingsmen, Hugh and Steuart Wilson, together with a horse named Guy. Posters advertising their meetings ('Principal Speaker Mr BROOKE. Questions invited') – were designed by Gwen Darwin, and Brooke threw himself into the minutest details of the tour with his customary furious energy and practical efficiency.

Beneath the planning, as so often with Brooke, there was a secret agenda, and, as so often, it revolved around his semi-secret passion for Noel. He intended to use the tour as an elaborate cover for meeting his beloved. As ever, he laid his plans with spidery care. At the end of April he had engineered a four-day walking tour in the wooded countryside around Noel's home village. His companion-cum-chaperone was Jacques Raverat. During this jaunt they dropped in on the Oliviers at Limpsfield Chart, and spent half a day with Bryn and Noel – the two less attractive sisters, Margery and Daphne, were, as Brooke well knew, safely an ocean away in Jamaica and would not return until October.

It was during this eventful spring that Brooke began to play one of those double games of love that he relished so inordinately. While continuing his obsession with Noel, he started a prolonged flirtation/pursuit of her beautiful, but less intelligent elder sister, Bryn. The unobtainable, elusive Noel absorbed the romantic, yearning side of his nature, while the overtly sexy Bryn was a magnet for his lust. This parallel pursuit was carried on often when both sisters were present, and he simultaneously corresponded with both, so the opening of the morning mail around the Oliviers' breakfast table must often have been an interesting occasion.

Brooke had to be back in Cambridge by 9 a.m. on 27 April after his exhausting walking tour, to take an oral examination. Jacques woke him at 4 a.m. and he passed through an 'absolutely empty & very beautiful & clean' London before taking the first train to Cambridge 'surrounded by milk-cans and the morning papers', as he told Bryn. After sitting his exam along with '50 other fools' he succumbed to a bad cold and headache. 'Still,' he reflected, the joy of meeting his two love-objects on their home ground meant 'it was all worth it.'

In mid-July, surrounded by clanking pots and pans, the caravan stuffed with books ranging from the poetry of John Donne to dry volumes on the Poor Law; with Dudley Ward on the box with the reins in his hands and Guy plodding grimly on with his muzzle in a nosebag, the private Fabian crusade got underway. The two friends set off from Winchester and meandered along the dusty byways of Hampshire and Dorset in the somnolent midsummer heat.

Brooke had already written to Noel warning of his intentions: 'I am coming to Petersfield. Is it permissible? The matter is this. Dudley . . . and I are going to start from Winchester in a cart . . . We can take Petersfield on the way . . . Jacques will be in Minorca and without him I should be too horribly frightened to come near Bedales.' In the absence of his usual Bedalian chaperone, Brooke had craftily enlisted the aid of a new friend, the melancholy country writer and future poet Edward Thomas, whose wife Helen was a Bedales teacher, and who lived near the school in a house built by another teacher, the architect Geoffrey Lupton. 'I thought of trying to get Thomas or Lupton to let Dudley & me slumber in their grounds that night, & give us a meal. If that is impossible, I suppose we shall just pass through the place and hang about for an hour or two, if it's decent or desirable. But I want to see Thomas!'

Brooke suggested that Noel obtain an exeat to visit them at Thomas's house high above the village of Steep. Failing that, he held out the hope that they would meet at the annual camp organized by the Oliviers, which would take place this summer at Buckler's Hard, on the River Beaulieu on the edge of the New Forest. 'Our cart will land us there . . . By God! Life will be good, in August! I shall make a special endeavour not to die during July.' Brooke made his plans even more plain to the absent Jacques: 'But all, almost, we want to do is to see the gorgeous Noel and talk with the tired Thomas.'

Not wanting to impose on the impoverished and permanently harassed Thomas, already the father of two young children, and with Helen Thomas heavily pregnant with their third, Brooke brought his charm to bear on Lupton, a follower of William Morris's Arts & Crafts movement, who built the Thomas's home, The Red House, and the library at Bedales, virtually with his own hands. As a result he and Dudley spent their first night on the road under Lupton's roof, and Noel Olivier joined them for tea, chaperoned by a school friend, Mary Newberry.

After this entertaining diversion from the stern central purpose of their tour, they set off once more, heading in a south-westerly direction; stopping and holding their public meetings as the mood took them. They divided responsibilities: it was Dudley's job to hand out leaflets drumming up interest, while Brooke made the main speech. He had a standard spiel, stressing the waste of letting between two and three million people idle in destitution while their energies could be put to productive use if the state put them to work. In his notes for the speech, we find pure Fabianism, as well as the doctrine of state-aided public works that was later to be associated with his Apostolic colleague Maynard Keynes. The influence of

Keynes and the Webbs is clearly visible in the doctrines Brooke preached on village greens and market squares that summer. Only at Wareham, in Dorset's Isle of Purbeck, did a downpour force them to abandon their itinerary and take refuge in the Black Bear hotel. Sadly, the rain continued, and they backtracked to Winchester with spirits somewhat dampened.

IO

'Life burns on'

While setting up his summer rendezvous with Noel, Brooke had not forgotten his parallel pursuit of Bryn. As usual he enlisted a third party as his agent in place to cover his covert actions. This time his fall guy was Bunny Garnett, the family friend of all the Oliviers. In order to ingratiate himself with Bunny, Brooke invited him to stay at the Orchard along with Bryn, seductively detailing its delights: 'apple blossom now, later . . . roses . . . bathing and all manner of rustic delight, cheeses, and fruit'.

Intrigued, Bunny obligingly showed up, and Brooke prevailed on him to organize a five-day cruise on the Norfolk Broads at the end of June, accompanied by Bryn and Noel, Godwin Baynes (now working as Medical Officer of Health for Hampstead) and an older family friend of the Oliviers, a Dr Rogers, to act as chaperone for the young people. Rogers had a wherry, the *Reindeer*, on which Brooke and Bunny shared a cabin next door to Bryn and Noel, whom they could hear giggling through the thin dividing wall.

An unsuspecting Bunny little realized his true role in Brooke's nefarious scheme:

> I was very happy and was aware that for some reason Rupert liked me. That holiday was the time of my closest friendship with him. His immense charm and intelligence had not yet been spoiled by success and by certain *idées fixes*, which later came to resemble hallucinations. With me, in our midnight cabin talks, he was simple, sincere and intimate, with a certain lazy warmth. It was only later that he was apt to utter warnings about the wickedness of other people.

Brooke passed his days in writing the essay, *Puritanism and the English Drama*, which he was entering for the university's Harness Prize, and in gazing adoringly at Noel and lustfully at Bryn. Flustered by these riches, he managed to leave a guinea razor on the boat when he returned to Grantchester to finish his essay and prepare for his propagandist excursion: 'So I have a beard and a headache & I work all night on black coffee,' he told Bryn, who had been dispatched with Dudley to scout for a suitable site for the Neo-Pagan summer camp.

They found what they were looking for at Buckler's Hard – an area of sentimental memories of Noel for Brooke. Bryn sent him a postcard showing a view: 'This place will do . . . It's not so full of yachts at present, & there is a splendid landing stage to dive from & hay-fields & two short rows of old red-brick cottages with a wide grass-grown street between.' The location provided all the suitable conditions for a Neo-Pagan gathering – the peaceful River Beaulieu for swimming and sailing (a lugger had been hired for the occasion), extensive woods and a convenient clearing for pitching the tents. Buckler's Hard had formerly been one of the main shipbuilding sites in southern England, and three of Nelson's battleships were constructed there. But the decline of wooden ships had left the place moored in time – an idyllic spot for an important milestone in Brooke's topsy-turvy emotional life. 'The place looks perfect,' Brooke wrote to Bryn. 'Can we get out of sight among the trees to avoid the gaze of the armoured cruisers?'

Present at the camp were Noel and Bryn Olivier, Ka Cox, Jacques Raverat, Godwin Baynes, Bunny Garnett and his friend Harold Hobson; Bill Hubback and his fiancée Eva Spielman; Sybil and Ethel Pye and their brother David; and a newcomer to the Neo-Pagan fraternity, A. E. ('Hugh') Popham, a Cambridge hearty who was patiently pursuing a long, and ultimately successful, project – the wooing and winning of Bryn Olivier. The group was joined by Brooke and Dudley Ward in time for Brooke's birthday. Photos of the camp show a cheerful and carefree Brooke, with bare legs, open shirt and tousled hair, writing, reading or merely gazing in adoration, his head on his hands, at a gypsy-scarfed Noel.

The opportunity he had been angling for for so long came when he found himself alone with Noel gathering firewood. Boldly, he unburdened himself of the nature of his feeling and made a full confession of love, coupled with a proposal of marriage. To his utter delight, Noel answered that she loved him and would indeed marry him – when she was older. Until then, she implored Brooke, who was ready to run back to camp and announce the glad tidings, their unofficial 'engagement' – more of a mutual understanding and a promise for the future than a formal betrothal – should remain a strict secret.

Reluctantly, Brooke agreed to keep the secret; but his bubbling high spirits could not be concealed from the others, and word got round that he and Noel had pledged their troth. It is hard to gauge the exact state of their feelings at this point – Noel was undoubtedly deeply touched by Brooke's evident devotion; but she remained cautious to the point of clamming up: not only did she distrust extremes of emotion as a sign of instability; she was also wary of Brooke's sudden and changeable enthusiasms in particular. A witness at the camp, Jacques Raverat, probably gives as good an insight as any:

> She accepted the homage of his devotion with a calm, indifferent, detached air, as if it were something quite natural. No doubt she was flattered by his attentions, for she cannot have failed to see something of his beauty and charm; also, she saw how he was sought out, admired, showered with adulation on every side. But he did not inspire respect in her; she found him too young, too chimerical, too absurd . . .

Brooke returned to Grantchester to find that his rooms at the Orchard were occupied by someone else, so he temporarily decamped next door to the Old Vicarage, thus spending his first nights under the roof of his beloved future home. His immediate preoccupation was a rerun of the Marlowe Dramatic Society's production of *Dr Faustus* for the benefit of a visiting party of German students. Wisely, knowing of his deficiencies as an actor, he had elected to play a minor role – the Chorus – and had handed over the part of Mephostophilis to a friend, Reginald Pole, a future professional actor. Brooke had been mugging up his part in Hampshire and Dorset, and contemporary photographs show him declaiming it in bare feet to a captive audience of Jacques and Dudley in the garden at Grantchester.

The production provided an excuse for a full-scale Neo-Pagan gathering: Justin Brooke came up to direct, while Bryn Olivier returned to re-create her much-admired role of Helen, and Noel accompanied her to understudy one of the seven deadly sins – Envy. Other sins were played by Ethel Pye, who, with her sister Sybil, carried a torch for Brooke; and the well-covered Ka Cox was rather cruelly given the part of Gluttony. The title role, as in the previous production, was played by the newly married Francis Cornford. After Brooke moved back to the Orchard, the Olivier and Pye sisters came to occupy the Old Vicarage for the duration of the rehearsals, which took place in Cambridge.

Brooke would ferry them back to Grantchester along the darkened Cam by canoe. In a nostalgic memoir of these summer days and nights, Sybil Pye recalled him instinctively gliding home along the river: 'He would know, he said, when we were nearing home, by the sound of a certain poplar-tree that grew there: its leaves rustled faintly even on such a night as this when not a breath seemed stirring.' In the evenings Brooke entertained his friends with readings from *Antony and Cleopatra* or Meredith's *Modern Love*. It does not take too much imagination to conjure up the picture of the star, under the low beams of the Old Vicarage, among an admiring circle of four young women, all of whom, to some extent admired or desired him. Sybil drew the scene:

> Our sitting room was small and low, with a lamp slung from the ceiling, and a narrow door opening straight on to the dark garden. On quiet nights, when watery sounds and scents drifted up from the river, this room half suggested the cabin of a ship. Brooke sat with his book at a table just below the lamp, the open door and dark sky behind him; and the lamplight falling so directly on his head would vividly mark the outline and proportions of forehead, cheek and chin; so that in trying afterwards to realize just what lent them, apart from all expression, so complete and unusual a dignity, and charm, I find it is to this moment my mind turns.

By day, they bathed in Byron's Pool, the women admiring Brooke's comely form. There is no record of whether he performed one of his regular party pieces before them – jumping into the water and then emerging almost immediately with a full erection. Decorously, the only Brooke performance recorded by Sybil came after a moonlight dip when he hung upside down from a branch of the rustling poplar to dry, the bough bending, and his long locks almost brushing the grass. Surprisingly, Sybil remarks that all this was done with a complete absence of self-consciousness on Brooke's part – although when she told him the scene reminded her of a Blake woodcut, a smile of self-satisfaction crossed his face. Brooke, she concluded, was at once both man and boy 'and we seemed [to be] looking at the very gestures of the child he must have grown from'.

In fact Brooke was always well aware of the effect his actions had on others, and obliquely boasted of his exhibitionism a few weeks later when asked by Lytton Strachey, absent in Sweden, to regale him with some juicy piece of scandal. Regretfully, Brooke replied that he had none: 'In my little cottage, and even more in the roamings of late months through the Country, and the Camp, I am so far away from such things. Anyhow my scandal is not your scandal . . . It wouldn't stiffen you even at all to hear of what it was the rosiest chatteringest delirium for me to do, – bathing naked by moonlight with the ladies.'

Although evidently a riveting reader of poetry and prose in private –
Sybil mentions another treetop performance when Brooke read to her and
Noel from *Paradise Lost* in the branches of a chestnut – Brooke's style on
stage was far less convincing. Even an uncritical admirer like Sybil admitted:

> Whether an audience irked him, I am not sure, but it is certain that we missed
> at the performance [of *Dr Faustus*] . . . all the charm of those rehearsals of his
> part, with lovely gestures, which took place in the Vicarage garden . . . Standing
> under a briar arch, with bare feet and shirt thrown open, he would appeal with
> passion to this person, giving chance observers all the joy an official audience
> was to lack.

A less besotted observer, Jacques Raverat, was also less than impressed – and
believed Noel to be likewise:

> He read [Noel] his poems . . . and others too – Donne, Milton, Swinburne – in
> his slow, slightly affected voice; she listened politely but a little bored and often,
> I think, completely mystified; she would have understood Chinese poems as
> easily. I still remember seeing [Brooke] when he was painting some piece of
> scenery, touch the tip of [Noel's] nose caressingly with his brush, as she came
> over to watch; she seemed to find this joke much more to her taste than serious
> readings or conversation. It was, it must be said, more suited to her age. In all
> she felt for him only a certain affection, tinged with a little disdain. But [Brooke]
> did not take it too hard. He was completely given over to his adoration of her;
> bitterness – along with desire – had not yet entered into his heart.

Jacques paints a picture of Noel at this time which gives us some idea of the
hold she had over Brooke:

> She had an admirable head, set on her handsome round neck, brown hair, flat
> complexion, the face very regular and unexpressive, even a bit hard. But it was
> lit up as if by the beam of a lighthouse when she turned her large grey eyes to
> you. One could hardly bear their gaze without feeling a kind of instant
> dizziness, like an electric shock. They seemed full of all the innocence in the
> world, and of all the experience also; they seemed to promise infinite happiness
> and wonderful love for whoever could win her.

The performance of *Dr Faustus* went off successfully on 17 August.
Afterwards the cast and their friends assembled at the Cornfords' new
home, Conduit Head, for a celebratory house-warming. Brooke,

dissatisfied with the plain black scholar's gown he had worn as the Chorus, changed into his old favourite – the transparent blue costume from *Comus*. Bryn Olivier was the rival belle of the ball, her beauty set off by gold powder in her hair. After a banquet of bread, cheese and beer, the jolly company set off down Madingley Road for a triumphal torchlight parade. Returning, they cast down the burning torches in a circle around the newly-wed Cornfords and danced in a ring around their hosts. Brooke, wearing a many-pointed crown, was the lord of the dance, as Sybil swooningly observed:

> the fitfullest gleam from the bonfire would catch and run up the tall points of his crown, giving it and his head a sort of ghostly detachment from his body, and marking vividly the peculiar golden quality of his hair. This hair, escaping from under the crown, flapped and leapt as the dance grew wilder: and all the while one was aware of that strange anachronism – the lighted eyes and serious face of a child's complete absorption, and again the detached watchful intelligence . . .

'If I were called in to construct a religion . . .' wrote Philip Larkin, 'I would make use of water.' The Neo-Pagans felt the same impulse, and their camps and rituals were tending to go beyond the frolics of a tight-knit group of friends and towards a mystical nature cult – perhaps as a sort of substitute for the religious orthodoxy of their parents' generation that most of them had rejected.

They were not alone in this tendency towards paganism. Germany was currently being swept by a similar cult – the *Wandervögel* ('Wandering birds') movement, in which bands of young people, attired, like Brooke and his friends, in open-necked shirts and shorts, and strumming guitars, made for the forests and mountains, where they would camp out around open fires, sing songs and commune with the spirit of the great outdoors. In their love of diving and bathing and camp-fires, the Neo-Pagans were tapping into the same *Zeitgeist* – enraptured with an idea of youth and freedom, and a hatred of age and stifling convention. But, as Paul Delany has pointed out in his study of the Neo-Pagans, there was something rotten at the heart of their myth.

Not only were they rejecting the main forces of the society around them – industrialism, urban life, modernity in all its ugly mediocrity – they also wilfully shut their eyes to the realities of human ageing and responsibility. There was no place for anyone over 30 in their world, and precious little for anyone under 15. That is why marriage, with its promise of children, was felt to be such a threat to Brooke, and why he could never come to terms with it.

The arcadian, rural England they dreamed of had already passed away, even as they discovered and celebrated it. And they made little attempt to understand the socio-economic basis on which their privileged lifestyle so insecurely rested: their camps, their holidays, their parties and pleasures, all depended on money provided by their despised parents, and labour by the despised underclass. Neo-Paganism was a theory of adolescence that failed to survive the merest brush with reality. For all his eloquently expressed horror of his parents and family life, Brooke – in his Fabian guise – was probably the one Neo-Pagan who came near to understanding the social reality of Edwardian life.

Meanwhile he returned to the Ranee at Bilton Road in a state of intoxicated ecstasy. The gloomy house – it was the first time, he pointed out, that he had ever lived anywhere as mundane as a house with a number – failed to stifle his effervescence: 'Life is splendid,' he told Dudley Ward. 'I cannot contain myself at meals. They suspect me . . . I roll about and gurgle inside. Life, Dudley, Life!' Perhaps it was Dudley's very orthodox dullness that made him the recipient of such declarations as 'It is absurd to say the world is dull. It is superb . . . SUPERB!' He told an adoring Sybil Pye: 'Since Monday I have read 11 plays, 3 novels, a book on Stocks and Shares and *Principia Ethica* [G. E. Moore's 'Bible' of Apostolic ethics, which apparently he had not bothered to consult before] . . . besides all the current magazines and papers. How gorgeous it is to work! Ha!'

The double game with Bryn and Noel continued, Brooke seemingly oblivious to the possibility that the sisters might compare notes. Knowing that Bryn was on the point of leaving for an extended trip to Jamaica, he wrote to 'beg, pitifully, on my knees' to see her before her departure, fearing that 'You will probably die there. Or return listless and married and unradiant. And anyhow it's so very long from now to next summer. And time skips by so, that you'll be fat & I blind & both old before we know it'. He proposed a joint outing to Hampton Court, or a month tramping across Gloucestershire or emulating the flamboyant Italian poet and lover Gabriele D'Annunzio in going 'aeroplaning at Brooklands . . . Will you be anywhere anywhen?'

Trustingly, Noel still held fast to their understanding made in the New Forest: 'if I think of it I just gloat & dance & other people dont notice it, except Bryn, who was always a sympathetic person.' The duplicitous Brooke responded on 6 September, remarking that his memory of their 'engagement' 24 days previously was growing hazy: 'Yet I refuse to disbelieve that something did, somewhere, happen . . .' But already he showed signs of wavering; pointing out that they were unlikely to meet before the following spring, he wrote: 'I may decay beyond recognition by next April: there are seeds of it in me already. I warn you, I am feeble . . . You see, I am feeble & mean & empty and a fool & a devil & rather a beast. And I feel that with proper treatment something might be made of me. Only, the proper treatment, I suspect, includes more of – you. And without that I, as I say, decay and decompose, – and occasionally dislike myself.'

Noel could not say that she had not been warned.

In the first week of September Brooke accompanied James to the annual Fabian summer school in Llanbedr. It was the last such organized socialist event that he would attend. Sleeping arrangements were rudimentary – he shared what he would one day call 'the rough male kiss of blankets' and a stable floor with James; the Welsh weather was typically atrocious; and the atmosphere was further dampened by the disapproving presence of Beatrice Webb, who felt, unfairly, that Brooke was only there for the social connections: 'We have had interesting and useful talks with these young men,' she wrote in her journal, 'but the weather, being detestable, must have made the trip appear rather a bad investment for them, and they were inclined to go away rather more critical and supercilious than they came . . . They won't come, unless they know who they are going to meet, sums up Rupert Brooke.'

For his part, Brooke was both more studious and more tolerant than the old dragon gives him credit for. His notes from Llanbedr show him taking a serious and informed interest in the topics under discussion, and he jibbed only when Beatrice Webb tried to organize enormous mountain hikes in the rain. He and Gerald Shove, another participant, formed an 'Anti-athletic League' which mutinously refused to walk more than three miles a day. He crossed swords intellectually with the Fabians' *grande dame*, as well, as James recalled: 'There was a remarkable scene in which Rupert and I tried to explain Moore's ideas to Mrs Webb while she tried to convince us of the efficacy of prayer.' Beatrice was evidently unimpressed: 'Why must these young men be so rude? . . . the egotism of the young university man is colossal. Are they worth bothering about?' she asked rhetorically.

Despite the mutinies by the younger Fabians against their elders – on one occasion things got so out of hand that the local police had to be called – Brooke seems to have enjoyed himself at the school. He told Geoffrey Keynes: 'I'm just back from doing my accursed duty at the Fabian Summer School. It was really rather fun. A thousand different people from different parts of life.' A new acquaintance at the school who impressed both Brooke and James – who would one day marry her – was Alix Sergeant-Florence, a Slade art student who was about to go up to Cambridge. Brooke reported to Noel: 'I went to the Fabian Summer School a week for conscience's sake. I rather loved it all. There was, I discovered, a Bedalian there . . . one Sergeant-Florence . . . I thought her rather fine . . .' Ka Cox, too, was given a glowing report: 'You ought to go there once to learn a little about Life, and to teach them – what? Anyhow it's not so bad as you think . . . I was acting on my conscience in going there, instead of reading peacefully. And acting on one's conscience is always rather fun.'

Brooke's relations with Ka, hitherto a peripheral concern, were taking a deeper turn. The woman to whom the other Neo-Pagans tended to turn in times of trouble, for her comforting, maternal tenderness, was herself in deep emotional waters. Jacques Raverat, who had long pursued her, had given up the chase and was concentrating on a receptive Gwen Darwin in London. Ka was hurt at the rebuff, and turned to Brooke for solace. Despite the blow, Ka took the news with commendable stoicism, and as ever, put the needs of others before her own bruised pride, even steeling herself to meet her friend and rival for a September visit to the Raverat family's château at Prunoy in northern Burgundy. As well as Ka and Gwen, Noel and Bryn were of the party, along with Francis and Frances Cornford. All in all, it was a gathering of Brooke's nearest and dearest female friends, and, fretting away at Rugby, he wanted very much to go too. He asked Ka for her counsel:

> it will be splendid for both parties – and for everyone else – if Brynnoel and France/is love each other. But that sort of joining-up is made easier by an extra person who knows and loves both lots and has a calmer, more intriguing and far-seeing mind than the romantic dreamer Jacques. So that I felt, though they of course would join, Francis' brooding and Frances' energy and Brynnoel's shyness and partly affected stupidity might just possibly make it less complete and happy than it would be under the benign encouragement of one so wise and so competent in both the languages and natures as (I was perfectly confident!) myself . . .

It is laughable that Brooke thought himself calmer and less of a romantic dreamer than Jacques, and in the end, some shreds of common sense prevailed. He realized that such a cat's cradle of emotions would be too much for him to handle, and reluctantly stayed away from Prunoy. He may also have been miffed by the latest put-down from Noel, who, reacting both to his warnings about his own emotional fluidity and to renewed intrigues to engineer a secret encounter in her well-guarded life, told him tartly: 'I am rather glad it was impossible to carry out those unspeakably horrid plots . . . If we cant meet without schemes I would rather, by far, not see you for half a year – when you will be "decayed" (I dont know what it means) & I shall have cut my hair, or put it up.'

Cut to the quick, Brooke was at first repentant: 'Oh, I loathe myself & I loathe you, that I upset you that day – made you "ill & mad" . . . I feel more & more flushed & foolish & gobbly & undignified & sinking into the unfathomable mud of your cool disdain . . .' Then his pride reasserted itself: 'No, damn you, I'm right. And you're a sentimental schoolgirl.' He then proceeded to let loose a torrent of emotional diarrhoea that must have terrified its young recipient:

> I could find you thinking yourself noble and high-minded and honest & open & self restrained & dignified & in general the ideal of the English public school clergyman ('playing the game' eh?), and me mean & hot-faced & undignified & sneaky & scheming & flustered & underhand & rotten & low; and (perhaps) I could leave you realising yourself a sentimental, flighty, priggish, silly, romantic, sloppy, infant and me an ordinary, commonsense, sane, business-like, ardent, middle-aged lover. But I won't. I won't argue on that basis. I bow to my fate. I realise that one of the disadvantages, for us common place, level-headed people, of falling in love with flighty, poetical, fantastic, unaccountable dreamers is that we have to fall in with their dear old silly poetry-book-cum-pulpit ideals . . . and go on without knitting. It is part of the penalty we pay. Perhaps it is worth it. So I'll always advertise extensively in the *Morning Post* whenever I'm going to meet you. And we'll all be healthy.

Brooke reminded Noel of the true spur to his 'fever', by (mis)quoting Marvell:

> But at my back I always hear
> Time's winged chariot hurrying near;
> And yonder all before me lie
> Deserts of vast eternity.

Brooke was feeling the eternal stresses of a young man in love with a chaste – or anyway immediately unavailable – young woman. Oddly, his raging frustration came out as transference. He invested Noel with some of *his* worst qualities: silliness, sentimentality, priggishness, being over-romantic, flighty and so on. Not surprisingly, she took fright at this storm of abuse and departed for Prunoy without further word, escorted, oddly enough, by

Ka Cox, resplendent in a navy-style blue cloak – leaving Brooke to grind his teeth in impotent fury in Rugby.

In the grand surroundings of Jacques' eighteenth-century château, with its castellated towers, huge windows, cavernous fireplaces and 700 acres of wooded grounds, the Neo-Pagans gave full rein to their fantasies of constructing a quasi-religious rite. Jacques reported: 'We talked a great deal of the urgency of some kind of ritual, mystery, initiation, symbolism and we planned a great litany of the four elements.' But then English scepticism crept in to curb his Gallic dreams: 'But I doubt whether it will ever come to anything. As Francis says, we are all much too rational and self-conscious . . .'

Back in Rugby, in late September, came cheering news that went some way to compensate Brooke for missing out on these thrilling diversions: he learned that he had won the Harness Prize, and with it a useful £70 to bolster his always tight finances. It was a boost, not only to his wallet but also to his ego, bruised by his disappointing performance in the Tripos. His prize-winning essay is an extreme – in places intemperate – attack on the stultifying influence of the Puritans on the English stage. He reserves his greatest scorn for the alleged hypocrisy of those Puritans who condemned the theatre for immorality.

But Brooke, for all his condemnation of Puritanism, was himself infected with the virus. Even his admiration for Shakespeare was tinged with disapproval of his vices: 'This glutton, drunkard, poacher, agnostic, adulterer and sodomite was England's greatest poet.' In the same notebook he gave his current opinion of the homosexual Cambridge clique in which he had moved in his early years at the university:

> I like telling the story of Shakespeare's love affairs. It shocks the Puritans, who want it hushed up. And it shocks the pro-Sodomites who want to continue in a hazy pinkish belief that all great men were Sodomites. The truth is that some great men are sodomites *and* womanizers, Shakespeare, [Michel] Angelo etc . . . Pure sodomy is a pretty affectation in the young, but if it is anything more, leads to secondratedness, sentimentality, fluff, gentle dilettante slush . . .

Brooke's farewell to the affections and affectations of his own youth seems to be already underway, although his 'conversion' to fully-fledged heterosexuality came within a year of his 'losing his virginity' with Denham Russell-Smith.

He tarried in Rugby to lecture a local women's group on Shakespeare, and to continue Fabian agitation for Poor Law reform. In the midst of this, he replied to a dispiriting letter from his early socialist mentor Ben Keeling, who had gone out into the real world and was finding it hard to maintain his youthful *élan* and idealism in the grim surroundings of managing a labour exchange, where he was also attempting to agitate for a socialist transformation of society. Rebuking Keeling for his 'pessimism', Brooke admitted his own ignorance of the world: 'I, writing poetry and reading books and living at Grantchester all day, feel rather doubtful and ignorant about "the world" – about England and men.' He acknowledged that his own innate optimism was 'a feeling rather than a reasoned belief'; but pessimism, he pointed out, could be equally subjective: 'caused by reason and experience, or more often by loneliness or soul-measles or indigestion or age or anything else'.

However, Brooke was clear about his own personal cure for 'soul-measles':

> The remedy is mysticism, or Life, I'm not sure which. Do not leap or turn pale at the word Mysticism. I do not mean any religious thing, or any form of belief. I still burn and torture Christians daily . . . I don't any more believe the world to be good. Only I do get rid of the despair that it isn't, and I certainly seem to see additional possibilities of it getting better. It consists in just looking at people and things as themselves – neither as useful, nor moral nor ugly nor anything else but just as being.

His response is essentially that of a poet:

> What happens is that I suddenly feel the extraordinary value and importance of everybody I meet, and almost everything I see . . . I roam about places – yesterday I did it even in Birmingham! – and sit in trains and see the essential glory and beauty of all the people I meet. I can watch a dirty middle-aged tradesman in a railway-carriage for hours, and love every dirty greasy sulky wrinkle in his weak chin and every button on his spotted unclean waistcoat. I know their states of mind are bad. But I'm so much occupied with their being there at all that I don't have time to think of that.

Brooke's poetic perception extends from people – whose physical imperfections he is always ready to dwell on at inordinate length – to the things of the world he was to celebrate in his poetry in long, ecstatic lists:

> Half an hour's roaming about a street or a village or a railway station shows so much beauty that it is impossible to be anything but wild with suppressed

exhilaration. And it's not only beauty, and beautiful things. In a flicker of sunlight on a blank wall, or a reach of muddy pavement, or smoke from an engine at night there's a sudden significance and importance and inspiration that makes the breath stop with a gulp of certainty and happiness.

Realizing that these flights might be too much for the essentially political Keeling to take, Brooke pulled up: 'I wish to God I could express myself . . . But the upshot of it is that one's too happy to feel pessimistic; and too much impressed by the immense value and potentialities of everything to believe in pessimism . . .'

This letter is the nearest we have to a statement of the philosophical beliefs and feelings that lay behind Brooke's poetry. For all its naivety, one can't resist being swept along by the sheer exuberance of his zest for life in its existential mess and absurdity, and share his delight in the transient beauty of the world. The document is also by implication a farewell to his rationalist Fabianism. He no longer hopes, he says to make a new world:

> It is not a question of either getting to Utopia in the year 2,000, or not. There'll be so much good then, and so much evil . . . The whole machinery of life, and the minds of every class and kind of man, change beyond recognition every generation. I don't know that 'Progress' is certain. All I know is that change is. These solid, solemn, provincials, and old maids, and business men, and all the immoveable system of things I see around me will vanish like smoke. All this present overwhelming reality will be as dead and odd and fantastic as crinolines or 'a dish of tay'. Something will be in its place, inevitably. And what that something will be, depends on me.

This passionate personal declaration of faith; disillusioned yet still hopeful, shows a maturing Brooke a million miles from the changeable child who writes to the Olivier sisters, so that it is hard to believe they are one and the same person. It is one more facet of the glittering chameleon who both beguiled and bewildered those who encountered him. By the beginning of October, Brooke had returned to the Orchard, from where, in his usual 'babbling Brooke' vein, he wrote to Bryn. The letter gives a good glimpse of the breakneck pace of his social life:

> I . . . am going to stay with Eddie Marsh on Thursday & Friday. On Thursday I'm going to let him take me to some theatre. May I come with you three [Gwen, Ka and Bryn] to the Promenade Concert on Friday, then? . . . I shall be galloping round picture-galleries, and the Exhibition . . . The Pyes had a fancy

they might be going to have you there the week-end, & me & Dudley & Jacques down for a walk on Sunday. But I guess they're disillusioned now. I think I shall come here for the week-end. Give my love to Noel. You don't know how funny it is to me to see you two . . . I can't come to Ka on Monday, even if she wants me, – though I am returning to London then. I have to dine with my amazing dining club that evening. But may I really come to Limpsfield on Tuesday or Wednesday (I don't mind which?) It's what I love to do most of all. Shan't I interfere with your packing? [for Jamaica] It will be splendid. I wag my head in an ecstasy of gratitude. I kiss your finger-tips. I salute you. And I'll hear about France. I've had a funny letter from old Jacques about it – full, too, of moral reflections on me. The old divil! It's so splendid to be going to see Margery & Daphne again: and so absurd that you should at the same moment be fading, decreasingly shining, away over streaky seas! What a spider God is! Life is glorious (I forget if I told you). You are superb. So am I . . . your eternally reverent Rupert.

Brooke's first visitor in the autumn was Edward Thomas, who took the opportunity to invite him down to his home near Bedales, at a time when he would be unencumbered by his family. He was followed by Dudley Ward, who put up at the Old Vicarage with two German girls, Clothilde von der Planitz, a dancer who was giving a performance in Cambridge, and her elder sister Annemarie, with whom Dudley was falling in love and would marry. The couple were not to know that they would one day live out their married life under the roof of the Old Vicarage.

Meanwhile Brooke had been having rows with his landlords, Mr and Mrs Stevenson, at the Orchard. Apparently the staid couple objected to the bohemian ways of him and his friends, especially to his habit of wandering round the village barefoot. 'I've had dreadful scenes with the Stevensons,' Dudley was informed. 'The village "talked" because of bare feet. So they [Clothilde and Annemarie] *must* keep their boots on. Otherwise they mayn't stay. This is true.' Brooke's next guest was the far-from-bohemian E. M. Forster, flushed with triumph over the publication of his new novel, *Howard's End*, with its injunction, which serves as a slogan for Brooke's generation: 'Only connect'.

Then Brooke was off to enjoy Edward Thomas's hospitality – and, as usual, to squeeze in a rushed, unsatisfactory meeting with Noel. But he relished his stay in Thomas's newly built house, with its view over the richly wooded hangers of the Hampshire Downs, a landscape that Thomas would one day make familiar in his own haunting poetry. At that time he was barely scraping a living as a hack reviewer of poetry and a harassed writer of pot-boiling biographies and country books. Poetry was an overriding interest, although he had yet to begin writing his own unique verse. Brooke read his latest poems to the older man, who observed him shrewdly:

> He stretched himself out, drew his fingers through his waved, fair hair, laughed, talked indolently, and admired as much as he was admired. No one that knew him could easily separate him from his poetry . . . he was tall, broad, and easy in his movements. Either he stooped, or he thrust his head forward unusually much to look at you with his steady blue eyes.

Thomas, in whom a native Celtic gloom allied with poverty to produce melancholy verging on suicidal depression, noticed an affinity of feeling with Brooke, who, he remarked, 'ranged between a Shelleyan eagerness and a Shelleyan despair'. No doubt Brooke told Thomas of his travails with Noel, causing the writer to comment that she was the 'least good-looking of the Oliviers' – an observation that a callous Brooke lost no time in passing on to Noel.

Buoyed by his new friend's advice and criticism, Brooke returned to Grantchester with renewed determination to revise and polish his recent poems and write the dozen or so more he would need before he could think of offering them to a publisher as his first collection. He did not find it easy to return to poetry after the excitements of the summer just ended, and in early November retreated further – to a hotel at Chatteris in the Fens, some 20 miles from his home. From here he told James Strachey: 'You've probably never tried to write poetry for three weeks and failed. Even if one succeeds it's wearing.'

But for once, Brooke was being overly self-critical. The poems he produced in the latter half of 1910 included several that were among the most successful he had written up until that time. These included 'Mummia', a recurring fantasy of necrophilia and cannibalism:

> As those of old drank mummia
> To fire their limbs of lead,
> Making dead kings from Africa
> Stand pandar to their bed;
>
> Drunk on the dead, and medicined
> With spiced imperial dust,
> In a short night they reeled to find
> Ten centuries of lust.

So I, from paint, stone, tale and rhyme,
   Stuffed love's infinity,
And sucked all lovers of all time
   To rarefy ecstasy.

Helen's the hair shuts out from me
   Verona's livid skies;
Gypsy the lips I press; and see
   Two Antonys in your eyes.

The unheard invisible lovely dead
   Lie with us in this place,
And ghostly hands above my head
   Close face to straining face;

[. . .]

Woven from their tomb and one with it,
   The night wherein we press;
Their thousand pitchy pyres have lit
   Your flaming nakedness . . .

This mysterious poem – opaque yet oddly memorable – marks a real departure in Brooke's verse. It is almost entirely shorn of the archaisms and plain silliness that marked his juvenilia, and is also refreshingly clear of his bitter little spurts of bile. For all that, its central image – that of drinking the dust of long-decayed lovers and thus re-creating their extinct passions – is grotesquely original. It is also marked by peculiar little personal touches: 'Helen's hair' is probably a recent memory of Bryn's gold-powdered locks when she played the doomed Queen in *Dr Faustus*; and 'Verona's livid skies' is a prophetic reference to the Italian city where Brooke and Ka would meet at the height of his crisis in 1912. As for 'Your flaming nakedness', this could be the fire-lit charms of Denham Russell-Smith's body, as seen by a lustful Brooke one year before, or a frustrated lover's vision of Noel bathing naked at Edenbridge or Grantchester. The private imagery of embracing Egyptian mummies was a long-held fantasy of Brooke's: he was to confide to Hugh Popham – again during the crisis year of 1912 – that he envied Hugh's newly acquired post at the British Museum, as he had often dreamed of sneaking into the place at dead of night to embrace a female mummy; although he had heard that most had died of syphilis, he said sourly, he hoped to find a clean one.

Just before leaving Ye Olde George Hotel at Chatteris, Brooke sent a copy of the poem to Noel, who had been ominously silent since receiving his raving letter of denunciation on her way to Prunoy. 'This is a very rough unfinished copy of the gift you don't write to me, – even ten words to say you exist . . . Farewell. Imagine, most unapproachable, a little figure stumping across the illimitable fens, occasionally bowing to the sun because it reminds him of you. Yours (what's good in him) your equal-inferior and lover Rupert.'

Noel replied in conciliatory vein: his 'awful' letter had, she confessed understandably, 'quite bewildered' her. She had resigned herself to the end of their affair after 'mourning you for 3 days and nights' and had 'started off with fresh and independent plans for life.' Noel admitted that her 'Purity' left her in a 'very unresponsive mood' to Brooke's passionate outbursts; but he should let her rest: 'I shall get better – or worse – soon.' Tantalizingly, she concluded:

> Dont write again about me, I am disgusted with myself – as a worm – at present; & anything which doesnt abuse & hate me seems unharmonious. If this is just the effect of being nearly 18, write to me about yourself, who are 23 (-4-5?.) & pull me out of it . . . Jaques [sic] also thinks Bryn is trustworthy & splendid. she is someone worth admiring; I dont think I can rely on anyone as I can on her. from Noel who is horrid.

The long-anticipated letter from Noel only served to agonize Brooke anew. Installed again at the Orchard in mid-November, he subjected her to a further emotional battering – despite knowing that his passionate incoherence only confused and disturbed her:

> Oh, Noel, I don't understand, I don't understand a bit. At least, I don't think I do. I can only guess – a million things. Oh, letters are hateful: writing is no use. It leaves everything dim. If one can *see* people and *talk* . . . If I could only talk to you, & ask you things. Two sensible people can say anything, – anything in the world – to each other. Forgive me for writing – for you asked me to 'let you rest'. It's filthy to bother you; yet it's right. For I don't understand – it may be my fault, or your's [sic], or letter writing's.'

After pages more of this emotional incontinence, a distressed Brooke concluded:

> This is damnably confused. Shall I 'sum up', as people do in papers on abstract subjects.

(1) I'm sorry to be disgusting and a nuisance.

(2) I don't think your letter hateful; but

(3) When you can, and even sooner than you like, I wish you'd write and tell me at least some of these things, –

(a) What in God's name I did or wrote:

(b) What the devil you mean:

(c) What the bloody hell is going to happen –

(4) Writing is awful: I wish I could see your face, and talk, to you.

–Oh, I won't 'classify' with 'unsuggestive' words, damn you! about instincts. I'll be as intelligent as I know how, & as well-meaning. I know you are you. But tell me what there is, more clearly, won't you? Ever Rupert.

Oh! Write! Write! Write! Noel!

Two things stand out clearly from this agonized morass: Brooke is as obsessive about Noel as ever; and neither is mature or ready enough to conduct a reasonable relationship, either by post or in person. Their feelings are too changeable, contradictory and infected by the frustration of being unable to meet except in clandestine circumstances. Perhaps it was best, as Brooke did, to let his poetry speak more clearly for him:

THE LIFE BEYOND

He wakes, who never thought to wake again,
  Who held the end was Death. He opens eyes
Slowly, to one long livid oozing plain
  Closed down by the strange eyeless heavens. He
    lies;
  And waits; and once in timeless sick surmise
Through the dead air heaves up an unknown hand,
Like a dry branch. No life is in that land,
  Himself not lives, but is a thing that cries;
An unmeaning point upon the mud; a speck
  Of moveless horror; an Immortal One
Cleansed of the world, sentient and dead; a fly
  Fast-stuck in grey sweat on a corpse's neck.

I thought when love for you died, I should die.
It's dead. Alone, most strangely, I live on.

Significantly, he did not send this sonnet directly to Noel, but, in childish petulance, sent it to Jacques at Prunoy, knowing he would show it to her.

Predictably, the 17-year-old was uncomprehending: 'I didn't understand
. . . I must have lost all the sense I ever had & I took it that you had gone
on to better things.' But somehow, the two star-crossed lovers patched
things up, and Brooke sent another sonnet in lyrical, rather than bitter
mood:

THE HILL
Breathless, we flung us on the windy hill,
  Laughed in the sun, and kissed the lovely grass.
  You said, 'Through glory and ecstasy we pass;
Wind, sun, and earth remain, the birds sing still,
When we are old, are old . . .' 'And when we die
  All's over that is ours; and life burns on
Through other lovers, other lips,' said I,
  'Heart of my heart, our heaven is now, is won!'

'We are Earth's best, that learnt her lesson here.
  Life is our cry. We have kept the faith!' we said;
  'We shall go down with unreluctant tread
Rose-crowned into the darkness!' . . . Proud we
    were,
And laughed, that had such brave true things to say.
—And then you suddenly cried, and turned away.

Brooke was deprecating about the poem – which has become, along with
the 1914 war sonnets, and 'The Old Vicarage, Grantchester', his most
anthologized piece: 'I have had two proofs of a bloody poem (8 months
old) sent me,' he told Noel in December. 'Here's the other. Ugh! . . . *don't*
go reading anything into it except itself. I've *never* seen you "cry & turn
away"!' Noel responded appropriately: 'I liked the old mummy poem
better than this "we flung us" one.'

'The Hill' is a very different sonnet from its sister piece, 'The Life
Beyond', with its 'shocking' Brookian images of decay and death: 'A
fly/Fast-stuck in grey sweat on a corpse's neck'. It could almost have been
written as a hymn to the Neo-Pagan lifestyle, with its breezy, overblown
rhetoric: 'Through glory and ecstasy we pass;/Wind, sun, and earth remain,
the birds sing still' and its undertone of regret at the passing of youth:
'—And then you suddenly cried, and turned away'.

Taken together, however, the two sonnets are an undeniable
demonstration of Brooke's ever surer grasp of his techniques and his

characteristic themes. Both, together with 'Mummia', betray the influence of the metaphysical poets and dramatists he was reading – Donne and Webster in particular. His confusion and frustration with Noel had, by some sort of inner alchemy, fused to produce real poetry, and he had reason to face the New Year with new-found confidence.

II

Munich

'On or about December 1910,' Brooke's friend Virginia Woolf (née Stephen) was to write, 'human nature changed.' She was probably thinking of the modernist era in art and literature, rung in by the likes of Joyce, T. S. Eliot and Ezra Pound – whose early poetry Brooke had favourably noticed in the *Cambridge Review* – and the Post-Impressionist exhibition organized in November of that year by Roger Fry, which introduced a bewildered London public to the sort of art that was already old hat in the rest of Europe.

But it was not only in the uplands of culture that new forces were astir that momentous autumn. It seems indeed that a new century was being born – ten years late, but this was England – in a climate of social and political upheaval. The death of King Edward VII in May had been a storm signal. His son and successor, George V, a bluff naval officer of severely limited mental horizons, was an unlikely figurehead for the changes that were unstoppably under way.

The old King's death had come in the midst of a constitutional crisis, caused by the overwhelmingly Tory House of Lords' point-blank refusal to pass into law a reforming budget proposed by David Lloyd George, the Liberals' radical Welsh Chancellor. The budget aimed to introduce rudimentary pensions and social insurance, to be financed by taxes which would fall heavily on the upper classes represented in the Lords. It was unprecedented for the upper house to refuse to pass a finance bill, and throughout a long summer, while Brooke and his friends frolicked by rivers, the crisis simmered on. Finally the King was constrained to promise his Prime Minister, Herbert Asquith, to create enough Liberal Lords to swamp the inbuilt Tory majority in the Lords should the Liberals win another general election on the issue of peers versus the people.

The election of December 1910 was fought out against an ominous backdrop that boded ill for the future peace and social cohesion of the country: among the bills that fell when Parliament dissolved was a measure giving women the right to vote. The leaders of the Suffragette campaign, who had been restrained and ladylike in their tactics so long as they could see themselves winning their battle by legal means, immediately switched to militancy. On 18 November determined followers of Emmeline Pankhurst, of the Women's Social and Political Union, rushed the House of Commons, battled with the police and were arrested *en masse*. To English gentlemen, it was a terrifying portent of what their hitherto docile womenfolk were capable of.

That same month England was racked by industrial strife: there were mass lockouts in the Lancashire cotton mills; lockouts in the shipyards of the north-east; and, most serious of all, a bitter strike in the coalfields of south Wales, which caused the Home Secretary Winston Churchill to send in troops to confront the starving miners of Tonypandy.

(Churchill's penchant for reaching for the trigger was shown again a year later, in December 1911, when he raced to Sidney Street, Stepney, where a group of anarchists from the Baltic, suspected of killing three policemen, were surrounded and shooting. Churchill called in the Scots Guards and personally supervised the subsequent siege, which ended with the anarchists dying amid the blazing ruins of their den. Newsreel cameras caught Brooke's patron, Eddie Marsh, in a bowler hat, nervously peering around a corner behind his chief as the bullets sang.)

The events of the end of 1910 were in Brooke's mind as he threw himself into a vigorous spate of intellectual work. He was wary of political commitment, and there were surfacing competing tugs on his loyalties: his Fabianism and his commitment to Poor Law reform, as well as the radical Liberal traditions of his family, should have placed him firmly on the Left and on the side of those agitating for change. On the other hand, he was steeped in gentility and the almost instinctive customs and traditions of upper-class, rural, collegiate England, and he was moving into increasingly grand circles in the upper reaches of the ruling caste. He knew nothing of the urban working class, and seems to have patronizingly despised what he did know. As for the rising voices of strident feminism, they simply terrified him.

His immediate concern was his academic future: he had received an offer of an English lectureship at Newcastle University; but his instinct was to refuse and try for a Fellowship at King's. To confirm his resolve he visited another of his elderly homosexual Cambridge admirers, A. C. Benson, one of a trinity of distinguished brothers who were all successful writers, in his rooms at Magdalene College on 9 November 1910.

Benson had first noticed Brooke when the young freshman presented 'a pretty picture' as the Herald in *Eumenides*. Meeting him again now, the elderly don, whose main claim to fame was as the author of the lyrics of that quintessential Edwardian Imperial hymn 'Land of Hope and Glory', noted that for all his fame and popularity, Brooke remained the fresh and unspoiled boy, neither egotistical nor self-regarding, and seemingly 'easily pleased' and happy for their talk to 'wander where it would'. Benson noted his guest's physical attributes in loving detail:

> He was far more striking in appearance than exactly handsome in outline. His eyes were small and deeply set. It was the colouring of face and hair which gave special character to his look. The hair rose very thickly from his forehead, and fell in rather stiff arched locks on either side – he grew it full and over-long, it was of a beautiful dark auburn tint inclining to red, but with an underlying golden gleam in it. His complexion was richly coloured, as though the blood were plentiful and near the surface; his face much tanned, with the tinge of sun-ripened fruit. He was strongly built, but inclined to be sturdy, and even clumsy, rather than graceful or lithe; his feet and hands were somewhat large and set stiffly on their joints; the latter had no expressiveness or grace and his feet were roughly proportioned and homely. Nor did he sit or move with any suppleness, but laughed, rather huddled, in his chair; while though his glance and regard were frank and friendly, his voice was far from beautiful, monotonous in tone, husky and somewhat hampered in the throat.

For all his literary felicity, it almost seems as though Benson is describing a rather large and overripe melon perched atop a recalcitrant block of timber.

Apparently reassured as to his future academic prospects at Cambridge, Brooke departed to prepare a lengthy paper he was due to deliver a month later as his valedictory address at the end of his year as President of the university's Fabian Society. He chose as his subject 'Democracy and the Arts'. The paper shows a seriousness and profundity of thought that would have amazed Brooke's more frivolous companions. The germ of his ideas originated in his violent antipathy to a lecture he had heard the previous year at the Fabian summer school. The lecturer was the drama critic and translator William Archer, to whom Brooke seems to have taken a strong dislike. (He described him as 'whiskers and no brains', and when asked what he thought of Archer's latest book, replied: 'Well, it weighs two pounds and thirteen ounces.')

Archer's thesis was that a fully functioning democracy would be death to the arts, which required a moneyed and leisured class of the idle rich both for patronage and appreciation. In setting out to rebut this, Brooke began by giving his own definition of democracy: 'The ordering of the national life according to the national will.' He scorned William Morris's vision of the worker of the future composing poetry while he laboured at his loom: 'Much of his own was. That may be why a lot of it is so dull.'

The artist and poet are answering a priest-like vocation, Brooke averred, and he poured contempt on the idea of the arts as an improving leisure activity that could be fitted in as part of the daily round: 'It is a thing we can't allow . . . the Civil Service poets, the stockbroker who does water-colours in the evenings, the music-master who has the holidays to compose in . . .' His vision of the place of the arts in society is unashamedly élitist and romantic, but also muddle-headed: for what else was Eddie Marsh but a civil servant with a spare-time interest in poetry? Gauguin – whose path to the South Seas Brooke would one day follow – was 'a stockbroker who painted' and Gustav Holst, the contemporary composer whose music now stands as a monument to Edwardian England, a 'music-master who had the holidays to compose in'. Brooke would have none of it. For him, art was 'an individual or unique affair' or it was nothing.

Rightly despising the notion of community art – 'you can't voice the soul of the Community any more than you can blow its nose' – Brooke was far-seeing in pointing out that modern society was swiftly extinguishing the old system of patronage and that the position of the artist was in mortal danger: 'Only the most fanatical and the most immediately popular survive – by no means the best types.' But surely it was not beyond the wit of man to devise an alternative?

> We can do something far better. Also we must realise that in a thousand ways new conditions and vast possibilities are round us and ahead. The circumstances of modern life offer new temptations and new dangers to the artist. Enormous potential art publics grow slowly before our eyes. And both they and the artist are increasingly helpless before the blind amoral profit-hunger of the commercial. We must not be unprepared for the effects these dark multitudes will have on the Arts . . .

Although Brooke would have been astonished at the acidic extent to which commercial values would have eaten into artistic ones by the century's end, he had unerringly put his finger on a trend that was gathering pace even as he spoke and warned. The admass culture of our day was but a gleam in the collective capitalist eye, but Brooke had spotted it. He cautioned against the innate tendency to idolize the past as a golden age – had not the eighteenth century, regarded as the pinnacle of the great age of letters, let Thomas Chatterton starve amidst its very plenty? The truth was, said Brooke, that there had never been a good time to be an artist or writer – they were perennial outsiders, and a danger to the good order of society.

Even patronage, held up as an ideal system that had produced the great works of Renaissance Italy and Elizabethan England had never worked well for long, said Brooke, drawing on his recent reading: 'most of the best writers lost all their shame (which doesn't much matter) and half their vitality (which does) in cadging and touting'. Patronage forced artists to be creeps and toadies, and the constant struggle for sheer economic survival soaked up creative energy: 'It is impossible to know how much more Milton and Marvell would have given us if they had had enough money to live on. If anything at all, the loss is enormous.'

But Brooke was determined to see a silver lining in the clouds – the products of mass education, he pointed out, were a potential reservoir for good; they need not be seen simply as the lowing, vulgar herd: 'The numbers of a potential literary public increase enormously year by year . . . this multitude of opening minds, may bring perplexity and apparent confusion of standards; but also (I say it soberly) the chance of a vast, unimaginable, unceasing addition to the glory of the literature of England.'

It was the duty of him and his audience, Brooke insisted, to pass on their privileges to the many: 'It is the future – their future fineness – we work for. It is only natural that the taste of the lower classes should be at present infinitely worse than ours. The amazing thing is that it is probably rather better.' Mentioning in passing a group of East End writers he had met in London, Brooke added: 'There is more hope in them . . . than in the old-world passion and mellifluous despair of any gentleman's or lady's poetry.' The freshest fruits of art and poetry must be looked for in the living, Brooke claimed, even a modern public abreast with Nietzsche, Van Gogh, Tolstoy and Ibsen were already falling behind the times: 'They are dead, my friends, all dead,' he said, adding ominously: 'Beware of the dead.' No art, however great, is immortal: 'If you write a poem on Tuesday it begins to die on Wednesday. Some take longer dying than others. That is all.'

Brooke went on to outline a positive proposal for a future socialist government that might be in existence, he hazarded, by the year 2050, and suggested that a panel of 30 or so members be set up to endow 30 creative artists with an allowance of £250 a year each. On a lower level: 'If the numerous universities of Great Britain could be given money to endow creative artistic work, it would be excellent.' Or, Brooke suggested, great and rich municipal authorities such as Manchester could endow their local artists and writers and thus be associated with the glory of 'the next great painter or dramatist'.

Brooke's words are an extraordinarily precise prophecy, almost a prescient vision, of what did in fact come about – not in the twenty-first century, but a whole century earlier under a Labour government in which one of the leading figures holding the state's purse-strings as Chancellor would be his friend and fellow-Fabian Hugh Dalton. And the first Chairman of the Arts Council – the body, as he envisaged, set up to endow needy artists and writers – would be none other than Maynard Keynes. Brooke's words to his small audience that cold December night in Cambridge sparked more fires than he could possibly have known. He concluded:

> To give vitality to the Arts it is necessary to direct a large proportion of our interest to contemporary art . . . it is our duty to be interested in contemporary art for the artist's sake, first that he may live, second that he may turn out better stuff. We shall – rather we will – find that the old unchanging ground for the artist stands fast, the emotions of the individual human heart. Imagination will only grow profounder, passions and terrors will come in stranger shapes. Tragedy and Comedy will not leave the world while two things stay in it, the last two that Civilization will cure us of, Death and Fools. In new shapes Hamlet and Othello and Macbeth will move among us, as they do today.

Brooke's address was not only a vision for the future, but a farewell to an important part of his past. He was leaving the Fabians in good shape – under his presidency, as he proudly boasted in a circular to freshmen, the Society had grown from 'a few individuals with a lust for martyrdom' into the university's biggest political association, with 105 full members who had signed the Basis and 142 associates. It now had an office in Trinity Street and a full-time paid librarian. On the other hand the campaign to reform the Poor Law on the lines laid down by the Webbs, to which Brooke had devoted so much time and energy, was clearly running out of steam, and much of the national impetus for social reform was now going into the fight to carry Lloyd George's reform budget through the reluctant Lords. Freed of his formal Fabian responsibilities – although he was never to formally quit the organization, he now lapsed from active membership – Brooke resolved to devote himself for the immediate future to private goals: winning his Fellowship by completing his thesis on Webster; finishing his first collection of poems; and studying German with a view to making an extended trip to the country in the New Year.

The end of the year saw another change in Brooke's domestic circumstances. He had clearly outstayed his welcome at the Orchard, where the Stevensons continued to voice their disapproval of his streams of visitors and his stubborn attachment to his bohemian ways. Fortunately, a new chance arose to move home without leaving his beloved Grantchester, to which he was increasingly devoted: Brooke prevailed on the owners of the Old Vicarage, next door to the Orchard, Mr and Mrs Neeve, to let him take over half the house as a permanent tenant. The Neeves needed the steady income that a tenant would bring to educate their teenage son and supplement their other chief source of cash – selling honeycombs from Mr Neeve's beehives to the Orchard tearoom at sixpence a comb. By Christmas Brooke was installed in his new – and final – home.

Reluctantly, he returned to Rugby to spend the first Christmas without his father in the company of the Ranee. But he soon became embroiled in the general-election battle. For the first time Labour were putting up a candidate in the constituency, and, in keeping with his Fabian principles, Brooke threw himself heart and soul into the fray on behalf of the socialists. He was given the task of organizing transport to the polls in the 90 far-flung villages of the constituency, but found himself facing an uphill battle since the Tories had commandeered all but 12 of the available cars in the area. He let out his frustrations in a letter to Ka Cox:

> Man after man we had to give up. Couldn't get them to the poll . . . the next day came pathetic letters, reproachful. 'We was waiting in the rain for three hours for that motor.' They can't afford railway fares . . . It is not true that anger against injustice and wickedness and tyrannies is a good state of mind, 'noble'. Oh, perhaps it is with some, if they're fine. But I guess with most, as with me, it's a dirty mean choky emotion. I *hate* the upper classes.

The result of the election was a virtual stalemate: the Tories succeeded in chipping away the Liberal majority, so the Asquith government depended on the support of Irish MPs – who exacted the promise of Home Rule as the price of their backing. The country now faced the prospect of more crises brewing.

Brooke, almost unconsciously, had been growing ever more dependent on the emotional support of Ka as his relations with Noel continued to run into brick walls. He had been hoping to persuade Noel to accompany him for a quiet holiday over the Christmas period for an 'H to H', as Ka called the heart-to-heart talks popular in their circle. His hopes were high as the ever-watchful Margery would be holidaying in the Swiss Alps with Daphne, and the distracting Bryn was in distant Jamaica. Noel, he presumed, would be at a loose end. He enlisted the aid of Ka as a prospective chaperone: 'You'll have to arrange about Noel,' he told her, 'unless you think she'd be a nuisance, and the conversation too much above her head. You'd be responsible (to Margery!) that that very delicate young flower keeps her pale innocence, and her simple trust in God unshaken by the world-worn scepticism of Jacques and me. You appear (which is the point) equal to that responsibility.'

At the beginning of December Noel had written expressing her eagerness to come to Lulworth, which Brooke, Jacques and Ka had settled on as their holiday destination, but she was leaving the final decision to her elder sister – 'Margery knows best' – who was acting as Noel's guardian in their parents' absence in Jamaica. Infuriated by Noel's passivity, Brooke replied, attempting to stiffen her resolve against Margery's interference:

I'm trying rather confusedly to urge you to make a protest against idiocy & wickedness. Don't show a Christian spirit. Thunder! Even if you're not used to thundering. You, you, can thunder. Is my advice impudent? No. Nothing's impudent, between us, now. And don't think it's all my hysterical selfishness. I'm right to begin with. Superbly right. And if you don't believe me, – everyone agrees, except cowards. Ka agrees, obviously. And she's fine, and wise. And think of Bryn! She's sensible. Margery *must* be made as sensible. You mustn't humour her. So make a push for it. And let me know what happens. Noel, I must see you. I love you.

In spite of the hysterical, hectoring tone, one can sympathize with Brooke's frustration, and his gathering rage against Margery's irrational attempts to control her youngest sister's life. Ironically, her 'idiocy and wickedness', along with her delusion that most men she met – including Brooke – were in love with her, were the early symptoms of a mental illness that would eventually be diagnosed as dementia praecox and lead to her lifelong confinement in psychiatric hospitals. By an even more bitter irony, it would fall to Noel, by then a qualified doctor, to sign the papers that certified Margery's insanity.

For the time being, Brooke remained fixated on Noel; but her continued elusiveness was starting to play on his own delicate mental balance. Writing from Rugby in mid-December he told her: 'I'm going to stop, and learn my German lesson . . . I seem feverish and horrible. Oh, I'm fretful and grimy and bad. But sometimes, I do assure you, I'm better than that. Though I'm hungering often for you, and though I'm of little faith, and full of jealousies and fears, sometimes I step back a bit and look at the world and me and you; and realise the glory.' Sexual deprivation, and the strain of the election, were playing their part in sapping Brooke's always limited mental and emotional reserves:

> Last week . . . I was working so hard at elections, all day & half the night, without moving, on occasional coffee and bread and butter. But that, or working, or writing, or meeting old friends in the streets, – it's all so vague and dreamy, compared with realities. For you're reality, and there I live – you coming up the Old Vicarage Garden, or in a field, or in camp, and the light on you, and the way you move, your mouth and hair and face and body, and the feel of your hands . . .

Desperately, feeling that Noel was starting to slip imperceptibly from his grasp, and their New Forest engagement was crumbling into dust and ashes, Brooke strove to bind her with the only weapon he had – words:

> It may be that I'm wrong, or hurting, writing so. For you've been mad, and I a fool, since. And what you are now, and are feeling, perhaps I don't know. For I can't see you; and how can I tell, how can I tell? But it won't be. I'll not have it. If we could meet, once, it would all be right . . . Noel, Noel, Noel, I'll not let you go. I'll hold you by the shoulders tight, tight, tight. I can almost feel you. You *shall* not *change*. Except to grow more glorious; for you'll burn more amazingly, and I'll do finer things, the finest in the world, for you. But oh! I must see you! Your lover Rupert.

But it was not to be. Noel replied to this torrent of aching eloquence with a dampener: her father had commanded her to go to Switzerland with her sisters and instead of resisting: 'I, as usual am damnably placid & indifferent, & wanting to do about three incompatible things at the same time.' This disappointment seems to have been a catalyst for Brooke, bringing to a head his simmering exasperation with Noel. She, he thought, had brought playing hard to get to an art form. Her hesitation and damnable placidity could no longer be blamed on her parents or sister – by her own admission they were part and parcel of her own sluggish emotions. Brooke, for his part, could not continue with his own feelings strained as taut as a high wire. He had to subside – or explode. He chose to confide in Ka.

'What hurts,' he told her, 'is thinking her [Noel] wicked. I do, you see.

Not very judicially, but I do. And what's to be done if you think a person you know so well is wicked?' The answer was staring him in the face. He squeezed in a Christmas trip to London and a hurried meeting with Ka. They visited a bookshop together, and when Ka asked him to choose a book as a Christmas gift from her, Brooke, beset with his own troubles, waved his arm irritably at a crowded shelf. Hurt by his indifferent gesture, Ka gently let it be known that if her present was a matter of indifference to him, it was very important to her. Brooke was mortified by guilt at his own insensitivity. The scales fell from his distracted eyes, as slowly it dawned on him that Ka, this quiet, lumpy woman who had already become a peripheral part of his life long ago, might, in fact, be more than 'the cushion' he liked to compare her to.

On his return to Rugby he wrote to try to explain his confused feelings: 'I'm red and sick with anger at myself for my devilry and degradation and stupidity. I hate myself because I wickedly and unnecessarily hurt you several times . . . I hurt you, I hurt you, Ka, for a bit, unforgivably and filthily and infamously; and I can't bear it; I was wild to do anything everything in the world to undo the hurt, or blot it out . . .'

After Christmas four old friends gathered at Cove Cottage and Churchfield House in Lulworth, the familiar one-street hamlet of terraced cottages, nestling between the sea and the whale-backed Purbeck hills of Dorset: Brooke, Jacques Raverat and Justin Brooke, and with them, revelling in the chance to love and mother three very needy males, the comforting, creamy presence of Ka. Caught in that empty, timeless cocoon between Christmas and the New Year, the four passed their time in relaxed fashion: walking the downs and the seashore by day; reading Shelley's *Prometheus Unbound* to one another in the evenings. But between the friends, emotional undercurrents flashed like electrical discharges: Jacques, in the emotionally heightened state that is a feature of the early stages of multiple sclerosis, seemingly forgot his interest in Gwen Darwin and once again asked Ka to marry him. She replied with a metaphoric pat on his head: 'You're too much of a baby.'

Brooke, brooding over Noel and the injustices he had suffered at the collective hands of the Oliviers, went off alone on long, silent walks, and finished a long letter to Bryn that he had begun at Rugby: despite his courtly, almost automatic compliments – 'I always think of you for an hour three times a week' – his bitterness ate through the brittle words; speaking of Noel he asked: 'Don't you think there's a chance of her turning out less pointless than the rest of you?' The letter gives a vivid picture of Brooke's less than festive Christmas at Rugby:

For Christmas Aunt Fanny came and stayed with us. She is a short wicked horrible middle-aged woman who believes in God. To keep her quiet I trooped off to Church on Christmas Day – a queer way of celebrating it. I hadn't been for years. Bryn dear, it was funny. I'd got over the bitter feeling I used to have when I was made to go. So I could enjoy it. All the old Christmas hymns turned up and fairly wrung my stomach with sentimentality. Most of the time, however, I was irresistibly driven to make up parodies on them – of a nature too obscene for me to write even to you, emancipated and unshockable!

He continues with a hint of his changing but still confused sexual interests, and his usual swipe at his old tormentors:

Also there was the lovely psalm about the King's Daughter, who was 'all glorious within; her clothing is of wrought gold' etc. All the bald Rugby schoolmasters around . . . sang it with fervour. I could see them calling up the picture of the King's daughter, very lovely & golden, riding out in the procession, in the sunlight. They all lusted for her – oh! just very slightly. Romance flitted in and out of the holly decorations; & their eyes looked far away. Beside each was his dumpy little middle-aged wife, quite placid; and the children. So it all faded again. Life is very wonderful; and all things are entirely for the best; and if; in twenty years or so, I meet you & find you a little dumpy middle-aged wife, I may kill you, just for sentimentality's sake, rather wonderingly.

As for church, I wasn't really very happy. A chinless man preached the sort of sermon a tapioca pudding might preach. However, there was a girls' school out to the left of me . . . and I stared at them for a long while, and longed for a dozen or so of them; and there was a beautiful choir-boy. Occasionally it seems a little tame. For I'd never bring myself to the point of just dashing into the girls' school and lugging the loveliest away. Yet that's just the only dignified thing to do, I suppose? But I just trotted home in my bowler hat & neat little stiff collar, without so much as winking at anyone on the way out of Church. (Aunt Fanny stayed to eat God.)

The vision of Brooke in bowler hat and neat stiff collar is a little hard to reconcile with the commonly accepted image of him in loose collar, 'poetic' puffed tie and with dishevelled hair – especially considering the mockery he continued to heap on such conventional figures, witness the smart little squib 'Sonnet Reversed' that he composed while still at Lulworth, on New Year's Day 1911:

> Hand trembling towards hand; the amazing lights
> Of heart and eye. They stood on supreme heights.

Ah, the delirious works of honeymoon!
   Soon they returned, and, after strange adventures,
Settled at Balham by the end of June.
   Their money was in Can. Pacs. B. Debentures,
And in Antofagastas. Still he went
   Cityward daily; still she did abide
At home. And both were really quite content
   With work and social pleasures. Then they died.
They left three children (besides George, who drank):
   The eldest Jane, who married Mr Bell,
William, the head-clerk in the County Bank,
   And Henry, a stock-broker, doing well.

The poem, successful in its cynical way, is really 'Menelaus and Helen' in a modern suburban setting. It demonstrates anew Brooke's disgust with the humdrum banality of modern life; and his execration of the capitalist, *rentier* class that he saw in full cry around him. And once again there is that lurking dread of marriage, children and responsibilities that he equates with ageing and death. And was there a personal touch in the final line? The poem was composed in the presence of Ka, whose own father, named Henry, was a stockbroker who had done very well indeed – enough to buy his daughter a substantial Surrey mansion and a lifestyle of horses, nursing her friends' emotional wounds, and indulging her Fabian ideals.

As the Lulworth break drew to a close, Brooke's thoughts turned to his imminent departure to Germany. He told Bryn: 'I go to Germany in a week. La! la! I hope to do infinite work there. I shall never return, and never see you again, – unless your ship touches at Munich. But perhaps Munich isn't on the sea. Send me, once, a card to say when you return, and on what day, with blanket + gun, we meet among the brigands in Spain . . . I will write to you from Munich . . . it will be all about Wagner, no doubt.'

As the prospect of a lengthy separation from Bryn, Noel and the rest of his friends sunk in, Brooke's mood waxed melancholy and philosophical:

I am overcome by the way things slip along and away, and the extraordinary chance that blew dust together & made me & the people I know & threw us together, and how little we know each other, and the queer way we smile at each other (or frown) and talk and fumble along, risking all sorts of dangers. I am impressed by it. I sit and gloom at people, with round eyes; and think how silly it is to be angry or to worry or to misunderstand, when we're all stumbling and groping in the dark. Also I think how silly it is to let things slide on and not to snatch at opportunities. One will be so sick one didn't. And only a fear of what a few people'ld say, or of telling the not-highly-thought-of Truth, stops one. I agree that these are sentimental truisms. But if they affect one's conduct, as some of them do & some may, I suppose they're important, in a way . . . I am as flat as the Fens, and as wearying to you as *Paradise Regained*. Farewell. You are splendid. Do not decay. I cast passionate hands towards you. Rupert.

Brooke returned to London with his friends. They were met by Ka's rival, Gwen, who accompanied Jacques and Brooke to Ka's Westminster flat. In an unpublished autobiographical novel, Gwen sketched the scene:

> They sat like mummies on the sofa while [Ka] lit the fire. [Jacques] thought there was something terribly feminine about her heavy form, as she squatted on the hearth, puffing with round cheeks; something eternally servile and domestic, utilitarian . . . 'She's a good woman,' said [Jacques] to [Brooke].'A good squaw,' said [Brooke]. These were almost the only words that were said . . . The fire and the tea melted them a little, but they would not talk; and directly afterwards [Brooke] said: 'Come on [Jacques]' and with a couple of gloomy goodbyes they left. In the street [Brooke's] arm came through [Jacques']. 'I like men,' [Brooke] said.

If this scene is a faithful account of what passed between the friends it indicates the growing emotional tension between Ka and Brooke, and the fading tension between Ka and Jacques. Brooke was coming to value Ka's sheer availability, as a creature comforter and helpmate, in contrast to Noel's maddening elusive evasions. Brooke could never do anything without complications, and as he reluctantly recognized the beginning of his great love for Ka – which, ironically, would only burst into full and frenzied life a year later, and again at Lulworth, under the spur of jealousy – his mixed-up feelings caused him to reach, as of old, for what he supposed to be the straightforward simplicities of male bonding.

In the meantime he sought a showdown with Noel before leaving for Germany. Perhaps hoping to jog her slumbering emotions into life, he travelled down to Limpsfield Chart and made a sort of confession of his growing attachment to Ka. Whatever his motives in making a clean breast – and he told himself that he only wanted to keep his relations with his beloved open and above-board – they must have served only to make Noel even more mistrustful of his mercurial emotions. He met up with her in London just before leaving for Munich, but, significantly, also saw Ka again, having supper with her just before he boarded the boat-train at Victoria.

It was to Ka, too, that his first letter was dispatched after his arrival at the Pension Bellevieu in Munich's Meresienstrasse. Typically, he was already regretting his weakness in leaning so heavily on his 'cushion': their supper, he said, was 'a mistake': 'I don't mind giving way to emotion if there's nothing else to do . . . But I'd made myself rather hysterical.' He half-apologized for walking away from her too abruptly before being overcome by tears. For Brooke, the bewildering cocktail of emotions he was experiencing was all too much. He was not exactly in love with Ka, he told himself – but if not, what was he? For the time being he shrugged his shoulders and gave way to the novel experience of enjoying himself in a foreign city.

Brooke had arrived in the Bavarian capital with a letter of introduction to a Professor Schick, an English specialist who would give him German lessons. Schick introduced him to a student, Ludwig Dellefant, who was eager to improve his English in return for coaching Brooke in German. Together the two young men wandered around the city's cafés and beer halls, and Dellefant introduced Brooke to the *Bursenschaften*, traditional students' associations where the Cambridge Apostles' evenings of high-minded talk over sardines and tea were replaced by the quaffing of vast quantities of foaming beer from stone mugs and the communal singing of raucous *Saufer-lieder* – drinking songs. Brooke was condescending about the company: 'The Germans consume an enormous amount of beer, but they don't get drunk in the same way that English undergraduates do,' he told his mother. '[They] are extremely simple compared with English undergraduates. They are more like very simple, fat, and hearty public-school boys; docile and sentimental.'

Behind the Ranee's back, his secret feelings about her were expressed in an aside to Jacques Raverat. Writing of a performance of Ibsen's *John Gabriel Borkman* that had much impressed him, he commented: 'Therein is a youth who will fly from his mother in order to *live* (it happens in Norway also).'

He was soon feeling homesick, an emotion reinforced by solitary trips to the Café Bauer, where he would read a day-old copy of *The Times* over an abstemious hot milk. His friends received long bulletins about his doings. Noel – like Ka – was informed that their last supper together in London had been 'a mistake'. But he made the best of their separation, he said, and maintained a stoutly stiff upper lip: 'I can take the wider view, and see all the splendour of you, and the blinding wonder that you love me, – that we love each other.' In a rare moment of perception he added: 'You must, after these months, be getting sick of my whinings. Ignore them!'

Turning from contemplating his navel, Brooke gave Noel a picture of his fellow-guests at the Pension Bellevieu that recalls the opening of his friend E. M. Forster's *Room with a View*: 'Two English ladies, a Romanian economist, his brother, professor of Physics in Bucharest, an Italian Count who is a cavalry-colonel, an Australian sheep-farmer . . . a Franco-German dancing master, and about eight Germans, male & female. One of the last is a dowager of sixty-five with white hair & a bright yellow face, that reeks of sin. She is the most hideous thing in the world; & fascinates me.'

He repeated what became a plangently enduring theme about his German hosts: 'They're Soft. That is all. Very nice, but . . . Soft. It comes out in their books, and everywhere. Their grasp is of a fat hand. Pictures, books, ideas, faces − it is all the same.' Damningly, he withered the *Wandervögel* worship of nature that was and is a truism of the German character: 'You hear and see a so fat, so greasy, so complacent and civilized German roll up his eyes and wheeze 'Ich habe gern die Natur' ['I love Nature'] − and the whole thing flies to pieces before you. You have a picture of that coated belly in the woodlands, waddling helter skelter from Pan, or Diana's hounds . . .'

Noel responded thoughtfully with a touchingly honest letter making it clear that despite all his theatrical protestations and scenes she loved him. Yet, cautiously, she was very conscious that she could not come up to his exaggerated estimations:

> Rupert, when he bowed his head & said the truth about what he felt; I understood & was sorry & I loved his head so I kissed it & then he & history made me believe that I was a lover as well as he. I'm not, Rupert. I'm affectionate, reverent, anything you like but not that. And so I get worried & sorry when you look devoted & I dont mind about Ka or German Duchesses at all, & I never feel jealous; only afraid of your loving me too much . . . I shall always love you. Noel.

Brooke's still-shaky command of German led to one comic misunderstanding with a fellow Pension guest who had allowed himself to fall in lust with Brooke. This man, the Romanian professor of physics, described to Noel as 'a nice little dark strange Slavonic creature', had invited Brooke to come and stay with him in the Balkans. But this half-serious plan was aborted when the professor came to Brooke's room to make his farewells before returning to Romania. Bidding goodbye, Brooke inadvertently called him '*Du*', in German the intimate form of 'you', and strictly reserved for close family, other intimates or lovers. The result was predictable, as Brooke related to James Strachey:

> There was, just for a fraction of a second, a dead pause . . . then I was confusedly conscious of a wrinkled dark nose – down there – a round Slavonic mouth; and an on-the-point-of-grabbing-left-hand and, concurrently, of myself, hat-on-head, half-way-through the door, screaming 'Leben Sie wohl, Herr Professor! . . .' & leaping downstairs, into the street . . . The Professor was left alone with the Stove. But whether he raped that, or merely abused himself in my bed, I don't know.

Beneath the hilarity, Brooke was unsure of his true purpose in Germany. His stay was supposed to turn him into a fluent German linguist and expert philologist; but he found it hard to concentrate on this – there were the distractions of the city: he supped enthusiastically of Munich's cultural feast, enjoying the première of Richard Strauss's *Der Rosenkavalier*, and dutifully watching Wagner's *Ring* cycle, although, as he told Noel: 'I shall never be *musikalisch*.' Ibsen was more to his taste. But, all told, it was far from the ideal study-trip or the rest-cure he had told Ka he was seeking: 'Rest means being where no-one knows you.' However, in the cosmopolitan society of pre-1914 Europe, disappearing was not so easy – Brooke even bumped into a Rugby contemporary in Munich – and his personality was so vivid that he made friends wherever he went.

Before leaving England, Brooke had deposited a putative collection of verse with E. J. Dent, a Cambridge don who had set up his own publishing company. In return Dent had provided him with a letter of introduction to Frau Doktor Clara Ewald, an artist who kept a Munich *pension*, and her student son Paul, who had spent a year in Cambridge. The Ewalds lived in Schwabing, the leafy suburb that was Munich's artistic quarter. Brooke got on so well with the Ewalds that he changed his lodgings early in February in order to be close to their home. Though he slept in the Ohmstrasse, he took most of his meals with the Ewalds in Friedrichstrasse, and exerted his matchless boyish charm over Frau Ewald to notable effect. She began an oil painting of him in a wide-brimmed hat that now hangs in London's National Portrait Gallery, and was sometimes constrained to command him to keep his unruly locks out of the jam pot.

Paul Ewald was useful in taking Brooke out of his introspective self and introducing him to some of Schwabing's more colourful artistic characters.

Pre-eminent among these was one Karl Wolfskehl, a sort of German Lytton Strachey, complete with long beard and pince-nez. Wolfskehl was a disciple of Germany's illustrious poet the legendary and reclusive Stefan George, whose circle, inevitably of handsome young men, regarded their master as a guru of mystic wisdom. Wolfskehl would intone George's gnomic verse in hushed salons at his home. He and Brooke shared an enthusiasm for Swinburne, who, Brooke alleged, he would recite 'in a vile German accent'.

February was the month of Fasching, the uproarious German carnival, which in Munich took the form of the Bacchus-Fest, when even staid citizens would unbutton their lederhosen and generally let their cropped hair down. In a final effort to propel Brooke into a more active role in the city's scene, Paul took his friend along. It was high time: when he wasn't attending high-minded evenings at the theatre or opera, Brooke generally kept to his room, reading. And he was distinctly underwhelmed by the current artistic explosion in the city, where the painters of the Blaue Reiter group – Kandinsky, Marc, Macke, Arp and Klee – were setting new limits for the avant-garde to follow. 'I move among the München P[ost] I[mpressionist]s,' he told Jacques.

> They got up an exhibition of their French masters here last year; and go on pilgrimages to all the places where Van Gogh went dotty or cut his ears off or did any of the other climactic actions of his life . . . They are young and beetle-browed and serious. Every now and then they paint something – often a house, a simple square bordered by four very thick black lines. The square is then coloured blue or green. That is all. Then they go on talking . . . it is all very queer and important.

In mocking modern art – belying his fine words to the Fabians about the 'duty' of backing contemporary art – Brooke was exposing his cultural conservatism – and the insularity that the Ewalds complained of in their English friend. In addressing his remarks to Jacques, he had chosen his confidant well: Jacques made something of a career of running down modernism in the arts and was a fervent Germanophobe into the bargain. Brooke received similar reassurance from Frances Cornford:

> It made me shake with joy to know that Cambridge and England . . . was all as fine as ever. That Jacques and Ka should be sitting in a café looking just like themselves . . . I fairly howled my triumph down the ways of this splendid city. 'Oh you fat muddy-faced grey jolly Germans who despise me because I don't

know your rotten language. Oh! – the people I know – and you don't. Oh! You poor things.' And they all growl at me because they don't know why I glory over them.

Thus armoured in his prejudices, Brooke ventured out into the teeming streets of the Bacchus-Fest. The idea was that every man should find his Bacchus-bride for the night, and sure enough, Brooke found his.

12

Elisabeth

True to his habitual form, Brooke was evasive to the point of duplicity in revealing anything about the young woman with whom he now had his first heterosexual love affair. The smokescreens he threw up to conceal the relationship succeeded in blinding and baffling his biographers over the decades, and it is only in recent years – in fact since the woman's death, aged 90, in 1980 – that the remarkable story of their liaison has gradually emerged from the shadows he cast over it.

According to Brooke's only extant account of their meeting – in a lengthy letter to Jacques Raverat – the pair bumped into each other by chance in the street during the Bacchus-Fest:

> Then there's me and the sculptress. I don't know what to make of that quite. To begin with you must know that we have carnival here in February. Joy. Youth. Flowers . . . The young lay round in couples, huggin' and kissin'. I roamed around, wondering if I couldn't, once, be even as they are, as the animals. I found a round, damp young sculptress, a little like Lord Rosebery to look on. We curled passionate limbs round each other in a perfunctory manner and lay in a corner, sipping each other and beer in polite alternation . . . We roamed and sat and even danced and lay and talked, and the night wore on. We became more devoted. My head was in her lap, she was munching my fingers, when suddenly I became quite coldly aware of my position in the Universe . . .

This account of a casual street pick-up is disingenuous at the very least. In fact the sculptress – whom Brooke calls 'Dutch' – was a Flemish Belgian named Elisabeth van Rysselberghe, two or three years his junior, who, like him, was in Munich to improve her German and partake of the city's lively artistic scene. She had been adopted by the Ewalds, who had introduced

her to Brooke as a suitable *Faschingsbraut* or 'carnival bride'. Her father was
a prominent neo-Impressionist painter, Theo van Rysselberghe, and her
mother, Maria, a writer, was a member of André Gide's circle.

Brooke's partly fabricated account of their carnival night continued:

> But then we put hands on each other's necks and shoulders for the millionth
> time and found them quite cool, and she raised her watery protruding eyes to
> mine, and I suddenly realized of her – and she of me – that she was in exactly
> the same state . . . was quite a conscious, sensible intellectual, real, modern
> person – might, in fact, in other circumstances, have been almost, not quite, one
> of Us – we found, in short – to quote one quite admirable sonnet I wrote on
> the whole thing next afternoon – 'that we, Were you (whoever you may be!)
> and I!' And as one can't very well begin a new game at five in the morning, we
> very solemnly and pathetically kissed each other on our quiet intellectual lips
> and so parted . . .

If we cut through the thickets of Brooke's ridiculously laboured prose,
what seems to have happened is this: the young couple ventured into the
swarming streets – possibly chaperoned by Elisabeth's mother Maria,
who was in Munich at this point – got excited by alcohol and the
anarchic party atmosphere, indulged in some mild petting, got more
excited, but chickened out of consummating their new-found
relationship and found their way to their respective homes in the cold
light of dawn.

But that was not the end of the affair by any means. We can piece
together what happened next through brief mentions in Brooke's letters
home from Munich. He tells Geoffrey Keynes: 'My life in München isn't
wildly thrilling. I don't emulate Dudley with women. I sit alone in a cafe
or my room and read or write . . . Of course there's Elizabeth [sic] . . . But
then there's always somebody . . . But there's never anybody quite like
Elizabeth . . . Oh! Oh! But as she's spoilt my life, and given me a devilish
cold in the head . . . let's pass to pleasanter topics . . .'

In mid-March James Strachey was told: 'I very nearly came to England
ten days ago. But I shan't now, of course. Mlle. van Rysselberghe has
appeared since then.' By now Elisabeth was alone in Munich, her mother
having departed. Brooke determined to screw his courage to the sticking
place and have full sexual relations with her. Elisabeth was an ardent and
romantic spirit, with a weakness for weaker men than her. She was strong-
minded, clearly falling in love with him, and obviously ready to 'do the
deed'.

By mid-April, Brooke was anxiously quizzing the worldly James about the availability and efficacy of contraceptive devices:

> James dear, The world moved very rapidly and I'd like to prosecute my academic enquiries. It's so difficult, here. You tell me the syringe (siringe?) is best. What I want to know is the exact name of the stuff. One's at such a disadvantage in dealing with a foreign chemist. And I don't want to poison anybody; least of all myself. In fact I want further information than one can get even from German textbooks – when one doesn't know the language . . . in fact if you could just forward any information you can heap together, – or even a neat little package . . . – might save a ball or two for the nation, at the risk of preventing a future Brother . . .

James dutifully responded to his friend's plea and made the necessary enquiries: 'I now know every detail of the whole sordid business.' With evident distaste for the messy goings-on of heterosexual intercourse, James proceeded to list details of the condoms, pessaries and syringes available to the wealthy and discerning ladies and gentlemen of the era. He advised against condoms: 'You get hardly any pleasure out of them and they are most likely to get torn in the excitement of the moment.' Pessaries were damned as 'unpleasant things . . . made of quinine and oil – and you shove it up the lady's cunt before you start . . . it makes a filthy soapy mess that comes out over everything'. James obligingly enclosed his own drawing of various syringes. His letter concluded with a self-parody: '"My dear boy", he wound up, "I recommend you to content yourself, if you're dealing with a girl, with 'playing about' with her – you can get plenty of pleasure that way. But if you must block someone, my final advice to you is – let it be a married woman."' Brooke must have known what would follow these headmasterly words of warning on the letter's final page: 'Oh, but isn't it all too incredibly filthy? Won't it perhaps make you sick of it? – Come quietly to bed with me instead . . .'

James's postscript was eerily prophetic, considering Brooke's future paranoid fears of his rival for Ka's love, Henry Lamb, who already had a formidable reputation as a fearless ladies' man and sexual athlete: 'I forgot to remind you of Henry's method – withdrawal before emission. But that requires an iron nerve – and if it fails . . .' Brooke's reply was brief and clipped: 'Many thanks. I don't admire your attitude. Cheer up, though: Elizabeth rather agreed with you & has funked it. (She's sorry now) . . .'

If Elisabeth did 'funk' it at this particular point, she was not alone in having cold feet. Brooke was already making her his unwilling partner in a push-pull game of love that was to become the characteristic hallmark of his future affairs. First of all he was the ardent pursuer: badgering Elisabeth to spend a romantic few days with him in Venice at the end of April. When she agreed, it was his turn to funk: he replied ostensibly full of desire, but the bulk of the letter was taken up with a sermon against the danger of pregnancy. Put off, Elisabeth withdrew her offer to 'give herself' to him. Reproachfully, Brooke chided her with her lack of courage: 'I can't help believing (am I right?) that if we'd met in Venice, that there, touching your hands, looking into your eyes, I could have made you understand, and agree. But I preferred to be honest. And so perhaps one of the best things in my life, or yours, is lost – for a time – through a desire for honesty.'

A novice in the lists of heterosexual love, Brooke had still to learn that honesty was not the best weapon in the seducer's armoury: he had told Elisabeth that their sexual encounter would be on a strictly no-strings basis, and a more experienced lover would hardly have been surprised at her reluctance to be used as a vehicle for Brooke to escape his burdensome virginity. As usual, Brooke had talked and walked himself into an unholy emotional mess.

When he came to take leave of Elisabeth before leaving Munich in late April, he told James:

> The parting with Elizabeth [sic] was most painful. I felt an awful snake. Especially when she said she would kill herself, and I felt frightened of the police . . . I am very bitter with myself and frightened of England. Of the scene when the maidservant suddenly brought two students to see the room, and found her with her hair down, weeping, at full length, on that plateau of a sofa, and me in great pain on one leg in the middle of the room, saying 'Yes . . . yes . . . yes', very wildly . . . of that I will tell you later. But, anyhow, do assure me that one ought to tell the truth: and that it's not honest to want to be raped.

Brooke's sexual inexperience had blown up in his face, leaving debris far messier than the soapiest pessary. Coldly and clumsily he had played Don Juan – and flopped miserably. His maladroitness may have stemmed from a secret fear of sexual failure with a woman. His sonnet 'Lust', which he claimed was inspired by Elisabeth, and which was to cause him much trouble with censorious publishers, hints at just such a problem.

> How should I know? The enormous wheels of will
>   Drove me cold-eyed on tired and sleepless feet.
> Night was void arms and you a phantom still,
>   And day your far light swaying down the street.

As never fool for love, I starved for you;
  My throat was dry and my eyes hot to see.
Your mouth so lying was most heaven in view,
  And your remembered smell most agony.

Love wakens love! I felt your hot wrist shiver,
  And suddenly the mad victory I planned
    Flashed real, in your burning bending head . . .
My conqueror's blood was cool as a deep river
  In shadow; and my heart beneath your hand
    Quieter than a dead man on a bed.

If Elisabeth had been left high and dry by Brooke's behaviour, she does not appear to have held it against him. She resolved to make another attempt to heat his 'conqueror's blood'.

13

Virginia and the Old Vicarage

Brooke's as yet abortive affair with Elisabeth was played out against the background of a cultural life in Munich that continued to be busy, as James Strachey heard from him: 'Fifth Symphony tonight. Tomorrow (Wagner's) *Lohengrin*. Friday Debussy. Saturday Schnitzler. Sunday *Valkyries*. Yesterday *The Wild Duck*. On Sunday I saw *Ghosts* for 6d: played as a farce. Mr Wedekind turns out to be a music hall singer: & has coffee at the next table after lunch. No other news. Rupert.'

This crowded cultural calendar shows Brooke supping both classic and modern fare – Frank Wedekind was the contemporary *enfant terrible* of German theatre, whose now-classic *Spring's Awakening* was an anarchic call to the young to rise and break the stultified grip of the older generation. Naturally its praise of parricide awakened a strong response in Brooke, who saw the play almost as often as he had seen *Peter Pan*.

Behind Brooke's back, as he grimly suspected, events and emotions in England were unravelling beyond his control. Another pair of his friends were about to break the unspoken rules of youth and seal the marriage knot. Ka's final rejection of his marriage proposal at Lulworth had propelled Jacques Raverat decisively back in Gwen Darwin's direction. The two shared an interest and ability in art, and, if not in love with each other, at least knew that they could live together in reasonable compatibility and contentment. Jacques apparently told Ka of his decision without emotion or rancour – merely remarking that he liked Gwen because she had 'bones in her mind'.

By the end of February their engagement was formally announced. The poisonously gossipy Virginia Stephen, a frustrated virgin if ever there was one, regaled her sister Vanessa with the complications of the *ménage à trois*: '[Jacques] says that now he is in love with them both, and asks Ka to be his mistress, and Gwen to satisfy his mind. Gwen is made very jealous; Ka evidently cares a good deal for Jacques . . . in my view J. is very much in love with K: and not much, if at all, with Gwen. Ought they to break off the engagement?' They did not, but married in June, enjoying afterwards a month-long painting honeymoon in Lulworth, of all places.

Brooke, learning in Munich of the betrothal, affected to be delighted at the union between two of his closest friends. 'It fills me with joy,' he wrote to Bryn in early March, while Noel was told: 'I'm going to write to Jacques and Gwen and tell them how great they are. I'm glad they're in love, and going to be married soon. You've heard? Quite sudden. And they're very radiant. And Ka's a little sad, but glad and very fine. And I wrote putting them all right . . . They and Ka worked everything out greatly. Be proud.' Brooke's self-assumed role as the ringmaster of his friends' complex emotional manoeuvres is remarkable in its arrogant – and naive – assumptions. If he was disappointed that Jacques and Gwen had defected to the married enemy, he hid it well – although he privately sarcastically referred to the match as the 'Moment of Transfiguration'. Most likely he was secretly envious of their evident happiness – and pleased that Ka would presumably now be more available for him to turn to and lean on.

He offered his services as an unbidden counsellor to the lovelorn trio. Gwen was told: 'You said you'd all three felt that week, as if you were in the hands of some external power, rushing you on . . . What? God? The Life-Force? Oh, my Gwen, be clean, be clean! It is a monstrosity. There is no power. Things happen: and we pick our way among them.' This otherwise sensible piece of advice is disfigured by Brooke's summons to cleanliness – a motif that was to become ever more obsessive in his life and letters. The evil demons of his lurking puritanism were beginning to awaken.

His advice to Ka, the most vulnerable member of the trio, and the one who had most clearly lost the game, was less clearly disinterested: 'Why are you sad? – Lust. But that's absurd. You'd never have gratified that anyway . . . even if, as I'll grant, a sort of lust-jealousy may plague you (an infinitely pale reflection of part of that plagues me every time I hear of anyone getting married!), that doesn't come to much.'

The miserable Ka was encouraged to buck her ideas up by the instant expert in married love. This was Brooke in his most insufferable Agony Aunt mode: 'Jacques and Gwen are in love and are going to marry. That is very fine . . . It is a risky business, as they're both so dotty. I hope Gwen won't hurt her wood-cuts with babies, or Jacques get domesticated. It's very splendid. They'll be in love for a couple of years. I hope they do it more gracefully than most.'

His vanity was further reinforced by news from James that he was the subject of hot gossip at home. James had bumped into their old school friend from Hillbrow, Owen O'Malley, who still seemed to be obsessed by Brooke – to the extent of accosting a girl at a ball who bore a vague resemblance to Brooke, with the line: 'Miss Brooke, I believe?' Interestingly, O'Malley also passed the rumour on to James that Brooke was in love with Bryn. At the same dance – a benefit for the Suffragettes – James overheard some guests discussing Brooke's love life. Outrageously eavesdropping, James heard someone say they were not surprised that people didn't fall in love with Brooke: 'He's so beautiful he's scarcely human.'

Brooke was in truth up to his old tricks of writing simultaneously to both Bryn – flirtatiously – and to Noel – more passionately than ever. Even when archly wooing the unintellectual Bryn, he could rarely resist a little sneer:

Life is very noble, in spite of the way one treats it. And even here there's the sun and a very beautiful city and lovely mysterious people in the darkness. Mostly I read the good John Keats. And once a week I sit in a corner of a café and brood over my sins and finally write a little poem. The little poems are not very good, nowadays. The elder ones are still with a publisher . . . the publisher thinks some of the poems too indelicate. Like you, he doesn't think it quite nice to talk about love & sea-sickness like that [a reference to 'A Channel Passage']. Oh, you healthy people! You may have a specious air of intelligence, Bryn, but never forget that you have really the soul of an old sheep . . .

But Brooke, too, had his philistine streak. After detailing his assiduous attendance at Munich's concert halls, he added:

But as I don't care for music, it none of it makes any difference. So I sit in a patient way while they perform *The Ring*, and know all the time I had better be reading *Endymion*, or watching people's faces. It's that – watching faces – that's really the chief thing in life, you know . . . Ho! I *do* like to see people who fairly burn with vitality . . . There are about 45 people in the world who are alive and the rest are mildewed corpses. But some of the corpses are better than the rest in that they can recognize the living. Such a corpse am I. One of the better ones. Lady, I take your congratulations with a little bow.

Naturally, none of Brooke's female correspondents – neither Bryn, Noel, nor Ka – was told of Elisabeth. His boasting of his amorous successes was confined to James, Jacques and Geoffrey Keynes. But his involvement with the Flemish temptress caused a hiatus in his stream of letters to Noel. Guilt-stricken, he wrote in mid-March: 'Noel, whom I love! I am a worm, a crawling thing "Buried and bricked in a forgotten Hell", because I have not written to you for months . . .' Having got his excuses out of the way, Brooke was soon back to ludicrous, self-parodying preening: 'I write damn good letters. I am a most clever creature, and can sometimes, write better than almost anybody in England. My God, I write well! And some of the letters I write to you – hoo, superb!' But all this was by way of praising Noel's own schoolgirl epistolary style: 'If I . . . could write you down one tenth as well as you . . . write yourself down – I'd be the greatest poet England ever produced.'

After burbling happily on in this vein for several pages, Brooke returns to his unvarying message: he is as ferociously 'in love and lust' with Noel as ever:

> I've such a passion to see you again, and talk, having kissed you. We've denied ourselves so much, there was Prunoy, and now Munich! We deserve something. And these hurried snatches at bliss – they don't admit of certain calmer longer glories. I must see you some time for a long while, day after day. Oh, Noel remember Grantchester! I want to sit and talk and talk and talk, and see you, in every light and mood and position . . . my dearest dearest – I love you. Rupert.

On 8 April Brooke temporarily left Munich and his tribulations with Elisabeth. His destination was the Austrian Imperial capital, Vienna, and his host was Ernst Goldschmidt, a fellow-Fabian and Trinity man, and a native-born Viennese described by Brooke to the Ranee as 'a very rich and clever Jew'. It is worth noting that it is about this time that occasional but persistent disparaging asides about Jews begin to creep into Brooke's letters. (He described one of his Vienna haunts to James as a 'Jews' café'.) James, ironically for a man who would one day become one of Freud's most devoted disciples, was at this time quite casually anti-Semitic in his comments. Such attitudes were the norm rather than the exception among the English upper and middle classes in the first half of the twentieth century. In continental Europe, particularly in Vienna, where a ragged tramp named Adolf Hitler was absorbing them at the time of Brooke's visit, such prejudice was even more vicious and virulent. In Vienna Brooke saw more theatre, including Arthur Schnitzler's *Die junge Medardus*, an epic which he described to Eddie Marsh as 'a Hebrew journalist's version of [Hardy's] *The Dynasts*; but rather good'.

After a week Brooke's visit was curtailed by the news that he was wanted on a mercy mission: his former Rugby form master and godfather, Robert Whitelaw, recently widowed, had been escorted by Alfred Brooke for a recuperative holiday in Florence. Alfred left him there, but the old man promptly suffered a collapse in health and Rupert was called upon to help him home. He spent a few days dutifully revisiting the Florentine galleries he had first seen as an eager youth. Again, the *pensione* where they were staying was irresistibly Forsteresque, as he told Marsh: 'Here I live in a pension surrounded by English clergymen and ladies . . . They are all Forster characters. Perhaps it is his *pension*. But to live among Forster characters is too bewildering. The "quaint" remarks fall all around one at meal-times, with little soft plups like pats of butter . . . So I am seeing life. But I am thirsting for Grantchester.'

Brooke's *Heimweh* was soon to be requited. He was on his way home. And was glad to be shaking Teutonic dust from his feet. He repeated to Eddie the same message he had already given Bryn and Noel: 'I have sampled and sought out German culture. It has changed all my political views. I am wildly in favour of nineteen new Dreadnoughts. German culture must never, never, prevail. The Germans are nice, and well-meaning, and they try; but they are *soft*. Oh! They *are* soft. The only good things (outside music perhaps) are the writings of Jews who live in Vienna.'

It is no accident that Marsh was the recipient of this nationalistic diatribe – his political boss, Winston Churchill, was about to take over as First Lord of the Admiralty, overlord of the largest navy in the world, and the ultimate arbiter of Brooke's own life and death when war with Germany arrived four years later. The political climate in which Brooke visited Germany was one of escalating tension. The country was not only a centre of the artistic and literary avant-garde; its politics were dominated by rising nationalism and a naval race with Britain – hence Brooke's reference to Dreadnoughts. Not the least important factor in the shift in his politics was his encounter with the reality of German power and vigour. His recoil from Germany and the Germans, despite, or because of, his frequent visits to the country, marked a decisive stage in his move away from Fabian socialism towards patriotic nationalism.

Yet there were limits to Brooke's metamorphosis from radical youth to conservative conformist: he was and remained a fierce, even a fanatical, atheist. As such he issued a stern rebuke to Gwen Darwin, who had written to him suggesting that the working out of the eternal triangle between herself, Ka and Jacques was akin to a ballet in which they all danced the steps allotted to them by some controlling force. To Brooke, a believer in the random workings of chance, this was all arrant nonsense, and he told Gwen so: 'Oh! Oh! I implore you to extend the flickering fingers of derision at the sky.' Inspired by his sojourn in Florence he continued:

> Did that vapid blue concavity make Brunelleschi build the Pazzi chapel? No! no! Derision's for God. But if it's really that madder horror, the Life-Force, that you're so anthropomorphically female to, even derision won't do. Laws do not wince. When you jeer, they wear the set, tired smile of a man who politely listens without hearing what you say . . . But there aren't laws. There aren't. Take my word for it. I saw – I lifted up the plush curtain and looked behind – nobody, only dust and a slight draught from the left . . . There are no laws; only heaps of happenings, and on each heap stands one of us and crows – a cock on a dung-heap or a beacon on a hill (in Lord Macaulay's poem) according to taste.

As the Florentine sky darkened, Brooke strove to sum up what he saw as the Neo-Pagan philosophy:

> The Puritans dimly try to build up the background: the hedonist flaps inconsistently for the thing. We go for both; we join up Puritan and Hedonist: we have (once more) only connected . . . The great thing about Life is to realize three qualities in things (1) this controllability I've mentioned; (2) Uniqueness; (3) Transience. All things are so; pins, moments, paramours, letters, intimacies, lamps, spinach. I saw Giotto's tower with the sun on it this afternoon. I saw Giotto's tower on April 28, 1911, with 6.0. p.m. sunlight on it. I needn't have done it. I splendidly came out of all the ages. I hurtled out of the darkness to do it. It was half a second – it changed as I looked; and so did I. It and I and the light won't be quite the same again. If you let the principles fairly sink in, and begin to realize Life, it leads to fainting in restaurants, screaming before a wallpaper pattern and madness in the end . . . You have no conception of the depths of horror of the mean and egoistic human heart.

Brooke drew his melancholy meditation on transience and time to an existential end:

> But perhaps you've already discovered the Great Secret – the Horror – that joy's as incommunicable as sorrow. Loneliness. Crying alone is bad enough: but that's an old story. It's when one discovers that one must always and for ever laugh alone . . . That's one of the things that, two by two, people sooner or later learn, and never tell for the sake of the young . . . It's so late: the stars over

Fiesole are wonderful: and there are quiet cypresses and a straight white wall opposite. I renounce England; though at present, I've the senile affection of a godfather for it. I think of it, over there (beyond Fiesole) Gwen and Jacques and Ka and Frances, and Justin and Dudley . . . good night, children. Rupert.

So the poet of England, sitting in a foreign field, against an appropriate background, struck another pose. For Brooke, England would be his friends, and the portable memories he had of them. A couple of days afterwards, Brooke steered his doddery godfather back to Rugby. It was the merry month of May and a final Neo-Pagan summer beckoned. He left for the Old Vicarage, Grantchester.

Brooke's new home was a rambling Restoration building, with three storeys made of red brick, complete with attics and dormer windows. A veranda covered with Virginia creeper gave on to the wild rear garden, with chestnut and box trees and various nineteenth-century features made of cement − a sundial, a disused fountain and a strange mock-Gothic folly. The long lawns running down to the river were pervaded by a rank smell of weed and wild mint. The vicarage had last been used as a clerical residence in the 1820s, since when it had been lived in as a private family residence, but was now in the hands of tenants, Henry and Florence Neeve.

For a rent of 30 shillings a week, Brooke was assigned three rooms − in the spring and summer he spent most of his time in the garden, writing or reading, with frequent trips to the river pools to bathe. In his early days there, his alfresco expeditions were encouraged by the presence of fleas and woodlice in his rooms − which Mrs Neeve attempted to keep down with insect powder. He would sleep on the lawn, waking to birdsong in the small hours with dew in his hair, before hurrying off to take an early-morning plunge. Jacques witnessed Brooke's war against the Old Vicarage's unwelcome wildlife: he caught him on all fours, stark naked, searching for fleas between the floorboards with a lighted candle. Jacques sensibly suggested applying more flea powder, but Brooke gloomily shook his head: 'It's no good,' he said. 'They rather like it. It just excites their appetite.'

The Neeves were more tolerant of their sub-tenant than the Stevensons had been, allowing him the privacy to come and go and entertain his many visitors as he pleased. Returning late at night from Cambridge by foot or boat, he would raid the pantry to carry off a slice of Mrs Neeve's prized home-made fruit pie, and for breakfast there would be lashings of honey from the hives Mr Neeve kept in the garden. Altogether it was a delightful nest for Brooke to enjoy the last summer of unalloyed happiness that he would ever know.

He summed up his delight in a letter to one of his oldest correspondents, his cousin, Erica Cotterill: 'This is a deserted, lonely, dank, ruined, overgrown, gloomy, lovely house: with a garden to match. It is all of five hundred years old, and fusty with the ghosts of generations of mouldering clergymen.' Despite his rationalist attitudes, Brooke was much possessed by the supernatural: his bedroom had formally been the vicarage's children's nursery, and he claimed he felt the tug of tiny hands as he climbed the stairs to bed.

One thing did not change from the Orchard: the constantly replenished stream of visitors who sought Brooke out in his rural hideaway. They were a disparate and sometimes ill-assorted crowd, for, as Jacques Raverat commented, Brooke liked to keep his friends in separate watertight compartments: 'He had two sets of friends that he was not interested in bringing together; for a long time he even tried to keep them apart. Was this because of his natural love of mystery, from fear of too great an incompatibility and mutual disdain, or did he fear a rapprochement at his own expense – that both sides might be exposed to a dangerous influence?'

One who crossed the lines between the groups was James Strachey; he was a social butterfly who corresponded as busily as Brooke – and with more venomous gossip – with the likes of Noel and Ka. Another was James's friend Virginia Stephen, who had known Brooke from his childhood but had faded from his intimate circle in more recent years. Now she was back – thanks to a friendship with Ka, who extended her comforting aid to nurture Virginia in her mental breakdowns, for, by 1911, the would-be author was describing herself as '29 and unmarried . . . a failure . . . childless . . . insane, too, no writer'.

Getting to know Ka, Jacques and Gwen, it was Virginia who formally dubbed them 'the Neo-Pagans' – a term she borrowed from the nineteenth-century Pre-Raphaelites and the homosexual social and sexual reformer Edward Carpenter. Virginia was at first envious and admiring of the Neo-Pagans' apparent freedoms – and their outdoor vitality; such a stark contrast to the sterile and waspish world of Lytton Strachey and E. M. Forster that she inhabited. For the wispy beards and bony chests of etiolated Bloomsbury, breathing the rarefied and stifling air of pure intellectualism, the lifestyle of the Neo-Pagans seemed at first a literal breath of fresh air. 'I mean to throw myself into youth, sunshine, nature, primitive art,' vowed Virginia. 'Cakes with sugar on the top, love, lust, paganism, general bawdiness . . .' Entranced by Ka, she gave her the affectionate nickname 'Bruin', suggesting at once her heavy sluggishness and her protective maternalism.

Safely installed at the Old Vicarage, Brooke lost little time in reassembling his friends. After dashing down to Limpsfield Chart to see Noel and Bryn (the latter back from Jamaica and hankering for marriage and children: 'I really must get married soon: I should make such an excellent mother . . . One can't go on living the life of the idle rich for ever,' she told Brooke), he gathered a party at Grantchester and the nearby Darwin home, Newnham Grange. Present were Jacques, Gwen and Bryn – and two interlopers, Virginia Stephen and the acidly observant philosopher Bertrand Russell, who recorded: 'I went to Grantchester . . . to tea with Jacques Raverat who is to marry Gwen Darwin. He had immense charm, but like all people who have superficial and obvious charm, I think he is weak and has no firm purpose. He is staying with Rupert Brooke whom I dislike . . . young people nowadays are odd – Xtian names and great familiarity, rendered easy by a complete freedom from passion on the side of the men.'

Virginia, too, soon came to regard her new-found Neo-Pagan chums with weary Bloomsbury cynicism: 'considering the infantile natures of all concerned I predict nothing serious. Ka will marry a Brooke next year, I expect. J. will always be a volatile Frog. Gwen will bear children, and paint pictures . . .' Her habitual squirts of poison and malice at anyone she suspected might be happier and more fulfilled than she was are clearly in evidence here; but she is prescient in predicting Brooke's tumultuous involvement with Ka, which would indeed reach its apogee in the following year.

Virginia was a guest at the nuptials of Jacques and Gwen in Cambridge as May turned to June. Brooke took the opportunity of inviting her to stay. Meanwhile close observation of his friends in their married bliss had sparked his always lurking jealous rage into rancid life. He let it out to his fellow-sufferer, Ka: 'I'd a bad touch of that disease you too'll have known. The ignoblest jealousy mixed with loneliness to make me flog my pillow with an umbrella till I was exhausted when I was shut into my lonely room to read myself to sleep . . .' It was not so much jealousy of Jacques' new-found regular sex with Gwen – Brooke had never fancied his friend, whom he described dismissively as 'a square-headed woman who cuts wood'. Rather it was the old anger at friends who deserted him and the single state for matrimony.

Brooke and Ka were drawn closer together in their mutual loss, and many of their friends shared Virginia's view that they would make a logical pairing in the kaleidoscope of shifting relations within the Neo-Pagan fraternity. Brooke, too, began to see the logic of emotional events. Cautiously he sounded Ka out with a catechism of the Neo-Pagan ethics that governed their set: 'We don't copulate without marriage, but we do meet in cafés, talk on buses, go [on] unchaperoned walks, stay with each other, give each other books, without marriage.' He coupled this with a warning about his own evasiveness: 'I'll try to cut off all the outside, and tell you truths. Have I ever seemed to you honest? That was when I got one layer away. There are nine-teen to come – and when they're off what?' Like the layers of an onion, which when peeled reveal yet another layer, Brooke had an obvious fear that his secrecy and subterfuges concealed a void. 'How many people can one love?' he demanded of Ka, 'How many people should one love? What is love? If I love at 6 p.m. do I therefore love at 7?' Like Noel before her, if Ka was considering a love affair with Brooke, she could not claim that she had not been warned of his waggling vacillations.

James Strachey was one of the catalysts working to break down the walls between Brooke's mutually exclusive circles. Just as his obsession with Brooke had caused him to become a Fabian without believing in the ideology, and to get his friends elected to the Apostles without much intellectual clout, so now he strove to bring Bloomsbury and the Neo-Pagans together in a wider circle orbiting around Brooke – with eventually disastrous results. Some of the Neo-Pagans were innately suspicious of this proposed merger – not least Brooke himself, as Jacques Raverat recalled:

> He did everything he could to hold off a rapprochement . . . he may have been right, but despite all his efforts he couldn't prevent it. Finally, James, whom he could not keep away, made the treaty of union between these two milieux, which had become too curious about each other, but which were deeply incompatible. The results were sometimes comic; but the rapprochement led Brooke into an ordeal that was sufficiently cruel and tragic to justify fully the instinctive fear he had of it.

James, an inveterate and interfering mischief-maker, kept up a correspondence with Ka and Noel, at least in part because he knew of Brooke's attraction to the two women. The perceptive Jacques saw through James's motives: 'He felt for our group, and perhaps especially for Ka, a kind of jealousy. He had the face of a baby and the expression of an old man; he seemed to take no pleasure or interest in material life or the physical world, and to exist only in the realms of pure intellect.' Although this assessment overlooks James's phenomenal skill as a serial seducer of both men and women – Brooke was one of his few failures – disdain and dislike of the younger Strachey was widely shared among the Neo-Pagans;

he was frequently compared to a self-satisfied and fastidious cat, and there was certainly something feline about his constant efforts to ingratiate himself into the good graces of Brooke and his friends.

Meanwhile, as spring turned to one of the summers that appeared so golden in retrospect to the world which followed the Great War, Brooke played the country gentleman and host at the Old Vicarage. The Oliviers' friend Sybil Pye, still as besotted with Brooke as she had been a year before, was one of the guests who bothered to note down her impressions – conscious perhaps that she was in at the birth of a legend. She admired Brooke's talent for easy social mixing. Early in June, when members of three separate May Week parties from Cambridge assembled in the Old Vicarage garden: 'he just moved from group to group, dissolving incongruities and creating links . . .'

Amid the social whirl there were also quiet, lazy days of study on the river: 'On some days . . .' wrote Sybil, 'he would take an armful of books into a canoe, and keeping a paddle in his left hand to steady it while the current drifted him along, would make rapid notes on scraps of paper from one book and another, and, in an easy mood, read out passages to enjoy the sound of the various forms and cadences.' Brooke's thesis on Webster, on which he was hard at work that summer, with completion due by the year's end, dictated the choice of writers:

> Spenser, Ben Jonson, Beaumont and Fletcher . . . and many lesser-known . . . all these keep an added gracious quality for those who heard them in this manner, among the dark reflected trees and the sudden wide openings across flat misty meadows . . . The affection he felt for the river is already familiar to readers of his poems. Each curve of its course, and each tree-clump that marked it, seemed known to him with a peculiar intimacy – like that which attaches sometimes to things constantly and affectionately handled.

Sybil noticed Brooke's surprising tenderness to animals – how he would break off from reciting poetry to rescue the frogs that infested the gardens from the slavering jaws of the Old Vicarage's resident dogs – a bull terrier named Pudsey Dawson by Brooke, and a puppy called Laddie. She also remarked his tendency to wear the same clothes continually. On being told that the black flannel shirt and red tie he was wearing were the same ensemble he had donned the previous year, Brooke remarked that he found it easy to clothe himself on £3 a year. Another observer, the Neeves' young son Cyril, recalled seeing the result of such parsimony: Brooke's white shirt-tail peeping out through a hole in the seat of his trousers.

Maintaining his friends in their separate boxes, Brooke was also careful to keep the Ranee in ignorance of his love for Noel. Writing in mid-May he told her of an impending visit by Mrs Brooke, adding: 'You ("that youngest Olivier girl – I hear she's left school") needn't meet my mamma.' But he tried to lure Noel up to his new demesne: 'Grantchester's much the same. Come back to it! Here'll be dog roses soon. Mrs Neeve, Byron's Pool, the Trees and the Village Idiot – all the old landmarks waiting for you.'

One who did accept Brooke's invitation was Virginia, who came for a five-day stay. Chastely she slept on the opposite side of the house from Brooke's quarters. Both were busy at their respective literary labours – Virginia was revising the text of what became her first novel, *The Voyage Out*, and writing reviews for the *Times Literary Supplement*, while Brooke was hard at work on Webster, and also writing and polishing his poetry. Virginia drew a portrait of the poet at work – biting his pencil, trying out words and lines aloud; and altogether giving the impression of a dedicated professional poet laboriously hewing art out of hard stone. 'His feet were permanently bare,' Virginia recalled in 1918 of her visit to Grantchester, and:

> he disdained all tobacco and butcher's meat, and he lived all day, and perhaps slept all night, in the open air ... Under his influence the country near Cambridge was full of young men and women walking barefoot, sharing his passion for bathing and fish diet, disdaining book learning and proclaiming that there was something deep and wonderful in the man who brought the milk and in the woman who watched the cows.

Despite her terror of sexuality, Virginia was evidently willing to flirt with Brooke, who thrilled her on one hot moonlit night by suddenly proposing: 'Let's go bathing quite naked.' She remembered the erotic occasion all her life – and privately told her friends how impressed she had been when Brooke performed his instant-erection trick. One mutual friend who saw Virginia after her visit – E. M. Forster – recorded in his diary: 'I shall see the goat [Virginia] today and hear how the Rupert romance is going on. She told me that he said he did not want to marry for several years at any rate but did want to copulate occasionally and promiscuously.'

Brooke was pursuing his project as outlined to Virginia with some enthusiasm. He was definitely lining up Ka as a future sexual partner, and – unknown to all his friends – Elisabeth van Rysselberghe had re-entered his life. Still entranced by Brooke, she had arrived in England ostensibly to improve her English, and was boarding with a clergyman's family in Teddington. The lovers' reunion took place in the Italian room at the National Gallery. But it was hardly the romantic idyll of which she had dreamed. Brooke was typically both callous and indecisive – at one time telling Elisabeth to book rooms for a dirty weekend, the next admitting that he was tired, confused and unable to decide what he really wanted to do. Unsurprisingly, Elisabeth was offended by his attitude and rejected sleeping with him on the cold terms he envisaged. But they continued to meet occasionally in London until she returned home in the autumn.

While Elisabeth had ruled herself out of the running, and Ka had to be played like a particularly lazy trout, Brooke had other amorous fish to fry – in particular Noel, with whom his endless game of emotional chess continued. She too could blow hot and cold, in late May writing: 'sometimes I hate your seeming to be in love with me, because you dont realise sufficiently how beastly I am, in most ways . . .' – which had the predictable effect of rousing his ire: 'Oh! Damn you! If people in love are blinded to the other person's real nature, I too am certainly not in love. For I see plainly that you're a codfish.' But he still danced to his young lover's tune, writing covertly to her in mid-June: 'Centre of the world, We are all sitting in the window of the Old Vicarage, for it's raining. Ethel [Pye] & Daphne [Olivier] opposite me: Hugh [Popham] to one side. But they don't know who I'm writing to. I read your letter during lunch, under the table . . .' After arranging to meet her fleetingly in London he concluded: 'Oh, I'm so keen to be seeing you again. You're very lovely & very kind & very good.'

Frequent forays to London were a feature of Brooke's summer, but his heart was increasingly in Grantchester. 'Oh, it is the only place, here,' Noel was told at the beginning of July.

> It's such a nice breezy first glorious morning, and I'm having a hurried breakfast, half dressed, in the garden, & writing to you. What cocoa! What a garden! What a you! And oh! damn! I've got to go into Cambridge & fetch out a punt for Dudley & his German women [Clothilde and Annemarie von der Planitz] . . . who are coming for the day. Damn them. Fetching a punt, entertaining them, & taking the punt back – there's a whole day gone. And I wanted to work.

Brooke revealed that he had just spent two days in London, seeing Diaghilev's legendary Ballet Russe, with Nijinsky as the principal performer. He was so enchanted with its glories that, as with *Peter Pan*, he became a serial attender, notching up 15 visits by the year's end.

But somehow, despite his grouchy complaints, Brooke went on attracting visitors to Grantchester as iron filings to a magnet. Among them was the 19-year-old Bunny Garnett, who has left a vivid account of his stay:

> One of the first things I noticed was a photograph of Noel in a silver frame on the table . . . Rupert could not have been more delightful. He was quite free from airs of superiority, which it must have been difficult to avoid with such a half-baked creature as myself. And he was quite free, also, from any affectations such as I noticed later. Instead he was easy, and kind, and hospitable, and yet happily preoccupied with his own work.

As soon as he arrived Bunny was honoured, too, with a midnight dip:

> We went about midnight to bathe in Byron's pool. We walked out of the garden of the Old Vicarage into the lane full of thick white dust, which slipped under our weight as we walked noiselessly in our sand-shoes, and then through the dew-soaked grass of the meadow over the mill-wall leading to the pool, to bathe naked in the unseen water, smelling of wild peppermint and mud.

During Bunny's stay there was a farcical episode involving Goldsworthy Lowes Dickinson, the homosexual don who had been one of Brooke's earliest Cambridge mentors. Invited to the Old Vicarage for dinner, 'Goldie' had stopped *en route* for a nude bathe. A puntload of young ladies happened along, and moored themselves between the unseen don, who had concealed himself in reeds, and his clothes. He was forced to wait while the party held a lengthy picnic, getting colder and colder and sinking deeper into the mud. He eventually arrived at the Old Vicarage caked in Granta ooze. A solicitous Brooke hurried off for blankets and hot milk to restore his patron's dignity and circulation.

As the summer reached its height, still the stream of visitors ran relentlessly on: Lytton Strachey came over from Cambridge for lunch; Geoffrey Keynes dropped by – he was fruitlessly pursuing Ka, and had commissioned a portrait of her by Duncan Grant, another visitor to the Old Vicarage. Grant painted in the summer house, leaving behind a clutch of pictures that remained forgotten until they were discovered in 1919. Other visitors included Maynard Keynes, Justin Brooke and Gerald Shove. Brooke's star was burning as brightly as ever, and attracting other planets to its fiery wake.

14

You and You

By the scorching July of 1911, as Britain's constitutional crisis simmered to boiling point, with the Tory Lords dividing into two factions – the 'hedgers', who were prepared to compromise and surrender to the government; and the 'ditchers', who wished to fight to the end – Brooke realized that his own life had come to a crossroads.

He saw that his long pursuit of Noel Olivier was getting nowhere, and that he was, however unwillingly, falling into some sort of love with Ka Cox. In the meantime he continued a parallel pursuit of both – inviting them to visit him at the Old Vicarage. But it was Ka who succumbed to a series of pleas like this: 'You *must* come this weekend. Then we'll talk: and laugh . . . Come! and talk! And love me – a little.' For Ka's edification he compiled one of his lists of 'the best things in the world':

(1) Lust
(2) Love
(3) Keats
(4) Weather
(5) go
(6) Truth
(5½) guts
(6) Marrons glacés
(7) Ka
(29) Rupert.

Ka was tempted, like many others, by Brooke's picture of the joys of his bucolic existence: 'There is no wind and no sun, only a sort of warm haze, and through it the mingled country sounds of a bee, a mowing machine, a mill, and a sparrow. Peace! And the content of working all day at Webster. Reading and reading and reading. It's not noble, but it's so happy. Oh, COME here!' Cautiously – and chaperoned by James – Ka met him in London for a performance of *Scheherazade*. He followed this up with more wheedling: 'Come. We'll be wholly frank! If you don't understand quite – nor, you know (don't tell anyone) do I. We'll explain and discuss, discover and guess, everything. Pride's irrelevant. Come! . . . O my dear, we'll, in any case, be so intimate, so damned intimate . . . You must come this week-end. Then we'll talk: and laugh. You'll have thought by then. Oh, come, come! . . .'

But Ka remained obstinately as elusive as Noel, for her family ties loomed large and she refused Brooke's urgent invitations in favour of looking after an aged aunt in Manchester. Playing hard to get always had the effect of further inflaming his passions, and he let loose a torrent of imploring adoration that cannot have left Ka in any doubt of his awakening feelings – which had been further exacerbated by a visit from those cooing newly-weds Jacques and Gwen Raverat that had left him 'drooping in front of the Old Vicarage and very sentimental and jealous'.

He felt he had only Ka's enveloping maternal warmth left to turn to:

Oh! Why do you invite responsibilities? Are you a cushion, or a floor? Ignoble thought! But why does your face invite one to load weariness on you? Why does your body appeal for an extra load of responsibilities? Why do your legs demand that one should pin business responsibilities on them? Won't you manage my committees? Will you take my soul over entire for me? Won't you write my poems? . . .

He makes it clear that he is in need of just the kind of support that only Ka can provide: 'Oh but I want to see you. Just now I'm scribbling this merely to say that I think you're the most lovely and splendid and superb and loved person, Ka.' In spite of the gradual peeling off of his friends into separate pairings – which left him, he confessed 'mourning and moping' – Brooke still saw himself as the ringmaster of the Neo-Pagan revels, a combination of squadron leader and spiritual guru: 'So I *must* meet you and we'll settle each other's business. I've got the rest off my hands! I've told Jacques about Marriage and Dudley about Women and Gwen about Babies and James about Wisdom, and I've brought Cambridge up to the level in European culture. Now for you! Besides . . .' he ended dolefully, 'we'd mitigate each other's loneliness.'

Finally, Ka caved in to this sustained emotional bombardment and spent two days at the Old Vicarage, sleeping, like Virginia, on the Neeves' side of the house. It wasn't quite the quality time alone that Brooke had promised – there were visits from Lytton Strachey, Lowes Dickinson and the Cornfords – but it was enough to confirm Ka's growing place in his heart.

Ka further entrenched herself in Brooke's affections by her homespun skills – noticing the paucity of his wardrobe, she sewed him a series of shirts. As unconventional in her own dress sense as Brooke, with her tight bodices and full skirts, and with her long, brown hair bound in a gypsy scarf, she artlessly showed off her ample charms. She accepted her role as repository of practical wisdom among the Neo-Pagans with quiet assurance, as her friend and love rival Gwen Raverat noted: 'Ka, where's the best place to buy sofa cushions? – Please, this Arab costume is too small for me, will you make it longer so that I can go to the Slade dance? – How does one send a parcel to Germany? – What do tortoises eat? . . .' All these and many similar questions she answered easily in the soothing, deep voice that many men appear to have found both reassuring and sexy. For, despite looks that could have been plain, Ka had no shortage of suitors among her male friends. They appreciated her unassertive emancipation and – not least – the inherited wealth that gave her financial freedom and independence.

And not only men – Ka attracted as many women friends, including Virginia Stephen, who got to know her at this time. Meeting Ka in January, by Easter Virginia felt close enough to her to contemplate a joint holiday, valuing her 'brightness', 'niceness', 'intelligence' and her 'trusty stable goodness'. She drew a pen portrait of Ka: 'Bruin going her way – with a beaver's tail and short clumsy paws . . . Ka came steadily along the road in time for lunch yesterday, with a knapsack on her back, a row of red beads, and daisies stuck in her coat.' But Ka's gentle passivity and lack of guile could – and did – land her in trouble. In her own way, despite her need to be needed, she was as unable to reciprocate Brooke's stormy emotions as Noel. This reverse side of her nurturing coin was at first hidden from him. When it gradually appeared it first exasperated him – '[She's] like a vegetable,' he jeered – but later, fatally, it was to estrange him.

For now, however, he needed her more than she him – he was the supplicant and she the object of his dawning love. After her Grantchester visit he teasingly told her that they were becoming an item in the gossip of their friends:

Ka, They've been talking, about You and Me. Talking! Awful. If you only knew what James said Virginia said So and So said! . . . these mediate ignorances!! But your repper [reputation], my dear, is going. Oh, among the quite Advanced. I, it is thought, am rather beastly; you rather pitiable . . . Isn't it too monstrous? They gibber night and morning, teleogically. 'How will it end?' They impudently ache for us. There are, you must know, only two 'endings' for this or any other case. (1) Marriage (2) Not. (1) is entirely good (2) entirely bad . . . They live for the future like puritans and judge by the end like parsons. Is there no SIGN to give them, that each minute is final, and each heart alone?

While appearing to ridicule the wagging tongues, Brooke was slyly validating what he hoped would become an affair, if not marriage. By teasing Ka with what people were saying about them, he was subtly suggesting that they should play out the roles their friends had already cast them for.

But where did this leave Noel and their 'engagement'? In mid-July Brooke visited the Oliviers at the house where they were staying in Rawlinson Road, Oxford, conveniently combining it with research on the Elizabethans at the Bodleian Library. Writing to Noel to arrange the trip, a harassed Brooke – 'working like a steam-roller' – let slip two pertinent pieces of information: 'a man has expressed a morose desire to print my poems immediately' and, perhaps of more interest to Noel:

> Ka comes from Newnham every day & we read Bergson together. I've got very fond of her. But as she's got a lot of old-fashioned and silly prejudices, the only thing they'll allow her to do is to marry & have children, & as she's very old . . . [Ka was four months older than Brooke, and hence 24 at the time of writing!] she'd better, I discovered, not waste time on me: she doesn't seem to be able to attend to two people at once. So woman. I must go & work . . .

If this was meant to reassure Noel, it was expressed with typical insensitivity and awkwardness. She responded with both sense and sensibility:

> Rupert, darling! [a uniquely fond endearment coming from the cool Noel] . . . I wish you wouldn't call Ka 'bloody'; she isn't, & it sounds as though you were angry with her; you have no cause to be . . . Oh, it would have been so much better, if you had married her ages ago! And you told me, once, that you could be very rich (& support a huge wife & family) if you wanted to. Perhaps you don't want to tho'[.] Love from Noel.

His knuckles duly rapped, Brooke turned his attention in August, as he entered his twenty-fourth year, to the other topic he had mentioned to

Noel: the publication of his first collection of verse. E. J. Dent having rejected the chance of bringing out the book, he had turned to another young publisher, Frank Sidgwick, who, knowing of Brooke via Lytton Strachey, had met him at his London office in mid-June and read the poems while on his honeymoon. The canny Sidgwick issued the traditional warning that poetry did not pay, but offered to publish the collection, provided Brooke stood guarantor against a probable loss on the venture. As the Ranee had already offered to subsidize the publication out of her pocket, Brooke gave the necessary assurance and signed the contract for the book in mid-August, with Virginia Stephen as his witness. He would receive a royalty of 15 per cent on every copy sold.

Frantically, Brooke set to work to knock his poems into shape. His major production of the year so far had been 'The Fish' – a long poem full of aquatic imagery that was a sort of wet run for his famous 'Heaven', a brilliant satire on religious belief in immortality. His poetic labour was witnessed by his friend and fellow-poet Frances Cornford: she said he made composition 'feel more like carpentering' – a hard physical effort. 'Sitting on the floor (he said he "couldn't think rhythmically sitting up") biting the end of his pencil, and jotting notes in the margin . . . he would say, without looking up "I like that" or "That's good."'

Frances was one of the many who fell for his still irresistible charm:

There was something dateless in his beauty which makes it easy to picture him in other centuries, yet always in England . . . It was a continual pleasure to look at him fresh each day – his radiant fairness, beauty of build, his broad head with its flung-back hair, deepset frowning eyes. The clear line of his chin and long broad-based neck on broad shoulders were so entirely beautiful that he seemed like a symbol of youth for all time . . . To watch him putting on his boots, frowning and groaning, with the absorbed seriousness of a child, with which he did all practical things – he would look up with a pink face and his pleasant hair tumbled and his sudden sharing grin which always had the loveliness of a child's.

But, besotted as she was, she was not so blinded by Brooke's 'radiance' that she missed the dark undertow to his sunniness that would eventually be his downfall: 'deep-ingrained in him, and handed down to him I should imagine through generations of English ancestors, was the puritanical spirit . . . nobody could miss it, whoever saw the scorn and sternness in his face when he spoke of things that he hated, things corrupt and unclean.' Unclean! Again that word that sounds a bell toll beneath Brooke's apparently easy hedonism. The black-clad Puritanism he was quick to mock in the Elizabethans was paradoxically built into his own genes by generations of clerical and schoolmaster Brookes and Cotterills. Under the slow-gliding waters of the Cam, the austere spirit of the Ranee was waiting to reclaim him. One day he would dive in and fail to surface.

Towards the end of August, Brooke began to badger his friends with anxious queries about that year's summer camp. Who was organizing it, Noel was asked. Would 'Bruin' be doing it? 'I'd hoped she were organising some party of wild adventurers & that my meek, silent, upturned face'd possibly secure an invitation . . .' In the event, a coincidence brought the two streams of his life, which he had striven to keep apart, together in one of England's last wildernesses, Dartmoor, which he had briefly visited two years before.

Lytton Strachey was the first to make his way there, journeying down in July to work in peace on his first book, *Landmarks in French Literature*, at Becky Falls in Devon. He found the isolated cottage in the rocky and remote location conducive to his literary labours, and summoned fellow-Bloomsburyites G. E. Moore and Leonard Woolf to share its delights. By chance, Bedales' annual camp was being held nearby, at Clifford's Bridge, where a long meadow bordered the River Teign. The Old Bedalian Justin Brooke arranged to take over the school's tents and camping gear for his friends, and swiftly invitations were issued for a long camp beginning in August. With the Bloomsbury party ensconced in the vicinity, it was fated that the two streams in Brooke's life were about to converge.

He was still mostly at Grantchester, trying his hand at translating a new enthusiasm – Strindberg, whose rampant misogyny and emotional dialogue must have appealed – under the tuition of a Swedish student at Newnham, Estrid Linder. Estrid photographed him hard at work in the garden of the Old Vicarage, bent over papers on the round table brought out from his room, with the ramshackle veranda of the house behind him. Bored by the solemn Swedish girl – 'Estrid's a limpet . . . she crawls,' he wrote to James contradictorily – Brooke was looking forward to the glories of Dartmoor, and was quick to round up his lady friends: he took advantage of a stay with Virginia at Firle, in Sussex, to invite her to the Clifford's Bridge camp, thus making the first daring cross-pollination between sterile Bloomsbury and the fertile Neo-Pagans; then rushed up to Woking to make sure of Ka, who was in residence at Hook Hill Cottage.

Virginia was another witness to Brooke's creative process as he sweated over his poems. 'Virginia,' he called suddenly. 'What's the brightest thing in nature?' 'Sunlight on a leaf,' she responded. 'Thanks,' he said simply, and at once the line went down in his poem 'Town and Country' as: 'Cloud-like we lean and stare as bright leaves stare.'

After collecting his ladies like an anxious shepherd – Noel, already on Dartmoor at the Old Bedalians' camp, resisted his proposal to meet secretly and 'dash across Dartmoor alone with light knapsacks . . . and careless hearts'. 'You must wait until I'm 21,' she replied – Brooke arrived in Devon on 27 August.

Participants at the Clifford's Bridge camp included Justin, James, Geoffrey Keynes and, surprisingly, Maynard, who was trying out life under canvas for the first time. On the distaff side there was Daphne, Bryn and Noel, Ka and Virginia – another camping virgin. Gerald Shove, staying at Becky Falls with Lytton, also put in a brief appearance. There were two newcomers, a doctor, Maitland Radford, one of many men in hot pursuit of Bryn Olivier; and Paulie Montague, an Old Bedalian Cambridge man from nearby Crediton, who entertained the campers with his virtuoso performances of Elizabethan songs, accompanying himself on his own home-made instruments.

Brooke arrived at the camp in a state of intellectual exhaustion. 'I've been working for ten days alone at this beastly poetry,' he told Ka. 'Working at poetry isn't like reading hard. It doesn't just tire and exhaust you. The only effect is that your nerves and brain go . . . I had reached the lowest depths possible to man.' On 30 August Paulie Montague issued a general invitation to his fellow-campers to walk over to his family home, Penton, and take tea, with his mother acting as hostess. It was to be a momentous occasion, for Brooke, eyeing his friends around the table, began to finalize the poem 'Dining-Room Tea', which he had begun in Munich. It is his own personal celebration of, and farewell to, his Neo-Pagan way of life.

Towards the end of the summer at Grantchester Gwen Darwin, sensing that the Neo-Pagans' fraternity and solidarity were beginning to fracture and slip away, had written:

I wish one of us would write a 'ballade des beaux jours à Grantchester'. I can't bear to think of all these young, beautiful people getting old and tired and stiff in the joints. I don't believe there is anything compensating in age and experience – we are at our very best and most livingest now – from now on the edge will go off our longings and the fierceness of our feelings and we shall no more swim in the Cam . . . and we shan't mind much . . . Do you know how one stops and sees them all sitting around – Rupert and Geoffrey and Jacques and Bryn and Noel – all so young and strong and keen and full of thought and desire, and one knows it will all be gone in 20 years and there will be nothing left . . . If one of those afternoons would be written down, just as it was exactly; it would be a poem . . . Oh it is intolerable, this waste of beauty – it's all there and nobody sees it but us and we can't express it . . .

Now, in 'Dining-Room Tea', Brooke was to attempt to answer Gwen's call, and produce his own Proustian effort to capture their golden hour in amber before time had its inevitable way with them:

> When you were there, and you, and you,
> Happiness crowned the night; I too
> Laughing and looking, one of all,
> I watched the quivering lamplight fall
> On plate and flowers and pouring tea
> And cup and cloth; and they and we
> Flung all the dancing moments by
> With jest and glitter. Lip and eye
> Flashed on the glory; shone and cried,
> Improvident, unmemoried;
> And fitfully and like a flame
> The light of laughter went and came.
> Proud in their careless transience moved
> The changing faces that I loved.

The poet concentrates on the scene until he is rewarded with the transformation that lifts the 'immortal moment' from time into eternity:

> I saw the marble cup; the tea
> Hung on the air, an amber stream;
> I saw the fire's unglittering gleam,
> The painted flame, the frozen smoke.
> No more the flooding lamplight broke
> On flying eyes and lips and hair;
> But lay, but slept unbroken there . . .

His friends' conversation turns to 'words on which no silence grew' and their transfigured faces are 'Holy and strange . . . Freed from the mask of transiency'. But it is only a mystic moment; inevitably 'mortal strength wearied; and Time began to creep'. As his world returns to the everyday:

The cup was filled. The bodies moved.
The drifting petal came to the ground.

The poet cannot communicate his vision. He remains roped in his isolation:

You never knew that I had gone
A million miles away, and stayed
A million years.

But despite his return to the prison of time and transience, nothing can rob him of his enduring sight of another reality:

I sang at heart, and talked, and eat,
And lived from laugh to laugh, I too,
When you were there, and you, and you.

Brooke lost no time in adding the hastily completed poem to the sheaf that he now posted to Sidgwick to form the manuscript of his definitive first collection. It was a worthy jewel in the crown. The task done, he felt free to relax and enjoy the exuberant pleasure of the camp.

They tarried in Crediton to enjoy a performance of a popular drama, *The Lyons Mail*, at the town's fair, and afterwards the joys of the fair's side-shows detained them for longer, so that it was late at night when they finally breasted the top of the valley which held their camp-site, and silently surveyed the white tents bright in the still moonlight. In their absence Ka and Virginia had arrived at the camp, tired and hungry after an eight-mile tramp from the nearest station. In the darkness they came upon a blackberry pie, made some days earlier by Justin Brooke and by now far gone in dissolution. They ate several mouthfuls before discovering its mouldy state – and only then found a note pinned to the flap of the kitchen tent, explaining their friends' absence.

The stay at Clifford's Bridge was an unusually lengthy one: the Neo-Pagans camped there for 18 days, although the visiting Bloomsberries – Shove and James Strachey – could not face more than a night or two in the great outdoors. James arrived late at night and, disdaining to disturb his friends, flung himself down in a heap of blankets under a gorse bush. There he was discovered at daybreak by Justin and Ka, rising at 5.30 to prepare the breakfast porridge. Always ready to poke fun at the faithful but sometimes comically absurd James, Brooke composed a couplet in his dishonour:

In the late evening he was out of place,
And utterly irrelevant at dawn.

Discomfited by this less-than-welcoming reception from the Neo-Pagans, James retreated to Lytton's lodgings at Becky Falls, where he was joined by his fellow-Apostle Gerald Shove, now known to Brooke, owing to his taciturnity, as 'the silent Shove'. Pictures taken at the camp portray a boyish-looking Brooke in a variety of poses: grinning maniacally at a tweed-suited Shove; alone in a field in a white, cable-knit sweater, with damp hair parted in the middle and gazing moodily at the ground; sitting cross-legged in shorts outside a tent; absorbed in writing, with a windswept Ka in squaw-like pose in the foreground; or looking solemn in shirtsleeves in front of a five-bar gate, accompanied by Virginia – grinning self-consciously in Neo-Pagan-style gypsy scarf – along with Noel and Maitland Radford.

Maynard Keynes, rather unexpectedly enjoyed his taste of open-air life when he turned up: 'Camp life suits me very well,' he told his father. 'The hard ground, a morning bathe, the absence of fresh food, and no chairs, doesn't make one nearly so ill as one would suppose.' Lytton Strachey, a martyr to piles, stayed in his cottage, characteristically commenting to Brooke that the ground 'was rather an awkward shape to sit on'. Their days passed in the usual round of activity – swimming in the river, with Brooke 'looking very beautiful', according to Paulie Montague's sister Ruth; and going on long hikes – on one enthusiastic occasion they made a 30-mile round trip to Yes Tor, breaking the journey with a visit to Lytton at Becky Falls, and organizing a woman-hunt with Bryn as their quarry on the way home. In quieter moments Brooke took up his work on Webster, which had been interrupted by his poetry, or read the passionate love-letters of Keats to Fanny Brawne.

Sexual and emotional currents criss-crossed the camp-site: Bryn took a dislike to Justin – a photo shows them sharing kitchen duty, with a grim-faced Bryn sitting as far as possible from an oblivious, grinning Justin. Bryn was fancied by Maitland, Brooke *and* Gerald Shove; and Brooke was also caught between his declining worship of Noel and his growing affection for Ka. When Ka left the camp early, he seems to have received some sort of rebuff from Noel, for, so he told Ka, he ended up by going off in a tearful huff and spending the night alone on a hill.

When the Neo-Pagans struck camp, Brooke went alone to stay with the Strachey brothers at Becky Falls. The meeting between Bloomsbury and the Neo-Pagans had not really worked: Bloomsbury, in the form of James,

Virginia, Shove and Maynard Keynes, had taken a look at their boisterous younger brethren and decided they preferred the more cerebral air of their accustomed lifestyle. But Brooke still felt he could keep a foot in each camp.

After five days scrambling over the rocks with the Stracheys, he headed for London, where an unwelcome, but not unexpected, piece of news awaited him. After attending a concert of Beethoven's Fifth Symphony with James, he met Dudley Ward at the National Liberal Club to introduce Bunny Garnett as a new member. It was then or soon afterwards that Dudley told him that he would be marrying Annemarie von der Planitz. Another desertion! Brooke endeavoured to make the best of it, and minimize the blow: 'Luckily it's not very definite,' he reported to Ka, one of the diminishing band of single heterosexuals in their circle. 'Dudley won't give up his freedom for some years yet. But I so idolized him . . . I felt so awfully lonely.'

On his return to the Old Vicarage in mid-September, the autumnal gloom that had descended on the damp riverside seemed to seep into Brooke's soul: what was to prove his last Neo-Pagan summer was over. His gloom was compounded by a letter from Frank Sidgwick complaining about 'Lust', the sonnet inspired by Elisabeth van Rysselberghe that he had included as an afterthought in the collection. Ostensibly his publisher thought it a bad poem; but really, Brooke suspected darkly, his objection was due to its title and sexual theme. He decided to stand firm and insist on the sonnet's inclusion.

He wrote to Sidgwick: 'Is the objection to "Lust" only that it's bad as poetry or also that it's shocking as morals? . . . If it's thought to be improper, it must be sadly misunderstood. It's meaning is quite "proper" and so moral as to be almost untrue. If the title's too startling "Libido" . . . could be substituted.' He added: 'My own feeling is that to remove it would be to overbalance the book still more in the direction of unimportant prettiness. There's plenty of that sort of wash in the other pages for the readers who like it.'

It is striking that Brooke is himself so critical of his own work that he attacks it even before publication for 'unimportant prettiness' – the very charge brought against him by unsympathetic critics ever afterwards. His reputation as a poet would probably stand much higher today had he had the wisdom to exclude such verse from the volume in favour of more unsentimental pieces – even if that would have held up publication for several years. Instead he let his desire for fame and his friends' acclaim get the better of him.

He masochistically continued: 'About a lot of the book I occasionally feel like Ophelia, that I've turned "Thought and affliction, passion, hell itself . . . to favour and to prettiness." So I'm extra keen about the places where I think that thought and passion are, however clumsily, not so transmuted.' After more haggling with Sidgwick, Brooke got his way. Ka was triumphantly informed: 'He wanted it left out. Said a woman's smell was excrement . . . This morning he's come down like a shot possum. Compromise: It's to be printed, but called "Libido" (Latin!) Let us pray.' In copies of the book that he distributed to friends Brooke meticulously crossed out 'Libido' in pencil and restored the original title.

Brooke now had less than three months left to complete the dissertation on Webster on which his academic – and financial – future depended. He knew that when the Michaelmas term began, the flow of visitors to Grantchester would resume and his chances of concentrating on his work would depart. There were other reasons, too, that encouraged him to desert the Old Vicarage: with the onset of autumn it had lost much of its summer enchantment; and if he lived in London the British Museum and its works of reference that he needed would be close at hand. Last but not least, Ka would be there, offering hospitality and – who knew? – the romantic comfort he craved.

But it was another, older form of comfort that he took up on a preliminary reconnaissance of the capital on 17 September, when he dined with Eddie Marsh, Duncan Grant and George Mallory – all three homosexuals. This, and the fact that Brooke took for his London *pied-à-terre* a studio in the Bloomsbury heartland at 21 Fitzroy Square, sometimes used by the lovers Duncan Grant and Maynard Keynes, caused the rumour mills to spin. Although Brooke defensively told the fiercely homophobic Jacques Raverat that the place was 'inconceivably disgusting', his residence there was enough to set Bloomsbury tongues wagging that the star of Grantchester had reverted to former sexual inclinations.

Writing later of this period, Virginia Woolf recalls being told by her sister Vanessa that James Strachey was 'in despair', because Brooke had 'been to bed twice' with a handsome Cambridge catamite of Maynard Keynes, Lytton Strachey and Duncan Grant named Arthur Lee Hobhouse, a youth elected to the Apostles on account of his looks rather than his brains. In the version of the rumour heard by Virginia, Brooke's bed partner was Mallory, the handsome mountaineer and another lover of Grant's. This Bloomsbury bitchery may have been inaccurate gossip relating to Brooke's years in Cambridge; but if it was true that he had indulged in dalliance with his male friends while increasingly involved with Ka, it suggests a degree of sexual confusion that was indeed to become apparent in the very near future.

Whatever the truth of the stories, Brooke's contact with his old pals was brief – by November the squalor of the studio in Fitzroy Square had driven him to nearby rooms, found for him by Ka, at 76 Charlotte Street. This was a convenient love-nest for them both, tucked away out of sight of their nosy friends' notice. By day, Brooke, armed with his newly acquired reader's ticket, laboured over Webster in the British Museum, while by night he played with Ka. The mild flirtatiousness of his by now daily letters to her is deceptive: 'Your body's strong and adequately divine; . . . you've an affectedly drawling laugh that puts several pounds on a sick man's weight, even down 85 miles of telephone; that if one sees you swing . . . across the street, the world's on the instant radiant and immortally good.'

The reality of their relationship that autumn comes out retrospectively in a letter written by Brooke the following year, when, driven half-mad by jealousy and regret over missed opportunities, he raves:

And then we had those nights – I had such lust for your fine body, far more (you *never* understood) than for Noel. I had passion for you, – and, as you know, other things, other ways of love, (I knew you –, Ka, – so deeply) as well. I was foolish and wicked, indeed. First, that I didn't chuck everything turn wholly to you, marry you, if you would . . . Then, I was a fool . . . I'd baby ideas about 'honour' 'giving' you a fair chance' 'not being underhand' 'men(!) and women(!) being equal' . . . I wanted you to fuck. You wouldn't, 'didn't like preventives'. And I respected you! . . . felt guilty and angry with myself when lust made me treat you 'unfairly!' I was getting ill and stupid . . . I was an object for pity – even love; not of course, lust. You gave me strength, comfort, rest – for a bit. I threw all my affairs – all the mess Noel and I had made – onto you.

What seems to have fuelled Brooke's rage later was not simple sexual frustration – by finding him his discreet rooms, he thought Ka was signalling her willingness to embark on a full physical affair, rather than just again showing her natural kindness, There seems also to have been a lingering suspicion that Ka was not aroused by him sexually – despite a sort of sentimental 'love'. Nothing is more irritating to the potentially ardent lover than the thought that his beloved thinks of him as a 'sweet boy', but looks elsewhere for sexual satisfaction. His nights with Ka seem to have been confined to heavy petting – with all its excitements and frustrations – and fretting arguments about sex and the constraints of the Neo-Pagan 'code' – that there should be intimacy between the sexes, but no copulation without marriage – and their bizarre belief that sexual intercourse was less a bodily act than a semi-mystical rite of passage that ushered participants from youth to adulthood.

At weekends Brooke found it necessary to escape back to Grantchester from the pressure of London. His letters to Ka from there sometimes contained droll accounts of domestic crises:

> 'Do you smell soot? I've been the last half hour with my arms up a chimney. The beam in the kitchen chimney caught fire. 'These old houses!' we kept panting. It was so difficult to get at, being also in part the chimney piece . . . an ever so cheerful and able British working-man and I attacked the house with buckets and a pickaxe . . . I was masterful at the always slightly wrong minute – but gave very decisive directions for the rest of the day.

Sometimes so dog-tired that he could barely lift his head, Brooke could nevertheless not resist another chance to stroll in the limelight – this time in the walk-on, non-singing part of a Nubian slave in a performance of *The Magic Flute* at London's New Theatre on 1 and 2 December. While waiting to go on stage he read about Webster in the Green Room. He had landed the part at the invitation of Clive Carey, a Cambridge acquaintance from whom he was receiving (abortive) singing lessons. One wonders why he bothered with such distractions at this turning point in his life.

On 4 December *Poems* by Rupert Brooke was published by Sidgwick & Jackson, in an edition of 500 copies. Brooke was too preoccupied by his work on Webster, then in its final stages, to show much exhilaration or even interest in the event. He told Sybil Pye dismissively that he would produce much better poetry in the next year or two when he was no longer bogged down with his academic tasks. He was not to know that the volume was the only collection of his poetry that would appear in his lifetime. Still less, that it would be one of the century's smash hits in terms of popular sales – it sold 100,000 copies by the beginning of the thirties, and made small fortunes for the Ranee and Brooke's literary heirs. For the moment, its impact was modest: it covered its £10 printing costs, and by the turn of the year had recorded a profit of £3.

Those reviewers who noticed the book were generally kind. Dealing with Brooke along with a clutch of other books of verse, as Brooke had predicted to Frances Cornford, the *Times Literary Supplement*'s anonymous critic praised his 'boyish' qualities, but deplored the 'disgusting sonnet on love and sea-sickness', which 'ought never to have been printed'.

However, the *TLS* admitted: 'We are tempted to like him for writing it. Most people pass through some such strange nausea as this on their stormy way from romance to reality.' The ultra-conservative *Morning Post* also highlighted 'A Channel Passage'. Noting Brooke's apparent dread of 'writing prettily', the critic demanded: 'What possible excuse is there for a sonnet describing a rough Channel crossing with gusto worthy of a medical dictionary?'

John Buchan's notice in the *Spectator* praised Brooke's 'strenuous originality', while the *English Review*, in a piece devoted exclusively to the poet, called 'A Channel Passage' 'a satiric masterpiece'. The weekly *New Age* perceptively picked up on the lack of experience informing his love lyrics, which it called 'frigid and unreal'. *The Nation*, which, like the *English Review*, had previously printed poems by Brooke, referred to the recently composed 'Dining-Room Tea' as showing a 'triumphant transformation of the commonplace into the unique'. The *Westminster Gazette*, Brooke's own house organ, which had been printing his poems and where he had been winning poetry competitions with monotonous regularity since his schooldays, predictably praised the book, but, like most of the others, jibbed at 'A Channel Passage': 'For obvious reasons it cannot be quoted here.' The *Observer* also noted and deplored Brooke's tendency to being 'nasty – as in his continual insistence on the physical unpleasantness of old age'. The review concluded favourably, however: 'it is enormously to his credit that he had managed to stagger free of convention'. The Liberal *Daily News* saw that Brooke's 'ugly' poems were merely 'an inverted reverence for beauty', while another sympathetic organ, the *Cambridge Review*, said his comparison of love and nausea 'ruined a promising book'.

Only one of Brooke's friends, Edward Thomas, reviewed his poems professionally. His article in the Liberal *Daily Chronicle* said: 'He is full of revolt, contempt, self-contempt, and yet arrogance too . . . Copies should be brought by everyone over forty who has never been under forty. It will be a revelation. Also if they live yet a little longer they may see Mr Rupert Brooke a poet. He will not be a little one.' Brooke's most hostile notice appeared in another Liberal newspaper, the *Manchester Guardian*, which accused him of 'a dislocation of the mind'. The paper was not to know that its gibe was about to become literally true.

It was not only the worries over Webster that were distracting and depressing Brooke as 1911 ended. Exhausted and nervous as he was, his delicate condition was not helped by rumours that had reached his ears that Ka was being seen around town in the disreputable company of that dangerously bohemian young painter Henry Lamb.

15

Lulworth and the Ka Crisis

Events in December 1911, the beginning of the supreme crisis in Brooke's life, began to rush up on him with frightening speed: first there was the appearance of his poems, to which, agitatedly absorbed in Webster as he was, he gave very little thought. Suddenly the Christmas season was upon him, and with it a slew of questions: where would he spend the festive season, and with whom? And what would he do in the New Year? Finally, and most disturbingly, why was Ka so suddenly quiet and removed? He had asked her to help him round up some suitable friends to see in the new year at Lulworth once again, in what he hoped would be a repetition of the close and quiet time they had enjoyed there with Jacques, Justin and Gwen the year before. He was feeling distinctly sickly, and was wanting the company of the old familiar faces; certainly he was in no mood for new friends, still less for uncomfortable emotional shocks and surprises.

To add to his doubts over Ka and Henry Lamb, he was also undergoing agonies of jealousy over Noel. At the Clifford's Bridge camp he had noticed that she had received a letter from an admirer and friend of hers at Bedales, the Hungarian aristocrat Ferenc Békássy. The letter left no room for doubt about the young man's feelings for Noel: 'Wherever I am and whatever I do, from writing poetry to flirting on various occasions – I always begin thinking about you. And really, there is no one else I care to be with so much . . . there is no one else I can talk with.' Almost certainly it was the sight of this letter that caused Brooke to flounce off in a storm of jealousy and spend a tearful night alone on a hill. But, in accordance with his normal pattern of behaviour, the knowledge that he had a rival in the field served to rekindle the dying embers of his passion for Noel; and throughout the autumn he bombarded her with letters that – while not as long as in former days – were equally emphatic in their declarations of love.

The refurbishing of his affair with Noel was made easier since she was closer to hand, having begun to study medicine at University College London. His letters hint gently at the hurt he had suffered at her hands in Devon:

> So Camp's faded from you, has it, 'except the smell and the scenery'? What do you mean when you say those things stay with you longer than anything else? I'm jealous again! Do they? There are a few things that stay longer. I'll not let you forget some things till you die – But anyhow, I rather vaguely protest, can't I be allowed to be part of the scenery? I so often was. And if I don't smell, I can, you know. I can buy stuff in a bottle and always sprinkle it on me, I mean. Anything, you see, not to be outdone by a rival.

Fired up by jealousy, he blames their geographical separation and mutual 'Incomprehension' for the recent *froideur* in their relations, but now:

> I'll give you the whole world, I love you so . . . To think of you is Heaven. Noel, whom I love, who is so beautiful and wonderful. I think of you eating omelette on the ground. I think of you once against a sky line: and sitting at Becky Falls: and bathing: and picking dewberries: walking: and on the hill that Sunday morning. And that night that was wonderfullest of all . . . You are so beautiful and wonderful that I daren't write to you: And kinder than God. Your arms and lips and hair and shoulders and voice – *you*. A million worlds and ages are smaller than that time. I daren't write. I could only repeat words. Beautiful, beautiful. They're silly. – I love you – There are no words. Goodnight Noel. Rupert.

After all her evasions, Noel was, ironically enough, probably more receptive to Brooke at this time than ever before – just at the moment when his affections were beginning to be engaged elsewhere. She accepted his invitation to hear a Wagner opera, during which he reminded her: 'You are lovely as the sunrise – and we have very few more years left to live.' With unaccustomed warmth, she responded: 'I get worse & worse & you more & more splendid. We must try again, another way. It cant go on – my being so filthy & you so fine – I cant bear the contrast, for one thing . . .' She proposed to recast their engagement to rule out physical demonstrations of love, and confine themselves to 'talking . . . Or something even stricter – something hard & restraining; awfully good for me! what about you?'

But such chastity was not good at all for an already severely deprived

Brooke, with the comforting charms of Ka so near at hand. He responded: 'I will pledge myself to no ordinance. For even though I only wanted to talk for the first three weeks: I might suddenly want to bite your fingers on the fourth. They're very nice. One can't bind oneself to want or not to want. By December I may not want to see you at all. Tra! la! Or the strain may be so great I shan't be able to bear it.'

Despite more meetings, teas and theatre visits in London that autumn, some carried on under the very nose of Ka, both at Fitzroy Square ('It's the dirtiest place in London, and the uncomfortablest') and his Charlotte Street bolt-hole that Ka had found, something intervened between them to thwart, yet again, their intimacy. The 'something' probably took place in November, since at the end of October he was still writing to her like a man possessed: 'There are things I've given you I can't get back again . . . I can't ever be separate from you. I can hurt you and be cruel and devilish and mean and tear you and destroy you and infect and poison you. But I'll never be free again . . . Nor you from me . . . (Oh, if you die before I've done loving you I shall go mad.)'

However, a month later things had drastically changed: 'I don't suppose that at any moment of your life any one's wanted to hurt you so much as I have for the past week.' By some hideous mischance, Brooke had happened to visit Ferenc Békássy, the 18-year-old ex-Bedalian who had fallen for Noel at school, and whose love-letter to her had thrown him into a frenzy in Devon. Békássy had gone up to Cambridge as a King's freshman that October. From curiosity, Brooke had visited him in his rooms for breakfast in late November, and to his utter horror, had seen a letter to the young Hungarian from Noel which by no means discouraged his hopes of winning her love.

Instantly he fired off what she called a 'little snappy post card' of protest to Noel, and at their next meeting perplexed her with his boorish, jealous petulance, eliciting the response:

> Rupert! This is awful! You mustn't go on like this, angry & wakeful & not working . . . your miserable-looking self . . . You mustn't be so dotty & queer. If you're grey & stern on Sunday I shall be affraid [sic] – and it's that fear (if anything) which makes me hate you; its when I feel that you are going to say horrors, & that you are thinking them, & that I can only shudder or squeak . . .

But she ended reassuringly: 'I'm not bringing Bekassy on Sunday. Love from Noel.'

Although Brooke recanted of his ill temper by return of post – 'Noel dear, I'm sorry. I'm all twisted and tired . . . I'm sorry. I'm a devil to treat you so. Oh, I've so little faith . . .' – the breach between them which had seemed to be healing was rapidly widening again to chasm-like proportions. Innocently, Noel was not to know that he was already exhibiting the symptoms – irrationality and insomnia – of the total breakdown that was about to tear his life apart.

On 15 December, with the Christmas holidays looming, the troubled lovers met at the Moulin d'Or restaurant in London and afterwards walked along the Embankment, wrapped in strained conversation about their future. Brooke, described by an anxious Noel a few days before as looking 'sad & worried enough to make me weep', declared that until Noel was prepared to make more of a commitment to the relationship, it could not continue. On this sad note they parted.

With her usual sensible attitude, Noel wrote to him on 20 December suggesting that his feelings were exaggerated, 'gloomy & continually irritated because, for about two months you have been working so hard & London is so awful & the last week you nearly killed yourself'. She pleaded for another chance before any irrevocable decisions were made. Brooke replied with his feelings clearly confused. He veered, he said, between wanting to go away for a year and having another shot at rebuilding their relations: 'It seemed incredibly stupid and wicked that we should mess it between us: or lose anything. Oh Noel, Noel, who's wrong and a fool – you? or I? or both?' Between the lines, Noel was asking for more freedom from his 'gnawing jealousies' – something that the increasingly frenzied Brooke would not, could not, grant. Almost beside himself with jealousy, exhaustion and confused fears for the future, he packed his papers at Grantchester and set off to see his mother. Ahead lay Lulworth – and the worst horrors yet.

In a poem roughed out before he left Grantchester, Brooke described the divided state of his soul:

> All night I went between a dream and a dream
> As one walking between two fires.

He thought he had left one fire behind, with the breach with Noel – but the warmth of Ka that he hopefully turned towards was to prove altogether too hot to handle.

From Grantchester he went via London – where he spent a last night at Charlotte Street with its piquant recent memories of the woman he was about to meet so explosively – to join the Ranee, who was staying at the

Beachy Head Hotel on the cliffs west of Eastbourne. It was at the hotel that he put the finishing touches to his dissertation. He was in a state of depression, telling Sybil Pye that it was only the art of the Ballet Russe – which he had continued to haunt through the autumn – that could redeem civilization. Then it was back to Rugby for Christmas.

With all his distractions, Brooke apparently failed to notice until it was too late that Ka had far exceeded her brief in extending invitations for the Lulworth party. She had visited him at Beachy Head and had informed him that she had merrily issued invitations to a far wider circle than Brooke had envisaged. By the time he wrote to Lytton Strachey from Rugby on 19 December, the cast of characters who would witness the drama of his life was almost complete. 'There's going to be a reading-party in dear old Lulworth. In January: . . . Ka and I. And perhaps his Lordship [Gerald Shove] and possibly Virginia. Will you come? Everybody will be writing plays. I suppose it will be dreadfully Apostolic . . .' Brooke had already issued a similar invitation to Maynard Keynes, and asked him to invite his lover Duncan Grant. As an extra inducement to the great economist, he assured him that there would be 'no Oliviers' – between them, Ka and Brooke had vetoed the troubling Neo-Pagan sisters.

But Ka had covertly been active: not only had she invited Lytton; she had also intrigued for him to ask Henry Lamb to join the group. She was plain about her motives, telling Justin Brooke that she wanted to flirt with the 'unpleasant but fascinating' painter, as she candidly but cruelly described Lamb to Brooke. Lytton was not averse to the idea: for he was already deeply in love and lust with Lamb himself. Having lost Duncan Grant to Keynes, Lytton had transferred his attentions to Lamb, and had recently returned from a visit to him in Brittany.

Although resolutely heterosexual, Lamb enjoyed teasing Lytton, and delighted in their banter – particularly about Lamb's ever-ready penis, which they referred to as 'the Obelisk'. He was the son of a mathematics professor at Manchester University. His brother Walter, a don at Trinity College, Cambridge, was an acquaintance of Brooke, and his sister Dorothy was a teacher at Bedales. Lamb had begun to study medicine, and had almost qualified as a doctor when, in 1905, he suddenly broke from his family's scientific bent and became an artist. In 1907 he married a fellow-Mancunian art student, Nina Forrest, who was always known as Euphemia. They immediately eloped to Paris, where Lamb got to know Augustus John and Duncan Grant. John had a strong influence on Lamb, who adopted the older artist's persona, dressing in arty clothes – corduroy jackets and floppy neckties – and sporting a scrubby beard. Lamb also followed the

21. 'The Patron': Eddie Marsh
posing as St Sebastian, 1912

22. Violet Asquith *(left)* and Lady
Eileen Wellesley at finishing
school in Dresden, 1903

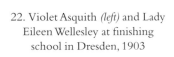

23. King's College, Cambridge, 1910 *(author's collection)*

24. *(Left to right)* Jacques Raverat, Ka Cox, Gwen Raverat, Frances Cornford, in Norfolk, 1912
(author's collection)

25. Bryn Olivier: 'I'm glad you're so beautiful', 1909 *(author's collection)*

26. Cathleen Nesbitt, 1912 *(author's collection)*

27. Elisabeth Van Rysselberghe *(Gallimard, Paris)*

28. 'Wash the mind of foolishness': Taatamata, a snapshot by Rupert, 1914
(King's College Library, Cambridge)

29. Taatamata *(far left)* and Rupert *(second from right)* outside their hotel in Tahiti, 1914
(King's College Library, Cambridge)

30. 'The Soldier': Rupert in Royal Naval Division uniform, 1914
(King's College Library, Cambridge)

31. 'The Argonauts': Rupert (*standing, left*) and his fellow officers aboard the SS *Grantully Castle*, Avonmouth Docks, 1915 *(King's College Library, Cambridge)*

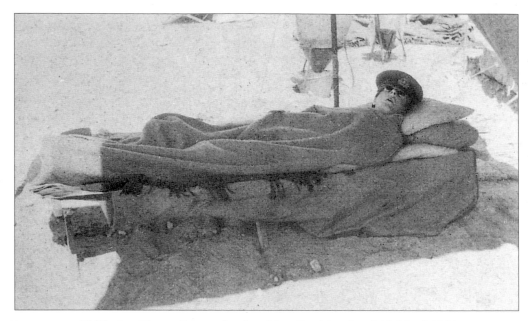

32. The Last Picture: Rupert, already stricken, lies sick at Port Said, 2 April 1915
(King's College Library, Cambridge)

33. 'Forever England': Rupert's original grave on Skyros
(author's collection)

master in matters of the flesh, becoming a recklessly dedicated womanizer. His wife promptly left him, although they formally remained married until his second marriage to Lady Pansy Pakenham some 20 years later.

Lamb returned to England, and by the end of 1910 had taken the redoubtable socialite Lady Ottoline Morrell as one of his many mistresses – much to the mortification of Lytton, who was already smitten by the wild bohemian. Lamb undoubtedly exercised a Svengali-like hypnosis over many women with his strongly masculine appeal – he had none of the mild effeminacy of Brooke, and his good looks were more straightforwardly sexy. He traded on his reputation as a heartless philanderer, causing Virginia Stephen to write of his 'evil goat's eyes'. By the end of 1911 his liaison with Lady Ottoline was running out of steam – she was a decade older than he, and was beginning her affair with Bertrand Russell. For his part, Lamb was wearying of her domineering possessiveness, which included providing him with a studio near her own house at Garsington, outside Oxford. But his relationship with Ottoline and the hard bohemian years with John's ménage had left him with a taste for the company of the well-off and the good things of life.

When he met Ka in the autumn of 1911, she looked like a heaven-sent opportunity to the worldly man on the make: wealthy, indulgent to her friends, vaguely bohemian, and above all sexually susceptible yet naive. He decided to move in fast, and did not hesitate when her invitation to join the Lulworth party reached him via Lytton.

This was the situation that faced Brooke when he arrived at Lulworth on 28 December. Almost all the odds were stacked against him: the personnel of the party was decidedly Bloomsbury rather than Neo-Pagan, with a trio of Stracheys (Marjorie, Lytton and James); Maynard Keynes and Duncan Grant. The only paid-up Neo-Pagans there were Ka and Justin Brooke. Two newcomers both posed a deadly threat to Brooke's peace of mind. First, there was the young Ferenc Békássy, his rival for Noel's affections. At King's Békássy had been taken up by the predatory Keynes, who was already angling for the youthful Hungarian to become the youngest-ever Apostle – a manoeuvre which bore fruit a month later.

Much more disturbing to Brooke, however, was the shattering news that Lamb was to join the party. It will be recalled that James Strachey had held him up to Brooke as a skilled practitioner of coitus interruptus, and Brooke must have seen him from the outset as a potent sexual threat – a ruthless philanderer whose experience and sexual expertise were sure to outshine his own. For once Brooke faced being eclipsed by a darker star than he.

No sooner had Brooke arrived in the familiar surroundings of

Churchfield House, the lodgings where the main participants were staying, than he took to his bed, ostensibly with flu aggravated by exhaustion. His friends noticed that he was silent and withdrawn, but they were growing used to his 'moods' and did not seem unduly concerned. The exact sequence of events that triggered Brooke's dormant neuroses into an emotional explosion is still the subject of rumour, but the general outlines are clear.

On Saturday 30 December Lytton received a telegram from Lamb, who had been visiting the Augustus John clan at nearby Parkstone. Lamb announced his imminent arrival at the local railway station at Wool, and Lytton obediently trotted off in a horse and carriage to meet him and bring him back to the Cove Cottage Inn. By all accounts, Ka was almost delirious at the prospect of the arrival of her new conquest. She was an outdoors woman, and loved Lulworth, as Gwen recalled of her exactly one year before: 'She pulled on great boots and laughed in the wind . . . I remember her, standing on the very edge of the cliff, her crimson skirt whirling in the wind, her head tied up in a blue handkerchief, and the gulls screaming below.' This year it would be Brooke doing the screaming.

Almost as soon as he arrived, Henry either carried off or was snapped up by Ka, and the pair disappeared for a long walk along the seashore. It is possible that they had sex there and then, but more probably confined themselves to mild petting. At any rate the effects on Ka were deeply stirring. Early the following day, Sunday 31 December, taking her courage in both hands, she braved Brooke's wrath and went to his room to tell all. She was falling deeply in love with Lamb, she confessed; and when a distraught Brooke demanded to know why, she advanced the lame reasons that he was older than them (by three years) and shared the same Christian name as her late and beloved father.

The effect of the news on Brooke was immediate and devastating: desperately he pleaded, even demanded, that Ka drop this mad infatuation with the man he would always henceforth refuse to name, merely calling him, with hatred and contempt, 'the creature'. (Jeeringly, Lamb would return the compliment, referring to Brooke as 'the cauliflower' – apparently a dig at his rural enthusiasms.) Forgetting in an instant his three-year romance with Noel and all its extravagant promises, Brooke abjectly begged Ka to marry him. Shocked that this proposal should be so obviously born of panic rather than passion, Ka curtly refused; and she also turned down flat Brooke's next demand – that she should never see Lamb again. She had every intention of doing so, she said defiantly; indeed she wanted to marry him when he was free.

Lamb himself had other ideas. He was ready for a flirtation, and if possible an affair, with Ka, but her sudden enthusiasm for him and for marriage thoroughly alarmed him. As soon as the weekend was over, he lost no time in slipping back to London, leaving Lytton as his agent in place at Lulworth to report the continuing reverberations of the explosion he had unleashed. Lytton, too, was worried by the evident consequences his malicious little games had had: pulling the emotional strings of his friends was meat and drink to him in his role as puppeteer-in-chief to the young literati. But this time the game had clearly got out of hand. Swiftly he used all his charm and guile to dissuade Ka from following Lamb to London, advising her instead to take up the role of nurse to Brooke, who was clearly in agonizing need of his ministrations.

Brooke, too, lost little time in following his rival's retreating footsteps and beating a path away from Lulworth, which, from a cosy cocoon of quietude, had become an amphitheatre of agony. On New Year's Day 1912, a Monday, Brooke accompanied James, who was taking a train to London. The two friends walked east along the top of the Purbeck hills, oblivious to the spectacular coastal scenery as Brooke agonized aloud over the weekend's events. When they reached the gap in the hills that enfolds the charming village of Corfe Castle, James caught the London train, leaving Brooke to push on, alone, along the ridge to Studland, the village set amid sand dunes where his old friends Gwen and Jacques Raverat were on a painting holiday.

Here Brooke repeated his tale of woe – a chronicle made the more poignant for Gwen and Jacques by their own recent eternal-triangle entanglement with Ka. Presumably on their advice, since they saw Ka and Brooke as natural partners, he returned to Lulworth in a desperate bid to patch things up with Ka, by now the only female left in the party, which, following more comings and goings, consisted of four homosexual Apostles – Lytton Strachey, Maynard Keynes, Gerald Shove and Harry Norton – and the increasingly incapacitated Brooke. Lytton's letters to Lamb told of the unfolding drama. On 4 January he wrote:

> Ka came and talked to me yesterday, between tea and dinner. It was rather a difficult conversation, but she was very nice and very sensible. It seemed to me clear that she was what is called 'in love' with you – not with extreme violence so far, but quite distinctly. She is longing to marry you. She thinks you may agree, but fears, with great conscientiousness, that it might not be good for you. I felt at moments, while she was with me – so good and pink and agreeable – that there was more hope in that scheme than I'd thought before. But the more

I consider, the more doubtful it grows. I can't believe that you're a well-assorted couple – can you? If she was really your wife, with a home and children, it would mean a great change in your way of living, a lessening of independence – among other things a much dimmer relationship with Ottoline. This might be worth while – probably would be – if she was an eminent creature, who'd give you a great deal; but I don't think she is that. There seems no touch of inspiration in her; it's as if she was made somehow or other on rather a small scale (didn't you say that?). I feel it's unkind to write this about Ka, and it's too definite, but I must try and say what I think . . . Henry, I almost believe the best thing she could do now would be to marry Rupert straight off. He is much nicer than I had thought him. Last night he was there and was really charming – especially with her. Afflictions seem to have chastened him, and I did feel – it was evident . . . they seemed to fit together so naturally – even the Garden-City-ishness.

'The Garden City' is Lytton's superior way of describing Brooke and Ka's shared Fabianism – a reference to the current socialist experiment in bringing high-minded, teetotal vegetarianism to suburbia in the form of the Garden Cities of Letchworth and Welwyn in Hertfordshire. More importantly, the letter clears Lytton of Brooke's subsequent charge that introducing Lamb into their charmed circle at Lulworth was all a vile homosexualist plot to destroy the pure relationship between Ka and Brooke. For a long time Brooke refused to believe the simple truth: that it was Ka's own work, and that Lytton had merely been a convenient tool, a tethered goat to tempt down the tiger – or in this case, the Lamb.

The following day, 5 January, Lytton sounded a note of alarm:

The situation, though, seems to be getting slightly grim . . . Rupert is besieging her – I gather with tears and desperation – and sinking down in the intervals pale and shattered. I wish I could recommend her to console him . . . As for Rupert – it's like something in a play. But you know his niceness is now certain – poor thing! I never saw anyone so different from you – in *caractère*. 'Did he who made the Lamb make thee?' I sometimes want to murmur to him. But I fear the jest would not be well received.

Lytton was right. A distraught Brooke was going from bad to worse. But if the puppet-master had seen some of his strings untied, he at once attempted to refasten them. By the following day, January 6, he was advising Lamb to drop Ka and allow Brooke to possess the field:

If you're not going to marry her, I think you ought to reflect a good deal before letting her become your mistress. I've now seen her fairly often and on an intimate footing, and I can hardly believe that she's suited to the post. I don't see what either of you could really get out of it except the pleasures of the obelisk. With you even these would very likely not last long, while with her they'ld probably become more and more of a necessity, and also be mixed up with all sorts of romantic desires which I don't think you'ld ever satisfy. If this is true it would be worth while making an effort to put things on a merely affectionate basis, wouldn't it? I think there's quite a chance that . . . everything might blow over, and that she might even sink into Rupert's arms. Can you manage this?

Lytton need not have worried. The cold-hearted and cynical Lamb was well capable of extracting himself from a situation in which his fishy emotions were not engaged. He cruelly asked Lytton to play Cupid between Ka and Brooke – and even offered to preside over their nuptials in a nearby Garden City. As for Lytton's motivation, it seems clear that he had briefly considered making Ka, with her recent experience of such triangular matches, the third point in a love triangle with Lamb – exactly the formula he later achieved with Dora Carrington and Ralph Partridge. Often attracted to heterosexual men, he saw that a sure way of keeping close to Lamb was to exert influence over the woman in his life. But on closer inspection, he decided that Ka was not intellectually or imaginatively fit for the post, and thought instead it would be more suitable to yoke her to a man without either bodily or intellectual attractions for him – Brooke.

On the same day as Lytton's last letter to Lamb, Brooke wrote from Lulworth to Noel. His tone is entirely different from his previous effusions – terse, anxious, with none of the playful silliness or ardent exaggerations of the past:

> I have been ill and feeling very tired: and as the days go by I get worse. Also, I can't get my plans settled even for the nearest future, and I don't know what I shall be feeling in even two or three days. It isn't your 'fault' this time! In addition to all the other horrors, there's now a horrible business between me & Ka, – we're hurting each other, clumsily, as one does. I'm worn out by it . . . I'm very sorry I've been such a nuisance, – to you & everybody. Please forget me entirely till I'm decent & well again if ever I am. Be – be Noel: which means such good & greatness. Good bye.

Seriously alarmed by Brooke's state, his friends at Lulworth – who would soon, owing to his deluded state, be rapidly turned into enemies

– sent for Gwen and Jacques Raverat from Studland. They collected him and conveyed him to London, where an urgent appointment was made with a Harley Street doctor specializing in 'nerves' – Dr Maurice Craig. Two months afterwards, when Brooke had regained some sort of precarious temporary equilibrium, he recalled his condition at Lulworth as he slid down the slope towards actual insanity: 'a week or so in the most horrible kind of Hell; without sleeping or eating – doing nothing but suffering the most violent mental tortures. It was purely mental; but it reacted on my body to such an extent that after the week I could barely walk.'

In this sad state he was taken to Dr Craig's consulting rooms. The doctor was something of a specialist, too, in counselling Britain's afflicted intellectuals – he was to be consulted by Leonard Woolf about Virginia's increasingly serious psychotic episodes. In the dawn of modern psychiatric medicine, the weapons at Craig's disposal to treat Brooke's condition were rudimentary: he diagnosed 'severe mental breakdown' – which was blindingly obvious to everyone – and added for good measure the extraneous information that his patient was 'hypersensitive and introspective' – again a deduction of almost Holmesian perspicacity. He prescribed complete physical rest, an absence of all mental work or intellectual effort, and a bizarre diet of milk, stout and a disgusting-sounding concoction described by Brooke to Hugh Dalton as 'compressed bullocks' blood!'

The regime was known as 'stuffing' and lasted for up to two months. The rationale was elementary: depressed people got thin and neglected to eat (Brooke had lost a stone over the previous month or so), and therefore the way to restore them to bodily health and mental vigour was to insist they ate as much as possible, as often as possible, and took little or no exercise. Brooke described it thus: 'My nerve specialist's treatment is successful and in a way pleasant, "aber etwas langweilig" ['but somewhat boring']. I have to eat as much as I can get down, with all sorts of extra patent foods and pills, milk and stout. I have to have breakfast in bed about 10 every day, go to bed early, never take any exercise, walk never more than two miles, and do no kind of brain-work.'

Where then could Brooke go to achieve the peace and careful supervision he needed? The answer was obvious: the Ranee was on the French Riviera on a long winter vacation. Informed of her son's condition, she summoned him to join her – an idea that had been in the air anyway, before Lulworth. He just had the time to squeeze in a brief visit to Noel at Limpsfield Chart, and then the Raverats put him on the boat train to Paris at Victoria. Ka, too, the ostensible cause of his collapse, was there. Using some emotional blackmail, he had managed to extract a promise from her to meet him in Munich at an unspecified time – but soon. As the train moved out, he clung to that hope – for the moment it was all he had to cling to. He was descending through the dark.

16

Madness

No one can say with certainty whether Brooke, in the months that followed Lulworth, actually crossed the thin line that divides the sane from the insane. His condition was too changeable, shifting, to be defined as insanity by any modern yardstick. There were times when he appeared well and seemed to be functioning normally. But there were other times when his behaviour was irrational, delusional, crazy – in a word, insane. It was not all waste. During this period, along with his raving, foaming denunciations of those who he believed had foully betrayed him, he wrote letters of passionate, poetic intensity – indeed, some of the most moving and eloquent love-letters in the language. If they were tinged with madness – as he himself believed – who are we to deny it?

The seemingly trivial incident that had touched off this psychotic episode cannot be considered in isolation. Brooke had suffered reverses in love before – indeed, his run-in with Noel over Ferenc Békássy could have been even more damaging than his quarrel with Ka over Lamb, given his long devotion to the youngest Olivier. The factors that made the Ka imbroglio act as a catalyst to push him over the edge were his fear that Lamb was a more potent and attractive proposition than he, who had been used to so much adulation for so long; and the uneasy suspicion, growing towards a manic certainty, that the whole business was some nefarious plot that had been carefully laid by Lytton and his Apostolic and Bloomsbury friends, in order to trap him and expose him as a fool. In this scenario Ka was not a forceful and independent woman with her own plans and hopes for her amatory and marital future, but at best a poor naive tool, or at worst a criminal whore who had dirtied his deepest love.

Brooke's rigidly moralistic principles rebelled at the thought that a homosexual like Lytton could take an interest in, and be adept at, influencing the love lives of heterosexuals. For him, homosexuality had its place – with his own history he could hardly deny it – but that place was to be strictly confined to the public-school dormitory or Oxbridge common rooms. It had to be cloaked in the secrecy that he had learned at his mother's knee. It is significant that he turned his rage, not on the obvious object – Henry Lamb – but on Lytton, who became the villain of the piece in his own disordered mind. Gradually this paranoia spread out like an evil stain until it touched not only Lytton, but his circle of friends, and beyond them whole strata of imaginary foes: feminists, Jews, pacifists, homosexuals – a world of enemies who were working to break down the world of purity, youth, freshness and frank honesty that Brooke imagined he embodied. Even after the acute phase of his paranoia had passed, these delusions remained, and in many ways he never recovered from that single disastrous weekend in Lulworth; certainly, when he emerged from the dark tunnel of his madness, he was not the same man who had gone into it.

Gwen and Jacques had been so worried by Brooke's evident unfitness to travel alone, that they arranged for one of the only people he knew in Paris – none other than his recent flame, Elisabeth van Rysselberghe – to meet his train and look after him before putting him on a connecting train to the Riviera. Given Brooke and Elisabeth's complex feelings for each other and their troubled sexual history, Elisabeth seems an odd choice of nurse to counsel the lovelorn and deeply disturbed man, but she rose to the occasion with disinterested devotion.

Late on the night of 9 January, Brooke's train pulled into the Gare du Nord, where he was met by Elisabeth, who took him to her parents' apartment in Rue Laugier. She put him to bed, and while he slept, she changed his money, reserved a seat on a Nice-bound train and wired the Ranee with the time of his arrival. Awaking after eight hours, he flipped through a book by André Gide, a travelling gift from Jacques – with no premonition that the solicitous woman whose hospitality he was enjoying would one day bear a child to the unconventional novelist.

He then gave way to his overriding obsession and started the first of many letters he would write over the next weeks and months to Ka: 'I want so to turn altogether to you and forget everything but you, and lose myself in you, and give and take everything – for a time. Afterwards – doesn't matter. But I'm so wanting that security of Heaven. I'll make myself so fine for you. And I'll find and multiply all the many splendours in you.' This passage presages many of the themes he would harp on continually in his correspondence with Ka. He openly needs her 'Heavenly' security; he has to 'make himself fine' for her – like a repentant drunk reforming, or an athlete preparing for some gruelling marathon; and he will be the one to discover Ka's 'splendours' – implying, perhaps, that she is incapable of doing so alone – it is to Brooke that the shining task belongs – whereas her role, presumably, is to be the passive vessel that receives his poured-out love.

As he looked ahead to his long journey south, only her vision would console him: 'If the carriage is hot and horrible tonight, I shall think of your eyes and hands and mouth and body and voice, and sleep instantly and happily'. Like a baby, one is tempted to silently add. But again, he returns to his insistent theme: this 'love' is to the greater glory of Brooke rather than its ostensible recipient. In by now familiar terms he tells her: 'I'll give you things you never dreamt of and you'll make me the wonderfullest person in the world . . . I love you so. I kiss your lips.'

Dimly realizing that Ka might be wondering exactly what his relations were with the woman who was caring for him – for jealousy can cut both ways – Brooke added reassuringly: 'I find myself so unmoved and kindly with her [Elisabeth]. Don't mind my being here for a day. I'm not loving Elisabeth.' The helpful Elisabeth conveyed him to the station and put him on the train for Nice that same night. He found himself sharing a carriage with a duchess and her maid, and the French painter Pierre Bonnard. An anxious Ranee, accompanied by Alfred, met him at the station and took him along the coast to Cannes, a balmy and genteel resort much frequented by well-heeled English visitors.

His mother had reserved a room with a balcony overlooking the sea at the Grand Hôtel du Pavillon, and Brooke lost no time in describing the view in another letter to Ka: 'Outside there are large numbers of tropical palms, a fountain, laden orange trees and roses. There's an opal sea and jagged hills with amazing sunsets behind.' The Ranee took charge of her son's care in typical no-nonsense fashion, but found the time to try to sell copies of his *Poems* to other English guests 'and bawling English with incredible success to crumbling foreigners'. As an awed Brooke reported: 'She has also entirely subdued eight solitary and separate maiden ladies in this hotel.'

Forbidden to read more than two hours a day, he passed his time in playing Patience and attempting to execute watercolours – and in writing an unceasing stream of letters to Ka:

I find myself – what *is* this degradation? – wanting you at each moment . . . I've such a longing to get out of myself, my tight and dirty self – to put it all out in the sun, the fat sun. And it's so hard to tell the truth, to give oneself wholly away, even to you. So one wants to chatter and pour everything out . . . and then perhaps the truth may slip out with it . . . I've never told anyone anything, hardly. 'Secretive'.

So the confession was torn out of him – in stark contrast to his simple, open-hearted image, as he well knew, the real Brooke was a covert creature of guile and malice – terrified of giving his secret self away to another. In his extremity he was driven to admit the truth of the repressions that were seething out of the depths of his mind, and to make a fumbling bid to reach and own up to the woman he had chosen, however unwillingly, for the dual role of passionate lover and comforting mother.

He wills himself to put some sort of restraint on his verbal outpouring – 'I *will* be continent' – and concentrate on getting well, but his best resolves are always at the mercy of his turbulent emotions: 'Sometimes as I lie and pant like an overfed puppy, thoughts of you and Munich and – I don't know what, storm so irresistibly in; and I can't help feeling such amazing energy and life in all my limbs and mind, that I'm racked to be up and off to meet you at the Hauptbahnhof.' Besides the symptoms of paranoid delusion, Brooke was displaying classic signs of manic depression. His ravings were also shot through with shafts of beautiful poetry: 'You go burning through every vein and inch of me, till I'm all Ka; and my brain's suddenly bursting with ideas and lines and flames, and my body's all for you. "Sh-sh". I hold myself in, and wait, and grow fatter . But I'm certainer than ever that I'm, possibly, opening new Heavens, like a boy sliding open the door into a big room; trembling between wonder and certainty.'

His self-analysis continued with the realization that he had fallen between the two stools of his desire: Ka and Noel, and possibly lost them both: 'I know now how beastly I was both to you and to Noel; and that one must choose, being human – one thing at a time. I couldn't give to either of two such people what I ought, which is "all". Now I've got a sort of peace, I think; because I shall be able.'

Every now and then, Brooke would come up for air from the depths in which he was drowning, and convince himself that he was swimming back to sanity and safety: 'I'm more sane, a little, about the world. Oh, far from sane: but better. I'm convinced that sanity is the most important thing there is. I'm so hampered and spoilt because there are things I dare not face, and depths I daren't look into.' The terror of lurking madness is a constant leitmotif – Brooke was plunging through the abyss of which Gerard Manley Hopkins had written:

O the mind, mind has mountains; cliffs of fall
Frightful, sheer, no-man-fathomed . . .
Hold them cheap may he who ne'er hung there.

It was Ka's so obviously solid sanity that was one of her main attractions for him. Afraid of being whirled away by the demons that beset him, Brooke clung to her voluminous skirts: 'By God, you're sane, with your splendid strength and beauty. But I've been half-mad, alone. Oh, it's all mixed up with this chastity, and everything's a whirl, and still I'm mad and tiny and frightened.' Recalling the agonies of Jacques Raverat, torn between Ka and Gwen, Brooke compared their cases and, naturally, emerged, in his own mind, as the winner: 'Jacques, being Jacques, went mad for half a year. I, being tougher and slower, defied chastity a bit longer, and then, naturally, would take it worse . . . It'll be a curious comment on civilization or women or something if I do go [mad].' It is a curious comment on Brooke's overweening egotism, that he should appear to think that the world's concerns revolved around his own emotional turbulence.

Like a rider on a switchback railway, he plunged and soared between highs and lows, sunny optimism and blackest despair: 'But I'm clambering to sane light. You've given me such sanity already – sometimes when you didn't know it. But you will give me more. I'll be able to do everything and look at everything if you'll give me that strength. Oh, give it me Ka!'

He fondly fantasized about Ka going on her humdrum rounds at home – attending a safe play in Oxford, and looking after her somewhat dependent sisters. In reality, while doing her best to humour him in her letters, Ka was continuing to pursue Henry Lamb. Unknown to Brooke, she had dinner with the painter while he was making his farewell visit to Noel at Limpsfield Chart, and she continued to haunt him all across artistic London, when Brooke happily imagined her looking forward to their reunion in Munich.

However, Ka, was a creature of her word, and on Monday 15 January, the same day that Brooke, leaning on his brother's arm, was allowed to take his first tottering steps outside the hotel, Ka was seen off by Justin Brooke at Victoria on her way to Germany. The mere knowledge that she was out of 'the creature's' way seems to have cheered Rupert, and his letters become quite chatty – telling her, with his usual bossy didacticism precisely what shows she should visit in Munich, and even patronizingly giving her a run-down on the correct way to board a Bavarian tram: 'It's so important. The gate *lifts*. You might have an accident.' In all this, Ka is treated like an incompetent, dim child, while Brooke is the wise father. The exact opposite of their real roles.

With their meeting in Munich now becoming a real prospect rather than a remote possibility, his thoughts began to focus on her sexual charms, and the chance that she would 'give herself' to him and relieve him of his burdensome heterosexual virginity, which was, at the age of 24, becoming such an embarrassment that it had played no small part in driving him mad. One letter dwelt on a memory of her in a low-cut dress: 'I looked at the firm and lovely place where your deep breasts divided and grew out of the chest and went down under your dress . . . and I was suddenly very giddy, and physically hit with the glimpse of a new sort of beauty that I'd not quite known of.' When Ka pointed out that up to the recent past he had given little idea of the physical passion for her he now professed so strongly, he replied in woolly confusion:

> It's funny, I still think, your idea that one doesn't – or that I didn't – love you physically, very strongly. When I felt last year, my whole conduct was wronging you, it wasn't, you know, that! It was that it'd come over me that I perhaps only loved you physically and very much as a friend, – that I'd still to "only connect" lust and an immense comradeship. But I didn't imagine I hadn't those, you know! It's possibly true that mere prettiness and champagne stir the penis most. But physical passion includes the penis but is more, it's hands and thighs and mouth that are shaken by it as well. And that's stirred by different things: strong beauty and passion and – undefined things.

In his case, the proverb that 'absence makes the heart grow fonder' was magnified tenfold: 'Loving you implies a geometrical progression . . . One gets worse and worse. You grow on one, so. It's a pervading, irresistible thing, "Ka".' A memory of Mrs Neeve and her insect powder at the Old Vicarage provided an image for his love: 'It's like having black-beetles in the house. "I've got Ka in the body . . . My dear, I've tried everything . . . Put down carbolic. My dear, Yes! . . ." So, I tell you, I get frightened. Where's it to stop? Am I to plunge deeper and deeper, for ever? Damn you! And it's so nice too – sometimes nice even if you don't care and won't have anything to do with me (save pity). That's queer. I'm happy; but also I'm frightened, Ka.'

The disturbing thing about this passage – and many similar ones could be cited – is the ease with which Brooke skips and slides between praising Ka and – literally – damning her. And then, a paragraph later, he is covering her with treacly praise once again, picking out a stray sentence from one of Ka's letters describing a meeting with Virginia Stephen: 'Who'd have thought that you had a prose-style that was a superior combination of the

Old Testament and poor Mr Wilde. "Virginia was more fantastic than an army of apes and peacocks." What an image! *What* a mind! God! I wish I could write like that!'

He imagines himself to be in telepathic contact with her: 'On Friday night I think you were being tired, somehow. I had the horrors, then; so I think may be something was happening to you. Were you . . . But I had the horrors. And again, curiously, this afternoon . . .' In this watchful, controlling mode, he even accompanied her in imagination as she crossed the Channel and 'crashed through Germany'. But unease was growing again. He left this letter open, and following a return of night terrors took it up again:

> Damn! A Bad Night. It followed on Depression yesterday. For five hours yesterday I was convinced that it was all something right inside the head, and that I was either going to have a stroke, or else going slowly mad. It may be true: and one's so damnably helpless. Any other illness, one can suddenly shut one's teeth and one's hands and throw it off. One can say 'I'm not going to be ill any more' and one isn't. But madness – means that it isn't up to 'one' to say anything. And yesterday (and part of today) I felt a cloud in my head and about me that seemed to mean it too certainly.

The recent memory of his father's death from a cerebral haemorrhage led to fears that he would go the same way. In a letter to James Strachey he repeats: 'I imagine . . . I shall get a stroke this summer.' But now there was also the all-too-present terror of his living parent to contend with. The Ranee was blissfully ignorant of the exact cause of her son's breakdown – she put it down to his overwork on his Webster dissertation. But his continual letter-writing, and the answers he received, could not be completely concealed and she began to sniff a rat – or rather a woman. With her ingrained anti-Olivier prejudice, she darkly suspected Bryn of impeding Brooke's recovery.

Following his normal course of conduct in the inquisitive presence of his mother, Brooke adopted several stratagems to avoid revealing the truth. He was not so ill that he did not relish the old pleasures of secrecy and deception when it came to dealing with his mother's nosiness. Pretending he was more well than he was, he even submitted to attending a classical concert at the Cannes Casino: 'It's part of a long scheme to hoodwink the Ranee.' The idea was to soften up Mrs Brooke sufficiently for her to give him permission (and money) to accomplish his planned mission to Munich – under the guise of visiting his Rugby friend Hugh Russell-Smith, who happened to be there. Meanwhile, Ka's 'kind cold letters', alternately dashing and raising his hopes, kept him in an agony of uncertainty.

Depressed by one of Ka's missives from Munich, in which, rather than offering him the unconditional support and adoration he craved, she quoted Frances Cornford's 'Young Apollo' verse about him as if to remind him of the Brooke he once had been, but no longer was, or wished to be, he responded with whining self-pity:

> I'm still mad and scary . . . Oh, Ka, I wanted to come so strong and clean and sane and well to Munich and to pay back a bit by helping you . . . I could. But I'm not getting better . . . And I don't want to come ill and foolish and beastly as I was, to weaken and worry you and sponge on your strength. And yet I *can't* keep always away and let everything drift by and get worse and worse, for not seeing you. What shall I do? I think the sight and presence of you might put me right again in a day or two. It's so ghastly lying here, struggling and thinking, fruitlessly, while these grey days go by . . .

Despite his insistence that he had no wish to sponge on Ka's strength, he incessantly harped on his obsession that she, and only she, could save him from madness or death: 'I've no faith and no strength. If only you were with me an hour, I'd get both; if you were with me a day, I'd be well again; a year, and I'd be the most wonderful person in the world . . .' He looked back in sadness at the carefree Brooke that Ka and Gwen had known in those already distant Cambridge days:

> Gwen once thought me 'sane' did she? I've always enjoyed that healthy, serene, Apollo-golden-haired, business. But, my dear, our relationship's based a bit deeper! My face – do what you like with it. But you, and only you in the world, understand my horrible nature. It's so importantly my humiliation and my – safety, joy, what is it called? I may be, and shall be, perhaps, sane and everything else one day. But, the dirty abyss I am now – I've let you see. Don't pretend you don't know me, fool.

There is a sinister foretaste here of Brooke's later rejection of the woman he now appeared to worship so abjectly. In his desperation he had indeed revealed the reverse of his 'golden boy' image – allowing Ka a long look into the seething, festering depths of his 'dirty abyss'. This was what he would never forgive her. Even now, as he closed his long, bruising letter, he wondered whether he had let her see too much: 'I suppose I oughtn't to post this. I think I shall. I'll write better . . . does one still say "with love"?'

On Saturday 27 January he wrote to James Strachey in quite another tone; but this letter too contained a revealing insight into his desperate mental condition: 'The Ranee, mixing my Ovaltine, was alarmed to see me get out of bed a few minutes past ten last night & stand, hands folded and head bent, on my lips nothing "roby [sic], – buzz . . . vacuum . . ." they framed. She made no comment. It's part (I've discovered) of the Treatment to pretend that nothing I do is out of the way. Daresay I often get out of bed in the worser moments.'

He told James that he doubted whether he would ever return to 'fair health' again. James had hardly helped Brooke's recovery by sending him a series of gossipy letters retailing the doings of the Apostles, including the election to their ranks of the young pretender to Noel Olivier's hand, Ferenc Békássy. This elevation of his rival, made at the behest of Maynard Keynes, who was in love with Békássy, was one more wedge hammered into the widening rift between Brooke and his oldest friends. But, he told James, he no longer cared: 'The gloom of Cannes is a trifle lightened for me by the reflection that "gott sei dank" ['thank God'] I've done with all that.' Brooke was washing his hands of his old self – he had yet to face up to the near impossible task of creating a new one.

Cautioning James – in vain, for his loose-tongued friend shared his family's love of malicious rumour-mongering – not to 'spread it to your grinning fellow-countrymen' – Brooke reported on the details of his painfully slow climb out of the abyss. During the fortnight he had been in Cannes, he said, he had regained seven pounds of the weight he had lost. But he was 'sick of this place' and his invalid existence. His overpowering desire was to cut loose from the soft tentacles of his mother, which seemed to be drawing him down into childlike dependence: 'I'm going to try more violent methods. Kill or cure, for me . . .' Ominously, there were also signs of his growing paranoia and a total rejection of the past that had made him: 'I shall, with great pleasure give orders that England is to be wiped out, *sunk*, and *deleted*.'

The hatred he expressed for his country was rather his sense of shame at the place that had witnessed his complete collapse, for which he refused to take any personal blame:

Was I fairly beastly in Lulworth & in London? I'm very sorry. I really wasn't responsible for my behaviour. I see now in a dim way that I have been infinitely ill for months and more than infinitely ill during this month. I got far worse after that Swanage journey . . . [a reference to the walk across the Purbeck peninsula that he had taken with James after Ka's announcement of her love for Lamb] I

didn't know one could be like that for days and days without intermission –
even Jews sleep. You were really well out of that grey hole. I was entirely
unpleasant to everybody. The lucky presence of Cox (an admirable nurse)
prevented me committing suicide in the drawing room, out of spleen . . .

Here again is a worrying storm signal of Brooke's worsening paranoia – his
surfacing anti-Semitism and his revulsion from Ka. His slights sit oddly with
the torrent of words of love that he was daily pouring out to her.

No sooner had he sent off this jet of spleen to James, than he began to
fret that his long letter to Ka had been a cry too far. Knowing her kindly,
nurturing nature as he did, he started to worry that she might suddenly
show up at Cannes, and expose his duplicity to the Ranee. That would
never do. He started to write another letter to her in calmer, more matter-
of-fact tones, reporting rosily on his daily doings. But the hysterical
undertone of guilt continued: he had been a 'devil of ingratitude' to her and
was 'dirty, dirty, dirty'. However, he had cleansed his filthy self with a nice
hot bath which had left him feeling 'radiant'.

I almost rushed to you. I looked at myself, drying, in the glass, and I thought
my body was beautiful and strong, and that I was keeping it and making it
splendid for you. And I know that if I rested for a night on your breasts, and
then caught fire from you, my mind and heart too would be able to give you a
million things that only I in the world knew of and could give. I was so happy.
I was happy thinking of Munich . . .

As he went from rampant narcissism to cringing abasement in almost the
same sentence, it was clear that Brooke was still very far from stability or
the glowing health he boasted of: 'And then at other times I lie and *ache* to
twist my thoughts on to Shakespeare, a poem, anything; and they always
go back to the blackness, till I can't bear it and from thinking of suicide
then, think of it immediate, to cut the thing clear and set you free from a
fool.'

Ill as he was, he was still slyly determined to outwit his mother and get
to Munich and Ka's imagined salvation by hook or by crook: 'Eh, I *do* want
your presence, you know, to keep me fine and sane, just now. But tonight
I *know* I shall get to Munich. I can see the Ranee thinks she's going to keep
a hand on me for a month or six weeks. But I give her ten days at the
outside. I shall have to be beastly to her, I suppose.'

He continued to fantasize about Ka's suddenly discovered charms: 'Oh
my dear Ka, Ka with that particular hair and head and neck, and a certain

walk, and a special way that clothes have of going down over the hip, and strong hands, and a hundred other things, Ka peering about and saying "Hoo!", Ka whom I know so very well, and whom I've been so beastly to, and whom I love so . . .' Imagining her 'peering about' in Munich, he gives a sketch of his own more prosaic life in Cannes – catching a glimpse of the Tory statesman Arthur Balfour and the novelist Arnold Bennett ('England in a nutshell') and taking tea with the Ranee – while all the time nerving himself up to break the news to his mother of his impending flight to Munich.

Among the news from Ka that was unnerving him was a worrying chance encounter with a young woman he had met there the previous year. The girl – Joanna – claimed to have been in love with Brooke and to have kissed his cheeks: 'Damn Joanna and my cheeks. I never even let her kiss them. Why am I old and dead and ugly, and why do they think me a lovely child.' As ever he was put out at being taken for younger than he was, and annoyed at the effeminacy noticed by the elderly residents of the hotel: 'old Mrs Woolaston . . . thought Alfred and I were twins aged eighteen, she confided in mother . . . after I'd tottered to bed. "He has a skin like a girl's – He looks very like a girl . . . in his Face" put in Miss Barclay. God! God!'

Like his beloved Keats, who had been given a nightcap sewn by Fanny Brawne to comfort him in his final, fatal exile in Rome, Brooke wore a loud yellow tie – a present from Ka – to remind him of his love. Naturally, it annoyed the Ranee: 'She says it is "so conspicuous"' – and naturally, Brooke concocted a lie to explain away the offending garment: 'It is understood that . . . I bought it at Liberty's on my way through.'

Suddenly his relative equanimity was shattered by a telegram from Ka in which, thoroughly alarmed by his self-portrait as a suicidal madman, she announced her intention to descend on Cannes to succour and console him. Thoroughly alarmed and panicked himself – how on earth was he to explain this to an increasingly suspicious Ranee? – he pretended the wire was from James, and sneaked away from his half-tearful mother to send his own telegram in a bid to put Ka off: 'For heaven's sake don't come on account of me or my letters[.] Was mad and wicked[.] Other letters on way[.] Am much better . . .' Suddenly the big, bold lover had become the quivering schoolchild, scared to death of his mother's anger.

He followed this with an abject letter of self-abnegation: 'Just back to find your telegram. And now from telegraphing; I must send this tonight, in case you don't come: as I hope. For I diagnose that my beastly letter upset you. I'm worthy of treading to death in dung. I *was* ill, and am a bit; but I'm much better. I *will* get to Munich in a week . . .' The next three days passed in an agony of suspense for Brooke, who, with no further word from Ka to indicate whether she had got his wire in time to forestall her mission of mercy, was dreading her appearance at any moment at his hotel: 'If you suddenly appear I know I shall cry,' he wrote pathetically.

But the knowledge that the woman he meant to make his mistress might suddenly materialize in front of his mother gave him the courage to face the Ranee. He told her he had gone out to consult the travel agents Thomas Cook about the times of trains to Munich. The Ranee was outraged, insisting that Brooke was not well enough to travel and should stay on with her in Cannes for at least a month: 'I felt the old helplessness before authority creeping over me: and wished you had emerged from the morning train. But I aped cold astonishment and colder reserve. And she began to crumble. I conveyed that I hated Cannes, her, the sea; that I should rest superbly in Munich, so quiet and healthy. So battle's joined. She wants to wire Dr Craig for a forbiddance. By God, I *will* come.'

As he locked horns in a battle of wills with his mother, Brooke was reinforced at last by a telegram from Ka saying that she was still in Munich but was ready to meet him at some halfway point between there and Cannes – Milan, perhaps, or Verona. Galvanized into action, he decided upon Verona, and booked the train for the following Tuesday, 30 January – exactly one month after Lulworth. He placed total reliance and trust in Ka – she would, she must, heal him: 'Ka! It will be good. I shall be infinitely gay and well. I look Italian. You look merely German. Oh, but to see you again and touch you! We shall be splendid . . . You're going to make me so amazingly strong and fine. And I'm going to give you undreamt things . . . You're to be the Ranee and Dr Craig and everything else!' Ka would have been hardly human if she had not been daunted by the burden of responsibility that Brooke was hanging on her sturdy shoulders in place of her favoured rucksacks. But her yearning to be needed came to the fore again. She – mother, lover and psychiatrist too – would not fail him in his hour of need.

The final days in Cannes passed in a whirl of letters and telegrams finalizing the details of their meeting, and pacifying the anxious Ranee. Brooke's penultimate letter to Ka was filled with erotic longing – the spur which must surely have put the touch of steel in him as he doggedly negotiated his departure with his mother: 'I think of your gently strong soft body – my thoughts are entirely indecent and entirely clean. I see you with your head thrown back. I put my bare arm round your bare back; and my arm's infinitely strong and the curves of your back are the loveliest things in the world.'

Desperately, the Ranee used the excuse that he was not putting on weight with the expected rapidity to demand that he delay his departure. But it was too late. His ticket was purchased. They were on their way. His last letter to Ka read:

> Damn! Weight only 1/2lb up, in a week. Ranee sicker than ever. Your telegram has just come. (Ranee intercepted, but didn't read, of course. She's sure something's *up*.) All's right, then. You'll get there at 10, wander till 11.55 and then meet me. Verona. Tuesday.
>
> From noon on Tuesday, you're in command.
>
> Auf wiedersehen!
>
> . . . Till Tuesday. R I kiss you.

As Brooke's train chugged east along the Riviera Corniche, and then cut north-east through the Alpine tunnels and into the valleys of northern Italy, he must have willed its wheels onward. He was going towards his girl, the woman he had convinced himself would solve all his problems. Like a bridegroom to a wedding, a warrior to the battle, a patient to the operating table that would cut out his pain, he looked forward to this meeting more than to any other of his life.

As he leaned out of the train window, straining for his first glimpse of her face, his tousled locks thrashing in the slipstream, small eyes screwed up against the tears, he was not to know that the meeting he rushed towards would be as ill-fated as that of Shakespeare's star-crossed young lovers in the same city. Just before noon his train pulled into Verona. She was there.

17

Herr und Frau Brooke

As the lovers embraced on the station platform it quickly became apparent to Ka that the Ranee had been right – Brooke was in no condition to be alone, to travel or to undertake many of the marvels of love he had promised her. For the present, her role would be the accustomed task of nursemaid to a sickly child. Brooke was no Romeo, and she no Juliet. Almost immediately she took him to a chemist's shop to purchase various pills, placebos and tonics to steady his jangling nerves. Instead of a planned romantic trip to Venice, she took her charge, after a brief and dutiful glance at Verona's historic sites, straight back to Munich.

As they arrived in the city, preparations were being made for the Faschings-Fest carnival – the scene of Brooke's inconclusive erotic encounter with Elisabeth exactly one year before. These memories must have added to the strain on him as he contemplated the woman at his side, so long desired, who, unlike Elisabeth, seemed fully prepared to go to bed with him in all seriousness. The question was: was he up to it?

With a practicality worthy of the Ranee, Ka installed Brooke in the lodgings he had occupied the year before, and primed his landlady with the task of continuing to fatten the calf-child with his diet of Ovaltine, sweet beer and bromides. Diplomatically, she herself was staying with friends nearby. Brooke's continued weakness and the frenetic atmosphere of Fasching were convenient excuses to hold off the consummation that he had affected to want for so long.

After a week of concerts, masked balls and gallery-going but, as yet, no lovemaking, they made a short trip to Salzburg, just over the Austrian border, on 9 February. Once again, his courage failed him: he took to his bed all right, but with a fever rather than Ka. She sat up with him all night, mopping his brow, and they talked, endlessly circling around their problems.

They returned to Munich, and on 13 February an apparently restored Brooke wrote to James, apologizing for being out of touch and mysterious about his movements: 'Secretiveness, I think, grows to a monomania, as the bonds of the body are breaking, and all comes in sight. Poor Dad, towards the end, used to hide little pieces of string. I took the most elaborate pains to prevent anyone knowing where I was . . . I knew Cox would be here, prattling eight letters a day to England.' Significantly, given his sexual travails, he compared himself to 'a chap at Rugger, kicked in the balls, doubling up and vanishing'. Again referring to Ka sneeringly by her surname, he none the less admitted his utter dependence on her: 'I lean with all my weight on Cox. It is infinitely wicked, but I'm beyond morals. I really rather believe she's pulled me through. She is stupid enough for me to be lazy and silly enough for me to impose on her.'

It seems that a bare fortnight in Ka's company has been enough to turn the fire-breathing lover into a cross between a sneering schoolboy and a milk-guzzling infant. This letter, the first of many in a similar vein disparaging Ka to his friends, sends a chill shudder down the spine. Brooke was kidding himself, as well, that he was 'beyond morals': he was no amoral seducer *à la* Lamb – rather more of a randy boy afflicted by a fatal strait-jacket of moral repression. It was a combination fatal to his own happiness, and to those who tangled with him. But, in his huffing, puffing way, he boasted to James that he would do great things between Ka's sheets – or rather, between her mountainous Bavarian bolsters: 'I'll tell you . . . authentically and as a not too strict confidence, there's very little doubt now, but that it's going to stand. It may be rather a grubby affair in some ways, but it'll possess some surprising features. And if it does come down, by God, you'll hear of it. I'll give you something to chat about. Damn it, one lives only once, one may as well flaunt.'

As yet though, Brooke had very little to 'flaunt' about. He closed his letter with a smutty couplet about a woman masturbating with a candle – but his sniggering ignored the fact that he had yet to give Ka the chance to do anything more satisfying. Sexual frustration was only one reason for the increasing tension she was under: ministering to a demanding, infantile invalid was bad enough, but his fragile state had also prevented her from telling him the truth about her continuing love for Henry Lamb; an admission which, in her honest way, she was determined to make at the right moment.

The moment was further delayed by the untoward arrival in Munich of Hugh Popham, the dull fellow who was Bryn's most persistent suitor. He insisted on dogging their footsteps, and, since their affair was still a secret from most of their friends, they had to endure this. In any case it may have been a relief to Brooke – yet another excuse to put off the moment of truth.

But for Ka at least, her moment came, as Neo-Pagan moments often seemed to do, on the platform of a railway station. It was in Munich as, having at last shaken off the insensitive presence of Hugh, they awaited a train to the lakeside resort of Starnberg on Saturday 17 February. As gently as she could, she told him not only that she still loved Lamb, but that they had spent a weekend in each other's company at a house party given by Lady Ottoline Morrell at her country home at Garsington. To add insult to injury, she added that Lytton Strachey had also been among the guests.

Brooke was stupefied with horror. He worked out that his telepathic feeling that 'something was happening' to Ka on the night of Friday 12 January had been precisely the time that she had begun her house party with Lamb on her last weekend in England. Once again, all the horrors of Lulworth came flooding back with redoubled force. The emotions he had felt then, and had only begun to slough off after a month of the most bitter suffering, returned in their naked fury: shock, disbelief, betrayal, jealousy, fear, rage, dismay – one by one, like falling clubs, they crashed into him with dull thumps. So Ka did not love him after all; she admitted that she had only come to Munich on a quasi-medical mission of mercy to succour a friend – not a lover – in his hour of direst need. Instantly, the slow and halting progress that he had made in Cannes, the crawling journey from darkness to light, was swept away and he was plunged back into the pit.

His reaction, too, was the same as at Lulworth: Ka must be his; this time he did not propose marriage, only a more radical measure would fit the gravity of the case: she must sleep with him, then and there. At last Ka acquiesced. Her motives can only be guessed at – concern for Brooke's renewed agony must have been one factor; so too was her own state of what Brooke had referred to as her 'extraordinarily randy state of virginity'. In any event it was this night, 17–18 February, that Brooke finally lost his heterosexual virginity. A month after the momentous night, Brooke, writing to Ka, recalled the encounter in lyrical terms: 'I remember the softness of your body: and your breasts and your thighs and your cunt. I remember you all naked lying to receive me; wonderful in beauty. I remember the agony and joy of it all: that pleasure's like a sea that drowns you wave by wave . . .'

But Ka's 'betrayal' had etched a deeper mark on his tender mind than the pleasure gained by possessing her could confer. Ka did not yet know it, but by yielding to his entreaties and emotional blackmail, she had tolled the death-knell for their relationship before it had really begun. Brooke would never forgive her for loving another man, but paradoxically he would not forgive her either for giving herself to him. Deep within his disordered brain, the logic went: 'Ka has given herself to me; therefore she will give herself to another – to any other; therefore she is a whore, a loose feeble-minded woman; therefore I cannot marry her or even have her as my mistress.' The working-out of this process was to take many more months of pain, and to leave searing and lasting scars on both the protagonists. Indeed, it can be argued that neither ever fully recovered.

Meanwhile Ka had the reality of Brooke's renewed collapse to cope with – news of her desire for Lamb, plus the shock of sexual intercourse, had unmanned him quite. By the time they returned to Munich, and dropped in on his former landlady, the artist Clara Ewald, Brooke was in a sad state. The painter was shocked at his condition, compared to the carefree youth she had known a year before – the boyish Brooke caught in her portrait of that time. Now she beheld a pale and sagging figure, like a straw doll with the stuffing knocked out. Ka plied him with pills and potions at regular intervals, but when he rallied it was only to cover her with abuse and raging imprecations about her 'betrayal'.

Ka decided that it was profitless for them to remain in Munich. After their disastrous 'honeymoon' she was exhausted: three weeks in the company of a man who was half sick and fractious child and half raging lunatic had drained even her deep wells of sympathy and compassion. James Strachey was in the awkward, but to him delicious, position of being the confidant of both parties: both wrote to him giving their sides of the unfolding story. Ka confided that she was bringing Brooke home because she was at the end of her tether; she had to feed and care for him like a baby, although he retained an adult's capacity to wound and disturb. Once the decision to return had been made, Ka made the necessary travel arrangements with her usual efficiency and they left Munich on 21 February, arriving at Victoria the following day.

Brooke calmed down somewhat during the journey, having extracted a promise from Ka that she would return with him to Germany – to stay with Dudley Ward in Berlin sometime in the spring, when they would have another shot at living together as 'Herr und Frau Brooke' far from the prying eyes of their family and friends. In the meantime Brooke would return to Rugby for more rest and recuperation under the watchful care of the Ranee. Once he had parted from Ka, he began to feel a sense of guilt over his behaviour towards her. Writing to James the same evening, he asked: 'You've heard Ka brought me back? Have you seen her? Will you? I was so unpleasant on the journey that she became infinitely tired. Now

Hester [Ka's sister] cries all day. I suppose we shall slay that immense woman (K.) before the end of it.'

Brooke confessed himself 'restless', and, cooped up as he was with the baleful Ranee, the need for his friends – even an equivocal companion like James – instantly reasserted itself. He asked James to come up to Rugby – 'With luck you might hit one of my chirpy periods' – but continued to forswear his old haunts: 'I'm not ever coming to London. England is inevedibly [sic] beastly . . . I loathe England & being in it.' Other friends who made the trek to Rugby to console Brooke were Geoffrey Keynes and Eddie Marsh. Both James and Keynes were cautioned to stick to Brooke's cover story concealing the truth of Ka from the Ranee. James was told: 'Will you kindly be Discreet in this house? I'll prepare a list [of lies]. The most notable recent point is that Ka's existence in Germany & voyage home with me is not known. O yes, & also you rang me up at 4.15 this afternoon.' (In fact the call had come from Ka.) Geoffrey was told: 'Mention *nothing* connected with my life, no names, nothing, for the Lord's sake. Relations between me and the Ranee are very peculiar. And one must be very cautious.'

Geoffrey, as an Old Rugbeian of conventional mien and manners, was already a favourite of Mrs Brooke. By contrast, she took an instant dislike to Eddie Marsh, perhaps sensing the homosexual interest that lay at the root of his regard for Brooke. This prejudice was to play an important part in the years following her son's death when she flouted his last written wishes and made Keynes his literary executor rather than Marsh, whose memoir of Brooke she vigorously obstructed and delayed.

Marsh had been dying to pay court to Brooke ever since the publication of his *Poems* the previous year. He had written a flattering, almost fawning, fan letter: 'I had always in trembling hope reposed that I should like the poems, but at my wildest I never looked forward to such magnificence . . . You have brought back into English poetry the rapturous beautiful grotesque of the 17th century . . .' He followed this up with a laudatory notice in the *Poetry Review*, although privately deploring, in a misogynistic way, Brooke's reference to a woman's sexual smell in 'Lust': 'There are some things too disgusting to write about, especially in one's own language.' Brooke, mystified, stoutly and rightly defended himself: 'The "smell" business I don't really understand . . . People do smell other people, as well as see and feel them. I do, and I'm not disgusted to think so.' Marsh also had his misgivings about 'A Channel Passage', although he manfully mastered his objection: 'so clever and amusing that in spite of a prejudice in favour of poetry that I can read at meals I can't wish it away'.

While Brooke had been descending into what he told Eddie had been 'a foodless and sleepless hell' after Lulworth, Eddie, too, had his own preoccupations. Following a government reshuffle after its summer victory over the Tory Lords, Winston Churchill had been moved from the Home Office to become First Lord of the Admiralty, with the task of dealing with the growing naval threat from Germany. Eddie had moved with him, and was now deeply entrenched in the political establishment. He was becoming too influential a contact for Brooke to neglect and, once back at Rugby, Brooke wrote a long letter of appreciation for his patron's efforts to promote his career as a poet: 'Your letter and review gave me immense and slightly pink-cheeked pleasure. It is absurdly kind of you . . .' and so on. This flattery laid on with a trowel re-cemented Brooke in his mentor's affections, and from now on they would become increasingly inseparable.

James came twice to Rugby. Despite, or because of, his own knowledge of the intricacies of his friend's involvement with Ka, he still tended his old flame for Brooke, which made the visits somewhat tricky occasions, as Brooke told Ka: 'It's nice having him here; although one's skating riskily, at times. Arguments on fucking . . . And there's James still in collapse because I said Madge, the second parlour-maid, was so natty.' On his second visit James was acting as chaperone to Ka herself, who made a good impression on the Ranee. The complications were obvious, but Brooke appears to have relished them, telling Ka: 'You, I, she [Brooke's mother], James: what a tangle of cross-motives & dissimulations it'll be! We'll want our clear heads. But it'll be fun.' His customary delight in intrigue and deception had clearly survived his mental collapse – although maintaining the fiction that he and Ka were 'just good friends' took some doing. It was at this time that his blush, 'as red as this blotting paper', nearly betrayed his real feelings to his mother. But the Ranee apparently remained convinced that the homely, unglamorous Ka was no siren for her son, and the intrigues continued, unabated, under her very nose.

But the accumulated strains were once more conspiring to undermine Brooke's fragile psyche as he brooded on the past and those who had wronged him. When Ka, in her honest way, informed him that she had once again bumped into Henry Lamb at a party, he exploded: 'I wish to God you'ld cut the man's throat . . . See very little of the man, for God's sake. And don't be more of a bloody fool than Nature made you.' His terror of Ka's infidelity – which, in his mind, had been proved by her willingly giving herself to him in Germany – prevented him from thinking clearly or naming the nameless things and dangers she was encountering in London. His defence was to attempt to persuade her that she, like him, was a nervous wreck, and should cocoon herself in a protective swathe of cotton wool from promiscuity and all temptation. Like some Old Testament prophet, he laid down his commandments:

> Ka, you've once given yourself to me: and that means more than you think. It means so very importantly that you're not your own mistress. And that, far more truly and dangerously than if I had you under lock and key – and with my 'physical superiority'. It means that you're not as free to do anything as you were. It means that you mayn't hurt yourself, because it hurts me, like Hell. It means you mayn't make mistakes, because I pay. It means you mayn't foolishly and unthinkingly get tired and ill and miserable: because you make me tired and ill and miserable.

He couldn't have stated in plainer terms what fears were plaguing him: without any engagement, he now regarded Ka as his private property, to be disposed of at his whim. Like for some fabled Oriental potentate, she was the chief ornament in his harem and was to be regarded as his prisoner just as surely as if he were her physical jailer. The mask of the progressive Fabian was well and truly cast aside in favour of the face of the stern Victorian patriarch.

Although he bombarded Ka throughout March, the month he remained in Rugby, with a deluge of letters as relentless as those from Cannes throughout January, their tone was very different. Sometimes, it is true, he was the sighing lover of old, but only when he remembered that he was supposed to be so. More often, the tone was that of the jealous, crabby complainant, alone against a world of enemies, and twisted with bitterness and a desire to wreak revenge on his foes.

One such target was Lytton Strachey, who was emerging more and more clearly through the red mists of Brooke's rage, as the villain who had masterminded the Lulworth débâcle: 'I'm glad Lytton has been having a bad time,' he told Ka, to whom the elder Strachey had been confiding his agonies over his unrequited love for Henry Lamb: 'next time you have one of your benignant lunches with him you can make it clear that I loathe him – if there's any chance of that giving him any pain.'

The corrosive emotions of hatred and revenge were beginning to replace any pretence of love towards Ka – he included her in his torrents of black bile at the whole pack of those who had witnessed his downfall at Lulworth, telling her bitterly:

> If I can still, at moments, hate you for having, in pitiful sight of a flirtation,

invited that creature [Lamb] to Lulworth, and then left the rest of us to go out [on] walks and out for meals with him; how do you think I hate Lytton, who hadn't even your excuse of ignorance and helplessness, for having worked to get the man down there, and having seen the whole thing being engineered from the beginning – and obligingly acquiesced in it as one of the creature's whims? You told me – in the first flush of your young romance – of the whole picture – Lytton 'hovering' (your word) with a fond paternal anxiousness in the background, eyeing the two young loves at their sport:– it was the filthiest filthiest part of the most unbearably sickening disgusting blinding nightmare – and then one shrieks with the unceasing pain that it was *true*.

Being unable to strike directly at Lytton, Brooke had to content himself with the first of an increasingly hysterical series of assaults on the (at first) uncomplaining James, which plainly reveal his galloping hysteria. 'God damn you,' ran one Rugby postcard to the younger Strachey. 'God damn everyone. God burn roast castrate bugger & tear the bowels out of everyone . . . You'd better give it up; wash your bloody hands. I'm not sane.'

Brooke was not the only member of the Neo-Pagan/Bloomsbury axis to have been undergoing a mental breakdown early in 1912. Virginia Stephen, soon to marry Leonard Woolf, had suffered one of the first of her increasingly devastating collapses. Hearing reports of this from James and Ka, Brooke wrote on 9 March from the midst of his own torment, to commiserate:

Virginia dear, I'm told – in the third-hand muffled manner I get my news from the Real World – that you've been, or are, unwell. It's not true? Let me implore you not to have as I've been having, a nervous breakdown. It's too unpleasant – but you're one of the few people who, of old, know what it's like . . . I feel drawn to you, in this robust hard world. What tormented and crucified figures we literary people are! God! How I hate the healthy, unimaginative hard shelled dilettanti, like James and Ka. It was a pity you couldn't come to the House party long, long ago at Lulworth – not that you'd have enjoyed it: it was too horrible. But you might have made all the difference. I fell into an abyss there . . .

It is notable how swiftly Brooke slides from a show of sympathy for his fellow-sufferer to a preening self-concern. Although Virginia wouldn't have enjoyed Lulworth, her presence might have saved *him*. As if to demonstrate the shallowness of his concern, he goes on to give Virginia – whose terror of sexual relations, possibly stemming from childhood abuse, he must have known about – a detailed account of a Rugby choirboy being gang-raped during a recent all-male church service in the town. From the callousness of his description – 'he has been in bed ever since with a rupture . . . He may live' – it is clear that his desire is not merely to shock, as of old, but to hurt and disgust. A new strand of sadism had wound itself into the complex fibres of Brooke's character.

The persistent note of sheer nastiness and utter lunacy is the dominant theme of his letters. Looking back in anger rather than regret at Lulworth, he minutely analysed what he considered Lamb's motives had been in targeting Ka. Lamb was, Brooke admitted:

> Someone more capable of getting hold of women than me, slightly experienced in bringing them to heel, who didn't fool about with ideas of trust or 'fair treatment' . . . You'd met the creature at some party. I have your account: 'very unpleasant' you wrote 'but fascinating'. 'Fascinating'!!! I dimly wondered . . . and passed on . . . The swine, one gathers, was looking around. He was tiring of his other women, or they of him. Perhaps he thought there'd be a cheaper and pleasanter way of combining fucking with an income than Ottoline. And his 'friends' had come to the conclusion he might be settled with somebody for a bit. He cast dimly around. Virgins are easy game. Marjorie Strachey, I understand, was the first woman he met. What was her answer? Ka was the second: an obviously finer object for lust, and more controllable. He marked you down.

With this partial, but not wholly inaccurate account, Brooke relishes his revenge and rubs Ka's nose in her own dirt: 'The creature slimed down to Lulworth; knowing about women, knowing he could possibly get you if he got a few hours alone with you (his knowledge turned out to be justified). I was ill. Influenza (or poison in the house) frustrated me that Sunday. I was in the depths, leaning utterly on you. Oh my God! how kind and wonderful you were then; the one thing in the world I had.' The mixture of self-pity and malice makes this and many similar passages wearisome and hard to swallow. And there are occasions when Brooke appears to have taken leave of his senses entirely. For example, a bizarre note to James Strachey at this time proposes that he, of all people, should join Brooke in kidnapping Bryn Olivier, taking her to Brighton's Metropole Hotel and 'going shares' with her sexual favours.

Ever since Lulworth Brooke had been incommunicado with the woman who had meant the most to him before he was swept away by his craze for Ka: Noel Olivier. In mid-March he somewhat sheepishly resumed contact with a letter calmly reviewing the tumult of the past three months; it began: 'Dearest Noel, I've treated you badly. Illness pain madness & the horrors must excuse me.' He gives a familiar account of his breakdown, touching on the months and years of strain that lead to his arrival at Lulworth 'half mad and ill'. He glosses over the Ka–Lamb–Brooke triangle and launches straight into a description of his nervous paralysis: 'I couldn't eat or sleep or do anything but torture myself.'

He claims, however, to be on the mend: 'I've got much better – My weight, which had gone down stones & stones, is now immense. I am very fat. I'm not clear yet, though. I've not begun to work at all. I shall go abroad again, sometime . . . and start working. At present my mind seems still dead. I don't see that I shall ever be able to write things again . . .' He seems half-hearted about resuming any sort of relations with his former 'fiancée': 'Perhaps you won't want to see me. You may be hating me by now.'

Noel, by now well used to Brooke's wails of woe, replied sympathetically enough: '*Mon pauvre* Rupert!' and so on, but she was guarded and equivocal, having been burned more than once, about re-entering Brooke's flickering fires: 'it must all depend so on our feelings, & I dont know what either of us will feel when (when?) next we talk.' By this time Brooke had learned that he would not win his Fellowship at King's that year – the vacant place had gone to a scientist, Hamilton Hartridge. The blow was expected, and Brooke was given a heavy hint that if he applied again in the coming year, his chances would be much greater. He took the news, preoccupied as he was by his personal woes, with equanimity.

By the end of March he felt more than ready to leave Rugby. He was not better – if anything, he was more disconsolate than when he arrived – but the tension of deceiving the Ranee under her own roof was too much. His nervous tension had gone; the elastic had snapped under the strain, and he was tired, listless, apathetic and tearful. The only bright spots on a grey horizon were a meeting with Noel and the other Oliviers at Limpsfield Chart, and Ka's promise that she would accompany him back to Germany. But the wind was changing in their relationship, and despite the almost automatic declarations of love and 'ferocious tempestuous oceans of lust', it was beginning to blow against Ka.

When he was capable of thinking, it was towards Noel that his thoughts once more turned, and he did not hesitate to tell Ka so. Angered by news that she had rushed to Henry Lamb's bedside after he had been injured in a fall from a horse, he wailed: 'Everything's gone from me, love for Noel, writing, everything – is swept away. I'm going to see Noel . . . I'm sick with a sort of fear . . . She . . . you don't know what she stands for – stood for to me – Do you I wonder understand about love, Ka?' And again: 'You have brought me, roughly enough, to see that women are lower, below men.'

In this lamentable condition, he escaped from Rugby at last, helped by his long-suffering rescuers, Jacques and Gwen Raverat: 'I can't sleep,' he had written to them, begging for aid: 'I'm leaving this Hell. I've got to defer the deluge a month or two yet. I'm going – I don't know where – with J. Strachey for the weekend . . . I'm entirely depraved and extremely unpleasant – but can I sleep in your Studio?' Before arriving at the Raverats' studio flat in Barons Court, west London, Brooke had planned tea with Noel and Bryn Olivier, but at the last minute Noel cried off – she was an increasingly sought-after star in her new college life and may have been scared to face Brooke in his stricken condition. Dinner with Ka the same evening hardly seemed like compensation.

Brooke was feeling friendless – he was eager to gather allies who would see the world through the black and twisted prism he had placed over it. In this situation he knew he could rely only on a tiny handful of his oldest and closest confidants. 'I can't bear that I should go about knowing some things alone,' Ka was informed. 'Jacques and Gwen and Justin – I feel I *must* tell them the horror, the filthy, filthy truth. It's unbearable, suffering alone . . .' Sure enough, when Ka left the Barons Court flat after they had dined *à quatre* on 28 March, Brooke unburdened himself of an edited version of his travails with Ka, leaving out the sex and painting himself in as favourable light as possible. The next morning, soothed by the Raverats' support, he left for a long weekend with James Strachey.

James had enticed Brooke south on the excuse of looking for a suitable site for an Easter reading party – Brooke now had a superstitious fear of Lulworth: 'Dorsetshire barred,' he told James firmly. Even as Brooke now was, James still hero-worshipped his old friend. On the spur of the moment they made for the Mermaid Inn (then called the Mermaid Club), in the quaint and ancient Sussex town of Rye. The Mermaid belonged to the family of a friend of James's, the future writer Richard Aldington, and its half-timbered walls and cobbled yard provided a cosy setting for a sorely needed restorative break. It was not to be: as though picking at a tempting scab, Brooke continued to bombard Ka with letters, mailing no fewer than five in the three days they were in Rye and sending another to Noel for good measure.

His first letter to Ka was laced with sexual longing: describing their fellow-guests at the Mermaid, he wrote:

There are two newly-married couples. The husbands have both retired, just now (9.0) How it brings the old days back, eh . . . Have they got Irrigators? Are they using Oatine? The dears! . . . I feel mentally better for being beastly to you . . . I'm loving you extraordinarily . . . Oh my God, I *want* you tonight. Your nakedness and beauty – your mouth and breasts and cunt. – Shall I turn in a frenzy and rape James in the night? I'd burn you like a flame if I could get hold of you.

That same evening Ka was again dining at the Raverats' home. Jacques refused to see her, in solidarity with Brooke; but Gwen was working on her susceptible friend on Brooke's behalf, and joining his crusade against 'these Stracheys'. 'They *are* parasites, you know,' she told Ka. 'I for one am a clean Christian and they disgust me.' Ka was bluntly informed that she had lost her fine instincts and forgotten God. She was 'arrogant' in thinking that she could manage her own life, since she didn't have the sense to govern her own instincts. Brooke, the Raverats insisted, lived only to marry Ka and make an honest woman of her – a travesty of the truth, for Brooke, in fact, was turning away from the whole idea.

Beneath the angry rhetoric, Gwen was worried that a single Ka was a sexual threat to her own marriage – there was no telling that she and Jacques would not resume their old liaison if she was not quickly tied down in matrimony. Largely ignorant of the extent of Brooke's psychosis, and the fact that he and Ka had already slept together, the Raverats based their prescription for their friends' future happiness mainly on false premises. Jacques believed that Ka had rejected Brooke's true love in favour of her lust for Lamb, a relationship that was 'neither convincing nor inevitable'. The simple obvious answer was marriage to Brooke.

Under the weight of these forceful arguments, Ka began to weaken. She started to believe the couple when they told her that Brooke loved her and she him. Marriage to Brooke would also satisfy her strong sexual hunger, they insisted. As if to confirm their argument, Henry Lamb was predictably beginning to tire of Ka's dumb love – just as Lytton had foretold. However, it was all happening too late – despite his lustful letters from Rye, Brooke, too, was tiring of Ka, and deeply resented the agony she had put him through and the fact that she had submitted to him sexually out of pity rather than love. Now that Ka was beginning to fall deeply for him, he was ready to bolt.

Brooke and James enjoyed their bracing days on Romney Marsh. They made a courtesy call on Henry James, whose country residence, Lamb House, was just up the street from the Mermaid – 'the Master' was not in

– and walked to the nearby picturesque village of Winchelsea. But then Brooke, having made arrangements to see both Ka and Noel on Monday – April Fool's Day – left Rye by train *en route* to Limpsfield Chart. His letter to Noel had a touch of the old tenderness: 'There is no doubt that you're the finest person in the world.' By contrast, when Ka, worn out by the nagging of the Raverats, called off their rendezvous in London, Brooke's response was a fierce burst of anger: 'Are you wanting to make me wild before I see Noel, lest I should be too nice to her? Or do you want to get rid of me by killing me – can't you do it quicker easier ways? . . . Gwen Jacques and a thousand more yourself me decency love honour good fineness cleanness truth –: you'd sacrifice them on your lust – and such lust – I'm frantic . . .' His incoherent fear and rage were prompted by his belief that Ka was deliberately avoiding him in order to remain in London and hang about Henry Lamb's haunts.

He remained with the Oliviers for four peaceful days. His regrets that he had alienated Noel's love in favour of a Ka whom he now perceived as unworthy of him were beginning to trouble him sorely. He now had another grievance to add to his heavy charge sheet against Ka: she had forced him to renounce his pure love for Noel, in return for a mess of pottage – or lust – from Ka. 'She [Noel] is amazing,' Ka was told. 'I didn't know such people existed. I go sick and blind to think she may be a woman' – that is, in Brooke's jaundiced eyes, a weak and feeble creature subject to the temptations of the flesh that Ka had already succumbed to.

Arriving at Ka's country home at Woking on Thursday 4 April, Brooke received a rude shock. Ka told him that she suspected their night at Starnberg had made her pregnant. The irrigator she had inexpertly used to protect herself against such an eventuality had evidently failed. The news stopped Brooke in his tracks. He did not know how to respond, but realized that it was best not to pester her with his wearying complaints and needs. 'I'm going to leave Ka alone,' he told Jacques the following day. 'I found her . . . pretty bad. To rest, as far as she will, is the best thing for her.' He said he was ready, at any rate, to do the decent thing by Ka, and marry her within a month.

The news was not altogether a bolt from the blue – in mid-March, barely a month after their night of passion, Ka's period was late, and Brooke was ruefully regretting 'mismanaging the machine' (the irrigator) and setting off Ka's 'well-known fecundity'. Now he was in the fix he had most feared – there was no question of an abortion or an illegitimate child for a woman of Ka's refined social class. Brooke, whether he liked it or not, would have to face up to his responsibilities, get married, settle down to some dullish academic post and play the dutiful, ageing bourgeois paterfamilias he had so frequently derided. The magic of youth would be gone in a puff of smoke. But there was one alternative, and it seems that Brooke did briefly consider it – suicide.

His options were closing in, and it is perhaps not surprising that, like some wounded animal, he should head for a familiar lair in a deep forest to hide from a suddenly threatening world. He travelled down to the New Forest, back to the remote woodland cottage of 'Beech Shade' near the hamlet of Bank, where he had secretly visited Noel in the first flush of his love for her, exactly three years ago. Now he was a very different man, in a sadly changed situation. But his first words from the place were addressed to Noel on Saturday 6 April:

> Mrs Primmer is well. The trees are there. The black hut stands. Also the holly-bush – And the room. Oh! Dearest Noel, you were good. It's incredible – I didn't know there were such things as you in the world. You . . . gave me immense strength compared to the weakness I've been in . . . it's madness to kill oneself when you're in the world. So I'm vacillating again . . . I do worship you so. I found Ka pretty bad. We had rather a rough time.

He hinted at the impasse in which he found himself seemingly trapped: 'I'm going through with all this business: & I don't know where I shall come out.' James was his companion in his solitude – mooching round making fatuous statements about the trees – and Mrs Primmer, his former landlady, fed him the fattening foods he had got used to. Not surprisingly, he told Ka that he wanted to stay there for ever. His mood grew nostalgic and wistful; a letter to Hugh Dalton, who had written to commiserate with Brooke for failing to win his Fellowship, recalled happy memories:

> Friend of my laughing careless youth, where are those golden hours now? Where now the shrill mirth of our burgeoning intellects? and by what doubtful and deleterious ways have I come down to this place of shadows and eyeless pain? In truth, I have been for some months in Hell. I have been very ill. I am very ill. In all probability I shall be very ill. It is thought by those who know me best (viz. myself) that I shall die. Nor do I greatly want to live.

Life had lost its savour for him, Brooke explained, his mind was 'worn and flabby' and he was just a tenth of the man he used to be. Physically, however, he had swelled: 'I am now enormously fat. Boys laugh at me in the street. But that is partly, also, on account of my manner. For I am more than a little gone in my head, since my collapse.' Brooke concluded with one of his vain, self-dramatizing promises: 'I go back to Germany soon. They are a slow race and will not know I am stupid. I shall never appear in England again. I shall never write poetry or limpid prose again.'

It is significant and typical that Brooke should now be appropriating the very real agony of his breakdown as a badge to add to his persona – he flaunts it to his friends in a mocking way. He is, as before, putting on a performance – but now, like a worn-out actor, he is merely going through the motions. This is demonstrated in another letter he wrote from Bank, to the poet James Elroy Flecker, an acquaintance and something of a rival from Cambridge days, now working with the consular service in Beirut and vainly seeking a cure for the tuberculosis that was to kill him. Describing what he called, with dramatic capitals, 'The Crash', Brooke relates his melodrama: 'Nine days I lay without sleep or food. Monsters of the darkest Hell nibbled my soul. They nibbled it away and therein that noblest part of it which men name the intellect. I am sodden and soft and dead, a don but less learned, a dotard but less energetic . . . I drift from place to place and eat enormously and sleep. I am utterly degraded and shall never climb from this morass.'

Brooke touched the bottom of his emotional swamp in the New Forest after James's departure. Desperate, he called on his Rugby friend Hugh Russell-Smith, and then apparently scoured the shops of Lyndhurst and Brockenhurst in search of a gun with which to shoot himself. Always terrified of being left alone, he had never felt more desperate or terrified. Since he had resolved to leave Ka in peace and Noel was unavailable, he had fallen back on Bryn Olivier and invited her down to Bank. Fresh from a rock-climbing holiday in north Wales with Bill and Eva Hubback and her future fiancé Hugh Popham, she answered his call, and joined him on 11 April.

It is something of a mystery why Bryn and Brooke had never got close before now, for in many ways they seem like an ideally matched couple. Both were exceptionally good-looking and the much sought-after stars of their respective social circles; both feared being valued by their brilliant friends for their looks rather than their intellects; and both mistrusted love and strong emotions. But now that Brooke had run through his other options, Bryn suddenly seemed like an attractive alternative to the complications of Noel and Ka. At the very least he was grateful for her solicitous concern and cheering company.

Months later, looking back at the four days they spent together at Bank, he told her:

Then there was Bank, Bryn. For three whole months I'd been infinitely wretched and ill, wretcheder than I'd thought possible. And then for a few days it all dropped completely away, and – oh! how lovely Bank was! – I suppose I should never be able to make you see what beauty is to me,– physical beauty –, just even the seeing of it, in spite of all the hungers that come – Bank passed & was good & is a lovely memory to you & me. A funny world!

Much though he may have wanted to possess Bryn under the greenwood trees of that idyllic spot, Brooke was held back by the thoughts of the hot water his passion had got him into over the past year. And fond though she was of Brooke, Bryn was too self-possessed and careful – and too much in solidarity with her sister Noel – to allow him an opening. Besides, her thoughts were beginning to turn towards marriage, and Brooke, unstable and inconstant, would surely not provide the solid rock she needed.

So they returned to London on 14 April *en route* to more rest and recuperation for Brooke with the Oliviers at Limpsfield Chart. They dallied in town that Sunday to take tea with Virginia Stephen, who maliciously reported the visit in a letter to Ka. Brooke, she said, was 'slightly Byronic' while Bryn, she cattily commented, 'has a glass eye – one can imagine her wiping it bright in the morning with a duster'. In a note dashed off to James from the National Liberal Club, Brooke begged his friend for £7 to fund his upcoming German jaunt – he had cleaned himself out with a cheque for £6 to Mrs Primmer, he moaned. But Bryn, he said, 'was infinitely sympathetic'.

More of that sympathy was doled out in buckets by both Bryn and Noel at their home. Brooke basked in their solicitude, but his peace of mind was broken again by a letter from Ka. Understandably peeved by his neglect of her while she was coming to terms with her probable pregnancy, she told him that she wished to back out of their agreed 'second honeymoon' in Germany. The letter sparked yet another explosion in its recipient:

I wonder why you want me to kill you now rather than later. Isn't it rather insolent of you, when I've rather resolutely gone away to get well *for* Germany, to make the beginnings of my success an excuse for trying to shirk Germany? . . . 'Not the right and only thing' 'not absolutely free' . . . 'it may bring the most awful misery' are your funny little reservations and irrelevancies . . . My dear, you don't seem to recognize where we are. I suppose its because you have had no pain worth calling pain. You twixt sentimentality and weakness . . . Oh Child, it won't do. You must realise that we're en route. You can't back out because you're tired or a little bruised.

Brooke's irritatingly patronizing habit of addressing women as 'Child' in his letters becomes ubiquitous from this point on: bizarre, too, is the irony of his upbraiding Ka for her weakness and inconstancy at sticking to an agreed course, when these are precisely the faults that he too will soon exhibit.

He flounced up to London ready to confront Ka; but she was nowhere to be found. One of his letters had missed her at Woking, the other had arrived in London but had been impounded by her sister Hester. By chance, she saw him on top of a bus in Trafalgar Square, and managed to track him down at the nearby National Liberal Club. They went out into the square for one of those tearful sessions at which Brooke was becoming a past master, with Ka leaning on the pediment of one of Sir Edwin Landseer's sculpted lions while her weeping subsided. Brooke succeeded in convincing her to accompany him to Berlin after all — not a difficult task, since her pulling out had been a manoeuvre to whet his interest in her, which seemed to be waning.

Now it was Brooke who came under pressure to abort the trip. The siren voices of the Oliviers pleaded in unison for him to stay in England. Noel told James, who had begun to pay court to her along with a myriad of other suitors, that she feared Brooke would return a fat, loud-voiced Prussian; while Bryn wrote him a note saying it was his duty as an English poet to stay where he was. The combined pressure did result in Brooke putting off his departure for one day and going instead to a show by Harry Lauder, but after returning to his club slightly drunk he wrote a mawkish letter to Bryn explaining why he felt he had to go.

'Your letter was incredibly nice to get . . . but I'm going. It's the will of God.' He explained soothingly that he would be back by the summer, and was going abroad to get 'disentangled' from his problems and complete his cure. 'I see, you see, that I must go abroad for these things. There's no point, after all, in my being in England. I'm rather unpleasant when I'm a whole person, and when I know what person I am, I'll come back.' Flirtatiously he implied that Bryn would be one of the magnets that pulled him back: 'I do like it so — that you do mind. It makes me happy. But you mustn't. I promise you I think everything's quite right . . .' He ended: 'I'm glad you're so beautiful.'

Then, after a 'shy and hurried' leave-taking with Ka, he was off, taking the night ferry from Harwich to Flushing (Vlissingen) on Saturday 20 April.

18

Three Women, a Play and a Poem

The Brooke who travelled to Berlin was still a deeply troubled, sick man. As his ship heaved across to Flushing, he felt he was falling, rudderless, into a vertiginous spinning void. A strange, drifting, almost insane letter to James Strachey, who had loyally financed the trip and seen him off at the station, described the crossing:

> One hour, one gaunt shrieking hour I dozed. You have talked to the Major, abused yourself, & slept, since Victoria. In a few hours you will have a late, bitter breakfast. And I, I have only that one intolerable ghost of an hour between me and yesterday. I hover eternally on the doubtful borderland between today and yesterday: a grayhaired embryo; a creature of no world; horrible. A bell clanged us out of delirium at 3.30. We put on our life belts – I snatched the Photos of my Letter of Credit – & went on deck. It was merely Flushing.

Writing on the train carrying him across the flat north German plains, Brooke keeps a tenuous toehold on reality with a description of a fellow-traveller:

> Mr D'Aucastre nods opposite. He has followed me like a dog, ever since he got over the shock of those first few minutes when, entering late & finding me in bed, my hair only visible, he thought he'd got into the lady's quarters. Charming, sterling fellow. He brushed my forehead lightly with his dreamy brown mustache once, & twice, & then skipped aloft to the upper birth [sic]. Uninterestedly and with a brown bag he spent those throbbing dreadful hours in abusing himself. Lucky fellow!

Sexual frustration, insomnia and hopeless emotional confusion combined to form a toxic brew robbing Brooke of any semblance of stability. But, now and then, perceptive rays of insight and grotesque originality leap off the page: 'Mr D'Aucastre (my last foot-hold over the abyss) sleeps opposite. He sleeps, always, with one eye, the right, not quite shut. A thin white line gleams, twixt lid and lid. The pupil is tucked away – he's genuinely asleep. It's a trifle like the moon we saw last night. What does it mean?'

An obsession with rancid sex – masturbation is always described as 'abuse' or, in private Apostolic jargon as 'pumpship' – has now congealed into open misogyny. Describing two women sharing his carriage, Brooke fantasized about their private thoughts:

> They bend their bodies and souls in vague meek inferiority. 'If it came to the Straight Thing between us' they continually think, 'you'd put us down, drive supremely home, & we'd open our legs, submit, accept mastery, whimper & smirk.' Oh! oh! I am touched almost to tears for them: because they never *quite* know what's up. Women aren't quite animals, alas! They have twilight, shadowy souls, like a cat behind a hedge . . . but how dreadful that the whole world's a-cunt for one. The clouds are but petticoats swirled so alluringly high . . . For THEM, do you think, are all the trees excitingly waving (trousers)?

Brooke signs off this strange, meditative missive with a gleam of self-recognition: 'Unter vier Augen ['under four eyes' – i.e. 'between you and me'] my dear chap. I'm more than a little tired.'

Reaching Berlin, Brooke installed himself as the guest of Dudley Ward, staying at a *pension*, but spending much of his time at Dudley's apartment, in Kantstrasse 14, in the central district of Charlottenburg. It was a crowded household, containing Dudley, who was working as Berlin correspondent of *The Economist*; his flatmate Alfred Reynolds, a *Daily Mail* correspondent and Cambridge writer; and the mothers of both Dudley and his fiancée Annemarie von der Planitz. The flat was in the final throes of preparations for Dudley's imminent marriage to Annemarie, and the fussing of the two mothers irked Brooke considerably – as he explained to Bryn Olivier, they were a little too like the Ranee for comfort:

> Her mother was being a nuisance – crying for her, fussing her etc. The usual mutter-liebe [mother-love] worry. (Mother lust, I once said, and was hit in the mouth.) But she's not as bad as Mrs Ward, who's been here a month, and is going to see the thing through. She is a silly little woman who can't speak a word of German and is absolutely dependent on Dudley all day. She objects to

German food in the restaurants, and can't think what she wants. She drags him round with her buying a hat, when he ought to be writing journalism. Reynolds . . . and I occasionally take her off his hands. From time to time she says 'I'm afraid I'm taking up a great deal of your time, Dudley.'

Although expecting Ka's arrival at any moment, Brooke kept up a postal flirtation with both Bryn and Noel Olivier. The plan was for him to find a house outside Berlin which he and Ka could rent as 'Herr and Frau Brooke' in an attempt at a second honeymoon after the fiasco of their previous German jaunt in February. He was, however, careful to gloss over this in his correspondence with Bryn, in which he is cursorily dismissive of Frau Brooke: 'Ka appears in Berlin, I gather, in a few days,' Bryn was told on 8 May. 'I shall wait and see her for a bit, to cheer myself up. Then I shall wander off probably, for a time . . .' The deliberate vagueness belies the fact that he was imploring Ka to make haste to join him:

> I am here because I love Ka and she is coming to Germany and we are going to live in a house together . . . You, you'll come, I know, and bring colour and things with you . . . You do want me a lot: and I you. And we know a great deal . . . I'm just passing through Potsdam. I've a fancy you may be, just now, in Grantchester. I envy you, frightfully. That river and the chestnuts – come back to me a lot. Tea on the lawn . . .

As was ever the case when he was abroad, Brooke had begun to wax nostalgic for England, and in particular, that corner of the country he had personally colonized: Grantchester. He already feared that the summer idyll he had briefly enjoyed in that blessed plot was irrevocably past – never again would he play host to flocks of visitors come to see him perform and dive naked into the embracing waters of Byron's Pool. The complications of real life, the deadening weight of adult responsibility, the entangling weeds of sexual confusion, were dragging him down.

Escaping from the frenetic preparations for Dudley's impending nuptials, Brooke, when not searching the surrounding countryside for a suitable love nest for himself and Ka, spent most of his time in the Café des Westens, a haunt of advanced intellectuals, where he tried half-heartedly to go native by smoking strong German cigars. It was here that his eddying nostalgia curdled with his coffee and gradually began to take on literary form in the shape of one of his most successful and best-known poems. He described the café's ambience to Bryn:

a café thronged by all the intellectuals, advanced, temperamentvoll [temperamental] picturesque, geniuses, and so forth. Long-haired and extraordinarily clothed people sit round little tables and shout – the words 'temperament', 'Kunst', 'Leben' [art, life], float out to you. Dudley . . . breaks off to call attention to the figures – a well-known Socialist leader; a woman with very flaxen hair and quite black eyebrows, who might be – anything; a very nice Russian professor; a Natur-Mensch [child of Nature] in a sack and sandals; a well-known model . . . A young shapeless dumpy foolish woman in a black satin sack got up to go. She was holding one scarlet tulip in her hand, and walked along smelling it. 'People here do the right things,' commented Dudley . . . 'but somehow it's the wrong people who do them.'

Some of these images – *'temperamentvoll'* Germans, tulips – wound their way into the nostalgic long poem about Grantchester that he now began, after half a year's abstinence from poetry, to compose in the café.

Nostalgia for an even more distant section of his life than Grantchester coloured a letter to James. Recalling their preparatory-school days at Rugby, he speculated that their form master, Mr Sandford, had worked himself up, while ostensibly angry over their Latin grammar, into a state of 'perfect orgasm and ejaculation of his rage. And, no doubt, there was a booming & swelling & throbbing below his flies, too. But for that, I never had the knowledge to look, in those days.' The sexuality of prep-school masters was also the subject of a poem very different from 'Grantchester', which survives in a letter to James but was torn out of his notebook by his censorious literary executors. Punningly called 'Ballade', it is a parody of the sort of 'facts of life' lecture delivered by embarrassed and red-faced paedophile prep-school masters beginning: 'Boys! mine is not a pleasant task today . . .' and ending:

> Prince, there is one fault you can hardly cure. Which, I regret . . . which makes me . . . to be terse! —
> (You often must have noticed, I am sure!) Between your legs there hangs a Bag, or Purse.

In mid-May Dudley departed for his marriage in Munich, and almost simultaneously Ka at last arrived in Berlin. Her mood was very different from the way it had been during their previous German encounter. The scales had fallen from her eyes and she was now disillusioned with Henry Lamb, who, she had at last grasped, was more interested in her as an occasional dalliance and provider of funds in hard times, than in making her his official mistress in place of the more brilliant and influential Lady

Ottoline Morrell. She was prepared to listen to Brooke's protestations of love and become both his fiancée and sexual partner.

Tragically for Ka, however, Brooke's mood had also changed. Now that he had gained complete sexual possession of her, and apparently seen off the threat of Lamb, his interest in her not only waned but changed into a sort of boredom that rapidly became disgust. The apparently bottomless well of the passion he had been fitfully proclaiming for the past four months had irrevocably run dry. The 'second honeymoon' proved even more of a disaster than the first.

While awaiting Ka's arrival, Brooke had dutifully attended the theatre to see plays by Shaw and Ibsen, and scribbled letters. His main occupation, however, was finishing the long poem that was destined to set in stone his reputation as a hymner of a mythical English pastoral paradise; and starting to write a short play – his first – which, in contrast to the poem, made no impact at all. Today it is regarded as little more than an historic curio, interesting mainly because it is Brooke's sole attempt to practise the dramatic arts that he had put so much labour into studying academically. The play, which he entitled *Lithuania*, had its origins, according to Brooke, in a story that Dudley Ward had heard in Berlin and filed as a stringer in the English press. Brooke outlined the plot to Bryn:

> When I was in England I saw a very good story in the paper, and cut it out to file it . . . When I came out here, I found it was Dudley who had sent it to England – out of a German paper. I got more details: and now I'm trying to write it as a play. The son of some poor Lettland peasants ran away. After twenty years in America, he returned, very rich. He thought he would play a joke on his parents and sister – the household. He went to the lonely village they lived in, and, having confided in the innkeeper, went to his home and pretended to be a rich stranger who'd lost his way and needed a night's lodging. They gave it to him. After he had gone to bed, they decided to murder him for his money. The father tried to go in and do it, but his courage gave; so he went down to the inn and drank himself into a fit state of mind. There, the innkeeper let out the joke. The father tore back the mile to his house: and found that the two women, who were strong, hadn't been able to bear the strain of waiting, and had just killed the man with a hammer. The mother went mad: the other two to Siberia. Bright little story.

This is the exact sequence of events that Brooke set down, unaltered, in terse dialogue. It is a slight piece, which he never managed to get put on in his lifetime, but which was produced at Chicago's Little Theater some six months after his death. It was a resounding flop. None the less, it does not quite deserve the oblivion to which even Brooke's slavishly sympathetic official biographer, Christopher Hassall, consigns it. Another Brooke biographer, the playwright Michael Hastings, praises its 'nicely cadenced sparse dialogue' and Brooke's 'good ear' and 'natural flair for voices from a stage'. *Lithuania* is also interesting for its insight into its author's psychology – given his bitterly misogynistic mood at the time, it comes as no surprise that his first and only play revolves around two murderous women and a helpless, sleeping male victim. Although Brooke claims the story was a real event reported in the press, it has the quality of myth – and indeed similar tales abound in European literature. It has elements of *Macbeth* and, of course, of that master of the grotesque, Webster.

But it was the other work he wrote in the Café des Westens that first made Brooke's name as a poet with a wide audience, and which still stands as his monument as a master of light verse. Thinking longingly of his lost paradise at Grantchester, he began:

> Just now the lilac is in bloom,
> All before my little room;
> And in my flower beds, I think,
> Smile the carnation and the pink;
> And down the borders, well I know,
> The poppy and the pansy blow . . .
> Oh! there the chestnuts, summer through,
> Beside the river make for you
> A tunnel of green gloom, and sleep
> Deeply above; and green and deep
> The stream mysterious glides beneath,
> Green as a dream and deep as death.

His thoughts turn to the last summer of his uncomplicated happiness, when

> . . . the May fields all golden show,
> And when the day is young and sweet,
> Gild gloriously the bare feet
> That run to bathe . . .

He skilfully employs half-rhyme and alliteration – 'green gloom', 'green and deep', 'Gild gloriously' – to paint a picture of summer sweetness, and then grumpily contrasts it with his present situation, where he sits 'sweating, sick and hot' surrounded by beer-swilling 'German Jews', where a conformist society is held in check and even Nature obeys well-defined rules:

> Here tulips bloom as they are told;
> Unkempt about those hedges blows
> An English unofficial rose;
> And there the unregulated sun
> Slopes down to rest when day is done . . .

Writing from a Germany already committed to an arms race that would lead to war in two years' time, Brooke thinks about an England that is languidly rousing itself to meet the threat. He ranges a corrupt, urban, stuffy Germany, nationalist yet cosmopolitan, against the purer rural values of an anarchic pastoral England where roses rather than guns are blooming. Asked to choose between the two, he knows where his heart lies: 'In Grantchester, In Grantchester!'

Brooke makes a detour into whimsy, describing the village's half-legendary past; a Grecian Arcadia with 'A Faun a-peeping through the green' and Naiads dancing to Pan's half-heard pipe. Grantchester is not only a desirable slice of English real estate, it is a magic kingdom where the poet can:

> lie
> Day-long and watch the Cambridge sky,
> And, flower-lulled in the sleepy grass,
> Hear the cool lapse of hours pass,
> Until the centuries blend and blur
> In Grantchester, in Grantchester . . .

Grantchester's eminent former literary denizens are summoned up in a parade culminating, by implication, in Brooke himself. Chaucer hears:

> his river still
> Chatter beneath a phantom mill.
> Tennyson notes, with studious eye,
> How Cambridge waters hurry by . . .

while 'His ghostly Lordship [Byron] swims his pool'. The poets are followed by former residents of the Old Vicarage:

> And spectral dance, before the dawn,
> A hundred Vicars down the lawn;
> Curates, long dust, will come and go
> On lissom, clerical, printless toe;
> And oft between the boughs is seen
> The sly shade of a Rural Dean . . .

Once again the procession of ecclesiastics suggests Brooke's ancestry, coming as he did, on both sides of his family, from countless generations of clerical Cotterills and episcopal Parker Brookes. Brooke's nostalgia becomes unbearable:

> God! I will pack, and take a train,
> And get me to England once again!
> For England's the one land, I know,
> Where men with Splendid Hearts may go;
> And Cambridgeshire, of all England,
> The shire for Men who Understand;
> And of *that* district I prefer
> The lovely hamlet Grantchester.

The list of ghostly Grantchesterians is succeeded by a roll-call of Cambridgeshire place-names, thrown in for comic effect in contrast to the sacred sward of his home hamlet:

> And Ditton girls are mean and dirty,
> And there's none in Harston under thirty,
> And folks in Shelford and those parts
> Have twisted lips and twisted hearts . . .

For all its farcical intent, the list demonstrates Brooke's obsession with 'dirt', women, the ageing process and ugliness. It is not clear, however, whether he counts himself among those with 'Splendid Hearts' or 'twisted' ones. The whole long poem shifts uneasily between its comic intentions and its more serious undertones. Just as his bathers gild their feet with flowers, so Brooke gilds the lily of his exaggerated lauding of Grantchester's virtues. We are not meant to take him seriously, surely, yet the suspicion lingers that this is just what we are supposed to do:

But Grantchester! ah, Grantchester!
There's peace and holy quiet there,
Great clouds along pacific skies,
And men and women with straight eyes,
Lithe children lovelier than a dream,
A bosky wood, a slumbrous stream,
And little kindly winds that creep
Round twilight corners, half asleep.

This demi-paradise is, naturally, inhabited by the purest of the pure:

In Grantchester their skins are white;
They bathe by day, they bathe by night.

And naturally they live by Brookian regulations:

The women there do all they ought;
The men observe the Rules of Thought.
They love the Good; they worship Truth;
They laugh uproariously in youth;
(And when they get to feeling old,
They up and shoot themselves, I'm told) . . .

– as the poet had so miserably failed to do the previous month in the New Forest. No matter, the touchstones of his heart, the well-springs nourishing this 'sentimental exile' – as he first entitled the poem – stand and stir him still:

Ah God! to see the branches stir
Across the moon at Grantchester!
To smell the thrilling-sweet and rotten
Unforgettable, unforgotten
River-smell, and hear the breeze
Sobbing in the little trees.

Was ever nostalgia for an unreal elysium so achingly invoked? As the poem builds to its climax, using the rhyme scheme of octosyllables in which he had made himself an expert, Brooke deploys all his skill, coupled with his genuine emotions of loss and guilt, to produce lines that transcend light verse and become, despite their mawkish content, true poetry:

Say, do the elm-clumps greatly stand
Still guardians of that holy land?
The chestnuts shade, in reverend dream,
The yet unacademic stream?
Is dawn a secret shy and cold
Anadyomene, silver-gold?
And sunset still a golden sea
From Haslingfield to Madingley?
And after, ere the night is born,
Do hares come out about the corn?

The rolling rhetorical questions plunge on, as Brooke reaches again for the sacramental elements which will either wash away his sins or drown him:

Oh, is the water sweet and cool,
Gentle and brown, above the pool?
And laughs the immortal river still
Under the mill, under the mill?
Say, is there Beauty yet to find?
And Certainty? and Quiet kind?
Deep meadows yet, for to forget
The lies, and truths, and pain? . . . oh! yet
Stands the Church clock at ten to three?
And is there honey still for tea?

'The Old Vicarage, Grantchester', the title Brooke eventually plumped for, is a prime example of what Orwell called 'good bad verse'. Ludicrously antiquated to a modern ear, and deliberately sentimental even as it was written, it nevertheless demonstrates a formidable skill in handling its material and tumbling line on memorable line. Not for nothing is it, despite its length, Brooke's most anthologized poem, apart from 'The Soldier'. No matter that the Grantchester elms are down now, victims of the humble bark beetle. No matter that the honey sold there today is produced far away in little processed plastic packets. Brooke has immortalized a place in a time that never was – a never-never land worthy of Peter Pan, where the clock does always stand at ten to three; a land of milk and honey, a refuge – and a salvation; but one he half-knew was already lost to him.

He made two fair copies of the poem, from the rough drafts scribbled in an accounts book given him by Maynard Keynes. One copy was posted to Bryn Olivier, tacked on, as if an afterthought, to a lengthy letter. He described it dismissively it as 'a silly quickly written thing – but it may amuse'. His true opinion of the poem is probably contained in the cable he sent to *Basileon* ahead of the poem itself: 'A Masterpiece on its way,' he told the editor of King's college magazine. In its own limited way, it was.

The Brooke Ka found waiting for her in Berlin must have been – for all his earnest importuning by post – a severe disappointment. She should have been warned by a letter in which he meditated sombrely on the essential loneliness of the individual, and the impossibility of a real marriage of minds: 'everybody's a pretty lonely figure, drifting in the gloom . . .' he said, citing his distinguished fellow-Rugbeian Matthew Arnold's famous lines about the God who bid the 'unplumb'd, salt, estranging sea' to flow for ever between the shores of two longing lovers. The same sentiment informed a more-or-less simultaneous letter to Bryn: 'We're all, you know, we human beings – tied fast to posts, each to a separate one, dotted about apart from one another, in the middle of the deserts. The vultures sit round in a large circle, waiting for the deaths. And occasionally we flap a hand or wriggle a nose to show we aren't dead. So I flap you so distant and grey a hand, Bryn, to show you I'm not dead.'

The 'deadness' he complained of was compounded in part by the collapse of his feelings for Ka, and in part by a smart rebuff Bryn had mailed him in a belated response to his drunken, maudlin hints that they might become a couple, contained in the letter he wrote from the National Liberal Club on the eve of his departure to Germany. It was far from a formal proposal of marriage, though that is how Brooke chose to represent it to James:

> I've just had a – 'a' – 'the' were better – letter from Bryn. Oh, my God. Frightfully nice of her, of course. And an absolute smack in the face for me. Refused – oh, Lord. There are some people (including all women) one should never propose to by letter. Remember that.
> 'Dear Rupert' it begins. So that's something. 'R' is dropped. The words are well-formed. The letters go stiffly up and down. Not much give and take about her, a graphologist would murmur. The spelling is inaccurate enough to be completely vulgar, but not sufficient to be – like Noel's – insane and rather fascinating. The whole page gives the impression of a thoroughly superior housemaid.

Brooke, when he wished, could be as bitchy as an ageing and on–the–skids opera diva overtaken by a younger rival. This state seized him most frequently in relation to those he professed to love the most.

He extends the attack from Bryn to all women: 'Did I ever tell you women were vague & sloppy? Not at all, James, not at all. Clear as Euclid. She sizes up and dismisses my letter to her. The emotional one. All things considered, disingenuous was, I thought, the word for it. So that's at an end.' Brooke, unable to be alone in agony, does not neglect to drag James down with him in the wreckage: 'It goes on to be pretty fairly beastly about you. But I mayn't say.' He caps this spit of venom with a breathtaking piece of hypocrisy: 'At Ka she [Bryn] gets in a nice hit or two. Females are at their best in malice.'

All in all, Bryn's breezy insensitivity to Brooke's suffering had driven him down to the depths of distraction. If he had hoped to leap like a crazed circus acrobat from the back of one galloping horse to another, just as he had abandoned Noel for Ka, Bryn had surely let him down. He ended the letter with a shriek of despair: 'Oh James: I think that Life's just too beastly to bear. Too utterly foul. But it's the irresistible, false fondness of the whole that pins me shrieking down.'

In a postscript, he sternly urges James: 'I'm almost completely hard now. Do be hard, James. Hard. Hard. *Hard*. Damn you. Hard as stone . . .' But in his own reply to Bryn, Brooke hid this new iron hand in a velvet glove of silky hypocrisy: 'I was pleased to get your last letter. Oh, and so nicely a long one . . . Oh you nice Bryn! I was immensely cheered . . .' After spinning this sugary candy-floss of untruth, he can't help getting to grips with his gripes:

> I'd planned, you know, such an outburst on you – against you . . . It'd just have shown you what a damned silly tight Weltanschauung you've got. Oh Lord, Lord, I did want to shake you! Oh my Bryn, meine Brunn, Brinna mia, mea Brynna, what do you think the world's made of? What do you think happens? What do you think counts? . . .

By the time this wheedling plaint was penned, Brooke's awkward 'second honeymoon' with Ka had come and gone. On her arrival he lost no time in whisking her off to the quiet village of Neustrelitz on 20 May; restless after a couple of days they moved on to the lakeside resort of Feldberg, and from there the unhappy pair journeyed to Müritz on the north Baltic coast near Rostock. Lacking much evidence apart from Brooke's spiteful little barbs in letters to his most loyal friends like Dudley and Jacques, we can only speculate as to what passed between he and Ka during this troubled fortnight. The atmosphere must have been artificial, owing to a pact as well as the troubles of the recent past. The strain contributed to one of Brooke's regular feverish collapses – and Ka, too, fell unaccustomedly ill.

The exact nature of this sickness is mysterious, but it is possible that it was a miscarriage. Almost certainly pregnant as a result of their first lovemaking at the end of February, she was no longer in that state by the end of May. What happened? An abortion is very unlikely, which means that Ka miscarried either in England while Brooke was in Berlin without her, or soon after joining him – perhaps as a result of more clumsy sexual fumblings between the inexperienced lovers. In any event the general misery of their trip in the mournful backwoods of Pomerania was mercifully cut short by a message from Ka's sister Margaret, summoning her home to comfort her after a broken engagement. True to form, Ka obediently returned. Brooke was glad to see her go.

Before parting, the couple agreed to stay apart for several weeks and separately consider their future. Brooke did not need the time – his mind was made up. Tired of Ka, and spurned by Bryn, predictably he turned his thoughts, like a dog returning to its vomit, to Noel. 'The crux is that that absolutely dead feeling I had when I was in Berlin before she [Ka] came, hasn't vanished,' Dudley learned in a letter that can hardly have enhanced the enjoyment of his Venetian honeymoon.

> I was afraid, beforehand, I might – when I saw her – be dragged down into that helpless tortured sort of love for her I had all the first part of the year, and had just crept out of. The opposite. I remain dead. I care practically nothing for any person in the world. I've anxiety, and a sort of affection, for Ka – But I don't really care. I've no feeling for anybody at all – except the uneasy ghosts of the immense reverence and rather steadfast love for Noel, and a knowledge that Noel is the finest thing I've ever seen in the world, and Ka – isn't. But that doesn't come to much.

Throughout his time in Berlin Brooke was continuing to correspond with both Bryn and Noel – playing a triple instead of his more usual double game. He was consumed with both guilt at having so woefully neglected the woman he now once again regarded as his true love during his Ka crisis; and a nagging certainty that his conduct had finally and irrevocably destroyed his credibility, and with it his last chance of regaining her love and respect. In an otherwise understandably incoherent and inordinately long letter to Noel on 2 May, he struggles to explain himself and make plain his hopeless complexity: 'One wants one thing now & one later, and most of the time one doesn't know what one wants.'

Even while awaiting Ka, he counsels Noel not to feel any sympathy for her about-to-be-rejected rival: 'it's fatal to be in the power of that sort of woman. I know this sounds beastly to you, you little fool . . . You don't understand. It doesn't matter about hurting Ka. You're not to talk about it . . . she's not fit for you to talk about . . . Ka's saved, it doesn't matter if she's suffered in the process. She's deserved a lot more than she had suffered and will suffer. If she's lost, the more broken up & spoilt she is, the better.'

Brooke's sheer stupidity and nastiness are shocking. This passage, and many like it, demonstrate, not only his hopeless, crack-brained confusion but also his lamentable lack of insight into female psychology. If he really thought that this was the best way for him to crawl back into Noel's good books – by simultaneously putting her on a pedestal and screeching at her for her lack of understanding, and by denigrating her cruelly spurned supplanter in his affections – he was not just a nasty piece of work but an utter fool. The charitable explanation is that he was still, simply – mad.

As if to confirm this diagnosis of his sickness he added: 'Ka's done the most evil things in the world. She has – or she's on the way to have – dirtied good & honour & all high things, & betrayed & degraded love. Think of the filthiest image you can for the fouling of the best things by the worst. Ka is doing that. For the sake of all those things, & for the sake of the Ka I used to know, & for the sake of the good love there was between us, I'd not care if I saw Ka *dying* of some torture I could inflict on her, slowly.' Having delivered this evil and insane rant, Brooke admits his sentiments are not noble and are unworthy of a fine or decent person: 'But *I'm* just a scuffling dirtied hurt maimed human soul . . .'

Admitting that he might 'sound silly', he portrays himself as 'the champion of good' and 'the instrument of punishing Evil'. As such, by some perverted twist of logic, he was a suitable partner for the degraded Ka:

> I've been in love with Ka: & I am in love with her in a way, & I shall be, I suppose; & I know her better than anyone does. She's better than you, than any of you, in many ways. She's, in most ways, unusually brave. You're all rather cowardly. She has feelings. None of you has any. But, I tell you, she's infinitely below any of you: and you, Noel, she's not fit – it's sacrilege & shame if she ever touches you. That's *truth*, you little fool. I may marry her. I may kill myself for love of her – but I *know* that's true.

Whether this farrago of hysterical and contradictory nonsense meant anything to its recipient beyond the clear fact that Brooke was beyond help and reason is unclear, but one factor that was goading him to the point of madness was Noel's refusal to descend to his histrionic level. The cool, almost cold-hearted, collectedness that she shared with Bryn here stood her in very good stead. Brooke would far rather have her hate him or love him than remain as she was: 'Oh, if you loved me, I couldn't write to you or be anything but dead to you. And if you cared not at all, I couldn't bother you. But as it is you're rather luckily between – interested in me, aren't you. "fond" & a little solicitous, as one might be for a favourite horse or dog. Damn you.'

But this long and frankly tedious tirade of abuse, self-pity and arrant contradictory twaddle was merely Brooke's peculiar way of wooing the lost Noel. He was preparing a peroration in which, he assured her, unless they got together the central meaning of his life would be missed. Times, dates, places and means are left typically vague – but they must unite: 'Noel, Noel, Noel; Noel with whom I've been through – all that these years have held – & to whom I can say anything; this is what, I sometimes know, you are to me. Soberly, greyly, clearly, as the dead see. I *see* that you're – that *you* & I is – the greatest potentiality for me – & for you, I think. Life together, somewhere & how, & for some period, the whole thing: being one. You, Noel & I.'

Anticipating her reaction, Brooke added an afterthought: 'It's a queer thing to be writing this, when I'm just going to live with – perhaps marry – someone else. It's unfair & insolent to you & unfair & treacherous to Ka (if anything can be unfair & treacherous to Ka.) But it's not either, really. Anyhow, it's true.' He finished his outpouring with a weak apology for being 'a nuisance'. 'Adroitly managed,' he explained, 'I'm capable of being quite sociable & friendly.' It doesn't seem to have occurred to him that not many people would be interested in 'managing' him – adroitly or otherwise.

The grey Berlin dawn was breaking through his windows as he finished his dark night thoughts. What he needed, he told Noel brokenly, was marriage or some equivalent: 'Care for me, care for me, Noel,' he pleaded pathetically as his sleep-starved hands spilt ink across his pillow, the smell of which reminded him of ants in camps gone by: 'I'm not fit to write.'

Noel replied with a brisk, no-nonsense letter recommending that Brooke emulate a lobster she had just seen being tranquillized in a medical lecture: 'They stood him on his head on a piece of glass over water and rubbed him up & down all along his back until he became languorous & finally slept, letting his pincers droop & his long red feelers lie flat. It looked dilicious [sic] for him. Get some one to treat you in the same way.' This piece of advice can hardly have failed to enrage Brooke still further. But it was not to be the last of his humiliations at the hands of the Olivier sisters. His ire was further stirred by Noel's casual news that she was seeing his closest friends, who were 'very pleasant to me'. She was posing for Gwen and Jacques, being courted by James in his new-found heterosexual guise and about to visit Virginia at her new house on the Sussex Downs. Brooke must have felt his solitary state still more keenly as he skulked in Berlin and its environs with the burden of Ka lying heavy on his hands.

He was cruelly cold and honest to Jacques in describing the breakdown of relations with Ka: 'there's some mud wall between us,' he reported from their lakeside retreat; 'my faculty for loving her got cauterized too far . . . [I am] as certain as I am about anything that I could make her promise to marry me within a month. Only I'm still dead.' The numbness, he continued in equally honest vein, extended far beyond Ka: 'I'd not have cared if the whole lot of you'd had your necks broken.' When Jacques replied by recommending two drastic alternatives Brooke told him: '"Marriage or Murder" you say. Well, we've tried both, in a way. I don't at all want either. Though it's true I don't want anything else . . . my love for Ka was pretty well at an end – poisoned, dead – before I discovered she was after all in love with me.' Now it was too late – Ka did not yet know it, and would for years be unable to accept it, but his love-hate for her had turned into that cold cousin – indifference. The embers of his passion were quite extinguished. 'I go about with the woman dutifully,' he told Jacques on 24 May. 'Love her? – bless you, no: but I don't love anybody. The bother is I don't really *like* her, at all.' The iron that had entered his soul over the past half-year had rusted right through: 'There is a feeling of staleness, ugliness, trustlessness about her,' he told Jacques charmlessly. '. . . Dirt. I've a sort of hunger for cleanliness.'

After parting from Ka, a numb and miserable Brooke trailed back to Berlin and the Wards' new apartment in Spichernstrasse to eke out a final fortnight before returning to England. On 30 May he reported ruefully to Noel the sad result of his 'second honeymoon': 'I just care about nobody & nothing in the world – least of all Ka. . . . I feel nothing for Ka except a great pity for her that she's so weak, and a dull uneasiness because she's unclean.' This pathological harping on dirt and uncleanliness was becoming a familiar feature of Brooke's rebarbative ramblings. A future Freudian like James, or a doctor like Noel, would have needed few further insights to understand the sickly state of his psyche. But he squeezed further pimples of pus in the direction of the man whose generous hospitality he was currently enjoying: 'For everybody I just feel blank. There's a man called Dudley – I remember, intellectually, that I like him very much – but actually I don't care twopence if he drowns in a Gondola in Venice.' 'I suppose you don't understand,' he added. But Noel understood all too well.

Brooke was eager to hear about Noel's weekend with Virginia – if only to warn her against the insidious influences of Bloomsbury that he believed had so corrupted Ka. 'They're mostly very amusing people as acquaintances, but not worth making one's friends because they're treacherous & wicked. So take care . . .' If ever there was a case of a pot calling a kettle black, this was it. Malice against Virginia, who was all too capable of holding her own in the vicious gossip stakes, naturally led Brooke on to his chief *bête noire*, Lytton. Defending James against Noel's suspicion that he was 'a worm', Brooke for once stuck up for his friend: 'It's not true.' But Lytton was another kettle of fish entirely: 'Lytton is filthy, & for God's sake don't touch him . . . but James is all right.' Of the rest of Brooke's diminishing circle of friends he could only recommend wholeheartedly his soul mates the Raverats: 'They're good people. I'm finding out how important goodness is: and how dreary mere cleverness.'

When Dudley and Annemarie came back from Venice, he felt more isolated and sorry for himself than ever. 'I'm writing in bed in the tiny room, scarcely bigger than the bed they allow me here,' he told Bryn. 'It's late . . . and those two little mice have scuttled off to bed; and I'm on my back writing by a lamp . . . I feel extraordinarily lonely. And very old . . .' Germany had done all it could for him, he added, describing his condition as 'strong and calm and flat'. His future aim was to 'settle in some obscure part of England for a bit, and write, and see a few people I love'. Fewer by the day, it might be added – it was high time for Brooke to replenish his dwindling stock of friends. But even as he proclaimed his return to health and sanity, he wavered. He continued to push his luck with Bryn: 'I feel so full of love and gratitude towards you', while in the same breath insulting her: 'You don't like things being put directly. Never mind. Poor Bryn. You must lump it.'

Balancing his mental books in Berlin, Brooke estimated he had been able to 'mark time – perhaps go down a bit – in general health and spirits . . . while something – my character? or mental equilibrium? or what? – was getting straight . . . So perhaps there is something to be said for the Universe.' He ended romantically: 'I blow a kiss to you, wave a pyjamad arm, West and a touch of North – is that right? Perhaps you're smelling a rain shower out of your window . . .'

Simultaneously he wrote to Ka proposing to fix a wedding day – an offer that was transparent in its half-heartedness: 'The end of July? Would that do? It's madness for me to make up my mind, now: isn't it.' Despite the spurt of creativity that had delivered 'Grantchester' and *Lithuania*, Brooke was leaving Germany depressed and dull. 'Oh God I hope I find rest and peace and kindness in England,' he told Ka. 'I feel as if all strength or all good were burnt out of me.'

His old friend Geoffrey Keynes, seeing 'Grantchester' in print in *Basileon*, wrote to congratulate Brooke, who replied: 'I may be there next week-end – shall we bathe? I haven't bathed since November. There's a lot to wash off.' The future doctor was asked if he had any cure for Brooke's 'syphilis of the soul'. If there was a remedy, Brooke mused, it might lie in some 'herb growing at the bottom of the river just above the pool at Grantchester, and that if I dive and find it and bring it up – it will heal me I have heard so. I do not know. It seems worth trying.' In fact the herb to cure Brooke's spiritual sickness would remain out of reach. He would continue diving for it – and emerging empty-handed – for the rest of his life.

An objective assessment of the state of Brooke's disordered soul on the eve of his return to England was offered to James. Shorn of the need to pose before any of the three women in his life, Brooke told his old friend:

> I fell (by May) completely out of love with Ka. I've got no emotions worth the name about anybody. I feel an affection for her, in a slight way: mixed with other feelings. I'm ready to flirt with Bryn or anybody else in the world. I DO love Noel in a dim & distant way: I feel a great deal of gratitude to her, with good reason, and a great worship/reverence for her – quite without any ground. I'm going to wait over the summer somewhere in England . . . & see if I get feelings of any kind and energy back. If I can work up enough love for Ka I suppose I shall marry her. But it seems unlikely enough as I am now. If we don't marry, she or I'll go off somewhere. So at least, its at present arranged. But she's very weak & changeable: no I suppose anything may happen to her: as she's got no one to look after her. All this is am strengsten [strictly] private.

Refreshing as it is to read a passage from a letter of Brooke's that is relatively rational and free of hysterical hatred, it is a rare oasis in a desert of spite. He was seriously alarmed by James's courting of Noel, and in the same letter strove creepily to put him off:

> She's a very ordinary person underneath the pink-brown mist, you know. And she's just a female: so she may let you down any moment . . . But I expect, really, she won't fall in love with anybody for at least two years. After that

there'll come a day when she'll suddenly feel a sort of collapse & sliding in her womb, & incomprehensible longings. Its when the ova suddenly begin popping out like peas. Then she'll just be ripe for anybody. But not for you, dear boy. Some rather small & very shiny man, probably syphilitic, & certainly a Jew She'll crawl up to him, will Noel . . . and ask him to have her.

This rich compendium of Brooke's prejudices, combining misogyny and anti-Semitism in a single sentence, is remarkable in its mixture of good and bad prophecy. Noel did indeed make a sudden late and largely loveless marriage – after rejecting many more romantic suitors. Her husband, however, Dr Arthur Richards, was not a Jew but a Welshman, and she did, eventually, enjoy a long-lasting affair with the patient James. Brooke would not live to see any of this.

His frantic jealousy of his friends' pairing off and sexual happiness was made worse under his very nose by the 'scuffling' of the 'little mice', as he termed the newly married Dudley and Annemarie. His reaction was to sip some bromide, turn over and go to sleep, he claimed. 'And when, in the morning, I find a towel in the bathroom bloody that was clean at midnight, I'm not in the least disgusted,' he added. This was Brooke's unsubtle attempt to put the fastidious James off the messier aspects of heterosexual life and 'go entirely back to balls (not mine)'. It was wasted breath: James was a patient philanderer and generally achieved his sexual goals. Brooke was a rare exception to this rule.

Dudley escorted Brooke from Berlin to Cologne on 20 June. There he met James by arrangement. James was reviewing an exhibition of post-Impressionist art for the *Spectator*. From his hotel, Brooke wrote to Bryn to press his suit more forcefully: 'You see, Bryn, life's very short and dull. And one really must take opportunities. – (I write quite without prejudice on this, as being too dead and dull to care about taking opportunities, or anything else –).' Despite his professed *Weltschmerz*, Brooke's message was the old familiar one of Marvell and Herrick. Bryn should gather rosebuds while she may, and stop being a coy mistress:

One doesn't have time to not be disingenuous. If you had eternity . . . I suppose you don't know how blank and dull life can be, and certainly don't know how much filthiness and horror there is in it, or you'd see the point of taking and acknowledging what decent good there is . . . My good woman, when one likes people, it isn't a disembodied spirit, or as a generalisation, or as a means to something, that one likes them – it's as themselves.

His postscript was a simple shout of joy: 'Glory! Glory! Glory! I am coming back!' Noel got the more intimate 'Noel, Noel, Noel, Noel, Noel, Noel, I'm coming home. I'm coming near you. I'm coming home.'

From Cologne they travelled to the Hook of Holland, *en route* spending a night in The Hague, from where Brooke wrote to Ka ominously: 'Please never think of me at all.' They came home on 25 June. During the journey Brooke eagerly devoured a book James had brought with him – Hilaire Belloc's account of a walk through rural Sussex, *The Four Men*. Its lyrical local patriotism deeply impressed Brooke, some lines sinking deep into his subconscious, to resurface again more than two years later in his most famous poem. The book redoubled his determination to return to his sorely missed Grantchester as soon as he could. The place might salve the heartsickness he expressed in a bitter little poem now fermenting in his mind. He called it 'Travel':

> 'Twas when I was in Neu Strelitz
> I broke my heart in little bits.
>
> So while I sat in the Müritz train
> I glued the bits together again.
>
> But when I got to Amerhold,
> I felt the glue would never hold.
>
> And now that I'm home to Barton Hill,
> I know once broken is broken still.

19

Broken Glass

On the evening that he arrived back in London, Brooke, as ever the indefatigable socialite, went to the theatre with the Cornfords. Frances had become something of a confidante to him during his emotional turmoils – sensible, stable, married and yet intensely interested in the man she had first marked out in his 'Young Apollo' Cambridge phase, she was an ideal substitute for the elder sister he had lost at birth. She shared his mother's bias against the Olivier sisters as heartless flirts; but, rejecting that view, Brooke flew to the defence of Noel, whom, he was more and more convinced, he had lost for ever: 'Among a hundred horrors I had been so wicked towards Noel, and that filled me with self-hatred and excess of feeling seeking some outlet.'

During the interval at the Court Theatre, Brooke encountered another sympathetic friend – Eddie Marsh – who invited him to stay at his apartment. The following evening, 26 June, Eddie and Brooke attended a London gathering of the Apostles which included E. M. Forster and Lytton. Thus Brooke found himself gazing balefully at the man, who had been thoughtlessly placed opposite him at the dinner table, whom he had cast in the role of demon. Afterwards a handful of Apostles accompanied Eddie and Brooke back to Raymond Buildings, where Brooke alarmed Forster by bursting into tears while on the phone to Bryn. He was still in an extremely shaky state, and realizing this, his fellow-Apostles rallied round to support a Brother in trouble. It was quietly agreed that Brooke should be invited to a succession of house parties and holidays that summer, which provided for him an almost unbroken chain of tactful buttressing.

Unaware of his friends' underlying plan, Brooke left London for the first of these events – a weekend party on the Thames at Goring, at the family home of Gerald Shove. Here he was surrounded by a sort of Praetorian

Guard of gay Apostles, who protected him from the contamination of women and the upset they inevitably caused him. There was Shove himself, and Eddie, and the other guests included a posse of admiring Cambridge dons – 'Goldie' Lowes Dickinson, Harry Norton and Jack Sheppard. Their soothing presence did not stop Brooke firing off letters to both Bryn and Noel. He had, of course, already squeezed in fleeting, separate meetings with both sisters – seeing Bryn in Trafalgar Square and escorting Noel to see Jacob Epstein's controversial memorial sculpture destined for Oscar Wilde's tomb in Paris.

Now Brooke was attempting to steer both sisters at once – a cracked cabman trying to yoke two fractious fillies to the same coach. He told Noel that she had looked 'incredibly beautiful' at Epstein's studio, and in the same breath invited Bryn out for lunch in London the following Monday. Being briefly dunked back into his homosexual Cambridge past was comforting, he told Noel: 'I like being here – the smells & feelings of summer bring things back – oh God. England's so nice.' But the atmosphere became too cloying and he longed to visit the Oliviers, which, after lunch with Bryn in London, is what he did. The atmosphere at Limpsfield Chart was not all it might have been, partly because of the rare presence of the 'Guv'nor', Sir Sydney Olivier, the stern Fabian and paterfamilias who somewhat daunted Brooke. Privately he called Sir Sydney 'the loony man' – a description that some might think would have been better applied to himself. However, Olivier was quite prepared to be charmed: like almost everyone else, he had been enchanted by 'The Old Vicarage, Grantchester', which Bryn had read out at the breakfast table after receiving it from Brooke in Germany. Brooke's problems lay more with Noel and Bryn, who were distinctly unimpressed by his continuing pose as the sick man of Europe. This no longer washed with the two stern sisters – they didn't mind if Brooke briefly 'crawled in' for the comfort he craved, Noel told James cruelly – so long as he soon crawled out again.

Then there was the Ranee to be faced: early in July Brooke journeyed to Rugby to make a dutiful call on his mother, but the atmosphere was inevitably tense – she was tight-lipped in disapproval of his constant gallivanting with his unsuitable friends, and curtailed his allowance for that year as a mark of her displeasure. Dispirited, Brooke left as soon as he decently could, and by 10 July was ensconced at the place he had dreamed of and longed after for so long: the Old Vicarage, Grantchester.

Some aspects of the old place were familiarly welcoming: 'You see, there *is* honey still for tea,' exclaimed Mrs Neeve as she bustled in with his tea-tray. His poem was already a talking point in the village. Other

Grantchester constants were less welcome: the interior wildlife had come back in force in his absence, and he found woodlice dropping into his golden locks. 'Mrs Neeve sprinkles yellow dust on my books and clothes,' he told Maynard Keynes, '. . . and says "They're 'armless, pore things!" But my nerve gives.'

Although back in the bosom of his much-missed home, Brooke was not as consoled for his soul-searing six months as he had hoped – there were too many ghosts around, he told Noel:

> The shock came when, having paced wonderingly through the garden and round my room, recognizing nothing . . . I mounted to my attic bedroom, & there were the two chairs, the table, the feather-bed, and, alone on the mantel piece largely framed, serene . . . you! I fairly broke down.'

Later, waiting for his supper, Brooke was startled to see what he took to be the ghost of himself:

> 'On the lawn, in the still light of the evening, I saw a figure in a chair, writing, at the little table. He had bare feet. His hair was fair & long & he kept putting his hand through it. What he was writing was not a letter, for there were several sheets, & he wrote on at an even pace – it must be Literature. He was dressed in grey.
>
> It slowly came on me that it was I at the table. I'd probably been here all the year, writing & wandering about. But who, or what had been in London & Lulworth & Cannes & Munich & Rugby & Berlin. Who was it watching myself from the window, then? Was it again I? Who was the chief I? Was there to be a fight? – At that moment the figure looked round . . .

This moment, like something out of a story by Poe or Maupassant, had a mundane end: the *doppelgänger* at the table proved not to be Brooke's own spirit, but Cyril Anthony Neeve, the young son of his landlady, who, Brooke alleged, had 'always modelled himself on me'. But the experience gave him a jolt – and soon there would be a real ghost to contend with.

Even his favourite element of water could not thoroughly cleanse his spotted spirit. 'I've bathed. It seemed to wash off a good deal. I do no work. And I'm terrified of being alone long. But I rest. I've made a vow some when to bathe again in that clean rocky place in Devonshire,' he told Noel, referring to a shared memory of Dartmoor. 'It was cleaner than elsewhere in the world, & it is made holy because your naked body has been in it. Perhaps I can get clean, if I bathe there again.'

Brooke's dread of being alone had developed into yet another of his many phobias, as he admitted to James on 10 July in a letter containing a momentous confession. He described being visited by Daphne, least inspiring of the Olivier sisters, and then having the 'horror' of an evening and night in solitary misery. After supper, unable to face this grisly prospect, he changed into his best grey suit and bicycled off to see his elderly Cambridge mentor, A. C. Benson. Finding he was out, he wheeled round, in increasing desperation, to see if any of his other donnish friends were about. After failing to locate a brace of philosophers – Bertrand Russell and G. E. Moore – and another pair of friends, he finally happened on a distant acquaintance, the historian E. A. Benians, who had grim tidings to tell: Brooke's friend and former lover, Denham Russell-Smith, had died of prolonged blood-poisoning that very morning. Stricken, he rushed home and dashed off his detailed description to James of his seduction of Denham at the Orchard. His matter-of-fact tone belies a grief that would have been sharper had his senses not been dulled by months of largely self-inflicted suffering and the sedatives he was taking to alleviate his dumb misery.

James was suitably sympathetic, offering to visit Brooke to share his sorrow, and hinting, none too subtly, that he would still like to take Denham's place in Brooke's Grantchester bed. Alone in the Old Vicarage, Brooke continued to brood over his loss, fancying that Denham had joined the long list of Grantchester spectres: 'I may see his ghost – I thought there was something last night. It's the only one I'm not afraid of.' There was little else to distract him from returning to his malevolent obsessions. While expressing perfunctory concern for Ka, who was waiting on tenterhooks in the country for him to decide on the future of their ill-starred relationship, he nevertheless told James: 'I suppose she'll soon go to hell.' His cold rage against Lytton showed no sign of abating. Accepting an invitation for a Scottish holiday with James, he cautioned: 'Uncle Trevor's cottage sounds almost too exciting. I suppose there's no danger of your brother Lytton being in it or anywhere near. Because I shan't come if there is.'

His 'bloody state' of gloom was increased by a bizarre medical puzzle: 'When I pumpship it's bright green. What does that portend?' A much more serious portent for his future then green semen came in a letter from Noel: 'You mustn't take on so about our having hooked in Hugh. We had to have him.' This refers to Brooke's having voiced jealous worries about rival suitors paying court to the Oliviers – James Strachey and Virginia's cousin Adrian Stephen to Noel, and Hugh Popham to Bryn. Noel continued: 'Margery was determined. She exclaimed vehemently the other day "I do wish Bryn wd marry Hugh!" & then there was no diverting her, but it must be carried through . . . He's just gone off, with Bryn accompanying him to the station, and one of my cigars to cheer him in the train. He's been very agreeable . . .' Just how agreeable, Brooke was shortly to discover.

During the course of his stay at Limpsfield Chart, Hugh Popham proposed to Bryn and was accepted. Bryn, having just passed her twenty-fifth birthday, had decided it was time to get married and settled on Hugh, who had begun a lifelong career at the British Museum, as a suitably stable suitor. She had seen far too much of Brooke at close quarters to have any illusions about his qualities as a prospective husband and father. However, she kept her engagement strictly secret from him, well knowing the likely effect on his fragile mental and emotional state, and only when he backed her into a corner did she disclose the news. For the time being, blissfully unaware, Brooke continued his archly suggestive postal flirtation with her, and began to plan a joint summer holiday together:

> Allerschönste [loveliest one], I'm so excited about August 4 – 11. I thought about sailing again, & get exciteder & exciteder.– I have had hundreds of proposals for those dates, – lots of other things to do —, as you said. But couldn't we do something remarkable — but it must include getting into the water a lot. (Lord! It's so hot!) . . . won't you explore the Ouse in a yawl? – What is a yawl? Or go to Ostend & give concerts on the beach or fly (in the air) . . . Do think of a thousand things to do in August, please – Perhaps I'll be real then – at last – instead of this palsied simulacrum – even now, about once every forty eight hours, for five minutes, I feel I could do everything in the world . . .

In reality, Brooke's chief activity was solitary, as he had told James, and daringly hinted to Bryn: 'I daren't tell you how I do occupy myself, you'd be shocked.'

But not as shocked as Brooke would be to learn that dull old plodding Hugh had pipped him to the post and carried off the prize. It was a classic case of the tortoise and the hare, and one more massive blow to his battered self-esteem. The blow fell at Everleigh, a remote village on the edge of Salisbury Plain, where Maynard Keynes had organized a rolling party for his friends at the end of July and beginning of August. The surrounding open downland appealed to the rising economist because he could indulge his new hobby of horse riding. He rented the village inn, the Crown Hotel, a hostelry with a private garden. The idea was for Maynard's friends to join him in relays in riding out on four hired nags, followed in the evenings by reading and parlour games.

The guests included Brooke – partly invited for charity in Maynard's capacity as the presiding deity of the Apostles, since he and Brooke were never really close – Geoffrey Keynes, Justin Brooke, James Strachey (though not Lytton, who was, Brooke would be grimly pleased to hear, enduring the horrors of a rainswept Scottish holiday in the company of a sick and irritable Henry Lamb) – and three Oliviers – Daphne, Bryn and Noel. The trinity was balanced by a trio of gay Apostles – Gerald Shove, Gordon Luce, a recently elected handsome young lover of Maynard's, and Frankie Birrell.

Maynard was grumpy at the intrusion of women into what would otherwise have been a cosily exclusive Apostolic occasion: 'I don't much care for the atmosphere these women breed,' he grumbled to his long-time lover Duncan Grant; but he put up with it with sufficient grace, even flirting with Bryn while riding, and consenting to read Jane Austen's *Emma* to his guests. As master of ceremonies, Maynard observed the antics of his most difficult guest with a somewhat jaundiced eye: 'Noel is very nice and Daphne very innocent,' he told Duncan. 'But Bryn is too stupid – and I begin to take an active dislike to her. Out of the window I see Rupert making love to her – throwing a tiny ball in her face, taking her hand, sitting at her feet, gazing at her eyes. Oh these womanisers. How on earth and what for can he do it?'

In fact, there was a clear reason beyond the obvious for Brooke's open flirting with Bryn – Noel was at Everleigh too, and he hoped to rekindle her interest in him by a display of outrageous attention-seeking with her more beautiful sister. In fact he was burning his bridges – annoyed at his behaviour, Noel left the party early, while Bryn, who had accepted his invitation to go boating, revealed that the companion she had asked along as chaperone was none other than – Hugh Popham. Brooke, nettled by the news, voiced vehement protests; he had discouraged 'Goldie' Dickinson, who had wanted to come along as chaperone, only to find him replaced by a rival for Bryn's hand. In addition, his odd notion that women were too frail to be allowed out on their own was aroused by Bryn's plan to leave Everleigh on foot and walk across country to Poole Harbour to pick up their boat. The Victorian lurking beneath the superficial veneer of a modern man in Brooke was outraged: what was quite natural to a free spirit like Bryn was to him an unseemly and dangerous provocation.

The pair wore each other out in a day-long argument over her plans – Bryn lamely tried to justify Hugh's presence on their trip on the River Beaulieu on the slightly suspect grounds that he knew how to handle boats. Brooke knew better: Hugh had in fact visited him in Grantchester only the previous week, and had confided that he had broken off a love affair with Gerald Shove's mother. The man was clearly another Henry Lamb – a practised seducer who could carry off Bryn as soon as look at her. Cornered, Bryn was at last compelled to admit the awful truth. 'I found it almost necessary to give him some explanation of you and bless me if I didn't make a comprehensive statement about my feelings and intentions such as would have amazed you to hear!' she told Hugh. 'So there's another peg to this queer web one has drawn over oneself . . . I'm sorry about Rupert, but he knows his own bloody character best, I suppose.'

Appalled, Brooke collapsed. This was nothing less than a reprise, albeit in a minor key, of the horror of Lulworth. Yet again a woman with whose affections he had carelessly toyed had been won by a rival he considered inferior in every way. His reaction, too, was the same: he fled to his bed and refused to stir, declining even to bid Bryn goodbye when she left the next day. Steeped in misery in his room that evening, Monday 29 July, he managed to pick up his pen: 'Dearest Bryn,' he began, 'I've been too much of a hopeless wreck all day to finish talking to you. I'd further things to say, too – but one can't say such things if one's a broken horror . . .'

At this point his friends, in a well-meaning attempt to revive him, got Brooke to come down to dinner, which was followed by a long poker game. At 1 a.m. he resumed: 'Now I'm going to take a lot of bromide, & I hope I shall sleep . . . I wish I'd said goodbye to you. God only knows if I shall see you again. I was too dead. I've not felt or heard or seen all day. I'm in a mist; going mad – But that's not what I'm writing about. If you like you may give Hugh my love: if you can do it prettily.'

Brooke had not lost hope that his wheedling charm could win Bryn back from the clutches of her fiancé: 'I do so wish I could see you again, before all closes down — that is, if I don't relapse into bed, & all that long desperate disease again.' Using heavy emotional blackmail, he begged Bryn to join him in Scotland after her sailing trip with Hugh: 'But that's if I'm a real person, not a wreck.' Having been invited to stay by both James and Gilbert Murray, a sympathetic Cambridge don, Brooke told Bryn that it was only her he wanted to be with, adding: 'We might have worked out something big – just in time, before life takes you too far in.' He closed with a typical self-pitying bleat: 'Oh, God; you can't think how dead I am & wretched. Forgive & relinquish this corpse.' But following this heavy hint that he was once again considering suicide – from which, he insisted, Bryn had narrowly rescued him in April at Bank – Brooke spoiled the effect of his theatrical climax with a bathetic curtain-call: 'Don't perhaps go too far out of reach. I shall write again, if ever I get back to sanity. Oh yes, Will you, or Margery, send my great BOOTS & my clothes brush here now?' A Hamlet bent on self-destruction does not normally, Brooke should have known, worry overmuch about footwear and specks on his garments.

He was now in a state of near-panic. He had apparently lost in one fell swoop both possible escape routes out of his crisis. Bryn was, as far as he knew, on a boat with Hugh – in fact, failing to find a maritime chaperone, they had gone rock climbing in north Wales with other friends – while Noel, accompanied by Daphne and a cousin of Ka's, Ursula Cox, had decamped to Switzerland. Pathetically, that same night he wrote to her attempting to retrieve something from the wreckage: 'Oh Noel if you knew the sick dread with which I face tonight – that bed & those dragging hours – And the pointlessness of tomorrow, the horror that it might just as well be this evening, or Wednesday, for all the pleasure, or relief from pain, I get out of it. The procession of hopeless hours – That's what's so difficult to face;– that's why one wants to kill oneself.'

He attempted to revive her affection by sentimentally calling up the best moments in their relationship:

Oh, Noel, Noel, Noel, my dearest; think! Remember all that has been! It's more than four years since that evening in Ben Keeling's rooms, & the days on the river – when we were so swiftly in love. Remember those days on the river; and the little camp at Penshurst, next year, – moments then; & Klosters; and the Beaulieu camp; & one evening by that great elm clump at Grantchester; & bathing in early morning by Oxford; & the heights above Clifford's Bridge camp; & a thousand times when we've gone hand in hand – as no other two people could; – & twice this year I felt your tears, Noel's tears, on my hand. There are such things, such things that bind us. Half what you have grown to be, is my making: half of what I am is yours. It's in the meeting of our hands, & lips, child. You *must* know it – I cannot live without you. I cannot indeed. You can make anything of me – For you I'll do anything, or make myself anything – anything in the world . . . You must see what we are, child – I cannot live without you. – But remember, I'm not only in love with you; I'm very fond of you – Goodnight child – in the name of our love Rupert.

In spite of this plea, sounding so passionately sincere, Brooke was continuing to investigate other escape routes. He had heard that Elisabeth van Rysselberghe was to visit England again, and wrote to her in hope of arranging a meeting: 'If I can't give you the love you want,' he told her, 'I can give you what love and sympathy and pity and everything else I have. And I have a lot . . . I've had a lot of pain, infinite pain – I know what it's all like . . .' But, he concluded honestly enough: 'I'm not worth your loving, in any way.'

Meanwhile there was one more painful duty to perform. At long last he had to face Ka in person. More than a month had passed since their separation in Germany. Ka had spent the time in the Sussex countryside, often in tears, waiting for Brooke's decision on their future. As for herself, she told Frances Cornford, chief confidante to them both: 'I love Rupert – I'm quite clear – and I'm waiting quietly now and getting as strong as I possibly can. To see if he has strength and love enough to heal himself and love me again.'

It seemed that she had taken Brooke's furious accusations to heart, for she was now accepting most of the responsibility for the breakdown of their affair:

> I have broken and hurt and maimed him – I see. O my dear – apart from me – it was wicked, it was awful to hurt so lovely a thing and so lovely a person. If I've destroyed love and strength in him (not for me particularly – but for everyone) there is no atonement and no help – I feel. I'm being very quiet – and I don't want to bother him now at all. He knows what it is and what there is to decide.

At last the shock of Bryn's desertion jolted Brooke to a decision. He wrote to Ka, who was staying with two aunts at the Swan Hotel in the small Gloucestershire town of Bibury before she too joined the Everleigh party – tactfully after his departure. They should meet alone, Brooke said, and work out their future together – or rather, he had decided, their future apart. On the eve of the meeting, 1 August, he wrote again to Noel from Everleigh:

> O child, I'm so miserable. Tomorrow Justin (who has his car here) is going to drive me to Ka's. I'm going to walk out, lunch somewhere with her; talk; & take a train on to Rugby. You see, it's no good putting it off. One can't go on waiting & waiting. It's a horrible strain on her. We decided, when she left Berlin, to wait a month or two, till we – especially I – were better & healthy & sane, & then see – see if I loved her, if we should marry. Well it's no good going on. I don't & can't love her. Things have begun to come back into that numb dank place that is the abode of my feelings: but not love for her. I couldn't ever live with her, I know – from experience even. I should go mad, or kill her, in a few months.

Finally, he assured Noel: 'I love someone else.'

Brooke felt huge guilt about the pain he was about to inflict on Ka, but his resentment of the pain he believed her to have put him through still rankled:

You see child – Noel – there's been so much between Ka & me. We've been so close to one another, naked to each other in our good parts & bad. She knows me better than anyone in the world, – better than you let yourself know me – than you care to know me. And we've given each other great love & infinite pain – and that's a terrible, unbreakable bond. And I've had her.

This terse admission of their sexual intimacy conveys the dual message that their lovemaking had formed a deep and unshakeable tie, and yet it had also rendered a relationship – let alone marriage – impossible. Ka was indelibly besmirched:

It's agony, *agony*, tearing out part of one's life like that – You see, I have an ocean of love & pity for her . . . I don't hate & despise her – By God, I'm infinitely far from it. She did once what I, you know, thought & think a mixture of a filthy ghastly mistake & an evil crime. I've 'forgiven' that ages ago . . . I'd give anything to do Ka good. Only . . . she killed somethings [sic] in me. I can't love her, or marry her . . .

At the same moment as he definitively washed his hands of the defiling Ka, Brooke was beseeching Noel for another chance: 'Noel, Noel, there's love between you & me, & you've given me such kindness & such sympathy – in your own Noel way – I'm wanting your presence so much – I'm leaning on you, at this moment, – stretching towards you . . . I do suck help from you, child; your hands & face, & mind.' But Noel was harder than Ka – no cushion she, still less a bottomless well of love from which Brooke could draw endless buckets of love and sympathy. Her oasis had dried up long ago.

On the morning of the dreaded day, Brooke found the time to scribble a hasty note in pencil to Bryn, thanking her for having safely sent on his boots and brush. He added silkily: 'Your presence is very lovely & comforting to me . . . and you've been very good to me. I'm apparently an ungrateful beast – I must see you again, once more – with love Rupert.' In a postscript he added: 'This is merely saying "do not entirely let me slip" – I've secrets to tell you.'

The second of August dawned hot and dry – a typical high-summer day of unforgiving heat. Brooke journeyed north from Everleigh with Justin at the wheel of his commodious Opel, the same car that had taken them to summer picnics around Cambridge in days of hope that already seemed a lifetime ago. Justin deposited Brooke at the roadside near Bibury, and then went to pick up Ka at the Swan. On returning he let

273

the two of them wander off into the surrounding woods and fields, and waited. One hour went by, then two. The airless heat lay heavily over the countryside, and it seemed that time stood still. No other car passed along the road, choked with white dust. A solitary farm labourer ambled by, touching his cap to the gentleman sitting patiently in the unfamiliar shiny car. 'The corn's gett'n' ripe,' he remarked in a broad Gloucestershire burr. After three hours Justin was relieved to spy two familiar figures approaching through the heat haze. Brooke and Ka were leaning against each other in mutual support. They looked pale and said little, but Justin noticed that Ka was holding her pince-nez. The glass was broken.

They dropped her back at Bibury, and drove on to the nearby town of Witney, where, the last Rugby train having long since departed, they were compelled to spend the night at an inn. That same evening Brooke wrote to the Cornfords to tell them what he had done: 'I can't love her, you see. So now all's at an end. And she's passed out of my power to help or comfort. I'm so sad for her, and a little terrified, and so damnably powerless . . .' It seemed, however, as if Brooke was more concerned about the agony he was going through in inflicting pain on Ka, than about the pain she was feeling:

> Oh Frances, it was Hell. Ka, whom I loved, whom I love so still, is in such hopelessness and agony. My God, it was awful. When one's seen people in pain like that, one can't ever forget it . . . I feel like a criminal (though I know I'm not). She spoke wildly – one does at first, I know – It was terrible. I'm aching so for her. She was so fine . . . She's in such agony. No one can help or comfort her. It tears me so, to think of her.

Although believing Ka to be beyond help, the next morning Brooke asked Frances to do what she could to comfort her: 'tell all the truth of how great you think her, and then lies. Pile it on, it doesn't matter if it's true – love and praise. It's the only sort of thing that helps human nature in these bloody moments . . . Not that anything'll do much. And it's impudent of me to write in this way. I'm all exhausted and worn with the pain of it.' Finishing the letter on the platform at Oxford station, where Justin had dropped him to pick up a Rugby train, Brooke added: 'It's incredible that two people should be able to hurt each other so much.' Then came a bleak postscript: 'I'm twenty five today.'

By the time she received the letter, Frances had already seen Ka's agony for herself. She wrote in her memoirs:

I remember her leaning her head right back against the wall while tears poured down her fair skin . . . saying 'You don't know how awful it is when one has broken down that wall of separation that one lives in and let another human being come right in, to have to live alone again.' She pushed out her big hands as if she was trying to push away the wall that had closed round her again.

For once Ka, the cushion who absorbed all the pounding her friends could offer, had split apart in all her naked vulnerability. She would never get over it.

In a swift note to James Strachey on that fateful morning of 2 August, Brooke dropped a heavy hint as to his future plans – he implied that he did not want to accompany him to Scotland after all, and added dismissively: 'Hadn't you better drop me?' It was becoming obvious that what he really wanted was nothing less than a clean sweep of his previous existence – a clearing out of all those who reminded him of the pain he had been undergoing for the past seven months. Having got rid of Ka, lost Bryn and probably forfeited Noel's regard into the bargain, he decided to rid himself of all those who would be less than wholly adoring or sympathetic. A core group of the Neo-Pagans – Justin, the Cornfords, the Raverats and Dudley Ward – would retain a precarious toehold in his affections; but all those who in his view were tainted by contact with the corrupt Bloomsbury clique would have to go. And that included his oldest and closest friend, James. As he explained to Jacques, what he found impossible to tolerate was 'the subtle degradation of the collective atmosphere of the people in these regions – people I find pleasant and remarkable as individuals'.

In his eyes, chief among those stained by this taint were his very oldest friends. Lytton, of course, took pride of place among the damned, and, by extension, James, especially when he had the temerity to defend his elder brother. Virginia Stephen, too, was to be cast out – particularly since she had recently become engaged to the Jewish Leonard Woolf; a move that fired into life both Brooke's latent anti-Semitism and his sexual jealousy: 'I thought the little man'ld get her,' he had written to James Strachey on hearing the news in Germany:

Directly he began saying he was the only man who'd had a woman she knew, and telling tales about prostitutes – oh you should have seen the lovelight dance and dawn in her eyes! *That* gets 'em. To him that hath shall be given: from him that hath not shall be taken away even that which he hath. Even that which he hath, James, one by one. Two, two for the lily-white balls: clothed all in hair, oh!

Duncan Grant and Maynard Keynes were also henceforth cast into the outer darkness, and a big question mark hung over Noel Olivier. Brooke watched her with grave suspicion for any sign that she was moving toward Bloomsbury's fatal orbit.

Rugby only held him for a day or two – his mother's cloying company he found increasingly irksome – and his restlessness now took on a manic quality as he rushed from place to place in a distracted search for relief with various hospitable friends and acquaintances. He appeared to be unable to remain anywhere for more than a few days at a stretch, and was uneasily aware that, wherever he fetched up, his presence was a strain. However, his fear of being alone outweighed such social embarrassment. The fact that those he stayed with were mostly married only served to underscore his solitary state. While at Rugby he had taken the opportunity to write to Noel again. He was still concerned about Ka, and, despite having made a definite break, he was again proposing to write to her to 'clear up points'. Like a dog with a bone he just could not leave well – or ill – alone.

'Ka keeps insisting that we must marry,' a patient Noel read. 'But it won't do. She wavers, at present at one moment she said I must marry somebody soon, – if not her, I must marry you. At another, she wanted me not to see you for some time, so that I might relove her . . . She's in a bad way. It half kills me every time I think of her . . . And the sort of friends she has – James, or Virginia – are useless: mere takers.'

Shrewdly Brooke noticed that his physical courage had diminished, along with his mental toughness – he noted that on his previous annual visit to the dentist he had endured hours of pain with an equanimity that drew admiration from his tormentor. 'This year,' he says of a visit to a dentist in Birmingham he made while staying with his mother, 'I found myself shivering & wincing before he touched me – it's bloody having all one's nerves gone.' He feared the effect such confessions would have on his already dwindled credit with Noel as a real man: 'I sometimes wonder if, being so romantic, you despise & dislike me for being whining, despondent, uneasy, glum, silly – miserable, for oh, a year perhaps . . . I'll be more competent when I get out of this bog.' But Noel's stock of patience was all but used up. On 2 August she had written briskly from her hotel at Kiental in the Bernese Oberland counselling: 'Rupert you mustn't die or go mad . . . Once you can see through this nightmare you'll see what infinite good is left for you, worth your living to be a hundred for. I'll leave you alone. It probably wont do me much harm, for you to stop pandering to my flat affection – it should never have counted . . . You MUST wake up. from Noel.'

From Rugby he travelled to Cambridge, anxious to have some news of Ka from the Cornfords. Frances, keen to alleviate the plight of both partners in the torturing tug-of-war, suggested that they go abroad separately, to forget each other and erase the pain among unfamiliar sights and sounds. France and Germany were no good, she advised a receptive Brooke. He must get away to the ends of the earth – Australia, perhaps, or how about picking oranges in the healing warmth of California? At any rate he must plunge into some sort of back-breaking physical work which might give his overstretched mental muscles some relief. Brooke pondered this well-meant advice for some months before acting on it; but Ka leapt at the chance, and within a few months was in Germany, before going on to Poland and Russia. Apart from one unfortunate chance encounter, she would not see Brooke for another two years.

Their physical separation did not stop them torturing each other by mail. Brooke brooded over the harsh words exchanged at their meeting in Bibury and wrote to her bitterly:

It's no good. I *can't* marry you. You must see. If I married you, I should kill myself in three months. I may, I daresay I shall, anyway. But if I marry you, I'm certain to . . . You had two ways before you, a dirty one and a clean one; coming to Germany was not even deciding; it was only giving the clean one a chance. You refused to marry me. You refused to forswear filth . . .

I felt ashamed because you were better and honester than I (ashamed and yet superior, because you are a woman). Yet it's not my lack of strength that makes me want not to marry you. It is my strength . . . When I found that I wasn't too dead for a sort of love, – but that it wasn't for you, that you had killed my love for you too dead – it seemed to me useless to prolong waiting any longer.

However much he dwelled on 'cleanliness', it seemed the one thing Brooke found impossible to do with Ka was make a real clean break.

By 9 August Brooke was at Beckhythe Manor, at Overstrand in Norfolk, the home of the academics Gilbert and Rosalind Murray. From here he wrote again to Ka, floating Frances's plan for a prolonged exile for them both: 'I suppose I might as well go. I feel more inclined to kill myself.' But he was still racked with indecision: 'At present my mind has about as much chance of deciding about going, or anything, as a river has of deciding where it shall run into the sea.'

Noel, too, received a letter from Norfolk, with an outline of Frances's scheme: 'She's Ka's only decent real friend: she's good, & not being a virgin, she understands things. She wants me to go abroad for a year – to

Australia or somewhere, & work manually . . . I don't know what to do.' But one drawback to his absence would be that it would leave Noel in mortal peril from the moral contamination he feared to the point of lunacy: 'I'm frightened of leaving you in that bloody place London. I'm afraid of evil coming to you. Your friends are a bloody useless & poisonous lot – your friends & mine. I'd rather be where I can help.' The strange *idée fixe* that only Brooke, like some latter-day Sir Galahad, could save his damsels from the rampant evil of the city, or to be more specific, of Bloomsbury, had taken firm root in his distressed mind. Dudley Ward was told: 'I daren't leave Noel for a year . . . Females are fools – virgin females. And the ideas about "sex" in all these circles are, as you know, monstrously false.' Brooke added for good measure that if Noel were seduced it would 'kill me'.

Detecting from Noel's cool tones from the icy slopes of the Swiss Alps that his suit with her was failing fast, Brooke switched from mawkish self-pity to whinging accusation – 'Noel, you have done me wrong. You owe me something' – before tipping over into hysteria:

> Oh, child, Noel, what *do* you want of me? . . . I can be anything with your desire & demand: & so wastingly nothing without you. Do you want eminence or money? They're the easiest things in the world. So you want liberty? You should have utter liberty. Are you tired of decency & do you want brutality? I could give it you, as much as you could swallow & more. Or strength? or kindliness? Or, being a woman, is it filth you're pining for? I assure you, there's no lack in me.

As raging jealousy grabbed him by the vitals, Brooke named his demons: 'Is it that you want, before you retire from modern virginity, to enjoy flirting & having James & Adrian & the rest dangling dolefully round? . . . You can get all that, married if you wish . . .' Admitting his 'desperation', he begged Noel to come away with him the following month. He was simultaneously, it almost goes without saying, begging Bryn to go away with him that same month. He promised, futilely, to get himself 'under control & behave decently' in the meantime.

Brooke seems finally to have taken leave of his senses during these desperate days. From Norfolk he returned to Rugby, whence he summoned James for a less-than-regal official dismissal. In a letter that should have warned James of what awaited him he ranted:

> To be a Strachey is to be blind – without a sense – towards good and bad, and clean and dirty; irrelevantly clever about a few things, dangerously infantile

about many; to have undescended spiritual testicles; to be a mere bugger; useless as a baby as means; & a little smirched as an end. You have – by heredity & more by environment – a little of the Strachey. Buggery, with its mild irresponsibility & simple problems, still hangs about you. You can't understand anything being really important – except selfishly – can you? So you'll not understand the possibility of 'He that is not with me is against me' being occasionally true.

What seems to have really angered Brooke was James's belated conversion to heterosexuality, with its awful possibility that his friend might successfully seduce Noel while his back was turned. To make matters worse, James had stubbornly defended his brother Lytton against Brooke's raving assaults:

It becomes possible to see what was meant by the person who said that seeing you & any member of the Olivier family together made them cold & sick.– It was wrong not to be able to distinguish between you & Lytton: but, if one's to believe you, not so very wrong. But then I suppose you can't understand anyone turning cold and sick to see anybody with anybody else – except through jealousy, and that makes hot –; can you? It doesn't happen in buggery.

James's conciliatory response seems to have sparked an even greater paroxysm of fury:

Listen. Men & women neither 'copulate' nor want to 'copulate': men have women: women are had by men. Listen. There is between men & women, sometimes, a thing called love: unknown to you. It has its laws & demands. It can be defiled: poisoned: & killed. Listen. It is not equally sensible to talk of your friend Lamb having nearly seduced Ka, & of Ka having nearly seduced your friend Lamb. Listen. Ka wrote to me that if she had done what she once contemplated, & what she was saved from by my love, she would have killed herself long ago.

There is about Brooke's whole lunatic performance a stench of sex gone bad. Mad with rage, he detests the homosexuality he once espoused; he considers himself a repository of wisdom on male–female relations; and he still sticks to his delusion that only his unique, disinterested devotion 'saved' Ka from a fate worse than death at the hands of Henry Lamb. James, the future Freudian, must have shaken his head with wonder. But, instead of giving his friend up as a hopeless case, he heroically made the tedious journey to Rugby in an attempt to reason with him. It was a mission that was doomed.

James had hardly set foot across the threshold when Brooke pitched into him with the familiar charges and wild accusations. A Brooke biographer, John Lehmann, who spoke to James at first hand, says that Brooke's raging became so intemperate that James felt he had to leave at once, retreating with 'Rupert's denunciations ringing in his ears'. Like Lytton, Duncan Grant and Virginia, James had to listen to foaming assaults on Lady Ottoline Morrell, whom Brooke had come to hate and fear both as Lamb's mistress and as the leading patron of Bloomsbury. As such he seemed to regard her as the malevolent spider at the centre of a web of uncleanliness. Some idea of the extremity of his feelings aroused by the extravagant Ottoline is gained from a letter to Ka the following April describing a brief encounter with the redoubtable lady: 'She stank, filthily. If ever she dared to mention you to me, I'd stop her bloody mouth by telling her what I thought of her. I only pray I shouldn't hit her . . . She's primarily & centrally filthy, nauseous, degraded. It made me feel dirty for days, having seen her . . . that slut.'

On 17 August, following his abortive visit, James wrote to Lytton, who had been regaling him with a tragicomic account of his disastrous Scottish holiday with Henry Lamb:

> I've been going through horrors too, and am pretty well wrecked now. It's all so senseless and unnecessary – but that doesn't prevent it reducing me to tears. One of the results is that I'm not now going away with Brooke. I don't mind telling you that it's now bestimmt [definite] and announced that he's 'abandoned' Ka and 'loves' Noel. The explosion with me, however, has had every motive assigned to it, except the obvious one. Oh lord there *have* been scenes. And the dreadful thing is that he's clearly slightly cracked and has now cut himself off from everyone.

Brooke appeared to agree: 'I've cut myself off from James (who I'm fond of),' he told Jacques, the friend who most nearly shared his anti-Bloomsbury, anti-Semitic paranoia. Still ignorant of the fact that he had become the chief hate-figure in Brooke's internal drama, Lytton, ironically, was chiefly concerned by the suspicion that his beloved Lamb was following Brooke down the slippery slope to insanity: 'Henry I suspect is daft,' he told Ottoline Morrell, who shared his passion for the wayward painter:

> That's the only explanation I can see for his goings on . . . oh dear, what a muddle of a world we drag ourselves along in, to be sure! I sit here brooding

over the various people – Woolf and Virginia, Duncan and Adrian, Vanessa and Clive [Bell] and Roger [Fry], and James and Rupert and Ka – and the wildest Dostoyevskian novel seems to grow dim and ordinary in comparison.

Having disposed of James, Brooke left Rugby to visit a more reliably supportive old friend, Justin Brooke, with whom he stayed at his palatial family home, Leylands, at Wotton in the Surrey countryside. He told Bryn of his plan to go abroad – although the destination had shifted to Canada: 'It's thought that it's the only way of saving my health & reason . . . I consort with the old now: & find a comparative peace and fitness in that.' Brooke was still wheedling for Bryn to join him on a walking tour before the summer ended and she embarked on marriage. He was, he said, 'available' after burning his boats with James: 'I have, in my course downhill, separated from him. I like him: but I disapprove of Stracheys & such like . . .' Half-seriously he threatened to 'shoot himself' unless she agreed to his proposal. But then came a spurt of malice: 'I suppose if you seem happy, I shall suddenly put a knife into you, out of sheer envy.' He hinted that he was relying on her to 'set me going again'. But this thin ray of hope, too, was not to be: a diplomatic bout of flu prevented Bryn taking up Brooke's invitation. As she explained to another victim of Brooke's wrath, James Strachey: 'no good could have come of my seeing him. He's evidently got to get through this – whatever "this" is, by himself. I can't help being slightly muddled by his rhetoric even after all these years and don't say the things I meant to when I'm with him, so what's the good? One comes away feeling baffled and exhausted.'

Bryn was not the only old friend to be running out of patience with Brooke's tantrums, inconstancy and sheer purblind, self-obsessed stupidity. James and Noel, too, had separately thrown in the towel. The only alternative left open for Brooke was to turn to new friends with only a sketchy knowledge of his dark history and tribulations. So he reached for the next link in the chain on which he hung over the abyss.

This was Rectory Farm, near Great Hampden in the Chilterns, the home of the poet John Masefield and his wife Constance. By this time Brooke had received another of Noel's coldly bracing letters from Switzerland in which she called him 'wrong and pathetic'. She added: 'Ka's probably right: that you ought to marry someone, she understands you. But if you cant, if there's no one that you can or will marry now, dont become dotty, like Margery is supposed to be, you MUST be able to do something to keep alive; without that. Be fine again, & dont spoil whats left by fury.' It was good advice, but wasted on Brooke in his present negation. At any rate it left him in no doubt that Noel had finally ruled herself out as his wife.

From Great Hampden he told Ka, ruefully but truthfully, that Noel 'rather dislikes me, and always will'. Revelling in his abject bitterness, he called the world 'a horror' and talked longingly of suicide: 'the days bring a sort of pain and nothing else; and I think I'm a little mad. My dear, it's nothing to do with you – I'm somehow rotten. And I guess it'll be better if I don't leave children – people like me – behind.'

By 21 August he was back in Rugby. On the way he had stopped off in London to see the lying in state of General William Booth, founder of the Salvation Army. Brooke's reaction to the hushed obsequies could have been a description of his own mood: 'Hysteria – hysteria gone stale in the air!' At Bilton Road he was plagued by 'ghastly' headaches, doubtless of psychosomatic origin, that prostrated him for 30 hours at a stretch.

In this pitiful condition, perhaps the lowest point he had touched, he forced himself to make a final throw of the dice with Noel. She had left Switzerland and was staying with Gwen and Jacques at the Raverats' grandiose château in Prunoy. From these loyal friends of Brooke, who would always believe that Ka was the right partner for him, Noel learned further wounding details of the full extent of the Ka–Brooke imbroglio. The news merely hardened her resolve to make a clean break with the hysterical and treacherous invalid. As she told her Bedales school friend Mary Newberry: 'He thought I wouldn't mind if he went off with Ka. But I did.' Her antipathy would have been stronger still had she read a letter that Brooke wrote at this time to Jacques in which he dubbed her 'one of these virgin-harlots of modern days; a dangerous brood . . .'. With unwitting irony he added: 'Margery is the only decent one of the family . . .'. In fact Margery was rapidly descending into the madness that would eventually devour her brilliant mind.

On 28 August Brooke wrote his make-or-break letter to Noel. He described himself as 'in far dissolution' and predicted: 'It is very probable that I shall smash up altogether this autumn. I think a great deal & very eagerly of killing myself, if my present state goes on. I spend an intolerable time in every kind of agony, day after day. I can do no sort of work, reading or writing . . .' But after this burst of self-pity he still had the energy to haul Noel over the coals of his misanthropic hatred: 'You are enabled, by initial stupidity and by years of careful & laborious practice, to despise me. There is the extraordinary spectacle of a silly little worm like you thinking me "unbalanced" and "pathetic".'

Brooke knew better. In a sad display of Lear-like impotence, he defied the world: 'I know, & a few more know, what I am & can be like. I know how superb my body is, & how great my bodily strength. I know that with my mind I could do anything. I know that I can be the greatest poet and writer in England. Many know it.' But, he insisted, he still needed Noel beside him as he performed these marvels: 'I could be anything in the world I wanted, with you. And nothing without you.' He actually proposed accompanying Noel to a summer camp, but lest she be tempted, capped the invitation with an arrogant burst of murderous rage against James: 'I find creatures like that, Stracheys & so forth, not only no good, but actually dangerous, spots of decay, menaces to all good. Even if one doesn't mind rats qua rats, one has to stamp out carriers of typhoid . . .' Absurdly, he then reflected: 'This isn't much of a love letter . . .' Even more astonishingly, this tirade of abuse was leading up to a postal proposal of marriage – something Brooke had carefully avoided throughout the four years of their tangled relations. 'You needn't tell me I've "fallen from love to love",' he began:

I know. I'm ashamed, & sorry. Oh God! I deserve reproaches. But I've paid enough, haven't I? for being unfaithful to you. I was evil. I'm sorry. I'll pay & pay. I've come back, child. I committed adultery. But what you threaten is divorce. It may not be. We've gone too far. We must marry. Not immediately, if you will. But we must. I'll give you everything in the world – You mustn't kill me. I must marry you.

In its bravura ignoring of reality, this was a typical Brooke performance. But his desperate plea fell on stony ground. On the last day of August, Noel replied that it was not the Ka affair alone or even at all that had put her off. Her disillusionment with him pre-dated Lulworth: 'It was last November that I decided and you found out I didn't love you – the idea of marriage & lots of thought about it has just strengthened my knowledge.' Yet, once this blunt and bare rejection was out, Noel bent over backwards to buttress Brooke and indulge his whims and fantasies. She would even camp with him, 'if you like', and she would not fall into the bad company he so paranoiacally feared: 'James . . . won't be allowed to do anyone any harm . . . In the winter I shall see only Bryn & Hugh & Margery & Ethel Pye & some old Bedalians, and Jacques & Gwen . . . but that will be all. You need have no fear of slug-like influences from the people Jacques calls "the Jews". (They comprise the Bloomsbury household & the Stracheys, I believe.)' Having mollified Brooke's morbid fear of cultural and racial contamination – he and Jacques referred to Bloomsbury as 'the Jews' even though Leonard Woolf was the sole Jewish member of the coterie – Noel also tried to calm his sexual jealousy of her other suitors: 'Especially I shal'nt see James, nor Adrian – that I have decided for my own good.' She ended the letter practically on her knees: 'Do write & say how I can be agreable [sic]. I'm humble. I'm penitent. I'm fond. & I want to be made use of, or kicked away for a cure, if I'm not wanted. Tell me what I can do.' Altogether, it was more than Brooke deserved.

At the end of August, looking back over the two months since his return from Berlin, Brooke surveyed a landscape of what he called 'waste'. He had torched the boat that could have carried him back to a past and happier existence, and one by one he had chopped off the four main props of his sexual and emotional life – Ka, James, Bryn and Noel – with a sort of cold, nihilistic fury. Now, like a chair without legs, he sat uselessly on the ground. He was left with the choice of sinking even lower or building his life anew.

20

New Friends, Now Strangers

It took some time for the fact of Noel's rejection to sink in. By the end of August Brooke was in Scotland, but not in the company of James, as had originally been planned, nor of Bryn, as he had so forlornly hoped. His host was yet another concerned Apostle, Harry Norton, who had witnessed Brooke's collapse at Lulworth. Staying at Moffat, near Dumfries, Brooke was not up to much beyond sleeping and eating; in his words he was 'loitering about in a stupor'. But he was stung by Noel's resolve and her claim that she did not love him: 'You lie, Noel,' he wrote angrily. 'You may have persuaded yourself you don't love me, or engineered yourself into not loving me, now. But you lie when you say you never did & never could. You did – Penshurst & Grantchester & a thousand times. I know you did; & you know it. And you could.' Even this plea failed to move Noel from her firm stance – although she softened sufficiently to agree to meet him, she held out no hope of a revival of their love.

On 17 September Brooke met Noel at her home, but all his desperate eloquence could not move her, and he returned to London that evening sick at heart. He was not to know that he had touched bottom and was on the brink of a revival after so many months of misery. He had been invited to stay for a week with Eddie Marsh at Raymond Buildings. Although Eddie had not played much part in Brooke's life during the long months of his breakdown – such emotional turmoil would have bewildered the rational, humorous and generous civil servant – he had continued to take a fond paternal interest in his favourite protégé's career. For example, in February a mutual friend had introduced Eddie to Harold Monro, the chief entrepreneur of contemporary poetry. Monro edited the influential *Poetry Review*, the house journal of English verse, and was about to open the Poetry Bookshop in Devonshire Street, probably the first shop in Britain devoted exclusively to the selling and promotion of poetry, including the unheard-of innovation of public readings by living poets and the provision of rooms above the shop where impecunious poets could stay.

Monro encouraged Eddie to write a long and laudatory appreciation of Brooke's poems in the *Poetry Review*. Eddie obliged with an extravagant plug, telling Brooke he hoped it would give his career a boost and make his name known to the 4000 fans of modern verse who bought the publication. He also showed Brooke's poems to leading contemporary critics, including Edmund Gosse and Austin Dobson, although he took care to steer them clear of what he called 'the ugly poems' like 'A Channel Passage'. At this time Eddie had only heard vague rumours of Brooke's condition in Cannes, and imagined him to be on some sort of rest cure after overworking. Comically, considering Brooke's real plight, he had written: 'I was delighted to hear rather vague reports that you are now bursting with health and had been revelling in the Riviera – I had a dismal picture of you in my mind, broken and prematurely aged by excess of milk and honey diet, mooning disconsolate in a depressing cosmopolitan watering place . . .'

Embroiled that spring in the latest of a succession of constitutional crises convulsing English political life – the government's Irish Home Rule Bill and Protestant Ulster's resistance to it – Eddie had still found the time to promote his young friend's verse, as E. M. Forster later recalled: 'Our oddest meeting was in a Belfast hotel, in the midst of a raging anti-Churchill mob. The lift descended into the lounge – there was a rush at it, but out got a slim figure [Eddie] who advanced toward me saying, "Have you wead Wupert's new poem?"'

Though grateful for his patron's shameless bugle-blowing on his behalf – the next Poet Laureate, Robert Bridges, was the latest target of Eddie's exhortation to read Brooke – the poet was too preoccupied by his personal problems to show Eddie 'The Sentimental Exile' (as 'The Old Vicarage, Grantchester' was originally titled when it appeared in *Basileon*). Eddie was slightly piqued when he found out, as he adored the poem to excess: 'It's lovely, my dear . . . the most human thing you have written, the only one that has brought tears to my fine eyes' he gushed to the author. It was he who pressured Brooke into changing the title to the one it bears today.

When Brooke arrived at Eddie's home on 17 September, he was given the key to the two-floor flat and invited to make it his London *pied-à-terre* in place of the National Liberal Club. He was glad to do so, and moved many books and other personal effects into the spare room, which was adorned by Stanley Spencer's striking painting *The Apple Gatherers* – the diminutive and eccentric artist being yet another of Eddie's innumerable protégés. Not the least of the charms of the flat was the comfortable presence of Eddie's housekeeper, Mrs Elgy, an apple-faced woman from Derbyshire. She found Brooke 'a stoojius type' who caused her little trouble, apart from his preference for eating his meals off a tray while sprawled on cushions on the living-room floor.

Brooke's initial stay as Eddie's semi-permanent guest lasted a week. On his first evening he went with his host to watch a fire that was consuming a timber yard behind nearby King's Cross station in a vast conflagration. On the way they stopped to pick up another of Eddie's poetic protégés – the Northumbrian poet Wilfrid Gibson, nine years older than Brooke, who had made a name for himself as a celebrant of the working lives of northern folk and had recently arrived in London in an attempt to make his way in the literary world. Arriving at the site of the blaze, the trio linked hands to keep from being swept apart by the huge crowd, and later, exhilarated by the disaster, they excitedly talked literature far into the night. It was Brooke's first meeting with a poet who would become close to him – he affectionately nicknamed him 'Wibson' – and would eventually be numbered among his three literary heirs.

A day or two later another late–night conversation resulted in the birth of a project that would have momentous consequences for the history of English poetry – and for the development of Brooke's own career. Arriving back home after a hard day at the Admiralty under the unforgiving lash of Winston Churchill, Eddie found Brooke lying half undressed on the bed but still wakeful. The insomnia that had plagued him since Lulworth was a hard habit to shift. Enchanted by the sight of the recumbent semi-naked Brooke, Eddie lingered to talk. The subject turned to poetry, and how best to foster the renaissance in English verse that they both believed was under way. Brooke facetiously suggested an anthology written entirely by himself under 12 different pseudonyms. Eddie countered with the idea of a genuine anthology written by their own friends.

They began to toss names about. There was Brooke's recent host John Masefield, whose violent narrative poem 'The Everlasting Mercy', dealing with earthy goings-on in rural England in a language shocking in its frankness, had been the poetry publishing success of the year. There was Gibson, the one-legged tramp poet W. H. Davies and Brooke's old friend James Elroy Flecker; as well as two acquaintances of Eddie's – Walter de la Mare, whose 'Listeners' had proved as popular with the public in its mysteriously romantic way as Masefield's saltier verses – and Gordon Bottomley, a fine writer confined to his Lakeland home by chronic illness.

And what about A. E. Housman, the austere author of the haunting *A Shropshire Lad*, or the brash and flamboyant young American Ezra Pound, who was making quite a splash in London's sedate literary scene? The more they considered the scheme, the more feasible and attractive it looked. Their shared aim – although Eddie approached it with a more conservative and cautious attitude than Brooke – was to demonstrate to the reading public that a new poetic wave had swept away the frigidity of the late-Victorian era and the artificial decadence of the Edwardian period that had so dominated Brooke's own juvenilia.

What they lacked was a name to grab public attention. Eddie suggested 'the Georgians', in honour of the new king. Brooke was scornful: it had too stuffy and respectable a ring about it; but he was stumped for an alternative, and the label stuck. They turned to the problem of finance, and Eddie suggested subsidizing the venture with the 'murder money' he had inherited as a result of the public sympathy that had followed the untimely assassination of his great-grandfather, the prime minister Spencer Perceval. He already drew on this cash to give handouts to the more cash-strapped of his protégés and was prepared to spend more to underwrite what became the first anthology of *Georgian Poetry*. They resolved to ask Monro to publish the book under the auspices of the *Poetry Review*, and, fired with enthusiasm, retired to bed long after midnight.

The next day a hastily arranged lunch party took place at Eddie's flat during which Eddie and Brooke outlined their scheme. Gibson was there, and Monro, along with his assistant Arundel del Re. Also present was John Drinkwater, an actor, playwright and poet who was a friend of Monro's; and another poet, Lascelles Abercrombie, may have joined the group. Both Drinkwater and Abercrombie had published their first well-received books of verse in 1908. The gathering agreed to help Eddie put together a collection of a dozen or so poets in an anthology to be published by Christmas. The royalties would be split between the *Poetry Review* and Eddie, who undertook to distribute them equally among the contributors. In blithely agreeing to fit the editing into his already hectically busy life, Eddie had little idea what he was taking on. There would eventually be five volumes of *Georgian Poetry* and much unsung work involved. But Eddie was a meticulous editor, whose main occupation in life would be as unpaid copy-editor to Churchill's voluminous writings – not for nothing was Eddie unkindly dubbed 'a valet to his hero'. He threw himself into the project with an energy and enthusiasm that surpassed Brooke's own.

After lunch the group walked around to the site of the Poetry Bookshop to see what they envisaged as the new clearing-house for the book, although most of the work would in fact be done at Eddie's flat. That evening Brooke looked up his old Rugby friend Denis Browne, now a composer and working as the organist at Guy's Hospital. He introduced Browne to Eddie and Gibson. Already the makings of what would become a new circle of friends was forming to replace those that Brooke had lost. Returning to Rugby after his momentous week in London, he reported to one of his old friends who had remained faithful, Frances Cornford: 'I've been meeting a lot of new poets . . . they were so nice: very simple and very goodhearted.' He noted the change that was already being wrought in his own condition: 'I do believe, just now, that God's giving me a kind of respite. He seems to have ceased to fiddle with me for the last week . . .'

But Brooke was still looking for an anchor to root him more securely in reality. What he needed above all, he told Frances, was to get married. 'I can't . . . be permanently and properly all right till I'm married. Marriage is the thing.' Unlike Byron, Brooke believed that love was more important to men than women. A woman could half-fulfil herself through children – but a man had only the hope of love. He ruefully quoted an observation of Bryn's that had been reported to him: 'Rupert holds such dreadfully conventional views nowadays.' Perhaps, he reflected, she was right, and maybe that was no bad thing after all.

Letters began to fly back and forth between Rugby and London, as Eddie reported on the progress of the project and Brooke responded with comments and criticisms. Their views about what was and was not worthwhile in contemporary poetry often clashed, but Brooke was careful not to push his luck too far, for Eddie was too influential and useful a friend to offend terminally: 'I can't set up to advise you, but I can taunt!' he teased.

The tireless Eddie went down for a weekend to visit the struggling young writer and critic John Middleton Murry and his talented girlfriend Katherine Mansfield. The couple had taken a cottage in the hamlet of Duncton, not far from Chichester in Sussex. Since June 1911 Murry and Mansfield had been editing *Rhythm*, an avant-garde arts review, produced in Chancery Lane a stone's throw from Eddie's flat. They too were added to the long list of bright young things deserving of encouragement and the occasional lob of Marsh money. Not the least of his services was to get them to take on the cash-starved Wilfrid Gibson as editorial assistant. Eddie secretly paid Gibson's salary, thus elegantly combining support for a struggling magazine with support for a struggling writer. It was an act typical of the extraordinary generosity which endeared him to many

grateful denizens of the world of arts and letters. Brooke was soon to follow
Eddie's footsteps in beating a path to the Murrys' door, and thus a new pair
of friends were added to a widening circle and a suddenly brighter world.

The beginning of October brought a reminder of the world he had lost.
On 3 October Bryn Olivier became Mrs Hugh Popham in a secular
ceremony in London, although Bryn, really quite conventional herself, had
wanted a white wedding. James, Ka, Noel and Bunny Garnett were among
the guests; but Brooke stayed away. However, on the eve of the wedding,
he wrote Bryn a remarkable letter of farewell that mixed renunciation,
recrimination and longing in equal portions. In its own way it was a
revelation.

'Dearest Bryn,' he began tenderly:

> I sit here, and, occasionally, think of you; and of the extraordinary mutations
> and incompleteness of life – the way we all drift and touch and swirl on under
> these gray & permanent skies. Oh dear, I get so solemn thinking of Eternity and
> Plus & Minus & the rest! Human Accounts are so devastating – all the things
> one didn't invest in, & so forth. And we're all twenty five, and we've done so
> little – this isn't cheering or polite, to an almost married lady. But I wanted to
> explain my mood. Otherwise you might think this too pompous . . .

Recalling their last, catastrophic meeting at Everleigh, Brooke admitted: 'I
fell into an abyss of despair that day, you happened to be going the next,
we happened not to meet in Scotland, through ill-luck – you're going to
be married, & I'm going – I really don't know, or, often, care, to what far
parts of the two worlds, material & spiritual, I may be going.' He again
touched on the theme of the eternal isolation of human beings, which he
had already offered to Ka as an explanation for the changeable nature of his
feelings. Bryn and Brooke, he slyly suggested, could have been different:

> It's not entirely an ordinary bump-&-part of the twigs on the stream. I mean
> that in this infinitely secretive & shy & ignorant world, where nobody says, at
> all, ever, what they're at, we had – whether through some greater honesty or
> friendliness in you, or daring in me – gone a faltering step or two towards
> hearing distance of each other. So I thought. But you, perhaps, are always as
> honest & intimate with everyone you know, and find them as honest & intimate
> with you – I don't know. I'm possibly queerer & shyer . . . I don't think that's
> so. Anyhow, I've more to be dishonest about.

So there Bryn had it – an honest admission of dishonesty – something she had long suspected in Brooke, but none the less refreshing to have from his own lips. Suspecting her derisive snort of 'I thought so!', Brooke continued: 'Oh but come, don't even you, my dear "sensible" unmorbid straightforward Bryn, think that everyone is infinitely incomprehensible & far & secret from everyone, & that approach is infinitely difficult & infinitely rare? One tells, some times, some people, a few things, – in a misleading sort of way. But any Truth! . . . oh, Bryn!'

At last Brooke was baring his soul to a woman he knew was already lost to him. Perhaps her very unavailability was a spur to sting him into truth – or rather his belief in the impossibility of truth:

> One of the great difficulties, & perils, you see, in ever telling anyone any truth, is the same as in ever loving anyone, but more so. It gives them a devilish handle over you. I mean, they can hurt. If I love a person & say nothing, I'm fairly safe. But if I tell them, I deliver myself bound into their hands. They can cry 'What bad taste, to feel & tell that!' or 'cheeky youth' or laugh 'I despise you' or 'Thanks for nothing'; or they can tell the public . . . But I don't care . . . I'm proud of myself. I'm proud of my relationship towards you, and my feelings towards you, and I wish it had gone further, but I'm proud anyhow. And even if you said you despised it, you couldn't make me not proud.

As he had done with Bryn's sister Noel, Brooke, well aware that his relationship with Bryn, if not entirely at an end, at least could never be the same, tried to sum it up through an evocation of shared good times:

> Well, then . . . I settle up so much nowadays with the Recording Angel. You may overhear: & be damned to you. I say to him 'They are really very important items on the side of Good, my relations with Bryn – all the various minutes, days, or months. They were very good. The time on the Broads. The various camps. There was always great delight in her presence, and in her appearance. Beauty like hers filled one with joy to see. Seeing her, knowing her so well, being with her, touching her, – among all the many other good & bad things in this one & only life of mine, those things were good, pure good . . .'
>
> Then there was Bank, Bryn. For three whole months I'd been infinitely wretched & ill, wretcheder than I'd thought possible. And then for a few days it all dropped completely away, and – oh! how lovely Bank was! – I suppose I should never be able to make you see what beauty is to me, – physical beauty –, just even the seeing it, in spite of all the hungers that come – Bank passed & was good & is a lovely memory to you & me. A funny world!

But Brooke was still not too pure for a postal flirtation:

And then, earlier & more definitely at Bank & after, there was what I told you of. You're beautiful. I've wanted you so passionately some times. I've known to myself how glorious it might be if ever we went away together. The joys of the body are infinite. And our clean and fine bodies! – Such thoughts were (I've told you) at the back of my relationship with you: hopes that it might come to that. (You would have had the strength to do it, & finely, if you'd wanted to; and there are so few people like that.)

And so, after suggesting the joys they had missed, he had to account for the fact that they had never come together. He attempted to do so:

I don't think I'm afraid of anything in the world. But I'm damnably shy. So I didn't ever (why doesn't one ever in this world) come, & say: – Also I was ill & less than fit for life, this summer. So things slipped along. I hoped that, when we were together in August, we might make something fine, together. And then, at Everleigh, you told me you were 'engaged'. I was glad enough of your happiness, for I love you a great deal. But it was also, to me, a 'blow'. I told you a lot, in that conversation that never got well finished. (It's so nice being able to talk to a person like you, after all, are: – i.e. talk freely. I dare say anything to you, now: or hear anything from you. We are a good pair.)

But now he is left holding dust and ashes:

We did well. We might have done better, I believe. But time past is past. Tomorrow, or whenever it is, you marry. I'm jealous of Hugh, a good deal, for marrying, living with, & copulating with you, & having your beauty & fineness. And I am envious of you both because you're happy & married, and I (though I'm well & cheerful now) am sad & very lonely. Perhaps you don't understand this. It shows that my nature isn't very nice. But there it is, you nice old Bryn, black lonely envy of you two. And if a spasm of it came on when I was seeing you, – & it quite probably might – I should hate both you and try, even, to hurt you.

At last, cleaned out, Brooke launched into his peroration:

Marriage is very lovely . . . I tell you so, & I know everything in the world, & I know that. 'I cannot say more than that I hope your married life will be as happy as mine' – imaginings of what it can be – for you, or me, or anyone: – each in his own way, of course. – Oh, that's all it is; good material. Each makes what he likes; as with all other good material – even love-affairs. But it is lovely.

Giving is lovely. Taking is lovely. Breakfast is lovely. I swear to you – Hush; Hush! I expect I only annoy you. You must be tired, just now, with all these arrangings and fusses. Please don't let that tiredness make you take this letter angrily. It would be so easy. We're beyond that. I've just put some of the thing, from my point of view, & God's. 'In its way, it's a kind of compliment.' And it's probably the only wedding present you'll get from me, until I'm a rich man: unless a friendly sort of love is any use. I don't know when I shall see you again, or what I'm going to do. Goodnight! Goodbye . . . I take hold of you with my arms & kiss your mouth – With all love Your devoted Rupert.

And so, with this extraordinary letter, Brooke bid farewell to Bryn – and to his old mode of life. He would see her again, but usually in the company of Hugh, and in a fairly perfunctory, steadily dimmer way. Perhaps because it lacked the deeply churning emotions that muddied his relations with Ka or Noel, his letter seems less hysterical, more open and objective. At last, we feel, the real Brooke may be getting a look-in, in all his confusions, hesitations and disarmingly declared duplicity and shallowness. To Bryn, scanning the letter as she prepared for a wedding to a man she was already regarding as dull, it must have been a disturbing goodbye.

After mailing the letter, Brooke went to spend the weekend with the Murrys in Sussex, where he and Murry strolled about the coastal marshes, discussing plans for the Georgians and Brooke's contributions to *Rhythm*. He delighted Katherine Mansfield with a macabre tale, which bears the mark of the same sort of myth that spawned *Lithuania*, about an old lady who sat motionless in her window for days, before neighbours broke in and found the lower half of her body had been gnawed away by her hungry cats.

Brooke returned to London to find preparations for the Georgian anthology in full swing. Over a meal at the fashionable Moulin d'Or restaurant, Eddie introduced him to Walter de la Mare, who would one day become, with Gibson and Lascelles Abercrombie, the third of Brooke's literary heirs, and would write the first book about him. It was another momentous week for meeting new people, for Eddie introduced him to the young philosopher, poet and artistic theorist T. E. Hulme, who was currently evolving a new anti-romantic aesthetic that would prove increasingly influential among the artistic and literary avant-garde, via such movements as Imagism in poetry and Vorticism in art. Influenced by Bergson, whom he had translated, Hulme was a tough-minded critical spirit, much possessed by the hard 'cindery' nature of matter, and instinctively distrustful of the lush romanticism that characterized many of the Georgians.

Then Brooke was off to Cambridge, to read a paper to the Apostles entitled 'In Xanadu'. The paper was something of a kick in the pants for his audience, since it represented his farewell to the milk-and-water philosophy of G. E. Moore that underpinned much of the Apostolic outlook. In contrast to Moore's emphasis on ethics based on cool, intellectual reason, Brooke declared, he now believed that 'goodness' was the most important quality a person could possess. He called it 'Moral Taste' and argued: 'It is the most important thing in a man – its possession the only thing I care for . . . its absence almost the only thing I hate.'

The Brothers must have sat up as they heard Brooke rejecting the cynicism of his youth: 'I think, now, that this passion for goodness and loathing of evil is the most valuable and important thing in us.' If ever one encountered evil, he concluded: 'One should count to five, perhaps, but then certainly hit out . . . It's the only battle that counts.' This was an open declaration of war on the moral relativism of the Strachey way of seeing things. Appropriately, Brooke also was about to address a rival Cambridge society calling itself 'the Heretics'. He too was now the holder of heretical opinions – or rather, heretical to his old friends who had long since rebelled against the values he claimed he espoused. Privately, it was not only Lytton's ideas that he wished to knock down – he was sorely tempted to do the same to the man himself.

After the meeting he dined with his Cambridge mentor A. C. Benson, who noticed a 'great weariness' overshadowing his young friend's former ebullience. Brooke referred only obliquely to the travail he had passed through, seeming most anxious to stuff its memory out of reach: 'He spoke of his trouble very seriously, and even with a sort of terror, as if he had for the first time realized that there might be . . . wounds which he could not cure.' The next day Geoffrey Keynes dropped in on Brooke at the Old Vicarage and confided that he was in love with Ka.

The change recently wrought in Brooke, part of which was an utter weariness with his long, sapping fever of love, is amply indicated by the fact that this news moved him not a jot. He even wrote to Ka recommending that she take Geoffrey's suit seriously: 'It doesn't distress me . . . he's a good person – and so unique in London . . . when I've thought of you, what you could be doing, I've sometimes thought "She may be with Geoffrey", and glowed with content . . . I wish you would [fall in love with him]. His devotion to you makes me rather happy.' Brooke added that he was seeking comfort with the old familiar faces – Frances, Gwen and Jacques – but was still liable to be thrown into a pit of black envy and rage by any indication – an arm around a neck or a touch of hands – that his married friends were happier than he was: 'I go sick with envy, and blind – and generally say something to hurt them.'

Another visitor to the Old Vicarage was his new friend Gibson. He watched Brooke in some astonishment, as he wrote a quartet of inferior poems that had been demanded by the *Poetry Review*. Such a literary cottage industry was unknown to Gibson, and he wrote to Eddie in wonder: 'I rather marvelled that poems could be written because Monro wanted them . . . It seemed queer – but never having seen poetry being written before, I didn't know – and anyhow from the spectacular point of view it was superb.'

Brooke was unabashed: he was prepared to do almost anything to thrust his name before the poetry-loving public. 'Have written four poems,' he wired Monro. 'Do you want more?' Meanwhile Eddie was feverishly at work lining up the Georgians. Some early choices – Housman and Pound – were ruled out, and some new ones – D. H. Lawrence and James Stephens – roped in. By the time of Brooke's next visit to Eddie's flat, on 1 November, the galley proofs of the poems were ready for his critical perusal. While in London he reviewed an exhibition of post-Impressionist art at the Grafton Galleries for the *Cambridge Review* – he was not overly impressed, except by Matisse and the work of Eric Gill, one of whose sculptures of a Madonna and Child he would acquire as a gift for Ka. He spared a few words for one of the portraits of Ka painted by Duncan Grant – without mentioning his own connections with artist and sitter: 'One always feels there ought to be more body in his work, somehow. Even his best pictures here are rather thin. But there is beauty in *The Seated Woman*,' the magazine's readers were told.

This duty over, and wearing one of the bold coloured shirts that Ka had sewn for him (this one sported green and purple stripes) he was off once more to Berlin, where he had been invited to recuperate by Dudley Ward and his heavily pregnant wife Annemarie. He soon fell into his accustomed state of mildly irritable jealousy when in the company of married friends: 'One suddenly finds oneself four million miles away from any human companionship, on the top of a frozen mountain, among stars and icicles.' Brooke's cure for his malady was simple: 'I shall work.' And work he did, this time without the distractions of love and letters that had marked his previous stay in the German capital.

He was not tempted to go back on his vows of August and recline on Ka's waiting bosom – not even when she wrote him that she had definitively broken with Henry Lamb, enclosing his last letter to her in proof. He sent it back to her. In desperation, Ka had even offered to fund his trip to the California sunshine, should he ever make up his mind to go. This too he refused: 'Oh child, oh my dear. I can't take money . . . Don't waste yourself or anything of yours on me . . . It would be wonderful, if you could be your lovely self again. It would give me a sort of peace, to know it.' Slowly, although he was still prone to erupt into little spurts of rage against Ka for the 'crime' she had committed against him with Lamb, the primary emotion he was coming to feel with her was guilt at his own behaviour.

His main work in Berlin was a reworking of his dissertation on Webster, on which, for a second year round, he was pinning his hopes of a Fellowship. An important late influence on the text was his conversations with T. E. Hulme, who had arrived in Berlin to attend an international philosophical convention. The two dissimilar men spent more than a week together, touring galleries, attending concerts and talking in Brooke's old haunt the Café des Westens. They were wandering near the Zoo station late one night, discussing Hulme's idea that material objects, especially man-made ones, born of the time in which they were living, were somehow more real than ethereal ideas or passing emotions, and as they talked a train thundered over their heads. At once an image was sparked in Brooke's mind, and this became his poem 'The Night Journey', which encapsulated both the sense of human will, as remorseless as a train roaring along its tracks, and man's essentially tragic solitude: 'the gloom'

> Is hung with steam's fantastic livid streamers.
>   Lost into God, as lights in light, we fly,
> Grown one with will, end-drunken huddled dreamers.
>   The white lights roar. The sounds of the world die
>
> And lips and laughter are forgotten things.
>   Speed sharpens; grows. Into the night, and on,
> The strength and splendour of our purpose swings.
>   The lamps fade; and the stars. We are alone.

Brooke's thoughts, as this poem indicates, were becoming resigned and fatalistic. Rationalizing the crisis of the year just ending, he told Frances that he had been the mere plaything of forces far stronger than himself. And it was with the idea of throwing himself further into fate's hands that, so he told Ka, he was seriously thinking of abandoning his dissertation and travelling to Russia as a correspondent if current tension between Germany and the eastern giant should burst into war. 'It would be fun,' he added, in a characteristic taste of the mood that would take him in the summer of 1914. 'In that case England wouldn't see me for a bit – for ever, if a bullet or the cholera were kindly . . . Be proud of the fineness we have done together. And think in years.'

In contrast with his previous deluge while abroad, he was sparing in the number of letters he wrote to friends. Noel received just one, in mid-November, its tone cool, tired and resigned. He recalled his disappointment at not having gone camping with her, as he had planned: 'It was somewhat melancholy unpacking the clothes I'd carefully packed for camp, all unused, and the books I'd thought might be nice to read there. I wept at the pathetic figure I'd made, trailing them round Scotland & London & God knows where . . . One is like a child, in the important little way one trots round with one's dreams – so unrelated to reality.'

He painted a patronizing portrait of his Berlin hosts: 'Dudley sits yonder clacking his typewriter; making history . . . his wife leads a quiet existence. She is very large with child. I hope it won't kill her – she's very tiny. I work indoors most of the time. Sometimes I go out of an evening to a theatre. And every other day I go out to lunch in a cafe, rather dignifiedly, to show I'm independent.' Although he lacked the energy to muster his furious forces of hate, bitterness against Bloomsbury still rankled. He referred to the area of London where his former friends lived as 'pestilential parts'.

A month later, on 12 December, he was back in London. His first night home he spent at Raymond Buildings catching up with the Georgian anthology. Eddie had been working like a Trojan in his absence, proofreading and 'puffing' the book extravagantly to his many influential friends. Advance copies were sent to all the main newspapers, not only in London and the provinces, but throughout the English-speaking world. Brooke, Monro and Lascelles Abercrombie helped Eddie package the review copies and post them off. As he awaited publication day, Brooke supervised the typing of the final edition of his dissertation, which incorporated the changes in the text he had made as a result of his intense conversations with Hulme. But there was another, less intellectual, preoccupation that increasingly took up his thoughts.

While staying at Raymond Buildings in September Brooke had accompanied Eddie to a fashionable first night – a production of Shakespeare's *The Winter's Tale* at the Savoy Theatre. He was much taken by Cathleen Nesbitt, the beautiful young actress playing the part of Perdita, and saw the play for a second time before his departure to Germany. Learning of Brooke's interest, Eddie had got to know Miss Nesbitt through the actor-manager Henry Ainley, with whom Cathleen was ending an unhappy love affair. He lost no time in inviting them to a supper party at his home to meet Brooke, who, so Cathleen recalled, was uncommunicative and rather tongue-tied. 'I saw a very good looking, very shy young man, sitting in a corner and I do remember being struck by his extremely blue eyes, and I sat beside him and he said "Do you know anybody here?" and I said "No". He said "Neither do I" and then we vaguely started talking about *Georgian Poetry* . . . I said there was an extraordinary poem called "The Fish" in it, and I quoted quite a bit of it and he blushed very scarlet and said 'You have very good taste – I wrote that . . .'

This momentous first meeting with Cathleen, on 20 December, was the beginning of perhaps the most uncomplicatedly happy love affair of Brooke's life. Sixteen months Brooke's junior, Cathleen had been born of Irish extraction in Cheshire and brought up chiefly in Belfast and France. She had made her stage début in 1910 and had toured with the Irish players in America, as well as appearing at Dublin's famous Abbey Theatre. Blessed as she was with a fine bone structure, a flawless skin, dark hair and luminously lovely eyes, it is scarcely surprising that Brooke was instantly smitten by her physical charms. Her membership of the Irish players, whose work he had seen and admired, and her more than professional interest in contemporary poetry, drama and literature, provided the bond of mutual interests. In addition, she possessed the inestimable advantage, given Brooke's present mood, of having no connection with his previous circle of friends, and complete ignorance of the crises that had so convulsed his recent life. Last, but by no means least, both were on the rebound from recent disastrous relationships.

There were shadows lurking in the sunlight: following up the supper party with a private lunch, Brooke made it clear to Cathleen that his bright and boyish appearance concealed a darker side. He was feeling 'neurotic and depressed', he let her know, and, to her disappointment, 'against love altogether'. For her part, she was by no means the sweet young innocent that – perhaps from over-identifying her with the role of Perdita – he assumed her to be.

The Winter's Tale was not the only play Brooke saw as 1912 ended – he and Hulme had been deeply impressed by Strindberg's *Dance of Death* in Berlin. Its powerful message of the hopelessness of male–female relations had appealed to the misogynistic impulses of both men. On a lighter note, just before Christmas Brooke attended the opening night of the show *Hullo Ragtime* at the London Hippodrome. As he had with *Peter Pan* and the Ballet Russe, he fell for the show, which he was to see at least ten times –

seven times in Cathleen's company. His latent anti-Semitism did not prevent him from enjoying the music of Louis Hirsch and the songs of Irving Berlin, nor the performance of Ethel Levey, the show's sexiest star, who, with bare arms and legs and a cropped head under ostrich feathers, belted out the show-stopping songs that seemed to herald a new and exciting age – barbarous, discordant, but indisputably alive. It was a melody Brooke was all too ready to hear.

He was soon tunelessly humming the ragtime tunes, which in their brash discordance, and bursting with American energy and panache, seemed to break asunder the genteel cords that had bound and limited his natural exuberance all his life. They were a message from the New World to what increasingly seemed an old and exhausted one, and, in their mindless optimism and cheerful inanity, they seemed to reflect Brooke's present hunger for change and amusement.

Having lingered in London long enough to see both *Georgian Poetry* and the ragtime craze launched on a waiting world, Brooke was in the more melancholy atmosphere of Rugby for Christmas, where he promptly succumbed to his usual seasonal ailment – flu. While there, he heard from Ka that she was about to depart for Germany, Poland and Russia. He was delighted that she was on the move: 'I'll sleep a fortnight without a care in the world,' he told her, 'if I can think you're out of England at last and without a care in the world.' Ka was angling for a goodbye meeting before she left, but Brooke was briskly discouraging of her pining. His language was insensitive, to say the least. Rather than 'loiter helplessly round London' he said she should better 'die en route'.

On New Year's Eve he returned to London, took Eddie to *Hullo Ragtime* and then joined the celebrating crowds waiting for the midnight chimes on the steps of St Paul's. Nineteen twelve was a year that Brooke was well pleased to see go. At least 1913 held out the promise of a better future.

21

Rotters and Fellows

The first anthology of *Georgian Poetry* had appeared in the dying days of 1912. Its appearance, so assiduously heralded by Eddie Marsh's tireless publicity efforts, was eagerly awaited. Herbert Asquith, it was reported, temporarily forgot the political crises with which he was beset, and dispatched a car to Bumpus, the Oxford Street bookshop, to pick up a copy on the day of publication. The story is almost certainly apocryphal, if only because Eddie would have made absolutely sure that the Prime Minister received a pre-publication copy. It was Eddie who had had the last word in the final selection of the poets and poems represented, riding roughshod over Brooke's objections to some of his choices. As a result, Brooke complained to Ka, there were 'too many rotters' in the book.

It is interesting to speculate whom Brooke meant by this gibe, since most of the Georgians were his own friends and acquaintances: there were six poems from W. H. Davies, most famous for his lines

> What is this life, if full of care,
> We have no time to stand and stare?

Brooke himself had five, as did Walter de la Mare; Gibson and James Stephens had three each; Gordon Bottomley, Flecker and Monro two; and a single poem or long extract from Lawrence, Masefield, Sturge Moore, Abercrombie, G. K. Chesterton, Drinkwater, and the now-forgotten Ronald Ross, Edmund Beale Sargent and R. C. Trevelyan – the latter an Apostle and likely 'rotter' – made up the rest of the book.

Eddie had exercised his editor's prerogative in providing a somewhat grandiloquent preface that amounted to a Georgian manifesto. It began: 'This volume is issued in the belief that English poetry is now once again putting on a new strength and beauty.' Eddie proclaimed the dawn of 'another "Georgian period" which may take rank in due time with several great poetic periods of the past . . .'. The reception of the book surpassed his and Brooke's wildest dreams – the first edition rapidly sold out, and would eventually sell 13,000 copies – an astonishingly high figure for verse. For Brooke personally, it placed his name firmly in the public domain as a promising and increasingly accomplished practitioner of poetry; while the royalties that flowed from the book were a very useful addition in his always straitened financial circumstances.

Brooke was not the only Georgian to be grateful to Eddie. A year after its publication, a surprised yet pleased Lawrence, for whom money would always be a worry, and whose single contribution, 'Snapdragon', is one of the few Georgian poems to have survived subsequent critical derision, wrote to Eddie to thank him for a much-needed royalty cheque: 'That *Georgian Poetry* book is a veritable Aladdin's Lamp. I little thought my "Snapdragon" would go on blooming and seeding in this prolific fashion.'

The Georgians were the complete creation of Eddie and Brooke's drive and energy. In no sense did the poets represent a coherent group, or even a united set of values or attitudes. Most have long since fallen into neglect; and those that survive in the public memory – Brooke, Masefield, Chesterton, Davies, De la Mare and Lawrence himself – are so different in theme and style as to be unclassifiable. De la Mare the mystical whimsyist; Davies the cracker-barrel sage; Masefield the muscular celebrant of the seafaring life; Lawrence the quirky free-versifier of genius; Chesterton the comic satirist – these poets are only Georgians in the sense that they were writing in roughly the same epoch, and, apart from Lawrence, using traditional forms.

Later volumes of *Georgian Poetry* edited by Eddie contained the Great War poets Sassoon, Blunden, Graves and Rosenberg – once again, a very diverse quartet, whom only the accident of enduring the common experience of combat in the trenches of the Western Front delineates as a group. Although Brooke eagerly used *Georgian Poetry* as a vehicle to promote his own career, his entanglement with the venture has done as much harm to his subsequent reputation as a poet as the uncharacteristically romantic and patriotic sonnets that he produced under the shock of the outbreak of war. In the light of the war, the Georgians came to be regarded as impossibly reactionary and backward-looking – celebrants of a mythical England of beer and cheese, rural backwaters and cosy firesides – utterly at variance with the modern reality of cities, cars, speed and violence. Looked at without that hindsight, however, they can be placed more fairly and squarely in their true context.

Following the fatuousness of the late Victorians and the preciousness of the early Edwardians, the poets in Eddie's anthologies did bring a breath of fresh air into what had become a stuffy hothouse. They were not a brick through the glass, but they were an opening of a door. They wrote about everyday things in plain language that was generally shorn of artifice and exaggeration. Their worst fault was sentimentality; but they cannot fairly be charged with failure just because they did not see the catastrophe lurking just around the corner. Few did.

Eddie's fifth and final Georgian collection, produced in 1922, coincided with the publication of Eliot's *The Waste Land*, that epochal moment in literary history that changed the course of poetry as Joyce's *Ulysses*, which appeared in the same year, changed the novel. Modernism in all its aspects swept aside the last vestiges of Georgianism, but the Georgians were as broadly representative of the decade 1910–20 as Eliot and Pound were of the twenties and the Auden school of the thirties. The poetry we remember of the years that contained the Great War is the poetry of the men represented in Eddie's anthologies – Brooke, Blunden, Sassoon, Graves and Rosenberg. The subsequent denigration of Eddie's unfortunate label 'Georgian' was itself overblown.

It was the war that altered perceptions. As the critic John Wain wrote: 'If the First World War had not happened, the new idiom in English poetry would have been a development of Georgianism . . . the seeds were there: the honesty, the dislike of cant, the "selection from the real language of men", the dissatisfaction with a narrow tradition of poetry laid down by the literary establishment.' Wain cites two poets, Edward Thomas and Wilfred Owen, both victims of the war, who exemplified this neo-Georgianism stifled at birth by the brutal fact of their deaths. 'If their flight had been longer, there would have been no need for a modern poetic idiom imported from France via America . . . Owen and Thomas, abetted by the excellent poets who survived the war, by Graves, by Blunden, by the older poets like Hodgson and De la Mare [all Georgians] would have made a living tradition out of English materials arising naturally from English life.'

As for Brooke's own role in the poetic politics of his time, it is much more radical than has been widely assumed. Just as his personal life has been misrepresented as clean and simple, so his poetry has been misread or simply dismissed as sentimental and reactionary. Nothing could be further from the truth. Like his friend Thomas and like Wilfred Owen he wrote of taboo themes – breakdown, physical decay, ageing, the banality and disgust of domestic life, the stultifying incompatibility of eroticism with marriage – using traditional forms. His early socialism was more progressive than the politics of the reactionary Eliot or the overtly fascist Pound, while his poetics were just as radical as theirs – albeit couched in traditional style over which he developed an awesome technical mastery. Eliot and Pound themselves recognized this. Brooke knew Pound personally, favourably reviewed his early poetry and recommended him to Eddie for inclusion in the anthology. Pound returned this high regard and referred to Brooke as 'the best of all that Georgian group'.

Only a predictable disagreement between the fastidious Eddie and the irascible Pound kept the work of the master of modernism out of a book that has been unfairly seen as the bible of backwardness in English verse. Eliot knew of and admired Brooke's critical work on Webster and drew on it and 'Grantchester' in his poetry. For his part, Brooke's critical eye was almost unerring when it came to separating the sheep from the goats in literature.

He demonstrated this early in the New Year when he left London on 1 January and took a train for Cornwall's far-flung Lizard peninsula, where the Cornfords had taken a house for their holidays. Here, ignoring the hustle and bustle of the household, he laboured over two critical articles on a poet he had long regarded with reverence: John Donne. His immediate inspiration was Stanley Spencer's painting *John Donne Arriving in Heaven*, which he had seen at the post-Impressionist exhibition at the Grafton Galleries. Writing at a time when Donne was by no means widely seen as the genius he was, Brooke presciently hailed him as the greatest love poet in English. During his fortnight with the Cornfords, Brooke also wrote a long poem called 'The Funeral of Youth', his first major poetic effort since 'Grantchester' and a clear sign that he had regained the stability and energy needed for creative work.

While in Cornwall he heard from Ka, who had arrived in Berlin and was waxing sentimental about their former haunts. Again he was harshly unsympathetic. In a brusque put-down aimed as much at Noel as at her, he told Ka: 'Love is being at a person's mercy. And it's a black look-out when the person's an irresponsible modern female virgin. There's no more to say . . .' She was advised to steer clear of 'reminiscence-ful' places and to 'Eat plenty'. He now came under renewed pressure from Frances Cornford to follow Ka's example and shake the clinging dust of England from his feet. Brooke, still irresolute, and awaiting the judgement of Cambridge on his Fellowship, postponed any decision, and hurried back to London to immerse himself anew in the giddy whirl of Eddie's social round.

After arriving at Raymond Buildings on 15 January he visited the Murrys – whom he dubbed 'the Tigers' – at the offices of *Rhythm* in Chancery

Lane. They asked him to join the board of the magazine, and he eagerly threw himself into this new project with his old energy, roping in his friends Denis Browne and E. J. Dent to write on music and unsuccessfully attempting to persuade Gwen Raverat to send one of her woodcuts. Gwen, staunchly reactionary in artistic as well as political matters, refused, as she distrusted *Rhythm*'s modernist and avant-garde tone. Brooke sprang to the defence of his new friends against his old. He told Gwen:

> I hope the things you hate in it, the 'modernness and desire to shock', will continue. Of course, it's modern. It's all by people who do good work and are under thirty-five. It shows there are such, and that they're different from and better than the *Yellow Book* or the Pre-Raphaelites or any other body. Do you think it ought to look as if it was written by Gosse and Tennyson and illustrated by Whistler and Madox Brown? . . . As for 'shocking', it's impossible to do much good or true work without shocking all the bloody people more or less.

This letter shows that Brooke, for all his recoil from Bloomsbury, had not retreated completely into reaction. The Murrys and other artists and poets he was now befriending, were just as radical and avant-garde as the Strachey set – but, in his view, they lacked the befouling personal deceits and general creepiness with which Bloomsbury was now irretrievably marked.

He accompanied Eddie on a tour of his protégés, visiting W. H. Davies at his Kentish retreat near Sevenoaks for tea after dropping in at the Sussex studio of Eric Gill in Ditchling. Here he purchased the Madonna and Child he had admired at the Grafton Galleries, intending to present it to Ka as a cross between a goodbye gift and a guilt offering. The eccentric sculptor, who combined incest, bestiality and pious Roman Catholicism in a weird personal creed, was not highly impressed by his visitors, describing Eddie and Brooke as 'aesthetic buggers'.

Back in London, there were more new and old friends to meet. Eddie introduced Brooke to the ambitious and rising young novelist Hugh Walpole, part of his discreetly gay network; and there was a lunch with Davies and De la Mare at the Moulin d'Or, followed by an evening with Pound and W. B. Yeats. On this occasion the great master of modern poetry praised Brooke's work, but advised him to abandon what he called 'languid sensuality' in favour of a 'robust sensuality'. And it was following this meeting that Yeats made his famous remark that Brooke was 'the handsomest young man in England', adding, less famously, that he also wore the most beautiful shirts. Brooke had Ka to thank for the garment in question. She had sewn and sent it to him in a bid to pacify his wrath at one of the worst moments of his madness the previous spring. He had responded in delight: 'The shirt's so extraordinarily nice. I've worn it ever since . . . It is, my dear, such a feminine shirt.' Now, bursting with pride, he wrote to tell her of the admiration of the great Yeats, who had even asked if he could get him one to match it. 'I promised to find out where he could get the stuff,' he explained, adding: '"You'll never get anyone who can make it as this is made," I flung at him as I vanished.'

Brooke also told Ka that though he thought of her continually, his aim was to make his life so 'chock-full' that he had no time to worry. Still driven by his restless demons, he left London on 24 January to stay with Jacques and Gwen Raverat, who had installed themselves at Manor Farm, Croydon, a hamlet some 15 miles south-west of Cambridge. While there, he put the finishing touches to *Lithuania*, which he had been working on intermittently since conceiving the idea in Berlin nearly a year before. Two other members of the original Neo-Pagan circle, who had remained loyal to Brooke throughout his crisis – Geoffrey Keynes and Justin Brooke – dropped in to pay their respects during Brooke's stay. From Croydon, he wrote to Eddie, falling back into his old habit of using a friend to covertly advance his love life, to suggest that Cathleen Nesbitt be included in an *après*-theatre outing they were planning: 'But no doubt it's quite impossible – I suppose she dines with Millionaires every night – I can see a thousand insuperable difficulties . . .'

Brooke returned to London four days later to attend a debate between Bernard Shaw and Hilaire Belloc, sponsored by the Fabians at the Queen's Hall. By chance, Noel Olivier was also there. Two days afterwards Brooke told Ka he had 'unluckily ran into that swine Noel. However we put up our noses and cut each other, which was good fun.' But from a letter to Noel herself, written on the night of the debate, a rather different picture emerges. If not exactly affectionate, the tone is one of tentatively fishing for some sort of reconciliation: 'Did you mind – or did you notice? – that I didn't write to you. I occasionally thought of it. But I nearly always was in a condition of hating you a great deal; so I didn't trust myself to write. I'm hastily taking advantage, now, of a friendly lapse . . .'

The letter goes on to reveal a continuing hatred of Noel's admirer Ferenc Békássy, who, in an effort to be friendly, had sent Brooke some of his poems for appraisal: 'I immediately hated him, & sent his poems back without comment.' Brooke sarcastically commiserated with Noel for 'so many people falling in love with you . . . I quite agree; Love's an entirely filthy business.' He remarks that, like Békássy, his feelings for Noel had been merely calf-love. 'Calf-love that goes wrong only hurts so-so – a remedial & finite business, merely a hand or foot off; not both legs.' While exhibiting bruised pride and hurt feelings, the letter is not entirely devoid of self-knowledge. Brooke is now ready to admit that a good deal of the blame for the rift between them lay with him: 'I have come more & more to see you've had a deal to bear from me in the past. I've always been horribly unpleasant. Good God! You were really very tolerant – Calf-love goes over, draggingly. It's a pity you've always elicited the worst side of me . . .'

Resuming the letter the next day after returning to Croydon, Brooke 'preaches' a little 'sermon' cautioning Noel against becoming too hard of heart, while he draws a fine distinction by praising her hatred of 'softness', which he shares. He as good as admits that his overblown rhetoric of hatred merely serves to protect his own vulnerability. 'I tell myself, and everyone else, most of the time, that you're the bloodiest & pettiest person in England. But I suppose I don't believe it. One has to say something, – in order to – well, you know as well as anyone the furtive way one builds up armour plating in personal relationships.' He ends by bestowing the same sort of benediction he had given to Ka when saying farewell: 'I don't care what happens, as long as you stay fine, are fine. If you betray that, I swear I'll kill you. One must invest one's money somewhere . . . Child I wish you well. Good be with you. Be happy, incidentally – I'm trusting you that you'll tell me if ever you want any help about anything or need anything or are in any difficulty. I'm almost infinitely powerful . . .'

Then, instead of leaving it at that, he returns to his bizarre obsession with Noel's personal security – his almost transparent tendency to wish to control her life and insulate her from the company he fears and detests:

So many people get kidnapped nowadays: & you're always drifting about alone. Please, I'm perfectly serious – be careful. – Don't ever, on any pretext, go off with people you don't know, however well authenticated, or get into cabs – it's impossible to be too careful. I demand this. Also, bewahr Dich Gott! [may God protect you] What I hope is that, at some crossing, when you're just going to be run over by a motor-bus one of these days, I may pull you out of the way, & get run over myself. It'd be a good way out of a bloody world for me: & I should go with the satisfaction of knowing that you'd feel horribly awkward for a great many weeks, or months. And how my book'd sell! with love Rupert.

To show that his hard-done-by feelings were lessening, Brooke sent Noel the two-volume edition of Donne's poems that he had reviewed for *The Nation* and *Poetry and Drama* (as the *Poetry Review* had just been renamed).

When Noel replied with a friendly note of thanks, he responded with a description of his social whirl in London, as though to let her know that he was enjoying life to the full without her:

> But you, poor brown mouse, can't, in the dizziest heights of murian imagination, picture the life of whirl glitter & gaiety I lead. A young man about town, Noel, (I've had my hair cut *remarkably* short-). Dinners, boxes at the opera, literary lunch-parties, theatre supper parties, (the Carlton on Saturday next) – I know *several* actresses. Last night, in the stalls at the Ballet, Eddie & I (I'd wired for my white waistcoat) bowed & smiled – oh, quite casually at
>   Queen Alexandra
>   The Marquis de Soveral
>   The Duchess of Rutland
>   Countess Rodomontini (or such)
>   Mrs George Keppel
> and a host more. And in the interval Mrs Humphrey Ward shook me very warmly by the hand, under the impression I was someone quite different from what I am. But as I'm an anti-Suffragist, I was, of course, rather flattered.

This display of schoolboy snobbery is both risible and typical of Brooke at his least sympathetic. Like an overawed teenager's bragging after his first grown-up party, his enthusiasm for a parade of faded Edwardian society figures, such as the late King's wife and mistress, and Mrs Humphrey Ward, the lady novelist who was Thomas Arnold's granddaughter and a leading light in the anti-Suffragette campaign, shows his weakness for consorting with the grand – a tendency Eddie was only too willing to exploit. Before Ramsay Macdonald took over the role, Eddie was the most assiduous duchess-kisser in London, and now that he had introduced Brooke into the capital's literary élite, his protégé was clearly ready for the next stage in his social elevation – the political and aristocratic worlds in which Eddie smoothly circulated when he was not wading into London's literary whirlpools. It was a world to which Noel, who belonged to another sort of élite, the progressive Fabian nexus, did not belong, and had little wish to. Once again Brooke was turning a tin ear to the subtle hints given out by those he most wished to impress.

On 8 February, still staying with the Raverats, Brooke went to Cambridge as the guest of Eddie's father, Howard Marsh, the Master of Downing College, to attend a college dinner at which he met two past masters of poetry: Sir Henry Newbolt, whose patriotic verses were once ranked with those of Kipling; and A. E. Housman. The following evening the melancholy Housman watched admiringly as Brooke played billiards with Professor Marsh. Jacques had heard that Annemarie Ward had given birth to a son, Peter, in Berlin. The news coincided with a letter from Ka in the same city, to which he immediately replied. Once again, he said, he had been stricken by jealousy at the Wards' marital happiness. The news had come as 'an awful blow,' he admitted. But he was still not ready to give in to love: 'Love *is* being at a person's mercy,' he gloomily maintained. But he promised Ka he would not fall again into the pit from which he had just crawled: 'I'm not ill, and never shall be again . . . If ever we meet again, it's got to be from strength – not weakness.' However lonely Ka felt amid the memories of Berlin and the Wards' example of the parenthood that had been snatched from her, Brooke could only offer words of comfort, not deeds. The decision he had told her of at Bibury was irrevocable: 'You don't know how I want to help you, child. I've loved you so and we're so closely entangled: I can't grow whole unless you do . . .' But Ka's pleas for his love was driving him to exasperated desperation: 'You're lonely. I can't bear it . . . I'd cut and tear myself all day, if it'd do anything. I'd cut my hand off. Oh my God, I can't have you going on like this . . .' Nevertheless he would have to go on grinning and bearing it – a task made easier by his growing enchantment with Cathleen Nesbitt, whom he was continuing to see in London.

Cutting between Cambridge and the capital, where the giddy whirl of parties, dinners and theatre visits continued without pause, Brooke was soon back in his alma mater to address the Heretics Society, ostensibly on the state of contemporary theatre. Under the thin veneer of a comparison between the two reigning giants of the Scandinavian theatre – Ibsen and Strindberg – he let loose a withering attack on the Norwegian master, with his sympathy for oppressed women. Scarcely concealing his pathological hostility to feminism, he charged Ibsen with a diseased, unhealthy morality, whereas he praised Strindberg for daring to 'declare that men are men and women women'. The strength of Strindberg, his 'wholesomeness', he claimed, lay precisely in the bitterness with which he denounced women. The Swede had been born into 'a community suffering from a "women's movement",' Brooke caustically continued. 'He not only stood for the tragedy of Feminism, but also for the revolt against it, and especially against its apostle, the great and dirty playwright Ibsen.'

These biting remarks were delivered in the soft tones Brooke employed when speaking in public; but the bitterness of his own condemnation of feminism was betrayed, according to one witness, by the way he tossed his lecture notes aside 'with a brusque flick of the wrist', as though he would consign uppity women and their treacherous male supporters to the same oblivion. Another personal prejudice came out in the same lecture when, speaking of the Ballet Russe, which he was about to revisit in London, he complained of Diaghilev's genius being 'handicapped by the extremely tawdry and inharmonious scenery and dresses of a Russian jew [sic] called Bakst'.

Having thumbed his nose at women and Jews in so public a fashion – a performance made still more piquant by the presence in his audience of women students from Newnham and Girton colleges – Brooke returned to London to step up his pursuit of one woman who, he felt quietly confident, would not disturb his fragile equilibrium with any untoward display of female revolt or unseemliness: Cathleen Nesbitt. By now he and the actress were on first-name terms. She was increasingly charmed by his looks, and still more by what she called 'his sense of fun and his fantastic enjoyment of life'. Their romance blossomed on outings to Kew Gardens and Hampton Court. Slowly, Brooke unburdened himself to Cathleen about the sad saga of his involvement with Ka, and she responded with the story of her own unhappy affair with Henry Ainley. Her confession inspired a poem, which he sent her on a postcard. The title, given his recent outburst in Cambridge, is ironic: 'There's Wisdom in Women':

> 'Oh love is fair, and love is rare;' my dear one she
> said,
> 'But love goes lightly over.' I bowed her foolish
> head,
> And kissed her hair and laughed at her. Such a child
> was she;
> So new to love, so true to love, and she spoke so
> bitterly.
>
> But there's wisdom in women, of more than they
> have known,
> And thoughts go blowing through them, are wiser
> than their own,
> Or how should my dear one, being ignorant and
> young,
> Have cried on love so bitterly, with so true a
> tongue?

Apparently in high spirits but gnawed inwardly by a cancer of guilt over Ka, Brooke had in effect taken over Eddie's flat for his own purposes. A slightly startled Eddie, returning on 1 March from a holiday in the Lake District, was bemused to find a note on the hall table from Brooke inviting him to attend a party in his own home. The 'party', Eddie discovered, consisted of Brooke and Cathleen, clearly on the closest of terms. The following day more friends congregated to hear Brooke read *Lithuania*, which he was seeking to have performed. The guests included his new friends Cathleen and Gibson, and an assortment from much earlier days – Geoffrey Keynes and Denis Browne as well as Duncan Grant – an interloper from Bloomsbury, presumably invited because he was close to Eddie. Also there, yet another of the seemingly inexhaustible supply of young writers at Eddie's door, was Brooke's former lover from Rugby, Michael Sadler, now calling himself Sadleir.

Eddie and Brooke again met Yeats, at the home of the Irish poet St John Ervine in Hendon, on 3 March. Two days later Edward Thomas visited Raymond Buildings for breakfast. In addition to this literary socializing, Brooke agreed to give a reading at the Poetry Bookshop, which had opened its doors in January. It was a disappointment, as only half a dozen people turned up to hear him read from Donne and Swinburne, according to Harold Monro's biographer. Brooke himself gave a characteristically inflated account of the occasion to Noel, telling her that 'thousands of devout women were there'. He added: 'An elderly American female cried slightly, & shook me by the hand for some minutes.'

On 7 March came the news that Brooke had been hoping for: his dissertation had won favour at Cambridge, and he had at last been elected a Fellow of King's. His spirits soared instantly, for the Fellowship solved several of his problems: as well as the status, privileges and perks that went with the position, it permitted him to face both his family and his friends in the knowledge that at last he had a solid place in the shifting quicksands of life. He needed no longer feel intellectually inferior to the Keyneses and Stracheys of the world; and the Ranee would have to drop her objections to his proposed overseas tour. Eagerly, Brooke telegraphed his acceptance of the offer to the Provost of King's, M. R. James. The telegram was handed to James as he was making his stately way into the college's incomparable chapel. Brooke always liked to make a bit of a splash. In celebration of the news, Eddie hosted a party in his honour at Raymond Buildings, Brooke's new-found respectability being ample reason to introduce him to a network of friends grander than he had ever met.

Around Eddie's table sat W. B. Yeats, the Prime Minister's daughter Miss Violet Asquith and her sister-in-law Cynthia Asquith, the aristocratic wife of Violet's brother, Herbert 'Beb' Asquith. To complete the trinity of distinguished young women there was the wife of Eddie's boss – Mrs

Clementine Churchill. Eddie chose his guests shrewdly. The two poets shared, beside their fondness for flamboyant dress and gesture, a certain snobbery that would make them both come to gaze adoringly at the somewhat decayed specimens of the old aristocracy. As for the women, the two Asquiths were exact contemporaries of Brooke; Mrs Churchill just two years older. Doubtless he dazzled them with a display of the fresh boyish stunt; and the unmarried Violet, in particular, would gradually come to be smitten by him. A distinctly horse-faced creature, Violet made up in brains what she lacked in beauty. Devoted to her father, she would go on to have a distinguished career as one of the last upholders of the classic Liberal tradition in the days of its long terminal decline. No doubt one of the topics of conversation around the table was a long tour of the USA and Canada from which Violet had recently returned. If so, it would have reinforced Brooke's hardening determination to follow in her footsteps.

Meanwhile he wrote a distinctly grumpy postcard to Noel who had had the temerity to mock his fear that she might be kidnapped: 'There is never a hint (unfortunately) of kidnapping; people don't like my looks. Still I hope it may happen one day.' To this light-hearted teasing Brooke responded: 'Don't joke about kidnapping.' In mid-March he handed over the key to Eddie's flat to John Middleton Murry who had arrived for an extended stay while Katherine was away, and travelled to Cambridge to formally accept his Fellowship. He knew that his life had finally turned a corner.

John Webster and the Elizabethan Drama, which had won Brooke the coveted Fellowship, is his finest sustained work of literary criticism. The dissertation is a thoughtful, authoritative piece of prose that did much to rescue the dramatist from obscurity and is still cited as an authority in critical works on the playwright. Weighing in at more than 30,000 words, it is an achievement that Brooke was right to feel proud of having produced with so much agonizing labour.

Brooke begins by pinpointing the first decade of the seventeenth century as the golden age of the Elizabethan era that produced the flower of the extraordinary upsurge in drama centring on the phenomenon of Shakespeare. In rebellious mode, he takes several cheeky swipes at the bard, calling his history plays 'childish' and his comedies 'failures'. He reserves his accolades for the great tragedies produced as the new century opened.

After this sweeping introduction, the main meat is reached as Brooke concentrates on Webster himself, the man of whose life we know next to nothing but who none the less produced some of the grimmest, most shocking plays in the history of the English theatre. Brooke defends him against charges of plagiarism, arguing that all writers of worth use notes and ideas drawn from the work of others. In a brilliant piece of literary detection he confidently cites Sir Philip Sidney, Montaigne and Donne as three of the influences on Webster's plays. 'The heaping-up of images and phrases helps to confuse and impress the hearer,' Brooke writes, 'and gives body to a taste that might otherwise have been too thin to carry. Webster, in fine, belongs to the caddis-worm school of writers, who do not become their complete selves until they are encrusted with a thousand orts and chips and fragments from the world around.'

The boost to his ego provided by the award of the Fellowship is immediately apparent in his letters. He tells Ka: 'ambition grows and grows in me. It's inordinate, gigantic . . . it doesn't even make me work. I just sit and think ambitious thoughts.' His success also helped him to free himself of the nagging guilt he still felt about Ka – at least to the extent that he now felt more free to intensify his pursuit of Cathleen, whom he began to bombard with streams of slushy, hyperbolic and self-consciously 'romantic' letters. His first effort is to impress her with his new importance as a don, beginning his letter with quotations from the lesbian poetess Sappho in Greek, followed by a snatch of German, and adding: 'that's for *you*. Just to teach you a befitting humility in the presence of the learned.' In Cambridge, he says, he had his first dinner in Hall on the dais with his fellow-dons: 'I dined solemnly with very old white-haired men at one end of a vast dimly-lit hall, and afterwards drank port somnolently in the common room, with the College silver and seventeenth-century portraits and a sixteenth-century fireplace and fifteenth-century ideas. The perfect don, I.'

After putting Cathleen firmly in her place, he turned on the oleaginous charm with the ease of a past master: 'If you don't know that you're the most beautiful thing in the world, either you're an imbecile, or else, something's wrong with your mirror.' Then he returned to his unhealthy fetish about kidnapping, with the twist that this time the abductor is to be himself:

It is very likely that one day I shall kidnap you into a motor as you're leaving the theatre, whirl you off to some very distant village on a high cliff over the sea, and immure you there in a cottage, feeding you on cream and beer and ambrosia and chops, but never permitting you to use up your transient and divine self in that bloody London. No one will know whither you've vanished. And I shall surround the cottage with a ring of cows; so you will not be able to escape. I shall wait upon you: and in the intervals look at you.

This fantasy – like a precursor of John Fowles's sinister novel *The Collector* – is almost too perfectly revealing and symbolic of Brooke's interior world. It is all there: his wish to dominate and imprison women; his inability to accept them as free, independent or equal beings; and his dread of the corruption of the city, and especially Cathleen's own profession – doubtless the Ranee had once told him that actresses were little better than whores – is pathetic in its manifestness. He has clearly cast Cathleen in the role of the Sleeping Beauty, with a touch of Snow White in the domestic arrangements, which in themselves – 'a ring of cows', cream, beer, ambrosia and chops – are the Georgian dream in miniature. His fear of change, decay and ageing is also apparent. He wishes to preserve Cathleen like Snow White and Sleeping Beauty: flawless – but lifeless too.

With Brooke, it never rained but it poured, and he now let loose a veritable Niagara of syrup:

> I adore you. I was in a stupor all yesterday; partly because of my tiredness, and partly because of your face . . . Why do you look like that? Have you any idea what you look like? I didn't know that human beings could look like that. It is as beyond beauty as beauty is beyond ugliness. I'd say you were beautiful if the word wasn't a million times too feeble. Hell! But it's very amazing. It makes me nearly imbecile when I'm talking to you – I apologise for my imbecility: it's your fault. You shouldn't look like that. It really makes life very much worth while. My God! I adore you.

The bombardment became relentless – at one point in March Cathleen received four letters in as many days; but she refused to take his effusions entirely seriously:

> I am infinitely thankful that you exist. Your eyes are quite well set in, and very lovely. They change a great deal, from the beauty of softness to the beauty of light; so that I don't even know what colour they are (I do, in a way): but they're always lovely. It was well thought that ripple in the middle. If you had had a straight unindividual nose, you might merely have been a goddess. You're something so far more wonderful and beautiful. The lines of your cheek and jaw – the Greeks may have *dreamt* of that, I think. They tried to get something of that effect in stone, once or twice – poor bunglers!

And so on. One wonders whether Cathleen noticed that his praise was almost entirely confined to her physical assets – there was very little about her mind, her spirit or her intellect.

But the effect on his own spirits was undeniable. From the depths of gloom in which he had languished for more than a year he was soaring up into the light. Time would prove that this buoyancy was as easily deflated as a punctured balloon – the wounds he had suffered and inflicted on himself simply ran too deep. But for now, the spring weather and Cathleen seemed to have shot bolts of energy into his jaded soul:

> I want to walk a thousand miles, and write a thousand plays, and sing a thousand poems, and drink a thousand pots of beer, and kiss a thousand girls, and – oh a million things: I daren't enumerate them all, for fear this white paper'ld blush. I wish I could get you from the theatre for a week, and we'd tramp over England together and wake the old place up. By God, it makes one's heart sing that such a person as you should exist in the world.

Cathleen told him, in a sensible understatement, that he got drunk on his own words. Stung, Brooke tried to cover his annoyance with joshing, patronizing bluster:

> It is a thing no lady should say to a gentleman. I daresay Irish girls are very badly brought up. I had a good mind to reply with a lot of dirty insults in German . . . Damn it, one must be allowed to comment on the facts of existence. I merely, offhandedly throw out a few facts: 'This book is red.' 'It is raining.' 'That tree is tall'. 'Consols are at 73.5/8.' 'There is no God.' 'Cathleen is incredibly, inordinately, devastatingly, immortally, calamitously, hearteningly, adorably, beautiful.'

When they met, the puffing, steaming, sighing lover became, if Cathleen's artless memoirs are accurate, a sweet and innocent boy. Roaming out of London, they would walk the Chiltern hills together; sometimes stopping at a favourite pub, the Pink and Lily, which Brooke had once visited with Jacques Raverat. Brooke had quipped:

> Never came there to the Pink
> Two men such as we, I think.

Jacques capped it with:

> Never came to the Lily
> Two men quite so richly silly.

According to Cathleen, their romance was innocent and non-sexual: 'we sort of lay down on a bank and held hands . . . he never kissed me or anything like that; just held hands and we felt our souls communing in the air, and we both turned round to each other and said Donne's "Exstasie" – this is it; we had a kind of excitement in the mere . . . feeling we had, and we could often come back, you know, from a day in the country . . . quite drunk with each other.'

Brooke and Cathleen also had urban assignations – he even faced his fears of her profession when they met for tea backstage at the Haymarket Theatre: 'Isn't that too romantic! I've never been into an actress's dressing-room in my life before . . . I'm terrified.' But, true to form, he was not about to put all his sexual eggs into one basket, even a repository as attractive as Cathleen. Simultaneously with his London liaisons with her, he was also secretly seeing his old flame, Elisabeth van Rysselberghe, who was living with a family in Swanley in Kent but came up to London for trysts with Brooke. Information about what took place at these meetings is scanty – at the end of February, a note to James Strachey, who was attempting to revive their friendship, turns down a meeting on the grounds that 'I'm unfortunately dining with Fräulein So & So' – probably a reference to Elisabeth rather than Cathleen. Brooke was again angling for full sexual possession of the Flemish woman, telling her that she had more physical passion than anyone he had ever known – and throughout the spring he pressed her to go to bed with him. The old pattern was repeating itself, as it had at Rugby with Sadler, Denham and Lascelles, and more recently with Noel, Bryn and Ka: Brooke was engaged in the simultaneous pursuit of multiple partners, in this case one woman to satisfy his ethereal, romantic side, the other his more earthy cravings. Predictably, his refusal to completely commit himself to either resulted in frustration and confusion.

Meanwhile he had the distractions of his busy social life in London to take his mind off his emotional imbroglio. He, Eddie and Denis Browne, to whom Eddie had taken a shine, saw the legendary ballerina Pavlova dance at Covent Garden, watched Forbes Robinson play *Hamlet* at Drury Lane and attended a fashionable soirée with one of Eddie's aristocratic friends, Lady Plymouth. Brooke conveys the flavour of his hectic life in a letter to Walter de la Mare: 'I shall be lunching at Treviglio's at 1.30 – 3.00 . . . & dining at the Pall Mall Haymarket at 6.45 . . . If you don't come up for lunch, drink coffee with me. Or come to tea at Gallina's, opposite the Royalty Theatre.' As Middleton Murry was still in residence at Raymond Buildings, Brooke's London base was temporarily 5 Thurloe Square, South

Kensington, the apartment of the artist Albert Rothenstein, whom he had met at Cambridge when Rothenstein had painted the scenery for the Marlowe Dramatic Society's productions.

His increasing celebrity had drawn the attention of fashionable photographers. Never averse to publicity, Brooke succumbed to one: the American Sherril Schell, whose images came to represent the face of the poet for posterity. Schell took a dozen exposures when Brooke visited him at his studio in Pimlico. Between poses, they discussed Brooke's enthusiasm for the Ballet Russe and *Hullo Ragtime*. The American found his subject eager to learn all he could about the USA, for Brooke had at last decided to take the plunge and follow Frances's advice to travel there. He was wearing one of his favoured blue shirts and a floppy silk tie of the same colour. Schell noted his myopic tendency to stop and focus on something, screwing up his small, deep-set eyes. His complexion, the photographer recalled, was tanned and ruddy rather than the delicate peaches-and-cream colouring he had been led to expect. The famously tousled hair was 'golden brown with sprinklings of red'.

The twelfth shot that Schell took became the most famous and derided of them all. At Brooke's own suggestion, he threw off his shirt, so that his torso, which, the photographer said, 'looked like Hermes', was pictured in profile with bare shoulders – a pose that his Cambridge friends derisively dubbed 'Your favourite actress' when the picture became a prized Brookian icon. (The original print is now in the National Portrait Gallery.) Even the loyal Jacques, writing to the equally devoted Geoffrey Keynes, described the pose as 'obscene'. Nonetheless, the picture eventually became the basis for Brooke's chiselled memorial tablet in the chapel at Rugby.

Writing to Cathleen a few days afterwards, Brooke gave his own verdict on the photograph: 'Very shadowy and ethereal and poetic . . . Eddie says it's very good. I think it's rather silly.' But, if this is so, the question it begs is: why had he suggested the pose? This letter to Cathleen was written from Clouds, the grand country residence of the aristocratic Tory politician George Wyndham, one of the privileged coterie of Edwardian social and political leaders known as 'the Souls'. Brooke had been invited down with Eddie as a weekend guest – another indication of the grand social circles into which his mentor was firmly guiding him.

One more such sign was the birthday dinner for Violet Asquith held at Downing Street on 15 April. Besides Brooke and Eddie, the guests included Bernard Shaw and his wife, J. M. Barrie, Edmund Gosse, John Masefield, the Cabinet Ministers Augustine Birrell and Lord Haldane, and Violet's brilliant eldest brother, Raymond. Brooke, aided and abetted by

Eddie, had now ascended into the highest stratosphere of the social firmament.

But by May he was ready to leave it all behind. Despite his declared devotion to Cathleen – 'You are incomparably the most lovable and lovely and glorious person in the world,' he wrote to her from Clouds, adding: 'The champagne was good. The port was very good. But I'm thirsty for you' – the tug of wanderlust was too great. 'I've got to wander a bit,' he added vaguely, although assuring her: 'You chain me to England horribly.' Beneath his social success and literary lionization he was still gnawed by guilt over Ka. There were other pressures, too, impelling his imminent departure. Eddie was to leave London in May on an extended trip on the Admiralty yacht *Enchantress* with Churchill and the Asquiths. Brooke had failed to get John Drinkwater to stage *Lithuania* at the Birmingham Rep. Also, despite intensive lobbying and after a printer disappeared leaving a trail of unpaid bills, the Murrys' magazine, *Rhythm*, was about to go under. It was transformed into the *Blue Review* but the new venture folded after only three issues. In short, Brooke's career was marking time, and it seemed a propitious moment to seek a new departure.

As if on cue, Naomi Royde Smith, the literary editor of the *Westminster Gazette*, whose columns Brooke's poetry had graced since his schooldays, commissioned him to write a series of travel pieces from the USA and Canada for a fee of four guineas per article, plus travel expenses. It was a timely offer, too generous to be passed up, and Brooke booked his passage for New York on the liner SS *Cedric* sailing from Liverpool on 22 May. His final weeks in England flashed by in a flurry of farewells.

Ka, too, was on the move. She had left Berlin and was in Poland, on her way to Russia. Stricken anew by first-hand reports of her fragile emotional state from Dudley Ward, who was visiting London, Brooke wrote to her: 'There are moments when I'm overwhelmed by the horror of your incapacity, and the pain's so great, that I want to tell the people that do care for you, that if anything goes wrong with you while I'm away I'll kill them (and you) when I come back . . . oh, I can't go on.'

All the old obsessions – the pathetic threats to 'kill' all and sundry; the crazed need for Ka and Noel to be 'looked after' in his absence – were rumbling away beneath the superficial veneer of Brooke's social success. The past was still too close and pressing for him to escape. Although he could not marry Ka, he told Frances that, 'because of the great evil she did me', he still felt a resentment of her as well as an overwhelming weight of responsibility for her present plight. In some senses his journey was an attempt to escape that burden, just as his departure to the wars in the east two years later would be a bid to evade the facts of growing up and growing old. 'I don't really feel going off to be nearly as "hellish" as you imagine,' he told Frances. 'I've really got quite callous in my feelings by now. I'm not excited by travelling. But I've the feeling of shaking the dust of a pretty dirty period of my life off my feet. And that makes up for any tear there may be.'

There were tears aplenty from Eddie when Brooke departed. As a farewell gift Eddie presented him with a complete edition of Jane Austen. Brooke took solemn farewells of his other friends. Edward Thomas was told: 'I leave the muses of England in your keeping . . . feed the brutes.' On 21 May, Brooke's last evening in England, Geoffrey Keynes, Gibson and Murry were among those who dined with him in a restaurant off Regent Street. The next morning two old friends from his youth, Denis Browne and St John Lucas Lucas, saw him off on the Liverpool train from Euston. At the port he found himself entirely alone and tipped a boy hanging about the quayside sixpence to wave him goodbye. The lad, named William, obliged. Brooke's last sight of England for more than a year was William's off-white handkerchief fluttering in farewell. A wave of mixed emotions: loneliness, guilt, nostalgia, hope – and perhaps a touch of fear – almost swamped him.

22

A New World

No sooner was Brooke on board the ship than he realized that in the rush of departure he had left behind the 67 letters of introduction to prominent people in the USA and Canada that he had assiduously gathered from friends and friends of friends in England. He wrote to Denis Browne asking him to forward them to his Broadway hotel, and then he used a good portion of the pad of writing paper Browne had brought him as a leaving present at Euston to write a lengthy screed to Cathleen. Before leaving England he had told her something of his troubled past:

> Dear love, I've been through evil places and I cling all the more graspingly to the peace and comfort I find more and more in loving you and being with you. It grows as I see love in you for me grow. Love in me grows slowly, and differently from the old ways – I thought the root was gone. But it's still there. It's the one thing I've got, to love you, and feel love growing, and the strength and peace growing, and to learn to worship you, and to want to protect you, to desire both to possess every atom of your body and soul, and yet to lose myself in your kindliness, like a child.

As if this threat to want to envelop and swallow her whole was not enough, Brooke went on to predict that all would anyway end in tears: 'It must be that, in the end, it wouldn't do, and we'd find that I didn't love you enough, or you me.' And yet there was a 'hope and a chance' that they might win through: 'We're so far towards it. The more I know you, the more I love. And the more I know and love, the more I find you have to give me, and I to give you. How can I let this growing glory and hope be broken, and let myself go adrift again? . . . I want to love and to work. I don't want to be washed about on these doubtful currents and black waves or drift into some dingy corner of the tide . . .'

Now that he was himself embarked on a real 'doubtful current', he found himself clinging to Cathleen's memory like a drowning man. To his delight, he found a letter and telegram from his beloved awaiting him in the purser's office, and wrote to tell her of his gratitude: 'You can't think how it cheered me up, this string of communication with you. It felt as if your love was so strong it reached with me all the way. It's queer. I do feel as if there was a lovely and present guardianship all the time. My darling, you give me so much more than I deserve. But it does make me feel so quiet and secure.'

But a sterner duty awaited – he knew that he owed Ka more than a letter – apology, explanation, contrition, even atonement. He hoped that Cathleen understood: 'Oh it's bitter destroying and breaking things two have built together – intimacies and trusts and friendliness,' he told her. 'It's like cutting something out of oneself . . . O child, its hard work cutting off from people one's been intimate with. (I told you I'd been with a girl I loved – and you'll not ever tell anyone about it, child: for its not wholly my secret) I've got, I feel, to stop even writing to her, for her sake, to give her a chance to get free . . .'

But Cathleen and Ka were not the only women on his mind. He used more of Brown's notepaper to write a revealing letter to Elisabeth van Rysselberghe. It seems that his determination to at last unburden himself had unlocked some long-closed chamber in the deepest recesses of his being; and now that he did not have to face the women in person he could at last afford to be fully, fearlessly frank. 'I'm in love, in different ways, with two or three people,' he told Elisabeth candidly.

> I always am. You probably know this. I'm not married to anybody, nor likely to be. A year and a bit ago I was violently in love with somebody who treated me badly. The story is a bloody one: and doesn't matter. Only, it left me for a time rather incapable of loving anybody. As for you, child: I have two feelings about you now, which alternate and mix and make confusion. I like to be with you . . . But quite apart . . . from all that, you – move me to passion . . . The fire in you lights the fire in me – and I'm not wholly responsible. Only, my dear, that's all there is: those two things. I don't want to marry you. I'm not in love with you in that way.

There, it was out – in its cold way, it was as near to a real declaration of truth as Brooke ever made to a lover. Unflattering it might have been, but at least he spared Elisabeth the illusion of lies. He concluded by offering to live with her for six months or so, sometime, somewhere. Meanwhile, as with Ka, he advised her to forget her love for him and concentrate on becoming independent. Tearing himself away from what he told himself was his past and his future amorous life, Brooke turned to the contemplation of his shipboard companions, and his first encounter with real Americans. He found their accent amusing, and mocked it: the 'Says . . .' and the 'Yeps . . .' and how he would find 'Amurrica Vurry different from England', and when one young man complained of English inequality, he forbore to mention segregated streetcars. He sampled his first American food. 'Today I ate clam-chowder,' he reported to Cathleen in wonder. 'That's romance, isn't it? I ordered it quite recklessly. I didn't know what it was. I only knew that anything called clam-chowder must be strange beyond words . . . Clam-chowder, my God! What am I coming to?'

One fellow-voyager who ate at Brooke's table was a theatrical entrepreneur named Klaw, an appropriately named grasper, just back from a trawl through Europe to add to the repertoire of the seven New York theatres he already owned. Another was one of those decadent *fin-de-siècle* poets Brooke had once so admired: Richard Le Gallienne, who was, he told Eddie, 'a really nasty man . . . he eyes me suspiciously – he scents a rival, I think. We've not spoken yet. His shoulders are bent. His mouth is ugly and small and mean. His eyes are glazed. His manner is furtive.' Le Gallienne's best-known eccentricity – the fact that he carried about with him at all times – despite the presence of a second Mrs Le Gallienne, an urn containing the ashes of his first wife, Mildred – inspired Brooke to write a cruel little satirical squib called 'For Mildred's Urn', which ended:

> Who knows, but in some happy hour
> The God, whose strange alchemic power
> Wrought her of dust, again may turn
> To woman, this immortal urn;
> May take this dust and breathe thereon,
> And give me back my little one.

Before docking, he found time to write a quick note to Noel, who had dined with him *à deux* at Treviglio's, his favourite Soho restaurant, on the eve of his departure, confiding that his old enemy, her eldest sister Margery, was slipping from eccentricity into a mental disturbance that would prove incurable. Callously, Brooke told her how ill he thought she had looked at their dinner: 'I do not desire you to be ill . . . a spasm of affection did shoot into my withered heart.' But he could not resist a few savage taunts, in a childish effort to convince Noel that in letting him go, she had parted with a pearl of great price: 'Three separate lovely young ladies have fallen in love with me,' he bragged. 'I have come to the conclusion that if I'm always so happy out of England, it is absurd ever to return.' Thus spake the poet who, more than any other, is identified by posterity as the patriotic embodiment of the essence of England, and who, in little more than a year, would pen a clutch of elegies to England as his swansong.

His first impression of America, or at least, of New York, after checking into the 'beastly' Broadway Central Hotel, was that he had landed on some alien planet. Life moved fast – the trams zinged along like streaks of fire, the skyscrapers seemed like great piled cliffs; hardly human at all. The faces seemed strangely ageless, without blemish or wrinkle, as if wrought from plastic. He admired the way the loose-limbed bodies moved freely, without a hint of English stiffness. The neon, the boys bawling baseball news, the continual noise and jangling telephones – all seemed strangely exciting, and reeked of a future he would know nothing of.

On 5 June, armed with one of his retrieved letters of introduction, this one from Goldsworthy Lowes Dickinson, he travelled to Staten Island, to meet one of 'Goldie's' friends, Russell H. Loines, an influential lawyer, who knew the city as well as anyone. Loines, with open-handed generosity, dropped everything to entertain this dazzling young visitor from England. He took him to Wanamakers department store, then whisked him up the River Delaware to shoot rapids in a canoe. Soon the self-pitying misery he had expressed from the anonymity of his hotel room – 'I don't know a soul in New York, and I'm very tired, and I don't like the food; and I don't like the people's faces; and I don't like the newspapers; and I haven't a friend in the world; and nobody loves me; and I'm going to be extraordinarily miserable these six months; and I want to die . . .' – was transformed. From an outdoor camp on the banks of the Delaware he told Cathleen, after paddling five hours in the sun: 'It was great . . . we came round a wild turn in the river, and there was a voice singing wonderfully . . . we saw a little house, high on the bank, with an orchard, and a verandah, and wooden steps down to the great river, and at the top of them was a tall girl, very beautiful, standing like a goddess, with wonderful red hair, her head thrown back, singing, singing . . .'

Back from this trip, he journeyed to Boston, cradle of the American revolution, which, paradoxically, he found full of 'a delicious, ancient Toryism'. He paid his respects to the matriarch of the city's ruling intellectual aristocracy, Amy Lowell, and then dropped in at the offices of the *Atlantic Monthly*, whose editor, Ellery Sedgwick, was awed by Brooke's Grecian looks:

A young man more beautiful than he I had never seen. Tall beyond the common, his loose tweeds accentuated his height and the athletic grace of his walk. His complexion was as ruddy as a young David's. His auburn hair rippled back from the central parting, careless but perfect . . . man's beauty is much more rare than woman's. I went home under the spell of it and at the foot of the stairs cried aloud to my wife, 'I have seen Shelley plain!'

It was time for English Cambridge to pay respects to its American counterpart. Brooke's next port of call was Harvard, to witness the university's baseball match against its traditional Ivy League rival, Yale. Conventionally enough, he compared the game to cricket, finding 'excitement in the game, but little beauty'. However, he adored the cheer-leaders, finding the rhythmic movements of their co-ordinated 'ecstasy' wonderfully American, with its combination of wildness and regulation. He also saw a parade of Old Harvardians tottering past, some of the alumni stretching back to the 1850s, with a poignant gap reflecting the fallen of the 1860s Civil War. He was oddly moved: 'Nobler . . . this deliberate viewing of oneself as part of the stream . . . the flow and transiency became apparent . . . In five minutes fifty years of America, go past one.' Asked by one Harvardian alumnus if he knew Matthew Arnold, he couldn't bring himself to pass on the news that the poet had died when Brooke was all of eight months old. A female acquaintance fiercely denounced democracy: 'They ought to take the votes away from these people, who don't know how to use them, and give them only to us, the educated.' For Brooke, who had always tended to H. G. Wells's hierarchical view of socialism, such élitism was becoming increasingly sympathetic.

Back in New York he steeled himself for the duty he had been ducking for too long: it was time to put things right with Ka. To gently but firmly detach himself from her clinging tentacles for good and all; for her own sake, as much as his. With a heart heavy with guilt and sadness he picked up his pen. 'My dear, I've been worrying so about writing. And almost every night as I crossed I dreamt about you. And you always seemed in pain,' he began. The best way of easing that pain was to close the books, settle up and make a clean break with the past and all its hopeless misery. His emotion lent eloquence to his words:

You *must* get right clear of me, cease to love me, love and marry somebody – and somebody worthy of you. Oh my dear, let's try to put things right together. It's so hard to know what to do – one's so stupid and blind and blundering. What I feel about you is this – I'm not arguing if it's true, I just state it as it comes to my heart – Ka is more precious than anything. She has marvellous goodness and greatness in her. She has things so lovely it hurts to name them. She is greater and better, potentially, than any woman I know: and more woman. She is very blind, and infinitely easy to lead astray. Her goodness makes her a prey. She needs looking after more than anybody else in the world. She's a lovely child. And with that in my heart I have to leave you. It's very difficult. Oh, Ka, you don't know how difficult it is! So have pity on me. And forgive my breaking out like this.

Even in the midst of tenderness and pity, he was unable to avoid self-absorption. After urging her to fall on her friends for comfort, he at last got round to an admission that he had played some part in the immolation of their relationship:

Dear child, dearest Ka, whom I've loved and known, you must get well and happy, and live the great life you can. It's the only thing I care for. Oh, child, I know I've done you great wrong. What could I do? It was so difficult. You had driven me mad. I'm sorry for the wrong. It's the one thing in the world I'm sorry for: though I've done a lot of evil things. I can't bear it that it is I have hurt you. But you'll grow, and be the fine Ka. In the end I know you, that you can't be broken or spoilt. I do know you.

And, knowing her as he does, he has to tell her that this is the end – an end to even written communication – but: 'In a few years we'll meet. Till then we can dodge each other. If we meet we're big enough to manage that. The creatures who watch won't get much change out of us.' In the meantime she will hold the place of honour in his heart:

There's one thing. Do you mind? I want to break the rule and give you a thing. A statuette of a mother and child . . . a tiny thing . . . I give it you; because you'll be the greatest mother in the world. And I'll not be anything but sad, till I've heard you're happy, and with a child of your own. Let it stand: not for what we did: but for what we learnt. I thought at one time I'd only learnt bad from you: now I know that before and after and over it all I learnt good – all that I have. I've got to leave you. But if ever it happens you're in ultimate need of help – it may – you know I'll come, at any time and from any place, if you want it. I'm very happy and well, travelling, and in the end I'll get back and work. Don't think of me. Please, Ka, be good and happy: and stick to and be helped by your friends. That's the last thing I ask. This is so bad a letter: and I wanted to make everything clear. Do believe. See what I've tried to write. Preaching and everything aside, let's just be Ka and Rupert for a minute: and say good-bye.

I'll be loyal to the things we've learnt together: and you be loyal. And life'll be good. Dear love, good bye. Rupert.

The effort required to write this had been phenomenal. And was not the Gill sculpture that he had bought long before, and secreted with Eddie against just such a moment, just too much an appeasement gift, designed to deflect Ka's righteous wrath? And what sort of sensitivity, knowing of Ka's miscarriage of his child, could conceive that a statue of a mother and child would be an appropriate commemoration of their love, so misbegotten? Soon after stumbling out into the teeming New York streets to post this offering, Brooke collapsed under the strain, but was promptly whisked away by Loines, who had taken over Eddie's accustomed role as mentor, to recuperate on Staten Island. Swiftly recovered, he resumed his literary rounds – introduced to Edward Arlington Robinson, he perceptively hailed him as a poet of genius. But, much to his American friends' dismay and bemusement, he was determined to leave for Canada: '"A country without soul" they cried and pressed books upon me to befriend me through the Philistine bleakness . . .'

Hardening his heart, he boarded the Montreal Express train on 29 June. As ever when alone, waves of homesickness threatened to overwhelm him. 'I shan't be really happy,' he told Eddie in a long letter penned on the train as it roared north, 'till I get back to you all.' A little later he defined who 'all' meant:

> I have a folk-longing to get back from all this Imperial luxury to the simplicity of the little places and quiet folks I knew and loved . . .

> Would God I were eating plover's eggs,
> And drinking dry champagne,
> With the Bernard Shaws, Mr and Mrs Masefield, Lady
> Horner, Neil Primrose, Raleigh, the Right Honour-able
> Augustine Birrell, Eddie, Six or seven Asquiths,
> and Felicity Tree,
> In Downing Street Again.

'Little places' – Downing Street? 'Quiet folks' – the grandest in London? One trusts he is being ironic.

Then, as now, the struggle to become England's Poet Laureate was a matter for popular speculation and faction fighting. The position was vacant after the death of the indifferent poetaster Alfred Austin, and Brooke was eager to give his views on the succession to Eddie. He believed the choice came down to three – either Yeats, Robert Bridges or Alfred Noyes – with Kipling and Masefield as outsiders. Brooke was not to know that the influential Eddie had already advised Asquith to appoint Bridges. Another of his protégés, Masefield, had to wait 17 years until Bridges' death before succeeding in Buggins' turn.

Unimpressed by a quick charabanc trip around Montreal, Brooke continued on the same day to Quebec, where he teamed up with a 'childlike' American businessman to tour the old city. He was hugely impressed by the St Lawrence, 'the most glorious river in the world', and was soon travelling up it through towering cliffs of black granite crowned with lonesome pines, to bathe in its tributary, the Saguenay. By 9 July he was back in Montreal, *en route* to the Canadian capital, Ottawa. Here he shamelessly exploited his contacts list: staying for more than a week under the roof of Duncan Campbell Scott, like Eddie, a civil servant with a part-time penchant for poetry. Although he found the Canadian, still in mourning for a beloved infant daughter who had died some years before, somewhat melancholy, Brooke enjoyed his hospitality, which included daily lunches at the Ottawa golf club. A set of pictures taken while he was there show a newly respectable Brooke, strangled by a high collar and tie, and looking handsome, but older, in a formal cutaway jacket and buttonhole.

Pursuing his newly acquired taste for cultivating the grand and the powerful, Brooke used a letter from Hugh Dalton's father, Canon Dalton, to arrange an interview with the Canadian Prime Minister, Sir Wilfrid Laurier, describing himself in his letter of introduction as 'an English Socialist . . . and writer'. He was treated to a lunch *à deux* with the Prime Minister and afterwards complained of his 'French sympathies' and his apparent unwillingness to contribute to an Imperial Naval expansion, but, for all that, he condescendingly pronounced Sir Wilfrid 'a nice old man'.

Soon he was underway once more, sailing up the St Lawrence and across Lake Ontario towards Toronto, where he arrived on 21 July. His host here was Edmund Morris, a painter friend of Scott's, and the kingpin of the local Arts and Letters Club, which received Brooke like visiting royalty in this provincial outpost of Empire where rumours of the Georgian poets were hot gossip and to see one in the flesh was a treat indeed. 'Oh Eddie, one fellow actually possessed my *Poems*,' Brooke proudly told his mentor. 'Awful Triumph. Every now and then one comes up and presses my hand and says "Wal, sir, you cannot know how memorable a day in my life this is." Then I do my pet boyish-modesty-stunt and go pink all over: and everyone thinks its too delightful. One man said to me "Mr Brooks (my Canadian name), Sir, may I tell you that in my opinion you have Mr Noyes skinned." That means I'm better than him . . .'

Brooke's painful self-consciousness passed unnoticed, though one observer did remark the contrast between his virile masculinity and his pink girlish blushes and habit of distractedly running his hands through his hair.

Letters were reaching him from England. One, from Noel, annoyed him mightily. Playing Brooke at his own game, she flirtatiously mentioned that she was still seeing two suitors – James Strachey and Ferenc Békássy – names that she knew would be like waving a red rag before Brooke. She admitted her share of fault for their undone relationship: 'I'm even sorry, about a few things. Sorry you got so injured. Sorry I wasn't nicer. But chiefly sorry, that the world's so difficult to fit in to. (And too much of a habit to get out of) . . . I do hope you accept my humiliation and my confession: that the world being what it is, you are right & I am wrong. And the Gods will treat us accordingly. Noel.'

To this he responded in a furious rage: 'You're a Devil. By God, you're a *devil*. What a bloody letter to write to me!' Calming somewhat, he noted with reasonable honesty on his progress in the New World:

> I was very happy in America, where I made a lot of friends; and occasionally miserable in Canada, where I scarcely know anybody. That's because I'm getting old and more dependent on human companionship. So once or twice I've been homesick. I'm alone you see. I've nothing immediate to worry me. I've had to cut away from Ka, & the thought of her hurts. But I try to pretend it's well with her. I'm not in love with you. I've no intention of playing le grand indifférent. I'm going to marry very soon and have a lot of children. I'm practically engaged to a girl you don't know to whom I'm devoted & who is in love with me. And if I don't marry her, I shall very swiftly marry one of two or three others, & be very happy.

Before posting this packet of sour grapes, he put the letter aside to attend to a more welcome correspondence: he had heard from Wilfrid Gibson, who, inspired by the runaway success of *Georgian Poetry*, was hatching a scheme with Lascelles Abercrombie to launch an anthology of their own from Gallows Cottage, the house Abercrombie had rented near Dymock, deep in the Gloucestershire countryside. Would Brooke consider joining them? Gibson wrote to ask. At the time, Gibson and Abercrombie were considered the coming names in English poetry, and their reputation had spread as far afield as Canada. Brooke regarded it as a great compliment that they should want to include him in their new venture. 'It's . . . rather a score for me,' he wrote to the Ranee from Toronto, 'as my "public" is smaller than any of theirs!' He replied enthusiastically, promising to send new poems from his travels.

All this time he had been dutifully sending his travel pieces to the *Westminster Gazette*. After a shaky start he hit his stride reporting a visit to Niagara Falls. He denounced with a shudder of disdain the puny human commercialization surrounding the great wonder of nature – the hotels, shops, sham legends, rifle-galleries – and then, still shuddering, he turned to the touts:

> There are touts insinuating, and touts raucous, greasy touts, brazen touts, and upper-class, refined, gentlemanly, take-you-by-the-arm touts; touts who intimidate and touts who wheedle; professionals, amateurs, and dilettanti, male and female; touts who would photograph you with a young lady against a faked background of the sublimest cataract, touts who would bully you into cars, char-a-bancs, elevators or tunnels, or deceive you into a carriage and pair, touts who would sell you picture postcards, moccasins, sham Indian beadwork, blankets, tee pees, and crockery; and touts, finally, who have no apparent object in the world, but just purely, simply, merely, incessantly, indefatigably, and ineffugibly – to tout. And in the midst of all this, overwhelming it all, are the Falls. He who sees them instantly forgets humanity. They are not very high, but they are overpowering . . .

Brooke was aware that his reaction to the might of the Falls – 'the real secret of the beauty and terror of the Falls is not their height or width, but the feeling of colossal power and of unintelligible disaster caused by the plunge of that vast body of water' – came perilously close to the conventional awe of the tourist. He was, he admitted to an old Cambridge friend, A. F. Scholfield, 'horribly impressed' by Niagara, despite all the sniffiness. Regrettably, he acknowledged, he was:

> a Victorian at heart, after all. Please don't breathe a word of it: I want to keep such shreds of reputation as I have left. Yet it's true. For I sit and stare at the thing and have the purest Nineteenth century grandiose thoughts, about the Destiny of Man, the Irresistibility of Fate, the Doom of Nations, the fact that Death awaits us All, and so forth. Wordsworth Redivivus. Oh dear! oh dear!

Resuming his letter to Noel 'with the spray of Niagara falling lightly upon me', he told her that, because he was 'the most conservative person in the world', he could not get out of the habit of being fond of her: 'You know how it is, affection – So many years of regarding you as queerly mine, & me as queerly yours, leave a mark.' Now, he claimed, he would be happy to just be friends, and not plunge back into being 'desperately in love with you.' He added, witheringly: 'I will *not* go into that Hell again. I've tried loving a woman who doesn't love me, you; and I've tried loving a woman who isn't clean, Ka; & it doesn't pay. I'm going to find some woman who is clean, & loves me.'

He realized that the letter was turning into a farewell; the last of his long goodbyes, just as his New York *cri de coeur* to Ka had been a closing of the accounts on that desperately damaging phase of his life. Both, in their way, represented a renunciation, and he could afford to be generous with his emotions. Above all, he was at last ready to rise above his past rancour:

> Noel, I will tell you a secret. No one ever knows where he or she is at. It's really so. In outline, you behaved precisely & boringly like any other girl in the world; as I did like any other boy – Really, child, – I think parts of you, & things you've done, wrong. But very slight affairs – you're just a little too irresponsible. That's all. The main evil was that we didn't, after all, love each other, and for that no one is to blame. Or, if anyone, I: for having been very often so very unpleasant; as I now see I was. Even that was inevitable to my age & temper, perhaps. But oh! how unbearable I was! You know, Noel, we were at odds about a good many things; & in almost all of them I've come to see that you were right. I don't know that you had thought much more wisely than my able self. You only had a cleaner mind and a better nature.

Having renounced the longest, and perhaps the deepest of all his relationships, Brooke, as was his custom, pronounced a benediction:

> My romantic darling, what *do* you want? To play Cleopatra? No, no, you're for better things, you childishist [sic] of children. You'll love somebody sometime: I've little doubt: & find it isn't whatever horror of delirium you suppose, but just great friendliness & trust & comfort – ordinary things. Nor do I doubt you'll marry – when I hear of it I'll have a bad hour or two, & then be too busy with my own love to think about it – & have children (it's always been my thought what lovely children you would have, most of all if they were mine). These things come round the corner on one.

He ended lightly: 'Noel, I always thought it was a funny name . . . not very English. Splendid Noel – silly little child – my friend, my penultimate word to you is, don't be a fool: my ultimate one, eat Ovaltine. With love Rupert.' In a postscript scribbled on 28 July he added: 'I always desire to repeat that tiresome demand that you should invoke my assistance whenever you need it – may it be taken as written at the end of each letter, till I revoke it?'

It was a less fraught farewell than his goodbye to Ka had been, and indeed, they would continue to communicate fitfully. But there was no doubt that he had mentally purged himself of his long and wasting involvement with both women. A fresh start beckoned, and a new frontier.

Appropriately, his next destination was the Canadian wilderness. From Sarnia, in the Great Lakes, he took a steamer across Lakes Huron and Superior. He found the vast expanse of water 'too big, and too smooth, and too sunny; like an American businessman'. From Port Arthur he travelled by train to Winnipeg, and then trekked into the virgin region around Lake George, where he stayed at a hunting lodge. He was impressed by the vast, untouched wilderness, where human habitation was rare; it seemed like a huge blank page awaiting its Wordsworth to 'give it a soul'. The space and the silence inspired profound philosophic thoughts: 'It is possible, at a pinch, to do without gods. But one misses the dead.'

In this empty amphitheatre, surrounded by mountains, forests and lakes, he spent his birthday, the last but one he would know. 'I never expected to pass my twenty-sixth birthday with a gun and fishing tackle, without any clothes on, by a lake, in a wood infested by bears, in a country where there aren't ten people within five miles and half of those are Indians.' He felt close to untamed nature, in a wilder way than he had at any Neo-Pagan camp. One night a trapper brought a huge dead deer by canoe to the lakeside log cabin where he was staying. By the light of a fire the great beast was strung up to a tree to be dismembered and dressed. 'For two hours we pulled and hauled at this creature . . .' he told Cathleen:

Then the trapper got an axe and hacked the beast's head off: with the great antlers it weighs some hundred pounds . . . I got cut and scratched and smeared with the creature's insides. It was a queer sight, lit up by the leaping flames of the fire, which the women fed – the black water by the lake, muddy with trampling at the edge, and smeared with blood, the trapper in the tree, this great carcass hanging at one end of the rope, my friend and an Indian and I pulling our arms out at the other, the head gazing reproachfully at us from the ground, everybody using the most frightful language, and the rather ironical and very dispassionate stars above. Rather savage.

On his birthday itself, he told Cathleen:

> Today, O my heart, I am twenty-six years old. And I've done so little. I'm very
> ashamed. By God, I'm going to make things hum, though. But that's all so far
> away. I'm lying quite naked on a beach of golden sand, some six miles away
> from the hunting-lodge, the other man near by, a gun between us in case bears
> appear, the boat pulled up on the shore, the lake very blue and ripply, and the
> sun rather strong ... we caught two pike on the way out, which lie
> picturesquely on the bows of the boat.

Gorged with venison, they spared a red deer they saw. 'I'm glad – I'm no
sportsman,' Brooke confessed. In his child-of-nature mode he picnicked off
fried eggs, cold caribou heart, tea and 'oh! blueberry pie'. He was acquiring
a taste for blueberries, for although, as he told Noel, 'materially they were
singularly tasteless', nevertheless they reminded him of camps gone by.
'Cooking and eating a meal naked,' Cathleen learned, 'is the most solemnly
primitive thing one can do.'

The next day he returned to Winnipeg, and left immediately for
Edmonton via Regina. Edmonton was a booming frontier town which had
sprung up out of the prairie over the past 12 years – mushrooming from a
population of 200 at the turn of the century to one of 50,000 at the time of
Brooke's brief visit. He was becoming adept at organizing his own
publicity, breezing into the offices of the local newspaper and offering
himself as a suitable subject for an interview: 'I just put a cigar in the corner
of my mouth, and undid my coat and put my thumbs under my arm-pits,
and spat, and said "Say, kid, this is some town!"' he told Eddie. The
reporter 'asked me a lot of questions, of which I did not know the answers.
So I lied.' One of the questions inquired about the growing arms and naval
race between Britain and Germany: 'When I come back I shall demand a
knighthood from Winston,' Brooke jested to Eddie. 'I've been delivering
immense speeches in favour of his naval policy.'

His next stop was another new frontier town, Calgary, in the Rockies.
The further west he moved, the more homesick he became. The new
frontier affronted his English sense of age and continuity. 'You can't think
how sick one's heart gets for something *old*,' he told Eddie in exasperation,
adding, with some exaggeration: 'For weeks I have not seen or touched a
town so old as myself. Horrible! Horrible! They gather round me and say "In
1901 Calgary had 139 inhabitants, now it has 75,000" ... I reply "My village
is also growing. At the time of Julius Caesar it was a bare 300. Domesday
Book gives 347 and it is now close on 390." Which is ill-mannered of me.'

The local paper, the *Calgary News Telegram*, carried an interview with Brooke with the headline 'General European War is opinion of Political Writer from Great Britain'. Brooke forecast that the coming conflict would also become a world war: 'a struggle in which practically every country will participate'. At a time when the Great War is supposed to have burst upon a complacent world with the shock of a summer thunderclap, his gift for prophecy proved uncannily accurate.

He was nearing the end of his odyssey across the continent. From a train crossing the Rockies near Banff in Alberta he wrote a rare note to James Strachey on 18 August. (On the same train a lady had offered him a packet of peanuts, and supposing him to be still a schoolboy, had worried about him getting back to England in time for the new term.) 'My dear boy,' he began, affectionately enough, 'I wonder how the world is treating you. I sometimes see the old *Spectator*, & often think of the old days.' He reported that he was 'awfully healthy and strong', adding: 'But the process you saw dawning has run its atrocious path. Poetry, even, has gone by the bawd. I'm relapsed comfortably onto the mattress of second class. Good. Perhaps my children . . .'

He spent four days at Chateau Lake Louise, where the main attraction was the young American widow of an Italian aristocrat, the Marchesa Capponi. Romance blossomed, and the couple corresponded affectionately. Whether Brooke graced the Marchesa's bed is uncertain, but she felt strongly enough about him to drop in on the Ranee during a visit to England while Brooke was still abroad.

He reached the Pacific at Victoria on Vancouver Island, where he was horrified to learn of the death by drowning of Edmund Morris, his recent host at Toronto. It was the second such untimely demise of a friend he had heard of since leaving England. Soon after his arrival, he had read that George Wyndham, whose aristocratic hospitality he had enjoyed at Clouds with Eddie, had collapsed and died during a visit to Paris with his mistress. 'It seemed abrupt,' he told Eddie. 'I wish he hadn't died.'

His encounter with the Marchesa Capponi may have given him more objectivity about Cathleen, for, in an unusually frank and bad-tempered letter to Eddie on 6 September, he wrote:

> My general position, you know, is queer. I've had enough and too much of love. I've come to the conclusion that marriage is the best cure for love. If I married, perhaps I could settle down, be at peace, and *work*. It's the only chance. Therefore, marry soon. Anybody. Cathleen's character is very good, and I'm very fond of her. Why not her? – On the other hand, she's an actress. Oh, hell,

she does mix with a rotten crowd. I hope to God she won't get spoilt. She's very simple – I hope I don't shock you, writing so coldly. I'm fierier, near her, I assure you . . .

In a guilty afterthought, he added, in parentheses: 'This is the sort of letter that doesn't look well in a biography.' Which is why it was excluded from Christopher Hassall's official study.

From Vancouver, Brooke crossed back into the USA by water to Seattle, where he caught a train to San Francisco. He was undecided on what to do: his homesickness was increasing; the six articles he had been contracted to write for the *Westminster Gazette* were written, and no more money would be forthcoming from that quarter. On the other hand, there was no pressing reason – apart from Cathleen – for him to return home. A $250 loan from Loines would fund further travel, so he decided to let fate decide. He spun a coin – and fate decreed that he travel on.

He booked a passage on the SS *Sierra*, which would sail on 7 October, bound for Honolulu. Meanwhile he was the guest of Loines's friend, Professor Chauncey Wells, of the University of California at San Francisco. He arrived in the middle of a heatwave – 21 September was the hottest recorded day since 1871 – and suffered accordingly. But Professor Wells was a charming and generous host, and Brooke began to relax. He gave a reading from *Georgian Poetry* at Stanford University, and, proudly reporting this to Eddie, added approvingly:

California is nice, and the Californians a friendly bunch. There's a sort of goldenness about 'Frisco and the neighbourhood. It hangs in the air, and about the people. Everyone is very cheery and cordial and simple. They are rather a nation apart . . . from the rest of the United States. Much more like the English. As everywhere in this extraordinary country I am welcomed with open arms when I say I know Masefield and Goldie!

He outlined his itinerary for Eddie: 'I leave for Honolulu on Tuesday. Then Samoa, Fiji, Tahiti, and a resting place at the bottom of the Pacific, all among the gay fish and lovely submarine flowers . . . you may figure me in the centre of a Gauguin picture, nakedly riding a squat horse into white surf.'

To the Marchesa Capponi he bemoaned the loss in British Columbia of a notebook containing '2 months notes on my travels, and unfinished sonnets . . . yessir isn't it too bloody. I've been prostrated by grief ever since.' His spirits lifted as soon as he had taken leave of his new friends and boarded the boat. Ahead lay the supreme sensual experience of his life.

23

Heaven on Earth

The year that Brooke spent out of England from June 1913 was by far the most productive, and probably among the happiest, of his life. Creatively, it is akin to Keats's 'marvellous year', which produced the odes, *Endymion* and his greatest sonnets. Brooke's four months in America and Canada had quite unexpectedly given birth, without painful labour, to a body of prose that is fresh and witty even today. His pieces for the *Westminster Gazette* were collected and published posthumously as *Letters from America* with a lachrymose and lengthy introduction by Henry James – the last piece of prose that 'the Master' wrote. Reading them today makes one regret the superb travel writer that the world lost in Brooke.

Perceptive, energetic, alive with colour, joy and reflections both wise and funny, they are still a pleasure. Brooke is acute in his observation of the tidal wave of commercialism that was gathering over the country, like some great cloud bank about to spew drenchingly forth. Business, with its handmaiden advertising, he pinpointed as America's new religion; although even he might have been taken aback by the proportions the worship of hype would attain by the century's end. He was perceptive, too, in recognizing another curse of the coming decades: the almost insuperable problem of racial harmony, even among superficially similar white peoples of European origin.

Writing of the English and French communities in Quebec, for example, he remarked: 'Inter-marriage is very rare. They do not meet socially; only on business, and that not very often. In the same city these two communities dwell side by side with different traditions, different languages, different ideals without sympathy or comprehension.' Although the racial divide had not, thus far, produced violence, Brooke likened it to a split personality, afflicted by 'debility and spiritual paralysis'. His own attitude to race was complex – in the essay 'Some Niggers' he jeered at the reflex racism of the traditionally missionary-minded whites he was travelling with in the South Seas and praised the looks of a young fellow-passenger who told him he was part Danish, part Chinese and part Hawaiian. But on the same voyage he was poisonous in his letters home about the Jewish politician Rufus Isaacs, who, despite his implication in the insider-dealing Marconi scandal, had been appointed Lord Chief Justice after serving as Attorney-General in Asquith's Liberal government. Brooke threatened to resign from the National Liberal Club in disgust. Apart from his anti-Semitism – which did not prevent him from having friendly relations with individual Jews he encountered, nor indeed from enjoying more-than-friendly relations with the Asquiths, who had ennobled Isaacs – Brooke was 'liberal' if patronizing in his attitude to other races, admiring the Polynesian culture he was about to fervently embrace, and enjoying the most physically satisfying sexual relationship of his life with a Polynesian woman.

His first brush with Pacific culture came on the first night out, when he sat on the deck under a moon and stars that looked both clear and close, and listened to the melancholy singing of a group of Hawaiians, accompanied by mandolins. As the *Sierra* steamed south, Brooke started to compose the sequence of poems that represent the peak of his poetic achievement. Simple, heartfelt, showing a carefully wrought mastery of form, they are yet another facet of his miraculous year that must have made him glad he had belatedly heeded Frances Cornford's advice to go west and heal himself in a culture far from home. The first such poem came to him as he gazed up at the moonlit Pacific skies from the ship's deck:

CLOUDS

Down the blue night the unending columns press
In noiseless tumult, break and wave and flow,
Now tread the far South, or lift rounds of snow
Up to the white moon's hidden loveliness.
Some pause in their grave wandering comradeless,
And turn with profound gesture vague and slow,
As who would pray good for the world, but know
Their benediction empty as they bless.

They say that the Dead die not, but remain
Near to the rich heirs of their grief and mirth.
I think they ride the calm mid-heaven, as these,

> In wise majestic melancholy train,
>> And watch the moon, and the still-raging seas,
>> And men, coming and going on the earth.

A second sonnet composed on the voyage turned on a lecture he had heard at King's about that very Edwardian sport of ghost-hunting. In contrast to the ethereal 'Clouds', in which the dead are imagined as majestic spirits, far removed from earthly concerns, 'Sonnet (Suggested by some of the Proceedings of the Society for Psychical Research)' conceives the departed as active sprites turning and running down 'by-ways of the air'. The poem, which seems to suggest a weakening in his previously staunch atheism, seems to look forward to a post-earthly existence in which souls will feel without hands, hear without ears, 'And see, no longer blinded by our eyes'.

The third sonnet that Brooke started to map out on board ship was the most directly personal. It was, as he candidly confessed to Cathleen, directly inspired by a memory of Noel (although he neglected to name her directly):

> I told you I was in love with a girl for three or four years, and then she got tired of it . . . Once, towards the grey end of that – I'd sort of put my love away, numbed it, for I saw things were going ill. But I was desolate and rather hungry. And one day – we were staying in the same house – we'd arranged to get up very early, and go out and pick mushrooms together in the summer dew, for breakfast (oh youth! youth!)-I crept along, having woken and being unable to sleep another hour, to her room some little while before dawn. She was sleeping. I knelt down by her and kissed her forehead to wake her, and put my head on her hand; and she woke, and felt fond of me I suppose, and pulled my head against her heart and held me a minute. And I thought I had found heaven. And all my love woke worse than ever. But she didn't mean anything, you know. Only she felt fond of me. But it made the breaking about nine hundred times harder; we both paid a lot for it, I most.

The sonnet this recollection inspired, 'A Memory (From a sonnet-sequence)', is simple, but touching and finely crafted:

> Somewhile before the dawn I rose, and stept
>> Softly along the dim way to your room,
>> And found you sleeping in the quiet gloom,
> And holiness about you as you slept.
> I knelt there; till your waking fingers crept
>> About my head, and held it. I had rest
>> Unhoped this side of Heaven, beneath your breast.
> I knelt a long time, still; nor even wept.

It was great wrong you did me; and for gain
Of that poor moment's kindliness, and ease,
And sleepy mother-comfort!
                                    Child, you know
How easily love leaps out to dreams like these,
Who has seen them true. And love that's wakened so
Takes all too long to sleep again.

Despite the sagging in the centre, the weakness of 'nor even wept' and the petulant whine of 'It was great wrong you did me', the peace of the beginning in the hushed and sleeping house is brilliantly and economically conveyed, and the line 'love leaps out to dreams like these' displays real flair. It was a love poem not quite devoid of sentimentality, but touching and poignant for all that.

The same letter to Cathleen that contained the rough beginnings of this Noel poem – '(Clumsy! Clumsy!),' Brooke scolded himself – also contained a Byronic epigram about love: 'For men catch fire quicker than women, though they may not burn so long. Lady, is it not true?' But he ended with a characteristic note of caution and control: men and women were like children, he said – especially women: 'My heart and my belief were so deadened, before I found you . . . You give me great riches . . . I pray you, love good and keep away from the evil things of the world, for my sake and for your sake and for our sake.'

The *Sierra* docked at Honolulu on 15 October. Brooke elected to stay at the Moana hotel on Waikiki beach, some five miles out of town. He was impressed by the luscious tropical vegetation – giant ferns, hibiscus and coconut trees – and while sitting in a wicker chair in front of the hotel he started yet another sonnet that harked back to Lulworth and Ka:

WAIKIKI

Warm perfumes like a breath from vine and tree
    Drift down the darkness. Plangent, hidden from
        eyes,
    Somewhere an *eukaleli* thrills and cries
And stabs with pain the night's brown savagery;
And dark scents whisper; and dim waves creep to me,
    Gleam like a woman's hair, stretch out, and rise;
    And new stars burn into the ancient skies,
Over the murmurous soft Hawaiian sea.

And I recall, lose, grasp, forget again,
  And still remember, a tale I have heard, or known,
An empty tale, of idleness and pain,
  Of two that loved—or did not love—and one
Whose perplexed heart did evil, foolishly,
A long while since, and by some other sea.

There are echoes here of his first serious poem, 'Seaside', written back in 1908, and also, surely, the susurration evoking the ebb and flow of tidal waters, that lies behind Matthew Arnold's great elegiac masterpiece 'Dover Beach'. The poem suggests that a new Brooke is emerging, chrysalis-like from the bitter husk that had encased him for so long. He had written several poems earlier in the year that share a common note of savage cynicism; suggesting that he was done with love and through with women. One of these ended:

Oh, it's not going to happen again, old girl
It's not going to happen again.

Even more bitterly, 'Love' concluded:

                                        love grows
      colder,
  Grows false and dull, that was sweet lies at most.
    Astonishment is no more in hand or shoulder,
  But darkens, and dies out from kiss to kiss.
  All this is love; and all love is but this.

'The Chilterns', too, which begins with a happy marching gait, concludes with cheery cynicism:

And I shall find some girl perhaps,
  And a better one than you,
With eyes as wise, but kindlier,
  And lips as soft, but true.
  And I daresay she will do.

Now he appeared to have sloughed off this brooding bitterness and could recollect even his unhappiest memories in some degree of tranquillity. In this spirit he sent Cathleen another sonnet:

ONE DAY

To-day I have been happy. All the day
  I held the memory of you, and wove
Its laughter with the dancing light o' the spray,
    And sowed the sky with tiny clouds of love,
And sent you following the white waves of sea,
    And crowned your head with fancies, nothing
        worth,
Stray buds from that old dust of misery,
  Being glad with a new foolish quiet mirth.

So lightly I played with those dark memories,
Just as a child, beneath the summer skies,
  Plays hour by hour with a strange shining stone,
For which (he knows not) towns were fire of old,
  And love has been betrayed, and murder done,
And great kings turned to a little bitter mould.

In the same letter he compiled a litany for Cathleen's sake of all the things he was missing: 'The Chilterns, Hampton Court, *Hullo Ragtime*, Raymond Buildings'. As ever, restless and unhappy alone, Brooke took a trip to the small island of Kanai, for whose owner he had acquired an introductory letter in San Francisco. During the visit he rode out on horseback to see a 200-foot waterfall, getting himself badly sunburned. He was back at Waikiki by 20 October, and a week later boarded another ship, the SS *Ventura*, which would carry him to Samoa, an island redolent with recent memories of another wandering writer – Robert Louis Stevenson.

On the last day of October the *Ventura* crossed the Equator and Brooke suffered the usual indignity of being thrown into a canvas bath. Two days later she docked at Pango in Samoa and he transferred to a local ferry that took him to Apia, the island's capital. In Samoa he acquired his first real taste of Pacific life, which pleased him more than the already commercialized Hawaii. He painted the scene for Cathleen:

After dinner six girls and six men came on board and performed a siva-siva on deck, before the astonished eyes of the American and Australian passengers. A siva-siva, my dear, is a dance. But not what you (poor stepper of hideous American stuff) or I or M. Nijinsky mean by dancing . . . both girls and men were naked to the waist, and glistening with coco-nut palm oil. The dancing was on a background of high nasal wailing – which seemed to be telling a story – hand-clapping, and convulsive rhythmic movements of the body . . . It was all very thrilling and tropical and savage. I felt ancient strange raucous jungle cries awakening within me ... The dancers vanished, after half an hour, precipitately into the darkness.

Without Brooke, the *Ventura* sailed on, bearing a precious packet of poems destined for Wilfrid Gibson and the first issue of the new magazine which came to bear the name *New Numbers*. From his new lodgings on Samoa he wrote to Eddie Marsh:

I live in a Samoan house, (the coolest in the world) with a man and his wife, nine children, ranging from a proud beauty of 18 to a round object of 1 year, a dog, a cat, a proud hysterical hen, and a gaudy scarlet and green parrot ... I am becoming indistinguishable from R.L.S. both in thinness, in literary style, and in disassociation from England. God have mercy on my soul! I have crossed the Equator, and so am a Man at last.

He paid his respects to the island's presiding literary spirit, making the arduous journey to the lonely summit where Stevenson is buried under his own epitaph:

> Under the wide and starry sky
> Dig my grave and let me lie.

A blurred surviving photograph from Brooke's camera shows him being carried across a stream on the shoulders of a strapping Samoan, clad in a white shirt and trousers and a tropical hat. He looks very happy – and he was. The charm of the South Seas was beginning to seduce his susceptible nature:

Oh, Eddie, it's all true about the South Seas! I get a little tired of it at moments, because I am just too old for Romance, and my soul is seared. But there it is: there it wonderfully is: heaven on earth, the ideal life, little work, dancing, singing and eating, naked people of incredible loveliness, perfect manners, and immense kindliness, a divine tropical climate, and intoxicating beauty of scenery.

Reluctantly tearing himself away from this demi-Eden to keep to his planned itinerary, he returned to Pango in mid-November and boarded the SS *Torfua* for Fiji. He knew that the letters he was writing would not reach England before Christmas, and nostalgically imagined what he was missing:

a chilly dampness in the air, and the theatres glaring in the Strand, and crowds of white faces . . . I can't help thinking of you trotting through crisp snow to a country church, holly decorated, with little robins pecking crumbs all around, and the church-bells playing our brother Tennyson's [a reference to the fact that Tennyson, like Eddie, had been an Apostle] *In Memoriam* brightly through the clear air.

By contrast, Brooke asked Eddie to picture himself: 'in a loin-cloth, brown and wild, in the fair chocolate arms of a Tahitian beauty, reclining beneath a bread-fruit tree, on white sand, with the breakers roaring against the reefs a mile out, and strange brilliant fish darting through the pellucid hyaline of the sun-saturated sea'. This, or something very like it – even down to the Tahitian beauty – was what Brooke was sailing towards. For once his lushest fantasies were in harmony with reality, and he lay back to let the warm winds and waters of this paradise 'wash the mind of foolishness', as he was to put it in one of his best Pacific poems.

There was more than a touch of the condescending imperialist in Brooke's attitude to the islanders whose hospitality he was greedily gulping down:

And Eddie, it's all true about, for instance, coco-nuts. You tramp through a strange vast dripping tropical forest for hours, listening to weird liquid hootings from birds and demons in the branches above. Then you feel thirsty. So you send your boy – or call a native – up a great perpendicular palm. He runs up with utter ease and grace, cuts off a couple of vast nuts and comes down and makes holes in them. And they're chock-full of the best drink in the world. Romance! Romance! I walked 15 miles through mud and up and down mountains, and swam three rivers, to get this boat. But if ever you miss me, suddenly, one day, from Lecture Room B in King's, or from the Moulin d'Or at lunch, you'll know that I've got sick for the full moon on these little thatched roofs, and the palms against the morning, and the Samoan boys and girls diving thirty feet into a green sea or a deep mountain pool under a waterfall – and that I've gone back.

Brooke had fallen hook, line and sinker for the tourist's picture-postcard view of the South Seas: the dusky maidens decked in flowers, the languid lagoons, the larder growing on trees. There is not much mention in his letters home of endemic poverty and disease – much of it brought to the islands by the colonial powers that had conquered and ruled them. The unconscious, patronizing attitude to the native peoples is less surprising – it was the common coin of the times. It must be remembered, however, that a tourist is exactly what Brooke was, for his wildly enthusiastic babble about the seductions of Samoa is based on a fortnight's stay – the length of the average package holiday of today. He saw the surface glories, and it must be admitted that they were enticing; and that his prose reports of them, shorn of his customary self-absorption in his own emotional state, make glittering, exciting reading. And so he rambled on.

On 19 November he made landfall in Fiji. He came close to some pointed social observation in a letter to Dudley Ward, in which, hoping to please his Germanophile friend, he praised Berlin's administration of its section of the Samoan islands for broadly letting the natives get on with their own lives, in contrast to the interfering French and the proselytizing Americans. He mentioned, too, how the plantations were worked by indentured Chinese coolie labour since the Samoan, sensibly, 'can, and will, live without working. He puts an hibiscus in his hair, twines a gaudy loin cloth round him, takes a few bananas and a coco-nut, and goes off bathing with the girls, singing as he goes. That is the end of life. Tra, la!' He summed up with an epigram: 'The South Seas are heaven, but I no angel.'

Fiji he found overcivilized, with its 'two banks, several churches, dental surgeons, a large gaol, auctioneers, bookmakers, two newspapers'. To the critic Edmund Gosse he wrote:

> Perplexing country! At home everything is so simple . . . there is only the choice between writing a good sonnet and making a million pounds. Who could hesitate? But here the choice is between writing a sonnet and climbing a straight hundred-foot coco-nut palm, or diving forty feet from a rock into pellucid blue-green water. Which is the better, there? One's European literary soul begins to be haunted by strange doubts and shaken with fundamental fantastic misgivings. I think I shall return home . . . One keeps realizing, however unwillingly, responsibility. I noticed in myself and in the other white people in Samoa, a trait I have remarked in schoolmasters . . . You know that sort of slightly irritated tolerance, a lack of irresponsibility, that marks the pedagogue? One feels that one's a White Man – ludicrously. I kept thinking I was in the Sixth Form at Rugby again. These dear good people, with their laughter and friendliness, and crowns of flowers – one feels one *must* protect them.

But it wasn't protection the Fijians demanded from Brooke – only a demonstration of his drawing skills with his long, prehensile toes that had so impressed Stanley Spencer. Having satisfied their curiosity, he left for a smaller island, Kandarva, sleeping on the deck of a cutter. On the island he was put up by the local chief, and dined on yam and turtle. He was even invited to play the island version of cricket – a more boisterous game than he was used to, with free fights replacing runs. After five days he returned to the capital, Suva, and fired off another ecstatic letter, this time to Denis Browne: 'Denis! . . . it is mere heaven. One passes from Paradise to Paradise . . . Life is one long picnic . . . These people are nearer to earth and the joy of things than we snivelling city-dwellers.' This letter suggested that he had become a real, rather than just a 'neo', pagan. He had lost, he claimed, all knowledge of art and literature, and much else that the world thought civilized, gaining in return a rich red-brown skin, a knowledge of how to mix tropical fruit cocktails, an ability to talk with all classes and conditions of man and an expanding repertoire of dirty jokes. 'Am I richer or poorer? I don't know.' Ironically, it would be Browne who would bury Brooke in another island paradise within 15 months.

But in the midst of all this richness, he was suffering from nostalgia for England. He told Jacques Raverat: 'I wander, seeking peace . . . several times I've nearly found it: once, lately, in a Samoan village. But I had to come away from there in a hurry . . . and forgot to pack it. But I'll have it yet. Fragments I have found, on various hills, or by certain seas . . . Oh, I shall return. The South seas are Paradise, but I prefer England.' He was looking forward, or so he claimed, to returning to a home, marriage and work, and conversation with his friends. In a passage which, with hindsight, reeks of horrible poignancy, given our knowledge of the future fates of both he and Jacques, who was already stricken with sclerosis, Brooke looked forward to a future in which 'I will have friends round me continually, all the days of my life, and in whatever lands I may be. So we shall laugh and eat and sing and go great journeys in boats and on foot and write plays and perform them and pass innumerable laws taking money from the rich . . . Won't 1914 be fun?'

He plunged into Fijian life – and death. At the beginning of December he accompanied the body of a Fijian princess to a neighbouring island for her funeral festivities after she died of pneumonia. A postcard to Cathleen reported the event – 'Tonight I travelled 70 miles in an auxiliary cutter with the corpse of a Princess' – and asked rhetorically: 'Have you ever done that?' Returning to Suva, he crossed the island accompanied by two faithful boys 'to carry my bag and rug and guide me'. During the course of the expedition, he told Cathleen, the 'boys', who were about Brooke's own age, became 'my sworn and eternal friends'.

One of them, Ambele . . . was six foot high, very broad and more perfectly

343

made than any man or statue I have ever seen. His grin stretched from ear to ear. And he could carry me across rivers (when I was tired of swimming them, for we crossed vast rivers every mile or two) for a hundred yards or so, as I should carry a box of matches. I think of bringing him back with me as a servant and bodyguard to England. He loved me because though I was far weaker than he, I was far braver. The Fijians are rather cowards. And on precipices I am peculiarly reckless. The boys saved me from rolling off to perdition about thirty times – and respected me for it – though thinking me insane. Would you marry me if I turned up with two vast cannibal servants black-skinned and perpetually laughing, all of us attired only in loin-cloths and red flowers in our hair? I think I should be irresistible.

Brooke continued this condescension towards the islanders in a long letter to Violet Asquith. With this new and influential correspondent came a return of his desire to shock those whom he thought a touch prim and proper:

It's twenty years since they've eaten anybody, in this part of Fiji, and far more since they've done what I particularly and unreasonably detest – fastened the victim down, cut pieces off him one by one, and cooked and eaten them before his eyes. To witness one's own transubstantiation into naked black man, that seems the last indignity. Consideration of the thoughts that pour through the mind of the ever-diminishing remnant of a man, as it sees its last limbs cooking, moves me deeply. I have been meditating a sonnet, as I sit here, surrounded by dusky faces and gleaming eyes: 'Dear, they have poached the eyes you loved so well . . .' I don't know how it would go on. The fourth line would have to be 'And all my turbulent lips are maitre-d'hotel . . .'

Quite taken up by the fantasy, he continued:

> The limbs that erstwhile charmed your sight,
> Are now a savage's delight;
> The ear that heard your whispered vow
> Is one of many entrees now;
> Broiled are the arms in which you clung
> And devilled is the angelic tongue; . . .
> And oh! my anguish as I see
> A Black man gnaw your favourite knee!
> Of the two eyes that were your ruin,
> One now observes the other stewing,
> My lips (the inconstancy of man!)

Are yours no more. The legs that ran each
dewy morn their love to wake,
Are now a steak, are now a steak! . . .

Beneath the gorgeous colour and exotic smells and sounds, Brooke dimly perceived the eventual fate of his new friends:

They are a dying race. We gradually fill their lands with plantations and Indian coolies. The Hawaiians . . . have almost altogether gone, and their arts and music with them, and their islands are a replica of America. A cheerful thought, that all these places are to become indistinguishable from Denver and Birmingham and Stuttgart, and the people in dress and behaviour precisely like Herr Schmidt and Mr Robinson and Hiram O. Guggenheim . . . it's impossible to describe how far nearer the Kingdom of Heaven – or the Garden of Eden – these good naked laughing people are than oneself or one's friends. But I forgot. You are an anti-socialist, and I mustn't say a word against our modern industrial system. I beg your pardon . . . I suppose you're rushing from lunch party to lunch party, and dance to dance, and opera to political platform. Won't you come and learn how to make a hibiscus wreath for your hair, and sail a canoe, and swim two minutes under water catching turtles, and dive forty feet into a waterfall, and climb a coco-nut palm? It's more worth while.

During the expedition Brooke cut his foot, and returned to Suva limping and with the wound turning septic. On 14 December he left Fiji on board a ship ironically called *Niagara*. The crossing to New Zealand was laboured, and he arrived in Auckland too late to catch the connecting ferry that sailed to his next scheduled port of call, Tahiti. He gave voice to his annoyance in a letter to Cathleen from the Grand Hotel: 'Why precisely I'm here I don't know. I seem to have missed a boat somewhere; and I can't get on to Tahiti till the beginning of January: Damn. And I hear that a man got to Tahiti two months ahead of me, and found – and carried off – some Gauguin paintings on glass. Damn! Damn! Damn!'

This reference is bizarre: there is no record of any Gauguins on glass being discovered by any visitor to Tahiti until 1917, two years after Brooke's death, when 'a man' did indeed find and purchase just such an artefact. Still more strange, the man in question was another star-struck English writer in pursuit of Gauguin's ideal of the simple, sensual life among the islands: W. Somerset Maugham. The writer, who had first come across Gauguin's work in Paris and developed an obsession with the artist, was mulling over the *roman-à-clef* which became *The Moon and Sixpence*, and travelled to Tahiti in search of Gauguin 'colour'. He got more than he bargained for, when, on a brief visit to the son of a man who had known the painter well, he saw the children of the house busily scraping paint from the glass panels of a rickety door. They had already 'cleaned' two of the panels and were just starting on the final one when interrupted by Maugham. On inspection, the panel proved to be one of the fabled 'lost Gauguins' that the painter had left scattered around the island: this one depicted Eve holding an apple. For the less than princely sum of $200 – the cost of a new door – Maugham persuaded his host to part with it, and so acquired an original Gauguin which hung in his writing room for the rest of his life, before he sold it in 1962 for $117,000.

When Brooke visited Tahiti it was only ten years since Gauguin's lonely, poverty-stricken death from syphilis; and he must have hoped that he could emulate him by living a passionate island idyll, and, if not actually stumble on a pot of gold in the shape of a lost masterpiece, at least imbibe some of the artist's questing, uncompromising spirit. Before following that dream, he had to kick his heels in Auckland over Christmas. He was not best pleased, describing New Zealand as 'a sort of Fabian England, very upper middle class and gentle and happy (after Canada), no poor and the government owning hotels and running charabancs. All the women smile and dress very badly, and nobody drinks.' He visited the capital, Wellington, to consult a specialist about his poisoned foot, and caught up with English newspapers at the Wellington Club, where, for the first time, he saw his own *Westminster Gazette* articles in print, and jealously read adulatory notices for Cathleen's appearance in a new play, *Quality Street*. Guilty as ever over the pleasures of the flesh, he told the actress: 'New Zealand turns out to be in the midst of summer . . . I eat strawberries, large garden strawberries, every day; and it's the middle of December! It feels curiously unnatural, perverse, like some frightful vice out of Havelock Ellis. I blush and eat secretively.'

Less selfishly, he wrote indignantly to his mother about the bitter strike of Dublin transport workers, led by the fiery Labour leader Jim Larkin, asking her to send two guineas in his name to the strike fund. 'I feel wild about Dublin,' he wrote. 'Of course the poor are always right against the rich . . . When *The Times* begins saying that the employers are in the wrong, they must be very unpardonably so and rotten indeed.' But the practical effects of state socialism around him puzzled him, as he told the Ranee:

> The queer thing is . . . that they've got all the things in the Liberal or mild Fabian programme: – eight hour day (and less), bigger old age pensions, access

to the land, minimum wage, insurance etc. etc. and yet it's not Paradise. The same troubles exist in much the same form (except that there's not much bad poverty). Cost of living is rising quicker than wages. There are the same troubles between unions and employers, and between rich and poor. I suppose there'll be no peace anywhere till the rich are curbed altogether.

The sleeping socialist in Brooke still stirred occasionally in its slumber. His rage against the rich – as witness his friendship with Eddie Marsh and the Asquiths – often did not survive his meeting flesh-and-blood members of the detested class. One such fleeting friendship was formed with Harold Ashworth, a Lancashire businessman, albeit of firm Fabian principles, whom he encountered on the ship that finally took him to Tahiti on 7 January. The meeting lingered on in Ashworth's memory, and after Brooke's death he wrote to the Ranee:

> many a time I would invoke his aid when my rather aggressive Radicalism brought the 'Smoke-room' men at me en masse. I never met so entirely likeable a chap, and when I could 'get him going' about his wanderings, or provoke him into discussions about literature, I was one walking ear! . . . I almost wept to know I could never again see that golden head and kindly smile – 'Young Apollo' I used to dub him in my mind, whilst the fresh wind tossed his hair, and his boyish eyes lit up with pleasure at some of my anecdotes of strange people and places . . . Your son was not merely a genius; what is perhaps more important, he had a charm that was literally like sunshine. To say that his manner is perfect is putting it quite inadequately . . . His memory is blessed by hundreds like me who were so fortunate as to meet him and were the better for that happy adventure.

Although Ashworth sounds like the worst sort of saloon-bar bore, Brooke evidently performed his fresh, boyish act – even to this tedious enforced companion – with ease and aplomb.

Another, and possibly more congenial shipboard companion was the famous contralto Clara Butt. Dwarfed by the statuesque singer, Brooke reported to another formidable female – his mother – in some awe: 'She's over six foot high and must weigh sixteen stone and has a bass voice like a man's.'

In Tahiti, he installed himself in early February in Mataia, some 30 miles from the capital, Papeete. He described his new dwelling for the Ranee: 'It is the coolest place I've struck in the South Seas . . . with a large veranda, the sea just in front, and the hills behind . . . there's a little wooden pier out

347

into the sea . . . with a dive into deep water. PS They call me "Purpure" here – it means "fair" in Tahitian – because I have fair hair.'

The nickname stuck – on his visit to Tahiti four years later, Maugham found the islanders did not remember Gauguin but still wept when they talked of 'Purpure', the golden-haired youth who had once lived among them. Brooke's magic, it seemed, even survived transplantation to a culture as far removed from genteel Cambridge as it is possible to get. The love affair was mutual: Brooke instantly fell head over heels in love with the island and decided to stay for a month at least. Nineteen fourteen, he told himself, did indeed promise to be an eventful year.

Accommodation at Brooke's *pension*, with French wine thrown in, came to just over six shillings a day, and armed with a cash injection that Professor Wells had wired to New Zealand, fell well within his budget. The place was run by a Tahitian couple, and his only fellow-guests were a pair of English ranchers from Canada on an extended holiday. Brooke soon fell into a pleasant routine of eating, swimming, working and sleeping, with occasional fishing trips and journeys into the surrounding hills. He described the country and its life as 'Greece without the intellect' and he found the native Tahitians – particularly the women – graceful and comely. Gauguin, he complained to Eddie, had grossly maligned the ladies in his work. One such beauty was soon to loom large in his life, and give him a better reason than shortage of funds to tarry in Tahiti for far longer than he had originally intended.

Her name was Taatamata, and little is known of her origins. One report claims she was daughter to the village chief, while another writer, Paul Delany, says 'she was vaguely attached to the hotel', adding unchivalrously: 'It would be unfair to call her a prostitute, but the English idea of virtue had no relevance to her life of easy sensuality.' What is certain is that Taatamata had charm and beauty in abundance, and that the combination beguiled an entranced a Brooke only too ready, at last, for real physical romance and uninhibited love. A handful of surviving photographs taken by him of his mistress show a lovely, half-smiling face beneath a wide-brimmed straw hat, with wavy black hair tumbling round her shoulders, and lithe limbs apparently willing to cast off the clothes that temporarily hide her charms. Her English was limited, and Brooke and she conversed in her pidgin English, his schoolboy French and one or two words in Tahitian that he quickly picked up. But these two beauties had little need for spoken words; within days, days that are significantly void of his endless chatty letters home, they had consummated their quick-flowering love, and a sated, utterly happy Brooke was writing perhaps his finest poem in praise of the woman he named 'Mamua'. He called it 'Tiare Tahiti':

> Mamua, when our laughter ends,
> And hearts and bodies, brown as white,
> Are dust about the doors of friends,
> Or scent a-blowing down the night,
> Then, oh! then, the wise agree,
> Comes our immortality.
> Mamua, there waits a land
> Hard for us to understand.
> Out of time, beyond the sun,
> All at one in Paradise,
> You and Purpure are one,
> And Taü, and the ungainly wise.
> There the Eternals are, and there
> The Good, the Lovely, and the True,
> And Types, whose earthly copies were
> The foolish broken things we knew;
> There is the Face, whose ghosts we are;
> The real, the never-setting Star;
> And the Flower, of which we love
> Faint and fading shadows here; . . .

Woven from octosyllables, the poem is at once a lyrical celebration of unrestrained simple love, and a mockery of the ideal of Platonic Love:

> Instead of lovers, Love shall be;
> For hearts, Immutability;
> And there, on the Ideal Reef,
> Thunders the Everlasting Sea!

Later there is a nod towards Marvell's plea to his coy mistress to make love while there is still time: for Brooke, Marvell's

> The grave's a fine and private place,
> But none I think do there embrace

becomes:

> And there's an end, I think, of kissing,
> When our mouths are one with Mouth.

He calls on his willing lover to join him in the only possible Paradise: here and now:

> *Taü here*, Mamua,
> Crown the hair, and come away!
> Hear the calling of the moon,
> And the whispering scents that stray
> About the idle warm lagoon.
> Hasten, hand in human hand,
> Down the dark, the flowered way,
> Along the whiteness of the sand,
> And in the water's soft caress,
> Wash the mind of foolishness,
> Mamua, until the day.

For the first time in his life, water became an enfolding warm embrace that united lovers, rather than a brisk, bracing douche to douse away uncleanliness. The cold showers of Rugby and the chilly disapproval of the Ranee had never seemed further away. No wonder that he dallied in Tahiti even after his self-allotted month had passed. At last, too, his fearful self-consciousness was erased. Here, where every body was beautiful, every face striking, and where shame and vanity were cast off as easily as clothes, he was just one of the crowd. No longer need he act a part, nor strut and fret.

Ignoring Eddie's squeak of protest that the stream of poems arriving steadily from the South Seas were all about 'Love', Brooke, writing on the veranda at Mataia, with the enticing Taatamata swaying and shimmying temptingly around him, embarked on yet another long poem, modestly entitled 'The Great Lover'. Pompously, it begins:

> I have been so great a lover: filled my days
> So proudly with the splendour of Love's praise,
> The pain, the calm, and the astonishment,
> Desire illimitable, and still content,
> And all dear names men use, to cheat despair,
> For the perplexed and viewless streams that bear
> Our hearts at random down the dark of life.
> Now, ere the unthinking silence on that strife
> Steals down, I would cheat drowsy Death so far,
> My night shall be remembered for a star
> That outshone all the suns of all men's days.

But this 'great lover' now indisputably a virgin no more, is not boasting: the loves he wishes to 'crown with immortal praise' turn out to be, somewhat bathetically, another of Brooke's lists of homely things he has enjoyed. Prosaic perhaps, but presented with a sensuality almost worthy of Keats in 'St Agnes Eve' – this is a list that we too can touch, handle, taste and smell:

> These I have loved:
>   White plates and cups, clean-gleaming,
> Ringed with blue lines; and feathery, faery dust;
> Wet roofs, beneath the lamp-light; the strong crusts
> Of friendly bread; and many-tasting food;
> Rainbows; and the blue bitter smoke of wood;
> And radiant raindrops couching in cool flowers;
> And flowers themselves, that sway through sunny
>   hours,
> Dreaming of moths that drink them under the moon;
> Then, the cool kindliness of sheets, that soon
> Smooth away trouble; and the rough male kiss
> Of blankets; grainy wood; live hair that is
> Shining and free; blue-massing clouds; the keen
> Unpassioned beauty of a great machine;
> The benison of hot water; furs to touch;
> The good smell of old clothes; and others such—
> The comfortable smell of friendly fingers,
> Hair's fragrance, and the musty reek that lingers
> About dead leaves and last year's ferns . . .
>   Dear names, . . .

Dear indeed, and Brooke has not finished yet. As he sits in the tropical, chirruping night; his mind clutters with images from the north, from damp, chill, sodden but beloved England:

>   Royal flames;
> Sweet water's dimpling laugh from tap or spring;
> Holes in the ground; and voices that do sing;
> Voices in laughter, too; and body's pain,
> Soon turned to peace; and the deep-panting train;
> Firm sands; the little dulling edge of foam
> That browns and dwindles as the wave goes home;
> And washen stones, gay for an hour; the cold
> Graveness of iron; moist black earthen mould;
> Sleep; and high places; footprints in the dew;

And oaks; and brown horse-chestnuts, glossy new;
And new-peeled sticks; and shining pools on grass;—
All these have been my loves.

Jesting and self-mocking he may have begun, but, as so often with Brooke, he has swapped horses in midstream, and the self-mocking laughter has become more than a little choked:

    —Oh, never a doubt but, somewhere, I shall wake,
And give what's left of love again, and make
New friends, now strangers . . .
                    But the best I've known
Stays here, and changes, breaks, grows old, is blown
About the winds of the world, and fades from brains
Of living men, and dies.
               Nothing remains.
O dear my loves, O faithless, once again
This one last gift I give: that after men
Shall know, and later lovers, far-removed,
Praise you, 'All these were lovely'; say, 'He loved.'

For Cathleen, and anyone else who enquired, he found excuses for staying on; Mamua was only hinted at. 'I've decided to stay here another month,' he told Cathleen in February:

for two very good reasons: (1) that I haven't enough money to get out, (2) that I've found the most ideal place in the world to live and work in. A wide veranda over a blue lagoon, a wooden pier with deep clear water for diving, and coloured fish that swim between your toes. there are also . . . scores of laughing brown babies from two years to fourteen. Canoes and boats, rivers, fishing with spear, net and line, the most wonderful food in the world – strange fishes and vegetables perfectly cooked. Europe slides from me terrifyingly . . . Will it come to your having to fetch me? The boat's ready to start; the brown lovely people in their bright clothes are gathered on the old wharf to wave her away. Everyone has a white flower behind their ear. Mamua has given me one. Do you know the significance of a white flower worn over the ear? A white flower over the right ear means 'I am looking for a sweetheart'. And a white flower over the left ear means 'I have found a sweetheart'. And a white flower over each ear means 'I have one sweetheart, and am looking for another.' A white flower over each ear, my dear, is dreadfully the most fashionable way of adorning yourself in Tahiti.

It was a heavy enough hint to his 'official' girlfriend that he had found love elsewhere, but it does not seem to have alienated the actress's sensible, tolerant affection for her wayward man.

Brooke was now burbling with joy:

> Good luck to everyone. Love to the whole world. Tonight we will put scarlet flowers in our hair, and sing strange, slumberous South Sea songs to the concertina, and drink red French wine, and dance, and bathe in a soft lagoon by moonlight, and eat great squelchy tropical fruits, custard-apples, papaia, pomegranate, mango, guava and the rest. Urana. I have a million lovely and exciting things to tell you – but not now.

Meanwhile he was learning the truth of Gauguin's summary of the easygoing Tahitian attitude to love: 'in Europe you fall in love with a woman and eventually end up having sex with her; while in Tahiti, you start with the sex, after which you may fall – often quite as deeply – in love too'.

Soon Brooke had a genuine reason to linger in his island paradise, for a worm, or rather a germ, had entered it. In mid-February, while diving near the pier he had lyrically written about, he spied a turtle and gave chase. In the excitement, he failed to notice a jagged coral reef, and ripped his leg on it. Coral is notoriously poisonous, and Brooke's immune system was notoriously weak: soon the five wounds – he would have noticed the Biblical parallel – were suppurating, and his primitive home treatment of dabbing them with iodine only made things worse. He was put to bed in a downstairs room at the back of the hotel, where Taatamata nursed him devotedly. By March, with the wounds still slow to heal, he travelled to Papeete accompanied by the loyal Taatamata.

He took the opportunity to post a package of poems to Eddie. Beside 'Tiare Tahiti' and 'The Great Lover', there was 'Retrospect' – a long and gentle meditation on Ka's 'mother love'; guilt about her was still gnawing him – and his masterpiece of satiric verse, 'Heaven', inspired by the many-coloured fish of the islands. It is a brilliant and devastating satire on religious belief, and almost unanswerable:

> Fish (fly-replete, in depth of June,
> Dawdling away their wat'ry noon)
> Ponder deep wisdom, dark or clear,
> Each secret fishy hope or fear.
> Fish say, they have their Stream and Pond;
> But is there anything Beyond?
> This life cannot be All, they swear,

For how unpleasant, if it were!
One may not doubt that, somehow, Good
Shall come of Water and of Mud;
And, sure, the reverent eye must see
A Purpose in Liquidity.
We darkly know, by Faith we cry,
The future is not Wholly Dry.
Mud unto mud!—Death eddies near—
Not here the appointed End, not here!
But somewhere, beyond Space and Time,
Is wetter water, slimier slime!
And there (they trust) there swimmeth One
Who swam ere rivers were begun,
Immense, of fishy form and mind,
Squamous, omnipotent, and kind;
And under that Almighty Fin,
The littlest fish may enter in.
Oh! never fly conceals a hook,
Fish say, in the Eternal Brook,
But more than mundane weeds are there,
And mud, celestially fair;
Fat caterpillars drift around,
And Paradisal grubs are found;
Unfading moths, immortal flies,
And the worm that never dies.
And in that Heaven of all their wish,
There shall be no more land, say fish.

He was suitably grateful to Taatamata for her tender loving care. He told Eddie that she was 'a girl with wonderful eyes, the walk of a Goddess, & the heart of an angel, who is, luckily, devoted to me. She gives her time to ministering to me, I mine to probing her queer mind. I think I shall write a book about her – only I fear I'm too fond of her.'

By the end of March he was back at Mataia, and feeling the tug of home. He knew that an earthly paradise, by its nature, is fragile and fleeting. That was its charm. 'Call me home, I pray you . . .' he wrote to Cathleen. 'I have been away long enough. I am older than I was. I have left bits of me about – some of my hair in Canada, and one skin in Honolulu, and another in Fiji, and a bit of a third in Tahiti, and half a tooth in Samoa, and bits of my heart all over the place.'

In the end it was not a call from Cathleen but the more mundane appearance of more money from Professor Wells that turned his reluctant footsteps homewards. The cash was enough to book a passage for San Francisco on the *Tahiti*, which was currently in Papeete. In a hurry, he said his sad farewells and boarded the boat on 5 April. As it steamed slowly across the broad Pacific he watched the green shores and mountain tops fade over the horizon: 'I suddenly realised,' he told Cathleen, 'that I'd left behind those lovely places and lovely people, perhaps forever. I reflected that there was surely nothing else like them in this world, and very probably nothing in the next.' His South Sea bubble had burst.

24

Homeward Bound

The magical spell that the South Seas had woven about Brooke during the six months he had spent there was slow to fade. As the *Tahiti* crawled slowly across the Pacific towards San Francisco, he lovingly imagined the bright Southern Cross that shone down on the ship also burning bright for 'those good brown people of the Islands', as he called them in a letter to Cathleen. He went on: 'And they're laughing and kissing and swimming and dancing beneath it. But for me it is set. And I do not know that I shall ever see it again . . . I'd told so many of those that loved me, so often "Oh yes, I'll come back . . . next year perhaps: or the year after . . ." that I suppose I'd begun to believe it myself.'

Although Brooke told Cathleen that he 'greatly desired' to see her, there was a certain stiltedness about his conventional declarations of adoration. He hinted at the reason: 'There are too many vagabond winds blowing through this evil and idle heart of mine, child. Do not let me wander. You are better than wandering.' He ended: 'English thoughts are waking in me. They'll fetch me back.' When the ship glided into San Francisco harbour, the sight of western civilization in all its vainglory induced another spurt of nostalgia for 'his' islands: 'How I hate civilization & houses & trams and collars,' he grumbled to Eddie. 'If I got on the *Tahiti* and went back again, shouldn't I find a quay covered with moving lights & lovely forms in white & pink & scarlet & green? And wouldn't Taatamata be waiting there to welcome me with wide arms?'

By the time he got round to writing to his confidants the Cornfords, whose daughter, Helena, had been born during his travels, his nostalgia and distaste had curdled into sour bile:

It'll be good to get back to theatres and supper parties & arguments & hedges &

roast beef & misty half-colours. But oh! sometimes – I warn you – I'll be having Samoan or Tahitian 'thoughts'. When everything's *too* grey, and there's an amber fog that bites your throat, & everyone's irritable and in a high state of nerves, & the pavement's greasy, and London is full of 'Miles of shopping women, served by men', and another Jew has bought a peerage, and I've a cold in my nose, and the ways are full of lean & vicious people, dirty, hermaphrodites and eunuchs, Stracheys, moral vagabonds, pitiable scum – why, then I shall have a *Sudseegedenke*, a thought of 20° South, a Samoan thought . . .

As this letter sadly shows, once the spell of the islands had worn off, the old, mad Brooke returned, with all his half-baked obsessions and prejudices intact. Addressing the Cornfords' infant daughter, he begged her: 'Helena, do not, as you grow older, become a feminist: become, I pray you, a woman.'

He again stayed with the hospitable Professor Wells and his family, who had accumulated a small mountain of mail for him, including a much-dreaded reply from Ka to his farewell letter, and a batch of unwontedly long letters from Noel, to whom he had last written affectionately from the *Sierra* on his way to Honolulu. Touched by this, Noel responded with several chatty reports on her doings. Wanting to be alone before dealing with his private correspondence, Brooke took the letters with him to his next American port of call, the Grand Canyon. His parting words to Wells were gloomy: 'We shall never learn to live decently together until it's too late.'

On 23 April he caught the train for Arizona. He had exactly one year left to live. Later on that ill-omened day, sitting on the rim of the vast canyon, he told the Marchesa Capponi that the canyon was 'very large and untidy, like my soul. But unlike my soul, it has peace in it.' He was near the border with Mexico, where the civil war that had followed the recent revolution was grumbling on – he thought briefly of crossing the border to flirt with danger, but turned north instead. There was troubling news, too, from Ulster, where the militant Protestants were threatening war rather than submit to Irish Home Rule. Brooke wrote lightly to Eddie: 'I do hope you're going to let the Orangemen slit all the priests' throats first; and then shoot them. I'll enlist on either side, any day.' It was increasingly evident from this ludicrous prattle that Brooke had acquired little wisdom during his sojourn in the islands, but, as he had written in the last line of 'Tiare Tahiti': 'There's little comfort in the wise.' To Hilton Young, a Cambridge friend, he wrote: 'I'm only coming back to put a bullet in [the Ulster Protestant leader] Sir Edward Carson and another in Mr Murphy, who smashed the Dublin strike. Then I shall bid farewell to plutocratic dirty

England: and back to the lagoons.'

Cathleen was primed for his return: he told her that he planned to arrive back in London on 15 June, but swore her to secrecy:

> It's very silly. But don't tell anybody the exact day I'm coming back. It's my fancy to blow in on them unexpected – just to wander into Raymond Buildings and hear Eddie squeak 'Oh, my dear, I thought you were in Tahiti!' It's *awfly* silly and romantic, but the thought does give me the keenest and most exquisite pleasure. Don't give away one of the first poets in England – but there is in him still a very very small portion that's just a little childish.

He was equally light and silly in his reply to Noel. Apparently cured of his sickly love for her, his letter chit-chatted about such vital subjects as the 'mat-like' and 'mouse-coloured' hair that had grown over his arms during his time in the islands. He ended, coolly, but revealingly:

> Noel, I am sick of immensity, I've seen the biggest buildings in the world, & the biggest lake in the world & the biggest volcano in the world & the biggest river in the world & the biggest canyon in the world & the biggest – I forget the rest. They are not interesting, or not for long. I desire small hedges & medium sized people & average intellects & tiny hills & villages and a little peace. I shall come back to England – I intend to live the rest of my life with my mother who is the only person I really like. But I shall take occasional holidays in London or Cambridge; so I may run across you again. Be good. Thank you for writing. With love Rupert.

It was his last letter to her.

On 29 April he arrived in Chicago, and took a room at the Auditorium Hotel in Michigan Avenue. This was next door to the city's Fine Arts building, which housed the recently opened Little Theater, a brave venture committed to putting on a mixture of classical and modern drama. Brooke's contact there was the theatre's founder, Maurice Browne, whose sister was married to Harold Monro who ran the Poetry Bookshop in London. Brooke felt an immediate rapport with Browne and his wife, the actress Ellen van Volkenburg. Browne knew roughly what to expect, having seen a photograph of Brooke during a trip to London the previous year. The image had bowled him over: 'The beauty of the man – I repeat the abysmal mythopoeic phrase: the beauty of the man – astounded me.' When Brooke breezed in in the flesh to greet Browne, his wife and his mother-in-law, Browne was not disappointed: 'Five minutes later the four of us were moving arm in arm down Michigan Avenue to drink beer. My memory of the next ten days is a riotous blur of all-night talks, club sandwiches, dawns over Lake Michigan and innumerable "steins".'

Brooke seemed particularly charmed by Browne's wife, and gave her several chains of South Sea shells and a copy of Belloc's beloved *The Four Men*. In a fond memoir of Brooke published in 1927, Browne recalled: 'The three of us would sit up night after night in our studio, talking, singing folk songs, reading poetry, surging across the tiny room like happy, healthy children. On three successive mornings we saw the sun rise.'

One of Brooke's appreciative audience, summoned by Browne to hear the glamorous visitor read his newly composed poems, was a lawyer, Arthur Davison Ficke, who, according to Browne: 'Came, saw, and fell.' This seems to be no more than the truth, judging by an elegy for Brooke that Ficke penned and published after his death. In it, he describes Brooke's last night in Chicago, when:

> High up above the city's giant roar
> We sat around you on the studio floor
> And you . . . like a boy
> Blushed suddenly, and looked at us, and smiled.

Brooke's winning ways had evidently made the transatlantic transition. If these Chicago nights sound like a hippie's memoirs, half a century early, it is still possible to be beguiled by their charm – and their all-too-evident innocence.

In contrast to most observers who heard him, Browne piously maintains that Brooke was an excellent reader of poetry: 'much better of course than the average professional reader or actor . . . quietly and shyly, with little tone-variation . . . emphasising rhyme and rhythm: reading, in fact, as a good lyric poet always reads good lyric poetry, taking care of the sound and letting the sense take care of itself'. He draws a vivid portrait of Brooke in full flight: 'sitting on the floor – his favourite position – with his knees hunched up, his arms around them, and his back against a wardrobe, blushing, with unfeigned pleasure, not embarrassment – when any of us became particularly inarticulate over some special loveliness'.

As ever, Brooke played the modest conqueror, taking the tribute of his awed subjects as his rightful due, but being careful not to make an un-English fuss about it: 'Rupert Brooke is walking down Michigan Avenue,' noted Browne, 'his right hand swinging his hat – some broad-brimmed, high-crowned, ridiculous feather-weight, plaited from South Sea straw, of which he was inordinately vain – his long legs striding carelessly and freely, his eyes fixed straight ahead, utterly unconscious of people and things, for he's talking, talking, as only he can talk.'

Brooke was a star before his time:

> Every woman who passes – and every other man – stops, turns round to look at that lithe and radiant figure. The wind, the dirty Chicago wind, is blowing Chicago dust and Illinois Central cinders through his hair – longish, wavy, the colour of his skin: a sort of bleached gold, both of them, from the sun of his lagoons, where day after day and month after month he had lived in a loin-cloth, spearing fish, writing poetry, making love.

Another American photographer, Eugene Hutchinson, followed his compatriot Sherril Schell in taking a set of pictures of Brooke, and was equally impressed:

> I found myself confronted by an unbelievably beautiful young man. There was nothing effeminate about that beauty. He was man-size and masculine, from his rough tweeds to his thick-soled English boots. He gave me the impression of being water-loving and well washed. Perhaps this was due to the freshness of his sun-tanned face and the odd smoothness of his skin, a smoothness you see more in women than in men . . . he seemed like a Norse myth in modern clothes – yet there was no vanity in the man.

Beneath this noble exterior, all the old rancid obsessions were bubbling and stewing. They came to the surface with a virulence that must have shocked these naive new friends during a discussion, on the empty stage of the Little Theater, of the artistic temperament: was it male or female? Brooke, who had been languidly leaning against a hollow property column, suddenly flared into life: 'He startled us by the vigour and decision with which he stated that, notwithstanding Havelock Ellis and Krafft-Ebing, this mixture of the sexes was all wrong,' a witness remembered. 'Male was male and female female, and any intermingling of the two was calamitous. In other words, this Shelley-like youth with his hyper-sensitive face and his girlish smoothness of skin and his emotional blue eyes was trying to tell us that manliness in men was the one hope of the world.'

With this parting shot, Brooke left Chicago, to arrive in Washington DC on 5 May. Here, by prearrangement, he met up again with the Marchesa Capponi, who showed him the sights of the American capital, in between bouts of flirtation that may have amounted to full-blown lovemaking. But he left the Marchesa in no doubt as to the underlying contempt in which he held her sex. After she had left Lake Louise following their encounter the previous year, he claimed, he had been disconsolately mooching around the local hills when he encountered a frightened group of seven young girls from his hotel. They had seen a bear, they told him, and wanted his protection on the dangerous walk back. He refused, allegedly telling them: 'I want to be alone. There are already too many females in the world. Go. And I hope you meet the bear.' In a macabre postscript Brooke told the Marchesa that he had not noticed any of the seven back in the hotel that night.

As ever, while in Washington he gravitated to the portals of the powerful. He dined with Sir Cecil Spring-Rice, the British Ambassador and author of the patriotic hymn 'I Vow to Thee My Country'. Having quaffed too deeply of the Embassy's champagne, he returned, slightly tipsy, to his hotel: 'I got excited . . . and had to have a bath and dance many obscene dances, in lonely nakedness, up and down my room, to get sober,' he confessed to Cathleen.

He brought forward the date of his return by a week, in order to travel with the Brownes, who were going to England on the liner *Philadelphia*, reaching Plymouth on Friday 5 June. Writing to tell the Brownes the news on 16 May, he added: 'I am infinitely homesick. I have made up a litany of all the places I know on the line between Plymouth and London – and there are many. I shall sing it, rather loudly, all that journey. So perhaps you'd better engage a separate compartment. What bleedin' fun!' He had received the results of his photographic session with Eugene Hutchinson, and did not much like what he saw: 'Is that the mouth that touched Tahitian lips, and drained the topless tankards of Berlin?' he enquired rhetorically. 'No, no, I have not changed so much – I return the infamy with a jeer.'

On 18 May he reached Boston – one of his first destinations after arriving in America one year before. He revisited Yale and made a round of farewells, including a stop-over on Staten Island to repay his debt to Russell Loines. He had told Eddie that his long sabbatical had achieved its objective in making him 'hard, quite hard'. This armour-plating was now used against Cathleen, who, predictably, was annoying him with her professional success. Brooke disguised his disapproval by pretending to disapprove of her choice of plays – a farce was beneath her, he felt. But the truth was, he would not countenance a woman with a life of her own. His petulance came out in a worrying echo of his tones towards Noel: 'You devil, you devil . . . you, the one lovely and wise person among all those painted shades . . . Why did I go away and leave you a year?' She was, he told Cathleen, at once a goddess and 'the bloodiest fool that ever plagued mortal poet . . . Forgive my anxiousness about you. It's partly because I'm lonely . . . I have staked very much on you, Cathleen.' Reading between the lines, it is clear that the root cause of his concern was not Cathleen's welfare, but his own. Again the green-eyed monster raised its ugly head:

> By God, London's a bad place. I know it. It's full of lust, and of hard mouths, and empty, empty eyes, and of din and glare . . . so little of beauty is left clean and standing by this ruinous age, and I have seen so many things crumble . . . I *will* not let you fade. If ever you wish to 'bedim the lovely flame in you' I will kill you, and myself too, before it can happen. What do I care for *you*, when there's Beauty to fight for.

Lest Cathleen be unduly alarmed by his anti-feminist raving, he added, in a rare moment of honest clarity: 'This is rant.' But he did not retract a word of it.

He spent his last five days in the New World in the McAlpin Hotel in New York's Greeley Square. He boarded the *Philadelphia*, still clutching his flamboyant straw hat. He also held a copy of D. H. Lawrence's masterpiece *Sons and Lovers* that Eddie had sent him for shipboard reading. He found the novel 'vivid – and hectic' and pronounced Lawrence 'a big man'. The voyage home passed merrily enough in the company of the Brownes. Ellen van Volkenburg kept a journal on the journey which records sudden snapshots of Brooke with a face 'as red as the curtains in the staterooms' after falling asleep in their deck-chairs, and notes that 'Mr Brooke eats ice cream with the air of a martyr and the look of a wicked baby'. The journal also records that: 'Mr Brooke is having sighs and eyes cast at him and even a married woman took a snapshot of him today because he has "such a noble head". A young girl two tables down from us gazes at him, awestruck, beautifully melancholy. When I told him of her adoration he remarked "How dull".'

Brooke was used to hero-worship; he had overeaten of the treacle of love, and it had made him sicker than any sea.

Bored by all the attention, he and the Brownes spent most of the time together on the deck:

> facing the stern with our backs haughtily turned to the rest of our fellow passengers who wandered past and eyed Mr Brooke with elaborate carelessness. He was in fine form, telling stories of the great and the near great . . . with just

the slightest touch of frosty snobbishness. I grew so interested in watching him that sometimes I forgot to listen. When he finished a story he would set his eyes ahead until the queer little cast came in one of them, run his fingers through his hair with ferocious energy, pause, grasp his nose between his thumb and forefinger, tweak it gently two or three times (you know, that 'quirky' way of his), stop, pull his Jaeger blanket high around his head (leaving none of it to protect his legs), and start on some fresh recollection.

On Friday 5 June they made landfall at Plymouth. Their first intimation of England was the strong smell of lush, new-mown Devon hay, wafting out across the sea: 'Mr Brooke is leaning over the taffrail sniffing ecstatically.' The news that greeted them in the port was that during their voyage across, another Atlantic liner, the *Empress of Ireland*, had gone down in the St Lawrence Seaway with severe loss of life. Also sent to the bottom on that same ship, by a strange twist of fate, was a flimsy little letter to Brooke from Taatamata. Even more extraordinarily, it would come to the surface in a year and somehow find its way to Brooke. By then, of course, it was too late for him to react to its contents – which hinted, its meaning garbled by the Tahitian beauty's emotions and exotic Franglais – that Brooke was to become a father. He had not only left his heart behind in the South Seas, but his genes too.

25

'If Armageddon's On'

Brooke had clearly thought better of his original plan to arrive in London unannounced: now he made very sure that there would be a welcoming committee to receive him, organized, of course, by the adoring Eddie, to whom he had sent a flurry of telegrams from New York and the ship giving the exact time of his arrival. But then, as now, it seems that English trains could be relied on only for their unreliability and, instead of the scheduled midnight, it was 2.45 a.m. on the morning of 6 June that his train rolled into London. In spite of the hour Eddie, Cathleen and Denis Browne were on the platform to greet him and take the sun-burned hero, radiant as ever, with his famous hair sun-bleached, back to Eddie's flat and one of Mrs Elgy's cold suppers. They talked until dawn, and then Brooke caught another train to pay his filial dues to the Ranee in Rugby.

His days in his native town were mainly taken up by the elaborate planning of a formal welcome-back dinner party which he had left Eddie to organize. Letters and postcards flew between Rugby and London in which Brooke requested that Eddie get hold of as many 'poets, actresses and lovely people' as he could. In an afterthought, he also asked for 'another gentleman' to balance the artists and actors, whom he said he found 'tiresome' as a group. There was another letter, in more flirtatious vein, to the Marchesa Capponi, which strongly suggests that their meeting in Washington had ended up in bed. 'You gave me great quiet and peace,' Brooke told the merry widow. 'You are very good to me.'

On his way to London he dropped in to greet the Raverats, who were still at Manor Farm, outside Cambridge. He found his friends entertaining a most distinguished guest: none other than the French novelist André Gide, whom they had met the previous March in Florence. The apostle of homosexual liberation had immediately fallen under the intellectual influence of his homophobic compatriot Jacques, and an enduring friendship was born. Piquantly, Gide was to play a prominent part in another aspect of Brooke's life – albeit posthumously – when he fathered a daughter by Elisabeth van Rysselberghe in 1923. Ironically, Brooke himself was still seeing Elisabeth in the weeks after his return to England. She had enrolled at the Royal Horticultural College, and they met for lunch at Simpson's in the Strand. Much to Elisabeth's dismay, she found her lover's ardour had cooled, and she never achieved her ambition of bearing a child by Brooke.

On 11 June Brooke returned in triumph to London and his homecoming party, which was preceded by a performance of the ballets *Les Papillons* and *Petrouchka* given in the presence of the dowager Queen Alexandra, Shaw, George Moore and other Edwardian luminaries. The late-night supper party that followed at Raymond Buildings almost overwhelmed Mrs Elgy's legendary catering ability: the guests were a veritable roll-call of Eddie's far-flung network of the artistic great and good, including the playwright, actor and producer Harley Granville-Barker; the painters Duncan Grant and Mark Gertler; the future politician Duff Cooper; Denis Browne, Maurice Browne and his wife Ellen van Volkenburg; the critic Desmond MacCarthy and his wife Lillah; Basil Dean, who would run ENSA in the Second World War; Cathleen Nesbitt and her former lover Henry Ainley; the novelist Hugh Walpole; and the *New Numbers* poets Wilfrid Gibson, John Drinkwater and Lascelles Abercrombie. Apart from Cathleen, Lillah MacCarthy and Ellen van Volkenburg, it was an overwhelmingly male gathering. The survivors gathered at dawn under the plane-trees of Gray's Inn Fields to see Brooke perform a Hawaiian siva-siva dance.

One friend whom Brooke had neglected to visit during the days following his return was Frances Cornford. The reason was that Ka Cox was staying with her to nurse her through an illness. But he did maintain contact by letter, defending himself from charges of misogyny inspired by his anti-feminist tirade from San Francisco. He did not hate women, Brooke explained; or at least, he did no longer, though there had been a time when he had 'rather despised them' for being 'fourthrate men'. 'But lately I've cheered up,' he added encouragingly. 'Noticing what supreme women they make . . . think of Gwen. Think of Ka (all her glory woman-ish, and what weakness she had feminist).'

Despite all the condescending praise, he did all he could to avoid Ka in person, knowing that she still, vestal virgin-like, tended the torch she continued to carry for him. When conscience at last compelled him to a strained meeting in a London teashop, he was full of foreboding: 'I know you're very sensible and all that, but I fear the feeling that the friendlier we got the more disturbing it'd be. It would put such a constraint, a bloody constraint on us . . . Do realize it, and, if you are likely to be upset by me, honestly don't arrange a meeting. There's trouble enough in the world.'

In the event, the awkward occasion passed off peacefully enough, although both parties wrote to the other expressing anxiety after the event. Their relationship, it seems, was one of those that could never end, this side of the grave.

This distasteful duty out of the way, Brooke resumed his social round, attending the première of Stravinsky's ballet *Le Rossignol* on 18 June and deepening his acquaintance with Lascelles Abercrombie, the main moving spirit, together with Gibson, in the *New Numbers* venture. He was taken by his fellow-poet's odd looks, described by Maurice Browne as 'small, dark, shy . . . with spectacles . . . greasy-looking hair . . . and a queer little green hat which tipped up preposterously in front'. Abercrombie, who was to grow close to Brooke in the last months of his life and would write a fervent obituary notice in his memory before learning that he was numbered among his hero's heirs, hit it off so well with Brooke at this meeting that Brooke gave up his bed at Raymond Buildings for the night – and slept on the sofa instead. He told Ka: 'I think he's very remarkable . . . he laughs very well.'

Two days later he and Cathleen visited their former haunt in the Chilterns, the Pink and Lily pub. They were joined by Eddie, and two of Brooke's oldest friends, Dudley Ward and Ben Keeling. Cathleen and the two long-time Fabians had to leave the party early – she to play the title role in a new production, J. M. Synge's *Deirdre of the Sorrows*. Afterwards, Brooke told her, he and Eddie 'walked by those glorious woods to Wendover (you know the Walk from Wendover, my dear) and drank much beer there, and ate, and started back, and slept in the heather, and walked on through arcades of mysterious beechen gloom and picked flowers and told stories and got back to roast beef and more beer and poems. I wish you had been there.'

Relations between Brooke and the woman he had swooned over so ecstatically the previous year were definitely cooler than before he had left England. And Cathleen was too perceptive not to notice the change. Long after Brooke's death she recalled that:

like all artists who have a neurotic strain he would always have needed [another woman]. I knew in the South Seas that he'd had a lovely girl there, and somewhere in Canada I always suspected there was a red-haired girl that he'd had an affair with . . . [a reference to the Marchesa Capponi]. When he wrote I could sort of read between the lines . . . I felt if I were married to him . . . I would probably suffer a great deal, because I thought there was no chance of his ever being a one woman man.

Late in June Brooke crossed the country on his first ever visit to the remote area on the Gloucestershire–Herefordshire border where the nest of poets who published *New Numbers* had rented their country cottages. He stayed for two days with Wilfrid Gibson and his wife Geraldine at the Old Nailshop in the hamlet of Greenway near Ledbury. The first two editions of the magazine, containing the best of Brooke's South Sea poems, had already appeared, and a third was in the production process, with Abercrombie's wife Catherine in charge of the subscriptions, her husband packing the publication into parcels and 'Wibson' himself licking the stamps – a process that gave him a mild dose of glue poisoning. Although his visit was brief, Brooke was delighted by the peaceful pastoral ambience in which his fellow-poets were steeping themselves. He described Abercrombie's Gallows Cottage to Russell Loines as 'the most beautiful you can imagine; black-beamed and rose-covered. And a porch where one drinks great mugs of cider and looks at fields of poppies in the corn. A life that makes London a very foolish affair.'

But despite this disdain for the metropolis, an eager Brooke was back in London by 26 June for a reunion of the Apostles at the Connaught Rooms. This was his last meeting with so many of the figures who had loomed large in his past life before the war intruded to drive a definitive wedge between the Cambridge–Bloomsbury ethos and Brooke's new, hard-edged views. His death, of course, permanently precluded any chance of subsequently healing the breach. Among the old friends soon to be enemies were several who would adopt a pacifist position in the whirlwind of war that was about to break over Europe: G. E. Moore, Gerald Shove, Harry Norton, James Strachey and Maynard Keynes. Perhaps significantly, it was not one of these, but his tutor at King's, Jack Sheppard, whom Brooke brought back after the meeting to stay the night at Raymond Buildings.

The following day Eddie at last engineered a meeting that Brooke had been urging upon him for weeks. He introduced Brooke to the *enfant terrible* of the English novel, D. H. Lawrence, who, together with his German wife Frieda, lunched with Eddie and Brooke at the Moulin d'Or and then visited an art exhibition in Holland Park. The two writers, with nothing in common save a Midlands birth, unexpectedly hit it off, and were observed in lively conversation punctuated by roars of laughter. The next day, 28 June, was not a significant one in Brooke's calendar; but during it the heir to the Austro-Hungarian throne, Archduke Franz Ferdinand, was shot dead in Sarajevo by a young Serbian nationalist, Gavrilo Princip. The event passed almost unnoticed, but the slow-burning fuses that it ignited among the allied European powers would blow the old order away before the summer was out.

Brooke was as yet too busy with his resumed London summer season of socializing to notice the distant rumbles of the gathering storm. There was dinner with the gifted young sculptor Henri Gaudier-Brzeska, who was likewise destined to die in the second year of the coming conflict. There was supper with the detested Lady Ottoline Morrell, soon to be one of the leaders of the pacifist faction. And there was a second poetry reading at Monro's Poetry Bookshop.

This event was to be much more successful than Brooke's sparsely attended session of the year before. Now, with *New Numbers* circulating, he was becoming a shining star in the poetic, as well as the social firmament. H. K. Sabin, a self-taught poet and printer, who witnessed the occasion, describes Brooke as 'beautiful as an annunciating angel', seated on the corner of a table, with a leg nonchalantly swinging, as he 'listened to the admirers who crowded round him'. Half a dozen had heard him in 1913, but this time a full house of up to 70 souls listened in rapt attention as Brooke read from his own poems. A poet named Eric Gillett, who was living above the bookshop at the time, describes Brooke fighting a heavy cold as he prepared for the reading: 'He came in and gave me his hand and told me he dreaded the thought of having to perform. After he had read a line or two in a low voice an old lady in the front row who carried an ear trumpet exploded "Speak up, young man!"'

Another witness who was less than enthralled by Brooke's questionable talent as a public reader was Amy Lowell, whom he had met briefly in Boston. She deplored the 'atmosphere of overwhelming sentimentality' in which 'Mr Rupert Brooke whispered his poems. To himself, it seemed as nobody else could hear him. It was all artificial and precious. One longed to shout, to chuck up one's hat in the street when one got outside.' Despite this comparative failure to work his customary magic, Brooke was soon back in the swing of London society. The poetry reading was followed by a theatrical supper party at the Savoy in the company of J. M. Barrie, Granville-Barker and Gerald du Maurier. Eddie's efforts to promote his treasured protégé knew few bounds.

A more reluctant and late-flowering literary lion than Brooke – indeed, hardly a lion at all, more of a lamb – was the wealthy young poet Siegfried Sassoon. Despite his diffidence about his own literary talent, Sassoon, who had been at Queen's College, Cambridge (he was a year older than Brooke) but had never met the shining star of King's, had taken roost under Eddie's capacious wings in the hope of promoting his own literary hopes. He too had come to live in Raymond Buildings – though on a different staircase to Eddie, who found the young man's intense shyness a barrier to giving his career his customary leg-up. But Sassoon's modesty could not prevent an understandable jealousy of what must have seemed to him the ease of Brooke's literary and social success. As a result, his attitude towards him, he confessed later, was one of 'admiring antagonism'. It was with mixed feelings, then, that Sassoon received a message from Eddie on 8 July inviting him to breakfast the next day to meet Brooke. He explained subsequently:

> The unromantic and provocative character of Brooke's 1911 volume had produced a vividly disturbing effect on my mind. Slow to recognise its abundant graces, I was prevented – by my prejudice against what I designated 'modern ugliness' – from perceiving his lovely and never prettified work as it really was . . . My unagile intellect was confused by his metaphysical cleverness. Interested though I was by the prospect of meeting the much-discussed young poet, I was unprepared to find him more than moderately likeable. Eddie's adoring enthusiasm had put me somehow on the defensive.

When they met over bacon and kidneys the following morning, Sassoon – at this time a decided but rather repressed homosexual – could not suppress an involuntary attraction for his fellow-poet, rhapsodizing about his 'living blue' eyes, his sunburned complexion and bare feet. Ignoring the presence around the breakfast table of the garrulous poet W. H. Davies and the taciturn painter Paul Nash, the two Cambridge contemporaries made polite literary conversation. Rupert's natural beauty was enhanced on this occasion by his poetic uniform of open-necked blue shirt, flannel trousers and unbrushed hair, which Sassoon prissily described as 'just a shade longer than it need have been'.

When Eddie had left for work at the Admiralty and the other two guests had departed, Brooke and Sassoon found themselves alone. Sassoon takes up the tale:

> We agreed that Davies was an excellent poet and a most likeable man. I then

asked him a few clumsy questions about his travels. His replies were reserved and unilluminating. One fragment of our talk which I clearly remember was – as such recoveries often are – wholly to my disadvantage. 'What were the white people like in the places you stayed at in the tropics?' I had asked . . . 'Some of them,' he said, were rather like composite characters out of Conrad and Kipling. Hoping it would go down well, I made a disparaging remark about Kipling's poetry being terribly tub-thumping stuff. 'But not always, surely,' he answered; and then let me off easily by adding, 'I used to think rather the same myself until Eddie made me read "Cities and Thrones and Powers". There aren't many better modern poems than that, you know.'

'I was conscious that his even-toned voice was tolerant rather than communicative . . .' Sassoon added. 'He may have been shy, but I am afraid he was also a little bored with me. I could only admit that I had never read it.' On this stilted and dispiriting note, the only meeting between two of the Great War's most prominent poets ended.

In spite of this unfortunate encounter, Sassoon kept the memory of Brooke burning bright. His voice, he remembered after Brooke's death, had:

almost meditative deliberation. His movements, too, so restful, so controlled, and so unaffected. But beyond this was my assured perception that I was in the presence of one on whom had been conferred all the invisible attributes of a poet. To this his radiant good looks seemed subsidiary. Here, I might well have thought – had my divinations been expressible – was a being singled out for some transplendent performance, some enshrined achievement . . .

When he left, after half an hour's desultory talk, Sassoon, sensitive and thin-skinned, imagined Brooke heaving a sigh of relief as he shut the front door on him, and got back to 'being his unimpeded self'.

The following day, 10 July, Brooke and Eddie dined with Henry James at his London home in Carlyle Mansions, and later received Stanley Spencer, who stayed the night on the sofa at Raymond Buildings. The next day Brooke left for Cambridge, and a meeting with another elderly admirer, A. C. Benson, who described him as 'more mature'. By 15 July he was back in London, and dining at Downing Street with Eddie and the Asquiths. Denis Browne performed on the piano and a King's contemporary, Steuart Wilson, sang accompaniments. By 24 July the international implications of the shots at Sarajevo almost a month before were becoming apparent: the previous day Austria had sent Serbia a harsh ultimatum, demanding not only the arrest of all those responsible for the assassination, and the suppression of anti-Austrian agitation, but the entry of Austrian officials into Serbia to supervise the suppression and the investigation of the crime. Not for the last time in the twentieth century, the Serbs rejected this interference in their internal affairs, and the interlocking alliances of Europe found themselves, via the terrible logic of military and diplomatic agreement, shut into a train speeding towards disaster. An agitated Eddie, who was privy to the unfolding catastrophe in the corridors of Whitehall wrote 'War Clouds' in large letters across his engagements diary.

That night, forgetting the tension, he took Brooke out to dine in the grand company of the Duchess of Leeds. Brooke found himself seated between two other aristocratic ladies, Lady Gwendoline Osborne and the young Lady Eileen Wellesley, daughter of the Duke of Wellington and a friend of Violet Asquith, with whom she had attended finishing school in Germany. Brooke and Lady Eileen, a round-faced, heavily built young woman, not dissimilar to Ka Cox in her physical appearance, felt an immediate attraction to each other. The young lady's aristocratic antecedents were clearly one element in the attraction. Who could resist a woman whose London home, the grand Apsley House at Hyde Park Corner, had been the residence of her famous ancestor, the 'Iron Duke', when it had borne the postal address 'Number One, London'?

After dinner with the Duchess of Leeds, the company moved on to Hyde Park Gardens, and the home of a most unusual soldier, General Sir Ian Hamilton, who combined literary ability and interest with a keen intelligence, great bravery and military irresolution. By yet another of those quirks of fate that wound through Brooke's life, this man would become his Commander-in-Chief during his final military expedition within nine months. After watching Hamilton's daughter, Marjorie, dance, Brooke, Eddie and Denis Browne – the last soon also to come under Hamilton's command – escorted Lady Eileen round the corner to her home in a four-wheeled carriage.

Hypocritically, Brooke was still denouncing the 'corruption' of London life in letters to the Raverats: 'the atmosphere is so *bloody* nowadays that only the stupid are fairly untouched, the sensitive wither like a bug-befouled leaf . . . Soho makes me sick.' It is with a sinking heart that the reader turns to the letters he was now writing to Cathleen: as with those to Noel and Ka, they are full of dire warnings against the corruption of the city and the immorality of the theatre, and dismiss any suggestion that Cathleen can look after herself. In fact, there are all the unmistakable signs that Brooke is tiring of his 'goddess' and looking for a way to dump her. When he met Lady Eileen – well-born, sophisticated, sexually experienced – the perfect excuse hove into view.

After telling Cathleen that she is 'mad' to trust the world and the people in it, he added: 'My dear, if you put cut flowers in red ink for water, the blossom goes red, and men are even more coloured and made by their surroundings than flowers, and women even more than men.' Attacking her chosen profession, he blurted out: 'I'd better state, before going further, that as a matter of fact I loathe women acting in public.'

As if to confirm his low opinion of the theatre, in the dying days of July Brooke encountered the man who epitomized all that he now told himself he loathed in London and England: Lytton Strachey. The unfortunate encounter occurred in the foyer of the Drury Lane Theatre, where Brooke had bumped into James Strachey and was chatting with him – possibly about the looming threat of war – when Lytton walked up. Facetiously James remarked: 'I don't think you know my brother Lytton?' Brooke's response was immediate. 'No,' he agreed, spun on his heel and stalked away. There was a stunned silence in the crowd around them, followed by the jangling of the bell summoning them for the second act. This was to be the last time that Brooke met the Strachey brothers, and the following day he made the breach irreparable by a final curt and priggish little note: 'My dear James, I have realized that, in the excitement of the evening, I may not have explained to you how much I was grieved at your opinions. I had hoped you had got rid of them. They seem to me not only eunuch & shocking, but also damned silly and slightly dangerous. R.B.' With this clear projection of his own confusions on to the baffled James, Brooke's oldest and deepest friendship came to its sad end.

As so often in his life, the slamming of one door opened another, and very shortly after the scandal in Drury Lane, on 30 July, he found himself among the most exalted company in the most elevated surroundings in England: meeting at last Eddie's revered 'Chief', Winston Churchill, at Downing Street. The international situation was more and more threatening: earlier that day Brooke was sitting with D. H. and Frieda Lawrence in the Ship restaurant, awaiting Eddie, who was un-characteristically late for lunch. At last he arrived, panting with excitement, to proclaim that the Foreign Secretary, Sir Edward Grey, had just averted war with Germany. Alas, Eddie's optimism was both premature and short-lived: the diplomatic disaster of mobilizations and unshakeable alliances continued its malign work, and by the time the subdued guests gathered at Number Ten that evening, a belligerent Churchill was offering to get

Brooke a commission if it should come to war. It was an offer that he would make good.

The next day Brooke travelled to Rugby, and on the morning of 1 August the Ranee brought him his newspaper in bed with the ominous news that Germany had declared war on Russia. From Bilton Road, he gave his initial reaction to Jacques Raverat, a fervent supporter of his native France and the allied cause:

> Everyone in the governing classes seems to think we shall all be at war. Everything's just the wrong way round. I want Germany to smash Russia to fragments, and then France to break Germany. Instead of which I'm afraid Germany will badly smash France, and then be wiped out by Russia. France and England are the only countries that ought to have any power. Prussia is a devil. And Russia means the end of Europe and any decency. I suppose the future is a Slav Empire, world-wide, despotic, and insane.

Still in Rugby, as if by reflex he began a long letter to the latest of his lady-loves: Lady Eileen. He described a long car trip with the Ranee and Alfred through the English heartland of Warwickshire, redolent with images and memories of Shakespeare, whose death-day he would so soon come to share. He ended: 'Please take care of yourself. Eileen, there's something solid & real & wonderful about you, in a world of shadows. Do you know how real you are? The time with you is the only waking hours in a life of dreams. And that's another way of saying I adore you. Goodnight. Rupert.' He was turning over in his mind his options should war come; but had not yet decided to accept Winston's offer. He thought aloud to Eileen: 'If war comes, should one enlist? Or turn war correspondent? Or what?' To Stanley Spencer – who would soon be doing his little bit in uniform alongside, of all people, his fellow-artist Henry Lamb – Brooke mused: 'If fighting starts I shall have to enlist, or go as a correspondent. I don't know. It will be Hell to be in it, and Hell to be out of it. At present I'm so depressed about the war, that I can't talk, think, or write coherently.' To Eileen he confessed that he was suffering an English melancholy: 'an uninspiring thing, a conglomeration of swear-words and uncharitable thoughts and awkward limbs. That am I.'

Brooke's first reactions to the approaching conflict, however under-standable, are somewhat surprising to those who have been schooled to think of him as an unswerving patriot, running lithely to answer his country's call. In fact, the war caught him on the back foot – awkward, stumbling and uncertain of what to do.

Still in Rugby for his twenty-seventh birthday – the last he would see – Brooke distractedly told Eileen of his nail-biting mood: 'It is raining. Every now and then one goes out and buys an evening paper to find the news. And the news is always a little worse . . . I can't sit still. I wish I could fly . . .' But no Peter Pan fantasy could rescue Brooke from the grim reality that was fast engulfing him. Significantly he compared his situation to a suitor awaiting the answer to a marriage proposal – clearly a fate that Brooke could only conceive of as worse than death: 'One feels as depressedly restless as in those dreadful pauses of a day or two after one's sent off a proposal of marriage, and before the reply comes. What *will* happen tomorrow? And whatever it is, won't it be dreadful?'

To Eddie he wrote, with a dreadful prescience: 'Do you have a Brussels-before-Waterloo feeling? That we'll all – or some – meet with other eyes in 1915? . . . and I'm vaguely frightened. I feel hurt to think that France may suffer. And it hurts, too, to think that Germany may be harmed by Russia. And I'm anxious that England may act rightly. I can't bear it if she does wrong . . .' By 'wrong' Brooke clearly means if the irresolute government followed the course that a pacifist minority of its ministers was urging upon it: to ignore its obligation to Belgium, whose neutrality had been violated by Germany, and stay out of a war that had by now consumed almost every other European power.

On 4 August, the day that Britain declared war on Germany, Brooke left for the coast, taking up an invitation to stay with the Cornfords and their infant daughter at Cley in Norfolk. The news of war did not reach the remote seaside resort until the following morning, but that night, he told Cathleen, he had a nightmare: 'Let my love wind round you and comfort you and be a guard over you and a sweetness and a glory for you.' Dumbstruck by the terrible news, neither Brooke nor his hosts spoke of what might happen until the evening when Brooke blurted out that the only thing that would make Ka happy would be 'that I should be blown to bits by a shell. Then she would marry someone else and be happy.' As a prophecy – apart from the manner of his death – it had Brooke's usual hallmark of uncanny accuracy. When Frances protested that he would not have to fight, he grimly informed her that they would all have to.

In an effort to cheer themselves up they took themselves off to the beach, where someone snapped Brooke, hair tousled amid the windswept dunes, reading to baby Helena, who had swallowed one of the South Sea beads he had bought for her. He stuck a flower behind his ear in pale imitation of a Polynesian. But, eerily, the flower he chose was a poppy – soon to be the symbol of the carnage of the war. On the beach he felt a chill

374

of premonition deeper than the North Sea winds that froze the water and forced him from it after a few minutes.

Although he remained in Cley for a few more days, his mind was elsewhere, his thoughts distracted. 'I feel dazed and troubled,' he confessed to Cathleen. 'The general uneasiness and tension of mind seems to take all the strength out of me.' He was not yet ready to follow Jacques, who had written, begging Brooke to use his influence to help him join up: Brooke tried to calm down his excitable friend:

> You mustn't get excited. I asked Eddie about interpreters' jobs. He didn't seem to think anyone was wanted just now. He promised to keep you in mind . . . One can't 'go and fight' in England. Volunteers are admitted neither to the navy nor the army. If we join the Territorials now, they give you six months' training, then let you garrison the chief ports and sea towns, *If* the Expeditionary Force leaves England – it *might* be worth doing . . .

Within a few weeks Brooke would be proved wrong – for the first time in English history mass armies of volunteers were being raised to fight the first mass war. Nor was he to know that his own posthumous image would be one of the most potent weapons used to tempt and shame young men into answering the call. But on one point his prophetic instincts did not desert him: 'Unless any country gets smashed,' he told Jacques, 'it'll probably be the people that hold out longest who win.'

Brooke toyed with various half-baked ideas to be of use: did the French need hands to gather in the harvest now that so many peasant-soldiers had been mobilized, he wondered. He also made a half-hearted effort to get a war correspondent's job, but there seemed to be no interest. Back in London on 10 August, and hurrying from office to office, he met the poet and journalist J. C. Squire in the street. Squire asked him what all the rushing was for. 'Well, if Armageddon is *on*,' replied Brooke, 'I suppose one should be there.'

He told Eileen of his frustration: 'It's not as easy as you think – for a person who has no military training or knowledge, save the faint, almost prenatal remembrance of some khaki drilling at Rugby – to get to the "front". I'm one of a band who've been offering themselves, with vague persistence, to their country, in various quarters of London for some days, and being continually refused. In time, one of the various doors we tap at will be opened . . .'

One door that Brooke tapped on did indeed open during these days of stress and exultation: the door to Eileen's bedroom, or rather, to Brooke's own; for it was most likely, during this period of frustration and hope, that the two of them became lovers in Brooke's room at Raymond Buildings. A shocked Mrs Elgy, as Brooke, half proudly and half ashamed confessed to Eileen, found some of her hairpins in his bed. At any rate, by the middle of August Brooke felt free enough to argue out his own internal debates with his new lady:

> One grows introspective. I find in myself two natures – not necessarily conflicting, but different. There's half my heart which is normal and English – what's the word, not quite 'good' or 'honourable' – 'straight', I think. But the other half is a wanderer and a solitary, selfish, unbound and doubtful. Half my heart is of England, the rest is looking for some home I haven't yet found. So, when this war broke, there was part of my nature and desires that said 'Let me alone. What's all this bother? I want to work, I've got ends I desire to reach. If I'd wanted to be a soldier I should have been one. But I've found myself other dreams.' It was that part, I suppose, which, when the tumult and unrest in me became too strong, sent me seeking for a correspondentship. At least, it was some individualist part of me which said 'It's the biggest thing in your seventy years. You'd better see as much of it as you can. Go, for some paper, immediately.' Base thoughts, those: when decent people are offering their lives for their country, not for their curiosity. You're quite right, it's a rotten trade, war-correspondent.

Once again, as at so many decisive junctures in his life, Brooke displays that essentially divided nature of his: keen sportsman versus decadent intellectual; puritan versus libertine; romantic versus cynic; socialist versus nationalist – now the detached observer jousts with the self-sacrificing warrior. But by mid-August Brooke's private war with himself seems to have been won – the man who had never wanted to be a soldier, but would write his most famous poem under that title, had decided to don the King's uniform and serve his country as a fighting man. But not, of course, as any old fighting man. He wanted to be special. He endeavoured to explain his frustration to Eileen:

> I came to London a few days ago to see what I could do that would be most use. I had a resentment – or the individualist part of me had – against becoming a mere part of a machine. I wanted to use my intelligence. I can't help feeling I've got a brain. I thought there *must* be some organizing work that demanded intelligence. But, on investigation, there isn't. At least, not for ages. I feel so damnably incapable. I can't fly or drive a car or ride a horse sufficiently well . . .

To add to his frustration, some of his friends had successfully got themselves into uniform: he watched Ben Keeling drilling with the Inns of Court Officers' Training Unit, and was filled with envy when he encountered Geoffrey Keynes in the uniform of the Royal Army Medical Corps. Desperately, he tried to pull strings, writing to Andrew Gow at King's, the friendly don who had been put in charge of processing applications for commissions from Kingsmen. On 22 August, the day after the tiny British Expeditionary Force had exchanged its first shots with the mighty German war machine near Malplaquet in Belgium, he wrote again to Gow from Rugby, where he had gone to inform a heartbroken Ranee that he was intent on joining up. Acknowledging receipt of an application form for a commission, Brooke told Gow that he was set on an active service posting, not a staff job. Asked why he wished to enlist, he noted simply: 'To Hell with Prooshians.'

Meanwhile he poured his frustration into journalism. The *New Statesman* published two pieces of his: the first, inspired by the news that the New Zealanders had taken possession of German Samoa, was called 'Not Counting Niggers' – an ironically titled tribute to the South Sea Islanders – while the second, 'An Unusual Young Man', was a lightly disguised slice of autobiography, describing his own feelings on the outbreak of war. He recalled his pre-war sojourns in Munich and Berlin, and how he had been seduced by the music and culture of Germany. How would he feel, he asks himself, at meeting the friends he had made then on the battlefield? But he would be fighting for England: its fields, lanes and 'holiness'. Already the lineaments of the soldier-poet are falling into place. By way of conclusion, he recalls his comment to Squire – however ambivalent his emotions: 'If Armageddon is *on*, I suppose one should be there.'

He was still at Rugby when the news came that he had been waiting for. Eddie wrote to say that Churchill was in the process of forming an entirely new unit – the first of the many private armies that the belligerent warrior politician would raise – to fight a new and unconventional sort of warfare. The Royal Naval Division, placed under the command of Major-General (later General) Paris, would comprise the Royal Marines, the Royal Naval Reserve and any suitable newly commissioned civilian officers. Intended for use as an amphibious force, the RND had naval ranks and was carried by sea, but fought on land.

If Brooke wished, Eddie wrote, Winston would fulfil his promise to get him a commission. Brooke had no doubts. Eddie pulled the necessary strings and within a brace of days the deed was done. There would be no nonsense about interviews or application forms – he was in. 'I'm glad I could do it for you, since you wanted it . . .' wrote the doting Eddie, 'but I feel I'm "giving of my dearest" as the newspapers say. Don't tell a soul that I did it all on my own or I shall be plagued to death.'

Now that Brooke was committed, he unburdened himself with a long confessional letter to Eileen, lest she labour under the illusion that he was really the stainless knight his sacrificial enlistment indicated. 'I am really rather horrible,' he admitted. 'Not especially fickle-hearted, but I *am* rather hard-hearted. I usen't to be. I think one of the things that appalls me is my extraordinary selfishness: which isn't quite the same as hardness of heart, though it helps. I mean, I just enjoy things as they come, and don't think or care how they affect other people.' And again the death-wish that he had expressed on the day war broke out enters the equation: 'I expect it will be the best thing for everyone if a stray bullet finds me next year.' Once more, although he again assumed his end would be violent, he was almost spot on about the date of his demise.

'And another thing,' he added, piling on the agony:

I'm really a wolf and a tiger and a goat. I am – how shall I put it – carried along on the tides of my body, rather helplessly. At intervals I realize this, and feel rather aghast. Oh, it's all right if you don't trust me, my dear. I don't. Never trust me an inch. Oh, I'm rather a horror. A vagabond, drifting from one imbecility to another. You don't know how pointless and undependable and rotten a thing you've got hold of. Don't laugh. I know it's funny. But it's all true.

The reality of the momentous step Brooke had taken began to sink in when he went to be fitted for a uniform. He told another lover, the Marchesa Capponi, that it brought the imminence of death home: 'It's terrible . . . but it will end all right, and lead to better things. A lot of people die, and others mourn them. But they'll do that anyhow. Death doesn't matter.'

By now it was late September, and he was rubbing shoulders with those directing Britain's increasingly desperate war effort. The huge scythe of the wheeling German attack on France had been blunted by the French before Paris in the battle of the Marne, and the Germans, blooded but unbowed, had changed direction and were now storming towards the Channel ports, opposed by the minuscule British Expeditionary Force, in the so-called 'Race to the Sea'. Lunching with Churchill and Eddie, Brooke was vouchsafed a glimpse of high strategy. To Cathleen, who was touring a play in the provinces, he boasted:

Winston was very cheerful at lunch and said one thing which is exciting, but a *dead* secret. You mustn't *breathe* it. That is, that it's his game to hold the Northern ports – Dunkirk to [Le] Havre – at all costs. So if there's a raid on any of them, at any moment, we shall be flung across to help the French reservists. So we may go to Camp on Saturday, and be under fire in France on Monday!

Brooke – still dressed in civvies – was already drilling at a depot at the Crystal Palace in south London. He hadn't joined the Army, he told Jacques, but the Navy: 'a more English thing to do, I think . . . I felt that if we were going to turn into a military nation and all the young men go in, I should be among them. Also I had curiosity.' It would have been easy – but facile – to remind Brooke of what curiosity did to the cat.

Eddie's action in using the old-boy network to secure Brooke a fast-track commission looks distasteful to us today, with the hindsight of what the next four years of slaughter would bring. But the mood of 1914 was one of patriotic exaltation. After half a century of peace, the Boer War apart, England was literally thirsting for war. Few knew, in that high summer, of the mud, blood and tears that lay ahead. The talk was all of being home by Christmas. In signing up Brooke – and Denis Browne, who also secured a commission in the RND through his good offices – Eddie was not acting as a pimp of death, but rather as a member of a gentleman's club securing admission for a promising new recruit. He was more devastated than anyone by the eventual result of his action. And, above all, it was what Brooke wanted.

Denis Browne was the first to get into uniform. He turned up on Sunday 27 September, resplendent in his new khaki kit. The previous day, his last as a civilian, Brooke had enjoyed a quiet lunch with Eddie and the new Poet Laureate, Robert Bridges. He was, he felt, one of an élite. Later on that Sunday, Eddie saw him and Denis off at Charing Cross station on their journey to the training camp. Both men were joining the Anson Battalion of the RND at Betteshanger, in the small Kentish coalfield. Sub-Lieutenant R. C. Brooke found himself in charge of the 15th Platoon in D Company, a unit of 30 men, mostly naval stokers from Northumberland, Scotland and Ireland. An unusual young man was going off to war.

26

The Soldier

As he was swallowed up by the vast maw of the military machine, Brooke's thoughts were still with the women in his life. To Cathleen he confided: 'Queer things are happening to me, and I'm frightened. Oh, I've loved you a long time, child: but not in the complete way of love. I mean, there was something rooted out of my heart by things that went before. I thought I couldn't love wholly, again. I couldn't worship – I could see intellectually that some women were worshipful, perhaps. But I couldn't find the flame of worship in me. I was unhappy. Oh, God, I *knew* how glorious and noble your heart was. But, I couldn't burn to it. I mean, I loved you with all there was of me. But I was a cripple, incomplete.'

He ended this letter with a reaffirmation of his love for Cathleen: 'I adore you . . . I worship the goodness in you . . . I feel like a sick man who is whole again. It comes on me more and more dazzlingly how you're the best thing in my life . . . Cathleen, if you *knew* how I adore you, and fight towards you. I want to cut away the evil in me, and be wholly a thing worthy of you. Be good to me, child. I sometimes think you can make anything in the world of me . . .' But there is, in the gaps between these fervent words, doubt. The nagging sense persists that Brooke protests too much. And Cathleen was too astute a woman to miss it. Years later she recalled:

> He was a great believer in goodness and solidity, and he felt he hadn't been either a good or solid person. He exaggerated of course when he wrote, but so many of the letters I got from the South Seas . . . said 'I need something to hold on to' and 'I don't live up to myself' and 'I'm only half a person' . . . strange things like that, which allowing for 50 per cent exaggeration, was still, I think, a kind of not quite certain of where he was going.

If uncertainty had been the chief leitmotif of Brooke's life since at least 1911, the war provided an answer to it. At last his duty seemed clear, his life appeared to be funnelling towards one inevitable conclusion. He did not attempt to resist, but flung himself, with a sense of almost blessed relief, into the fray. The fact that most of his friends were doing the same thing enhanced his sense of solidarity with destiny – and the fact that those he had already written off as enemies – the Stracheys and the rest of the Bloomsbury set – were not, merely served to confirm his resolve. At last, after all the indecision, he knew what he had to do. Cathleen knew it too: 'I don't think it was, in a sense, so much an escape, as an odd fulfilment that he didn't have to think about what he was doing with his life, because I think he took very seriously what one ought to do.'

It was a time to tie up the loose ends of his life. To Ka, who, in spite of all, still held out hopes that somewhere they could make a future together, he wrote with 'deep and bitter shame': 'through me you have been greatly hurt, and two or three years of your life – which can be so wonderful – have been changed and damaged. And I'm terribly ashamed before you.' He strove to alleviate her grief and desperation that, after all they had been through, things had come to nought: 'Till I think you're complete I shan't be happy. When you're married and happy, I shall believe that the world *is* good. Till then I shall be conscious of – general – failure.'

The least problematic of his relationships was the most recent – that with Lady Eileen – and because of their lack of history, he was able to write freely, with a carefree, careless joy:

> Well, child, if you're happy with me: that's something, isn't it? I'm certainly happy with you. We can have fun together, can't we? and supposing I go off & get blown to pieces – what fools we should feel if we hadn't had fun – if we'd foregone our opportunities – shouldn't we? . . . It's so good being with you. You give me – much more than you know. Be happy, child . . . I kiss you good night . . . All Heaven be about you.

If these simultaneous professions of love reveal Brooke's familiar emotional confusion, it was not a state he was destined to endure for long: the white-hot blade of war was about to cut through the Gordian knot of his tangled feelings and make all simple once more. Mars was to replace Venus as his presiding deity.

Military life was not unfamiliar to one who, as Brooke had, had been through the joys of an English boarding school. He was well used to the bugle calls at unconscionable hours, the duties, the rotas, the winds whistling through unheated huts. Only the 35 men in his platoon were as unlike Rugby boys as it is possible to be: he confessed himself unable to remember their names; and their Celtic or northern dialects were a mystery to him; nevertheless, he admired their physical strength and simplicity. With more than a touch of homoeroticism he wrote to Eileen:

> . . . occasionally I'm faintly shaken by a suspicion that I might find incredible beauty in the washing place, with rows of naked, superb men, bathing in a September sun or in the Camp at night under a full moon, faint lights burning through the ghostly tents, and a distant bugler blowing 'Lights Out' – if only I were sensitive. But I'm not. I'm a warrior. So I think of nothing, and go to bed.

His first days of service life passed in a busy whirl of kit inspections, route marches through the muddy Kentish lanes, boxing, soccer, drill and (for officers only) a bath in Betteshanger rectory. At 5 a.m. on Thursday 1 October a call roused them from sleep, and they all thought they were bound for France; but it was a false alarm. But on the following Sunday the reveille call was for real and they marched off to Dover, lustily belting out music-hall songs like 'Who's Your Lady Friend?' Reaching the port, they were greeted by the townspeople, cheering noisily and thrusting the fruit of Kent – apples – into their hands. Girls sprinted into the ranks to steal kisses, and tears were shed. Marshalling his platoon, Brooke was seized by gloomy reflections: 'I felt very elderly and sombre and full of thoughts of how human life was like a flash between darknesses,' he recalled later. The officers stocked up with provisions for the crossing at a local hotel, and then their requisitioned troop-ship stole out into the choppy grey Channel to rendezvous with two destroyers that were to escort them across the dangerous waters. By the morning they were off Dunkirk. They spent the next day unloading equipment in a vast customs shed, and as night fell word spread that, as expected, they were bound for the great Flemish port of Antwerp, which was already under bombardment by the Germans' big guns.

Senior officers, in a misplaced attempt to instil a spirit of grim determination into the men, told them there was little chance of survival, and advised them to use the time before they entrained in writing farewell letters to their nearest and dearest. 'So we all sat under lights writing last letters: a very tragic and amusing affair,' Brooke subsequently reported to Cathleen:

My dear it *did* bring home to me how very futile and unfinished life was. I felt so angry. I had to imagine, supposing I *was* killed. There was nothing but a vague gesture of goodbye to you and my mother and a friend or two. I seemed so remote and barren and stupid. I seemed to have missed everything. Knowing you shone out as the only thing worth having . . .

We have to imagine the scene: the arc lights on wires dancing as the autumnal evening wind got up, throwing flickering shadows across faces squinting against the acrid fumes of strong tobacco smoke. Brooke among the rest, struggling to order his thoughts, and make a sudden sense of the life that just a few weeks ago he had mentally measured in decades rather than days. Small wonder that he wished to leave little consoling lies behind: like a drowning man, he clutched at the straws of comfort.

But even *in extremis*, the mocking, facetious side of him leapt out to seize the sad absurdities of the situation: 'Men kept coming up and asking things. One said "Please, Sir, I've a bit o'money on me. It's not much to me: but it'd be a lot to my wife: we've got fourteen children: and supposing anything happened to me. I wouldn't like them bloody Germans to get hold of it." What should he do? We arranged that he should give it for the time to the parson . . .' His role as an officer resembled his brief stint as a schoolmaster – once more trust was placed in him. He felt the weight of responsibility and braced himself under the burden.

They steamed east through the night and arrived in the morning to an Antwerp delirious with joy at the anticipated relief: '. . . everyone cheered and flung themselves on us and gave us apples and chocolate and flags and kisses, and cried "Vivent les Anglais", and "Heep! Heep! Heep!"' The last time Brooke had been in the city it was as a King's freshman, accompanied by his brother Alfred, now serving as a volunteer with the Post Office Rifles, and he had deplored the activities of rioting strikers. But there was no time to relish the irony. They were about to be flung into a battle that was already lost. The dithering at Dunkirk had wasted precious hours, and the Belgian army was in pell-mell retreat before the inexorably advancing Germans. With the suburbs of the city already in flaming ruins, the brigade-strength detachments of the RND were too puny a force to have any hope of stopping the steamroller.

As they marched towards the Front they were met by the dispiriting sight of wagon-loads of dead and dying men. For the first time Brooke and his men tasted the real horror of war. Stragglers on horseback and horse-drawn limbers towing guns in retreat added to the depressing sight; but before these impressions could fully sink in, they wheeled into the grounds of a château on the outskirts of town. In the darkness Brooke glimpsed little pools glimmering through trees, and ornamental statues. His men set about digging latrines in the rose gardens, before trying to snatch some sleep among the shrubbery. 'It was bitter cold . . . it seemed infinitely peaceful and remote. I was officer on guard until the middle of the night. Then I lay down on the floor of a bedroom for a decent night's sleep. But by 2 the shells had got unpleasantly near. A big one . . . burst above the garden; but too high to do damage.'

Among the officers gathered in the château were those who were to remain with Brooke to the end. There was Denis Browne, who had been with him in his beginnings; and an Asquith – Arthur, the Prime Minister's third son, universally known as 'Oc', who had interrupted a civil service career to volunteer the previous month; and somewhere in the darkness – Brooke had last glimpsed him embarking his men at Dover – was Patrick Shaw-Stewart, a small, fine-featured man, and a brilliant Eton and Balliol scholar, with aristocratic connections and a promising career with Barings Bank. This was the nucleus of the group of officers who would gather around Brooke's radiant figure and accompany him across the seas to his death. Of the trio in the shell-shocked château that night, only one, Oc Asquith, would survive the war, and he would lose a leg.

Meanwhile the night, horrible with whining shells and crashing artillery fire, imposed its own imperious duties. At dawn, sleepless, they scrambled off and marched towards the gunfire, with orders to relieve the Belgians holding Fort 7, an obsolescent structure built in the 1860s. As the shell bursts came ever nearer, Brooke passed the test of courage that every fighting man must face to his own satisfaction. 'It's queer to see the people who do break under the strain of danger and responsibility,' he reflected later. 'It's always the rotten ones. Highly sensitive people don't, queerly enough . . . I don't know how I should behave if shrapnel was bursting on me and knocking the men around me to pieces. But for risks and nerves and fatigue I was all right. That's cheering.'

Once in the trenches they dug in and watched aeroplanes lazily avoiding shrapnel bursts in the skies high above their heads. 'A dozen quiet little curls of white smoke would appear round the creature – the whole thing like a German wood-cut, very quaint and graceful and unreal.' This sense of the 'unreality' of war, which Brooke mentions several times, seems like a distancing device to throw a filter between his sensitive nature and unbearable reality.

During a long day of waiting, news came through that the Brigade's baggage, waiting at a nearby station, had been totally destroyed by a

German bombardment. Up in smoke went Brooke's luggage in the general conflagration, including a precious pair of field-glasses – a gift from E. M. Forster – and a couple of sonnets he was working on. Both items were to be speedily replaced. Also hit by shells was the château of Vieux-Dieu, where they had spent the previous night, and the general ghastliness of the scene was given an infernal quality by cascades of blazing petrol, released from ruptured tanks struck by the shelling. Like a hammer being brought down on a line of nuts, the chain of forts the RND were holding were being reduced to rubble piecemeal by the guns of Herr Krupp, and their position was clearly becoming untenable.

The order went out for a general withdrawal under cover of darkness, and the Brigade, weary and shell-shocked, began a 25-mile foot-slogging march of retreat. Illuminated by the blazing lakes, blinded by smoke and horrified by the sight, sound and smell of horses and cattle cooking in the burning fuel, they staggered back to the banks of the River Scheldt, where two German saboteurs were caught in the act of attempting to blow up a pontoon bridge. Both were shot out of hand. Once across the river, the march mingled inextricably with a pathetic human tide of Belgian refugees, all desperate to escape the advancing enemy.

Recollecting the retreat in relative tranquillity a few days later, Brooke told a Californian acquaintance, Leonard Bacon, that the march had become like a scene from a Dantesque hell, lit by 'hills and spires of flame'. But the columns of humanity spilled by the war, the dreadful flotsam of conflict, were a 'truer Hell' than the hottest fires:

> Thousands of refugees, their goods on barrows and hand-carts and perambulators and wagons, moving with infinite slowness out into the night, two unending lines of them, the old men mostly weeping, the women with hard drawn faces, the children playing or crying or sleeping. That's what Belgium is now: the country where three civilians have been killed to every one soldier. That damnable policy of 'frightfulness' succeeded for a time. When it was decided to evacuate Antwerp, all of that population of half a million, save a few thousands, fled. I don't think they really had any need to. The Germans have behaved fairly well in the big cities. But the policy of bullying has been carried out well. And half a million people preferred homelessness and the chance of starvation, to the certainty of German rule. It's queer to think that one has been a witness to one of the greatest crimes of history. Has ever a nation been treated like that? And how can such a stain be wiped out?

Brooke's anguished, outraged question would be echoed time and again through the terrible century that had just begun. Victorian smugness, the belief in peaceful, inevitable progress, crumbled like a sandcastle when it encountered the harsh realities of human savagery. All at once, or so it seemed, the things that had occupied Brooke's mind for years past – personal relations, the war between the sexes, art, literature, socializing – faded into insignificance. All doubts and ironies disappeared, shrivelled by the terrible things he saw through that night of hell on the road back to the railhead at Saint-Gilles. He had found a cause, and it was one that, together with most active members of his generation, he was quite ready to die for.

'The eye grows clearer,' he told Bacon, 'and the heart. But it's a bloody thing, half the youth of Europe, blown through pain to nothingness, in the incessant mechanical slaughter of these modern battles. I can only marvel at human endurance.' His brush with danger, and his first sustained look at the brutish face of war, give the lie to those who jeer at Brooke for mouthing slushy sentiments without having experienced the horrors of the trenches. He was a faithful echo of the frenzied mood of patriotic self-sacrifice that had gripped every European power. Even Sassoon, whose later war poetry, informed by his disgust at the suffering of his comrades, is the quintessential voice of protest against the waste and futility of war, wrote early poems hailing the bullet and the bayonet, and acquired the nickname 'Mad Jack' for the ferocity of his private war against the Germans.

During the long march Brooke saw many strange and terrible sights – railway stations with their tracks torn up; London buses rushed over to transport troops with their adverts and indicator boards intact; broken-down carts full of hopeless humanity awaiting the Germans – but the most profound change of all was the transformation going on within him – from doubter to passionate warrior; from light-hearted curiosity to furious duty; from cynical lightweight to earnest and deadly serious patriot: from a young man who liked kissing, to a soldier whose sole purpose in life was to kill and be killed. He had awakened, by the strangest irony of all, just when he was about to fall asleep for ever.

At dawn they reached their destination, and wearily slumped into the trains that would carry them to Bruges and safety. In the ancient city of circular canals they ate and slept properly for the first time in five days, before entraining for Ostend the following morning. Their odyssey had lasted just six days. Arriving back at Dover in a morning mist on 9 October, the officers were given leave. Brooke left at once for London with Oc Asquith and made straight for Churchill's office at the Admiralty to give a first-hand report on the blooding of the First Lord's military brainchild. In battle-stained uniforms, they spilled out the story of the expedition's failure.

It would not be the last time that Churchill would preside over an inglorious evacuation of a British army from a Channel port.

Brooke washed off the grime of a week's warfare in Eddie's bath at Raymond Buildings. When his patron returned from a long day at the Admiralty with the anticipated news of the fall of Antwerp, he continued to babble compulsively about his baptism of fire. Perhaps as a reaction to the bottled-up nervous tension, he found he could barely keep his eyes open with a recurrence of his childhood complaint, conjunctivitis. His leave extended, he went up to Rugby and enthralled a half-horrified Ranee and curious neighbours with more accounts of his military adventure. He wrote to friends, asking them if they could make good the luggage he had lost: binoculars from the Marchesa Capponi, clothes and a sleeping-bag from Frances Cornford.

He was back in London on 16 October for a curious appointment with Hugh and Bryn Popham. His old flame had had the first of her three children with Hugh, which was disturbing enough; but the shock was compounded when he encountered Noel as he arrived. For their part, the Olivier sisters were struck by Brooke's unfamiliarly close-cropped military haircut, and his silent and subdued manner. The meeting was Brooke's last encounter with the two women who had unwittingly caused so much havoc in his life. But if he was taciturn in the Oliviers' company he was loquacious elsewhere, and seemed to have a compulsion to hunt out friends and tell them of his experiences. He had a fleeting last meeting with James Strachey, and looked in at the Poetry Bookshop to talk with Harold Monro, who found him haggard, his eyes still pink, and unable to talk of anything save the war.

Then he was off to Great Yarmouth on the Norfolk coast to bid farewell to Cathleen, who was touring a play in the resort. Together they walked along the seashore, reading their beloved John Donne aloud. Afterwards, back in her digs, they sat in front of a fire of sea logs, spitting blue and green flames, and Brooke asked her to read him something 'quite beautiful'. She pulled down her well-thumbed volume of Donne and read 'The Anniversarie', with its haunting lines:

> Here upon earth, we'are Kings, and none but wee
> Can be such Kings, nor of such subjects bee.
> Who is so safe as we? Where none can doe
> Treason to us, except one of us two.

Brooke's spongy memory soaked up the lines; and they went to seed one of the group of sonnets he had begun to work on, which were destined to ensure his lasting fame – or infamy – as either Michael Holroyd's 'chauvinistic fugelman of 1914' or, in Winston Churchill's altogether more flattering view, 'one of England's noblest sons'.

Brooke was already far gone in the process of identifying his own obsessions and concerns with those of the greater community of the nation. It had come as a blessed relief to him to cast off the clothes of selfishness and bathe in the common pool of a cause in which he was merely one of a number. For him, the idealized figure of Cathleen symbolized what he was going to war to defend; he told her explicitly: 'I feel so happy in this new safety and brightness . . . Do you know what a trust you hold for the world? All those people at the front who are fighting – muddledly enough – for some idea called England – it's some faint shadowing of the things *you* can give that they have in their heart to die for.' He was Arthur to her Guinevere.

Back at Betteshanger on 18 October, Brooke heard a garbled rumour from Denis Browne that the Old Vicarage was to be demolished. In alarm, he asked Frances to investigate the report, and appealed to Gwen Raverat to go and make a painting of the house as a sad memorial to a lost epoch. With relief he learned that the reports of the house's end were false, and he declared his intention of buying the freehold should he survive the war. In his heart, however, he must have known that the prospects for this were rapidly diminishing. Meanwhile he turned again to Ka for aid – not for emotional support, but for the sort of assistance that her friends always relied on her for: sheer, hard-headed practical help. What he needed, he told her, were the sort of simple, concrete things similar to the list he had enumerated in 'The Great Lover', but even more banal: a tin mug, toilet paper, a cake of sweet-scented soap. She would know, he concluded patronizingly, where to acquire such items quickly and cheaply.

Meanwhile the Anson Battalion was on the move from Betteshanger, transferring by rail to naval barracks in the port of Chatham. It was not a happy unit: there were grumblings in the ranks and among the officers over their insensitive and overbearing CO – the man who had cheerfully told them before the Antwerp expedition that they were all going to their deaths. Brooke, Asquith and Browne discreetly lobbied the authorities through Eddie to have the man removed before the Battalion 'floundered in a morass of incompetence'.

Brooke fired off a long letter to his old Cambridge friend E. J. Dent, who had written to ask him to contribute to a fund to send a bronchial friend to winter in the warm climate of California – just as Brooke had done the year before. In his reply, Brooke was withering: it was not the time, he told Dent, to be wintering in Los Angeles, and if anyone had cash to spare 'he should be trying to assist . . . some of the outcast Belgian widows and children'. He added that he had seen such victims of the war: 'I can't help feeling, I mean, that there's bigger things than bronchitis abroad. I know a girl who is consumptive. Her doctor said she'd probably die if she didn't spend the winter in a sanatorium. She's doing Belgian refugee organization and clothing in London, and is going to stay at it.'

Now that he had embraced his country's cause with his whole heart, there was no holding him back. Scornfully, he recommended that Dent's friend should disregard his 'weakness'. He continued:

> In the room where I write are some twenty men. All but one or two have risked their lives a dozen times in the last month. More than half have gone down in torpedoed ships and been saved *sans* their best friends . . . I feel very small among them. But that, and the sight of Belgium . . . make me realize more keenly than most people in England do – to judge from the papers – what we're in for, and what great sacrifices – active or passive – everyone must make. I couldn't bear it if England daren't face or bear what Germany is facing and bearing.

This attitude of 'Don't they know there's a war on?' became more and more pervasive. It seemed that even in his most generous and self-sacrificial moments Brooke could not pass up the temptation to sneer at and scorn those denied his own courage and commitment. And, along with his usual insight and prescience about the long struggle that was now beginning – in stark contrast to the prevailing 'it will all be over by Christmas' belief – there was a sense of snobbery that Brooke and his comrades-in-arms were members of a self-chosen élite somehow more worthy of the title 'Englishmen' than those who did not see things his way.

The roll-calls of casualties at the front were ominously lengthening – some Rugby contemporaries were already dead – and, at the end of his letter to Dent, Brooke noted the death of a French poet who was, like him, a socialist turned patriot: Charles Péguy. He was, he owned, almost ashamed not to have gone west with him: 'I am envious of our good name.' His new-found stern resolution came out clearly in a letter to Cathleen from Chatham: after again deploring her stage career – 'If you were a man there'd be no excuse for you to go on acting. You'd be despicable' – he launched a full-frontal assault on non-combatants, ending belligerently:

'The central purpose of my life, the aim and end of it, now, the thing God wants of me, is to get good at beating Germans. That's sure.' Underneath the bluster, though, there were still hints of the doubting, questing Brooke of old: 'What it [his life's purpose] . . . was I never knew, and God knows I never found it. But it reached out deeply for other things than my present need. There was some beauty and holiness in it I should have taken hold of.' There is poignancy in the realization that Brooke knew surely that there would be no more time to answer these questions. He had boarded a train there was no getting off.

He had already begun work on the series of five sonnets that are his main claim to fame and yet the most serious bar to the appreciation of his worth as a poet by a modern audience. In their mystic mood of exalted, almost religious patriotism and sacrifice, the sonnets published under the title *1914 and Other Poems* are both untypical of Brooke and prone to his worst poetic vices of windy linguistic flatulence and vague, empty rhetoric. Nevertheless, they undoubtedly hit the authentic spot in expressing the prevailing mood of millions of people in that short and shining moment when the war seemed glorious, peace a bore and the national cause simple, generous and right. And, not least, they gave lines to the language that are still remembered and quoted down to this day. Of how many other poets who died in their twenties can this be said?

The first of the sonnets in order of composition, though Brooke numbered it second of the sequence was 'Safety', inspired by his meeting with Cathleen at Great Yarmouth and her reading of Donne. As he told her a day or two later, when sending her the poem: 'I feel so happy in this new safety and brightness . . . You don't mind me printing ours, because it's private, nobody knows it's ours.' It is the only one of the poems specifically addressed to an individual:

> Dear! of all happy in the hour, most blest
>   He who has found our hid security,
> Assured in their dark tides of the world that rest,
>   And heard our word, 'Who is so safe as we?'
> We have found safety with all things undying,
>   The winds, and morning, tears of men and mirth,
> The deep night, and birds singing, and clouds flying,
>   And sleep and freedom and the autumnal earth.
> We have built a house that is not for Time's throwing.
>   We have gained a peace unshaken by pain for ever.
> War knows no power. Safe shall be my going,
>   Secretly armed against all death's endeavour;

Safe though all safety's lost; safe where men fall;
And if these poor limbs die, safest of all.

After a very shaky start – the absurdly shouted 'Dear!', like a porter running
after a lady who has forgotten a tip, and the archaic 'most blest' – the poem
comes perilously close to becoming a list *à la* 'The Great Lover' in its
middle lines: 'winds, and morning, tears of men and mirth' and so on. Even
a sympathetic critic, John Lehmann, remarks fairly: 'Every image in these
lines is obvious and of the most general kind, and contributes nothing
concrete to the idea, or makes any imaginative discovery that can be called
in any way original: it is little more than a lulling incantation of clichés.'

'Safety' finds what power it possesses only in its second stanza, and it is
the power of paradox. A house has been built that will endure even time's
slow gnawing; the lovers have discovered a peace invulnerable to pain;
against this even the might of war is powerless; even if the lover fails to
return from the war, this will not be a failure but a secure victory over the
two great enemies of love and life. Ironically, for the one-time militant
atheist, the sentiments are profoundly Christian: time and death are both
outfaced: where are their sting and victory? Essentially these simple themes
are to be repeated, with only slight variations, in the other four sonnets.
Almost simultaneously with 'Safety' Brooke wrote the sonnet 'Peace' –
though perhaps the title 'War' would have better expressed its sentiments.
In it he gave expression to the spirit of stern resolution, and also relief that
a peace that had stagnated into corruption had been broken by the
thunderclap of war:

Now, God be thanked Who has matched us with His
    hour,
  And caught our youth, and wakened us from
    sleeping,
With hand made sure, clear eye, and sharpened power,
  To turn, as swimmers into cleanness leaping,
Glad from a world grown old and cold and weary,
  Leave the sick hearts that honour could not move,
And half-men, and their dirty songs and dreary,
  And all the little emptiness of love!

Oh! we, who have known shame, we have found
    release there,
  Where there's no ill, no grief, but sleep has mending,
    Naught broken save this body, lost but breath;

> Nothing to shake the laughing heart's long peace there
>   But only agony, and that has ending;
>   And the worst friend and enemy is but Death.

It opens with an ejaculation that is very like the booming first words of the stirring Lutheran hymn: 'Now Thank We All Our God'. Like 'Safety', it draws on profoundly Christian imagery: the sleeping prince roused to new life from sottish slumber. But the new life that is beckoning is actually death – though Brooke cloaks the jump into extinction in an undeniably beautiful and economic image: 'To turn, as swimmers into cleanness leaping'. Of course, it is irresistible to point out that the 'cleanness' into which his swimmers are gaily leaping would actually become the slime-filled shell holes of Passchendaele. What is even more striking is the explicitness with which Brooke acknowledges that the war is a convenient way of purging his sexual sins and emotional guilt – the contrast between cleanness and dirt is specifically underlined, as is the orgasmic 'release' that 'we' (actually he) has found. The first stanza ends with a final reckoning with Bloomsbury and the Stracheys – for who else are the 'sick hearts that honour could not move' (to join up with him) and who else are the 'half-men' with their 'dirty songs', celebrating 'the little emptiness of love' – an emotion that he can at last, in all good conscience, joyfully reject.

The second stanza, like 'Safety', celebrates paradox: sleep (i.e. death) mends all ills, heals all griefs; and, if the body is broken and breathing stops, so what? But the couplet

> Nothing to shake the laughing heart's long peace there
>   But only agony, and that has ending

and the last line are a weak ending to a poem that begins with such a stirring bugle blast.

Brooke was not alone in his volte-face from socialism to super-patriotism: half Europe was seized by the same cosmic convulsion. Only one member of the mighty German Social Democratic Party – the future communist leader Karl Liebknecht – voted in the Reichstag against the War Credits, causing the Kaiser to exult: 'I see no more parties – only Germans.' In France, as the workers answered the ancient call of La Patrie, Charles Péguy, before he died on the battlefield, found time to call for the pacifist socialist leader Jean Jaurès to be shot, and another super-patriot promptly obeyed the command. A young leader of the Italian socialists, Benito Mussolini, resigned from the party to begin a violent and ultimately successful campaign to bring his country into the war. In Britain, those members of the Labour party like Ramsay Macdonald, who held fast to their pacifist creed, were outnumbered and howled down. The call of country and nationalism proved far stronger than the recent and nebulous concepts of international workers' solidarity. It would take the fearful bloodletting of the next four years to prompt second thoughts, but by then, for Brooke and millions more, it would be far too late.

As he received news of the casualty lists from France and Belgium at Chatham, Brooke was working on a third sonnet, aptly titled 'The Dead':

> Blow out, you bugles, over the rich Dead!
> There's none of these so lonely and poor of old,
> But, dying, has made us rarer gifts than gold.
> These laid the world away; poured out the red
> Sweet wine of youth; gave up the years to be
> Of work and joy, and that unhoped serene,
> That men call age; and those who would have been,
> Their sons, they gave, their immortality.
>
> Blow, bugles, blow! They brought us, for our dearth,
> Holiness, lacked so long, and Love, and Pain,
> Honour has come back, as a king, to earth,
> And paid his subjects with a royal wage;
> And Nobleness walks in our ways again;
> And we have come into our heritage.

The bugle call, that ancient military instrument, which opens the poem, lends an archaic touch; and there is an appropriately medieval whiff of Agincourt in the opening lines that recalls Henry V's pep talk before the battle, when he speaks of the tiny élite – 'be they ne'er so vile' – who have found rank and majesty by taking part in the fight. The colour of the poem is red – the analogy of blood and wine; the mention of gold and royal wages – and at the end the idea is repeated that dirt and dishonour are being richly purged and cleansed by the holy douche of war and death.

The rhetoric of the poems is repeated in Brooke's letters to friends pleading with them to join him in fighting the good fight. Or, if they are disqualified by age or pacific opinions, like his mentor Goldsworthy Lowes Dickinson, they are bidden to at least give him their blessing: 'I hope you don't think me very reactionary and callous in taking up this function of England,' he told 'Goldie' in a note during a brief valedictory visit to King's: 'There shouldn't be war – but what's to be done but fight Prussia?

I've seen the half million refugees in the night . . .' Another old friend, Rosalind Murray, who had married the philosopher Arnold Toynbee, and just given birth to a son, the future critic, communist, journalist and drunk Philip Toynbee, was told with sad lack of prescience: 'Perhaps our sons will live the better for it all.' Brooke's uppermost thought, when he thought he was going to die at Antwerp, Mrs Toynbee was informed, was: 'What *hell* it is that I shan't have any children – any sons. I thought it over and over, quite furious, for some hours.'

Brooke did not yet know it, but the death he had escaped at Antwerp, was already being replanned for him, in a very familiar setting: the Admiralty and Number Ten Downing Street, where Winston Churchill had already seized on the absurdly ambitious plan to short-cut the stiffening stalemate on the Western Front by some amphibious operation to strike elsewhere at a vulnerable soft underbelly of the Central Powers. His first scheme was to land a Russian army on Germany's Baltic coast, backed up by the Navy and the RND. When Russia's crushing defeat at Tannenberg precluded this, and Turkey entered the war on Germany's side, he switched his support to a scheme for relieving pressure on Russia by forcing the narrow straits of the Dardanelles into the Black Sea, and, as a possible bonus, seizing the then Turkish capital, Constantinople.

It was the sort of madcap idea that was to appeal irresistibly to Churchill throughout his career: impatiently, he always disliked the long slog, in war, as in politics, and was forever searching for the short-cut, the audacious surprise blow. This one would have the advantage of employing the Navy and the RND – both his babies – linking up with Russia and possibly knocking Turkey out of the war, and opening up a route into Europe's heart, all at a single stroke. Meanwhile, as he laboured to convince his sceptical Cabinet colleagues, the RND, lacking an immediate function, marked time.

In November Brooke was posted to Portsmouth with the RND's Nelson Battalion, and thought, in his frustration, of applying for a transfer to the Army, which was at least seeing immediate action in France. Impatient for an invasion, he wrote to Jacques Raverat that the English needed a salutary blooding: 'The good ones are alright . . . but there's a ghastly sort of apathy over half the country. And I really think that large numbers of male people don't want to die. Which is odd. I've been praying for a German raid . . .'

Suddenly there came a ray of hope: Oc Asquith told him there was a vacancy in A Company of the RND's Hood Battalion, commanded by Bernard Freyberg, a massively built and exceptionally brave and brilliant

New Zealander. As soon as he applied, he heard by telegram from Eddie that not only himself, but also the brother officers he had been with at Antwerp, were being transferred *en masse* to the Hood Battalion, under the command of a professional CO, Colonel Arnold Quilter. As a gift, Brooke brought with him a mass consignment of winter woollies, sent by his Aunt Fanny 'on behalf of the Mayor and Corporation' of her native Bournemouth. Marching through Bournemouth on the way to the Hood Battalion's training camp at Blandford in Dorset, he saw a playbill advertising *Butterfly on a Wheel,* starring Cathleen Nesbitt. Stung by her obvious refusal to heed his hints about giving up the stage, he wrote petulantly: 'I hope you'll be giving up this beastly stage business soon.'

Arriving at Blandford on the last day of November, he was placed in charge of No. 3 platoon of Freyberg's A Company, responsible for some 30 men. In a letter to Russell Loines in New York, he gloried in the transformation wrought in those of his friends who had joined the colours:

> ... it's astonishing to see how the 'intellectuals' have taken on new jobs. Masefield drills hard in Hampstead ... Cornford is no longer the best Greek scholar in Cambridge. He recalled that he was a very good shot in his youth and is a Sergeant-Instructor in Musketry. I'm here. My brother is a 2nd Lieutenant in the Post Office Rifles ... Among the other officers in this Division are two young Asquiths ... a New Zealander [Freyberg] who was fighting in Mexico and walked three hundred miles to the coast to get a boat when he heard of the war, ... Denis Browne ... a youth [Shaw-Stewart] lately through Eton and Balliol ... a young and very charming American John Bigelow Dodge who turned up to fight 'for the right' – I could extend the list. It's all a terrible thing. And yet, in its details, it's great fun. And – apart from the tragedy – I've never felt happier or better in my life than in those days in Belgium. And now I've the feeling of anger at a seen wrong – Belgium – to make me happier and more resolved in my work. I know that whatever happens I'll be doing some good, fighting to prevent *that.*

Life at Blandford was run on austere naval lines: Brooke slept in a wooden hut with seven other officers; leave in town was referred to as 'going ashore'; and, in a well-meant bid to make the wintry conditions more homely, Brooke began to pester those practical women, the Ranee and Ka, with requests for extravagant creature comforts for his comrades. He sent Ka the measurements of the hut windows with a plea for her to sew suitable curtains – and did she know where a deck-chair was to be obtained? She should rope in the Oliviers to help her, he said imperiously: 'That's what you civilians are for, isn't it?' He also got Eddie to wangle Denis Browne a posting to the battalion from nearby Portland – ironically, for this ensured that Denis, too, would go to his death on the Dardanelles expedition. Ka dutifully responded to Brooke's importunities, sending a parcel of maps and pins for the brothers-in-arms to follow the war's course.

As winter drew on, the weather worsened, and mud became the bugbear of their existence on their frequent route marches: 'My God, this mud!' Brooke complained to Ka in comic exasperation. 'We hope to get Winston down into it. Then we may obtain alleviation.' His relentless requests for practical help to his former love went on unabated: her next task was to discover how many Christmas Turkeys would feed 250 hungry stokers, and what such a lavish gift would cost. In another mission of mercy she supplied the red curtains he had requested, and the Ranee sent a chest of drawers. His quarters cosily furnished, he hunkered down for the festive season. His health, as usual in moments of high stress, was giving him trouble: in fact he was never really to be fully well again. His throat, a perennial weak spot, was permanantly sore, its rawness exacerbated by the coke fumes from the hut stove.

It was not only his body that was failing the exorbitant demands of its owner – his mind, too, was troubled. In a letter to Dudley Ward he confessed:

> Last night I rolled about in this so-called bed. I've been bad lately with [typhoid] inoculation, a cough and things. And I dreamt I landed at Papeete, and went up between the houses, and the air was heavy with sunshine. I went into the house of a half-caste woman I know and she gave me tea, and talked . . . And at last I said 'and how and where's Taata-mata [sic]?' and she said: 'Oh – didn't you know?' And I said 'No'. She said 'She's dead.' I asked (knowing the answer) 'When did she die?' 'Months ago, just after you left'. She kept evading my eye. After a long silence I asked (feeling very sick) 'Did she kill herself?' The half-caste nodded. I went out of the house and out to the lagoon, feeling that a great friendliness – all the place – had gone against me. Then I woke with a dry throat, and found a frosty full moon blazing in at the window, and the bugle hammering away at the 6.30 Reveille. Perhaps it was the full moon made me dream, because of the last full moon at Mataia (about which there is an unfinished poem, now in German possession). Perhaps it was my evil heart. I think the dream was true. 'There's no health in me' as we used to say to some Confession in Chapel. And now I'm not only sicker with myself than ever: but I've also got another bad attack of *Heimweh* for the South Seas.

Brooke need not have worried: Taatamata was not only alive – if reliable rumours are true, she was about to give birth to Brooke's child, perhaps conceived under the very full moon he dreamed about. His psychic connection with her – probably activated by conversations with his company commander, the bluff Freyberg, who knew the Pacific islands well – was about to be concretely revived by a letter from the woman herself, although he would never know of the daughter he had left behind. All this makes Brooke's regrets about not marrying and leaving a child behind all the more poignant. He told Dudley:

> I agonise every night. At times I want to wire to almost anybody 'Will you be my widow?' And later, I sigh, that I'll be free and the world before me, after the war. It's partly dependent on my premonition. If I think I'll survive, I plump for freedom. When I feel I'll be killed (which is my general feeling and deepest), I have a revulsion towards marriage. A perplexing world.

But the question was beginning to obsess him, as he put it to Jacques, in his sleeping-bag between thoughts on the attack and his men's boots. Then he would doze, to be awoken by the orderly's gruff 'Six-thirty, and you're Orderly Officer today, sir.' And another dim and drizzling day would be ushered in with a 'queer green chalky dawn'. Even his imagery is becoming corpse-like.

There were, at this stage in his life, practically speaking, four candidates for the role of Brooke's widow: Cathleen, Eileen, Ka and his latest interest – not least for her connections with the highest corridors of power – Violet Asquith. In November he had begun a regular, light-hearted correspondence with the equine Violet, who was more in love with his handsome persona than he could ever be with her. She came down to the camp to visit her brother Oc and Brooke, and finding them both sickly, removed them to convalesce at Lady Wimborne's conveniently close country house at Canford. Here Brooke showed her the drafts of his war sonnets, which had now become four, with the completion of the weakest of the poems, also called 'The Dead', which was Brooke's own favourite, although it is generally judged the worst of the bunch:

> These hearts were woven of human joys and cares,
>   Washed marvellously with sorrow, swift to mirth.
> The years had given them kindness. Dawn was theirs,
>   And sunset, and the colours of the earth.
> These had seen movement, and heard music; known
>   Slumber and waking; loved; gone proudly
>   friended;

Felt the quick stir of wonder; sat alone;
    Touched flowers and furs and cheeks. All this is
    ended.

There are waters blown by changing winds to
    laughter
And lit by the rich skies, all day. And after,
    Frost, with a gesture, stays the waves that dance
And wandering loveliness. He leaves a white
    Unbroken glory, a gathered radiance,
A width, a shining peace, under the night.

Once again lists of tedious nouns slap feebly around like dying fish searching for meaning. Brooke's wit and precision have entirely deserted him here in favour of a few flaccid metaphors almost entirely devoid of any sense.

Christmas was spent in a state of simmering discontent among his landlocked stokers, who do not seem to have entirely taken on board the correct war spirit. Brooke tried to alleviate their boredom with games like draughts and hoops, supplied by his well-meaning Uncle Alan, the Dean of King's. Ka came up trumps with a huge batch of mince pies for the men, and many in the unit got slightly drunk. The day before Christmas Eve, while still staying at Canford, Brooke scribbled down a single line in his field-training notebook: 'If I should die, think only this of me.' It proved to be the opening line of his fifth and final war sonnet – and the most famous poem he was to write in his short, truncated life. He continued to develop it over Christmas, and when he had shepherded the last of his drunken stokers to bed on Christmas Day, he had an hour to himself to finish and polish it, as he proudly reported to Eileen Wellesley.

Old habits die hard, and, although he continued to correspond with Cathleen and Eileen, a large number of letters flowed to and fro between Brooke and Violet Asquith, who at least had the virtue of novelty – and she was, of course, the Prime Minister's daughter. At the end of his busy Christmas Day, he found time to reply to one of her own hopelessly indiscreet letters, in which, writing from the moated and crenellated Walmer Castle in Kent, she had excitedly reported on a top-secret meeting between her father, the War Minister Lord Kitchener and General Sir John French, commander of the British armies in France. 'Your Walmer week-end sounds too thrilling for belief,' responded Brooke. 'I wish I'd been there. But one can't get away from this mud-heap very easily. My throat collapsed again and left me voiceless . . .' Two days later, on cue, Violet invited him to Walmer. Brooke, predictably, was tickled pink: 'Can you really find room for me among all those Field Marshals? And may I wear my oldest khaki and finish a sonnet?'

Granted New Year's leave, he saw in the last year of his life, as he had so many others, at home in Rugby with the Ranee. But on 2 January he arrived at Walmer – scene of the death of Eileen's forebear the Duke of Wellington – to take up Violet's invitation. Two days later he was in London, and in a brief reprise of his former socializing, lunched at the Admiralty with Denis Browne, Winston Churchill and the Prime Minister. That evening he attended a variety show at the Ambassadors' Theatre with Denis and Eddie, accompanied by Oc and Violet Asquith; followed by supper at the Carlton Grill. The next day, while he was staying with Eddie, word came that his Cambridge contemporary James Elroy Flecker had succumbed to TB at a Swiss sanatorium. Although Brooke had not known the poet well, he was hit hard by the news and penned an obituary tribute in *The Times*. He told Eddie bitterly: 'What a bloody jest: and a bloody world.' To Eileen he was even more prescient: 'He was my friend. Who'll do *The Times* for *me*, I wonder? Damn them.' That question was to be answered much sooner than he perhaps imagined.

On his return to Blandford Camp yet another shock awaited him. A letter had arrived from Taatamata in faraway Tahiti, and, still more astonishingly, it had been lying at the bottom of the Atlantic Ocean for the intervening months, since it was posted as long ago as May, just after he had left the island. The letter had been on the doomed *Empress of Ireland*, whose loss Brooke had learned of as he docked at Plymouth six months before. Divers had recovered it from the wreck, and, faded, dog-eared, but still legible, it had found its way to him. As he commented to Dudley after retailing the letter's strange odyssey: 'I think life's far more romantic than any books.'

The letter itself, couched in Taatamata's quaint marriage of English and French, was both touching and ambiguous:

My dear Love darling, I just wrote you some lines to let you know about Tahiti to day whe have plainty people Argentin Espaigniole, and whe all very busy for four days. Whe have good times all girls in Papeete have good times whit Argentin boys. I think they might go away to day to Honolulu Lovina are giving a ball last night for them. beg ball. they 2o'clock this morning. I hope to see you here to last night. Lovina make plainty Gold Money now. About Mrs Rosentale she is went to [illegible]. whit crower by Comodore before they go away to whe have been drive the car to Lage place. Enton and I. Mrs Rosental Crower Williams Banbridge to whe got 12 Beers Bred Sardines only whe tout come right away to lage the car Break and whe work down the beach. have drinking beer. Music and whe come away 5 o'clock morning . . . pas dormir. I wish you here that night I get fat all time Sweetheart you know I always thinking about you that time when you left me I been sorry for long time. whe have good time when you was here I always remember about you forget me all readly oh! Mon cher bien aime je l'aimerai toujours. Le voila Cela partir pour San Francisco je lui ais donne quel cadeau pour lui he told me to send you his regards je me rapeller toujour votre petite etroite figure et la petite bouche qui me baise bien tu m'a perceau mon coeur et je aime tourjours ne m'oubli pas mon cher maintenant je vais finir mon lettre. parceque je me suis tres occupee le bateau par a l'instant. 5 heurs excuse me write you shot letter. I hope you good health and good time. I send my kiss to you my darling xxxxxxxxxxxxxxx mlle kiss Taatamata

There was more than enough here to make Brooke 'gulp', as he put it to Dudley. Apart from the obvious fact that his lovemaking had pierced Taatamata to the heart, there was the hint that he had left a more tangible souvenir of his sojourn behind in Tahiti than fading memories: 'I get fat all time Sweetheart.' What did that throw-away phrase mean? We do not know whether Brooke, puzzling out the faded script by the flickering lights of his hut, took in the full import of the words – although later events would seem to suggest that he confided his story to Dudley, a long-time confidant in the affairs of Brooke's heart.

But now the only thing to do was to grit his teeth, shove the letter away in his pocket and get on with his military duties, which meant acquiring a new sniper's telescopic rifle for his platoon at a cost of eight guineas; he appealed to his mother to go halves on purchasing the deadly weapon. Meanwhile, unknown to Brooke, his fate was being decided in Whitehall. Ever more urgent appeals were coming in from Russia for a diversionary attack to remove pressure on their hard-pressed fronts. On 2 January the Russian Chief Commander, the Grand Duke Nicholas, the resolute uncle of the weakling Tsar, sent an appeal which tipped the balance: he pointed out that a successful forcing of the Dardanelles straits would also benefit England and France, releasing unlimited supplies of Russian wheat, to replace the already U-boat-threatened Atlantic route from the USA. Kitchener went to see Churchill at the Admiralty to discuss the Russian plea. The War Supremo, whose influence over the civilian politicians was at this time immense, was converted. 'The only place that a demonstration might have some effect . . .' he told Churchill, 'would be the Dardanelles.

Particularly if, as the Grand Duke says, reports could be spread at the same time that Constantinople was being threatened.' Britain's Naval Supremo, the First Sea Lord, Admiral Jackie Fisher, was equally enthusiastic, and gave the project his customary energetic endorsement, promising a squadron of antiquated battleships to help force the straits.

At Churchill's prompting, the commander of the Mediterranean Fleet, Admiral Carden, drew up a detailed plan of operation, which was submitted to the War Council in London on 13 January. Churchill's eloquence carried the day, and the plan was approved without dissent. The RND would accompany the Fleet as the spearhead of the assault. Churchill knew full well that his brainchild would take severe casualties, but, as he grimly wired to Carden: 'Importance of results would justify severe loss.' Two days after the War Council had approved the operation, on 15 January, the RND Commander, General Paris, gathered his officers around him at Blandford to brief them on the broad outlines of the planned attack. He told them their training would be intensified, and that they would be on their way to the eastern Mediterranean in six weeks. 'God knows how I shall live through the interval,' Brooke wrote to Ka impatiently.

There is no doubt that Brooke realized the implications of the intended operation: he knew that he had only a faint chance of returning from the expedition alive; but, as he told John Drinkwater: 'I'd not be able to exist for torment if I weren't doing it . . . Better than coughing out a civilian soul amid bed-clothes and disinfectant and gulping nieces in 1950 . . .' The same fear of and contempt for old age that had inspired the Clevedon pact was at work again, and he proclaimed himself ready to die – along with the best of his generation: 'I had hopes that England'ld get on her legs again, achieve youth and merriment, and slough the things I loathe – capitalism and feminism and hermaphroditism and the rest. But on maturer consideration, pursued over muddy Dorset, I think there'll not be much change . . . Come and die. It'll be great fun.'

In an effort to shame Drinkwater into quitting the theatre and joining up, he added: 'The theatre's no place now. If you stay there you'll not be able to start afresh with us all when we come back. Péguy and Duhamel; and I don't know what others. I want to mix a few sacred and Apollonian English ashes with theirs, lest England be shamed.' Brooke's self-identification with his native soil, so evident in the final and most famous of his war sonnets, 'The Soldier', is becoming ever more apparent.

By the end of the month sickness was once more laying him low. 'I've deplorably got a cold again,' he ruefully reported to Violet on 24 January. 'I'm in bed with it, stupid beyond military crassness, irritable, depressed &

uncomfortable.' But Brooke's irrepressible energy, bubbling up like a geyser, could not be kept down for long. Despite being confined to Blandford's 'miasmic' huts, he found time to look over a nearby country house, Stourpaine House, which Jacques Raverat was considering buying, and sent his friend an unfavourable surveyor's report – there was water in the cellars. Next, with a spark of his former social egalitarianism, he was lobbying Eddie at the Admiralty for a pay rise for his miserable stokers.

By now the handful of poems that were to make Brooke, in the hour of his death, famous to a wide public, were in print. He had sent them to Wilfrid Gibson for the latest issue of *New Numbers* and the galleys had come back to Blandford with his admiring approval. Deprecatingly, Brooke began to send copies out to his friends. The crowning sonnet, 'The Soldier', the one he had begun at Blandford and finished at Walmer, sums up the series:

> If I should die, think only this of me:
>   That there's some corner of a foreign field
> That is for ever England. There shall be
>   In that rich earth a richer dust concealed;
> A dust whom England bore, shaped, made aware,
>   Gave, once, her flowers to love, her ways to roam,
> A body of England's, breathing English air,
>   Washed by the rivers, blest by suns of home.
>
> And think, this heart, all evil shed away,
>   A pulse in the eternal mind, no less
>   Gives somewhere back the thoughts by England
>   given;
> Her sights and sounds; dreams happy as her day;
>   And laughter, learnt of friends; and gentleness,
>   In hearts at peace, under an English heaven.

One can well understand why this handful of words – of which no fewer than six are 'England' or 'English' – caught the national mood of the moment. Brooke had flung his fistful of images into the air and rearranged them with the sure touch of a master: the plangent repetition of the sacred word 'England', the sure and careful progression of thought are seamless, and it is still possible to read today and feel the faint shape of a lump forming in the throat. What stirs the doubts is not the sentiments themselves, but, as ever, Brooke's own personal identification with them. He is mingling his own body and spirit with a mystical England, and the sticky paste that forms

leaves a weird after-taste. This is not only a modern criticism from a
contemporary taste informed by the poetry of disillusion that was to follow
from Sassoon and Owen, Rosenberg and Gurney. One of Brooke's
contemporaries, destined, like himself, to die before the year was out,
Charles Hamilton Sorley, put his finger unerringly on the weakness, the
Achilles' heel on Brooke's flawless body:

> He is far too obsessed with his own sacrifice, regarding the going to war of
> himself (and others) as a highly intense, remarkable and sacrificial exploit,
> whereas it is merely the conduct demanded of him (and others) by the turn of
> circumstances, where non-compliance with this demand would have made life
> intolerable. It was not that 'they' gave up anything of that list in one sonnet: but
> that the essence of these things had been endangered by circumstances over
> which he had no control, and he must fight to recapture them. He has clothed
> his attitude in fine words: but he has taken the sentimental attitude.

Although a minority view at the time, this has come to be the commonly
accepted opinion of the war sonnets; a sequence which it is hard to view
dispassionately outside the steamed-up context in which they were written.

Brooke himself, either with false or genuine modesty, affected to think
little of the poems that, together with his death, would lift him from life to
legend: he deprecated all except the last two: 'God they're in the rough,
these five camp children,' he told Cathleen; '4 and 5 are good, though, and
there are phrases in the rest.' One of the main themes of 'The Soldier', his
identification with the land he loved, and his mystical incorporation of it in
his own mortal flesh, was derived from his favourite book, Hilaire Belloc's
The Four Men, an account of a four-day walk through the author's beloved
Sussex countryside. It ends:

> He does not die that can bequeath
> Some influence to the land he knows,
> Or dares, persistent, interwreath
> Love permanent with the wild hedgerows;
> He does not die, but still remains
> Substantiate with his darling plains.

Now, having already written his own hymn of praise to his own patch of
England in 'Grantchester', Brooke extends the local patriotism to his whole
country. The uniqueness of England persists, even when buried in a foreign
field. His much-praised body and spirit continues, albeit as 'a pulse in the
eternal mind'. Worthy or not, it is his shot of light, 'England seeming to

flash like a line of foam', as he goes eagerly towards the darkness.

The cold that had laid him low, refused to go away and he was granted sick-leave. He journeyed to London and was cared for by a concerned Eddie. Almost speechless, he roused himself to watch the artist Sir John Lavery paint a portrait of the reigning Queen of London society, the beautiful Lady Diana Manners, in a red gown. He dined the next day with Eddie and Churchill at Admiralty House, but his condition was not improved by this socializing and the Asquith family offered to look after him at Number Ten Downing Street. He remained at the nerve centre of British power for nine days, occasionally receiving visitors, the most distinguished being Henry James. After a week he felt well enough to venture out on his own for a poignant final meeting with Ka Cox. He had forgotten it was her birthday. 'I feel so angry and ashamed,' he wrote to her in retrospect. 'I've grown older and evil and selfish, but the only thing I do want in the world is that I should do you as little harm or hurt as possible, to give you what little good I may . . .' It was an old and plangent theme, made poignant only by the knowledge in hindsight that it would be the last time he would voice it to its familiar recipient.

As soon as Brooke was well, he was packed off to Walmer Castle for some sea air to help his convalescence, but he was back in London by Valentine's Day and once again dining at the Admiralty with Churchill and Eddie. Eddie left early, but Winston was in garrulous mood and the two men sat up late talking. Brooke told Churchill that he did not expect to survive the coming expedition; but the ever-ebullient Winston told him to put his faith in the destructive power of the Navy, which within a few days was to begin the preliminary pounding of the Turkish forts along the Dardanelles straits. 'He was rather sad about Russia,' Brooke reported to the Ranee, 'who he thinks is going to get her "paws burned" . . . but he was very confident about the Navy and our side of Europe.'

He saw Churchill again almost as soon as he arrived back at Blandford. The First Lord came down on a long-promised inspection of his military baby, choosing a day when rain lashed the exposed Downland, and Brooke and his comrades stood in ranks 'a battalion of Lears, lashed by pitiless rain, for half an hour'. The next day he wrote to Violet Asquith, thanking her for being an 'angel' to him in his sickness. He described Churchill's implacable demand for the battalion to be put through his paces, despite the 'mud, rain & a hurricane'.

'We were hurried,' he went on, 'to an extemporised performance, plunging through rivers and morasses. It was like a dream. At one point I emerged from the mud, with my platoon, under the wheels of a car, in the midst of a waste. And in the car were what I thought were two children, jumping about clapping their hands shrilling and pointing. It was Eddie & Clemmie [Clementine Churchill].' He added hopefully: 'It is rumoured that Winston was "pleased", & impressed by our superiority to the other Brigades: & that we shall go out *as* a Brigade. Which gives us more chance of survival.' The communication ended with a touch of gallows humour: 'This is a letter of a sublieutenant – as dull as ditchwater. I wish I had even my civilian bright little interest in *anything*. I'm a machine, a clod, a platoon officer . . . a tittle, an omicron, a jelly, a dry anatomy, a less-than-protoplasm . . . There's a fine sun & a clean wind . . . come and view my buffalo-like health, your handiwork. Rupert.

On 20 February Violet replied from Walmer. The previous day, the battle of the Dardanelles had begun with 40 ships bombarding the coastal forts. She added: 'I have just . . . heard that you are *going* on Sat. I can feel nothing but grey, iced terror for you all – but I know how happy you and Oc will be & try and feel glad for you – it is very difficult.' Brooke had already heard the news. That same day Colonel Quilter assembled his officers to tell them they would be sailing for the Mediterranean in a week. The weeks of waiting were over, and relief was instantaneous. 'It's too wonderful . . .' Brooke told Dudley in ecstasy, 'the best expedition of the war. Figure me celebrating the first Holy Mass in St Sophia since 1453.'

Optimistically, they were told they would be part of a force that would not only break through the Dardanelles and link up with the Russians, but take Constantinople into the bargain. As usual with ambitious military operations, outlandish optimism was at a premium: they would only be taking equipment for a fortnight's fighting; they were told they would be home within six weeks. 'At any rate,' Brooke told his mother with forced cheer, 'it will be much more glorious and less dangerous than France.' He failed to pass on the appreciation that, as the spearhead of the landing, the unit could be expected to take casualties of 75 per cent. His chances of surviving the expedition, already remote, were diminishing daily.

With less than a week to go until departure, preparations moved into feverish gear. He filled in the time between last-minute kit inspections and lectures on the maintenance of weapons, with brushing up his Greek. Earlier he had written to Cathleen of his sense of identification with an old England stretching back into the mists and myths of antiquity:

Where our huts are was an Iberian fort against the Celts – and Celtish against Romans – and Romans against Saxons . . . Last week we attacked some of the New Army in Badbury Rings – an ancient fort where Arthur defeated the

Saxons in – what year? Where I lay on my belly cursing the stokers for their slowness, Guinevere sat, and wondered if she'd see Arthur or Lancelot return from the fight, or both, or neither, and pictured how they'd look; and then fell a-wondering which, if it came to the point, she'd prefer to see.

Brooke, too, may have wondered which of his women, should he 'return from the fight', he would most want to see. Writing to one of them, Violet Asquith, he continued his sense of identification with the myths and legends of a heroic past, but this time the locale switched from ancient England to the Classical world he had learned about at Rugby in his youth:

Oh Violet it's too wonderful for belief. I had not imagined Fate could be so benign. I almost suspect her. Perhaps we shall be held in reserve, out of sight, on a choppy sea for two months. Yet even that. But I'm filled with confident & glorious hopes. I've been looking at the maps. Do you think perhaps the fort on the Asiatic corner will want quelling, & we'll land & come at it from behind & they'll make a sortie & meet us on the plains of Troy? It seems to me strategically so possible. Shall we have a Hospital Base (& won't you manage it!) on Lesbos! Will Hero's Tower crumble under the 15″ guns? Will the sea be polyphloisbic & wind dark & unvintageable (you, of course, know if it is)? Shall I loot Mosaics from St Sophia . . . & Turkish delight? & Carpets? Shall we be a Turning Point in History? Oh, God! I've never been quite so happy in my life, I think. Not quite so pervasively happy; like a stream flowing entirely to one end. I suddenly realise that the ambition of my life has been – since I was two – to go on a military expedition against Constantinople. And when I thought I was hungry, or sleepy, or falling in love, or aching to write a poem – that was what I really, blindly, wanted.

It is very revealing – and very Brookian – even down to the throw-away afterthought that seeks to cancel all that has gone before: 'This is nonsense. Goodnight. I'm very tired.' One last time the babbling Brooke of yore rises to the surface in a series of iridescent yet evanescent bubbles. The schoolboyish burbling might occasion a smile if we did not know the tragic outcome of his Trojan fantasies. The fact that he was destined to die, and be buried, on the very island where Achilles was born, is just one more twist of fate so typical of Brooke.

British hopes were pinned on the expedition as a semi-chivalrous diversion from the depressing slogging match on the mud-locked Western front, and a big send-off was planned. Not only Churchill, but the King himself, came down to review the Hood Battalion before its departure. The big day was Thursday 25 February, and the previous evening a select band of friends, including Eddie, Violet and Clemmie Churchill, were entertained to dinner in the officers' mess. The day dawned clear and cold, with 'a brilliant sun sparkling on frost – air like crystal', according to Violet's diary. After the last of his many breakfasts with Eddie, Brooke joined his platoon.

Clemmie and Violet on horseback cantered along the serried lines of men drawn up on the Downs. 'Oc, Rupert, Johnnie Dodge & Patrick [Shaw-Stewart] standing like rock before their men,' Violet noted admiringly, adding: 'Rupert looked heroic.' She continued:

> Poor little Eddie was heartbroken at losing the Hood – & a rather pathetic figure
> . . . Clemmie & I cantered about till the King came – then there was a formal
> march past – they all looked quite splendid sweeping past in battalion formation
> – & I had a great thrill when the Hood came on preceded by its silver band –
> & Quilter roared like a lion 'Eyes Rrright' & all their faces turning. I hadn't
> realised what a different colour men of the same race can be – Patrick was
> arsenic green – Oc primrose – Kelly slate-grey – Rupert carnation pink – Denis
> Browne the most lovely mellow Giorgione reddish-brown.

The march-past was followed by a lunch of grapefruit, marrons glacés, foie gras and champagne. But Violet found the bubbly turned quickly flat: 'It somehow wasn't quite the fun it ought to have been,' she recorded. 'I had a tightening of the heart throughout.' After lunch Brooke said a last goodbye to Eddie, who, driving alone to London, turned and waved as he sped out of sight.

On Saturday 27 February the Hood Battalion left Blandford. Violet witnessed the striking of the last of Brooke's many camps. She found wagons piled high with blankets and packing cases 'becalmed in a sea of mud'. She also found Brooke in a foul mood – one of his fellow-officers, Frederick 'Cleg' Kelly, an Australian-born Oxford 'hearty' who had thrice won the Diamond Sculls at Henley Regatta, had got hold of his sonnets and shown them round the mess with antipodean ribaldry, much to Brooke's dismay.

Brooke gave Violet those of his personal possessions that he did not want to take with him, among them Ka's 'futurist' curtains, but seemed to her 'very tired – & the bubble of excitement momentarily gone off him. He had his hair cut very short – by order – and his sun-helmet was too small for him & wldn't go on.'

Soon after seven that evening the Hood Battalion, wearing their pith-helmets, marched ten miles to the railhead at Shillingstone, where they

entrained for Avonmouth, the cheerless modern port of Bristol. Late that
night they boarded their troopship, the 7612-ton converted Union Star
liner the *Grantully Castle*. A last package arrived on board from Eddie,
containing a mysterious gift for Brooke – a good-luck charm in the form
of an amulet. Eddie's note explained: 'My dear, this is from a very beautiful
lady who wants you to come back safe – her name is not to be divulged. I
have promised that you shall wear it – and I beseech you to make my word
good. It's a very potent charm . . .'

Loading the ship with equipment, mules, and men took most of the
night, but at 5.30 the following morning Brooke retired to his cabin to
snatch some sleep. He was not too exhausted to resist the habit of a lifetime,
and scribbled a quick farewell note to Ka, telling her he was off to take
Constantinople. 'Isn't it luck?' he burbled. 'I've never been so happy . . .
Goodbye. Please keep well.' As he wrote, the Prime Minister's daughter,
staying the night outside Poole, was writing him what started as a goodbye
note but became a love-letter: 'When I have asked myself . . . why I loved
being with you so . . . one of the reasons . . . was that I have never spent a
moment with you anywhere – not at a pounce table – or a music hall – or
a Downing St lunch! – that wasn't permeated by & shot through with
colour – & a sense of adventure – the feeling one lives for – the Dardanelles
in fact.'

The shy confession of love was followed by a hasty, blushing
acknowledgement that she realized Brooke did not return her feelings: 'but
that didn't matter to me. I was too happy to have any vanity about it.' She
ended 'tearfully': 'Goodbye beloved Rupert – bless & keep you – if
thoughts could save you should be very safe.'

Clutching the letter to deliver in person, Violet drove to Avonmouth to
bid goodbye to Brooke and her brother. Brooke wangled a few hours'
shore leave by swapping his watch with Cleg Kelly, and he, Oc and Violet
went off to lunch at the nearest hotel. Violet's diary recorded: 'After lunch
Brooke's main idea as usual was to get as warm as possible – he is a real
lizard – and we coiled ourselves almost in the fire-place.' After a few hours
they wandered off to find a chemist to get a prescription made up for
Patrick Shaw-Stewart, who was suffering from a poisoned throat. Waiting
outside the pharmacy, and making desultory conversation, Brooke showed
Violet his latest poem: 'The Treasure', which begins with the striking line:
'When colour is gone home into the eyes.' 'He said in his usual intensely
quite modest eyed way – "A [I] think the first line's perfectly divine."'

With a feeling that a knife was suspended above them, Violet
accompanied Brooke and Oc back on board. A series of imperious siren

blasts told her the knife was falling: it was time for civilians to go ashore. 'Rupert walked with me along the narrow crowded decks – down the little plank stairs – then I said goodbye to him. I knew by his eyes that he felt sure we should never see each other again.'

She watched as the gangway was raised and the liner moved slowly away from the quayside. The Battalion's trumpeters played a salute on their silver instruments as the ship cleared the harbour mouth. 'The decks were densely crowded with happy confident faces – the thought of the Athenian expedition against Syracuse flashed irresistibly thro' my mind.' Violet's premonition was understandable – but unfortunate – the expedition she refers to was a raid against Sicily in 413BC, during the Peloponnesian War; it ended with the complete annihilation of the Athenian force. Through eyes misted with tears, she watched until the ship became a distant blur. She had seen Oc waving goodbye, but not Brooke: 'I think he purposefully stayed away,' she wrote sadly.

Escorted by two destroyers, the *Grantully Castle* sailed down the Bristol Channel: to port, if Brooke had been watching, lay the cliffs near Clevedon where they had all carelessly vowed to defeat middle age. Now he was sealed in another pact. It was to prove a far surer way of defeating age, and of finding the only end of age.

27

A Body of England's

Brooke endured several days of seasick misery as the liner lumbered down the Bay of Biscay before he found his sea legs. Then it was into a routine of coaxing his stokers into having their vaccinations and coaching them in semaphore. By 4 March they were through the Straits of Gibraltar and passing along the southern coast of Spain. That day he wrote to Violet with a touch of his travel-reporter's eloquence, describing the smell and sense of the Spanish land mass:

> There was something earthy in the air, & warm – like the consciousness of a presence in the dark – the wind had something Andalusian in it. It wasn't that wall of scent and invisible blossom & essential spring that knocks you flat, quite suddenly, as you've come round some unseen corner in the atmosphere, fifty miles out from a South sea island. But it was the good smell of land – & of Spain, too! and Spain I've never seen, & never shall see maybe. All day I sat & strained my eyes to see, over the horizon, orange groves & Moorish buildings & dark eyed beauties & guitars & fountains & a golden darkness. But the curve of the world lay between us . . .

The ship sailed on, tacking close to the coast of Africa as it neared their first port of call, the British island base of Malta. The two musician officers – Denis Browne and 'Cleg' Kelly – did their best to entertain the stokers with renderings of popular songs on the liner's piano. The further east they sailed, the more the reality of what they were engaged on sank in. There was little hard information, and in its absence rumour flourished. Brooke told Violet: 'We're in the dreamiest, most utter, most Trustful, ignorance of what's to come. Some even say it'll all be over before we get there. I hope not: & certainly think not. Impossible. I rather figure us scrapping forlornly in some corner of the Troad [the area around ancient Troy] for years & years. Everyone will forget all about us. We shan't even be told when peace is declared . . .'

Responding tactfully to Violet's recent declarations of love for him, Brooke claimed to have been too involved in his work – 'entirely surrounded by the horizons of the day' – to withdraw and think. 'Perhaps I never have, even in peace. I'm a hand-to-mouth liver, Gods help me.' Then he let her down gently with soft lies, similar to those he had told before, so often, and to so many: 'It has been very good being with you. I had rather be with you than with anyone in the world. And you've been very kind to me.' Then, recalling perhaps, his situation, and that there was no more need for lies, honesty overcame him:

> Do not care much what happens to me or what I do. When I give thought to it at all, I *hate* people – people I like – to care for me. I'm selfish. And nothing but harm ever seems to have come of it, in the past. I don't know. In some moods that thought seems wrong. Generally right. I don't know the truth about that – or about anything. But somewhere, I think, there's bad luck about me. There's a very bright sun, & a lot of comedy in the world; so perhaps there's some point in my not getting shot. But also there's point in my getting shot.

The Brooke who was going to his death was as confused and, deep beneath the bright and brittle charm, as sad a man as ever. But he concluded brightly: 'Anyway, you're very good to me. The Staff-Captain is going to seal up the mail-bag. Goodbye. Rupert.'

He had begun to write what he knew would be his last letters. He prioritized them: only the best, the closest and the oldest friends: Ka, Dudley, Jacques, Eddie. Many were excluded: the Strachey and Keynes brothers; the Olivier sisters – his last word to Noel, back in January, had commented cynically on the fact that his rival Ferenc Békássy had enlisted, but on the other side, going off with money from Maynard Keynes, to fight and die for his native Hungary. 'Dreadful if you lost all your lovers at once,' Brooke had remarked, adding: 'Ah, but you won't lose all!'

His mind turning to the practicalities of his posthumous life, he explicitly instructed Dudley and Eddie to deal with his letters and literary manuscripts. Dudley, as always, was detailed to clear up the amatory messes Brooke had left behind:

> I want you, now – I've told my mother – to go through my letters (they're mostly together, but some scattered) and DESTROY all those from (a)

Elisabeth van Rysselberghe. These are signed E.V.R. and in a handwriting you'll pick out once you've seen it. They'll begin in the beginning of 1909–1910, my first visit to Munich, and be rather rare except in one or two bundles. (b) Lady Eileen Wellesley: also in a handwriting you'll recognise quickly; and generally signed Eileen. They date from last July on . . . Indeed, why keep anything? Well, I *might* turn out to be eminent and biographable. If so, let them know the poor truths . . . try to inform Taata of my death. Mlle Taata, Hotel Tiare, Papeete, Tahiti. It might find her. Give her my love . . . You'll have to give the Ranee a hand about me: because she knows so little about great parts of my life . . .

Although prepared to lift the curtain a fraction on the dark secrets of his inner life, Brooke was still – even in the valley of the shadow of death – too terrified of his mother for plain honesty; and this despite his injunction to Dudley to 'Let them know the poor truths'. If he was frightened of revealing the truths of his sexual liaisons with white women – Elisabeth and Eileen – he balked completely at the relationship with a Tahitian semi-courtesan. As they neared the coast of Tunisia, ancient Carthage, he wrote to Dudley: 'It is my watch. I have just picked my way over forms recumbent on the deck, and under hammocks, visited twenty sentries, smelt the stale smell of sleeping stokers, and noticed the beginnings of the dawn over Africa. The sky is a grim silver, and beyond Carthage there's a muffled half-moon whirling faintly round in clouds.' Dudley's wife had sent him a gift of handkerchiefs, which, he feebly jested would come in useful for binding his stumps if his legs were lopped off by Turkish scimitars. He concluded grimly with a sober assessment of the odds they were facing: 'There are a quarter of a million Turks ahead. We are ten thousand. This is some expedition.'

On 8 March they put in at the Fish Dock in the harbour at Valetta. Brooke was officer of the watch, and remained on board writing to Eddie while the stokers went ashore for an uproarious day's leave. 'War seems infinitely remote,' he told his mentor, assuring him that the five-pointed-star amulet given by the anonymous lady well-wisher – almost certainly Lady Eileen or Cathleen – was hanging round his neck along with his identity disc. 'Please thank Anonyma and say I'm quite sure it will bring me luck. But what 'Luck' *is* we'll all wait and see. At least, we'll all wait, and you'll see. perhaps. I can well see that life might be great fun: and I can well see that death might be an admirable solution . . .' Here once more is the terrible admission, unspoken but unmistakable, that Brooke's sense of failure and unworthiness is so strong that death seems a simple and even desirable 'solution'; that the puzzle of life is too complex and messy to be patiently teased out, and must be severed by a bullet.

Eddie had procured for Brooke, as a going-away gift, a history of Turkey and the Crusades, and, predictably enough Brooke and his comrades saw themselves as latter-day Crusaders, off to liberate the Holy Places of Christendom from the Infidels. He told Jacques Raverat:

> the early Crusaders were very jolly people. I've been reading about them. They set out to slay the Turks – and very finely they did it, when they met them. But when they got to the East, to the Levant and Constantinople, were they kind to their brother Christians they found there? No. They very properly thwacked and trounced them, and took their money, and cut their throats, and ravished their daughters and so left them: for they were Greeks, Jews, Slavs, Vlachs, Magyars, Czechs, and Levantines, and not gentlemen. So shall we do, I hope.

The minds of Brooke and his band of brother officers were transported more and more back to the Classical world they had imbibed over dusty school benches years before: '. . . we've been gliding through a sapphire sea, swept by ghosts of triremes and quinqueremes, Hannibal on poop, or Hanno . . . soon – after Malta – we'll be among the Cyclades. There I shall recite Sappho and Homer. And the winds of history will follow us all the way.'

Relieved of his duties, Brooke went ashore with Oc and Denis. Valetta reminded him of Verona, which he had seen with Ka on that glorious day of reunion after his confinement at Cannes – it seemed a lifetime ago, although it was just three years. While dining, the last member of 'the Argonauts', as they were coming to think of themselves, joined them. Charles Lister was the delicate only son of Lord Ribblesdale and a contemporary of Patrick Shaw-Stewart at Eton and Balliol. Serving with the General Staff but eager for glory, he was persuaded by his friends to transfer immediately to the Hood Battalion.

As they got up steam to leave Malta just before midday on the following morning, the officers got their first glimpse of Britain's allies, in the shape of a French warship, and Denis Browne assembled the Battalion's band and belted out a rendition of the Marseillaise to greet their comrades-in-arms. Two days later, on 11 March, they arrived off the Greek island of Lemnos, the main assembly point for the assault. The anchorage at Mudros Bay was already crowded with Allied shipping, including the brand-new British battleship the *Queen Elizabeth* and her elderly counterparts the *Nelson* and the appropriately named *Agamemnon*. Next morning they were joined by an antiquated Russian cruiser, the *Askold*, whose five slim funnels, sticking up like cigarettes in a pack, caused some wag on the ship to nickname her 'the Packet of Woodbines'.

They remained on Lemnos for a week, kicking their heels, while the rest of the expedition assembled. They were all bewitched by the 'isles of Greece/where burning Sappho loved and sang . . .'. Brooke scanned the horizon with the Marchesa Capponi's powerful binoculars: 'We saw,' he told Cathleen Nesbitt, 'they *said* we saw – very far away, Olympus . . . But with strong field-glasses I could not certainly see the gods . . . its head was shrouded in mist. Also there was, I think – Parnassus . . . and my eyes fell on the holy land of Attica. So I can die.'

His impending death was weighing sombrely on his mind. On 10 March, *en route* from Malta to Lemnos, he wrote what was intended as his final farewell to Ka, consciously couching it with an eye to posterity and Parnassus:

> I suppose you're the best I can do in the way of a widow. I'm telling the Ranee that after she's dead, you're to have my papers. They *may* want to write a biography! How am I to know if I shan't be eminent? And take any MSS you want. Say what you like to the Ranee. But you'd better not tell her much. Let her be. Let her think we might have married. Perhaps it's true. My dear, my dear, you did me wrong: but I have done you very great wrong. Every day I see it greater. You were the best thing I found in life. If I have memory, I shall remember. You know what I want for you. I hope you will be happy, and marry, and have children. It's a good thing I die. Goodbye, child. Rupert.

On 18 March came the orders they had been waiting for. They were to sail into Turkish waters. In a postscript to Ka, Brooke described the day that followed: 'Off we stole that night through the phosphorescent Aegean, scribbling farewell letters, and snatching periods of dream-broken excited sleep.' Reveille sounded at 4 a.m. the following morning: 'We rose and buckled on our panoply, hung ourselves with glasses, periscopes, revolvers, food and the rest, and had a stealthy large breakfast. *That* was a mistake. It is ruinous to load up one's belly four or five hours before it expects it: it throws the machinery out of gear for a week. I felt extremely ill the rest of that day.'

Unbeknown to the Battalion, the previous day had seen a decisive defeat for the Allied plan: Churchill had ordered a full-scale naval assault on the forts on either side of the straits in preparation for getting the assembled troops ashore, against the advice of his admirals, one of whom, Carden,

collapsed with a nervous breakdown and was removed from command.
Their forebodings proved only too well-founded: the Anglo-French fleet
came up against a chain of unswept mines, and two British and one French
battleship were sunk, with great loss of life. Brooke described the
anticlimactic sequel to Ka:

> We paraded in silence, under paling stars, along the sides of the ship. The
> darkness on the sea was full of scattered flashing lights, hinting at our fellow-
> transports and the rest. Slowly the sky became wan and green and the sea opal.
> Everyone's face looked drawn and ghastly. *If* we had landed, my company was
> to be the first to land . . . We made out that we were only a mile or two from
> a dim shore. I was seized with an agony of remorse that I hadn't taught my
> platoon a thousand things more energetically and competently. The light grew.
> The shore looked to be crammed with Fate, and most ominously silent. One
> man thought he saw a camel through his glasses . . . There were some hours of
> silence. About seven someone said 'We're going home'. We dismissed the
> stokers, who said, quietly, 'When's the next battle?'; and disempanoplied, and
> had another breakfast. If we were a 'feint' or if it was too rough to land, or, in
> general, what little part we blindly played, we never knew, and shall not. Still,
> we did our bit: not ignobly I trust. We did not see the enemy. We did not fire
> at them; nor they at us. It seemed improbable that they saw us. One of B
> Company . . . was sick on parade. Otherwise, no casualties. A notable battle.

In fact the Battalion had been the victim of the sort of bungling that was to
characterize the whole Gallipoli operation, which should, in hindsight,
have been called off at this point, as the element of surprise was lost and the
Turks, with German help, were busily strengthening the peninsula's
defences. Instead General Sir Ian Hamilton was hurriedly appointed
to command another attempt, and the whole Allied force withdrew to
regroup, but not, alas, to rethink. The Battalion endured another week of
waiting on Lemnos, before sailing for Egypt, to disembark at the unlovely
town of Port Said on 28 March.

They pitched their tents – the last of Brooke's camps – on a stretch of
dirty sand just outside the town. Brooke shared his with his Company CO,
Bernard Freyberg, the ebullient American Johnny Dodge and a Lieutenant
Nelson, rumoured to be a descendant of his famous namesake who had
trounced the French – now Britain's allies – in these waters a century
before. After two nights under canvas, Brooke, Shaw-Stewart and Oc
Asquith were given 48-hour-leave passes for Cairo. They took the train
to the capital and stayed in the famous Shepheard's Hotel, dropping in
on some of Oc's well-born friends among Cairo's ruling British

administration, including the famous adventurer Aubrey Herbert. They saw the usual tourist sights, visiting the Pyramids and the Sphinx, where Brooke was photographed in a pith helmet astride a camel. The next day he braved the hawkers bargaining in the bazaar, acquiring a few trinkets. By the time they returned to camp that evening, he was beginning to feel distinctly queasy.

In the morning there was a route march across the desert sands, and by midday he was exhibiting the symptoms of sunstroke: a high temperature, nausea, diarrhoea and a headache. Charles Lister took him by taxi to the best hotel in town, the Casino Palace, but he was not excused duties, and spent the next morning practising shooting with his platoon. Shaw-Stewart had come down with similar symptoms, and their illness was vaguely put down to 'a touch of the sun' or the dysentery that often afflicts unacclimatized Britons in the Tropics. That night he vomited, and the next morning, feeling ghastly, he slept outside his tent in search of a breath of fresh air in the stifling desert heat.

On 2 April the whole Division was due to be reviewed by the newly arrived Commander-in-Chief, General Sir Ian Hamilton. Brooke lay under a green awning outside his tent, his head throbbing and his ears singing. Denis Browne took a picture of him – the last of his life – asleep on his cot, with peaked cap and sunglasses, his mouth open. After completing his review, Hamilton, who had been enjoined by Churchill and the Asquiths in London to do what he could to preserve Brooke, called on the sick man. He noted the meeting in his diary: 'He looked extraordinarily handsome . . . quite a knightly presence stretched out there on the sand with the only world that counts at his feet.' Sitting at Brooke's bedside the General offered him a 'cushy billet': a job on his personal staff on the *Queen Elizabeth*. Brooke refused. 'He very naturally would like to see this adventure through with his own men,' Hamilton reported back to Eddie Marsh, another admirer with his own reasons for wanting to keep his beloved boy safe from harm: 'It was very natural and I quite understand it – I should have answered the same in his case had I been offered a staff billet.' According to Hamilton, Brooke told him that though he realized the privileges he would be passing up by his refusal, he felt bound to undergo the ordeal of the landing 'shoulder-to-shoulder with his comrades'. If he survived, well, he might take the General up on his offer. This, the poet-General approvingly remarked, would enable him to 'keep an eye on the most distinguished of the Georgians'. On this note they parted.

Brooke gave his own account of this momentous meeting – his last chance to save his own life, as he must have thought, even though the fatal illness that was to destroy him was probably already under way – in a letter to Violet Asquith when he was feeling somewhat restored on 9 April:

> . . . just now – for these six days – I've been a victim to the sun. He struck me down, all unaware, the day before Sir Ian inspected us. I lay, racked by headaches & diarrhoea, under an awning on the sand while the stokers trudged past. Afterwards, Sir Ian came to see me a moment. A notable meeting, it was generally felt: our greatest poet-soldier & our greatest soldier-poet. We talked blank verse. He looked very worn & white-haired. I thought him a little fearful – less than cock-sure – about the job.

Before leaving the Division to return to his headquarters, the Commander-in-Chief drew Colonel Quilter to one side. 'Mind you take care of him,' he said. 'His loss would be a national loss.' Fortified by the visit, Brooke willed himself to get up that same afternoon and return to the Casino Palace, where Shaw-Stewart was still sweating out his fever. Brooke, whose own temperature was an alarming 103 degrees, joined him. Next morning he waved aside a doctor, who wanted him admitted to hospital, and consulted instead the Regimental Medical Officer, who prescribed a strict diet of arrowroot to counter the diarrhoea. He and Shaw-Stewart spent the next six days in the jelly-brained vacuity of convalescence, lying under their mosquito-nets, letting their beards grow and only stirring to stagger down the corridor for frequent visits to the toilet. He mustered the energy to write a couple of comic verses on their plight with the refrain: 'This is the seventh time today.'

As their condition slowly mended, they improved their diet to include by degrees chicken broth, fruit and finally fish. But, if Brooke's martial spirit was still willing, the flesh was most definitely weak: 'I shall be able to give my Turk,' he told Violet, 'at the utmost a kitten's tap. A diet of arrowroot does not build up violence. I am as weak as a pacifist. The better able to survey & note maybe . . .' Ominously, since his arrival in the hotel, he had been bothered by a swelling sore on the left side of his upper lip. He shrugged it off, and it seemed to improve with the departure of his fever; but it was to prove to be the first onset of the condition that would kill him – probably the bite of one of the fearsome Egyptian mosquitoes, which, a few years later, would also claim the life of Lord Carnarvon, co-discoverer of the tomb of Tutankhamun, in almost identical circumstances.

Brooke posted the gifts he had brought in the Cairo bazaar the day he had been struck down: a tear bottle for his mother and an amber necklace for Cathleen, along with reassuring little notes. Colonel Quilter visited the sickbay, and, alarmed by Brooke's thin appearance and shaky state, recommended that he stay behind for a fortnight's convalescence after the Battalion sailed in two days' time. Quilter was mindful of Hamilton's injunction, but again Brooke refused the chance to preserve his life. The day before their departure he shaved and sent Eileen Wellesley a pair of semiprecious stones.

The next day, 10 April, at 6 a.m., Brooke and Shaw-Stewart were back on board the *Grantully Castle* as she slowly steamed back to the Aegean. Brooke, still feeling distinctly seedy, remained in bed for three days. He had the leisure to write in his journal a beautiful passage of reflections on the environment:

> There are moments – there have been several, especially in the Aegean – when, through some beauty of sky and air and earth, and some harmony with the mind, peace is complete and completely satisfying. One is at rest from the world, and with it, entirely content, drinking to the full of the placidity of the loveliness. Every second seems divine and sufficient. And there are men and women who seem to do what one so terribly can't, and so terribly, at these moments, aches to do – store up reservoirs of this calm and content, fill and seal great jars or pitchers during these half-hours, and draw on them at later moments, when the source isn't there, but the need is very great.

He also found time to write more letters. To Jacques, in a spirit of farewell, he wrote: 'I turn to you. Keep innumerable flags flying. I've only two reasons for being sorry for dying – (several against) – I want to destroy some evils, and to cherish some goods. Do it for me. You understand. I doubt if anyone else does – almost . . .' Eddie dutifully sent him a clipping from *The Times* which reported that, on 5 April, Dean Inge of St Paul's, a sombre cleric known as 'the gloomy Dean', had read 'The Soldier' 'from the pulpit of the great cathedral', commenting that the young Brooke would, he ventured to think, 'take rank with our great poets'. The Dean qualified his praise by deploring the lack of conventional Christian sentiment in the sonnet. Being 'a pulse in the eternal mind', he thought, did not exactly qualify as the ever-present certainty of the Resurrection being celebrated that Easter Sunday. As the Dean closed his remarks by praising Brooke's 'pure and elevated patriotism' a pacifist in the congregation rose to his feet and denounced the war. It was already clear that Brooke, in the eyes of the general public, was either damned or praised solely on the simplified view of what he thought of the war.

Eddie also brought news of a review in the *Times Literary Supplement* heaping praise on the latest issue of *New Numbers*, which contained the war sonnets. The *TLS* critic said that 'the very blood and youth of England seem to find expression' in the poems, which 'speak not for one heart only, but for all to whom her call has come in the hour for need and found instantly ready . . . no passion for glory here, no bitterness, no gloom, only a happy, clear-sighted all surrendering love'. Thus, before he was dead, the rudiments of the legend that would gather around Brooke were already taking their place.

Inspired by the news of *New Numbers*, Brooke took up a letter to its co-editor, Lascelles Abercrombie, describing his recent sickness, which he still put down to 'sunstroke [which] is a bloody affair. It breaks very suddenly the fair harmonies of the body and soul. My head was shattered in three parts, and my diarrhoea was part of the cosmic process.' He hadn't, he said, the time or detachment to write, though he had been jotting down a few aimless lines, detached 'from the ambient air . . . collaring one or two of the golden phrases that a certain wind blows from (will the Censor let me say?) Olympus, across these purple seas. In time, if I'm spared, they'll bloom into a sort of threnody – really a discussion of England – which I have in my head . . .'

Brooke and his fellow-officers who ate at the same table in the mess – Lister, Asquith, Shaw-Stewart, Kelly, Browne and Dodge – had devised an ingenious way of getting round the censor and letting their friends in England who shared the benefits of a Classical education know where they were. They were derisively nicknamed the Latin Club by their less well-educated comrades, but actually their discourse was of Ancient Greece, and, using Shaw-Stewart's edition of Herodotus as a crib, they had devised a code using Homeric illustrations. By now they had been diverted from Lemnos, whose harbour was chock-a-block with Allied shipping, and were heading for the nearby island of Skyros, Achilles' refuge from the Trojan wars and the island where his protector, King Lykomedes, had treacherously slain Theseus, King of Athens. Drawing their pitchers of sustenance from these ancient tales, their minds ticked over in neutral. In his last letter to his mother Brooke described the future as 'an absolute blank' but added: 'if anyone in this war is lucky, we who are on this job are'.

It was during these last days of peace on the wine-dark sea that Brooke wrote his fragmentary final poem on a new note of resignation and quiet thought – far from the stridency of the sonnets. It is as good a note as any on which to pass into eternity:

I strayed about the deck, an hour, to-night
Under a cloudy moonless sky; and peeped
In at the windows, watched my friends at table,
Or playing cards, or standing in the doorway,
Or coming out into the darkness. Still
No one could see me.

                    I would have thought of them
—Heedless, within a week of battle—in pity,
Pride in their strength and in the weight and firmness
And link'd beauty of bodies, and pity that
This gay machine of splendour 'ld soon be broken,
Thought little of, pashed, scattered . . .

                    Only, always,
I could but see them—against the lamplight— pass
Like coloured shadows, thinner than filmy glass,
Slight bubbles, fainter than the wave's faint light,
That broke to phosphorus out in the night,
Perishing things and strange ghosts—soon to die
To other ghosts—this one, or that, or I.

They reached Trebuki Bay, the largest natural anchorage in the Aegean, on the south coast of the hourglass-shaped island of Skyros on 17 April. Pacing the deck together that evening, Brooke and Lister noted the strong smell of flowering sage and thyme that drifted across the wind from the dark island. Brooke remained on ship the next day, while the others explored the island. He wrote to his friend Sybil Pye, who, one voice in a gathering chorus, had expressed her admiration for his sonnets. Eddie was told:

> I cannot write you any description of my life. It is entirely featureless. It would need Miss Austen to make anything of it. We glide to and fro on an azure sea and forget the war – I must go and censor my platoon's letters. My long poem is to be about the existence – and non-locality – of England. And it contains the line:
>
>   In Avons of the heart her rivers run.
>
> Lovely isnt it [sic].

The following day, 19 April, Brooke went ashore to lead his platoon in a

Battalion exercise. The stokers could not resist the temptation of expending some of their ammunition in shooting snakes, or attempting to organize a tortoise race. They marvelled at the island's wild beauty: tumbled pink and white marble rocks, interspersed with patches of wild flowers: scarlet poppies, ilex and everywhere the ubiquitous scented herbs thyme, sage and mint. The exercise was by way of a warm-up for a full Divisional Field Day, a war game planned for Tuesday 20 April, held in a dried-up river valley under the shadow of Mount Khokilas, the highest point on Skyros. Operations paused for lunch, and Denis Browne led his companions to an olive grove he had discovered a mile inland where they rested under the shade. Brooke, already tired, remarked on the peace and beauty of the place. Browne, Lister and Shaw-Stewart were to remember this comment when it came to selecting the site for Brooke's last resting-place.

As they assembled at the beach, Freyberg, a strong swimmer, suggested swimming back to the ship, but Brooke said he wasn't up to it, and took a fisherman's boat back laden with their clothes. The final phase of his illness was beginning, and his race was almost run. The Battalion's officers treated two of their comrades from a neighbouring ship, the *Franconia*, to dinner that evening; but Brooke was notably quiet amid the noisy festivities, and told Shaw-Stewart at the end of the meal that the hock they were drinking was making his lip swell again. At ten o'clock, pleading tiredness, he went to bed.

Oc Asquith looked in on his cabin the next morning and found that Brooke's lip had swelled still further. He complained, too, of pains in his back and head, but lay in bed all day before sending for the Divisional surgeon, Dr McCracken, that evening. The doctor found that Brooke had a temperature of 101, and ordered hot compresses for his swollen lip. Denis Browne looked in on Brooke later, armed with *The Times*'s report of Dean Inge's sermon on 'The Soldier'. Brooke said he felt very bad and asked Denis to leave the light off. He tried to rise to his usual flippancy by saying he had already read the piece and was sorry the Dean had unfavourably compared his sentiments to those of the Prophet Isaiah. But Denis saw that he was too sick for jokes and left him alone to sleep. By the next morning, 22 April, the Battalion's doctors realized that Brooke was seriously – perhaps fatally – ill. His continuing pains in the back and now the chest gave warning that a bacterial infection was running rampant through his always frail, but now dangerously depleted, body. An anxious Denis called in on Brooke three times in the course of the day, but on each occasion found him semi-conscious.

At 3 p.m. McCracken called a conference with his fellow-physicians,

Drs Gaskell, Casement, and Schlesinger, whom Denis had known at Guy's Hospital. They were joined by Dr Goodale, the *Grantully Castle*'s surgeon and a bacteriologist, who confirmed the fear that Brooke was suffering from acute blood poisoning, and, moreover, had virtually no chance of survival. The onset of the illness had been brutally swift, and Brooke's jest about Dean Inge were the last conscious thoughts he formulated as words before lapsing into a comatose state. The source of the toxins that were destroying him, the doctors agreed, was the sore on his lip, which was probably an infected mosquito bite. In the days before antibiotics, once septicaemia had declared itself there was next to no chance. Brooke's friends were advised to prepare themselves for the end.

They resolved to go down fighting. As the doctors decided to conduct an exploratory operation on Brooke's neck, to take a swab for analysis from the abscess that had formed on the side of his face and was quickly spreading down his neck to his torso, someone remembered that an ancient French hospital ship, the *Duguay-Trouin*, built in Brest in 1878, was anchored in the bay nearby. Facilities would be better there than on the cramped and stuffy *Grantully Castle*. The decision to transfer Brooke was rapidly made and executed, and he was stretchered into a pinnace. As he was lowered into the boat, he recovered consciousness momentarily, pushed the blankets off his face and recognized Denis, who was gently lifting him down. 'Hello,' he said, trying to force a smile. It was his last word.

The staff on the *Duguay-Trouin*, who were preparing for battle casualties, and had only one other patient to deal with, put Brooke into an airy cabin set on the aft sun-deck of the ship. Having seen him installed, Oc Asquith and Denis left the hospital ship around six and went to the *Franconia* to send the first news of Brooke's illness to the outside world. One cable went to Hamilton at Lemnos, the other to the Admiralty in London. Signed by General Paris, the RND Commander, the marconigram to Hamilton described Brooke's disease as 'Diplococcus, morphologically resembling Pneumococcus', adding: 'Condition very grave. Please inform parents and send me instructions re disposal of body in case he dies and duplicate them to *Duguay-Trouin*.'

At the Admiralty, Eddie received the news he had long dreaded. He instantly wired the Ranee in Rugby: 'I have had bad news admiral telegraphs Rupert on board french hospital ship duguay trouin with septicaemia condition very grave please inform mother and telegraph instructions if anything special end of telegram. Churchill is telegraphing for further report is there anything you wish wired I have strong hope Marsh.'

Churchill himself wired his cousin, who was serving in the Aegean: 'Personal. From First Lord to Major John Churchill. Endeavour if your duties allow to attend Rupert Brooke's funeral on my behalf. We shall not see his like again. W.S.C.'

As these messages hummed across the wires, the dying man at the still centre of the storm moved peacefully towards the shade. Oc and Denis crossed back to the *Duguay-Trouin* soon after 9 a.m. on Friday 23 April, St George's Day and the birth- and death-day of William Shakespeare. Now another poet was about to join the bard on Parnassus. They agreed to mount a vigil at the bedside, Oc taking the first watch. 'He was unconscious,' he told his sister later; 'at least, twice, when I spoke to him, he seemed to make an effort in his throat to speak: but no words came.'

At noon Oc was relieved by Denis, who at 2 p.m. was told by the French head surgeon that Brooke was sinking fast. Denis departed post-haste for the *Franconia* to fetch the chaplain 'for his mother's sake'. The chaplain, 'Failes by name, came back with me and saw him, but he was unconscious so after saying a few prayers he went away.' Oc had rejoined the small group attending Brooke, and Denis sent for Dr Schlesinger, who confirmed that it was simply a matter of hours. On learning this news, Oc hurried off again to make preliminary arrangements for the funeral as word was spreading that the Division was due to sail for the Dardanelles the next morning. Meanwhile an enquiry had arrived from Hamilton at Lemnos. The surgeon told Oc to answer simply: '*Etat désespéré.*' When he received the message, Hamilton wrote to Eddie: 'Alas, what a misfortune . . . he was bound, he said, to see this fight through with his fellows . . .' Privately, he recorded in his diary: 'War will smash, pulverize, sweep into the dustbin of eternity the whole fabric of the old world; therefore the firstborn of intellect must die. Is *that* the reading of the riddle?'

Alone, Denis sat on with his dying friend. 'At four o'clock he became weaker, and at 4.46 he died,' he wrote in his subsequent account, 'with the sun shining all round his cabin and the cool sea breeze blowing through the door and the shaded windows.' The surgeon immediately wrote out a death certificate, giving the cause of death as a malign oedema caused by rapid septicaemia. This bald and brief statement of fact has given rise to much speculation as to the exact cause of Brooke's death. It has been suggested that some long-dormant infection – possibly of venereal origin and dating back to his sojourn in the South Seas – was triggered into fatal virulence by the stresses of his service life and his exposure to the soup of tropical infections in Egypt. All this must remain speculative. The only certainty is that Brooke had a long-standing constitutional weakness and a disposition to fall victim to various infections, particularly when he was emotionally or physically overstretched. His delicate constitution was an obvious target for the virulent mosquito that probably bit him in Cairo or at the Pyramids, and once the poison was firmly in the blood, his resistance – already depleted by the relatively recent coral poisoning in the Pacific – gave way at once, allowing the disease to run its swift and fatal course.

At 5.15 p.m. Oc returned and held a hurried conference with Denis. They decided that Brooke would not have wanted to be buried at sea, and, in view of the impending departure for the Dardanelles, decided to bury him that same evening on Skyros – in the olive grove where they had rested only three days before.

Two hours after Brooke's death a grave-digging party led by Freyberg, Browne and Lister went ashore and climbed to the olive grove, following the course of the dried-up river bed. Denis selected the grave site beneath an olive tree, which seemed to be 'weeping' over the head of the tomb. He cleared the ground with Brooke's fellow-officers before handing over to stokers from A Company to do the spade work.

Back on the *Duguay-Trouin*, the French medical staff washed Brooke's body and dressed him in his uniform, before laying him in a plain oak coffin provided from the ship's stock. Oc, who was in charge of the arrangements, personally burned Brooke's name and the date of his death into the wooden lid with a soldering iron. They covered the coffin with 16 palm fronds and the Union Flag, and placed Brooke's pith helmet, pistol and holster on top, stepped back and saluted. Senior British officers arrived on the French ship, including General Paris and Brooke's CO, Colonel Quilter. As a French guard of honour presented arms, the coffin was lowered into a boat. A large escort of pinnaces and launches from other ships in the fleet set off for the shore. A French officer described the funeral procession: '. . . they glide over the water like a holiday procession . . . music sounds as they pass; the huge ships one after another send them hoots in harmony, but the atmosphere is solemn and still. The night is soft with a sheen of moon, and starry. The island's perfume drifts through the night, becoming stronger and stronger.'

A party of a dozen burly Australian pallbearers waited on the dark shore, commanded by Shaw-Stewart. As clouds moved across the moon, they inched their way by lamplight up the stony river course towards the olive grove. It took the cortège nearly two hours to negotiate the difficult path in the darkness, with sentries holding lamps posted every 20 yards to light their way. The procession was led by a stoker with a lantern, followed by Brooke's platoon sergeant, Saunders, holding a large wooden cross that had been made by the men of the platoon for their departed officer. Shaw-Stewart came next, with a group of men bearing rifles to form a firing party, followed by the coffin, which was accompanied by Paris and Quilter.

The grave was dug and ready when the grave-digging party spied the bobbing lights of the cortège approaching up the valley just before 11 p.m. Seeing the size of the coffin, Oc leapt into the grave with a spade and hastily lengthened it. The earth walls were lined with olive branches and sprigs of pungent sage. Chaplain Failes recited the burial service of the Church of England and the coffin was lowered into its resting-place. At last Brooke had arrived at the end of his journey. What remained in the memory of those who saw it were sensual, immediate things: the flaring lamps, the dark clouds scudding across the moon's face, the insistent smell of sage, thyme and mint. That night Kelly noted in his journal that the smell of the herbs 'gave a strong classical tone, which was so in harmony with the poet we were burying that to some of us the Christian ceremony seemed out of keeping. One was transported back a couple of thousand years, and one felt the old Greek divinities stirring from their long sleep.'

Shaw-Stewart's firing party fired three volleys over the grave. The shots rolled around the surrounding hills, sending wild goats running with a jingle of bells. The ceremony over, the parade presented arms and broke up, stumbling back to the beach the way they had come. Only five of the Argonauts – Browne, Freyberg, Asquith, Lister and Kelly – remained behind to gather the loose, sharp-sided pink and white marble rocks that lay scattered profusely around and heap them in a cairn over the tomb. A small cross was placed at the foot of the grave, and a large one, bearing Brooke's name in large black letters, was planted at its head. On the back, the unit's Greek interpreter, an islander from Lemnos wrote:

> Here Lies
> the servant of God
> Sub-lieutenant of the
> English Navy
> Who died for the
> deliverance of Constantinople from
> the Turks.

As they walked away from Brooke, only six hours after he had ceased to breathe, leaving him alone with the goats and shepherds in his corner of a foreign field, more than one of his friends felt an overwhelming sense that they had been not just at a death, but at a birth: the beginning of a legend.

Kelly spoke for them all when he wrote in his journal:

> I have had a foreboding that he is one of those, like Keats, Shelley and Schubert, who are not suffered to deliver their full message . . . No more fitting resting place for a poet could be found than this small grove, and it seems that the gods had jealously snatched him away to enrich this scented island. For the whole day I was oppressed with the sense of loss, but when the officers and men had gone, and when at last the five of us, his friends, had covered his grave with stones and took a last look in silence – then the sense of tragedy gave place to a sense of passionless beauty, engendered both by the poet and the place.. . . I copied out the contents of his notebook before going to bed . . .

So Kelly, who had angered Brooke back at Blandford by filching his sonnets and mockingly showing them around the mess, was moved to copy in awe the contents of Brooke's last jottings. Among the fragmented lines and unfinished poems were a few words, in which, prophetic as always, the poet seemed to foretell his own end:

> He wears
> The ungathered blossom of quiet; stiller he
> Than a deep well at noon, or lovers met;
> Than sleep, or the heart after wrath. He is
> The silence following great words of peace.

Epilogue: Man and Myth

'Rupert Brooke is dead,' thundered *The Times* on Monday 26 April 1915.

A telegram from the Admiralty at Lemnos tells us that this life has closed at the moment when it seemed to have reached its springtime. A voice had become audible, a note had been struck, more true, more thrilling, more able to do justice to the nobility of our youth in arms engaged in this present war, than any other – more able to express their thoughts of self-surrender, and with a power to carry comfort to those who watched them so intently from afar. The voice has been swiftly stilled. Only the echoes and the memory remain, but they will linger. During the last few months of his life, months of preparation in gallant comradeship and open air, the poet-soldier told us with all the simple force of genius the sorrow of youth about to die, and the sure triumphant consolations of a sincere and valiant spirit. He expected to die; he was willing to die for the dear England whose beauty and majesty he knew; and he advanced to the brink in perfect serenity, with absolute conviction of the rightness of his country's cause, and a heart devoid of hate for his fellow-men. The thoughts to which he gave expression in the very few incomparable war sonnets which he has left behind will be shared by many thousands of young men moving resolutely and blithely forward into this, the hardest, the cruellest, and the least-rewarded of all the wars that men have fought. They are a whole history and revelation of Rupert Brooke himself. Joyous, fearless, versatile, deeply instructed, with classic symmetry of mind and body, he was all that one would wish England's noblest sons to be in days when no sacrifice but the most precious is acceptable, and the most precious is that which is most freely proffered.

The tone is unmistakable: reading the initials 'W.S.C.' at the foot of the tribute is superfluous – the rolling, grandiloquent prose style could have come from no other pen. Though a shattered Eddie Marsh wrote the original draft, the piece bears all the hallmarks of Churchill's mind and pen. The short tribute followed Eddie's official obituary (now Brooke knew who would 'do' him for *The Times*, the question he had posed in a letter to Eileen Wellesley after writing his obituary of James Elroy Flecker only months before); ironically both that obituary and the letter had been written under the roof of his obituarist and first biographer, Eddie. Churchill's fulsome, but essentially false, tribute set the tone for the orgy of grief and lamentation that followed the news from Skyros. Beneath the clamour of loss, the private words of Brooke's friends were drowned beneath an outpouring of sentimental elegy from those who had never met the real man. For every flowery adjective marshalled by Churchill to lay upon the dead poet's tomb one could substitute another that would be equally, and usually more, true. 'Joyous' certainly, but also, like Churchill himself, bleakly and blackly depressive. 'Fearless' yes, but also doubtful. 'Versatile', perhaps, but also set in long-meditated bigotry and con-servatism. 'Deeply instructed', of course – equipped with all that a Rugby and Cambridge education could provide; but also woefully ignorant of the processes of real life and the way that most people actually behave. 'Classic symmetry of body and mind' is hardly an adequate summation of a mind whose intellect and emotions were rarely in synch, whose intellectual rigour was matched by childish spleen, prejudice and self-absorption. Ready for the final sacrifice, to be sure, but as much from a deep desire to escape the complexities and compromises of existence than to lay down his life for others.

But all these qualifications and counter-arguments were for later. For now, the expression of national mourning held the field, and within the short compass of a weekend Brooke the man vanished in a ray of Aegean sunshine, his human frailties buried under a ton of marble rocks. The man became a myth: the process was egged on by some of those who should have known better, but, in the shock of the moment, lent their voices to the chorus of approval. His oldest friends, for the most part, held their peace, but those who had got to know him after the watershed year of 1912 made up for the brevity of their acquaintance with the loquacity of their extravagant eloquence. For example, the day after Churchill let loose the flood-tide of eulogy, Lascelles Abercrombie wrote an obituary in the Conservative *Morning Post* that opined: 'Not since Sir Philip Sidney's death have we lost such a gallant and joyous type of the poet-soldier.' The war sonnets, the paper's readers learned, were not only 'among the few supreme utterances of English patriotism' but were 'incomparably the finest utterance of English poetry concerning the Great War' and 'the work of a talent scarcely . . . to be equalled today'. Abercrombie spared no cliché in his drooling encomium: Brooke was compared to Sir Philip Sidney, who, killed at Zutphen in 1586, was loved by the Gods and so died young; his poetry was as 'effortless and eager as the winged songs of Spring-tide'; and so on.

In the days that followed, a cacophony of other newspaper voices added their notes to the choirs of praise. *The Sphere*, too, drew the comparison with Sidney, inaccurately claiming that Brooke was 'the only English poet of any consideration who has given his life in his country's wars'. *The Star* said he was 'the youth of our race in symbol', while the *Daily News* said: 'To look at he was part of the youth of the world' – a statement at once obvious and meaningless.

More than one of Brooke's friends perceived that his death had already taken on the quality of myth. Gilbert Murray, writing in the *Cambridge Review*, said: 'I cannot help thinking that Rupert Brooke will probably live in fame as an almost mythical figure'; while Walter de la Mare, a writer who, as one of Brooke's three designated heirs, had more reason than most to be grateful to the dead poet, wrote in Brooke's old paper the *Westminster Gazette*: 'Nature is as jealous of the individual as of the type. She gave Rupert Brooke youth, and may be . . . in doing so grafted a legend.'

Brooke's death was first reported as being caused by sunstroke; and writing to Brooke's old enemy Lady Ottoline Morrell, just after hearing the news, D. H. Lawrence, with his own quirky but heartfelt touch of genius, exclaimed:

> He was slain by bright Phoebus' shaft – it was in keeping with his general sunniness – it was the real climax of his pose. I first heard of him as a Greek god under a Japanese sunshade, reading poetry in his pyjamas at Grantchester – at Grantchester upon the lawns where the river goes. Bright Phoebus smote him down. It is all in the saga. O God, O God, it is all too much of a piece: it is like madness.

Henry James, hearing the news, merely hung his head and murmured: 'Of course, of course.' Later he told Marsh: 'What a price and a refinement of beauty and poetry it [Brooke's death] . . . gives those splendid sonnets – which will enrich our whole collective consciousness.'

Even Brooke's spurned friends – those he had scorned in the years before his death – were horror-struck: Lytton Strachey wrote to Duncan Grant on 25 April: 'It was impossible not to like him, impossible not to hope he might like one again.' The same day Maynard Keynes told the same correspondent: 'And to-day Rupert's death. In spite of all one has ever said, I find myself crying for him. It is too horrible.' James Strachey, writing to Harry Norton on 3 May, was more circumspect:

> Yes. It's horrible. But somehow I haven't personally felt as much as I should have expected . . . I've hardly seen anything of him in the last three years – and that softens things. It's more like losing the possible chance of making friends with him again than an actual loss. I cried a lot more over him when he went off in 1912 than last week. Other people feel it shockingly. Poor Eddie, whom I interviewed at the Admiralty the other day, seemed almost done for. And Ka one doesn't like to think of. Then there's Mrs B. – Alfred being in France. The only actual collapse I've heard of is most unexpected and queer. Daphne Olivier went quite mad last night.

Indeed the women in Brooke's life seemed to feel his death more tellingly than the many men who mourned. Ka's pain is evident in the brevity of her letter to James in response to his condolences on 28 April: 'My dear. There really isn't anything. Give my love to Noel. Ka.' Violet Asquith heard the news while staying at the vice-regal lodge in Dublin. She was devastated:

> . . . it was not only for me that I minded but for the world – that this perfect thing should be no more – this being without compare. It was like Spring being dead – or music – or flowers – like seeing some marvellous vase shattered before one's eyes. And I wanted so much more of him for myself. Never to be able to dip into his mind – never to be able to look into his eyes again. I went alone to St Pauls at 12. It rained all day. After tea I saw Eddie – quite broken poor darling. It is the first thing that has given me control – the feeling that he was feeling it FOR me – it somehow seemed to lighten the weight & dull the edge.

Eddie was inconsolable. He wrote to the Ranee, who bore her loss with stubborn silence and pride: 'It is the greatest sorrow I could have, and I dare not think what it must be to you – I have never known or heard of anyone like him – his genius and his beauty, his wisdom, honour, gentleness and humour made him such a man as seldom lived. Everybody loved him, there was no one who had so many devoted friends and so many charmed acquaintances.'

But Eddie and the Ranee had to brace themselves for further loss. Back in the Aegean, early in the morning after Brooke's death and burial, the Fleet sailed again for the fatal straits of the Dardanelles: on board the *Grantully Castle* Denis Browne and 'Cleg' Kelly sorted through Brooke's possessions – his compass was given to Charles Lister, who, as a newcomer, did not have one. The rest – silver watch, amber cigarette holder, a locket and identity disc, along with Brooke's clothes, letters and papers (minus copies of his final notebooks which were carefully made by both men) – were packed up for dispatch to Rugby.

Brooke's bequests, written in full knowledge of his impending likely demise, must have seemed simple to him, but he could not have known of the complications they would cause. While explicitly appointing Eddie as his literary executor – 'This is very odd. But I suppose I must imagine my non-existence, and make a few arrangements. You are to be my literary executor' – he qualified the instruction by asking Eddie to let his mother keep his papers until his death (minus the love-letters and other revealing material that he had already instructed Dudley to abstract from Grantchester and destroy before the Ranee could clap eyes on them). Then he further muddied the waters by asking Eddie to let Ka and Alfred have any papers they might wish to keep. He ended his confusing letter, which amounted to a will and testament:

> You must decide everything about publication. Don't print much bad stuff. Give my love to the *New Numbers* folk, and Violet and Masefield and a few who'd like it. I've tried to arrange that some money should go to Wilfrid and Lascelles and de la Mare . . . to help them write good stuff, instead of me. There's nothing much to say. You'll be able to help the Ranee with one or two arrangements. You've been very good to me. I wish I'd written more. I've been such a failure. Best love and goodbye. Rupert.

As an afterthought he added: 'Get Cathleen anything she wants.'

Brooke's financial affairs were in chaos: his mother found he had a huge overdraft of £300 at Barclays bank in Cambridge, and owed rent to the Neeves at Grantchester. Fortunately, his galloping popularity ensured that sales of his posthumous *1914 and Other Poems* – rushed out by an enterprising Frank Sidgwick within months of his death – were stratospheric; and their continuing popularity – even at his critical nadir the public appetite for Brooke's poems ensured that they never went out of print – gave his three designated heirs a healthy addition to their income for the rest of their days.

The Grantully Castle was only one ship in an armada of 200 Allied vessels sailing towards the Dardanelles. The RND sheared off to make a diversionary attack. When they were 6000 yards from the shore Denis

Browne finished his letter to Eddie Marsh with a paean of praise to
Freyberg: 'He loved and understood Rupert intuitively in spite of the
differences in their temperaments, and last night, when we were making
the grave, he was as tender as a woman, and as strong as a giant.' The gallant
Freyberg distinguished himself again during the landings, winning the DSO
for swimming ashore alone, and lighting flares to guide his troops in. The
Hood Battalion lost 11 of its 15 officers during the war: Freyberg, though
severely wounded at Gallipoli, survived to become a general by the war's
end. Asquith, too, survived, despite the loss of a leg, to become Britain's
youngest general, and so did Johnny Dodge, who stayed in his adopted
country at the war's end to become a London stockbroker.

Of the others, Denis Browne was the first to follow Brooke, as he
predicted to Eddie at the beginning of June: 'I've gone now, too; not too
badly I hope. I'm luckier than Rupert because I've fought. But there's no-
one to bury me as I buried him, so perhaps he's better off in the long run.'
He died on 7 June. Charles Lister, who, like Brooke, had spoken in longing
terms of 'fighting on the plains of Troy', survived until the autumn. 'Cleg'
Kelly was the next to go, dying at Beaumont-Hamel on the Somme, the
battle that also took Oc Asquith's brilliant elder brother, Raymond. Patrick
Shaw-Stewart died the following year on the Western Front. By the war's
end only two of the five officers who had buried Brooke were still alive.
The war took other friends too – Ben Keeling, another socialist and patriot;
Hugh Russell-Smith, close friend of Rugby days; and in June 1915 – the
same month that saw the death of Ferenc Békássy, fighting against the
Russians with the Hungarian cavalry – a fresh blow struck at Bilton Road,
Rugby: Alfred Brooke was killed by a stray shell at Vermelles in France. In
his last letter home he had implored his mother not to believe the
sentiments voiced in Brooke's notorious sonnets; war, he said, was hell.

As the casualty lists lengthened, the first signs of a reaction against the
cult of Brooke's death began to faintly glimmer. Unsurprisingly, and
cautiously at first, they began to surface in Cambridge. Writing in the
Cambridge Magazine a month after Brooke's death, Harold Monro protested
courageously against Brooke being used as a 'poster-poet' to boost
recruitment for the war: 'One fears his memory being brought to the
poster-grade. "He did his duty. Will you do yours?" is hardly the moral to
be drawn. Few people trouble to know much about poetry – but everyone
takes an intelligent interest in death . . . His whole poetry is full of the
repudiation of sentimentalism. His death was not more lovely than his life.'

Jack Sheppard, Brooke's former tutor, complained in the *Cambridge
Review* that his friends owed a duty to Brooke not to comfort themselves

by dwelling on a 'mythical being who was not the real Rupert'. Gwen Raverat, too, privately protested – in a letter to Stanley Spencer – that the Brooke they had known was being taken from them and twisted into a lie to suit the needs of the hour. The myriad articles she had read about their friend, she said, 'might have been written about King David, or Lord Byron, or Sophocles, or any other young man that wrote verse and was good looking . . . they never got the faintest feeling of his being a human being at all'. Among the vague abstract sentiments that were being voiced, the flatulent poetic tributes that were being penned, there was very little concrete personal reminiscence about the 'real Rupert': most likely because, for those in the know, the 'poor truths' about him were too rawly painful to be told.

Meanwhile the cloying sentimentalists had the field to themselves; and their ranks were swelled by some friends of recent vintage like Wilfred Gibson, who wrote a poem – only a marginal improvement on the tide of verse tributes that the abrasive editor of *The Nation*, H. W. Nevinson, complained was deluging him:

THE GOING

> He's Gone.
> I do not understand.
> I only know
> That as he turned to go
> And waved his hand
> In his young eyes a sudden glory shone
> And he was gone.

Frances Cornford chimed in with her own poem, 'Rupert Brooke', which ends:

> O friend we have loved
> Must it be thus with you? – and if it must be
> How can men bear laboriously to live?

When he had got over his immediate grief for Brooke and Denis Browne, Eddie took leave from the Admiralty, and, after calling on Mrs Brooke to pay his condolences and help her open the boxes of her son's possessions – 'I had never seen such grief' – went to stay with the Gibsons at their country cottage, where, as Gibson's poem 'The Golden Room' recalled, Brooke had enjoyed the company of his fellow-poets only a year before:

Do you remember that still summer evening
When in the cosy cream washed living room
Of the Old Nailshop, we all talked and laughed –
Our neighbours from the Gallows, Catherine
And Lascelles Abercrombie; Rupert Brooke;
Eleanor and Robert Frost, living awhile
At Little Iddens, who'd brought over with them
Helen and Edward Thomas? . . .
'Twas in July
Of nineteen fourteen that we talked
Then August brought the war, and scattered us.
Now, on the crest of an Aegean isle,
Brooke sleeps, and dreams of England: Thomas lies
'Neath Vimy Ridge, where he, among his fellows,
Died, just as life had touched his lips to song . . .

Here, working eight hours a day in the attic, Eddie finished in eight days a 150-page memoir-cum-biography of Brooke, which, written in the first flush of grief for his dead friend and much altered by the censorious hand of the Ranee, is little more than a parade of surface facts, spiced by extracts from his letters: all designed to show Brooke in the flattering, one-dimensional light Eddie preferred to remember.

The path to publication of the memoir was slow because it did not meet the Ranee's high expectations of what a memorial to her beloved son should be. She was mistrustful of Eddie by instinct, and her hostility was heightened by the fact that Brooke had appointed him as his executor: in her view, Eddie had snatched her son into the corrupting world of high politics and higher society; and she was not minded to lose him again now that he was dead. On the contrary, her view of Brooke as 'just a fresh, charming boy' was all the more enhanced by the fact that his living reality was not there to contradict and escape her, as he had maddeningly done so often in life. With icy determination, she swooped to reclaim her boy from the world's clutches.

The Ranee, almost demented with grief after Alfred's death – 'there is nothing nobler in England now than your sorrow,' Abercrombie told her – vetoed the publication of the memoir, ostensibly on the grounds that it included some casual juvenile remarks by Brooke mocking schoolmasters, and hence, by implication, her husband. Eddie was irritated by her nit-picking: 'How Rupert could be produced by a woman without sense of humour, or beauty, and narrow to that degree I shall never understand,' he wrote to Frank Sidgwick.

Exasperated, but determined, Eddie produced a second version of the memoir tailored to meet the Ranee's requirements. But Mrs Brooke turned it down a second time in order to solicit the views of Geoffrey Keynes, always her favourite among Brooke's friends, and her own choice to oust Eddie as executor. Keynes himself had known the Ranee since she was his housemistress at Rugby and loved her dearly – almost as deeply as he resented Eddie's friendship with Brooke.

After some months the Ranee had a change of heart: she accepted a much bowdlerized third version of the manuscript, which excluded a few 'damns' and almost all mention of Cathleen Nesbitt, whom she considered, like all actresses, to be 'fast'. Maddeningly, she then changed her mind yet again and wrote a scorching letter to Eddie questioning his right to write the memoir because he was (a) too old; (b) 'almost a stranger' to the family; and (c) 'almost absurdly inaccurate' in his facts. As the kindly Eddie had gone out of his way in his busy life to boost her son's reputation and had been consideration itself to Mrs Brooke in her bereavement, it beggars belief that he persisted with the project in the teeth of such insulting discouragement, but persist he did. Gritting his teeth, he wrote back in tones of injured moderation pointing out that if his memoir did not appear, years after it had been announced, the task would fall to other, even more untrustworthy and possibly less friendly hands.

Chastened, the Ranee consented to a fourth version, happy at least in the knowledge that she had prevailed on Eddie to slur over all the central crises of Brooke's life. After three years of this vexation, Eddie himself was on the verge of a breakdown as his work at last went to press. It appeared in 1918, in a different world from the one in which Brooke's poems had been written. A hecatomb of corpses, and a great gulf of disillusion, now lay between the war sonnets and the poetry of Siegfried Sassoon or Wilfred Owen.

If Cathleen Nesbitt felt marginalized in Eddie's memoir, being referred to mysteriously as X, one can only guess the feelings of Brooke's last lover, Lady Eileen Wellesley, who was not mentioned at all. By July 1915 she was gossiping about her love affair with the freshly dead Brooke to her society friends. Violet Asquith's sister-in-law Lady Cynthia Asquith noted in her diary on 3 July: 'Eileen Wellesley claims very serious love affair with Rupert Brooke saying that quite unsuspected of everyone else they used to meet in Richmond Park and Eddie's flat. No doubt Rupert Brooke had the thoroughly polygamous instincts of most poets.' Eventually Eileen was to sell Brooke's love-letters to her in order to buy a car.

As the adulation of Brooke subsided under the increasingly heavy weight of the war and its unimaginable tragedies and losses, his friends were left to debate his legacy. Virginia Woolf spoke for many of them when, in an unsigned review of the memoir for the *Times Literary Supplement* in August 1918, she called it 'incomplete', pointing out that the most intimate (and interesting) parts of his letters had been rigorously excluded. She damned with very faint praise indeed, concluding by archly suggesting that only his friends could have known the real Brooke – Eddie, by virtue of his age, being excluded from this inner circle – and that the friends weren't telling.

Indeed they were not, at least in public. Privately, however, it was a different matter. Virginia, in contrast to her cool and polite *TLS* article, privately called the memoir 'a disgraceful, sloppy, sentimental rhapsody' which left Brooke 'tarnished'. Before she wrote the review, she met James Strachey to discuss their joint views of Brooke: 'We couldn't say much . . . save that he was jealous, moody, ill-balanced, all of which I knew, but can hardly say in writing.'

Coincidentally, much of the meeting had been taken up with discussion not of Brooke but of the news that Ka had just got engaged to be married to a young and weedy-looking Navy officer, unknown to their circle, named Will Arnold-Foster. Ka, it was generally agreed, had never and would never, get over her love for Brooke. Staying with Frances Cornford soon after his death, she had pathetically shown her Brooke's last letter from the Aegean, drawing attention to the line 'You were the best thing I found in life'. During the war she had plunged into work, trying to forget her grief. For six months she ran a camp for Serbian refugees in Corsica, then returned to London and worked as a civil servant organizing Allied shipping. During this time she met and, despite her old friends' disdain, married, her Will. After the war they moved to Cornwall, where she stayed in distant touch with her friends – and, in accordance with Brooke's wishes, had children and was happy. Or ostensibly so. Virginia thought differently:

> Her own identical life ended when Rupert died. So I think. After that she was acting a part very carefully and deliberately chosen. Maternity, Will, public life; hence some squint; she was never natural; never with me at least. And I was self-conscious; remembering how she had seen me mad. She used to come to Asheham, or Holford: condescending, patronising, giving up her own pleasures to tend me and help L[eonard] . . . But . . . that was her role: to help; to lift lame dogs; to entertain; to arrange; manage; receive confidences . . . after Rupert's death she was playing a part. Yet this is superficial, for there was a trustiness in her; a stable goodness; a tenderness.

After years of blameless life and toil – raising her children; presiding over her local magistrate's bench; supporting her husband in his thankless attempts to promote the rural Labour party; even, on one occasion, enjoying a family day out with the cause of all her trouble, Henry Lamb, and his new family – Ka died of a heart attack, aged only 51, on 22 May 1938.

Two of the Olivier sisters – those least important in Brooke's life, Margery and Daphne – were afflicted, like Virginia, by mental illness. Margery's madness was already well advanced in Brooke's lifetime. She imagined most men she met to be in love with her, and eventually attacked her father violently. Noel signed the certificate confining her to an asylum, and she remained in such care until her death in 1974, outliving her younger sisters. Daphne recovered from her breakdown, which had been touched off by Brooke's death – both she and Margery, like Brooke, were treated with the 'stuffing' method. Marrying relatively late, she and her husband, Cecil Harwood, opened England's first Rudolph Steiner school. She divided her time between teaching and bringing up her five children, and died of cancer in 1950.

Brynhild, too, was a victim of cancer. After she had had three children by Hugh Popham, his dullness finally dawned on her and she began an affair with a younger man, Raymond Sherrard, in 1918, a liaison which scandalized her friends and family. Hugh divorced her and she married Sherrard, and had three more children in conditions of growing poverty as her husband's business ventures failed. In 1933 she developed lymphatic cancer, and died, after an agonizing illness, on 13 January 1935. The ruthless Noel evicted Sherrard and his children from the farmhouse at West Wittering on the Sussex coast, and used the place as a holiday home.

Noel herself qualified as a doctor and married a colleague, Arthur Richards, in 1920. They had a son and four daughters. Late in the day, she too, like Bryn, grew bored with her conventional husband, and in 1932 started an affair with her former suitor, James Strachey – which, had he known of it, would doubtless have caused Brooke a wintry smile. The relationship lasted for a decade, and then Noel resigned herself to middle age. In contrast to Ka's correspondence, her letters to and from Brooke remained unavailable until they were edited for publication by her granddaughter in 1991. In retirement Noel remained active, enjoying frequent visits to the London theatre, where she would speak of her long but ultimately fruitless liaison with Brooke with affection and regret. She died on 13 April 1969, aged 76, of a stroke while pruning a vine at the Sussex home she had inherited from Bryn.

Elisabeth van Rysselberghe had been the recipient of one of Brooke's shipboard farewells. He was cruelly dismissive, telling her that he was destroying her letters and that she should forget him. She, like so many others, continued to mourn his bright but brittle spirit for her whole long life, despite bearing a child to André Gide, of all people. She kept a photograph of Brooke by her bedside, and maintained that they had enjoyed a passionate physical affair – a claim which seems, on the scanty evidence available, quite plausible. After giving birth to Gide's child, Catherine, Elisabeth married another man in 1931 and spent the rest of her life in seclusion in the South of France. She died in 1980, aged 90.

Dudley Ward, in his quiet way the most loyal of Brooke's friends, faithfully executed the task of extracting and destroying the embarrassing love-letters from Elisabeth and Eileen, from the mass of Brooke's voluminous papers, before handing them over to the Ranee. He was aided and abetted by the equally loyal Jacques Raverat. Becoming a career civil servant and eventually head of the British branch of UNESCO, Dudley enjoyed a marriage to Annemarie von der Planitz which survived two world wars and produced one son, Peter, who still lives at Cley, in Norfolk, where Brooke was staying when the Great War broke out. Dudley inherited the Old Vicarage, Grantchester, and, along with Geoffrey Keynes, was the chief keeper of the poet's flame. One of his strangest duties was to investigate reports from distant Tahiti that Brooke had fathered a child by Taatamata only a few months before his own death.

Discreet as ever, Dudley approached this delicate mission with great caution, using second and third parties as his agents. He waited until the Ranee died in 1930 before broaching the matter with contacts who knew or lived in Tahiti. Via Viscount Hastings, a sometime Tahitian landowner, an approach was made to the film producer Norman Hall, who had got to know the islands while making *Mutiny on the Bounty* with Charles Laughton. Hall was able to confirm that Taatamata was still alive (she had erroneously been reported to have fallen victim to the epidemic of Spanish flu that swept the island in 1918). Hall apparently also discovered that Taatamata had indeed borne Brooke a child, a daughter named Arlice Raputo, who spent her life in the islands and is said to have died, childless, in or about 1990. Taatamata, who was last reported alive in the early 1930s, apparently ended her days in Moorea.

Whispers of scandal followed Brooke even in death. In 1947 Maurice Browne, who worshipped his friend's memory and staged an unsuccessful production of *Lithuania* at his Little Theater in Chicago in 1915 after Brooke died, wrote to Eddie to complain of rumours circulating in the

USA that the cause of Brooke's death had been syphilis of homosexual origin. A cautious Eddie, not wishing to be drawn into such gossip, passed the letter on to the staunchly heterosexual Geoffrey Keynes, who by then had long usurped his position as Brooke's literary executor. Keynes quashed the suggestion, as he did any idea that Brooke was not a straight-batting heterosexual all his life.

Eddie continued to act as a patron of the arts and artists until he was bombed out of Raymond Buildings in the Second World War. The main occupation of his days after he retired from the civil service was as copy-editor, unpaid, to the copious writings of his old master, Winston Churchill. At tense moments of the war they would exchange letters arguing about the placing of commas. Eddie Marsh died in 1953.

Justin Brooke, the mentor of Brooke's entry to the world of the theatre, also succumbed to nervous trouble, broke with his wealthy tea-producing family, but struck out on his own, made a successful second marriage and became a prosperous and socially minded fruit farmer in East Anglia at the height of the agricultural depression in the 1930s. A keen attender at Bedales reunions and camps into his seventies, he preserved, in his unintellectual way, the optimism and youthful zest of the Neo-Pagans for longer than anyone. A cheerful libertine, he said of Ward's and Keynes's fears that Brooke would be publicly perceived as the same if his letters were published in full: 'So he was!' Despite his incapacity for close and deep friendship, he is one of the most attractive of the figures in Brooke's charmed circle.

Frances and Francis Cornford were able to do what Brooke had asked several of his friends to – name a son after him. Their boy, Rupert John Cornford, disappointed them in several ways – not least by never using the first of his forenames. In his own way as brilliant a Cambridge star as Brooke had been, John Cornford espoused communism and poetry, and was the first Briton to die in the Spanish Civil War, aged 21. His heartbroken mother, who died in 1960, continued the family's close links with Cambridge. Of all her copious poetry, the only lines remembered today, apart from the epigram on Brooke that she so vehemently rejected, are:

> O fat white woman whom nobody loves
> Why do you walk through the fields in gloves . . .
> Missing so much and so much?

Jacques Raverat, like Brooke, succumbed prematurely to disease – in his case the undiagnosed multiple sclerosis that had threatened his delicate balance since his early Cambridge days. The cause of his ailment was only discovered when he tried to enlist for both Britain and his native France in the war. After the diagnosis, his collapse was rapid, and a year after Brooke's death he was in a wheelchair. Despite this adversity he fathered two children by Gwen, continued to paint and corresponded feverishly, notably with André Gide and Virginia Woolf. With the latter he effected a reconciliation between the Neo-Pagan and Bloomsbury spirits before his death on 7 March 1925. His widow contrasted his end unfavourably with Brooke's: 'Jacques wouldn't have gone and died like Rupert,' Gwen wrote of his long and savage struggle against his malady. 'And yet, somehow life has seemed duller since Rupert died.' Gwen came back to Cambridge from France after Jacques died, and resumed her successful career as a woodcut artist. She published a best-selling family memoir of the Darwins and dons in Cambridge, *Period Piece*, in 1952, and died by her own hand five years later, aged 72. In a letter to Virginia she wrote an epitaph for the Neo-Pagans:

> . . . anyhow, it's all over long ago; it died in 1914 I should think – though it was sick before – Neo-Pagans, where are they? Here's Jacques and me very old in Vence, and Ka so pathetic and lost in Cornwall; and do the Oliviers exist or not? Frances I believe carries on the tradition in the fields of Cambridge – at least as far as neo-paganism can be combined with evangelical Christianity . . . and all the others are dead, or have quarrelled or gone mad or are making a lot of money in business. It doesn't seem to have been a really successful religion, although it was very good fun while it lasted.

Of Brooke's oldest friends, one, Geoffrey Keynes, married yet another Darwin, Margaret, and fulfilled his destiny as a successful surgeon, pioneering radical surgery for breast cancer, and working for the Army's medical services in both world wars. He was knighted for his work. Never as brilliant nor as unconventional as his elder brother Maynard, Geoffrey was nevertheless an honourable, decent man, who died full of years and honours, the patriarch of an impressive family dynasty, as late as 1982. His habitual honesty deserted him in only one particular: when it came to telling the truth about Brooke, whom he idolized to his dying day. 'Rupert was quite the most wonderful person I have ever known,' he told a biographer of Brooke's circle, Paul Delany, towards the end of his long life. Geoffrey so wished to believe in his own mental portrait of Brooke, so bound him up with his own golden youth, that he was prepared to suppress the truth about him; and as long as he lived he was in an excellent position to do so.

Keynes could never conceal his furious jealousy that it was Eddie Marsh – compared with himself, a relative newcomer in Brooke's life – who had been clearly named by Brooke in his 'will' as his literary executor. Indeed, by the time he came to write his own autobiography, *The Gates of Memory*, in his mid-nineties, his memory had tricked him into charging Eddie with 'taking it upon himself' to become his friend's executor, who had 'appropriated' Brooke's literary archive. Keynes made no secret of the fact that he despised both Eddie, who, he said, 'lived in a sexual no-man's land' and his memoir: 'a . . . trifle, totally inadequate as a portrait of its subject . . . [a] pretty sketch [which] should never have been printed'. When named in the Ranee's will, contrary to Brooke's last wishes, as literary executor in Eddie's stead, Keynes made fast tracks round to Eddie and collected Brooke's papers, which, after 15 years of intermittent warfare with the Ranee, he was only too glad to yield up to him.

From this time on, Brooke's 'repper' was safe in the hands of a man who, together with his joint trustee, Dudley Ward, would allow no critic, nor criticism, to breathe upon the pristine mirror portrait of Brooke that they had created and now lovingly burnished. Keynes edited a carefully 'weeded' edition of Brooke's huge correspondence in 1968. Brooke's posthumous reputation suffered denigration mainly because he was unfairly identified with the five untypical sonnets he had written on the very verge of death. Well-meant attempts to honour his memory appeared merely to add to the false and misleading cult of piety tinged with homoeroticism that gathered around his head like a cloud of gnats.

In March 1919 a marble plaque was unveiled on the wall – just in the spot where he had once predicted he would appear – of Rugby chapel. The plaque was based on the bare-shouldered photographic portrait by Sherril Schell that had been christened 'Your favourite actress' by irreverent Cambridge wits. The eulogy was spoken by General Sir Ian Hamilton, and Walter de la Mare delivered a lecture that was turned into the first slim book about Brooke: *Rupert Brooke and the Intellectual Imagination*. Brooke's poem 'The Soldier', carved by Eric Gill, was affixed under the plaque. Another stone cutting of the poem was placed at the foot of the elaborate marble tomb that Mrs Brooke caused to be placed over his original grave after the war, a sarcophagus so heavy and out of keeping that it seemed as though the Ranee was making absolutely sure that Brooke would not escape her in death, as he had so frequently done in life.

In April 1925, ten years after his death, yet another one of the war sonnets was inscribed on the memorial to the Royal Naval Division in Horse Guards Parade. The unveiling was performed by Churchill, who spoke warmly once again of the poet and the poetry. Ironically, the memorial was swept away in the Second World War, when it was cleared to make way for the building of Churchill's underground bunker, the Cabinet war rooms. The final indignity heaped upon Brooke's corpse was the unveiling of a grotesque memorial in Skyros, the village capital of the island where he died. Allegedly modelled upon a Belgian male prostitute by its sculptor, the tall bronze nude bore little resemblance to Brooke. When Geoffrey Keynes visited the place in 1949 to lay a wreath, he was met by a demonstration by local boys protesting at the domination of Greece by British and American imperialism and bearing placards reading: 'Rupert Brooke died for Liberty'.

Today Skyros is home to an Anglo-Greek holistic holiday centre where courses are offered in esoteric subjects like shamanism, 'how to love yourself' and creative writing. The centre's brochures call Skyros 'the island of Achilles – and of Rupert Brooke'. Course students visit Brooke's grave by taxi. In the sixties, when it was more remote, the present Poet Laureate, Andrew Motion, visited the place – and nearly died of thirst trying to locate it. When he got there, he was intrigued to see a long line of ants emerging from a crack in the tomb: 'There,' I thought, 'goes the last of Rupert Brooke.' Ironically, considering the cause for which Brooke died, tension between Greece and Turkey has made access to the grave easier: Trebuki Bay, where he died on board the *Duguay-Trouin*, is now a front-line Greek naval base, and a new road to it passes by the tomb. Brooke's name is revered in Greece in the same breath as that of Byron – another good-looking, romantically confused, sexually ambivalent, Midlands boy. Both died of disease while fighting the Turks in Greece.

In October 1930, the year before the absurd monument in Skyros went up, the Ranee died in Rugby and was buried alongside her husband and eldest son Dick in Clifton Road cemetery. The original wooden cross from Skyros was also brought home to the family plot. Keynes found himself presiding over continued steady sales of Brooke's poetry, which, by the 1980s, had sold a million copies. Slowly and methodically, Keynes began to collect Brooke's letters for projected future publication. Meanwhile the first biographers, as Brooke had predicted, were beginning to gather. As they did so, some of his prose was posthumously published. His *Letters from America* reveal a promising travel writer whose prose can suddenly shine like a raindrop on the edge of a leaf. His essay *John Webster and the Elizabethan Drama* crucially influenced the young poet T. S. Eliot, who wrote the lines celebrating the Jacobean's 'possession by death' after reading Brooke's work.

After short tributes by De la Mare and Edward Thomas, the first person to go into print in hard covers about Brooke was another American, Maurice Browne. His brief account of Brooke's stay in Chicago on his return from the South Seas, *Recollections of Rupert Brooke*, published in 1927, only just steered clear of sentimentality but nevertheless offered up some glimpses of a living man. Yet another American, Arthur Stringer, was the first to complete a fully-fledged life of the poet, *Red Wine of Youth*, published in New York in 1948. Horrified that such a 'sub-literate' production might pass down as a picture of Brooke accepted by posterity, Keynes and Ward commissioned the poet and opera librettist Christopher Hassall to write an official biography. Ward had already vetoed Keynes's bowdlerized edition of Brooke's letters, on the grounds that the 700-page manuscript, even in its neutered state, was too revealing of the real Brooke's embarrassing lapses from the plaster saint image. But both Keynes and he agreed that Hassall would be a safe choice as a biographer, if only because Hassall's previous book, a huge 1955 biography of Eddie Marsh, had, through all its 700 pages, managed to steer resolutely clear of such ticklish topics as its subject's homosexuality.

Hassall, after years of labour, produced another opus of more than 500 pages, which nevertheless managed to leave out all the salient facts of Brooke's life, while faithfully following him almost day by day and even hour by hour. If ever there was a case of not seeing the wood for the trees, then Hassall's biography is it. Hassall, also, like Keynes, an honest and honourable man, was hobbled by the need to please the Trustees – the hero-worshipping Keynes and the neurotically suspicious and over-loyal Ward. In addition, he did not have the advantage of access to Brooke's letters to Noel and Bryn. His self-censorship did the rest. So while the Lulworth breakdown is reported in vague terms, the full picture is denied us: reading Hassall is like watching a film through a thick gauze bandage: shapes and shadows and intriguing sounds flash through, but the real meaning is lost. None the less between the lines of what did get printed, hints were there in plenty of richer seams for a bolder biographer to mine.

A few years later, after Hassall had died prematurely of a heart attack in 1964, just before his *magnum opus* was published, a young and bold writer took up the challenge. Michael Hastings, a playwright of the Angry Young Man generation, initially interested in writing a documentary play about Brooke, produced instead *The Handsomest Young Man in England*, utilizing, for the first time, the wealth of photographs of the Neo-Pagans at play that had been left behind. Published in 1968, when another sort of youthful rebellion was shaking the world, Hastings's book is perceptive, fair and sympathetic to Brooke and his friends, but damning and devastating in his critique of their delusions. With all the confidence of youth, Hastings, who enjoyed the confidence of a septuagenarian Noel – he wooed the old lady with trips to the theatre – lambasted what was left of the legend; performing a necessary demolition job on both the remnants of the golden-boy myth and the excessive anti-Brooke reaction that had damned his work to the limbo of the great unread in the eyes of serious critics. Hastings explained exactly why the Brooke myth had arisen, pointing out how perfectly the poet embodied a pastoral dream of innocence and youth, and a pre-modernist England of teas and camps and cricket that lay just over the horizon of living memory, and seemed yearningly attractive to a crowded country of new towns, cars, radios, TVs and sodium lights, where executive estates were rapidly eating up the fields where Brooke and his friends had romped, and toxic pollutants were poisoning the rivers where they once leapt into cleanness. Finally, Hastings dared to hint that the reluctance of the handful of Brooke's surviving old friends – Keynes, Frances Cornford, Cathleen Nesbitt and Noel Olivier – to speak to outsiders or expose the full truth about Brooke's confusions, complexes and cruelties had much to do with their fears of destroying a myth upon which their own lives rested.

The year before Hastings's book appeared, perhaps the closest friend of all – James Strachey – died. James had enjoyed one of the most interesting and varied lives of all Brooke's friends; and one of the most self-fulfilled. Resigning from the *Spectator* because of what Brooke called in his last, insulting letter his 'damned silly, eunuch, and slightly dangerous' pacifist ideas, he spent the Great War doing relief work for the Quakers. After a brief post-war stint as a drama critic, James married Alix Sergeant-Florence in 1920, and the newly-weds went off to Vienna to be analysed by Sigmund Freud. It was the beginning of a lifetime's vocation: he and Alix became leading Freudian analysts themselves, and were the first translators of Freud's work into English. James's interest in drama matured into a consuming passion for music and opera, and he became a founder member of Glyndebourne. Behind the scenes he also continued to express his views of Brooke, remarking on the occasion of Hassall's biography: 'Rupert wasn't nearly as nice as people now imagine; but he was a great deal cleverer.' Michael Holroyd, in his massive life of James Strachey's brother Lytton, gives an unforgettable portrait of the ageing James and Alix, living alone near the Thames at Marlow, weighed down with a monstrous mountain of Bloomsbury papers, and living frugally off bread and cheese and wine diluted with water until only the faintest Brookian blush of red was left in the glass. James died in 1967, just after learning he had been awarded a prize by the Society of Authors for his immense labours in translating Freud.

By the eighties, only Cathleen Nesbitt and Geoffrey Keynes were still alive of Brooke's friends. Cathleen, who married once – unhappily, after her romance with Brooke – had continued, despite all his injunctions, to appear on stage until the end of her long life, in 1980. The ruins of her breathtaking beauty can still be viewed in the 1972 film *The French Connection* – and she, like all the others, never forgot Brooke. Also in 1980 John Lehmann, a writer and editor who had first heard of Brooke while an office boy at Leonard and Virginia Woolf's Hogarth Press, published *Rupert Brooke: His Life and His Legend*, an elegantly written short biography that at last had the courage to engage with Brooke and the reality of his life with a fair degree of frankness, while still remaining deeply sympathetic to the poet. Starting from the central crisis at Lulworth, which he rightly saw as the watershed in Brooke's life between the carefree innocence of youth and the complexity and compromises of maturity, which he struggled towards but never reached, Lehmann, homosexual himself, stressed Brooke's insecurity over his sexuality, and, like Hastings, endeavoured to rescue the good from the bad in his poetry.

In 1987 came the most controversial book yet about Brooke. *The Neo-Pagans: Friendship and Love in the Rupert Brooke Circle* was written by Paul Delany, a British-born Canadian professor of literature who sums up a contemporary view of Brooke with wit, brevity and understanding. At last, with the restraining hand of Geoffrey Keynes removed by his death, aged 95, Delany was able to give chapter and verse from those of Brooke's letters that Keynes had silently and surgically vasectomized. These references included Brooke's homosexual confessions and his rancid spleen against Bloomsbury. At long last, unsightly warts had been planted on the features of the 'handsomest young man in England'. From praise of Ka's 'cunt' to raging abuse of those he believed had wronged him, Brooke comes over as an astonishingly modern figure: flawed, self-pitying, with his emotions in such a hideous mess that he actually welcomed his death in war.

Delany roundly denounces the Neo-Pagan dream as profoundly reactionary: 'Nostalgic, anti-industrial, dedicated to leisure ... and an Arcadian England'. He sees the 'dew-dabbling' delight in camping and nude bathing as essentially childish escapes from a world where someone else is always there to cook and clean. Brooke himself is represented as a failure in national nerve and imagination rather than the simplistic hero

445

hailed by Churchill. And yet, and yet – Delany has the honesty to admit that there is something about Brooke and the Neo-Pagans that 'still has the power to charm, resist it or debunk it as we may'.

If Delany has written the last critical word on Brooke, biographical surprises continue to leap out: the belated publication of his correspondence with Noel, under the misconceived title *Song of Love*, appeared in 1990, edited by Noel's granddaughter, Pippa Harris. The letters reveal a light and witty Brooke – albeit an irritatingly self-obsessed man, with the maddening habit of referring to every female as 'Child'. Also on show is a surprisingly mature and sensible Noel, if on occasion displaying the icy, hard streak that seems so characteristic of the Oliviers. Another collection of letters, between Brooke and James, filled in more pieces of the puzzle when it was published in 1998 under the title *Friends and Apostles*.

A self-confessed uncritical fan of Brooke, the disc jockey Mike Read, published the sensational claim in a 1997 biography, *Forever England*, that the poet had had a daughter by Taatamata, backing up the story with a fuzzy photograph of Arlice Raputo, the woman in question. As Tahitian birth records are so scanty, the claim must remain unproven – but not unlikely. If true, it is appropriate that the one uncomplicated physical passion in Brooke's life – and with a woman as unlike his mother as it is possible to be – should have borne such fruit.

The current keepers of Brooke's reputation: the Trustees who have succeeded Keynes and Ward as guardians of his Estate, are the poets and biographers Jon Stallworthy and Andrew Motion. It may seem strange that two distinguished professors and poets should concern themselves with such an unfashionable figure as Brooke. But, as Delany indicates, it is undeniable that Brooke exercises the sort of lasting appeal of a Shelley, Keats or Byron – poets whose deaths in foreign fields seem as symbolically potent as the verse they left behind.

In a time of renewed interest in a world that has just slipped over the horizon of living memory, it seems likely that Brooke's life and legend will loom larger as he recedes into history.

A few years ago I beat a path to Skyros, and read those words of the poem carved on the grave's thick foot. The silence beat down like sunlight. Insects clicked and lizards scuttled, and time, as Alan Moorehead wrote of the graves of Gallipoli, went by 'in an endless dream'. Idly, I picked up one of the sharp marble rocks, those pink and white chunks, that still litter the place.

There shall be
In that rich earth a richer dust concealed; . . .

The richer dust of Brooke's reality that lay undiscovered for decades in the shallow grave of his manufactured myth has at last broken through a crumbling legend of lies. The man who was fashioned into smooth marble has become a man again. And not before time.

A Note on Sources

I have decided not to burden further an already lengthy book with a detailed list of the sources of each and every quotation. Instead I will here outline the archives, libraries and the most important of the many books I have consulted, so that the interested reader will be able to locate the material on which I have drawn.

The primary source of original written material on Rupert Brooke is the Rupert Brooke Archive of King's College Library, Cambridge. This is a massive and still-growing collection of documentation and photographs recording in microscopic detail almost every aspect of the poet's life from infancy until death (and beyond – there is much on the upkeep of his grave in Skyros). The archive contains school reports, early poems, manuscript notebooks, locks of hair and, above all, letters to and from Brooke. Foremost among the correspondents whose letters to and from Brooke I have quoted are Ruth Mary Brooke, Francis and Frances Cornford, Erica Cotterill, Ka Cox, Hugh Dalton, Arthur Eckersley, Geoffrey Keynes, John Maynard Keynes, St John Lucas Lucas, Eddie Marsh, Cathleen Nesbitt, Jacques and Gwen Raverat, and Dudley Ward.

The letters to and from Noel and Bryn Olivier remain in private hands. Those to and from Noel appeared in *Song of Love* (Bloomsbury, 1990), edited by Noel's granddaughter, Pippa Harris.

The letters to and from James Strachey are held in the Berg Collection of the New York Public Library. They were edited by Keith Hale and published under the title *Friends and Apostles* (Yale University Press, 1998).

Letters to and from Lady Violet Asquith were included in *Champion Redoubtable* (OUP, 1998), edited by Mark Pottle.

Brooke's *Collected Poems* are still in print from Faber, in an edition that also includes Eddie Marsh's memoir. Faber also issued Geoffrey Keynes's voluminous though still incomplete *Collected Letters* (1968) and continue to issue reprints of Christopher Hassall's official life, *Rupert Brooke: A Biography*, which first appeared in 1964.

Other useful Brooke biographies are (in order of publication):

Michael Hastings, *The Handsomest Young Man in England* (Michael Joseph, 1968).

John Lehmann, *Rupert Brooke: His Life and His Legend* (Quartet, 1980).

Paul Delany, *The Neo-Pagans: Friendship and Love in the Rupert Brooke Circle* (Macmillan, 1987).

Mike Read, *Forever England* (Mainstream, 1998).

The secondary sources relating to Brooke's friends and various aspects of his life such as Rugby and the public-school tradition, Cambridge, the Apostles, the Great War and Bloomsbury are, of course, extensive. Indispensable titles include:

Keith Clark, *The Muse Colony: Dymock, 1914* (Redcliffe Press, 1992).

Keith Clements, *Henry Lamb* (Redcliffe Press, 1984).

Cyril Connolly, *Enemies of Promise* (1939).

George Dangerfield, *The Strange Death of Liberal England* (1935).

Paul Fussell, *The Great War and Modern Memory* (OUP, 1975).

David Garnett, *The Golden Echo* (1953), *The Flowers of the Forest* (1956), *The Familiar Faces* (1962).

Michael Holroyd, *Lytton Strachey: A Biography* (1963; new edition Chatto & Windus, 1994).

Michael Holroyd, *Augustus John: A Biography* (Heinemann, 1974).

Geoffrey Keynes, *The Gates of Memory* (OUP, 1981).

Peter Miller, *Rupert Brooke: A Brief Biography* (Warwickshire County Council, 1987).

Alan Moorehead, *Gallipoli* (1956).

Cathleen Nesbitt, *A Little Love and Good Company* (Faber, 1975).

Peter Parker, *The Old Lie: The Great War and the Public School Ethos* (Constable, 1987).

Ben Pimlott, *Hugh Dalton* (Cape, 1985).

Gwen Raverat, *Period Piece* (Faber & Faber, 1952).

Timothy Rogers, *Rupert Brooke: A Reappraisal* (1971).

Richard Shone, *Bloomsbury Portraits* (Phaidon Press, 1976).

Jon Silkin, *Out of Battle: The Poetry of the Great War* (OUP, 1972).

Robert Skidelsky, *John Maynard Keynes: Hopes Betrayed 1883–1920*.

Frances Spalding, *Duncan Grant* (Chatto & Windus, 1997).

Alix & James Strachey, *Bloomsbury/Freud: The Letters of James and Alix Strachey 1924–25* (Basic Books, 1985)

Arthur Stringer, *Red Wine of Youth: A Life of Rupert Brooke* (Merrill, 1948).

Virginia Woolf, *The Diary of Virginia Woolf, Vol. 1: 1915–1919*. Edited by Anne Olivier Bell (1977).

Index